THE ULTIMATE EU TEST BOOK

Administrators 2019

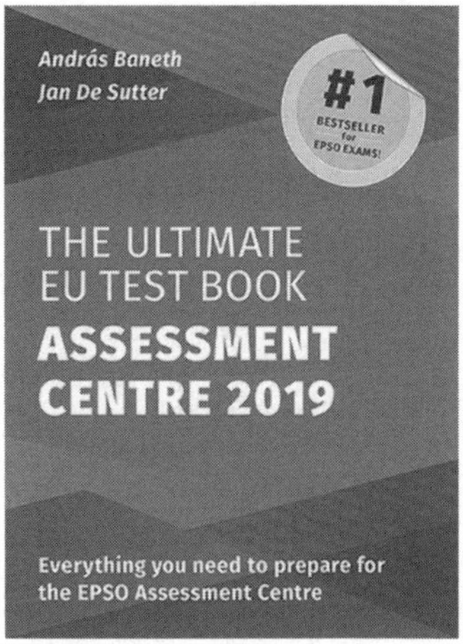

The Ultimate EU Test Book Assessment Centre 2019

By András Baneth and Jan De Sutter

This book has become the absolute must-have for candidates hoping to succeed at their EPSO Assessment Centre. The 2019 edition is up-to-date with all the latest developments including for the first time the just-introduced Motivation Interview.

- How the Assessment Centre works
- What the competencies are and how EPSO measures them
- The exercises in detail
- How to behave, what to do – and what not to do
- Comprehensive guide to competency anchors and indicators
- Competency passport and recruitment
- Packed with sample exercises and presentations
- Relevant for all EPSO competitions

€39
Local prices may vary

ISBN: 9781999959548

The Ultimate EU Career Development Book

By Jan De Sutter

This book shows you how to evaluate and improve your personal performance in the EU core competencies, for job satisfaction and career advancement.

It is designed for all EU staff at all levels, permanent, temporary or contract and is supported by a free online toolkit.

Author Jan De Sutter is a former EU official and now a professional coach and trainer working with EU staff and EPSO selection competition candidates..

€35
Local prices may vary

ISBN: 9780993454936

Also from John Harper Publishing

The Ultimate EU Test Book is available in separate editions for
- ADMINISTRATORS,
- ASSISTANTS,
- ASSESSMENT CENTRE.

Also in the series is THE ULTIMATE EU CAREER DEVELOPMENT BOOK

Full details may be found at **www.johnharperpublishing.co.uk**

To keep up to date with developments on EPSO exams and any updates on The Ultimate EU Test Book, visit **www.eu-testbook.com**, from which you can also link to the Ultimate EU Test Book Facebook page to gather information from and make contact with others taking the exams.

THE ULTIMATE EU TEST BOOK

ADMINISTRATORS 2019

András Baneth

JOHN HARPER
PUBLISHING

The Ultimate EU Test Book Administrators 2019
ISBN 978-1-9999595-5-5

Published by John Harper Publishing
27 Palace Gates Road
London N22 7BW, United Kingdom.
www.johnharperpublishing.co.uk

Sales and distribution: Turpin Distribution Services Ltd.

The Ultimate EU Test Book – edition history
First edition, November 2005
Second edition, May 2007
Third edition, March 2008
Fourth edition, April 2009
Fifth edition, March 2010
Assistant edition 2011, November 2010
Administrator edition 2011, February 2011
Assistant edition 2012, October 2011
Administrator edition 2012, October 2011
Assistant edition 2013, January 2013
Administrator edition 2013, January 2013
Administrator edition 2015, December 2014
Assistant edition 2015, December 2014
Assessment Centre edition, May 2015
Administrator edition 2016, February 2016
Assistant edition 2016, February 2016
Assessment Centre 2018, February 2018
Administrators 2018, March 2018
Assistants 2018, March 2018
Assessment Centre 2019, November 2018
Administrators 2019, March 2019

Typeset mainly in 9 & 10/11pt Palatino

Printed and Bound by Short Run Press, Exeter, United Kingdom.

TABLE OF CONTENTS

INTRODUCTION

Purpose of the Book

The purpose of *The Ultimate EU Test Book* is to help candidates prepare and practise for the European Personnel Selection Office (EPSO) competitions, so as to be eligible for jobs in the EU institutions.

EPSO competitions (often called by their French name, *concours*) are divided into two main types: those for Administrator (AD) level positions and those for Assistants (AST), with a sub-category being Secretaries (AST-SC). The AD level includes Linguists and many Specialist roles.

While the structure of competitions shows some variability (in essence, the more specialised and specific the role, the greater the weight put on applied specialised and specific job-related knowledge), the core elements of competitions are the reasoning tests (psychometric tests) and as the final stage the assessment of a candidate's "competencies" at the Assessment Centre.

The resoning tests, which for the vast majority of candidates constitute the first phase of the exams, make up the "pre-selection" round. This comprises a range of psychometric tests, administered on a computer, which measure candidates' skills in numerical, verbal and abstract reasoning and (possibly) situational judgement tests. Nowadays almost everybody must take all of these tests.

For most candidates, it is the pre-selection round that proves the stumbling block, and in the big "generalist" competitions a large majority fall at this hurdle. For this reason, the focus of the *The Ultimate EU Test Book Administrators 2019* is on the pre-selection tests. Successive chapters explain what the various types of test involve, the skills needed to tackle them, and the errors to avoid – and in each case this methodology is followed by extensive practice questions with detailed explanations of the answers. All the questions have been specifically designed to mirror Administrator-level competitions.

Only a minority of candidates make it as far as the Assessment Centre phase, and they are in reach of becoming "laureates", eligible to take up permanent posts in the EU institutions. A more specialised book, with guidance and practice exercises specifically for those who reach the Assessment Centre, is now available: *The Ultimate EU Test Book Assessment Centre 2019*.

Overview of the chapters

Chapter 1 provides an overview of EPSO selection procedures for Administrators, including what is tested, where and how, as well as issues such as the language rules and the relative chances of success in different competitions. **Chapter 2** then takes a step by step look at typical competitions, generalist, linguist and specialist. Topics include timelines for what tests are taken when, the importance of understanding the scoring rules, commonly made mistakes to avoid, and recruitment. Also covered are internal and CAST competitions, which can provide an alternative route to AD permanent official jobs and also AD-type contract roles.

Few candidates instinctively feel comfortable with the full range of pre-selection psychometric tests: everyone has their strengths and weaknesses, and there are also many hazards in tests which people think they are good at. **Chapter 3** offers a brief overview of what these tests are and why EPSO uses them, with a much fuller look at each test type in the following chapters. Candidates who do not reach the required level in these tests will not be offered the chance to proceed further in the competition. It is therefore vital to study carefully the methodology to learn the principles and shortcuts involved and then make sure to practise to increase your speed, accuracy and ratio of correct answers.

With **verbal reasoning tests**, a common problem is that candidates consider them relatively "easy", without being aware of the traps they contain. In an EPSO competition you are presented with a short text and have to say which one of a series of statements is correct, based on the information in the passage. The nub of the problem for many proves to be the requirement "based on information in the passage", because the statements always include superficially attractive answer options which "seem" right, but in fact cannot be properly based on what the passage actually says. Sometimes, too, the correct answer is a statement which seems rather bland or even immaterial but is in fact soundly based. **Chapter 4** explains the common errors candidates make, and then **Chapter 5** provides a full test exercise with questions designed to probe your ability to spot the hazards.

In the case of **numerical reasoning tests**, the questions are not designed to assess your high-level mathematical skills: nothing is required beyond the maths you will have learned at school. What is tested, however, is your ability to grasp the essence of a problem quickly – to work out what data in the jumble of information in the tables or charts is actually needed to solve the problem, and to calculate in the fastest and most direct way possible. Sometimes, indeed, no or scarcely any real calculations are needed at all, if you know how to see this. For this reason, **Chapter 6** focuses on the fundamental types of calculation needed and how to speed up your application of these.

Chapter 7 then provides a series of targeted "warm up" exercises for specific types of numerical reasoning operations. In this chapter you are immediately given the answer explanations along with the questions so you can "walk through" the reasoning involved. **Chapter 8**, in contrast, follows with a full test where the answers are separated off from the questions, and the operation types are all mixed together, to simulate a real test.

You are not alone if your first reaction to **abstract reasoning tests** is one of anxiety or even dismay, as you try to work out which in a series of shapes is "next in the series". However, as **Chapter 9** shows, such tests involve in a systematic way the application of often quite simple rules – and the key thing is to learn to spot what those rules are. Chapter 9 explains the patterns and operations test designers use, and then in **Chapter 10** you can test yourself in applying those rules in practice. In each case, the answers explain the rules so if you get the answer wrong, you can work backwards from the rules to see where you made your mistake.

Chapter 11 explains the principles and methodology of **situational judgement tests** (SJTs), which are based on real-life workplace scenarios, where a complex interplay of factors is often involved. SJTs are used selectively by EPSO, most importantly in the annual AD5 graduate competition. Here you are being measured against the "competencies" EPSO uses more intensively at a later stage at the Assessment Centre. Unlike with the verbal, numerical and abstract reasoning tests, there is not a simple "right" or "wrong" answer with SJTs – rather there is a progression from a "most" to a "least" appropriate or effective response to a given situation. **Chapter 12** gives you the opportunity to see how your responses match those set as standards in a test exercise. While, unlike with the other psychometric tests, you cannot simply improve your SJT scores by learning and practising techniques, how you do in the test should help guide you as to what interpersonal or other skills you need to think about and work on.

The Assessment Centre exercises are very different from the reasoning tests and are covered in *The Ultimate EU Test Book Assessment Centre 2019.*

Keep up to date!

As is emphasised at many points in this book, you must always check carefully the exact rules for your competition (as announced in the Notice of Competition), because the shape of competitions, including such important matters as the weighting of marks between different tests, can vary. Make sure also that you keep up-to-date with the EPSO website and, for more informal but often useful news and tips, www.eu-testbook.com and *The Ultimate EU Test Book* Facebook page.

András Baneth
Brussels, February 2019.

ABOUT THE AUTHORS

András Baneth wishes to express his appreciation to all those who have over the years contributed ideas and content to *The Ultimate EU Test Book*, including Barnabas Bóta, Zoltán Csipke, Delphine Galon, Márton Magyar, Christine J. Ruzicka, Thomas A. Williams and many others. Special thanks are due on this edition to András Kőrizs, Anna Schmidt and Veronika Koseluk.

ANDRÁS BANETH, an SHL-certified assessor, is a trainer, consultant and partner at Arboreus Online EU Training. He is also managing director of the Public Affairs Council's European office. His bestselling *Ultimate EU Test Book* has helped thousands of candidates prepare for EPSO competitions since 2005. András has a wide knowledge of EU policies, institutions and communication, his career having included seven years' experience at the European Commission and the European Court of Justice, where his roles included coordinating briefings for Commission President Barroso and serving as member of the *cabinet* of Commissioner Kovács. He holds an M.A. in law and political sciences and the degree of Master of European Public Administration from the College of Europe, Bruges, Belgium. He is always open to invitations to speak about EU careers, strategic communication or public affairs. His personal website is available at www.baneth.eu and his direct e- mail is andras@baneth.eu

GÁBOR MIKES is the former managing director of Arboreus Online EU Training and an expert on successful methodologies, including both the theory and practice of passing pre-selection tests. With an M.A. in English Language and Literature and former Kellner Scholar at Trinity College in Hartford, Connecticut (USA), Gábor has worked at an NGO specialising in EU affairs communication and at Ericsson, the Swedish telecom giant. Gábor has held dozens of training courses for hundreds of people around Europe on verbal, abstract and numerical reasoning, many of whom are now working for various EU institutions.

ZOLTAN ARANY-SZABÓ is senior French-language psychometric expert at Arboreus EU Training, and works for the Court of Justice of the European Union in Luxembourg. He previously taught professional translation in various universities and led training courses in French organised by EU Training on verbal, numerical and abstract reasoning.

BENJAMIN WILLIAMS is an HPC Registered Occupational Psychologist and a Chartered Associate Fellow of the British Psychological Society (BPS). Ben has led the design and implementation of Assessment Centres for over 300 public and private sector clients across Europe and the Middle East. He has developed practice materials for the EPSO assessments for over a decade. Ben began his career reading Experimental Psychology at Oxford University followed by a Masters in Organisational and Occupational Psychology. After his studies, Ben worked for three large consultancy firms before launching Sten10, a firm that specialises in designing bespoke people assessments.

1. What Are Administrators and How Are They Selected?

Who are the Administrators?

The administration of the European Union offers a huge range of jobs under an at times bewildering variety of names. There are Administrators (AD), Assistants (AST) and Assistants-Secretaries (AST-SC). There are different staff categories such as contract agents and temporary agents (both of various types), local agents, seconded national experts, parliamentary assistants and different types of paid traineeships. There are "profiles" and "function groups" for particular types of jobs. To make it even more complex many of the titles are peculiar to the EU administration and not found in other walks of life. And of course all these job titles exist in a range of national languages.

All about EU careers

For a full picture of the careers available in the EU administration, read **Working for the EU: How to Get In** by Johannes de Berlaymont.

This explains the many types of jobs available, the routes in (including little known side routes), and the best strategies for building a career.

At the heart of the system, however, are the Administrators. About 56 per cent of the staff of the European Commission, by far the biggest of the institutions, are Administrators and it is the AD-level grades who are the engine room of EU policy making and delivery. The Administrators are at the core of the vision of a European administration of permanent civil servants serving the Union. **Administrator level jobs start at grade AD5** (there are no AD 1 to 4 grades) and go all the way up to AD 16 (Director-General). Most Administrators start at AD5, though for some more specialised roles, where candidates typically have to have had several years of relevant experience, first appointments may be made at AD6 or AD7.

While AD5 posts are described as "entry-level" it would be a mistake to imagine that most AD5s are fresh-faced young graduates straight out of a university first degree course. The average age of recruitment of AD5s in the Commission, for instance, is 34, so a majority have significant previous work experience, including many who have held traineeships or temporary posts in the institutions.

The greatest concentration of Administrator jobs is, not surprisingly, in the "EU capital", Brussels. This is where the European Commission and the Council of the European Union are based and it is also the key location of the European Parliament even though its official seat is Strasbourg. There are however Administrator-level jobs in many other locations: Luxembourg, especially, where many "back office" functions are located (as well as many translator jobs) but also in agencies around the Member States as well as representations of the Commission and Parliament in every Member State capital (and some other cities). Furthermore, there are jobs in the EU delegations all around the world.

The "classic" Administrator job is the civil service generalist moving through their career from one task to another as a permanent official. But many specialist roles also exist. For example, two of the biggest categories of AD-level jobs are highly-specialised – linguists and lawyer-linguists – and there are many other specialist AD jobs as will be seen below.

How are Administrators Selected?

A very important distinction in the EU administration is between "selection" and "recruitment". It is the various EU institutions and other bodies who actually recruit. However for permanent official Administrator jobs they recruit from lists of eligible candidates who have been "selected" by succeeding in competitions. Most recruitment is via so-called **open competitions**, i.e. competitions that are open to any EU citizen with the relevant qualifications, subject to a few criteria.

> ***Key point***
>
> There are numerous career options in the EU administration. But to become a permanent official, an EU civil servant, now usually involves succeeding in an EPSO open competition.

Open competitions (and some closed internal ones) are run by the **European Personnel Selection Office (EPSO)**. EPSO became operational in 2003 in an effort to make the hitherto fragmented personnel selection procedures of the institutions more consistent, efficient and transparent. EPSO organises competitions for all the EU institutions with the notable exception of the European Central Bank.

There is a way to become a permanent official without taking an EPSO open competition, which is via an **internal competition**. However such internal competitions, open only to people already working in another capacity in the institution concerned, are unpredictable as to when they will occur. Traditionally they have been most frequent in the European Parliament, where they tend to occur a couple of times per mandate and may be organised without the involvement of EPSO. In late 2018, however, the European Commission launched a very large internal competition seeking candidates for a wide spectrum of positions. Despite these exceptions it is true to say that, broadly speaking, the usual direct route nowadays to secure a job as a permanent AD official is through succeeding in an EPSO open competition.

> ***Key point***
>
> EPSO organises competitions for contract agents. However only a limited number of candidates with the right qualifications and experience are invited to the pre-selection tests.

Selection of Contract Agents

The original conception of an EU administration of permanent officials has been eroded with the creation of the category of **Contract Agents for Specific Tasks (CAST)**. These roles in effect have come to substitute for some permanent official posts, providing the institutions with greater flexibility as these roles are not "jobs for life" in the way of permanent officials. However, as contract agents have come to take on ever greater shares of the workload many of these positions have de facto become semi-permanent, with much of the job security and many of the benefits of the permanent officials.

There are two types of CAST posts. So-called **3(b) contract agents** are found in the larger institutions and have contracts of defined duration. They have the advantage of usually being eligible for internal competitions. Type **3(a) contract agents** are usually employed in the agencies and although they may get an indefinite contract after extension they are not able to compete in internal competitions.

EPSO is involved in the selection of contract agents, though its role is very different than in the case of the permanent officials. This is described more fully in chapter 2. Suffice it to say at this point that the CAST competitions organised by EPSO will involve the types of verbal, numerical and abstract reasoning tests covered in this book.

A further category in the EU administration is that of **temporary agents**, of which there are multiple types. Unlike with contract agents, EPSO is not usually involved in their selection, although rare exceptions are possible. Temporary agents may, however, (depending on their category), have the opportunity to participate in internal competitions which can be organised by EPSO on behalf of the institutions, enabling them to become permanent officials.

> ***Key point***
>
> CAST candidates need to receive an invitation from an EU institution and not from EPSO. Many candidates are unaware of this.

The decentralised agencies, employing mainly contract and temporary agents and now found in nearly all Member States, sometimes select staff directly and sometimes make use of EPSO. Vacancies are usually posted on the EPSO website.

EPSO Procedures

The EPSO system has evolved considerably over time, most notably with the establishment of a new system of assessment of reasoning skills and competencies in 2010. This opening chapter gives an outline of the EPSO selection system and what it tests: who can take part in competitions and the rules applying, the skills and competencies that are tested, how the competitions are administered, the language rules, and other practical matters.

Chapter 2 then explains the sequence of competitions step-by-step, looking in more detail at what is tested at each step and how.

The System in Outline

The EPSO system of testing has two primary components.

1. **Computer-based tests using multiple-choice questions (MCQs)**. These typically occur as the first element of testing and include numerical, abstract and verbal reasoning questions as a general rule and sometimes situational judgement tests as well. Linguist tests will also include language comprehension tests. This is what is referred to as the **"pre-selection"** stage.
2. The **Assessment Centre**, where candidates are evaluated by human assessors in a series of planned exercises.

While these are the two primary components the mix of tests between the two will vary from competition to competition and the annual graduate Administrator competition also includes an intermediate test using an e-tray exercise.

Generally speaking, ALL eligible applicants for Administrator profiles, get the chance to take the computer-based MCQs as the first round of testing. There is one notable exception: for specialists these tests are sometimes deferred to the Assessment Centre. In that case some candidates are eliminated before taking any tests. This is done on the basis of a "**Talent Screener**", where the assessors look first at the candidates' relevant experience and qualifications in that specialised area.

Although ratios vary, typically about 3 times the number of successful candidates sought are invited to the Assessment Centre. This means that for the more popular competitions only a small minority will ever make it that far; for some specialised competitions, however, a significant proportion will reach the Assessment Centre.

The system is a complex one and there are variations which are discussed below.

Applications in General

EPSO will not consider any ad hoc applications or CVs that are submitted outside the framework of an official competition, not least because EPSO itself is not recruiting new staff: it "only" selects applicants who can later be hired by EU institutions and bodies. On the other hand, vacancies for non-permanent posts or a limited number of senior positions (Director level and above) that do not require the selection procedure described below are regularly posted on the EPSO website with links to the given agency or body where applications should be submitted directly. (You can find more information about non-permanent jobs below and a list, updated daily, on *http://www.eutraining.eu/eu_jobs.)*

> ***Key point***
>
> EPSO does not recruit; it selects those who are available to be recruited but the actual recruitment is done by the various EU institutions and bodies.

Planning and Transparency

One of the key aims of EPSO is to make selection as transparent as possible by giving more information to candidates about the stages and methodology of the system, along with detailed and timely feedback about the applicants' very own performance in the tests.

It is in this framework that strategic human resource planning is now used in all institutions, meaning that each Directorate General, service or high-level administrative unit must signal a forecast of its staffing needs for the upcoming three or so years. This is to help EPSO to plan competitions and to try to avoid situations, such as used to occur, when a successful laureate received no job offer for months or even years. Planning is further reinforced by analysing employee fluctuations, political developments (e.g. the creation of the European External Action Service) or other factors affecting staff turnover or intake.

Nowadays, while being selected by EPSO is not a guarantee of being recruited, there is a much better match between the numbers of successful candidates and the jobs actually available. The steps you need to take to maximise your chances of getting recruited are covered in our book *Working for the EU : How to Get In* (see page 1 above).

Increasing transparency is an ongoing effort that includes disclosing the names of Selection Board members, communicating test results and Assessment Centre reports to candidates and helping candidates plan their preparation efforts by providing a relatively precise timeline of exam schedules.

Skills vs. Knowledge

The most significant element in the current selection system is the shift from the old pre-2010 system of testing knowledge about the EU institutions and policies to an emphasis on **reasoning skills (psychometric tests) and competencies ("soft skills")**. Broadly speaking, reasoning skills are tested in the first pre-selection phase of competitions and the competencies at the final Assessment Centre stage. The reasoning tests are of three types, verbal reasoning, numerical reasoning and abstract reasoning, which are described in full later in this book.

EPSO has created a **competency framework** against which candidates are evaluated. This is to assess the all round suitability of candidates to the EU working environment, alongside any specific skills they need for the particular job profile. The weight given to these general "core competencies" varies by competition and is greatest for generalist roles. The testing of competencies is mainly at the Assessment Centre but this may also be done to some degree at pre-selection in the form of situational judgement tests, also covered in this book.

Core Competencies

According to EPSO, the following are considered as core competencies (which are required for all profiles independent of the competition):

- **Analysis and Problem Solving** – Identifies the critical facts in complex issues and develops creative and practical solutions
- **Communicating** – Communicates clearly and precisely both orally and in writing
- **Delivering Quality and Results** – Takes personal responsibility and initiative for delivering work to a high standard of quality within set procedures
- **Learning and Development** – Develops and improves personal skills and knowledge of the organisation and its environment
- **Prioritising and Organising** – Prioritises the most important tasks, works flexibly and organises own workload efficiently
- **Resilience** – Remains effective under a heavy workload, handles organisational frustrations positively and adapts to a changing work environment
- **Working with Others** – Works co-operatively with others in teams and across

organisational boundaries and respects differences between people

- **Leadership** – Manages, develops and motivates people to achieve results (only for Administrator grades)

For senior or management-level posts (usually AD9 and above), one or two further competencies may be identified for specific job profiles or competitions, depending on the analysis of the given position. The above general competencies are always tested by two different exercises to ensure their validity and reliability as organisational psychologists and human resource experts have created a specific method to ensure the above quality criteria. (For more details on what each competency means and how it is measured, see *The Ultimate EU Test Book Assessment Centre 2019*.)

Duration

EPSO has tried to streamline and professionalise the selection procedure as much as possible. This in practice means that instead of being on an ad hoc basis, competitions are in principle announced each year on a regular, cyclical basis (although other factors sometimes prevent this), complemented by exams for specialists based on a need basis. The annual cycles usually start with the announcement of the major generalist (graduate) **Administrator** competition in March, followed by the publication of competitions for **linguists** (AD and AST) around July, and closing with the call for application of **Assistants** in November or December. It is essential to check the EPSO website for the latest information on the schedule as changes in policy or priorities may always happen and smaller scale/specialist competitions may be announced at any time. EPSO publishes a table on its website showing upcoming competitions as well as those already announced.

Each cycle is theoretically intended to be completed within a year from announcement until the publication of the reserve list, though in practice the timescale is usually longer. In reality a typical AD competition lasts thirteen or fourteen months from beginning (Notice of Competition) to end (Reserve

The 2018 Graduate (Generalist) Administrator Schedule step by step

March 2018

Notice of competition

↓

June/July 2018

Pre-selection tests

↓

October 2018

Intermediate Test

↓

January/February 2019

Assessment Centre

↓

May 2019 (Estimated)

Reserve List

↓

Recruitment

List). Of course, actual recruitment takes longer still. However, it is possible to plan ahead your preparation as it is fairly clear what type of competition is to be announced and when. The chart on page 6 shows the timings for the 2018 AD5 generalist competition, the biggest AD competition of the year.

On a related note, it is advisable to focus your efforts exclusively on preparing for the next upcoming competition phase (pre-selection reasoning tests or Assessment Centre competency tests) and not the entire procedure as such from the very beginning. This book accordingly concentrates on the pre-selection phase while the very different tests used at the Assessment Centre are covered in *The Ultimate EU Test Book Assessment Centre 2019*.

Soon-to-be Graduates Welcome

The "cut-off date", meaning the date by which a candidate must meet all eligibility criteria, especially that of possessing a degree or other qualification, is often moved to a later specified date instead of the application deadline for a given competition. This is true for most of the Administrator and AD linguist exams. However, always check this requirement in the Notice of Competition to ensure that you are eligible for the competition.

Take a practical example. Let's say EPSO announces a competition in March 2019. The way the system works means that if you are a graduating student and you expect to receive your degree in June 2019 but the EPSO exam, where a university degree is a pre-requisite, has its application deadline in April, you can still apply, as long as the degree is obtained by the time of the date specified. The rationale behind this is to offer soon-to-be graduates the opportunity to apply in their last year of studies, thus broadening the scope of the candidate pool.

Candidates with Special Needs

European Union institutions have always been keen to respect the principles of equal opportunities and non-discrimination given this policy's pivotal place in the EU Member States' legislation and obviously inside the institutions themselves. Therefore in the EU selection procedure candidates with special needs, such as seriously limited eyesight, physical disability or other issues that require adaptation in the test centres, should notify EPSO well in advance to make sure that both their access to the testing and the scoring of their exams are adapted to their condition. Supervised one-on-one tests or other measures may exceptionally also be made available to encourage such candidates to apply.

Chances of Succeeding

An obvious basic question for candidates is *"what are my chances of succeeding?"*

There are two factors of supply and demand involved in answering this question.

The first factor, the demand, is **the number of successful candidates EPSO is looking for**. The driver of this is the institutions. After a period of buoyant growth, largely due to the accession of 12

> ***Key point***
>
> Around 20 percent of Commission staff are 55 or older. Because of the numbers coming up to retirement age, the institutions need to keep recruiting just to stand still.

Key point

You can often increase your chances by applying for a more specialised competition where the number of candidates relative to the number of posts available is lower.

new Member States in 2004/2007, staff numbers were subject to a theoretical 5% cut in the period 2013-17 as the EU came under pressure from the Member States to control its spending. In practice, however, total staff levels remained almost unchanged as recruitment for some specific tasks like Croatian accession added headcount. And of course even during that period competitions continued as new types of post were created, people retired or moved on and had to be replaced, etc. While downward pressures on budgets continue, this underlying need to continue recruiting will remain.

However, while aggregate demand is one thing, the detail at the level of specific job profiles is another. One year might have a large competition to select specialists in a particular field, or translators for a particular language, and another none at all for those profiles. The numbers sought in such competitions can also vary widely, depending on the needs of the institutions.

Competition	Reference	No. of successful candidates sought	No. of applications
AD5 Irish language translators	EPSO/AD/361/18	72	190
AD5 Italian language translators	EPSO/AD/345/17	14	2332
AD7 Irish language lawyer-linguists	EPSO/AD/350/17	8	26
AD6 Food Safety Policy and Legislation	EPSO/AD/341/18	35	799
AD5 Graduate 2018	EPSO/AD/356/18	158	22,666
AD7 Financial Economics	EPSO/AD/339/17-1	55	905
AD7 Spanish language lawyer-linguists	EPSO/AD/332/16	8	619
AD6 Building Management Engineers	EPSO/AD/342/17	24	1044
AD5 Administrators in the Field of Audit	EPSO/AD/357/18	80	4755
AD6 Administrators in the Field of Data Protection	EPSO/AD/360/18	30	970

Key point

Numbers for very specialised competitions can be very small. For example, the 2017 AD7 Irish lawyer-linguists competition had only 26 applications for 8 reserve list positions. But of course the more specialised the competition, the more likely it is that most of the candidates will be highly qualified in that specific field.

The second factor is the **supply of candidates.** This is influenced by such considerations as the strength of the job market in the different Member States and the level of specialisation required. By definition, an AD5 competition open to graduates with no prior experience from any of the Member States is going to attract more applications than a competition for nuclear specialists, or for lawyer-linguists in the Finnish language.

The table on page 8 shows the relationship between the number of successful candidates sought by EPSO and the number of completed applications in some recent or ongoing Administrator competitions. As you can see, most competitions attract a large number of applicants relative to the number of successful candidates sought.

However while most EPSO competitions are intensely competitive, some are not, and a few can be categorised as distinctly uncompetitive because of the obscurity of the profile being selected. Look at the figures in the table for the 2018 competition for AD5 Irish-language translators. This competition sought 72 successful candidates but (despite the deadline being extended) attracted only 190 applications. Compare that to the 2017 AD5 for Italian-language translators where only 14 successful candidates were sought but there were 2332 applications!

Most likely few of the candidates for the Italian-language competition had an alternative option. But if you do have one, you should be aware of it. Imagine you are an Italian native speaker who also has a very good command of Maltese and there are competitions for both languages. In an EPSO competition your nationality is not relevant so you can apply for either. Your first instinct might be to choose the Italian-language competition, simply because it is your native language. However, the EU has a similar need for Italian and Maltese language translators but there are 127 Italians for every 1 Maltese. It is obviously the case, therefore, that there will be many more Italian candidates and you would be better off choosing the Maltese competition.

As a general rule, the more specialised the competition the better your chances of success. There is one main proviso to that statement, however. It is also the case that the more specialised the competition, the more likely it is that the other candidates will be highly qualified in that specific field and also highly motivated. In contrast, for example, you can be sure that for a big competition like the AD5 graduate, open to all-comers, a lot of the candidates will simply be "having a go" and poorly prepared. Indeed, a proportion will not even turn up to the pre-selection tests (which are usually held on a weekday, but occasionally on Saturdays) if they decide their chances are not good enough for it to be worth taking a day off from work or other pursuits.

5476 of the people who completed the first part of the application form for the 2018 AD5 graduate competition never finished the second part, meaning nearly 20% dropped out at the very first hurdle!

Beyond that, of course, comes the issue of preparation. Where there are two candidates of potentially equal ability, the one who is best prepared, who has practised for the tests and understands what the examiners are looking for, will be the one who wins out.

You must therefore always consider carefully which competition profile to apply for. For example, if you have a qualification in human resource management and relevant professional experience, you can sit both an Assistant exam and also an Administrator exam (if your qualification is a university degree), and may also be eligible for a specialist competition if that fits your profile.

Another aspect to consider is the **long-term repercussions of your choice**: not only will your competition profile determine the required professional knowledge but it will also affect your recruitment prospects once placed on the reserve list. It is for obvious reasons that EPSO creates sub-profiles and specialist profiles in the selection process: if an expert on environment law is sought, those on a lawyers' reserve list may have better chances of being offered a job than those on a Public Administration list (though this is not a formal rule and depends a lot on other external and individual factors as well). Important to note, however, is that de facto *anyone* can be recruited from ANY reserve list as long as their personal profile and the function group (Secretary, Assistant or Administrator) matches the specific vacancy's requirements, though EU

Key point

Moving from Assisstant to Administrator grades is not a straightforward matter. So be careful about taking an AST competition if you are really set on an Administrator job.

institutions try to respect an internal policy of not "poaching" candidates from other reserve lists than the one from which they are meant to recruit.

What is also important to bear in mind is that **the hierarchical division into Administrators and Assistants is quite rigid**. The EU administration is nothing like a private sector company where talented individuals can be fast tracked out of one type of job into another on a quickly moving escalator. Everything to do with promotions and career progress follows very defined rules. Although there is a procedure for moving from AST to AD, known as "certification", this is by no means straightforward. So if your goal is to get an Administrator job be cautious about taking an Assistant competition just because you think it will be easier. Note also that, for Assistant competitions, EPSO may require specific qualifications among the "essential selection criteria" and this may prove an obstacle to passing such a competition.

Deciding on which profile to sit is therefore a tough decision for many, given its repercussions on the chances to succeed. Nevertheless, *you can apply for an unlimited number of competitions* (provided the Notice of Competition does not specifically exclude this). **Candidates are often not aware that they can apply for multiple profiles** so do be alert to this possibility. As long as you are aware of these aspects, you can evaluate the position better for yourself – this will, in fact, be your first numerical reasoning practice exercise!

Feedback and Complaints

When discussing feedback and complaints, it must be borne in mind that given the significant number of candidates, both are handled in an automated way in the first place until human intervention is required.

Feedback (on test results) is only given in an automated format for the pre-selection phase while those who take part in an Assessment Centre are given more comprehensive feedback in the form of a written report called a **competency passport**, which is provided for everyone regardless of whether they passed or failed (see below for more on this). EPSO also often requests feedback online or immediately after the computer-based test on screen, so as to improve its procedures.

Only well founded and serious complaints can be taken into account by the Selection Board, for the above reasons. This also means that individual cases are always examined by the Selection Board or exceptionally by EPSO as a body. Moreover, complaints can only concern the lack of respect for the exam rules or other administrative procedures and they can hardly ever relate to "revision" of the scores or exam results. As an example, if you missed the pass mark by one point, you cannot argue in favour of leniency or flexibility unless there was an error in one of the exam questions and it must be "neutralised" for all candidates (more on this below). Another scenario when your complaint may be substantiated is when an exam rule was not respected, e.g. your relevant qualification was not accepted by the Selection Board even though the issuing university is accredited and recognised by your Member State.

As mentioned above, the first place to lodge a complaint with is the Selection Board where strict deadlines apply (usually within 10 days from the communication of the results), but both the Ombudsman and ultimately, the Civil Service Tribunal may deal with the case. While the Ombudsman can only deal with "maladministration" (this term refers to a situation when an EU institution or body fails to respect the exam rules or procedures – as opposed to individual exam results or evaluations of the Selection

Board), the EU Civil Service Tribunal does examine individual cases on their merits but acts only as a second level judicial review body after the Selection Board has refused your formal complaint. It must nevertheless be borne in mind that these are long and cumbersome procedures that are only worth the effort if you are truly and reasonably convinced that you have been discriminated against or that your application's treatment can be challenged on legal grounds.

Another important aspect is that regardless of any failed efforts to pass the exams you can, as mentioned above, apply for new competitions without any limitations. If you do not pass an exam, EPSO does not retain your scores or keep a file on your results, therefore *you can start with a "clean slate" if you decide to have another go at passing the exams*, and you may even apply in parallel for multiple competitions (provided you meet the eligibility criteria and there is no clause in the Notice of Competition forbidding this).

The Selection Boards

Selection Boards have traditionally been composed of EU officials who volunteer to take part in such tasks. Their background, motivation and interests vary greatly which ensures objective and fair treatment based on strict guidelines that each of them must follow. Selection Boards, including most assessors, are still chosen from among volunteering active and even retired personnel, though some expertise, especially in developing multiple choice tests and administering the exams in various locations around the world, is now provided by external contractors. EPSO has been trying to professionalise the Selection Boards by extending the scope of their members' assignments for several months or even years instead of using them on an ad hoc basis, thus ensuring the accumulation of more insight and knowledge on their part, and also by providing proper training before their assignment commences.

Members of the Selection Boards generally perform the entire administration of an exam while being independent from EPSO and, legally speaking, they are the ones who are solely responsible for the administration of a competition and not EPSO. Each competition has its own Selection Board, which takes on tasks such as preparing the tests, admitting candidates on the basis of their files or marking the exercises. In a case brought before the European Court of Justice, a candidate in the 2010 Administrator exam challenged the Selection Board's ability to control and supervise the computer-based tests created and run by an external company. He won the case, requiring a re-run of the 2010 Administrator exams in 2013. This case demonstrates the importance of the Selection Board and their duty to supervise all elements of the competition.

You, of course, may never approach a Selection Board member for any additional information other than that formally communicated to you, even though the board members' names are always made public on EPSO's website for reasons of transparency. Some candidates think that a quick online search to find the professional background of board members could help identify their favourite topics (e.g. if a member works in DG Competition of the European Commission, it may have some bearing on the questions they ask), though this is rarely the case especially since the Assessment Centres have a very different approach in testing candidates.

Venues and Costs

The **pre-selection** exams take place all over Europe and in several other locations around the world. Where citizens of all Member States are eligible for a competition (which is the normal situation), there will be exam centres in each country's capital, and in case of bigger countries, also in other large cities.

As almost all exams under the EPSO system are administered on computers, exams

> ### Key point
>
> Pre-selection tests can be taken in your home country, at your own expense. Assessment Centre tests are usually in Brussels and your expenses are paid.

are generally held over a certain period of time at the designated centres.

Candidates are required to pick and book a date and venue online that suits them most within this period, though you must be very careful in your first choice as revisions or changes are almost never allowed after the booking period is over (the very few exceptions may include issues such as childbirth or medical events).

After you validate your application (i.e. submit it formally online), you then have to wait until EPSO closes the application period and opens the booking period. Both these phases have strict timescales. The minute the booking period is opened, be sure to sign up as soon as possible given that the most popular places and time slots tend to fill up fast, and to avoid any last minute internet blackout or server crash that may prevent you from securing your place in time.

No contribution is made by EPSO towards any travelling or subsistence expenses associated with the pre-selection phase of the exam. As these exams take place in your own country or at multiple venues elsewhere in the world, travelling from your home to these centres is always on your own budget.

For the assessment phase, you will be given a specific date some time in advance with limited or no option to amend it unless compelling events prevent you from attending and you can duly justify the reason.

Assessment Centres are located centrally in Brussels though exceptionally and only for lawyer-linguists, there is an Assessment Centre in Luxembourg too. Candidates who need to travel there are reimbursed for their travel costs and also given a daily subsistence allowance for hotel and food costs. The specific rules are always communicated in advance either as early as in the Notice of Competition or later to those who actually make it through to the assessment phase. The underlying principle is that nobody should suffer any disadvantage in attending the competitions due to budgetary issues. The same rule of equal opportunities applies for those flying in or travelling to a specific job interview unless a telephone or videoconference is a feasible alternative.

Motivation

Before applying, it is useful to reflect on what factors motivate you in wanting to work for an EU institution. Usually it is a mixture of various considerations – such as the desire to work on international affairs in a multicultural environment, belief in European integration, the opportunity to travel, getting an attractive salary and benefits, having an interesting and varied job, speaking and learning foreign languages, job security etc.

Being aware of which factors are the most important for you personally can help in identifying which profile to apply for – and it should also help in the structured interview, if you get to the Assessment Centre, when assessors try to find out more about your personality. "Being part of something larger than yourself" is a vital aspect that you may also emphasise in your application's motivation section. Also on this topic, for the 2018 AD5 generalist (graduate) competition EPSO introduced an "EU Motivation Interview" at the Assessment Centre, to assess candidates' commitment to the "European idea".

The Candidates

It is very hard, if not impossible, to outline a "typical" candidate profile given the large number and diverse backgrounds of applicants. However, I have formed the impression that most of the serious applicants have some key things in common. They:

- Are interested in EU affairs, committed to European integration and wish to work for a "good cause"
- Are flexible and willing to work abroad in a multi-cultural environment
- Have a strong motivation to study for and pass the exams to get into the EU institutions
- Understand and accept that EU institutions are different from the private sector inasmuch as they are a hybrid of a diplomatic corps, an international organisation and a government administration that is based on a hierarchic model

The above qualities will also be looked at by assessors if only on an indirect or informal level. EU institutions deal with such a wide variety of issues that you can certainly find the job that best suits your interests and personality if your motivation is right.

There is no minimum age as such for candidates, this in effect being determined by the requirement of a degree/diploma or work experience. Obviously the EU is keen on ensuring a level playing field in terms of candidates' backgrounds, ensuring equal opportunities for all based on merit, regardless of whether they belong to any particular religious, sexual, ethnic or other minority, social segment or age group.

Whatever your age, you will be required to pass a medical check that will serve as a benchmark for your social security and health insurance file before taking up an EU job. This also serves to ensure that you are physically capable of doing the job you are to be required to perform.

Quotas

It is frequently asked whether the EU institutions apply a quota system for allocating posts to a certain number of officials from each Member State. This is a somewhat delicate issue given that EU civil servants work for the EU not for their national governments so in theory their nationality should be irrelevant. In practice however the situation is rather different.

In fact, the Staff Regulations, the legal document that lays down the conditions of employment of staff in the EU institutions, provide that officials are to be "recruited on the broadest possible geographical basis from among nationals of Member States of the Union". This reference to "the broadest possible geographical basis" explains the special competitions in recent years e.g. to select candidates exclusively from Croatia based on their recent accession to the EU, but such targeted competitions are the exception, not the rule.

> ### *Key point*
>
> Eight countries were identified, because of their under-representation, as "focus countries" for EPSO communication efforts for the 2018 AD5 generalist (graduate) competition. These were the Czech Republic, Denmark, France, Germany, Ireland, Netherlands, Poland and Sweden.

Apart from such special circumstances, where new Member States are starting from a base of zero, the "broadest possible geographical basis" provision in practice means there is an ongoing effort to maintain an allocation of posts that more-or-less reflects the proportion of each Member State's population in the EU as a whole. This is true for all grades, including senior management. Yet, despite this principle, there are no hard-coded quotas for Irish or Cypriot or any other citizens given the merit-based competition system. Natural imbalances therefore always exist and they could only be challenged by the introduction of specific staff allocations, which would then likely infringe upon the principle of non-discrimination based on nationality. This is certainly not an easy issue to handle politically as it touches on the very essence of the principles guiding European integration.

An issue that is likely to come to the fore in the coming years is the under-representation of the older (EU-15) Member States among younger officials in the AD5-8 bracket. As older officials, where the EU-15 are over-represented retire, this imbalance will transfer itself up the ranks as time goes by.

Languages of the candidates for the 2018 Graduate Administrators competition

Languages Declared at B2 level or above (percentages), in rank order

English	97.86
French	51.30
Spanish	27.98
Italian	26.73
German	19.33
Greek	10.50
Dutch	8.40
Romanian	6.80
Portuguese	5.04
Polish	3.89
Bulgarian	3.12
Croatian	2.58
Hungarian	2.12
Czech	1.75
Swedish	1.65
Slovakian	1.34
Lithuanian	1.28
Finnish	1.12
Slovenian	0.99
Danish	0.89
Latvian	0.60
Gaelic (Irish)	0.41
Estonian	0.39
Maltese	0.34

Language Rules

Generally speaking, other than for linguist competitions, you will be asked for knowledge of two official languages: one at C1 level (thorough knowledge) and one at a minimum of B2 level (satisfactory knowledge). **These are your so-called language 1 and language 2.**

The levels are defined in the "Common European Framework of Reference for Languages".

One of the most common misunderstandings regarding EU competitions is the exact meaning of your first and second language. In practice the term "language 1" usually but not necessarily means your mother tongue, *as long as it is an official EU language*. The reason why this latter point needs to be emphasised is because a Lithuanian candidate, for example, may have Russian as their mother tongue but that cannot be offered as their language 1 choice since it is not an official EU language.

In some cases, especially for enlargement-related or linguist exams, the candidate's citizenship or the given competition's specific language profile automatically determines the required first language. Examples would be competitions for Croatian Administrators and Assistants requiring the first language to be Croatian; or having French as the compulsory first language for translator exams in the French language. In other instances you are free to choose your language 1 as long as the above rules on citizenship and the official EU language requirements are respected. Thus, for instance, if you have Luxembourgish citizenship, your "first language" may well be French or German as Luxembourgish is not an official EU language.

It is important to note that "mother tongue" can also mean that if you have a perfect command of a language that you "learned" – and if you are confident that your speaking and writing is close to perfect in that language, you can indicate it as your first language. For example, if your citizenship is Slovak but

Competition	Reference	2nd language requirement	Notes
Administrators (AD 7) in 1. Financial economics 2. Macroeconomics	EPSO/AD/339/17	English, French or German	
AD5 Graduate Administrators 2018	EPSO/AD/356/18	1 of the 5 languages selected (the 5 declared by most candidates, subject to the needs of the service)	See the first "Key point" on page 16! You must declare a minimum of 2 languages at stage 1 of the application. You can ONLY complete part 2 of the application if you have declared one of the 5 selected languages
AD5 Administrators in the Field of Audit	EPSO/AD/357/18	English or French	
AD7 in 1. Customs, 2. Taxation	EPSO/AD/363/18	English or French	
AD6 Building Management Engineers	EPSO/AD/342/17	English, French, German	
AD6 Food Safety Policy and Legislation	EPSO/AD/341/18	English, French, German, Italian	The European Food Standards Agency is in Italy and agencies will use local languages as well as the EU working languages.
AD6 Administrators in the Field of Data protection	EPSO/AD/360/18	English or French	

you speak Greek perfectly, and you wish to apply for an exam where one of the first language choices is Greek, feel free to do so. But bear in mind that your second language must also be at a high level.

Language 2 is in fact normally your first foreign language. Traditionally you have only been allowed to choose between English, French or German. However following a ruling by the European Court of Justice (which actually led to the cancellation of the AD5 generalist competition in 2016) EPSO is now offering in the generalist competition as language 2 the five languages most frequently declared by candidates at B2 level or higher in the first part of their application form for the competition in question (meaning it can vary from one competition to another).

The first time this new procedure was applied, for the 2017 AD5 generalist competition (EPSO/AD/338/17) the following 5 languages were declared by the most people: English, French, Spanish, Italian and German (in that order, from highest to lowest number), which was as might have been expected. Exactly the same happened in the 2018 competition (see table on page 14).

How this rule will be applied in future is uncertain because for the most recent Secretaries/Clerks competition more candidates actually declared Greek than German as one of their languages. However, it is worth pointing out that the Notice of Competition in this case (as in others) states that while EPSO intends to offer as language 2 "the 5 languages most frequently declared by candidates" this would be only *"while also taking into account the needs of the service"*. Therefore there is discretion in deciding which languages will be treated as language 2 – and it seems unlikely, for instance, that this would ever be interpreted as meaning that the Assessment Centre should be offered in Greek.

For linguist exams the second language is usually the one for which candidates are sought. For example, if EPSO announces a linguist exam for Bulgarian translators, the first language is required to be Bulgarian, the second language would likely be English, French or German, with a third language (in fact, second foreign language) requirement as well. Note that there is no requirement of Bulgarian citizenship as the goal is perfect command of a language regardless of which EU citizenship you may have. This is a fundamental rule in the system: the citizenship requirement is almost always decoupled from the language requirements.

> ### *Key point*
>
> For the AD5 graduate competition (as of 2018) you have in the first stage of the application process to declare a minimum of 2 languages. These can be ANY of the official languages. EPSO then says what the 5 most-declared languages are (with a proviso that this must be subject to the needs of the service) and you can ONLY proceed further in the competition if your language 2 is among those 5. In other words, there is no point in declaring Estonian and Lithuanian, or Croatian and Portuguese, as your 2 languages in part 1 because none of those will ever qualify as a language 2.

EPSO now provides for abstract reasoning, verbal reasoning and numerical reasoning tests to be done in your first language. This shows that the aim of such tests is not to test your linguistic knowledge but to assess your psychometric reasoning skills. Situational judgement tests and other tests (e.g. domain specific tests for specialists, Assessment Centre exercises and others), however, are in language 2 and as these are linguistically very demanding your language 2 has to be very good.

Once recruited, AD level officials will also need to demonstrate their ability to work in a second foreign language (their "third language") before their first promotion. The language 3 level required of existing officials is, however, in practice fairly unexacting compared to the language 2 requirements of candidates in EPSO competitions.

Another crucial piece of advice to bear in mind is that once you know which language you will be assessed in (i.e. the choice for language 2; in case of linguists/interpreters, your first language will also be tested), read all preparation materials only in that/those language(s). Needless to say, French, German and all other names of EU institutions, abbreviations, programmes and concepts may differ significantly from each other, and you certainly do not wish to mix up the European Council with the Council of Europe because of a language issue.

> ### *Key point*
>
> Your language 1 will most likely be your native language – but it doesn't have to be, and in some cases it might not be the best option. Imagine your native language is French but you have a good command of German and you are entering a competition where either can be chosen as language 2. You might decide to do the pre-selection tests in German and keep your native language for the Assessment Centre, where more sophisticated and interactive linguistic skills are required.

	Administrators (AD)	Linguists (AD)	Assistants (AST) Secretaries (AST-SC)	Specialists (AD or AST)
Minimum Qualification	Degree (min. BA level or 3 years of studies, EPSO may require it to be related to the chosen sub-profile, e.g. Audit)	Degree (min. BA level or 3 years of studies)	Relevant high school diploma or post-secondary qualification (a minimum of 3 years study-related work might also be required)	Same as for ASTs and ADs
Work Experience	None (AD5); 3 years (AD6); 6 years (AD7); 12 years (AD9) (exception: see Specialists' column)	None (AD5); 6 years (AD7); 12 years (AD9)	None to 3 or 6 years, depending on the qualification (AST3 and above and SC1 and SC2 unless relevant diploma available)	Same as for ASTs and ADs (with possible exceptions, e.g. AD7 lawyer-linguists may need only 3 years of work experience instead of 6). Experience required may also depend on qualifications
Type of Qualification (in many cases, though not always, qualifications are eliminatory, so make sure to read EPSO's Notice of Competition carefully)	Arts, Law, Economics, Political Science, Statistics etc.	Language Studies, Interpreting	Clerical Studies, Arts, Finances, IT, Technical skills etc.	Lawyers, Linguists, Engineers, Scientists, Doctors, Veterinaries, etc.

Important note: the terminology relating to qualifications varies greatly from country to country – what is called a "degree" in one country is a "diploma" in another, and so forth. For a country-by-country list of what EPSO regards as examples of qualifications corresponding to those required by the Notices of Competition, see http://europa.eu/epso/doc/diplomes-fortheweb_en.pdf

Please note that the above table is for information purposes only and the actual requirements may differ; please always consult EPSO's official communications for up-to-date information

Formal Criteria

As a candidate applying for EU exams, you must meet certain formal (objective) criteria. These, as a general rule, say you must:

- Be a citizen of a Member State of the European Union (though exceptions might occur as in the case of enlargement-related competitions)
- Be entitled to full rights as such a citizen (e.g. no legal limitations as a result of criminal acts or other issues) and meet the character requirements for the duties involved
- Have fulfilled any obligations imposed by the laws on military service (only relevant for those Member States where such service is compulsory, and even there you may prove that you were exempted from the service)

Key point

The "minimum qualifications" in the table above can be a bit misleading. Most Assistants these days will have college degrees and the majority (but by no means all) of newly appointed AD5s will have post-graduate degrees.

- Have a thorough knowledge of one of the official languages of the European Union and a satisfactory knowledge of a second (this is the minimum requirement but further linguistic prerequisites may be set out in the given Notice of Competition as also mentioned above)
- Have the sufficient minimum education and/or work experience as set out in the Notice of Competition (see the table on page 17)

These formal criteria are required for ALL profiles, regardless of the specific provisions of the competition; if you do not meet the eligibility criteria and this is discovered later you will be disqualified however well you do in the tests.

Choosing a Profile

Choosing a profile is determined by both objective and subjective factors: depending on your qualifications and work experience (which are "objective" facts you cannot change overnight), you may be limited to only one "choice"; it may nevertheless happen that you are formally eligible for multiple profiles and it remains your individual choice which one to sit for. For example, a lawyer with three years' experience and fluent knowledge of three languages would potentially be eligible for a whole range of profiles. In that case the choice would be determined by career aspirations and perhaps the relative chances of success in different competitions.

Multiple Applications

A general approach taken by many candidates is to apply for all competitions they are eligible for, this way increasing their chances. This is also an excellent way to practice the tests you need to pass and it is a highly recommended strategy. You should, however, be very careful not to apply for two competitions in parallel that are mutually exclusive and you should not create two accounts (profiles) on EPSO's website, because this will lead to disqualification from the competition.

Such rules are usually indicated in the Notice of Competition and are limited to the sub-profiles of a given exam. Thus an Administrator (AD5) competition in the annual cycle may have multiple domains such as Public Administration, Law, Economics, Audit, Finance and Statistics, where candidates are required to pick only one of these options. Apart from the risk of being disqualified from both, it is also technically impossible to choose two domains at the same time given the features of the online application form. If in doubt whether you may run parallel applications for different competitions (for example an AD or AST exam and a specialist exam), better to ask EPSO than lose out on both counts.

2. Administrator Competitions Step by Step

Introduction

Having looked at the principles and procedures of EPSO competitions, we can now move on to the specific phases of the competitions in more detail.

For the AD5 generalist (graduate) competition the phases are:

1. Notice of Competition, Self-Assessment, Registration
2. Pre-selection Phase (first round of exams)
3. Intermediate test
4. Assessment Centre (second full round of exams)
5. Reserve List, Recruitment

The various phases can look different depending on the competition. For linguists, for example, phase 3 would be translation tests, while the sequence for specialists can be different because of the use of the Talent Screener.

Below we provide an outline of each of the stages and tests, along with some practical advice. Later chapters in this book provide very detailed coverage and practice materials for the critical pre-selection phase.

On the next two pages you will find charts showing the tests used at each stage of competitions for some sample profiles. Bear in mind these are just samples and you will need to check the Notice of Competition for the exact tests use at each stage in your competition.

Phase 1: Notice of Competition, Self-Assessment, Registration, Talent Screener

The Notice of Competition

The Notice of Competition (NoC) is a special administrative notice addressed to all EU citizens and it is therefore published in the Official Journal of the EU (EUR-Lex) both in print and online. It is important to underline that the NoC is the only official source of information, therefore if you see any contradicting or different interpretation in the

Sample AD5 Graduate Administrator Competition

PRE-SELECTION

Verbal reasoning
Numerical reasoning
Abstract reasoning
Situational judgement

↓

INTERMEDIATE TEST

E-tray exercise

↓

ASSESSMENT CENTRE

Oral presentation
Case study
Group exercise
Competency based interview
Motivation interview

↓

RESERVE LIST

Sample AD6/AD7 Specialist Competition

PRE-SELECTION

(a) if number of applications above threshold set by EPSO

Verbal reasoning
Numerical reasoning
Abstract reasoning

(b) If below threshold, these tests will be at the Assessment Centre

↓

TALENT SCREENER

Comes first if (b) above applies

↓

ASSESSMENT CENTRE

Case study
Group exercise
Competency based interview
Interview in the field

↓

RESERVE LIST

Sample AD5 Translators Competition

PRE-SELECTION

Verbal reasoning
Numerical reasoning
Abstract reasoning
Language comprehension (languages 2 and 3)
Main language skills (language 1)

↓

TRANSLATION TEST

Language 2 to 1
Language 3 to 1

↓

ASSESSMENT CENTRE

Oral presentation
Group exercise
Competency based interview

↓

RESERVE LIST

Sample AD7 Lawyer-Linguist Competition

PRE-SELECTION

Verbal reasoning
Numerical reasoning
Abstract reasoning
Language comprehension (language 2)

↓

TRANSLATION TEST

Legal text from language 2 to 1

↓

ASSESSMENT CENTRE

Oral presentation
Group exercise
Competency based interview
Field specific competencies

↓

RESERVE LIST

AD 5 is the grade at which graduates begin their careers as administrators in the European institutions. Administrators recruited at this grade can undertake, under supervision, three main types of work in the institutions: policy formulation, operational delivery, and resource management. We are particularly looking for candidates with a potential for career development.

The general role of administrators is to support decision-makers in fulfilling the mission of their institution or body.

Their main duties, which may vary from one institution to another, include:

- devising, implementing, monitoring and control of programmes and action plans,
- managing resources including staff, finances, and equipment,
- assisting decision-makers by means of written or oral contributions,
- drafting policy analysis briefings,
- external communication as well as internal reporting and communication,
- relations with external stakeholders and with the Member States,
- inter-service and inter-institutional coordination and consultation regarding policy,
- coordinating working groups set up by the Member States, the institutions and other external stakeholders,
- drafting contracts, preparing calls for proposals and invitations to tender, and participating in evaluation committees for monitoring selection procedures and the allocation of proposals.

press or on a website, make sure to check the original authentic source which is always referenced on EPSO's website.

The NoC is a rather extensive document that sets out all the formal eligibility criteria, language requirements, deadlines and other practical arrangements linked to the competition. Just as important, the NoC contains a wealth of information that you can use to your benefit by reading it attentively, such as the size of the reserve list (so you can estimate your chances and thus decide which sub-profile or domain to apply for).

The basic "job description", also detailed in the NoC, is particularly interesting as it is not only an indication of what sort of tasks you would need to carry out once employed; from it you can also deduce lots of hints about the topics to cover when preparing for the domain-specific parts of the assessment phase, especially the case study.

Above, by way of illustration, are extracts from a **Notice of Competition for a generalist Administrator competition**, where the main aspects of the role are described.

It is crucial to understand and analyse every detail provided in the NoC. This will also help you avoid seemingly evident pitfalls that might lead to disqualification (such as a requirement to submit a certain certificate or sign a submitted document) – you would be surprised to know how many people get rejected on formal grounds by accidentally overlooking a date, a provision or a prerequisite.

Self-Assessment

Self-assessment as a tool is widely used in international organisations and multinational private sector companies and EPSO makes use of it as well. The objective is to ensure candidates realise what EU jobs are really about and dispel misconceptions at the earliest stage. This is intended to reduce non-eligible applications and candidate frustration.

Self-assessment, which is not to be confused with the Talent Screener used for specialists, is non-eliminatory, meaning that you cannot pass or fail based on your answers.

> **Key point**
>
> Competitions are often heavily oversubscribed. The incentive for EPSO is to reduce numbers to manageable proportions. Don't give grounds to be thrown out of a competition just because you made a careless mistake in your application form.

Registration and Application

Registration is done exclusively online on the EPSO (EU Careers) website at the start of the procedure. The first step is to create an **EPSO account or profile**, which is an online personal profile where your correspondence with EPSO will take place. If you change your postal or e-mail address during the procedure or any other contact information becomes obsolete, make sure to update your online account immediately.

If, after registration, the confirmation e-mail does not arrive in your inbox within a few hours, check your spam or bulk mail folder as it may have been misfiled by your e-mail application; should you still not receive anything, ask EPSO for technical assistance. Make sure, however, that you do not register twice as it may lead to potential disqualification if other signs show you had second thoughts when doing so.

What you need to do at the application stage will depend on your competition. Confirming your eligibility for the competition (e.g. your citizenship, level of education achieved) and declaring your language 1 and language 2 is standard, but other aspects do vary. As with everything to do with EPSO competitions, you have to carefully observe the rules laid down in the Notice of Competition.

If you are entering an **AD5 generalist competition** the application process is straightforward because every eligible candidate will be invited to the pre-selection computer-based testing. You only have to make sure that the information you provide is accurate because if it isn't you may end up being disqualified from the competition through sheer carelessness. You can also submit your application in your language 1.

For **linguist competitions** you will have to complete your application form in language 2 and may also have to provide additional information relevant to the competition but, assuming you are eligible, you can expect to be called to the pre-selection round of MCQ tests – i.e. there is no elimination by Talent Screener (see page 24).

Declarations in the application form are made "on your honour" and proof of what you claim is not required at the application stage. However there is absolutely no point in trying to "put a gloss" on what you claim (e.g. pretending to have a higher level of proficiency in language 2 than you really have, or claiming a period of work experience that was longer or with more responsibility than was really the case). The whole process of selection is a rigorous one and you will be found out – and might end up being disqualified from a competition where you could have succeeded on the basis of truthful statements and your own merits.

Finally, an obvious point but a necessary one. *Don't leave your application to the last minute.* You will end up panicking about finding a missing piece of information you need for the form or losing the internet connection at a crucial moment. If you rush the process and make a mistake you will not be able to correct it once you have validated your application. And if you miss the deadline, that's it; there is no provision for late applications.

Talent Screener

If you are entering an **AD6 /AD7 specialist competition** you will have to provide additional information about your diplomas and work experience and answer questions specific to the field you are applying for. This is the **Talent Screener** and it is absolutely crucial that you not only provide correct information but also don't miss anything that could help your application (including relevant information you have provided in other parts of the application form). The reason for this is that you may not get a second chance to go further – the Selection Board may very likely make the "first cut" of candidates simply based on the Talent Screener. Even if it doesn't, and all candidates are called to a pre-selection round, the Talent Screener will be used as a basis for your assessment at the Assessment Centre. The Talent Screener must also be completed in your language 2 so that the Selection Board can make an objective comparison of all the candidates. Sometimes the entire application form for specialist competitions has to be done in language 2.

Phase 2: Pre-Selection

> ***Key point***
>
> Pre-selection is the point where the majority of candidates fail. The core Administrator pre-selection tests are the main subject of this book.

Having taken the above steps and provided that you meet all formal eligibility criteria, you should receive an official invitation to the pre-selection phase, communicated to you in your online EPSO profile. Once this eagerly awaited message arrives, you should get on with your preparation immediately (if you haven't already started) as the booking period may open straightaway and the exam be imminent.

Once the booking is open, you can choose a venue and a time from the available exam centres and time slots. If you live outside Europe, you can choose an exam centre outside the Member States; EPSO has extended the reach of exam centres to other continents via international test centres in China, the USA and elsewhere, which is a welcome development (though it does not necessarily apply for all exams).

When choosing an exam centre, make sure you are fully aware of the logistical issues: print the map of its location, find out which public transport goes there on the exam day, make sure that no strike or service interruption is foreseen for that day, and have a fallback plan in case you are running late, such as the phone number of a reliable taxi company.

My general advice for test-takers is to start practising as early as you can; preferably straight after deciding to sit an EPSO exam. In the pre-selection phase, competition is usually fierce and you must achieve the highest possible score in demanding psychometric tests. (Note, however, that for certain specialist competitions, the "pre-selection" phase is the Talent Screener, and the psychometric tests are part of the Assessment Centre.)

> ***Key point***
>
> Pre-selection tests of the type described in this book may be given at the Assessment Centre in some competitions for specialists. It depends on the number of candidates.

I strongly advise creating a concrete study

The 2018 Graduate Administrator Competition

No. of applications

22,666

↓

No. Invited to intermediate test

1639

↓

No. Invited to Assessment Centre

365

↓

Reserve list

158 (proposed)

The 2017 AD7 Financial Economics Competition

No. of applications

905

↓

Talent Screener

463

↓

No. Invited to Assessment Centre

158

↓

Reserve list

55

plan where you allocate sufficient time for the upcoming weeks and months for practice, revision, simulation and preparation. Simply saying "I'll find the time whenever I have nothing else to do" will not lead to tangible results, as watching the next episode of *Game of Thrones* will always seems more fun than dealing with rhombuses in abstract reasoning quizzes.

Scoring

As can be seen from the table on the next page, the rules for scoring vary from one competition to another. Making sure you know and understand the rules for your particular competition is essential if you are going to focus on the critical areas for practice.

As the table shows, the various tests have "pass marks". **Three important aspects of pass marks need to be taken into account**.

- **A pass mark is precisely that, a pass mark. Anything below it is a fail**. If you don't achieve the pass mark in any test where one is stipulated, then you are out of the competition however superbly you might perform in all the other tests. Thus in preparing for a competition you cannot afford to ignore your

Competition	Reference	Verbal Reasoning	Numerical Reasoning	Abstract Reasoning	Situational Judgement	Note
AD 7 in 1. Financial economics 2. Macroeconomics	EPSO/AD/339/17	20 questions. 15/30 combined with abstract reasoning	6/10	10 questions. 15/30 combined with verbal reasoning	Not used	
AD5 Graduate Administrators 2018	**EPSO/AD/356/18**	**5/10**	**5/10**	**10/20**	**24/40**	**Pass mark needed in all tests but only abstract + SJTs count to score**
AD5 Audit	EPSO/AD/357/18	5/10	5/10	10/20	24/40	Pass mark needed in all tests but only abstract + SJTs count to score
AD7 in 1. Customs, 2. Taxation	EPSO/AD/363/18	10/20	10 questions, 10/20 combined with abstract reasoning	10 questions, 10/20 combined with numerical reasoning	Not used	
AD6 Building Management Engineers	EPSO/AD/342/17	10/20	10 questions, 10/20 combined with abstract reasoning	10 questions, 10/20 combined with numerical reasoning	Not used	
AD5 Italian language translators	EPSO/AD/345/17	20 questions. 15/30 combined with abstract reasoning	4/10	10 questions. 15/30 combined with verbal reasoning	Not used	Computer-based language test MCQs also used
AD7 Danish lawyer-linguists	EPSO/AD/349/17	10/20	10 questions. 8/20 combined with abstract reasoning	10 questions. 8/20 combined with numerical reasoning	Not used	Computer-based language test MCQs also used
AD6 Food Safety Policy and Legislation	EPSO/AD/341/18	10/20	10 questions. 10/20 combined with abstract reasoning	10 questions. 10/20 combined with numerical reasoning	Not Used	
AD5 Graduate Administrators 2017	**EPSO/AD/338/17**	**10/20**	**5/10**	**10/20**	**Not Used**	**Pass mark needed in all tests but only abstract + verbal count to score**

areas of weakness in a vague hope that you will be saved by doing well in other areas.

- A pass mark is a **minimum requirement** and NOT a ticket to go on to the next stage of a competition. EPSO will be selecting the "best X" candidates for the next stage. So, for example, if EPSO is planning to invite 120 candidates to the next stage and 500 candidates achieve the pass marks in every test, only the 120 with the best scores will get the invitation.
- **The results of two tests may be combined** to create a pass mark for the combined tests. For example, looking at the table on the page opposite, for the AD5 Italian language translators the marks for the verbal reasoning and abstract reasoning tests were added together to produce a combined pass mark. So, if a candidate was very good at verbal reasoning and got 15/20 and very poor at abstract reasoning and got no marks at all they would still reach the pass mark because their combined score for verbal and abstract reasoning was 15. This can take a little bit of the pressure off candidates if they find that the results of one of their strongest tests are to be combined with one of their weakest. Of course, in the case of the translators they would still have the problem that other candidates might themselves get 15/20 on verbal reasoning but also accumulate points on abstract reasoning, thus getting a higher combined score. As already said, it is not just a matter of achieving the pass marks, you have to be among the "best X" in scores.

Another important factor is that in totalling your scores EPSO *sometimes disregards altogether the results of some tests*, provided of course that you have reached the pass mark in those tests.

Look, for example, at the scoring rules for the 2018 AD5 graduate competition. You had to achieve the pass mark of 5/10 in both the verbal and numerical reasoning tests. However, when it came to determining the "best X" scores, EPSO disregarded the verbal and numerical reasoning scores and simply added together the scores for abstract reasoning and situational judgement. With those rules, it made sense for a candidate to make sure they were "good enough" to get the pass marks in the verbal and numerical reasoning and then focus all their efforts and energies on becoming the "very best possible" in the other two tests. In the real world it is hard to become brilliant at everything so how your competition is scored should influence where you make the most intensive effort to improve.

Finally, you should be aware that EPSO *can and do change the scoring rules from one similar competition to another*. Just because a particular type of competition was scored one way one year it does not mean the same rules will apply the next. A notable example was the scoring for the AD5 graduate Administrator competition pre-selection round in the 2017 and 2018 competitions (see the table). For 2018 the abstract reasoning and situational judgement test scores were the ones added together to decide the "best X". In 2017, in contrast, it was the abstract and verbal reasoning and there was not even a situational judgement test at all! While the EPSO system is relatively stable compared

Scoring Rules of the 2018 AD5 Graduate Competition

Pass marks were 5/10 for both the verbal and numerical reasoning tests, 10/20 for the abstract reasoning and 24/40 for the situational judgement test. The minimum pass mark had to be reached in ALL the tests but ONLY the abstract reasoning and situational judgement test scores were used to qualify for the next stage, the intermediate test.

The minimum score of candidates invited to the intermediate test was 49.

Key point

How your competition is scored should decide where you make the most intensive preparation effort.

with the huge upheaval of 2010 everything is by no means set in stone and you therefore need to keep alert as to what changes are made.

Computer Screens

As all tests in the pre-selection phase are administered on computers located in accredited exam centres, you should be prepared for the difficulties this entails. Reading a text is always slower on a computer screen than on paper, speed being also influenced by the font size and screen resolution. Adding comments on screen is technically not available, therefore you need to take notes on the scrap paper or erasable slate that the exam centres provide. (This is even more relevant when it comes to the case study, which is formally part of the Assessment Centre, even if it is usually organised separately for logistical reasons.) For the numerical reasoning test an on-screen calculator is available and candidates are also provided with a fairly standard physical calculator such as a Sharp EL-240 SA or similar.

Computer-based exams do have a few advantages however. The display of the available time (which is not meant to put pressure on you but rather to help time management); the automatic registration of answered and unanswered questions (which should help you keep track of the questions); the flexibility of choosing a convenient exam day for all candidates (as opposed to having a single exam day for all candidates); and the faster (and more reliable) correction of your answers given the electronic evaluation, are among the advantages of computer based exams.

Verbal and Numerical Reasoning Tests

The verbal and numerical reasoning tests, along with abstract reasoning, are commonly known as **psychometric tests**. These are one of the most popular methods to evaluate cognitive skills and the intelligence of prospective employees. They are widely used by multinational companies and civil service recruiters around the world given their flexible application, cost-effectiveness and proven relevance to gauge candidates' skills. The relevant chapters of this book provide a full methodology and hundreds of practice exercises: what follows here is more of a description of how these tests are administered along with some general advice on how to tackle them.

Verbal reasoning tests are essentially reading comprehension tests where you are required to answer a question based on a text. A fundamental rule is to only consider information contained in the text.

Numerical reasoning, on the other hand, is a calculation exercise using statistical charts, tables and graphs, based on which you are required to find a certain percentage, figure, or decide on relative values (e.g. "Based on the table, which country had the highest birth rate in 2008?"). Questions can be tricky as sometimes no or minimal exact calculation is required given that you can simplify the riddle by applying calculation methods and shortcuts. A comprehensive toolkit is offered in the relevant chapter of this book.

EPSO has been using verbal and numerical reasoning tests for some years in its competitions and they have proven to be one of the most challenging parts of the exam procedure. While EU knowledge, as tested before 2010, could to some degree be memorised by dedicating sufficient time to this end, succeeding in verbal and numerical reasoning requires a completely different approach. Learning the methodology, and then plenty of practice in using it, is therefore crucial to succeed.

As mentioned in the section on languages above, since 2011 all verbal and numerical reasoning tests can be taken in your first language (along with abstract reasoning, but there the choice of language has no relevance). Linguists can expect to have two or three different verbal reasoning tests: one in their main language (which depends on which linguistic profile they had applied for, e.g. Bulgarian translator or German interpreter); while the other two depend on the source languages available for that given exam (English, French and German have privileged status and almost always appear among the languages).

Work as hard as you can to improve your overall vocabulary in the exam's language by reading quality news websites, boost your spelling skills for complex words, your understanding of measurement units (billions vs. millions, how many litres in one cubic metre, etc.) and revise basic mathematical operations. In addition to the extensive resources in this book, you will find tests in 19 different languages on the EU Training website.

Abstract Reasoning Tests

Abstract reasoning is another test type that various international employers commonly use; it is a common feature of popular IQ tests as well. Abstract reasoning is different from the other two tests as it requires no linguistic skills: there is only one main question for all tasks, such as "Which figure is the next in the series?"

Using these questions for personnel selection is practical for EPSO given that there is no need to translate the exercise into any language and also because abstract reasoning tests have been scientifically proven to be culture-neutral while effectively testing candidates' so-called "fluid intelligence". This latter term refers to the capability to solve new problems and understand the relationship between various concepts, independent of any acquired knowledge.

The main skill you need to efficiently resolve abstract reasoning tests is "imagination" – that is, the ability to mentally rotate, flip or turn certain figures according to a certain logic or rule. This rule is one of the main challenges of this question type as you should be able to "dissect" a figure and identify its component elements. Those capable of performing such tasks are likely to be able to cope with unknown or new situations in the workplace: this skill therefore does have more practical value for predicting actual job performance than may seem at first glance. You can find a large number of abstract reasoning test questions along with an in-depth methodology in chapters 9 and 10 of this book.

Situational Judgement Tests

The objective of situational judgement tests (or SJTs for short) is to create **realistic work-related scenarios** in which you must determine the most appropriate course of action given the parameters and situation.

An important element of SJTs is that there are no absolutely "right" or "wrong" answers when using your judgement. Rather, judgement is about your ability to assess a given situation and make clearly defined decisions on how to proceed from there, based on your own unique set of experiences in life and understanding of the EU institutions' culture and ethical rules, while applying a certain common

> **Key point**
>
> Many AD competitions do not involve situational judgement tests as such. The competencies they measure are instead evaluated at the Assessment Centre. Very importantly, however, such tests are regularly used for the big "generalist" AD5 graduate competitions: Although dropped for the 2017 competition they were used again in the 2018 competition (see table on page 26).

sense to workplace situations. This is closely linked to the competencies, summarised in chapter 1, that EPSO is seeking to find in future EU officials.

Since there are no right or wrong answers as such, the decision whether one answer is better than another lies in the hands of the test administrators; however, the benchmark for deciding the value of each answer is the competency list that EPSO has established and against which it evaluates candidates. This is explained more fully in chapter 11.

It is important to point out that while real world situations can certainly be summarised into brief sentences or paragraphs, rarely do we come across situations in life that resemble these questions precisely. For example, you could be confronted with a colleague who may be stealing but who may also be a friend, or someone with whom you are in direct competition for a promotion. Such factors would certainly influence your judgement and response.

Professional Skills Tests

Skills specifically related to the field of the competition (for specialists and linguists) may be tested either at the pre-selection stage or the Assessment Centre, or both. For convenience these types of tests are discussed in a separate section below.

Notification of Results

After the pre-selection phase, or in the case of specialist profiles, after the successful sifting-in of your CV, candidates are notified both of their positive or negative results. The scores and the answers you had given are communicated to you in all cases though for practical reasons EPSO cannot disclose the multiple choice questions themselves, only the answers you had marked.

Since the number of applicants in the pre-selection phase can run into the tens of thousands, EPSO decided to require the submission of supporting documents only for those who have passed the pre-selection or were specialists short-listed on the basis of their CV. This means that even those who have already cleared the first hurdle may not take their eligibility for the assessment phase for granted.

> **Key point**
>
> The feedback from EPSO on your pre-selection test results is of limited value if you have failed the test and are planning to retake. EPSO tell you what the correct answer options were and what you chose but because they don't repeat the actual questions it is impossible to work out where you went wrong. You need to practise with the tests in this book to see where you are making mistakes.

Phase 3: Intermediate Test

The intermediate test is a fairly recent addition to the EPSO selection process and consists of an e-tray exercise. It was brought in specifically for the AD5 graduate competition, always the biggest of the year in terms of number of applications, but may also be used in other big competitions (e.g. the 2018 AD5 in the field of Audit). The test takes place on computers at testing centres around the Member States.

The intermediate test is designed to compensate for a fairly obvious difficulty with

> **Key point**
>
> The intermediate test provides a useful "second chance" in some competitions with a lot of candidates. But you still need to get a very good score in the pre-selection tests.

the pre-selection tests in generalist competitions where there are very large numbers of candidates. If there are many thousands of candidates – bearing in mind that an AD5 graduate competition will attract well over 20,000 – of whom only a small proportion will be invited to the Assessment Centre, there is a risk that only those who are exceptional performers in tests like abstract reasoning will ever be seen for personal evaluation by the assessors. Such candidates may not always be the ones possessing the ideal range of "soft skills" – the EPSO competencies, listed in chapter 1 – that are needed for a "rounded" EU civil servant.

It is logistically impossible (and would in any case be prohibitively expensive) to invite thousands of candidates to an Assessment Centre, so the intermediate test is a filtering process, designed to let some of those who did well, but not quite well enough, in the pre-selection tests have a second chance. The e-tray exercise, like the pre-selection tests, is computer-based so is logistically practicable but it shifts the emphasis to real-world office skills, calling to some degree on the competencies that will be thoroughly measured at the human level at the Assessment Centre.

The general principle is that EPSO will invite to the intermediate test around 10 to 11 times the number of candidates sought for the reserve list. Thus, for example, of the 22,666 who applied for the 2018 AD5 graduate competition, 1639 were invited to take the intermediate test as compared with an intended reserve list of 158 successful candidates. Similarly, for the 2018 AD5 in the field of Audit, 803 of the 4755 candidates who applied for the competition were invited to the intermediate test as compared with an intended reserve list of 80.

Three important points should be noted about the intermediate test.

- Firstly, as the above figures show, although the intermediate test provides a useful second chance for those who might not be absolutely brilliant at, for example, numerical or abstract reasoning, the great majority of candidates in such competitions will nevertheless drop out at pre-selection. In other words, *you still need to get a very good score in the pre-selection tests* so cannot in any way ease back your preparation for those tests in the hope of "saving yourself" at the intermediate test.

- Secondly, once the intermediate test is reached, *your pre-selection scores are forgotten*. In other words, even if you had the maximum score on everything in the pre-selection tests, this will not help you if you do badly in the intermediate test.

- Thirdly, the intermediate test e-tray is, formally speaking, part of the Assessment Centre. This means that if you do get to the Assessment Centre proper, *your e-tray scores will be added to the scores you get in the Assessment Centre exercises* in evaluating how you do in the competencies of analysis and problem solving, delivering quality and results, prioritising and organising, and working with others. So, once again, you can't afford to do "just enough" – you must aim for the best score possible.

The e-tray exercise is covered in full in *The Ultimate EU Test Book Assessment Centre 2019.*

Phase 4: Assessment Centre

Generic Assessment Centre Exercises

An Assessment Centre is used as the **second full round of exams** for Administrators (including linguists) and Assistants (but in most cases, the first round for specialists). At the Assessment Centre several trained observers called "assessors" evaluate your performance throughout half a day or a full day of exercises that have been developed specifically for this purpose. EPSO uses multiple types of exercises based on their competency framework: the idea is that each competency (listed in chapter 1, such as "Delivering quality and results") will be tested by two types of exercises to make sure that the observations are valid.

The core generic exercises currently used at the Assessment Centre for Administrators are:

1. The Case Study
2. The Group Exercise
3. The Competency-based Interview
4. The Oral Presentation

The above exercises are generic in the sense that they test personal behaviours and qualities in ways which are relevant to the wide range of roles that candidates may be called on to undertake in the course of their career.

A new test of "EU motivation", basically evaluating your commitment to working for the EU was introduced for the 2018 generalist Administrator competition.

In addition to these "core" elements of assessment, for more specialised roles the competition will involve other tests focusing on specialised knowledge, as will be explained in the following section.

All about the Assessment Centre

The exercises used at the Assessment Centre and the competencies they measure are fully described in *The Ultimate EU Test Book Assessment Centre 2019.*

These exercises are very different from the psychometric (reasoning) tests we focus on in this book. They are instead designed to test the "soft skills" like "working with others" needed to perform effectively as an EU civil servant.

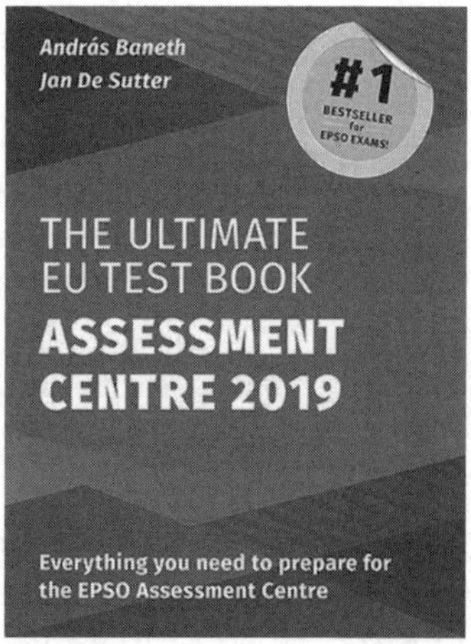

AD Professional Skills Tests

Candidates in linguist and specialist competitions face a double challenge. They have much the same range of reasoning tests and Assessment Centre exercises as generalists but are also intensively tested in their skills specific to the profile they are applying for.

Linguists' Skills Tests (Translators, Interpreters, Lawyer-Linguists)

Linguists are typically tested in their language skills in three phases, the pre-selection round, a second round of translation tests in an accredited EPSO centre, and then the Assessment Centre. But they also must tackle the other types of tests faced by all candidates. This means, for example, that however good at translating texts a translator might be, they will not get past the first pre-selection round of computer-based tests unless they achieve the necessary marks in their verbal, numerical and abstract reasoning tests. The pass marks may not seem particularly daunting per se (e.g. 4 out of 10 in numerical reasoning – see sample scoring in table on page 26) but it is not just a question of achieving the pass mark because only the "best X" number of candidates with the highest total marks will be invited to the next stage of translation tests. Beyond that, they will also be tested in their generic competencies at the Assessment Centre, so if their "soft skills" are unsatisfactory then, again, skill in translating texts will not save them. This underlines the importance for linguists of preparing "across the board", especially as language skills rather than the other tests may be their real strength.

> **Key point**
>
> It doesn't matter how good a translator you are if you can't pass the verbal, numerical and abstract reasoning tests.

Linguists need to offer 3 languages and the language requirement will be quite precise. For example, in the 2017 AD5 translators competitions, for the German-language translators your language 1 had to be the language of the competition (i.e. German), language 2 had to be either English or French and so too did language 3. In other words, the only 3 languages you could offer were English, French and German. If you were an Italian language candidate your language 1 had to be Italian, language 2 one of English, French or German and language 3 one of English, French or German. Similarly, for the 2016 AD7 lawyer-linguists competition your language 1 had to be one of the languages of the competition (in this case Spanish, Greek, Italian, Lithuanian, Maltese or Swedish), language 2 had to be English, and language 3 one of French, German, Italian, Polish or Spanish.

The most widely applicable combination of languages is native language (if not English or French) + English + French. The key is knowledge of the working languages. There is no point being able to offer half-a-dozen languages if they do not include at least one and usually two of the working languages.

For the 2017 AD5 translators competition at the pre-selection computer-based testing round candidates faced (as well as verbal, numerical and abstract reasoning in their language 1 – the language of the competition) tests in their two source languages (languages 2 and 3). Provided they achieved the pass mark in numerical reasoning, the numerical reasoning score was not added in to the calculation of their total score.

As the next phase, the translators faced translation tests from languages 2 and 3 into language 1 and again the "best X" were invited to the Assessment Centre where they took the competency exercises (oral presentation, competency-based interviews and group exercise, but no case study) in their language 2, the scores in those exercises then

Create your own competency passport!

You can carry out your own self assessment using the EPSO competencies at:

www.johnharperpublishing.co.uk/the-ultimate-eu-career-development-toolkit/

This tool kit will automatically generate your own personal competency passport. It's a great way to start your preparations for an Assessment Centre and is absolutely free to use.

being added together with those brought forward from the translation tests.

In the lawyer-linguists competition mentioned above, at the first round a language comprehension test was taken in language 2 and verbal, numerical and abstract reasoning tests in language 1. Those invited to the next round, the translation test, had to translate a legal text from language 2 into language 1. At the Assessment Centre, in addition to a general competency-based interview and group exercise in language 2, candidates had to summarise in language 1 a legal text in language 3 and do an oral presentation including their field-specific competencies (i.e. knowledge of EU law in particular) in their language 1.

Specialists' Tests

As noted previously, for specialists, the pre-selection verbal, numerical and abstract reasoning tests may be moved into the Assessment Centre stage, depending on the number of applicants.

As a general rule, EPSO says that if the number of specialist applicants (e.g. nuclear scientist, cohesion policy expert, competition lawyer etc.) exceeds X times the number of places available on the reserve list, it will organise a pre-selection round for them as well. If not, then these tests will be included in the assessment phase. The use of the Talent Screener means that in that case all those applying will not necessarily be called to any test at all. This is different to other Administrator competitions where the default rule is that every candidate who meets the formal eligibility criteria will be invited to take the pre-selection tests.

Specialist knowledge is tested in the assessment phase mainly in the form of a practical exercise, a special field-specific and targeted interview, and/or in the framework of the case study. This latter is closely related to the competition profile and the sub-profile or domain that the candidate chose at the time of application.

The importance of field-specific knowledge in specialist competitions is reflected in the fact that this may account for 55% (or even more in some cases) of the final score at Assessment Centre, as opposed to 45% for the "general" competencies.

Specialist knowledge is tested for all profiles, as no capable candidate who otherwise lacks the proper knowledge of the chosen field can be recruited, given EPSO's wish that all new officials should be operational from "day one". Moreover, even specialists need a solid understanding of EU institutions, procedures and stakeholders, which can add valuable points to your performance in the assessment phase of the exam. For instance, if you are familiar with the overall context of the EU's environmental policy, know which institutions and agencies are involved, which are the formal rules to enact policy in this field, which European associations and NGOs are taking an active part in influencing decision-makers and what the strategic thinking is on this policy's future, you are immediately in a position to make more out of the group exercise, the case study or the oral presentation than many other candidates who lack such knowledge would be able to do.

CAST Permanent Selection

Key point

CAST Permanent competitions offer an alternative route to an Administrator type of job without being a permanent official. But you still have to pass the EPSO verbal, numerical and abstract reasoning tests.

So-called "CAST Permanent" competitions ("Calls for expressions of interest") are organised by EPSO and attract many applicants as an alternative to the open competitions for permanent officials.

Contract Agents for Specific Tasks are divided into four "function groups" designated with Roman numerals, I to IV. **Function Group IV** is the highest. Function Group IV contract agents will include profiles such as administration/human resources, budgeting and financial planning, law, political affairs/EU policies, translators, and communication, which are very much classic Administrator tasks. CAST positions have in effect increasingly been used to cover roles which might otherwise have been taken by permanent officials: more than one-fifth of the European Commission staff are now contract agents.

Type 3(b) contract agents, found in the lager institutions, have contracts for fixed periods but with the advantage that they are usually eligible to take part in internal competitions for permanent posts, and internal competitions are generally easier than open ones. Thus a 3(b) contract agent post can potentially be a stepping stone to a job as an Administrator permanent official.

Type 3(a) contract agents, found for example in the executive agencies, have contracts that become indefinite on second renewal, providing job security. Although this type of contract does not give access to internal competitions, in practice long careers are possible for 3(a) contract agents.

In some respects the CAST Permanent procedures are very different from the competitions for permanent officials.

- There is **no planned number of successful candidates** to fill a more-or-less defined number of actual jobs. Instead this is a way for the institutions to have a reservoir of candidates they can call on from time to time as need arises. There is therefore no way at the time of applying to calculate your chances of succeeding.
- There is **no deadline for applications**; the whole process is very open-ended and you need to renew your application (to show you are still interested/available) every six months.
- Applying for a competition **does not mean you will actually be invited** to take any tests. Instead, only candidates short listed (pre-selected) by the recruiting service on the basis of information provided in applications will be invited, as and when vacancies arise. As there are often large numbers of applicants, this means you may never get to take any tests.
- **If you pass the EPSO tests, the recruiting service will then use its own selection procedure** to see if you are suitable for the post. If you pass the tests, the recruiting service is obliged to interview you. Once you have passed the EPSO tests you are available for further testing/recruitment by other services too, so you do not have to start the process all over again.
- The computer-based multiple-choice tests administered by EPSO are similar to the "regular" EPSO competitions. They include numerical, verbal and abstract reasoning tests (in your language 1) and a specific competency test for the pro-

file and function group you have applied for (in your language 2). Languages 1 and 2 are defined as in the regular competitions. These tests are, however, **held on a rolling basis at intervals** (usually every one or two months) rather than in one window as with regular competitions. The recruiting service will not wait for you so if you are offered the chance to take the exam, you should do so as soon as possible.

The EPSO CAST tests are easier in the sense that your marks just produce a straight pass or fail – you do not have to be among a "best X" top slice of candidates, which is a big challenge in many regular competitions. For example, the pass marks in a currently open CAST Permanent procedure, which started back in January 2017, are 10/20 in verbal reasoning and 10/20 in abstract and numerical reasoning combined. Thus you can afford to do rather poorly on abstract reasoning, say, as long as you can compensate for this in numerical reasoning, and you don't have to worry about the impact on your aggregate score. You also have to get a pass mark in your specific competency test (16/25 for FG IV).

> **Key point**
>
> In CAST Permanent competitions if you get a pass mark in the EPSO verbal, numerical and abstract reasoning tests it remains valid for 10 years. That is different from the regular open competitions each of which is a stand-alone.

If you pass the EPSO tests your scores are not taken into any further account (and remain valid if successful for 10 years for the numerical, verbal and abstract reasoning and 5 years for the competency test). It then becomes a question of whether you can pass any additional tests or interviews required by the recruiting service. It is also possible that if you fail the EPSO tests you will get a further chance to take them after 6 months, if the recruiting service liked your profile enough. In other words, all through the process the recruiting service is very much in the driving seat, to a far greater extent than in the regular open competitions.

Assessment of Heads of Unit

The assessment for Head of Unit and Director posts has traditionally been carried out via an Assessment Centre. Potential Heads of Unit should prepare along the same lines as Administrators, even though the competency model against which they are evaluated is somewhat different, having a strong focus on management-related issues. This means that questions testing the candidate's skills in variously managing people, time, teams, finance, operations and conflict feature prominently in the competency based interview and possibly impact other exam items such as the group exercise and the case study as well. Moreover, candidates for these exams are advised to be familiar with the EU Financial Regulations and general principles of handling budgets and funds. Besides the Assessment Centre, these candidates would also have normal interviews with the recruiting services as the second step in the procedure.

Assessment Report

After both the Assessment Centre and other forms of assessment, a report with a **competency passport** will be drawn up by the assessors to evaluate you against the pre-established competencies. This also means that first and foremost you will not be judged against other candidates but rather against the objective behavioural criteria

EPSO seeks in candidates. The ranking of suitable candidates will come afterwards and will be influenced by your performance in professional knowledge metrics.

Based on a streamlined and structured methodology, assessors draw up a report that summarises your performance, along with your strengths and weaknesses. EPSO provides this report to all candidates regardless of whether or not they were successful in the assessment phase. This report can add a lot to your self-development as it provides a comprehensive analysis of your personality traits as observed during the assessment. It can also be very helpful in deciding which of your skills or competencies may need to be developed.

Phase 5: Reserve List, Recruitment

For those candidates who successfully passed the Assessment Centre, a notification including the words "we are happy to inform you" arrives in their virtual EPSO account's mailbox. This also means that your name will be published in the reserve lists that appear in the EU's Official Journal and on EPSO's website (unless you opt out) and your competency passport, based on the above assessment, will be added to your profile once you take up employment. Those who did not succeed this time should not despair as they can re-apply for any later exam with the advantage of being familiar with the working methods of the system.

Validity of the Reserve List

Once a reserve list is published, it is always clearly indicated when it expires, meaning until which date you can be recruited from it. However, EPSO has in practice regularly extended the validity period of a reserve list to make sure that all available candidates are recruited from it.

The idea is to have the Administrator and Assistant competitions' reserve lists valid until the next annual cycle results in a new list; for linguists it is the same approach but instead of the next annual cycle, it will be the next competition in the same language that replaces the previous list; for specialists, the lists are valid for at least three years as long as they still contain recruitable (available) laureates.

Recruiter Portal

Once on the reserve list, candidates (or as they are called at this stage, "**laureates**") are available for recruitment by the institutions. The recruiter portal enables recruiters to generate multi criteria searches for candidates across the lists of available laureates. The recruiting services also have access to the competency passports of laureates. It is advisable to upload your CV into the portal to share more information about yourself.

Job Interview

When you pass an EPSO competition, EPSO will activate a "show vacancies" button in your account, which will allow you to see the available vacancies. Once on the reserve list, you can try to lobby for yourself by indicating your exam's reference number and presenting your CV to targeted Heads of Unit; this, however, is of mixed effectiveness: while it works for some, it may yield no result at all for others. Those candidates who are already working in one of the EU institutions (e.g. as a temporary agent) can also-have direct access to the internal vacancy list. Application to these posts is sometimes limited to "internal" candidates; however, sometimes "external" candidates are also considered if they meet the specific requirements of the post.

Finally, if you have a chance to make personal contacts, it can go a long way as you can make a good impression on a Head of Unit or demonstrate your abilities instead of depending on an impersonal message. Friday afternoons may be your best bet to manage to talk to or meet with a person in charge, but you may need to travel to Brussels at your own expense in the hope of effective networking. And if you know people in the institutions, personal recommendations can also be very useful.

Any time between a few weeks and several months, you may receive a phone call or e-mail asking whether you would be interested in an interview for a position at x or y EU institution. Always make sure your contact data is up-to-date and that you regularly check your EPSO profile as well in order not to miss such important events.

Once offered the chance to attend a job interview, it is highly recommended to participate even if the job itself may not be the most appealing. You can always decide to decline and wait for a better or different offer, but it is better to have such options than decline flatly in the first place and take a gamble. You can also gain useful interview experience and find out more about the position; you might even realise that the job is in fact meant for you.

The job interview itself is different from other parts of the selection competition as it is focused on your suitability for the specific position and it may only include some basic general EU questions. If you apply for a consumer health expert position, for example, you can expect a number of technical questions on this specific topic but nothing on e.g. the Treaty of Lisbon or the EU's immigration policy (unless the job in question is in the Commission's DG Home).

Your interviewers will most likely speak in English, French or German, unless you are applying for a translator or interpreter post where the rule is rather your second language (if different from the above three). Be aware, however, that questions may be put to you in any other language specified in your CV. Should you feel that you need to further clarify matters, take care not to patronise the interviewer and that your body language is also entirely respectful.

Travelling

You will most likely need to travel to Brussels or Luxembourg for the interview unless a video- or phone-conference call can be arranged at the EU representation or delegation office of your country of residence. Should you need to travel, all costs will be reimbursed and you will be given a modest daily subsistence allowance as well (based on strict formal conditions), but be prepared to receive the reimbursement only several weeks later.

Recruitment

If your interview was successful, you will be offered a job first by phone or e-mail, then formally by letter. Should this not arrive in time, make sure you ask your future EU institution's HR department or the unit in which you will work to send it to you.

A medical check is required of all new recruits. It takes place after a successful interview. Usually you will have received an "intention of offer" letter or email which will say that the service wishes to hire you, but this can be rescinded in the (rare) case of an unsuccessful medical check.

Generally you can agree on the starting date of employment with your future boss, so you can look for accommodation (if in Belgium, try *www.immoweb.be* or the

European Commission's Intranet also has a fine small ads section with real estate ads) and arrange paperwork in due course.

Moving costs are paid for unless you have lived in the country where you were recruited to for more than a certain period of time (e.g. if you had done an EU traineeship at the Commission in Brussels right before you got recruited, this may prevent you from having your moving costs paid, though the rule is generally six months of residence and for traineeships, the duration is five months). The detailed rules can be found in the EU officials' Staff Regulations.

Knowing Your Goals

Having bought this book shows that you are serious about starting an EU career. But it is still worth thinking on an ongoing basis about your goals. As well as working hard on the detail of the EPSO tests you face, you also need to make sure you are prepared to take a step back to *think strategically and long-term.*

The "holy grail" for most who seek a career in the EU administration is to become a permanent EU civil servant, an Administrator in one of the "core" EU institutions. It is this status that opens the widest opportunities, with the highest salaries and benefits, and opportunities for roles with great responsibilities and recognition. To achieve this goal, there is really only one *direct* route, and that is to pass an EPSO open competition. But even that route, though direct, is not really short: as we have seen above, from the time of submitting your application to getting on a reserve list can easily be 12 to 15 months, even if you pass your first competition, and then further months can go by before you actually get a job.

As always, the most direct route is not necessarily the easiest. The competition is fierce. This is especially so if you aspire to be a "generalist" Administrator. If you are looking for a more specialist role – and, of course, have the specialist skills – the competition may be a bit less intense, but it will still be considerable. If you take an open competition and pass it first time, you will have done well.

In practice many of those who do make it to become permanent EU civil servants are not starting from point zero. They have, rather, started in one of the many types of temporary or contract roles within the institutions and then proceeded by "stepping stones", sometimes taking an internal competition or an open competition where they benefit from the experience they have gained from working in the institutions.

There are plenty of people in the institutions who have "hopped" from one supposedly short-term stepping stone to another, never actually becoming permanent civil servants as such but in practice having many of the benefits and much of the security of permanent officials as their accumulated experience becomes increasingly valuable to the institutions that employ them. You can be sure that with the ever-increasing use of contract posts in the institutions, this sort of "semi-permanent" status will become ever more a feature, a sort of grey zone which is not exactly one thing or another.

You need therefore to consider your options carefully. Are you absolutely wedded to the idea of being a permanent civil servant? While the ideal, this is also the hardest goal to achieve. Might it make more sense to try in parallel to get a contract/temporary post? You will then be on the "inside", able to take advantage of opportunities that come along that are closed off to outsiders. There is absolutely nothing to prevent you from exploring multiple options simultaneously – indeed it is positively recommended. A CAST position might not be your ideal but there are many good jobs available in this category and it can also be a good springboard.

You will also need to think about where the jobs are. If you are aiming for a career in Brussels, you need to target career paths that will take you there. Bear in mind that most EU jobs do not involve working on top-level policy documents at the Berlaymont with EU Commissioners waiting in the wings. There are many back office roles which are essentially just the same as working in any large public administration. If you "want Brussels" you may need to explore many options before you get to where you want to be. That could well involve working in the "bubble" of NGOs, public affairs firms, consultancies, national and regional representations and media that surround the institutions.

Understanding how the system works and opportunities arise, the indirect "back routes" that most people do not know, the role of networking to be in the right place at the right time, and the need to always think strategically, are all of vital importance. Plenty of potentially excellent candidates never get the careers they are looking for because they do not understand this. This is a large and complex subject, and beyond the limits of this book. So do take the opportunity to read *Working for the EU: How to Get In* by Johannes de Berlaymont because it is packed with the information you need to help you with this.

Finally, bear in mind that, even if you decide at some point that the EU is not going to be where your career path takes you, the work you have done in preparing for and taking EPSO competitions will not be wasted. The EPSO tests are something of a "gold standard". Many big employers use tests with many similarities to those used by EPSO, so you will have a head's start in tackling them.

Our Top 10 Tips

Obviously there are many aspects to succeeding in an EPSO competition, and the importance of the different aspects can vary from one competition to another. However, we have picked out our "top 10 tips" – key things to keep in mind that apply to pretty much all competitions.

1. **Think strategically and learn how the system works.** Are you taking the right competitions, can you get more experience that will help you, can you get a temporary position that will qualify you for internal competitions? Sometimes there is a back door as well as a front door. Read *Working for the EU: How to Get In* as soon as you can!

2. **Don't hesitate to apply for multiple competitions,** if you are qualified for them. Each competition is independently organised and previous unsuccessful attempts, however many, don't count against you. You will also very likely get better at it the more competitions you take. Also consider becoming an EU trainee, available to 1200 people each year at the Commission, and several hundred options at the European Parliament, European Court of Justice and other institutions as well.

3. **Try to calculate the odds, by reference to previous similar competitions.** By all means go for a competition which has very long odds, but if you can qualify for an "easier" competition, it makes sense to try for that instead or as well. And remember that if you pass a CAST competition, your numerical, verbal and abstract reasoning scores remain valid for 10 years.

4. **Always read carefully the Notice of Competition.** Never assume you know what's in it because you have done a similar competition in the past – the rules can and do change, sometimes in big ways. Candidates can easily get confused about matters that are actually clearly spelled out in the Notice of Competition.

5. **Observe the competition rules strictly.** The information you provide to EPSO must always be accurate so never make claims that are not true. Bear in mind that the deadlines are inflexible – and you need to be proactive in checking your EPSO account, because EPSO doesn't "chase" you.

6. **Make sure you understand the scoring system for your competition.** Which elements require just a pass mark, which ones require you to be in the "best X"? Which elements are totalled and which are stand-alones? The rules vary from competition to competition and you need to understand which tests are most likely to be critical for you.

7. **Never rely on just doing well in some tests** – you must prepare across the board because you will have to reach pass mark targets in everything even though some tests will carry more weight than others. But proceed one step at a time – for example, while it is worth knowing what the Assessment Centre exercises are at the outset, there is no point in preparing for them in detail if you are going to fail your pre-selection tests.

8. **Practise as much as possible** with the aim of mastering the main techniques to make them instinctive. This will save you vital time under pressure because there is very little time for thinking in EPSO reasoning tests. This is especially relevant to numerical and abstract reasoning.

9. **The best advice is usually to "get in" first.** If you succeed in becoming a laureate, you don't have to take the first job offer that comes along. You may have very good personal reasons for rejecting it. But remember that it is far easier to move on once you are already inside the system. And that second job offer may never come, or only come several months later when your personal situation may have already changed.

10. **Finally, don't ever regard not succeeding in your EPSO competition as some sort of personal failure.** Not only are the mathematical odds very tough, you are up against ambitious and well prepared people from all over Europe. In most competitions a "second team" of candidates who just missed out could be selected who would be virtually as good as the "first team". The EU simply doesn't employ enough people to take in all the talent on offer. And remember, your experience with the EPSO system will also stand you in good stead to tackle the similar tests organised by many other employers.

3. Verbal, Numerical and Abstract Reasoning Tests in EPSO Administrator Exams

Introduction

EPSO has, since its inception, used verbal reasoning and numerical reasoning tests in the pre-selection or admission phase of open competitions (while for some specialist profiles these are required in the assessment phase). Although such tests do not require specific knowledge, they have been dreaded by many candidates – and for good reason. From 2010 onwards, the so-called abstract reasoning test also became part of the pre-selection stage of the competitions.

When it comes to abstract, verbal and numerical reasoning tests (commonly referred to as "psychometric tests"), a number of questions arise:

- What exactly are these tests like?
- What do they measure?
- What is the concept behind their design?
- What is the rationale for their use?
- What are the factors determining success?
- How are these tests scored?
- And finally: how to prepare and practice for them?

An Overview of the Three Test Types

Each test type will be described in detail in the relevant upcoming chapters, but it is important to first get a sense of what these tests are like in general terms.

Format

All three test types, verbal, numerical and abstract reasoning, are in multiple-choice format. Based on EPSO's practice, all three "reasoning" tests have either four or five answer options for each question or text passage. In both cases, there is always only one correct answer and no penalty for wrong answers.

Verbal Reasoning

Verbal reasoning tests are designed to measure a candidate's ability to comprehend complex texts on various topics. These may vary from the description of an EU policy through current news, culture, history, or even natural sciences – in other words, the topic can be almost anything.

The length of the text is typically around 150 words and you are normally asked to decide which of four answer options is correct, based on the information in the text.

The answer options will then measure whether you:

- understood key concepts
- have the necessary vocabulary to comprehend a wide range of topics (believe it or not, this may be an issue in your native language as well)
- are able to deduce arguments from the text
- can accurately interpret key indicators (such as chronology, causality, quantities) in the text

For more information and practice tests, turn to chapters 4 and 5.

Numerical Reasoning

Numerical reasoning tests are designed to measure a candidate's ability to interpret data and numbers, with a special emphasis on the relationship between various data sets and on performing quick calculations based on intuitive insight. This means in practice that the focus is not on complex mathematics but on identifying how one can arrive at the correct answer in the most efficient way.

The data on which the test question is based is usually a table with several rows and columns. The rows usually indicate various groups (countries, age groups, regions, industries, and so on), while the columns often contain various metrics (GDP, average income, amount transported, percentages, and so on). Alternatively, the data can also be presented in the form of a chart or several charts (pie chart, bar chart, etc.), or any combination of the above-mentioned items.

The test question usually seeks either a figure ("200", "0.3", "45%", "1/5", etc.) or one of the groups in the data set ("France", "People aged between 15-64", "Europe", "Agriculture", etc.) as the answer.

By arriving at the answer in a timely manner, you can demonstrate your ability to:

- identify relevant data
- understand the relationship between various metrics
- determine the level of accuracy needed to answer the question
- perform quick mental calculations, and
- make fast but relatively accurate estimates

For more information and practice tests, turn to chapters 6, 7 and 8.

Abstract Reasoning

Abstract reasoning tests always involve geometric shapes. Although there are test types where the shapes are three-dimensional, EPSO has so far decided against using such tests and therefore candidates will only be given questions with two-dimensional objects.

The figures in the questions can be geometrical ones, such as circles, rectangles, triangles, lines, and combinations of these, but they can also be the simplified representations of real-life objects, for example bodies, faces, vehicles, animals, and so on. Another important aspect is to avoid any gender, nationality or other bias regarding candidates' abilities to solve them; EPSO (or, more precisely, the company that has created the tests) also makes sure that those with visual challenges are not being discriminated against either.

The tests are designed so that there is a linear relationship among the items in the set of illustrations included with the question. The figures in the test item form a series going from left to right and the test-taker is expected to select which of the five answer options would come next in the series.

Abstract reasoning tests measure your ability to:

- interpret abstract concepts that do not carry actual real-life meaning
- draw conclusions in new and unfamiliar scenarios
- discover relationships between seemingly unrelated concepts, and
- use your so-called "fluid intelligence" and apply it to any intellectual problem

For more information and practice tests, turn to chapters 9 and 10.

Why these Tests are Used

When someone first looks at verbal or numerical reasoning test questions, and especially in the case of abstract reasoning, a thought that often comes to mind is ***"How is this related to my potential performance as an Administrator in the European Commission?"*** It is a fair question and one which deserves a good answer.

According to one approach, these tests are generic indicators of intelligence. Their results are standardized and are simply good predictors of performance in any work situation where intelligence, creativity and independent thinking is required. While this is certainly true, it is also easy to identify much more concrete work scenarios where the "skills" measured by these tests can actually be put to good use.

As mentioned above, **verbal reasoning** tests measure a general ability to interpret texts, regardless of the topic. One can easily imagine the wide array of topics, formats and styles an Administrator at the European Commission or the Committee of the Regions will be expected to read about and make sense of in the course of their career. One day you might be reading about some new internal procedures to follow, the next day you might be asked by your superior to skim through a report on the effects of the increasing price of fertilizers on the Latvian farmers' standard of living. Regardless of the topic, one thing is certain: you will need to be able to make sense of the text in a timely manner, draw the right conclusions, avoid common misunderstandings and eventually summarize your findings. Sounds familiar? Hopefully it does as this is exactly what you will be expected to do in the verbal reasoning test as well.

The same goes for the **numerical reasoning** tests. You might also be given a statistical report one day at work. It may contain a mind-numbingly large number of tables and charts, and although you are looking for one single figure or piece of data, it's just not in there. There may be a wealth of other (irrelevant) data, but not the bit you are looking for though you are expected to come up with an answer based on that report and nothing else. What you will need to do is sort through all the data, disregard everything you do not need and find a way to "extract" the useful information. This is exactly what you will do when taking the numerical reasoning tests.

When it comes to **abstract reasoning**, the above analogy will of course not work. Not even in an institution with as widespread responsibilities as the EU will you face a situation where you need to select a shape with four circles and one rectangle (as opposed to two rectangles) in order to get through the day! You do, however, stand a good chance of going to your office one Monday morning and facing a situation or being given a task that will be completely unfamiliar; it might be about something you have never even heard about. Situations like this are the ones where the above-mentioned "fluid intelligence", the ability to manage the "unfamiliar" and apply logic, patterns and common sense becomes useful and that is exactly what abstract reasoning tests measure, as proven by various psychological experiments.

The Factors Determining Success

Just as is the case with any other test, success and good performance in EPSO's pre-selection exam is determined by several factors. We will now briefly discuss the four most important ones:

- Motivation
- Habits and hobbies
- Educational background
- Preparation and practice (most important)

Motivation

EPSO's pre-selection exam is certainly an event that one must prepare for and set aside significant amounts of time for this purpose: expect to experience a lot of stress both in the process of preparing and in the exam itself. In short, it takes time and effort, and it is easy to be distracted or discouraged on the way. This is exactly why having a clear and strong motivation is so important.

One essential component of self-motivation is knowing why you are expected to carry out a given task and how you can benefit from the effort that must be dedicated to it. Even if performing well at these tests is just a means to an end, it is still much easier to put in the required effort if you have a clear sense of why you are expected to do them and understand their objective benefits, such as getting an EU job or performing much better in job tasks requiring psychometric skills.

The above section on how these test types can be related to actual work situations may be thought of as one component of the motivation needed to succeed – knowing why you are expected to do these tests at the exam rather than something else.

Motivation is also about setting clear and attainable goals. There is an acronym that nicely sums up this challenge: being SMART.

A SMART strategy is one that includes goals that are:

Specific – "I will practice X hours a day for X days a week in order to get the job I have always wanted. Each week I will do X number of tests and revise X previous tests. I will also start reading about EU affairs to familiarise myself with the institutions."

Measureable – "I will improve this or that much every week, and will be able to get X per cent at these tests by the time of the exam. I will do a benchmark test against which I can measure my progress."

Achievable – "I have never been particularly good with numbers so I will not try to score 100% at numerical reasoning, but I will make sure to score as much as possible above the 50% threshold and to make it up in the other test types."

Relevant – "I will do all of the above because my goal is to work in the Directorate General for Development of the European Commission. I would also like to get this job so I will have the financial means to pursue my long-time dream of visiting a friend in Australia. Even if I find these tests challenging or tedious at times, I understand that they are required for the exam and in any case I can improve my skills too."

Time-bound – "I will set aside this amount of time for the next X months to achieve this or that goal. I will have a clear timetable for the next two months where I indicate the days and hours I plan to spend on practicing. I will be able to stick to my schedule because I see the end of the tunnel."

Educational Background

Educational background is another important factor in success. In addition to the obvious fact that the quality of education one received can make a huge difference, there are various fields of study that provide a more relevant background for performing well at these tests than others. Mathematics or other disciplines that make use of logic and deduction may help in solving the test questions better under time pressure.

Obviously, your educational background is not something you can change at the time you decide to participate in an EPSO Administrator competition. If you have a more relevant background, so much the better – though if you do not, there is certainly no reason for despair either: there are numerous important factors in success, all of which you can improve significantly (see relevant tips below and in each consequent chapter).

Habits and Hobbies

Before turning to the "controllable" factors mentioned above, we must also mention that there are certain hobbies and activities that, if you are a fan of them, may provide some temporary advantage. When it comes to verbal, numerical and abstract reasoning, people who have done crossword puzzles, Sudoku and other mind games might be at some advantage.

Preparation and Practice

The factor, however, that is the single most important one is what this book is all about: ***the quality and quantity of preparation and practice you complete in the run-up to the exam.***

In the following chapters, we will introduce in detail:

- the three test types and how they are designed
- the typical problems and challenges they pose
- the methods and skills that can greatly improve your performance
- the best ways to approach and interpret the test questions, and
- the optimal way to prepare and practice for these tests

With a clear grasp of the methods that can be used to efficiently take these tests and with the right amount of focused practice, powered by the correct motivation, even those candidates who feel that such tests are not their strong suit can improve significantly and pass this stage of the exam.

How these Tests are Scored

When you are preparing for the exam, you might often wonder exactly how well you are expected to perform in order to succeed. To answer this question, let us overview the marking system for these tests. The score candidates receive will have to satisfy two conditions:

Pass Mark – this is a simple "objective" barrier, usually 50% (but in some profiles, this is lowered to 40% for certain test types) that must be reached in each test separately, to be considered for the shortlist. It often happens, however, that for Administrator exams EPSO will set a pass mark for two or more tests combined (e.g. they will consider your numerical and abstract reasoning test scores as one and establish a 50% pass mark for the aggregate score of these two tests) – this is a somewhat easier situation because you can compensate for poorer performance in one test by excelling in the other one(s).

The Best X – this is a "relative" barrier, meaning that in addition to scoring higher than the objective pass mark, you must also be among a given number of best-performing candidates in all the tests combined. Some of the test results may be excluded from this relative barrier, meaning that numerical reasoning, for example, sometimes doesn't count toward your total score: all you need to do is achieve the pass mark.

Mixed Version – EPSO may also use the "pass mark" approach to create a larger pool of potential candidates and then "sift in" a certain number whose qualifications or professional experience (in the case of "specialist" Administrator exams) match various objective, pre-determined criteria, though the "best X" may also be factored in the decision.

In Practice

- Although you can hope to compensate for your weakness in one test type by performing better in another and thus still reaching a relatively high overall score, this option is limited by the requirement to reach the pass mark in each test separately (except for the cases outlined above when two test types have a combined pass mark)
- A "good" score in the context of one group of candidates (e.g. those who sit exams for the human resources sub-profile) might be an insufficient score in another group (e.g. those who have chosen the financial management sub-profile) – so examples of "successful scores" from the past are not really relevant

The figure below shows what is known as a "bell curve". Although it is just an illustration and it is not based on statistics, it quite accurately shows the typical distribution of scores candidates get at such tests. As we can see, there are few candidates with very low scores and very high scores. Most of the candidates will get scores in a very narrow range, for example between 60% and 70%, or 70% and 80%.

If "successful" candidates are selected by the best X number of participants in the exam, you must certainly score higher than others. ***Looking at the bell curve, it is easy to see that only a few percentage points of improvement can mean that you have beaten a large number of additional candidates!***

Why is this important? The way we must approach this information is that the goals you set when you start preparing and practicing for these tests do not have to be unrealistic or unattainable. Also, you can take comfort in the fact that every small improvement will make a huge difference at the exam and will improve your chances exponentially – all thanks to the bell curve.

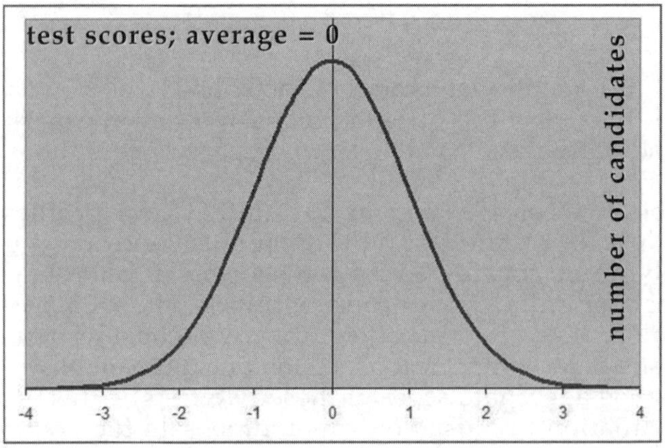

In the following chapters, we will see what the best methods and skills to achieve success are, accompanied by a large number of quality practice tests.

After all, the best way of learning things is by doing them a lot.

4. Succeeding in Verbal Reasoning Tests

In the world of standardized testing, the term "verbal reasoning" is commonly used to designate various test types relating to the interpretation and comprehension of texts. Although EPSO uses currently only one of these verbal reasoning test types, some of the models below measure skills that underlie the verbal reasoning tests EPSO uses to test candidates. It is therefore worth taking a quick look at each of them:

- **Spelling tests** are designed to test a person's ability to spell words correctly and also to differentiate between words with similar spellings yet completely or partially different meanings (for example, "steal" and "steel" or the correct spelling of "miscellaneous")
- **Word meaning tests** measure a person's vocabulary and their ability to select the best definition for words that have complex meanings (for example, to correctly identify the meaning of "exasperation" or "innuendo")
- **Word relationship tests** are designed to test a person's ability to determine the relationship between two concepts based on the analogy of another pair of concepts (for example, "what law is to anarchy, medicine is to …")
- **Comprehension tests** measure a person's ability to comprehend complex texts and determine whether statements about a text are correct, incorrect, or impossible to tell (this is the "classical" type used by EPSO)
- **Verbal deduction tests** are the most advanced form of verbal reasoning exercises – they measure the reader's ability to make correct and logical conclusions based on the information provided (for example, a text describing the mating habits of penguins followed by various questions such as "What are the right conditions for penguins to start mating?", "How do male penguins draw attention to themselves?" etc; this is a somewhat different approach from the "Which of the following statements is false?" question)

EPSO's verbal reasoning tests are closest in design to the comprehension test type. It is, however, easy to see how good performance in a comprehension test is based on the candidate's ability to identify correct spelling, the meaning of complex expressions and the relationship between various concepts. In this respect, this type of test is at the top in a hierarchy where success in comprehension depends on skills stemming from good performance on each of the lower levels.

In the following, we will overview several issues to look out for in a text, as well as a number of methods and skills that, once mastered, can greatly improve your performance. These include:

- How verbal reasoning tests are designed
- The role of familiar and unfamiliar topics
- Sources of information
- Assumptions
- Correct versus incorrect statements
- Near-equivalent versus identical statements
- Omission of information
- General versus particular
- Determiners and quantities

- Frequency
- Verbs: time and mode
- Causality versus chronology

We must mention here that a few of the methods and tips discussed in this chapter are discussed in the context of English-language test questions – this does not mean, however, that they cannot be applied in taking tests in other languages as well. In addition, the overwhelming majority of test-taking strategies discussed here are language-independent and are extremely useful in taking these tests in any language.

We will also discuss the best way to deal with each test question, the suggested order of reading the various components of the test (the text, the question and the answer options) and the recommended methods to practice for the test.

The sample test below is representative of the type of test questions EPSO currently uses as well as the expected level of difficulty at an EPSO competition. It consists of:

- A passage of text of between 100 and 200 words
- A standard question asking which of the supplied statements is correct or true
- Four statements as answer options, one being the right answer, i.e. the only correct statement

A Sample Test

Bacteria growing in near darkness use a previously unknown process for harvesting energy and producing oxygen from sunlight, a research team discovered. The discovery lays the foundation for further research aimed at improving plant growth and harvesting energy from the Sun.

"We have shown that some cyanobacteria, also called blue-green algae, can grow in far-red wavelengths of light, a range not seen well by most humans," said a researcher. "Most cyanobacteria can't 'see' this light either. But we have found a new subgroup that can absorb and use it, and we have discovered some of the surprising ways they manipulate their genes in order to grow using only these wavelengths," he said.

The experiments revealed that these cyanobacteria replace seventeen proteins in three major light-using complexes while also making new chlorophyll pigments that can capture the far-red light. The scientists also discovered that the organisms accomplish this feat by quickly turning on a large number of genes to modify cellular metabolism and simultaneously turning off a large number of other genes.
(*Science Daily*, 26 August 2014)

Which of the following statements is correct?

A. The mechanism by which some cyanobacteria capture far-red light may in the future be used to harness solar power.
B. Blue-green algae utilise far-red light by substituting three light-using proteins for chlorophyll pigments.
C. Some cyanobacteria cannot activate the genes necessary to absorb far-red light because they lack the necessary proteins.
D. The light-absorbing process described requires replacing 17 proteins but does not necessitate major genetic changes.

We will now consider the factors and methods listed above one by one. Before we do that, however, it is essential to gain some insight into how verbal reasoning tests are designed by their authors – if you understand the concepts and strategies behind the creation of verbal reasoning tests, taking those tests will become incomparably easier.

How are verbal reasoning tests designed?

When psychologists whose specialty is the creation of psychometric tests design verbal reasoning items, they essentially follow two design steps:

1. Selecting an appropriate piece of text.
2. Authoring appropriate answer options.

Let us see what considerations go into each of these two steps.

1. Selecting an appropriate piece of text

When selecting excerpts for a verbal reasoning text, several factors are considered, such as:

- Does the text include a good variety of verbs, nouns, adjectives, and so on?
- Is the difficulty of vocabulary appropriate for the purposes of the test (e.g. for assessing Assistant or Administrator candidates for an EU job?)
- Is the text free of jargon?
- Are abbreviations explained at least once in the text?
- Is the text free of topics that might be objectionable from a political, moral or ethical point of view?

The difficulty of the text and its vocabulary is a complex issue: suffice it to say that such things are considered as the length of the sentences (in number of words) or the length and complexity of the words themselves.

2. Authoring appropriate answer options

The creation of the answer options is the most difficult and most important task in the design of verbal reasoning tests. Let us overview what kind of answer options exist – being aware of the types of answer options that you might face will be highly useful in the EPSO pre-selection as well.

"Correct" or "True" statements: Such statements are clearly and demonstrably correct based on the information in the text. No outside knowledge is required to prove their correctness; it is possible to determine that on the basis of the excerpt and by drawing well-founded conclusions. Obviously, each verbal reasoning test item features only one such statement, and that statement will be the right answer. It is worth noting that the difficulty of the test item can be greatly influenced by how this statement is formulated:

- Does the right answer use similar expressions to those found in the text? The more similar the wording, the easier it is to spot that it is the correct statement.
- Is the right answer simply a reworded version of a statement in the passage, or is it a conclusion that can be drawn by utilizing several pieces of information from various parts of the excerpt?

"Incorrect" or "False" statements: Such statements are clearly and demonstrably incorrect based on the information in the text passage. It is important to point out that these statements are not simply unfounded (that is, no evidence exists as to whether they are correct or incorrect) but can be clearly disproved by utilizing information in the text. The difficulty of spotting such statements is, again, dependent on several factors:

- Is part of the statement correct? If so, it may be more difficult to realize that it is an incorrect statement, because only part of the information contained in it makes it so.
- Is the topic of the text expected to be familiar to test-takers? If so, it is much easier to decide a statement is incorrect, because most candidates will know it to be false and it will immediately "stand out".

You may now think that the above two statement types are all there is to verbal reasoning tests, but we will see very soon that there is one more statement type which makes the whole thing much more complicated. Nevertheless, we can already see that the degree of difficulty of test items that utilize only these two statement types can also vary greatly based on the factors listed above.

"Insufficient information" or "Cannot say" statements: This is the type of statement which usually causes the greatest confusion and represents the most dangerous trap when taking a verbal reasoning test. "Insufficient information" statements can belong to one of two categories:

- Statements that are *incorrect* if assessed using outside knowledge: such statements are easier to handle, because they will "feel" incorrect – you might know the statement to be incorrect based on your knowledge of facts, but it is impossible to classify the statement as incorrect based solely on information in the test passage. Fortunately, you are not expected to do that – just remember that **any statement which cannot be clearly proven by information in the excerpt is "incorrect"** in the context of a verbal reasoning test
- Statements that are *correct* if assessed using outside knowledge: such statements are the hardest to spot because they will "feel" correct upon first reading. The reason they are dangerous is exactly because you instinctively want to agree with the statement you know to be true. The important thing to remember here is that the **only correct statement in a verbal reasoning test is one that is fully supported and proven by information in the text passage.**

We can now easily realize that verbal reasoning tests can be designed using any mixture of the above statement types.

Here are a few:

- 1 true statement, 3 false statements: this is probably the easiest type, as true and false statements are easier to spot
- 1 true statement, 2 false statements, 1 "insufficient information" or "cannot say" statement: this test would be a bit harder, because in addition to the correct answer, one additional answer option might at first "feel" correct – remember the tips above and you will be able to easily avoid this trap
- 1 true statement, 3 "insufficient information" statements: this is the "crown jewel" of verbal reasoning tests – the most difficult type. This is because due to the nature of the statement types used, you might feel that *all four statements* are correct upon first reading, but, again, you can discard those with insufficient information by remembering the principles described above

Based on experience and consulting with occupational psychologists, the great majority of verbal reasoning test questions that you will encounter at an EPSO Administrator competition will feature at least one "insufficient information" statement and it is quite likely that you will face at least a few questions where three of the four answer options will be of this type. You should, however, be aware of the existence of the other combinations listed above as well – better safe than sorry, as the saying goes.

Let us now consider a concrete example and return to the sample test item above. Let us analyze the answer options based on the criteria we established.

A. The mechanism by which some cyanobacteria capture far-red light may in the future be used to harness solar power.

This is a true statement:

- the passage describes the way certain bacteria can absorb and use far-red light
- the passage states that this discovery lays the foundation for further research
- one of the future research areas mentioned is harvesting the energy of the sun
- we can draw the well-supported conclusion that the mechanism may in the future be used to harness the power of the sun

B. Blue-green algae utilise far-red light by substituting three light-using proteins for chlorophyll pigments.

This statement is false. Although all of the components of the statement have a basis in the text passage, things are completely mixed up. The number of proteins is 17, three is the number of light-using complexes. Also, chlorophyll pigments are not substituted, rather, new ones are grown. The only correct part of the statement is the one that states that it is blue-green algae that can utilise far-red light.

C. Some cyanobacteria cannot activate the genes necessary to absorb far-red light because they lack the necessary proteins.

This is a typical insufficient information type statement which is made even more difficult by the fact that the claim it makes feels logical and true.

- it is true that some cyanobacteria cannot use far-red light
- it seems logical that this may be caused by the necessary genes not being activated
- it also seems logical that this might be because the necessary proteins are missing

What we have to realise here is that we used several unfounded assumptions to arrive at this conclusion. In reality, we have no idea what causes some cyanobacteria not to be able to absorb far-red light, and we are not given enough information to make claims about what proteins are necessary to activate which genes.

D. The light-absorbing process described requires replacing 17 proteins but does not necessitate major genetic changes.

This statement is false. While it starts out making a correct claim (the process does require replacing 17 proteins), the last paragraph of the passage is in clear contradiction to the second part of the statement: it describes major genetic changes taking place in these bacteria and a large number of genes are activated and turned off to achieve this ability.

Now that we have analyzed the above four statements, we can see that our sample test item contains one true statement (the right answer), one "insufficient information" or "cannot say" statement, and two false statements. From a design perspective, the above test item is of medium difficulty, and the EPSO verbal reasoning test for Administrators will include items of comparable or greater difficulty.

Let us now turn our attention to the factors listed a few pages earlier – familiarity with such techniques as verb time and mode or generalizations will help you quickly determine which category each statement in a test belongs to, allowing you to find the correct answer in record time.

The Role of Familiar and Unfamiliar Topics

The topics of the texts in the verbal reasoning test can be varied. They may be closely EU-related (descriptions of policies, EU news) or they may be completely unrelated, dealing with history, art, nature, science and technology, music, and so on. Based on their interests or hobbies, most candidates have one or several preferred topics; however, the topic of the text should be completely irrelevant from the point of view of performing well in the test. While it is troubling to be faced with a topic that is completely alien to you, a familiar topic has its own dangers, because you must only use the information in the text, not your own knowledge.

Let us consider the pros and cons of familiar and unfamiliar topics.

As we can see, there is no significant argument either for or against wishing for familiar topics. Each has its distinct pitfalls and advantages.

As an example, if a candidate is very interested in space exploration and reads a text on a topic they know a lot about, for instance the New Horizons spacecraft launched to explore the solar system and beyond, it may seem a comfortable situation but may also backfire. Having a deep knowledge of a topic may make it hard to separate the information in the text from the information we already have about the subject – and, as we will see, it is one of the main mistakes test takers commit. In the above example, the candidate may, for instance, be aware that New Horizons initially travelled faster than any other space probe launched previously. This could lead the candidate to choose a statement about the spacecraft's speed as being correct when it is actually a "cannot say" statement because the speed is not mentioned in the text or any reference is ambiguous.

On the other hand, many candidates panic when faced with a text about a subject they have never been interested in. There may even be words and expressions that they have never even heard of. Yet it often happens that it is exactly the distance from the topic and "objectivity" that allows us to consider only the information in the text and select the right answer quickly and systematically.

Familiar Topic (space exploration)		**Unfamiliar Topic (e.g. molecular biology)**	
Pros	***Cons***	***Pros***	***Cons***
Mainstream vocabulary	*Bias*	*No bias*	*May be colloquial*
Familiarity	*Technical vocabulary*	*May be everyday topic*	*May include exotic vocabulary*
No colloquialisms	*Assumptions*	*No assumptions*	*Not familiar*

Sources of Information

When we discussed the familiarity of the subject, we touched upon the fact that it is crucial to always keep in mind what information we use when assessing whether statements in the answer options are correct.

Let us consider the following sentence from an imaginary verbal reasoning text passage: *"nearly one in five European adult males still smoke cigarettes on a daily basis"*.

Now let's look at a theoretical answer option where pre-existing knowledge could cause a problem: *"Almost 40 million European adult males still regularly smoke cigarettes."*

If the candidate happens to know that there are approximately 200 million adult males in Europe and uses that knowledge when taking the test, they might end up selecting the above answer option as correct – and lose a point, because the statement cannot be correct if the text does not contain information about the adult male population of Europe.

It is thus crucial to remember that statements in the answer options must be assessed based solely on the information in the text.

It can be particularly dangerous when a statement includes information of the sort that it may seem "everybody" knows, not just that is familiar to you because of your own specialist knowledge. Examples of this would be: "The German economy is bigger than that of Greece"; "the Olympic Games are held every four years"; "more of the Earth's surface is ocean than land". Be very alert to this risk. The test questions in the next chapter have many such examples.

Assumptions

In the previous example, we saw a situation where an assumption (regardless of whether true or false) was made about a statement based on "outside" knowledge. Let us consider another example.

"Performing specific physical exercises daily decreases the chances of developing certain movement-related difficulties in old age."

A possible answer option: *"Cycling for 30 minutes every day decreases the chances of developing rheumatism later."*

One might be tempted to select the above answer option as correct. If we do so, we make two assumptions:

1. Cycling is one of those specific physical exercises that are useful for such purposes.
2. Rheumatism is one of those movement-related difficulties that can be prevented in such a way.

Whether the above answer option is indeed the correct one depends entirely on what other information regarding the specific physical exercises and the types of movement-related difficulties is included in the text. For example, if there is no mention of cycling in the text, considering it as one of those exercises will be a false assumption which will cause us to lose a valuable point in the test. Also, it is merely our interpretation (assumption) that rheumatism is a movement-related difficulty that can be prevented this way – unless the text itself gives that information.

Correct versus Incorrect Statements

Although the verbal reasoning test in EPSO competitions almost exclusively includes items where the question is of the *"Which of the following statements is correct?"* type, it is important to mention another possibility – when the question is *"Which of the following statements is incorrect?"*.

The same principles that we discussed apply in this situation as well, but we will need to look for the false statement – that will be the right answer. It is also important to point out that if the question is seeking the incorrect statement, we can still encounter "insufficient information" statements – in this case, however, such statements will often be designed to "feel" incorrect – thereby leading you to think that they indeed are. Just remember: if you are expected to pick the incorrect answer option, look for a statement that can be clearly and unambiguously disproved based on the information in the text passage.

As a final point, it is worth mentioning something that may seem obvious, but must be noted. It is crucial to always carefully read the question (the one immediately after the text) and keep in mind whether you are supposed to look for the correct or incorrect statement. As simple as this may sound, many candidates have lost points in verbal reasoning tests by not taking the extra two seconds to read the question, especially under the stress and time pressure of the exam.

Near Equivalent versus Identical Statements

Consider the following example.

"Not many inventions last for more than a hundred years without major modifications. One of them is the barometer."

A possible answer option: *"Since it was invented, the barometer has not been modified."*

The statement in the answer option is very similar to the information in the excerpt. It uses many of the same words, and it essentially conveys a fairly similar meaning. Yet in the context of a verbal reasoning test, we cannot infer that "without major modifications" is equivalent to "has not been modified". The former implies *little* has been changed, the latter that *nothing* has been changed in the design of the barometer.

It is always dangerous to look for similar words and expressions in the answer option. Similarity can hide small but important differences in meaning and can prevent you from reading on and seriously considering other answer options among which the correct one can be found.

Another piece of advice is to always look for prefixes or adjectives that change the meaning or the scope of a statement, such as "some", "hardly", "almost", "not always", "any", "completely", "at all", "partially", "to some extent", "mostly", "generally", "exclusively", "sometimes", "largely", "arguably", "seemingly" and others (see more examples below).

Although since 2011 this problem has eased as you are now able to take the verbal reasoning test in your native (official EU) language, it is still worth taking some time to think about words and expressions in your own language that slightly modify the meaning of the sentence in which they are included. This is especially true because we use our native language much less consciously than a second language and slight shifts in meaning are often overlooked in everyday speech.

Omission of Information

Here is an excerpt from another text:

"Shakepeare's plays are still well-liked by audiences. In 2010, almost 100 countries had theatres where a Shakespeare play was in the programme and tickets to these productions were sold to nearly 15 million people."

A possible answer option: *"There are still theatres that stage Shakespeare productions."*

Note that this answer option has a completely different approach than the excerpt from the text. Having read the text, readers might be inclined to look for answer options that emphasize how well-liked Shakespeare's plays still are. Our example answer option does not do that, it simply states that Shakespeare productions are still being staged in an unspecified number of theatres.

At first reading, the statement in the answer option seems to be in conflict with the excerpt by not conveying the popularity of these plays. Yet it is a perfectly valid and correct statement.

We must, then, remember that the fact that a statement fails to convey all the information that was included in the text about something does not mean that it is an incorrect statement. In short and all other factors being equal, omission of information is not necessarily disagreement or contradiction.

General versus Particular

Another typical mistake many candidates make has to do with the difference between general categories and particular instances. This mistake can take one of two forms:

- Generalisation
- Over-specification

Let us consider an example.

"The oceanic climate is one of the wettest ones in the world. Average precipitation is significantly higher than in continental habitats. Some areas of the Atlantic Ocean do not go a full week without rain for decades."

A possible answer option: *"Oceanic areas do not have completely dry weeks for decades."*

The above statement is an example of a generalisation where a statement made about certain instances of a category (in this case, Atlantic areas) is assumed to be correct about the entire category (that is, all oceanic climate areas).

Let us consider another example.

"Some oceanic areas have wetter winters and springs while others experience more rainfall in the summer and autumn."

A possible answer option: *"The amount of rainfall in oceanic areas differs by season, depending on the geographical location."*

The above answer option is correct in stating that the amount of rainfall differs by season, but it is overly specific in stating that this depends on the geographical location – this is unfounded information not included in the text.

Determiners and Quantities

We now come to more language-specific problems. While most of the points raised so far are valid in all languages the test is administered in, there are always language-specific issues to consider. If the test is administered in English these tips will be directly useful to your preparation.

If you take your test in another language, the following few sections can serve as a guideline along which you can consider the peculiarities of your own language and come up with a list of things to look out for. A good way of doing this is to read newspaper articles with higher than usual attention – professional journalists are always careful about how they formulate their statements and use many of the linguistic devices demonstrated here to make their statements more accurate.

Determiners and words expressing certain or uncertain quantities can be hard to notice; many candidates tend not to attribute much meaning to them in everyday situations even though they may greatly alter the meaning of a statement in the context of a verbal reasoning test.

Be mindful of the exact meaning of some of the most common determiners:

- "the" usually signifies one concrete object or person, or one concrete group: "the apple","the fruit", "the pencils [on the table]", and so on.
- "a/an" and nouns without any determiner usually refer to one unspecified object or person, or an unspecified group of objects or persons: "an apple", "a fruit", "people in the United Kingdom", and so on.

When the answer option lacks the determiner found in the text or features a different one, we must always be suspicious and consider whether this distinction changes the meaning of the statement.

A similar pattern can be observed when it comes to quantities: "some", "many", "several", "a number of" refer to an unspecified number of objects of persons. "All", "the entire", "every", and "each" signifies that the statement is about every single member of a group, or an object in its entirety, without exception.

It is important to bear in mind that these determiners of quantity are not interchangeable and if the text mentions "many countries", an answer option that extends that claim to "all countries" will not be correct.

Frequency

A very similar situation can be created by the use of adverbs signifying the frequency at which an action takes place. Always pay special attention to the use of the adverbs "sometimes", "often", "usually", "frequently", "never", "hardly ever", "occasionally", "always" and so on.

Although the only two concrete indicators are "never" and "always", and it is very hard to define the difference between "sometimes" and "occasionally", we must be mindful of the fact that they do carry meaning and can significantly change the meaning of a statement.

The same also can be said about adjectives and adverbs expressing chronology:

- "before", "previously", "earlier", "prior to that" are hints that one event took place sooner than another one
- "meanwhile", "concurrently", "simultaneously", and others indicate that two events occured at the same time

- "after", "subsequently", "followed by", "later", and similar words help us establish that one event followed another event in time

Think of the following statements: "I occasionally go to work after eating breakfast" and "I sometimes eat breakfast after going to work". The implied sequence of actions and their frequencies are very different. Another example is "Birds have colourful feathers" versus "Some birds have colourful feathers": the scope and extent are very different.

Verbs: Time and Mode

Closely related to the previous point, the tense of verbs also plays a crucial role in re-creating a series of events. Take an example:

"Until his brother successfully launching his internet startup, Gerorge was the richest member of the family thanks to his burgeoning career as a successful attorney."

A possible answer option: *"George is the richest member of the family."*

The above option is incorrect because according to the text, he had been the richest member of the family only until his brother successfully launched his internet startup. This fact is indicated by the use of the expression "until" and also the past tense.

Verb mode also plays an important part in determining whether a statement is correct:

- Probability – "would happen" does not necessarily mean that something "will happen"; "would have happened" commonly means that the event did not in fact happen at all
- "Could happen" indicates that a certain event is only one of several possible outcomes
- "Should do something" indicates that a certain course of action is recommended or likely, but not necessarily unavoidable or mandatory
- "About to happen" shows that an event was going to take place but may or may not have actually happened
- "Was about to" (e.g. "he was about to go home when") refers to an intention or plan that was likely to take place when a certain event interrupted it or took place

Causality versus Chronology

As a last point, we must mention two phenomena that are frequently confused. Let us look at an example.

"The San Francisco Zoo has been visited by record numbers of visitors ever since 2005. In 2012, it received a gold medal from the World Zoological Society."

A possible answer option: *"Record numbers of visitors go to see the San Francisco Zoo every year, which resulted in it receiving the Gold Medal from the World Zoological Society."*

The statement in the above answer option incorrectly makes the assumption that there is a cause-and-effect relationship between the record number of visitors to the zoo in recent years and the receipt of the gold medal. As far as the statement goes, the relationship between the two things is merely chronological. There is no evidence that the gold medal was awarded because of the high number of visitors: it could just as well wave been given as a commendation for good animal keeping conditions or other factors, we simply do not know.

It is easy to mistake a merely chronological relationship for a cause-and-effect one, but one thing that will help decide is the verbal clues mentioned above. Since test-makers tend not to include ambiguous information in tests, we can always count on indicators of a cause-and-effect relationship ("led to", "consequently", "resulted in") or a mere chronological relationship to appear in the text.

Methods for Approaching the Test Questions

Let us return to our sample text:

> Bacteria growing in near darkness use a previously unknown process for harvesting energy and producing oxygen from sunlight, a research team discovered. The discovery lays the foundation for further research aimed at improving plant growth and harvesting energy from the Sun.
>
> "We have shown that some cyanobacteria, also called blue-green algae, can grow in far-red wavelengths of light, a range not seen well by most humans," said a researcher. "Most cyanobacteria can't 'see' this light either. But we have found a new subgroup that can absorb and use it, and we have discovered some of the surprising ways they manipulate their genes in order to grow using only these wavelengths," he said.
>
> The experiments revealed that these cyanobacteria replace seventeen proteins in three major light-using complexes while also making new chlorophyll pigments that can capture the far-red light. The scientists also discovered that the organisms accomplish this feat by quickly turning on a large number of genes to modify cellular metabolism and simultaneously turning off a large number of other genes.
> (*Science Daily*, 26 August 2014)
>
> *Which of the following statements is correct?*
>
> A. The mechanism by which some cyanobacteria capture far-red light may in the future be used to harness solar power.
> B. Blue-green algae utilise far-red light by substituting three light-using proteins for chlorophyll pigments.
> C. Some cyanobacteria cannot activate the genes necessary to absorb far-red light because they lack the necessary proteins.
> D. The light-absorbing process described requires replacing 17 proteins but does not necessitate major genetic changes.

When somebody first looks at a verbal reasoning test like the one above, the natural instinct is to start reading the text, then read the question, and finally read the four answer options. If we wish to consider all the factors we discussed in this chapter and make mental "notes" of them by underlining the key expressions in the text using the above method, it would look like this:

Bacteria growing in <u>near</u> darkness use a <u>previously</u> unknown process for harvesting energy and producing oxygen from sunlight, a research team discovered. The discovery lays the foundation for <u>further</u> research aimed at improving plant growth and harvesting energy from the Sun.

"We have shown that <u>some</u> cyanobacteria, also called blue-green algae, <u>can</u> grow in far-red wavelengths of light, a range not seen <u>well</u> by most humans," said a researcher. "Most cyanobacteria can't 'see' this light either. But we have found a <u>new</u> subgroup that <u>can</u> absorb and use it, and we have discovered <u>some</u> of the surprising ways they manipulate their genes in order to grow using <u>only</u> these wavelengths," he said.

The experiments revealed that these cyanobacteria replace <u>seventeen</u> proteins in <u>three major</u> light-using complexes <u>while</u> also making new chlorophyll pigments that can capture the far-red light. The scientists also discovered that the organisms accomplish this feat by <u>quickly</u> turning on a <u>large number</u> of genes to modify cellular metabolism and simultaneously turning off a <u>large number</u> of other genes.

Which of the following statements is correct?

A. The mechanism by which some cyanobacteria capture far-red light <u>may in the future</u> be used to harness solar power.
B. Blue-green algae utilise far-red light by substituting <u>three</u> light-using proteins for chlorophyll pigments.
C. <u>Some</u> cyanobacteria cannot activate the genes necessary to absorb far-red light <u>because</u> they lack the necessary proteins.
D. The light-absorbing process described requires replacing 17 proteins but does <u>not</u> necessitate <u>major</u> genetic changes.

The underlined expressions are "suspect phrases" because of the various factors we discussed.

But what if most of the factors that we concentrated on when reading the text for the first time later turn out to be completely irrelevant because the answer options do not relate to those bits of the text? In order to avoid wasting time on irrelevant information, it is a good idea to read the question and the answer options first, looking for keywords and key concepts, and then read the text, already focusing on and searching for those bits that we know we need to answer the question.

Our mental notes using this recommended method would therefore look like this:

> Bacteria growing in near darkness use a previously unknown process for harvesting energy and producing oxygen from sunlight, a research team discovered. The discovery lays the foundation for further research aimed at improving plant growth and harvesting energy from the Sun.
>
> "We have shown that some cyanobacteria, also called blue-green algae, can grow in far-red wavelengths of light, a range not seen well by most humans," said a researcher. "Most cyanobacteria can't 'see' this light either. But we have found a new subgroup that can absorb and use it, and we have discovered some of the surprising ways they manipulate their genes in order to grow using only these wavelengths," he said.
>
> The experiments revealed that these cyanobacteria replace seventeen proteins in three major light-using complexes while also making new chlorophyll pigments that can capture the far-red light. The scientists also discovered that the organisms accomplish this feat by quickly turning on a large number of genes to modify cellular metabolism and simultaneously turning off a large number of other genes.

Using this method, we can immediately discard option B when we read that chlorophyll pigments are not substituted, but capture far-red light. Option D can be discarded when we read that significant genetic changes take place to allow for the absorption of far-red light. Option C is a bit trickier, but when we realise that the text passage does not actually explain why certain cyanobacteria can not absorb far-red light, the entire explanation given in the statement becomes an unfounded assumption and we can discard that quickly as well.

Let us summarize the above method in a few points:

1. Read the question first – are we looking for the correct or incorrect statement?
2. Read the answer options and make a mental note of the important keywords and themes included in those statements.
3. Read the text by focusing on the themes and keywords you made a mental note of when reading the answer options.
4. If you encounter a statement in the text that is clearly in agreement with an answer option (or in clear disagreement, if you are looking for the incorrect statement), and you are sure about your assessment, you can even stop reading and move on, thereby saving precious time.
5. If you are not sure about your assessment, you can continue reading and then eliminate the answer options one by one. This is where your knowledge of the possible statement types (true, false, insufficient information) will prove extremely useful – if you apply this knowledge right, and factor in the methods we discussed in this chapter, no amount of "witchcraft" on the part of the test item's author will confuse you.

Practice Methods

As a last point, it might be useful to make a few suggestions as to what the best methods are for preparing for the verbal reasoning test.

- Start practicing by taking your time, reading all kinds of high level English texts, making mental notes of the "suspect phrases" we covered in this chapter
- Continue by doing the same, this time with the actual test questions in this book (for

the sake of practicing, you may wish to underline or outline these concepts and also write down in your own words why a certain answer option is wrong)

- Once you have established the necessary routine in identifying the key phrases and concepts, you can start timing yourself – begin by simply measuring how much time it takes for you to answer one test question
- Check how much time you will have at the exam, and how many questions you will need to answer (**as a general rule, you will have 35 minutes for 20 questions**).
- Start decreasing the amount of time you let yourself use for answering one question – ideally, by the time of the exam, you should be able to answer more questions in the given time than required in the exam (this is necessary because you cannot re-create the stress of the exam, which can decrease performance, not to mention the slower pace when reading texts on a computer screen for the pre-selection exams)
- Try to re-create as much of the atmosphere and infrastructure of the exam as you can – do not interrupt the test, go to a quiet place, use an alarm clock, and so on
- If you have access to such a service, practice tests online, e.g. the *www.eutraining.eu* site – since the EPSO exam will also be computer-based, and it is a good idea to get used to the "interface" before going to the exam. Most such websites also offer the opportunity to revise the practice tests you took and look at detailed statistics, comparing your performance to others and measuring your improvement in a test type over time – experience shows that such statistics can have an extremely positive psychological effect as well as help to reveal the weaknesses and strengths of your skills in various tests.
- Try to read as much as possible on screen and measure the time it takes to read texts of comparable length (e.g. one page copied into Word) so you can measure and improve your performance.

For advice and tips on tackling verbal reasoning questions – see the previous chapter.

For the answers to this test – see at end of questions.

5. Verbal Reasoning Test

180 QUESTIONS – ANSWERS follow questions

In each question below, you have to decide which of four statements, A, B, C or D is correct, based on the preceding passage of text.
***There is only one correct answer to each question**, which is "True" in terms of the information given in the text: the other statements will either be "False" or "Cannot say" from the information given in the text.*
*Each question must be considered without reference to any other knowledge you may have of the subject matter – **only information included in the passage itself may be used** in deciding your answer.*
For practice purposes, you should try to complete 20 questions in 35 minutes.

1. **English has been the unofficial language of pilots for many years, but a tragic accident in the Canary Islands in 1977 emphasized the need for a universal aviation language. In this case, two 747 jets—one Pan Am, one KLM—collided on the runway at Tenerife airport. At one point, the KLM pilot told the tower in a heavy Dutch accent either "We're now at take-off" or "We're uh…taking off." The tower didn't understand the message and told KLM to standby, but a simultaneous communication from Pan Am garbled the instruction. Reviews by the National Transportation Safety Board (NTSB) of the cockpit recorder transcriptions determined that the KLM pilot's use of non-standard phraseology during the critical moments leading up to the accident contributed to the disaster. (*mentalfloss.com*)**

A. English was chosen as the universal aviation language because it is so widely spoken.

B. It took a tragedy before people officially adopted English for use in aviation.

C. The tragedy in the Canary Islands demonstrated the importance of standardised language.

D. The Dutch pilot's inability to speak English resulted in the tragedy on the Canary Islands.

2. **Most of us consider our personality to be an integral and unchanging part of who we are – perhaps the essence of that thing we call the self. In 1887, psychologist William James went so far as to argue that it becomes "set like plaster" by the age of 30. His idea stuck. Psychologists have long debated how to measure personality, settling eventually on the "big five" traits. But at least they were able to agree on a definition: personality refers to an individual's thought patterns and behaviours, which tend to persist over time. Now mounting evidence is undermining that notion. Personality is far more mutable than we thought. That may be a little unsettling. But it's also good news for the almost 90 percent of us who wish our personalities were at least a little different. (*newscientist.com*)**

A. By the time people reach the age of 30 their personalities are mostly set in stone.

B. William James was the psychologist who defined the "big five" psychological traits.

C. Nearly everyone wishes that their personality was strikingly different.

D. Personalities are now believed to be much more malleable before and after the age of 30.

3. **One theory regarding Edgar Allen Poe's death is that he may have been a victim of a violent crime. Because the tavern where Poe was found prior to his death was being used as a polling place (it was common practice in the 19th century for voting to take place in drinking establishments), it has been proposed that he may have been caught up in an unusual form of electoral fraud known as "cooping." In a cooping scheme, gangs working for corrupt politicians would grab unwilling bystanders off the street and force them to vote repeatedly for a certain candidate. Victims were often beaten or forced to drink alcohol to make them comply. Disguises were used to allow the victims to vote multiple times. This could explain the bizarre outfit that Poe was wearing when he was discovered. (*Britannica.com*)**

A. Voting usually took place in drinking establishments in the 19th century.

B. Poe's mysterious death may be explained as the product of electoral fraud.

C. In the 19th century, people were allowed to vote on multiple occasions in elections.

D. When Poe was found it was discovered that he had voted on multiple occasions.

4. **Chromatic aberration, also known as "colour fringing" or "purple fringing", is a common optical problem that occurs when a lens is either unable to bring all wavelengths of colour to the same focal plane, and/or when wavelengths of colour are focused at different positions in the focal plane. Chromatic aberration is caused by lens dispersion, with different colours of light travelling at different speeds while passing through a lens. As a result, the image can look blurred or noticeable coloured edges (red, green, blue, yellow, purple, magenta) can appear around objects, especially in high-contrast situations. (*photographylife.com*)**

A. Chromatic aberration is caused by lens dispersion in lenses that are inexpensive.

B. Chromatic aberration is also called purple fringing because that is the most common colour.

C. Lenses unable to bring all colour wavelengths to the same focal plane produce colour fringing.

D. The effect of chromatic aberration will not be seen in situations featuring low contrast.

5. **Education does not stop. Professors must update and develop their technical skills throughout their careers. But as they progress, few take the time – or are offered the opportunity – to become educated in how to be an effective leader. As a consequence, academic teams waste time dealing with unproductive interpersonal issues, lack of motivation and unnecessary conflict. When things do not run smoothly, the costs in terms of money, productivity and retention of talent are high. Leaders should inspire others to achieve goals. Professors lead research teams and manage teaching staff. They also have to lead intellectually, making advances in engineering and science that benefit society. The importance of leadership skills grows as scientists gain seniority. Even well-meaning professors can create chaos by bossing people and failing to take into account the emotions of others.**

Equally, those who take a back seat can create teams that are much less effective. (*nature.com*)

A. Academic teams fail due to the conflict caused by poor leadership that does not tackle inter-personal issues and low motivation.

B. It is important that senior academics build strong leadership and technical skills in order to be effective in their roles.

C. An abundance of opportunities for promotion explains why academics do not focus on developing their leadership skills.

D. Seniority is not relevant when considering the leadership skills necessary for scientists whereas the ability to read emotions is.

6. **At the *ludi meridiani*, or midday games, criminals, barbarians, prisoners of war and other unfortunates, called *damnati*, or "condemned," were executed. (Despite numerous accounts of saints' lives written in the Renaissance and later, there is no reliable evidence that Christians were killed in the Colosseum for their faith.) Some damnati were released in the arena to be slaughtered by fierce animals such as lions, and some were forced to fight one another with swords. Others were dispatched in what a modern scholar has called "fatal charades," executions staged to resemble scenes from mythology. The Roman poet Martial, who attended the inaugural games, describes a criminal dressed as Orpheus playing a lyre amid wild animals; a bear ripped him apart. Another suffered the fate of Hercules, who burned to death before becoming a god. (*smithsoniamag.com*)**

A. Historical evidence proves that no Christians were killed at the Colosseum, along with war prisoners and barbarians.

B. All *damnati* were forced to participate in staged executions involving characters and scenes from mythology.

C. During the morning games, spectators could witness wild beast hunts involving fierce animals such as lions and bears.

D. As part of their execution, a criminal could find themselves facing a wild beast or sword fighting another person.

7. **Dr Caroline Lyon, Professor Chrystopher Nehaniv and Dr Joe Saunders have carried out experiments as part of the iTalk project with the childlike iCub humanoid robot to show how language learning emerges. Initially the robot can only babble and perceives speech as a string of sounds, not divided up into words. After engaging in a few minutes of "conversation" with humans, in which the participants were instructed to speak to the robot as if it were a small child, the robot adapted its output to the most frequently heard syllables to produce some word forms such as the names of simple shapes and colours. Dr Caroline Lyon said: "It is known that infants are sensitive to the frequency of sounds in speech, and these experiments show how this sensitivity can be modelled and contribute to the learning of word forms by a robot." (*Science Daily*)**

A. According to Dr Caroline Lyon, our current knowledge of how infants perceive language can help robots learn word forms.

B. When robots are starting to learn language skills, they readily recognize individual speech units including words.

C. Experiments that are part of the iTalk project have shown that robots develop language skills more quickly than humans.

D. After a few minutes of "conversation" with humans, a robot will adapt its output to the most frequently heard inflections.

8. **Leonardo da Vinci's *Vetruvian Man* is the attempt to illustrate the idea, set down by Vitruvius in the *Ten Books*, that the human body can be made to fit inside a circle and a square. This was more than a geometrical statement. Ancient thinkers had long invested the circle and the square with symbolic powers. The circle represented the cosmic and the divine; the square, the earthly and the secular. Anyone proposing that a man could be made to fit inside both shapes was making a metaphysical proposition: The human body wasn't just designed according to the principles that governed the world; it *was* the world, in miniature. This was the theory of the microcosm, and Leonardo hitched himself to it early in his career. "By the ancients," he wrote around 1492, "man was termed**

a lesser world, and certainly the use of this name is well bestowed, because ... his body is an analogue for the world." (*smithsonianmag.com*)

A. Viewing the body as a miniature representation of the world was the key to Leonardo da Vinci's success as an artist.

B. According to ancient thinkers, the circle symbolizes the non-spiritual while the square symbolizes the spiritual.

C. *Vetruvian Man,* as an attempt to fit the human body inside a circle and a square, reflects Leonardo's belief in God.

D. *Vetruvian Man* is a statement of the metaphysical idea that the human body is a microcosm of the world.

9. Quantum cryptography is, in principle, a foolproof way to prevent hacking. It ensures that any attempt by an eavesdropper to read encoded communication data will lead to disturbances that can be detected by the legitimate users. Therefore, quantum cryptography allows the transmission of an unconditionally secure encryption key between two users, "Alice" and "Bob", in the presence of a potential hacker, "Eve". The encryption key is communicated using light signals and is received using photon detectors. The challenge is that Eve can intercept and manipulate these signals. When quantum hacking occurs, light signals subvert the photon detectors, causing them to only see the photons that Eve wants Bob to see. (*Science Daily*)

A. In quantum cryptography, the encryption key is transmitted with photon detectors and received with light signals.

B. Quantum cryptography uses light signals that can be captured and manipulated by a would-be hacker.

C. Quantum hacking, in which light signals subvert photon detectors, is the least common form of hacking.

D. If a hacker attempts to access data encoded with quantum cryptography, legal users have no way of knowing.

10. The European economy is largely linear by design. This design results in avoidable environmental and human health impacts, inefficient use of natural resources and over-dependency on resources from outside Europe. Moving to a circular economy would alleviate these pressures and concerns, and deliver several economic, social and environmental benefits and affect current trade practices. In the past the creation of waste in connection with production and consumption was accepted as a necessary evil. Today, that apparent common sense is increasingly being challenged: circular economy, zero waste, closed-cycle, resource efficiency, waste avoidance, re-use, recycling – all these terms can be attributed to the ideal of achieving a world largely without waste, with a responsible attitude to resources, materials, products and the environment. (*European Parliamentary Research Service*)

A. There is universal agreement that the manufacture of goods in the European economy will always create waste.

B. European member states have agreed to pursue a closed-cycle economy based on the ideal of a world largely without waste.

C. Progressing towards the model of a circular economy could help Europe use raw materials more efficiently.

D. Moving towards a circular economy would cause a fall in trade between Europe and the rest of the world.

11. The Higgs boson is one of the final puzzle pieces required for a complete understanding of the standard model of physics – the so-far successful theory that explains how fundamental particles interact with the elementary forces of nature. The so-called God particle was proposed in the 1960s by Peter Higgs to explain why some particles, such as quarks – building blocks of protons, among other things – and electrons have mass, while others, such as the light-carrying photon particle, do not. Higgs's idea was that the universe is bathed in an invisible field similar to a magnetic field. Every particle feels this field – now known as the Higgs field – but to varying degrees. If a particle can move through this field with little or no interaction, there will be no drag, and that particle will have little or no mass. Alternatively,

if a particle interacts significantly with the Higgs field, it will have a higher mass. The idea of the Higgs field requires the acceptance of a related particle: the Higgs boson. (*National Geographic*)

A. The Higgs boson helps explain why, in the standard model of physics, some particles have mass and others do not.

B. According to the Higgs theory, a particle with high mass could travel through the Higgs field with few interactions.

C. Without the existence of the Higgs field, atoms, electrons, and chemical bonds would have difficulty forming.

D. Higgs boson particles attach themselves to fundamental particles like quarks, electrons, and atoms, causing drag.

12. **When [Arthur Conan] Doyle graduated from Stonyhurst College in 1876, his parents expected that he would follow in his family's footsteps and study art, so they were surprised when he decided to pursue a medical degree at the University of Edinburgh instead. At medical school, Doyle met his mentor, Professor Dr. Joseph Bell, whose keen powers of observation would later inspire Doyle to create his famed fictional detective character, Sherlock Holmes. Doyle became increasingly invested in Spiritualism or "Psychic religion," a belief system that he would later attempt to spread through a series of his written works. By the time he received his Bachelor of Medicine degree in 1881, Doyle had denounced his Roman Catholic faith. Doyle's first paying job as a doctor took the form of a medical officer's position aboard the steamship Mayumba, travelling from Liverpool to Africa. (*biography.com*)**

A. Arthur Conan Doyle's renunciation of his Roman Catholic faith was largely due to the influence of his father.

B. Following family tradition, Arthur Conan Doyle studied art before he decided to pursue a medical degree.

C. The powerful observational skills of Sherlock Holmes were modeled on a doctor he met while aboard the Mayumba.

D. After receiving his medical degree, Doyle served as a medical officer on a steamship for his first paying position as a doctor.

13. **Warm-blooded birds need about 20 times more oxygen than cold-blooded reptiles, and they have evolved a unique lung structure that allows for a high rate of gas exchange and high activity level. Their unusual thigh complex helps support the lung and prevent its collapse. But the scientists said that every other animal – including humans, elephants, dogs, lizards and, in the ancient past, dinosaurs – that has walked on land has had a moveable thigh bone that was involved in the animal's motion. The implication of these facts, the researchers said, is that birds almost certainly did not descend from theropod dinosaurs such as the tyrannosaurus or allosaurus. The scientists' findings add to a growing body of evidence in the past two decades that challenge some of the most widely held beliefs about animal evolution. (*Science Daily*)**

A. Scientists have concluded that dinosaurs such as tyrannosaurus are probably not the ancient ancestors of birds.

B. Cold-blooded reptiles have a special structure in their lungs allowing them to exchange gases at a rapid rate.

C. Dinosaurs had a flexible thigh bone that allowed them to walk on land with more efficiency than elephants.

D. Birds were able to survive what likely killed the dinosaurs because their thigh complex prevented lung collapse.

14. **Van Gogh's art helped him stay emotionally balanced. In 1885, he began work on what is considered to be his first masterpiece, *Potato Eaters*. His brother Theo, by this time living in Paris, believed the painting would not be well-received in the French capital, where impressionism had become the trend. Nevertheless, Van Gogh decided to move to Paris, and showed up at Theo's house uninvited. In Paris, Van Gogh first saw impressionist art, and he was inspired by the color and light. He began studying with Toulouse-Lautrec, Pissarro and others. Van Gogh was passionate, and he argued with other painters about their works, alienating those who became tired of his bickering. In February 1888, Van Gogh boarded a train to the south of France. He moved into the "little yellow**

house" and spent his money on paint rather than food. He lived off of coffee, bread and absinthe, and found himself feeling sick and strange, even sipping turpentine and eating paint. (*biography.com*)

A. Despite Van Gogh's love of passionate argument, he maintained friendships with Pissarro and other painters.

B. Van Gogh was emotionally volatile and had turbulent relationships with other painters throughout his life.

C. When Van Gogh first moved to Paris, he was introduced to impressionism and was inspired by the colour and light.

D. Despite his brother's initial scepticism, Van Gogh's first masterpiece, *Potato Eaters,* was well received in Paris.

15. Until recently, black holes were thought to come in only two sizes: small stellar varieties that are several times heavier than our sun, and supermassive black holes that pack the gravitational punch of many millions of suns – large enough to swallow our entire solar system. Notorious for ripping apart and swallowing stars, extra-large black holes live exclusively in the hearts of most galaxies, including our own Milky Way. The new middleweight black hole is between these two types – equal to the matter of about 90,000 suns. Supermassive black holes might form when a single intermediately sized black hole gobbles enough matter to grow into a supermassive black hole with at least a million solar masses. Or perhaps a number of intermediate black holes merged in the early universe to form the supermassive black holes we see today. Either way, without further surveys, it's impossible to tell how common middleweight black holes are across the universe. (*National Geographic*)

A. A supermassive black hole may have formed when a group of intermediate black holes merged in the early universe.

B. Intermediate black holes, equal to the matter of about 90,000 suns, are instrumental in the formation of solar systems.

C. Supermassive black holes live at the centre and outskirts of most galaxies, dismantling and consuming stars.

D. Based on existing research data, it is possible to forecast the number of intermediate black holes that exist in the universe.

16. The challenge to "transform Europe into a low-carbon economy and increase its energy security" is one of the Grand Challenges facing European policymakers. The EU has set itself a legally binding goal to cut greenhouse gas emissions from all primary energy sources by at least 20% by 2020, compared to 1990 levels. It will also push for an international agreement to succeed the Kyoto Protocol aimed at achieving a 30% cut by all developed nations by 2020. In October 2009, EU leaders endorsed a long-term target of cutting up to 50% of carbon emissions from primary energy sources by 2050, compared to 1990 levels. In parallel, the European Commission has put forward a Strategic Energy Technology Plan "to accelerate the development and deployment of cost-effective low carbon technologies". Both actions, which originated from the Climate Action and Energy Commissioners, respectively, coincide in the need for appropriate research, such as that done by the European Research Council. (*European Research Council*)

A. The European Research Council has been asked by the European Commission to fund appropriate research into cost-effective low-carbon technologies.

B. In 2009 the EU agreed to adopt a legally binding target of reducing its greenhouse gas emissions by 50% by 2050, compared to 1990 levels.

C. The Strategic Energy Technology Plan being put forward by the European Commission was originated from the Commissioner for Energy.

D. The EU is negotiating with all developed nations with the aim of achieving a cut of 30% of their greenhouse gas emissions by 2020.

17. Videogame technology is proving to be a valuable tool for helping people of all ages improve lifestyle and health habits and manage disease. New research is showing that so-called "exergames" significantly benefit older adults by providing them with cognitive stimulation and a source of social interaction, exercise, and fun. Thus, the games help lead them to fuller, more

independent lives for a longer time. "The elderly often forsake their lifelong activities in exchange for the safety, security, and care of institutional living," says Editor-in-Chief Bill Ferguson, PhD. "This trade-off need not require the sacrifice of physical activity and fitness. Furthermore, videogames offer an escape from routine. All of these benefits can improve the well-being of elderly adults." Digital games offer a home-based method of supporting behavior modification, motivating patients to take better care of themselves and to self-manage chronic conditions. (*Science Daily*)

A. According to Bill Ferguson the elderly must give up physical activity and fitness for safety and security.

B. Elderly adults living in assisted care facilities reap greater benefits from exergames than do their peers living in their own homes.

C. Elderly adults who regularly use exergames are more mentally healthy and more fulfilled socially than those who do not.

D. Videogame technology can benefit the elderly by helping to motivate them and manage some of their chronic conditions.

18. René Lacoste's mechanical mind never really lagged behind his athletic pursuits. A tenacious perfectionist, he had once been criticized by a coach for overtraining. His tendency to wear out practice partners proved so frustrating that Lacoste created the world's first tennis ball machine, a hand-cranked device he called "lance-balle." His inventive mind worked in areas outside of tennis, too. Between the mid-1960s and late 1980s Lacoste filed 20 new patents. But a clothing line that bore his name proved to be Lacoste's greatest post-game success. As a player, Lacoste went against traditional on-court fashion, opting to compete in short-sleeved knit shirts rather than dress shirts. Sensing a market for this look, Lacoste formed a small company to manufacture the apparel soon after leaving the game. By 1950, Lacoste's shirt, with its signature crocodile emblem on the left breast, entered the U.S. market. (*biography.com*)

A. Gifted in tennis, mechanical engineering, and fashion design, Lacoste's main passion was always invention.

B. After his tennis career, Lacoste's greatest success was his invention of the world's first tennis ball machine.

C. Lacoste was a perfectionist, quickly went through practice partners, and wore short-sleeved knit shirts on court.

D. The Lacoste name and crocodile symbol conquered the US market and became status symbols in the world of fashion.

19. Cleopatra's father had thrown in his lot with Pompey the Great. Good fortune seemed eternally to shine on Pompey, that brilliant Roman general, at least until Julius Caesar dealt him a crushing defeat in central Greece. Pompey fled to Egypt, where, in 48 BC, he was stabbed and decapitated. Twenty-one-year-old Cleopatra was at the time a fugitive in the Sinai – on the losing side of a civil war against her brother and at the mercy of her brother's troops and advisers. Quickly, she managed to ingratiate herself with the new master of the Roman world, Julius Caesar. Caesar arrived in Alexandria just days after Pompey's murder. He barricaded himself in the Ptolemies' palace, the home from which Cleopatra had been exiled. From the desert, Cleopatra engineered a clandestine return, skirting enemy lines and Roman barricades, arriving after dark inside a sturdy sack. Over the succeeding months she stood at Caesar's side – pregnant with his child – while he battled her brother's troops. With their defeat, Caesar restored her to the throne. (*smithsonianmag.com*)

A. After Caesar returned Cleopatra to the throne, she went on to rule the Mediterranean region for many years.

B. In 48 BC, the Roman general Pompey the Great escaped to Egypt, where he was stabbed and beheaded.

C. In 48 BC, the young Cleopatra was living in the Sinai following a civil war victory against her brother.

D. The young Cleopatra was able to quickly win the favour of Julius Caesar, a new leader in the Roman world.

20. George Frideric Handel's *Messiah* was originally an Easter offering. It burst onto the stage of *Musick Hall* in Dublin

on April 13, 1742. Handel's superstar status was not the only draw; many also came to glimpse the contralto, Susannah Cibber, then embroiled in a scandalous divorce. [Handel] was born in Halle, Germany, into a religious, affluent household. His father, Georg Händel, a celebrated surgeon in northern Germany, wanted his son to study the law. But an acquaintance, the Duke of Weissenfels, heard the prodigy, then barely 11, playing the organ. The nobleman's recognition of the boy's genius likely influenced the doctor's decision to allow his son to become a musician. By 18, Handel had composed his first opera, *Almira*. During the next five years, he was employed as a musician, composer and conductor at courts and churches in Rome, Florence, Naples and Venice, as well as in Germany, where the Elector of Hanover, the future King George I of England, was briefly his patron. (*smithsonianmag.com*)

A. Handel was born into a religious family, the son of a successful surgeon who wanted him to study law.

B. Handel mostly preferred to work for one or two main benefactors, rather than seeking patronage more widely.

C. On its opening night of April 13, 1742, the *Messiah* drew crowds solely because of Handel's dazzling reputation.

D. Contralto Susannah Cibber drew crowds not because of her voice but because of the scandalous divorce she was going through.

21. Suzanne de la Monte, M.D., has found a link between brain insulin resistance (diabetes) and two other key mediators of neuronal injury that help Alzheimer's disease (AD) to propagate. The research found that once AD is established, therapeutic efforts must also work to reduce toxin production in the brain. Alzheimer's disease is one of the most common degenerative dementias, and more than 115 million new cases are projected worldwide in the next 40 years. There is clinical and experimental evidence that treatment with insulin or insulin sensitizer agents can enhance cognitive function and in some circumstances help slow the rate of cognitive decline in AD. Alzheimer's and other neurodegenerative diseases destroy the brain until the patients finally succumb. In order to effectively halt the process of neurodegeneration, the forces that advance and perpetuate the disease, particularly with regard to the progressive worsening of brain insulin/IGF resistance, must be understood. (*Science Daily*)

A. The underlying causes of brain insulin resistance (diabetes) and Alzheimer's disease are almost identical.

B. If Alzheimer's disease is diagnosed early, the rate of neurodegeneration can likely be decreased effectively.

C. Clinical and experimental evidence suggests that insulin treatment can improve cognitive function in Alzheimer's patients.

D. Alzheimer's disease is the most common degenerative dementia and more than 115 million new cases are projected worldwide in the next 40 years.

22. A painter, sculptor, printmaker, ceramist and writer, Gauguin stands today as one of the giants of Post-Impressionism and a pioneer of Modernism. He was also a great storyteller, creating narratives in every medium he touched. Some of his tales were true, others near-fabrications. For instance, the lush Tahitian masterpieces for which he is best known reflect an exotic paradise more imaginary than real. The fables Gauguin spun were meant to promote himself and his art, an intention that was more successful with the man than his work; he was well known during his lifetime, but his paintings sold poorly. Certainly the artist would have been pleased by the renewed attention; his goal, after all, was to be famous. He dressed bizarrely, wrote self-serving critiques of his work, courted the press and even handed out photographs of himself to his fans. He was often drunk, belligerent and promiscuous – and possibly suicidal. (*smithsonianmag.com*)

A. Gauguin's Tahitian masterpieces provide a remarkably accurate and detailed record of the lush tropical environment.

B. Gauguin used his gift for telling stories to please his friends and fans and to advance the cause of art in general.

C. Along with painting, Gauguin spent time drinking, promoting himself, telling stories, and engaging in sexual relations.

D. Gauguin never made much money selling his paintings because of his strange and provoking behaviour with the press and the public.

23. When cats are on what they perceive to be safe ground they can and do behave affectionately towards their owners. They show this in a whole variety of ways including: raising their tails upright when they see us, rubbing their heads or flanks on our legs, licking us when they're sitting next to us, and purring when we stroke them. How do we know that these are signs of affection? Well, it has to be said that we will never know precisely what's going on inside a cat's head (or a dog's for that matter), but we do know that these are the ways in which cats indicate their affection for other cats. The fact that cats get along with other cats at all is something of an achievement for a species that was exclusively solitary just 10,000 years ago. Our domestic cat's wild relatives, the Arabian wildcat Felis lybica, spend most of their lives alone. During the breeding season, males consort with females for just a few days of the year, but otherwise avoid other cats as much as possible, unlike male lions and cheetahs, both of which are able to form "brotherhoods", competing with other groups for the attention of females. (*theguardian.com*)

A. Male lions and cheetahs are similar to domestic cats in that they have evolved over the years to have specific behavioural tendencies towards one another.

B. 10,000 years ago the Arabian wildcat Felis lybica spent most of its time alone until the breeding season meant it sought out a mate with which to breed.

C. It is not possible to know precisely what goes on in the mind of a cat but we can make assumptions by observing their behaviour.

D. Unlike lions and cheetahs the Felis lybica form groups, which allow them to compete effectively with big cats for the attention of females.

24. Fake news flourished in the 19th century. One such fake correspondent was Theodor Fontane, a German pharmacist-turned-journalist who would go on to write some of the most important German Realist novels. In 1860, Fontane joined the staff of the Kreuzzeitung, an ultra-conservative Berlin newspaper. The paper assigned him to cover England, and for a decade, he published story after story "from" London, spellbinding his readers with "personal" accounts of dramatic events, like the devastating Tooley Street Fire of 1861. But during the entire decade, he never actually crossed the English Channel. Fontane sifted through existing accounts to get a sense for what readers already knew about the catastrophe. He cut up the old articles, picked out the most relevant texts, and glued them together for his own account. Then, to elevate the drama, he wrote some new passages with details and characters that were completely fabricated. (*theconversation.com*)

A. In 1860 the German writer Theodor Fontane created the journalistic practice that we now call fake news.

B. During the decade that he wrote about English affairs for the Kreuzzeitung newspaper, Theodor Fontane never left his home country.

C. All of the details in the story written by Theodor Fontane about the Tooley Street fire were invented.

D. The journalistic practice that we now call fake news was widely practised in a previous century.

25. Morse gave up painting entirely; relinquishing the whole career he had set his heart on since college days. No one could dissuade him. He had to attend to one thing at a time, as his father had long ago advised him. The "one thing" henceforth would be his telegraph, the crude apparatus that was housed in his New York University studio apartment. Later it would be surmised that, had Morse not stopped painting when he did, no successful electromagnetic telegraph would have been developed when it was, or at least not a Morse electromagnetic telegraph. Essential to Morse's idea, as he had set forth earlier in notes written in 1832, was that signals would be sent by the opening and closing of an electrical circuit, that the receiving apparatus would, by electromagnet, record signals

as dots and dashes on paper, and that there would be a code whereby the dots and dashes would be translated into numbers and letters. (*smithsonianmag. com*)

A. Morse made many attempts to develop a code for his telegraph before finding one that worked.

B. Morse planned for telegraph signals to be sent by the opening and closing of an electrical circuit and recorded by electromagnet.

C. Morse pursued the design of his electromagnetic telegraph even as he was working as a commissioned painter.

D. Although his telegraph was not immediately successful, Morse continued to refine his invention, undeterred.

26. Peat wetlands in northwest Europe are well-known for their bog bodies. The wetlands provide cold, acidic, oxygen-free conditions, which prevent decay and mummify human flesh. The two new Irish bog men were named after the places where they were found: Croghan Hill and Clonycavan. Oldcroghan man was preserved so perfectly that his discovery sparked a police murder investigation before archaeologists were called in. Radiocarbon dating showed that he lived between 362 BC and 175 BC, while Clonycavan man dates from 392 BC to 201 BC. A team led by researchers at the National Museum of Ireland studied the two bodies. The scientists say the fingerprint whorls of Oldcroghan man are as clear as any living person's. While both bog men appeared to be aristocratic dandies of their day, they still met horrible deaths. Oldcroghan man shows signs of cruel torture before he was beheaded. Meanwhile, Clonycavan man suffered three axe blows to the head, plus one to his chest. (*National Geographic*)

A. The two new Irish bog bodies show signs of torture, indicating that they were killed as part of a ritual to pagan gods.

B. The two bodies were found preserved in the cold, acidic conditions of the bogs Croghan Hill and Clonycavan.

C. The two bog bodies were apparently men of low social rank, which may explain why they were buried in the bog.

D. Oldcroghan man and Clonycavan man offer evidence of Iron Age burial modes occurring across Western Europe and beyond.

27. Scientists have long known that the body rids itself of excess copper and various other minerals by collecting them in the liver and excreting them through the liver's bile. However, a new study suggests that when this route is impaired, there's another exit route just for copper: a molecule sequesters only the copper and routes it from the body through urine. The researchers found this additional copper escape hatch by studying an animal model of Wilson's disease, a rare disorder most often diagnosed in children. People with this disease accumulate abnormally large amounts of copper in the liver, eventually leading to liver damage and failure. Micronutrients such as copper, zinc and iron are indispensible for human development. Copper is required for embryonic development, respiration, and cardiovascular function, among other processes; too little copper can be fatal whereas too much can cause neurological impairment and organ failure. (*Science Daily*)

A. Individuals with Wilson's disease were either over or under exposed to the micronutrient copper before birth.

B. In individuals with Wilson's disease, liver cells die off at increasingly rapid rates without regenerating.

C. Too much of the micronutrient copper leads to death, but too little leads to neurological damage rather than death.

D. Collection in the liver and excretion through the liver's bile is just one way that excess copper exits the body.

28. In 2001, the Human Genome Project and Celera Genomics announced that after 10 years of work at a cost of some $400 million, they had completed a draft sequence of the human genome. Today, sequencing a human genome is something that a single researcher can do in a couple of weeks for less than $10,000. Since 2002, the rate at which genomes can be sequenced has been doubling every four months or so, whereas computing power doubles only every 18 months.

Without the advent of new analytic tools, biologists' ability to generate genomic data will soon outstrip their ability to do anything useful with it. Researchers talk about a new algorithm that drastically reduces the time it takes to find a particular gene sequence in a database of genomes. And in fact, the more genomes the algorithm searches, the greater the speedup it affords, so its advantages will only compound as more data is generated. (*Science Daily*)

A. A lone scientist is able to sequence a human genome over the course of a few weeks for less than $10,000.

B. Celera Genomics finished a draft sequence of the human genome after 10 years of work for less than $10,000.

C. The new algorithm reduces the time it takes to locate a gene sequence by utilizing related species' genomes.

D. Since 2002 the rate at which scientists can sequence genomes has doubled.

29. Since they became widely known in the late 1920s, the mysterious desert drawings known as the Nasca lines have puzzled archaeologists, anthropologists, and anyone fascinated by ancient cultures in the Americas. For just as long, waves of scientists – and amateurs – have inflicted various interpretations on the lines, as if they were the world's largest set of Rorschach inkblots. At one time or another, they have either been explained as Inca roads, irrigation plans, images to be appreciated from primitive hot-air balloons, or, most laughably, landing strips for alien spacecraft. Almost all of these iconic animal figures, such as the spider and the hummingbird, were single-line drawings; a person could step into them at one point and exit at another without ever crossing a line, suggesting to archaeologists that at some point in early Nasca times the lines evolved from mere images to pathways for ceremonial processions. (*National Geographic*)

A. Since the 1920s due to the influence of popular culture, amateurs proposed that the Nasca lines were alien spacecraft landing strips.

B. Recently scientists have proved that the Nasca lines were initially images that evolved into ceremonial pathways.

C. Inca roads, irrigation plans, and landing strips are three interpretations of the single-line Nasca drawings.

D. The Nasca lines, including the spider and hummingbird, always served the dual purpose of irrigation and ceremony.

30. Italy managed to borrow in the financial markets at slightly lower rates Friday, despite a downgrade of its sovereign debt by a credit rating agency that threatened to deal a new blow to its efforts to escape the debt crisis. The Italian Treasury sold out its offering of €5.25 billion, or $6.4 billion, with three-year government bonds at 4.65 per cent, the lowest rate since May but still at a high price by historical standards. Moody's Investors Service lowered Italy's government bond rating Friday by two steps to Baa2 from A3, citing concerns that Italy faces higher financing costs and an increased risk of being locked out of lending markets as it battles contagion emanating from Greece and Spain. Nicholas Spiro, managing director of Spiro Sovereign Strategy, a London-based consultancy specialising in sovereign credit risk, described the Italian auction as a "mixed bag" but called the outcome more positive than negative. (*New York Times*)

A. Moody's Investors Service downgraded Italy's government bond rating because of the country's unsuccessful efforts to escape the debt crisis.

B. Despite the auction, the stakes for Italy remain high because the country is too big for the euro zone to bail out.

C. The Italian Treasury sold three-year government bonds at 4.65 per cent, a price that is high by historical standards.

D. Italy may become caught in a downward cycle, with recessionary trends adding an unsustainable debt burden.

31. Nothing about elephants is small, and their pregnancies are no exception. Before giving birth to a 110-kilogramme calf, mothers carry the foetus for 22 months, the longest gestation period of any mammal. And whereas most mammals have only one corpus luteum – a temporary gland that controls hormone levels during pregnancy – elephants have as many as 11. Now, by giving 17

elephants blood tests and ultrasound scans throughout their pregnancies, researchers have discovered a key to this remarkable form of motherhood. The researchers found that the animals formed, on average, five corpora lutea during each menstrual cycle. And surprisingly, whereas one corpus luteum was derived from an egg-generating follicle, as happens in mammals such as humans, the rest of the structures formed from separate follicles at a different point in the reproductive cycle. The observation could lead to methods for controlling elephant ovulation or timing artificial insemination. (*sciencemag.org*)

A. Young female elephants that have not yet reached sexual maturity are not able to develop multiple corpora lutea.

B. Multiple corpora lutea form from separate follicles in female elephants in order to maintain steady hormone levels.

C. Female elephants form about five corpora lutea during each menstrual cycle, all from one egg-generating follicle.

D. Elephant mothers carry the foetus for 22 months, which is the longest gestation period among mammals.

32. Physicists are often interested in mathematically describing how a system behaves: for instance, a formula tracks the motions of the planets and their moons in their complicated dance around the sun. Researchers work out these equations by measuring the objects at various points in time and then developing a formula that links all of those points together, such as filling in a video from a set of snapshots. With each new variable, however, it becomes tougher to find the right equation. Computers can speed things up by sifting through potential solutions at breakneck speed, but even the world's top supercomputers meet their match with a certain class of problems, known as "hard" problems. These problems take exponentially more time to solve with every additional variable that is thrown into the mix – an extra planet's motion, for instance. (*sciencemag.org*)

A. With each variable that is added, so-called "hard" problems take exponentially more time to solve, even for computers.

B. As researchers work to describe a system mathematically, each variable makes it easier to find the correct equation.

C. Problems considered "hard" can still be solved at breakneck speed by the best supercomputers of the world.

D. Any algorithm that turns data into a formula describing a system over time can't be simplified to run on a computer.

33. This new, irrational art movement would be named Dada. It got its name, according to Richard Huelsenbeck, a German artist living in Zurich, when he and Ball came upon the word in a French-German dictionary. To Ball, it fit. "Dada is 'yes, yes' in Rumanian, 'rocking horse' and 'hobby horse' in French," he noted in his diary. "For Germans it is a sign of foolish naiveté, joy in procreation, and preoccupation with the baby carriage." Romanian artist Tristan Tzara, who later claimed that he had coined the term, quickly used it on posters, put out the first Dada journal and wrote one of the first of many Dada manifestoes, few of which made much sense. But the absurdist outlook spread like a pandemic – Tzara called Dada "a virgin microbe" – and there were outbreaks from Berlin to Paris, New York and even Tokyo. And for all its zaniness, the movement would prove to be one of the most influential in modern art, foreshadowing abstract and conceptual art, performance art, op, pop and installation art. (*smithsonianmag.com*)

A. The irrational art movement of Dada appealed particularly to those who could not make sense of the events of the early 20th century.

B. The first of many Dada manifestoes, issued by Romanian artist Tristan Tzara, were all highly logical and meaningful.

C. The term "dada" means "hobby horse" in French and for Germans it has associations with joy in procreation.

D. The element of Dada that paved the way for abstract and conceptual art was its absurdity and irrationality.

34. The international Cassini mission has concluded its remarkable exploration of the Saturnian system in spectacular style, by plunging into the gas planet's atmosphere. Confirmation of the

end of mission arrived at NASA's Jet Propulsion Laboratory at 13:55 CEST (Central European Summer Time) with the loss of the spacecraft's signal having occurred 83 minutes earlier at Saturn, some 1.4 billion km from Earth. With the rocket propellant for manoeuvring the spacecraft fully expended as planned touring Saturn and its moons for the last 13 years, the mission concluded with the intentional plunge into the gas planet. This ensures that Saturn's icy moons, in particular, ocean-bearing Enceladus, do not risk being contaminated by microbes that might have remained on board the spacecraft from Earth, and are left pristine for future exploration. (*European Space Agency*)

A. The Cassini spacecraft plunged onto Enceladus after its signal was lost.

B. The Cassini spacecraft travelled more than 1.4 billion km during its mission to explore Saturn.

C. The Cassini spacecraft discovered an ocean-bearing icy moon.

D. Scientists want to avoid future exploration of Saturn's moons, to avoid contaminating them with microbes from Earth.

35. In 1565, ambitious for the English throne, Mary Queen of Scots married her cousin, Henry Stewart, Lord Darnley, a grandson of Margaret Tudor, but became disgusted by his debauchery, and was soon alienated from him. The birth of a son, the future James VI, failed to bring a reconciliation. While ill with smallpox, Darnley was mysteriously killed in an explosion at Kirk o' Field (1567); the chief suspect was the Earl of Bothwell, who underwent a mock trial and was acquitted. Mary's involvement is unclear, but she consented to marry James Hepburn of Bothwell, a divorcé with whom she had become infatuated. The Protestant nobles under Morton rose against her; she surrendered at Carberry Hill, was imprisoned at Loch Leven, and compelled to abdicate in favour of her son James VI. After escaping, she raised an army, but was defeated again by the confederate lords at Langside (1568). Placing herself under the protection of Queen Elizabeth, she found herself instead a prisoner for life. (*biography.com*)

A. Mary Queen of Scots married James Hepburn of Bothwell with whom she had a son, the future James VI.

B. In 1567 Mary's husband, Lord Darnley, was in strange circumstances killed in an explosion while sick with smallpox.

C. Queen Elizabeth I had Mary arrested and imprisoned because she saw her as a serious threat to the throne.

D. After gathering an army, Mary Queen of Scots successfully defeated the confederate lords at Landside in 1568.

36. Neurosurgeons and researchers are adapting an ultraviolet camera to possibly bring planet-exploring technology into the operating room. If the system works when focused on brain tissue, it could give surgeons a real-time view of changes invisible to the naked eye and unapparent even with the magnification of current medical imaging technologies. The pilot study seeks to determine if the camera provides visual detail that might help surgeons distinguish areas of healthy brain from deadly tumors called gliomas, which have irregular borders as they spread into normal tissue. Because tumor cells are more active and require more energy than normal cells, a specific chemical (nicotinamide adenine dinucleotide hydrogenase or NADH) accumulates in tumor cells but not in healthy cells. NADH emits ultraviolet light that may be captured by the camera and displayed in a high-resolution image. The camera employs the ultraviolet technology used in space to study planets and distant galaxies. (*Science Daily*)

A. Neurosurgeons do not use images taken by the ultraviolet camera in making decisions or to aid surgical technique.

B. Healthy cells require more energy than tumor cells and typically display irregular borders as they grow.

C. The ultraviolet camera will revolutionise how brain tumors and other neurological disorders are treated.

D. Ultraviolet technology used to study galaxies and planets could be adapted for the benefit of neurosurgery.

37. It was hailed in 2010 as the most "alien" life-form yet: bacteria that reportedly,

and unprecedentedly, had rewritten the recipe for DNA. And the secret ingredient was arsenic. Researchers led by then NASA astrobiologist Felisa Wolfe-Simon had found the organism, dubbed GFAJ-1, in arsenic-rich sediments of California's Mono Lake. They later reported that the bacterium thrived in arsenic-rich, phosphorus-poor lab conditions. The team concluded that GFAJ-1 must be incorporating arsenic into its DNA in place of phosphorous, which is essential for the DNA of all other known organisms. The find was exciting to astrobiologists, who had previously speculated that extraterrestrial life might survive in unexpected places if only such a swap were possible – arsenic and phosphorous being chemically similar. But when the amount of phosphorous was reduced even further than in Wolfe-Simon's experiments, GFAJ-1 stalled. The new conclusion: the arsenic-loving life-form does in fact need phosphorous to grow, but shockingly tiny amounts of it. (*National Geographic*)

A. Wolfe-Simon and her team concluded that GFAJ-1 was able to incorporate hosphorous into its DNA in place of arsenic.

B. Wolfe-Simon and her team found the GFAJ-1 organism in sediments of Mono Lake.

C. GFAJ-1's ability to exchange phosphorous and arsenic would confirm the existence of extraterrestrial life.

D. The fact that GFAJ-1 requires miniscule amounts of phosphorous for growth confirms the extraterrestrial life hypothesis.

38. **By the time Paul Morphy was felled by a stroke on July 10, 1884, he had become an odd but familiar presence on Canal Street in New Orleans: a trim little man in sack suit and monocle, muttering to himself, smiling at his own conceits, swinging his cane at most who dared approach. Sometimes he would take a fancy to a passing woman, following her for hours at a distance. He lived in fear of being poisoned, eating only food prepared by his mother or sister, and he believed that neighbourhood barbers were conspiring to slit his throat. His family tried to have him committed to an asylum, but he argued his sanity so convincingly that the authorities declined to admit him. It had been a quarter-century since he became a world-renowned chess champion, and for the last decade of his life he was loath to discuss the game at all. (*smithsonianmag.com*)**

A. Morphy's obsessions and paranoia, which bordered on madness, were probably the necessary counterpart to his genius.

B. Morphy wore a monocle, believed that barbers would cut his throat, and ate only food that his family prepared.

C. In his later years, Morphy came to believe that time spent playing chess was nothing more than wasted time.

D. Morphy's behaviour eventually became so disturbing that his family had him committed to a mental asylum.

39. **Research shows a twenty-fold enhancement in harvesting light by combining graphene with metallic nanostructures, and this new discovery could pave the way for advances in high-speed internet and other communications. By putting two closely spaced metallic wires on top of graphene and shining light on this structure, researchers generated electric power. This simple device is actually an elementary solar cell. Such graphene devices can transfer data tens and potentially hundreds of times faster than communication rates in the fastest internet cables; this is due to the uniquely high mobility and velocity of electrons in graphene. But the major stumbling block towards practical applications of these otherwise promising devices has been their low efficiency. The problem is that graphene – the thinnest material in the world – absorbs little light, approximately only 3 per cent of the total light shined on it, while the rest penetrates the graphene without contributing to the generation of electrical power. (*Science Daily*)**

A. Graphene devices can transfer data so fast that they will replace existing internet cables.

B. A graphene solar cell can be made only by placing graphene on top of a metallic wire and then shining light on it.

C. Graphene devices owe their incredible speed to the high mobility and velocity of graphene's electrons.

D. Graphene devices are promising to communications because of their high efficiency and lightning speed.

40. Shrapnel from mortars, grenades and, above all, artillery projectile bombs, or shells, would account for an estimated 60 per cent of the 9.7 million military fatalities of World War I. And it was soon observed that many soldiers arriving at the casualty clearing stations who had been exposed to exploding shells, although clearly damaged, bore no visible wounds. Rather, they appeared to be suffering from a remarkable state of shock caused by blast force. This new type of injury, a British medical report concluded, appeared to be "the result of the actual explosion itself, and not merely of the missiles set in motion by it." In other words, it appeared that some dark, invisible force had in fact passed through the air and was inflicting novel and peculiar damage to men's brains. "Shell shock," the term that would come to define the phenomenon, first appeared in the British medical journal *The Lancet* in February 1915, only six months after the commencement of the war. (*smithsonianmag.com*)

A. Shell shock causes no visible wounding but those who suffer from the condition display symptoms similar to a concussion.

B. From early in World War I, soldiers appeared at casualty clearing stations suffering from an unusual state of shock.

C. The term "shell shock" was coined by military doctors in the barracks before appearing in the February 1915 edition of *The Lancet*.

D. About 60 per cent of the 9.7 million World War I military deaths were due to what would become known as shell shock.

41. Overexploitation, pollution, habitat loss or emerging diseases have led a large number of species to extinction. This has made zoos and wildlife enclosures expand their goals beyond entertainment and fun; their participation in conservation and research programs is important for the recovery of multiple species. To ensure success, staff need to know the specific requirements of each species. In the case of the Iberian ibex, different mange outbreaks caused dramatic declines of some ibex populations, which led managers and researchers to explore strategies aimed at preventing and controlling this disease and to reduce its impact on ibex populations. The objective of the Iberian ibex stock reservoir El Toril, as a key part of a general management plan, is to keep in captivity a sex and age structured representation of the free-ranging population, with most of its genetic variability, destined for conservation programs. (*Journal for Nature Conservation*)

A. Iberian ibex are being kept in captivity at El Toril in order to preserve the species from threatened extinction.

B. The ibex being kept at El Toril are planned to have a similar mix of hereditary characteristics to those which still roam free.

C. Mange outbreaks have increased in the Iberian ibex population due to overexploitation, pollution and habitat loss.

D. Ibex bred at El Toril have been successfully released into the wild.

42. From the Middle Ages to the Baroque period, tapestry enjoyed a prestige far beyond that of painting. Royalty and the church commissioned whole series of designs – called cartoons – from the most sought-after artists of their times: Raphael, Rubens, Le Brun. Later artists from Goya to Picasso and Miró and beyond have carried on the tradition. Still, by 20th-century lights, tapestries fit more naturally into the pigeonhole of crafts than of fine arts. In their Golden Age, however, tapestries were seen to offer many advantages. They are portable, for one thing, as frescoes and wall paintings on a similar scale are not. For another, tapestries helped take the edge off the cold in large, drafty spaces. They had snob appeal, since only the richest of the rich could afford them. To hang tapestries was to show that you not only could appreciate the very best but that cost was no object. The materials alone could be worth a fortune, not to mention the massive costs of scarce, highly skilled labour. (*smithsonianmag.com*)

A. During their Golden Age, tapestry cartoons could be licensed and woven in multiples by different artists.

B. After the 18th century, there was a great decline in the creation of tapestries as oil painting became in vogue.

C. Tapestry was associated with the peasant classes during the Middle Ages through the Baroque period.

D. Tapestries were favoured at one time for their convenience, ability to block cold air, and role as status symbols.

43. An interesting pattern over the last four decades is that inequality has grown much faster for households with children than it has for households over all – an indication that changes in family structure (as opposed to wages and employment alone) have increased inequality. Bruce Western and Tracey Shollenberger of the Harvard sociology department compared households at the 90th percentile and the 10th percentile. In 1970, the top households had 8.9 times the income of the bottom. By 2011 they had nearly 11.7 times as much – inequality between them grew 31 per cent. But among households with children it grew 121 per cent – the ratio went from 4.8 in 1970 to 10.6 last year. Most of that growth, it should be noted, occurred by 1994, while births to unwed mothers have continued to rise. And though no one has suggested that it is the sole or even main driving force behind the increases in inequality, rates of single parenthood are important but sometimes overlooked. (*New York Times*)

A. Children raised in single-parent households have more difficulty moving up the income ladder than their peers.

B. Single parenthood could be an important factor in inequality, and it's one that can also be ignored or missed.

C. A pattern emerging over the last forty years suggests that inequality has increased due only to wages and unemployment.

D. Between 1970 and 2011, income inequality between the top and bottom households grew by 121 per cent overall.

44. In 1956, Mandela and 150 others were arrested and charged with treason for their political advocacy, though they were eventually acquitted. Meanwhile, the African National Congress (ANC) was being challenged by the Africanists, a new breed of Black activists who believed that the pacifist method of the ANC was ineffective. In 1961, Mandela, who was formerly committed to non-violent protest, began to believe that armed struggle was the only way to achieve change. He co-founded Umkhonto we Sizwe, also known as MK, an armed offshoot of the ANC dedicated to sabotage and guerilla war tactics to end apartheid. He orchestrated a three-day national workers strike in 1961 for which he was arrested in 1962. He was sentenced to five years in prison for the strike, and then he was brought to trial again in 1963. This time, he and 10 other ANC leaders were sentenced to life imprisonment for political offences, including sabotage. (*biography.com*)

A. Mandela first began to consider guerilla war tactics shortly after he was arrested and charged with treason in 1956.

B. Umkhonto we Sizwe changed its pacifist tactics after Mandela was put on trial.

C. Mandela was arrested in 1962 and later sentenced to life imprisonment for sabotage and other political crimes.

D. The Africanist Black activists accepted the leadership role of the African National Congress and its pacifist method.

45. For centuries, scientists have tried to solve the mystery of how the colossal stone statues of Easter Island moved. The multi-ton behemoths travelled up to 18 kilometres from the quarry where most of them were carved, without the benefit of wheels, cranes, or even large animals. Scientists have tested many ideas in the past, figuring that the islanders must have used a combination of log rollers, ropes, and wooden sledges. Now a pair of archaeologists have come up with a new theory: Perhaps the statues, known as moai, were "engineered to move" upright in a rocking motion, using only manpower and rope. Last year, Hunt and Lipo showed that as few as 18 people could, with three strong ropes and a bit of practice, easily and relatively quickly manoeuvre a three-meter, five-ton moai replica a few hundred meters. No logs were required. (*National Geographic*)

A. Islanders designed the moai specifically so the statues could be moved using rope and a rocking motion.

B. Islanders used wheels, cranes, and strong animals to move the stone statues from the quarry.

C. All of the stones were carved at a rock quarry and then moved 18 kilometers to their resting places.

D. As few as 18 islanders could have moved the stone statues with three ropes using a rocking motion.

46. The Thames has been synonymous with rowing for almost three centuries. In August 1715, half a dozen "watermen" – oarsmen who ferried passengers on the river – convened beneath London Bridge for Britain's first rowing race. Nearly 200 years later, at the London Summer Olympic Games in 1908, spectators thronged the banks of Henley-on-Thames, site of the annual Royal Regatta, as British scullers competed against crews from seven countries, including Canada, Hungary and the Netherlands. Eton College, the nearly 600-year-old prep school whose graduates include novelist Ian Fleming, Prime Minister David Cameron and Prince William, is famed for its fanatic devotion to rowing. Dozens of Etonians have gone on to row in the Olympics, including four-time gold medalist Sir Matthew Pinsent, now 42. Before the 1990s, Eton's crews practiced and competed on the Thames, but today recreational boat traffic makes rowing there too dangerous. (*smithsonianmag.com*)

A. Britain's first rowing race took place in 1715 with six watermen gathering on the Thames beneath London Bridge.

B. Etonians have rowed in the Olympics, and students of the College continue to row on the Thames even today.

C. Olympic boating events are no longer held on the Thames due to varying currents that would cause unfair conditions.

D. At the London Summer Olympics in 1908, the British crew was more successful than those of Canada and the Netherlands.

47. With his work "Reason's Oxymorons" that premiered at the Lyon Biennial art festival in 2015, Kader Attia created an expansive video installation. It contained interviews with philosophers, ethnologists, historians, psychiatrists, psychoanalysts, musicologists, patients, healers, and fetishists. Its volumes are edited following different themes like "Genocide," "Totem and Fetish," "Reason and Politics," or "Trance." Each individually and also as a whole they make up an essay on the psychiatric pathology as it is perceived in traditional Non-Western cultures, on the one hand, and in modern Western societies, on the other. In its mix of rational explanations and irrational representations of what the West calls psychiatry, the work is particularly concerned with the question of the unrepairable, inherent in the idea of "repair" and it calls into question the ambivalence of the psyche of modern Western societies towards traditional Non-Western societies. (*europenowjournal.org*)

A. Kader Attia's work "Reason's Oxymorons" functions as a video library and explores the causes and effects of psychiatric illness.

B. "Reason's Oxymorons" explores the theme of "Genocide" and the way that it was perpetrated historically by Western societies on non-Western societies.

C. Kader Attia has explored the theme of psychiatric pathology using the experience of experts and individuals who have undergone treatment.

D. "Reason's Oxymorons" relies on absurd images of psychiatrists to question the idea that some mental illnesses are fundamentally unrepairable.

48. Researchers used data from the UK's census to examine how health varied across the country, finding that people were more likely to have good health the closer they live to the sea. The analysis also showed that the link between living near the coast and good health was strongest in the most economically deprived communities. The results show that on average, populations living by the sea report rates of good health more than similar populations living inland. The authors were keen to point out that although this effect is relatively small, when applied to the whole population the impacts on public health could be substantial. Along with other studies the

results of this work suggest that access to 'good' environments may have a role in reducing inequality in health between the wealthiest and poorest members of society. (*Science Daily*)

A. In the UK, living further inland affords higher health benefits than living by the coast.

B. Researchers believe that some of the features and benefits of living by the sea can be transferred to other locations.

C. Living near the coast confers good health because it offers stress reduction and cleaner air compared to inland locations.

D. In the UK, the connection between living near the sea and good health was found to be strongest for the poorest people.

49. Painter, provocateur, risk taker and revolutionary, Gustave Courbet might well have said, "I offend; therefore I am." Arguably modern art's original enfant terrible, he had a lust for controversy that makes the careers of more recent shockmeisters like Jeff Koons, Damien Hirst and Robert Mapplethorpe seem almost conventional. As a rebellious teenager from a small town in eastern France, Courbet disregarded his parents' desire for him to study law and vowed, he wrote, "to lead the life of a savage" and free himself from governments. He did not mellow with age, disdaining royal honours, turning out confrontational, even making salacious canvases and attacking established social values when others of his generation were settling into lives cushioned with awards and pensions. As the standard-bearer of a new "realism," which he defined as the representation of familiar things as they are, he would become one of the most innovative and influential painters of mid-19th-century France. (*smithsonianmag.com*)

A. Although Courbet originally stated his intent to live the life of a savage, he softened considerably in his later years.

B. Courbet's rebellious spirit and corresponding vision were precisely what made him such a brilliant modern artist.

C. Courbet's sometimes salacious paintings were intended to change the public's taste and way of seeing.

D. Courbet rejected his parents' wish that he study law, instead becoming a key figure of new realism in modern art.

50. John Gotti, born in the Bronx on October 27, 1940, was the Boss of the New York City Gambino crime family. He was known for his outspoken personality and flamboyant style, resulting in the nickname, "The Dapper Don." Between 1957 and 1961, Gotti pursued a life of crime on a full-time basis. His arrest record included street fighting, public intoxication, and car theft. By his 21st birthday, Gotti had been arrested five times, but served little gaol time. On March 6, 1962, Gotti married 17-year-old Victoria DiGiorgio. At the time of their marriage, DiGiorgio had already given birth to their first child, Angela, and was pregnant with their second. Gotti briefly tried his hand at legitimate jobs for the sake of his family: first, as a presser in a coat factory, and then as an assistant to a truck driver. In 1992, Gotti was convicted of 13 murders and various other charges and was sentenced to life in prison without parole. He died there 10 years later. (*biography.com*)

A. Although Gotti was arrested five times by the time he was 21, he left crime entirely when he married Victoria DiGiorgio.

B. Born in the Bronx, Gotti was known as "The Dapper Don" and at one time worked in a coat factory.

C. Although Gotti was arrested many times, no court ever punished him for a crime.

D. By the time he was 21, Gotti had served five years in prison for public intoxication, street fighting, and car theft.

51. A battle-scarred, eighth-century town unearthed in northern Germany may be the earliest Viking settlement in the historical record, archaeologists announced recently. Ongoing excavations at Füsing, near the Danish border, link the site to the "lost" Viking town of Sliasthorp, which was first recorded in AD 804 by royal scribes of the powerful Frankish ruler Charlemagne. Some 30 buildings have been uncovered since excavations began in 2010. Chief among them is a Viking longhouse measuring more than a hundred feet (30 metres)

long and 30 feet (9 metres) wide. The longhouse's burnt-out remains seemingly bear witness to a violent attack: Arrowheads found embedded in its charred wall posts suggest the communal building was at some point set on fire and shot at, Dobat said. A caltrop – a type of small, spiked iron weapon that was scattered on the ground for the enemy to step on – was also found at the entrance. Other finds include precious jewellery, glass beads, and silver coins. (*National Geographic*)

A. The "lost" Viking town of Sliasthorp, located in Germany near the Danish border, was once visited by Charlemagne.

B. Scribes of the Frankish ruler Charlemagne first recorded the Viking settlement of Sliasthorp in AD 804.

C. The caltrop is a type of large arrowhead weapon that sticks into the walls of wooden buildings like Viking longhouses.

D. Arrowheads found in scorched wall posts of a Viking longhouse indicate that Danish warriors attacked the building.

52. Just days after a poacher's snare had killed one of their own, two young mountain gorillas worked together Tuesday to find and destroy traps in their Rwandan forest home, according to conservationists on the scene. Bush-meat hunters set thousands of rope-and-branch snares in Rwanda's Volcanoes National Park, where the mountain gorillas live. The traps are intended for antelope and other species but sometimes capture the apes. Adults are generally strong enough to free themselves. Youngsters aren't always so lucky. Just last week an ensnared infant named Ngwino, found too late by workers from Karisoke, died of snare-related wounds. Her shoulder had been dislocated during escape attempts, and gangrene had set in after the ropes cut deep into her leg. The hunters seem to have no interest in the gorillas. Even small apes, which would be relatively easy to carry away for sale, are left to die. (*National Geographic*)

A. It is almost always the young male gorillas who dismantle the snares because it is their role to protect the clan.

B. Volcanoes National Park employees look for and dismantle snares, and young gorillas often help them with the task.

C. Poachers in Rwanda set snares to capture young mountain gorillas because they can sell them for large profits.

D. While adult gorillas are often strong enough to free themselves from the snares, young ones often cannot.

53. Rhinovirus infection is linked to about 70 per cent of all asthma exacerbations with more than 50 per cent of these patients requiring hospitalisation. Furthermore, over 35 per cent of patients with acute chronic obstructive pulmonary disease (COPD) are hospitalised each year due to respiratory viruses including rhinovirus. A new antiviral drug to treat rhinovirus infections is being developed by Melbourne company Biota Holdings Ltd, targeted for those with these existing conditions where the common cold is a serious threat to their health and could prove fatal. A team of researchers is now using information on how the new drug works to create a 3D simulation of the complete rhinovirus using Australia's fastest supercomputer. (*Science Daily*)

A. Every year, nearly one in four patients with COPD are hospitalised due to respiratory viruses such as rhinovirus.

B. The antiviral drug being developed by Biota Holdings Ltd disables rhinovirus by binding to the shell that surrounds it.

C. Using Australia's supercomputer technology allows researchers to monitor how a drug will work at a molecular level.

D. For individuals with asthma and COPD, respiratory viruses such as rhinovirus can be extremely serious and even fatal.

54. Climate change has had a significant impact on the timing of river floods across Europe over the past 50 years, according to a new study. In some regions, such as southern England, floods are now occurring 15 days earlier than they did half a century ago; however, around the North Sea, in the Netherlands, Denmark and Scotland, the trend is towards later floods. The scientists believe this is due to changes in the North Atlantic Oscillation (NAO), the weather phenomenon that

pushes storms across the ocean into Europe. The study has been published in the journal Science. Floods caused by rivers impact more people than any other natural hazard, and the estimated global damages run to roughly a 100 billion dollars a year. (*BBC News online*)

A. Scientists have found that climate change is usually resulting in later flooding in Europe.

B. Floods caused by rivers result in estimated damage of nearly 100 billion dollars to European economies every year.

C. Changes in the North Atlantic Oscillation may be causing later river floods in northern European countries.

D. In southern England river floods are now occurring at a much earlier time than river floods in Scotland.

55. The third plague pandemic lasted roughly from 1855 to 1959 and marked the first time that bubonic plague reached all inhabited continents, leaving more than 12 million dead. Plague made its first major appearance in the Crown Colony of Hong Kong in 1894. It then spread first to India (1896) and then, rapidly, on a global scale; between 1898 and 1900 alone it struck Hawaii, California, Manchuria, Australia, Madagascar, Paraguay, Portugal, Scotland, Egypt, and Japan. During its course the third plague pandemic functioned as a catalyst for major public health and urban planning reforms, colonial policies, geopolitical struggles, and medical theories and techniques. This was not simply on account of the mortality and morbidity crisis in different parts of the world induced by plague. It was also because incidents of this pandemic were systematically photographed and documented from beginning to end, with images from local outbreaks making newspaper headlines across the globe. (*Royal Historical Society website*)

A. The third plague pandemic spread quickly around the globe due to colonialism and global conflict.

B. The third plague pandemic started in Hong Kong in roughly 1894 and then spread to India in 1896.

C. The third plague pandemic was widely documented during the course of 1855 to 1959.

D. The third plague pandemic reached Europe in 1898 when outbreaks occurred in Portugal and Scotland.

56. A recently published study examined how decision-making would be affected by a human-like aid. The study focused on adults' trust, dependence, and performance while using a computerised decision-making aid for persons with diabetes. The study is one of the first to examine how the design of decision-support aids on consumer devices can influence the level of trust that users place in that system and how much they use it. Many people interact with computerised decision aids or automation on a daily basis, whether they're using smart phones, digital cameras or global positioning systems. When automation is only reliable sometimes, a person's level of trust becomes an important factor that determines how often the aid will be used. The research findings have revealed that the inclusion of an image of a person can significantly alter perceptions of a computerised aid when there is no difference in the aid's reliability or presentation of information. (*Science Daily*)

A. An individual's level of trust in computerised decision aids has influence on how they use a device.

B. An individual's level of trust in computerised decision aids is highly influenced by the design used.

C. Research shows that computerised decision-making aids that include an image of a person change how such an aid is perceived.

D. Research shows that human-like computerised decision aids may reduce decision-making reaction time for adults.

57. In all, Francis of Assisi, noted ascetic, holy man and future saint, found that he bore five marks: two on his palms and two on his feet, where the nails that fixed Christ to the cross were traditionally believed to have been hammered home, and the fifth on his side, where the Bible says Jesus had received a spear thrust from a Roman centurion. This was the first case of stigmata – the appearance of marks or actual wounds paralleling those Christ

received during Crucifixion – described. Later stigmatics (and there have been several hundred of them) have exhibited similar marks, though some bear only one or two wounds, while others also display scratches on their foreheads, where Christ would have been injured by his crown of thorns. Through the centuries, stigmata has become one of the best-documented, and most controversial, of mystical phenomena. The extensive record makes it possible to compare cases that occurred centuries apart. At least ten more were recorded in the 13th century. (*smithsonianmag.com*)

A. Stigmatics bear the five marks that mimic those wounds that Christ received during the Crucifixion.

B. Among the stigmata marks borne by ascetic and holy man Francis of Assisi were scratches on his forehead.

C. Stigmata is a controversial mystical occurrence that has been reportedly experienced by several hundred individuals.

D. Francis of Assisi, who has been recognized as a saint, was the first person to bear the wounds of Christ.

58. Modern cats diverged in skull shape from their sabre-toothed ancestors early in their evolutionary history and then followed separate evolutionary trajectories, according to new research. The study also found that the separation between modern domestic cats and big cats such as lions and tigers is also deeply rooted. Scientists studied the skull shape of extinct sabre-toothed cats, modern (conical-toothed) cats and prehistoric 'basal' cats (ancestors of modern cats). This is the first time these three different types of cats have been analysed together in a single dataset. The researchers quantified skull shape by taking various measurements, adjusting these measurements for size differences, then investigating the distribution of cat skulls in shape-space. They found an early and conspicuous divergence between the conical-toothed cats and sabre-toothed cats, with all sabre-toothed cats being more closely related to each other than they were to modern conical-toothed cats. (*Science Daily*)

A. Their parallel evolutionary trajectories underlie the close connection between modern big cats such as lions and tigers and modern domestic cats.

B. Despite the divergence between the skull shapes of extinct sabre-toothed cats and modern domestic cats, these two different types of cats are closely related to each other.

C. Skull shape indicates that all types of sabre-toothed cats were more closely related to one another than to modern conical-toothed cats.

D. The skull shapes of sabre-toothed and conical-toothed cats indicate that they followed different evolutionary trajectories.

59. Future high-energy accelerators will need stronger magnetic fields and the magnets of the future will most probably be manufactured from high-temperature superconductors (HTS). These materials are thus named because they exhibit superconducting behaviour at higher temperatures than niobium-titanium and niobium-tin, which are both known as low-temperature superconductors (LTS) and must operate at extremely low temperatures to reach and retain their superconductive state. In the Large Hadron Collider, which is the world's largest and most powerful particle accelerator, for example, the niobium-tin magnets are cooled to just 1.9 Kelvin (–271.3 °C) using liquid helium as a coolant. Above a critical temperature and above a critical magnetic field, the superconductors fail to maintain their superconductive state, and stop operating correctly (they are said to undergo a "quench"), which is very undesirable behaviour for a magnet, because it results in the appearance of voltage and a rapid temperature increase. (*European Organization for Nuclear Research*)

A. Niobium-tin magnets are likely to undergo a quench when operating at a temperature of 1.9 Kelvin (–271.3 °C).

B. Niobium-titanium and niobium-tin are both low-temperature superconductors used in the magnets of the Large Hadron Collider.

C. Liquid helium is used as a coolant in the Large Hadron Collider because alternative coolants cannot achieve a temperature of 1.9 Kelvin (–271.3 °C).

D. Low-temperature superconductors only work properly within a critical range of temperature and magnetic field.

60. The massive population decline of Lord Howe Island stick insects began with a shipwreck in 1918, on their namesake Lord Howe Island, a small, lush landmass jutting out of the ocean off the east coast of Australia. The ship contained a horde of rats that quickly invaded. With no larger mammals to predate on the rats, their population exploded. The stick insect was eventually classified as extinct in 1983. In 1960, a group of rock climbers visited another small volcanic rock island nearby, named Ball's Pyramid. It was there that they found what appeared to be the dead remains of the "extinct" stick creatures. It wasn't until 2001 that researchers returned to Ball's Pyramid. Atop a tea tree, 213 feet above sea level, sat a few living examples of what appeared to be Lord Howe Island stick insects. However, the identity of the insects has been the subject of debate. Visually, the captive-bred stick insects looked different. It wasn't until genome sequencing was conducted on both museum specimens and the captive-bred stick insects that scientists realised they had a less than one percent genetic variance—enough to officially classify them as the same species. (*nationalgeographic.com*)

A. In 1960 stick insects were found on Ball's Pyramid, a rocky outcrop on Lord Howe Island.

B. The rock climbers retrieved samples of what appeared to be the extinct stick insects.

C. Until the rats came along, the Lord Howe Island stick insects had no large predators.

D. The scientists compared the extinct samples to the living stick insects to find they are of the same species.

61. The biggest known crocodile has been found – and the 8.3-metre-long predator likely swallowed early humans whole, a new study says. *Crocodylus thorbjarnarsoni* lurked in deep lakes near present-day Lake Turkana in Kenya between about two and four million years ago. According to research, the ancient animal would have resembled a heavyset Nile crocodile, some of which can reach up to 6 metres long. Other species in the wider category of crocodyliforms – part of a group that includes modern-day alligators, caimans, and more – are bigger, such as the 12-metre-long SuperCroc. The prehistoric reptile likely got so big from eating plentiful large prey – including our ancestors, who at the time stood about 1.2 metres tall as adults. When *C. thorbjarnarsoni* gobbled an early human, "the whole thing [probably went] down the gullet, so nothing gets fossilized," said Hastings, who discovered a prehistoric crocodile species in 2011. (*National Geographic*)

A. The giant *Crocodylus thorbjarnarsoni* likely ambushed our 1.2-metre tall ancestors when they went to collect water.

B. *Crocodylus thorbjarnarsoni* is the biggest species in the category of crocodyliforms, which also includes caimans.

C. *Crocodylus thorbjarnarsoni,* the largest crocodile known, is a distant ancestor of the Nile crocodile.

D. The 8.3-metre-long *C. thorbjarnarsoni* lived about two to four million years ago in lake waters of present-day Kenya.

62. In 1848, the British East India Company sent Robert Fortune on a trip to China's interior, an area forbidden to foreigners. Fortune's mission was to steal the secrets of tea horticulture and manufacturing. The Scotsman donned a disguise and headed into the Wu Si Shan hills in a bold act of corporate espionage. Although the concept of tea is simple – dry leaf infused in hot water – the manufacture of it is not intuitive at all. Tea is a highly processed product. At the time of Fortune's visit the recipe for tea had remained unchanged for two thousand years, and Europe had been addicted to it for at least two hundred of them. But few in Britain's dominions had any firsthand or even secondhand information about the production of tea before it went into the pot. Fortune's horticultural contemporaries in London and the directors of the East India Company all believed that tea would yield its secrets if it were held up to the clear light and scrutiny of Western science. (*smithsonianmag.com*)

A. Robert Fortune's "corporate espionage" trip to China was the first attempt by the British East India Company to steal the secrets of tea horticulture and manufacturing.

B. Tea is nothing more than an infusion of dry leaf in hot water, and the process of manufacturing tea is just as simple.

C. In 1848 when Robert Fortune visited the Wu Si Shan hills of China, the recipe for tea had not changed for two thousand years.

D. In 1848 within the British East India Company, only a few people had firsthand or secondhand knowledge of tea production.

63. Text messaging may offer tweens a quick way to send notes to friends and family, but it could lead to declining language and grammar skills, according to researchers. Tweens who frequently use language adaptations – "techspeak" – when they text performed poorly on a grammar test, said Drew Cingel, a former undergraduate student in communications, Penn State, and currently a doctoral candidate in media, technology and society, Northwestern University. When tweens write in techspeak, they often use shortcuts, such as homophones and omissions of non-essential letters and initials, to quickly and efficiently compose a text message. "Overall, there is evidence of a decline in grammar scores based on the number of adaptations in sent text messages, controlling for age and grade," Cingel said. Not only did frequent texting negatively predict the test results, but both sending and receiving text adaptations were associated with how poorly they performed on the test, according to Sundar. (*Science Daily*)

A. Research shows that tweens who text daily with friends and family are better adapted socially but perform less efficiently on grammar than their peers.

B. Studies show that how tweens perform on a grammar test is unrelated to how many text adaptations they send and receive.

C. Research shows that tweens who use techspeak when texting could experience a decline in grammar and language skills.

D. According to research, the use of techspeak is the primary reason for the decline in grammar scores among tweens.

64. Embedding family doctors in casualty departments to free up emergency staff slashes waiting times and hospital admissions for children, but increases antibiotic prescriptions, a study has shown. The measure follows an ongoing increase in casualty department admissions as they struggle to cope with the numbers. Two researchers had this to say: "The results presented in this study highlight both advantages and challenges", said Professor Taylor. "During this period patients seen by the family doctor were significantly less likely to be admitted, exceed the four-hour waiting target or leave before being seen. However, they were more likely to receive antibiotics."

"The most common medical presentations in emergency departments are breathing difficulty, febrile illness, diarrhoea and vomiting, abdominal pain, seizures and rash, all of which could be potentially serious", said Professor Carroll. "Long wait times and overcrowding in emergency departments are associated with delays in delivering urgent treatments such as antibiotics for sepsis." (*www.telegraph.co.uk*)

A. It is likely that casualty departments will reduce the use of family doctors after this report.

B. Professor Taylor and Professor Carroll disagree on the value of the increased use of antibiotics in casualty departments.

C. Family doctors working in casualty departments have had some positive effects, according to research.

D. Embedding family doctors in casualty departments has led to a major increase in the use of antibiotics in hospitals.

65. The job of a renaissance court portraitist was to produce likenesses of his sovereigns to display at the palace and give to foreign dignitaries or prospective brides. It went without saying the portraits should be flattering. Yet, in 1590, Giuseppe Arcimboldo painted his royal patron, the Holy Roman Emperor Rudolf II, as a heap of fruits and vegetables. With pea pod eyelids and a gourd for a forehead, he looks less like a king than a crudité platter. Lucky for Arcimboldo, Rudolf had a sense of humour. Arcimboldo served the Hapsburg family for more than 25 years, creating oddball "composite heads" made of sea creatures, flowers, dinner roasts and other materials. Part scientist, part

sycophant, part visionary, Arcimboldo was born in 1526 in Milan. Giuseppe's father was also an artist, and Giuseppe's early career suggests the young man designed cathedral windows and tapestries rife with angels, saints and evangelists. Though apples and lemons appear in some of the divine scenes, the produce is, comparatively, less remarkable than that of the fruit portraits. (*smithsonianmag.com*)

A. Giuseppe was not only a visionary painter and a scientist, but evidence suggests that he also designed tapestries.

B. Giuseppe most likely learned from his father how to paint sea creatures, flowers, dinner roasts, pea pods, gourds, and more.

C. In 1590, Arcimboldo painted Holy Roman Emperor Rudolf II at the emperor's request.

D. From the beginning of his career as an artist, Arcimboldo used only fruits and vegetables as the elements of his works.

66. What does a robot feel when it touches something? Researchers published a study showing that a specially designed robot can outperform humans in identifying a wide range of natural materials according to their textures, paving the way for advancements in prostheses, personal assistive robots and consumer product testing. The robot was equipped with a new type of tactile sensor built to mimic the human fingertip. So, is touch another task that humans will outsource to robots? Fishel and Loeb point out that while their robot is very good at identifying which textures are similar to each other, it has no way to tell what textures people will prefer. Instead, they say this robot touch technology could be used in human prostheses or to assist companies who employ experts to assess the feel of consumer products and even human skin. (*Science Daily*)

A. A robot with a special tactile sensor that simulates the fingertip of a human can outperform humans in identifying materials.

B. Robots with a special tactile sensor could be used to advance some types of health products or assist with testing consumer products.

C. Robots with a special tactile sensor are able to identify many materials including plastic, wood, wool, silk, and polyester.

D. Robots with a special tactile sensor can outperform humans at jobs that deal with texture comparison and people's texture preferences.

67. A new study concludes that among older adults – especially those who are frail – low levels of vitamin D can mean a much greater risk of death. The randomised, nationally representative study found that older adults with low vitamin D levels had a 30 per cent greater risk of death than people who had higher levels. Overall, people who were frail had more than double the risk of death than those who were not frail. Frail adults with low levels of vitamin D tripled their risk of death over people who were not frail and who had higher levels of vitamin D. Because of the cross-sectional nature of the survey, researchers could not determine if low vitamin D contributed to frailty, or whether frail people became vitamin D deficient because of health problems. However, Smit said the longitudinal analysis on death showed it may not matter which came first. (*Science Daily*)

A. Individuals who are frail develop vitamin D deficiency primarily because of their health problems.

B. Frail older adults with low vitamin D levels are three times as likely to die as those who are not frail and have higher levels.

C. According to the new study, older adults with low vitamin D levels faced a lower risk of dying than those with higher levels.

D. According to most studies, researchers have concluded that low vitamin D levels contribute to frailty in older adults.

68. Mariza, the internationally known Portuguese singer, is captivating yet another audience with the haunting sounds of fado – the music called the soul of Portugal and often compared to American blues. As her voice fills the hall – alternately whispering and shouting, rejoicing and lamenting – the wildly receptive audience confirms her rising reputation as the new queen of fado, and the genre's increasing world appeal. The roots of fado, Portuguese for fate or destiny, are a mystery. But musicologists see it as an amalgam of cultures, especially African and Brazilian,

stemming from Portugal's maritime and colonial past, combined with its oral poetry tradition and, possibly, some Berber-Arab influence from the long Moorish presence that spanned the 8th through the 13th centuries. In the 19th century, fado became popular among the urban poor of Lisbon. It was sung in bars, back streets and brothels. (*smithsonainmag.com*)

A. The urban poor of 19th-century Lisbon were drawn to fado because they could sing it any time or place.

B. According to musicologists, fado comes from just Portuguese, Moorish, and Berber-Arab cultures and oral poetry traditions.

C. Fado music is currently more popular around the world than it was among the urban poor of 19th-century Lisbon.

D. Fado, which means "fate" or "destiny" in Portuguese, is called the soul of Portugal and is compared to American blues.

69. Autism spectrum disorders, including Asperger syndrome, have generally been associated with uneven intellectual profiles and impairment, but according to a new study of Asperger individuals, this may not be the case – as long as intelligence is evaluated by the right test. Both autistic and Asperger individuals display uneven profiles of performance in commonly used intelligence test batteries such as Wechsler scales, and their strongest performances are often considered evidence for deficits. However, this study reports that Asperger individuals' scores are much higher when they are evaluated by a test called Raven's Progressive Matrices, which encompasses reasoning, novel problem-solving abilities, and high-level abstraction. By comparison, scores for non-Asperger individuals are much more consistent across different tests. (*Science Daily*)

A. A recent study of Asperger individuals suggests that the measure of intelligence is exactly quantifiable.

B. Asperger individuals score higher than non-Asperger individuals on the Raven's Progressive Matrices test.

C. In general Asperger individuals score more unevenly on different types of intelligence tests than their non-Asperger peers.

D. High-level abstraction and the ability to solve novel problems are considered higher forms of intelligence.

70. Few insects capture the imagination like bees do. Honeybees (*Apis mellifera*) in particular, with their social hierarchy and sweet product, have long been part of our literary and agricultural heritage. Honeybees are the workhorses of modern farms, which rely on them to pollinate crops. That dependence has made reports of declining bee populations and colony collapse all the more alarming. Although bees are known to be affected by environmental shifts, including habitat loss and climate change, public attention has been focused on a class of pesticide called neonicotinoids, or neonics. But the link between these pesticides and colony collapse remains obscure. Daunting as the prospect is of losing our main pollinators, the furore has masked wider issues. Not only honeybees are at risk – solitary bees face greater threats. Like humans, bees have microbes in their guts that provide a host of benefits, and studying the honeybee provides insights into how biological and synthetic systems interact. (*nature.com*)

A. The interaction of biological and synthetic systems within the gut of a bee can prove as harmful to a bee as it is for a human.

B. The decline in the honeybee population means they may be wiped out altogether in some areas.

C. Solitary bees face the same threat as honeybees as environmental changes lead to the loss of their natural habitat.

D. Neonicotinoids have been linked with the decline in the number of bees, however this link has not been categorically confirmed.

71. Superconductivity is one of the most fascinating phenomena known to humankind. When a superconductor is cooled below its 'critical temperature', the fluid of electrons, which is responsible for the conduction of electricity through the material, undergoes a radical re-organisation. The electrons form 'Cooper pairs' and these Cooper pairs condense into a single, collective quantum state, which means they all behave as a single entity. This allows the manifestation of quantum-mechanical effects, which

are normally confined to the world of sub-microscopic particles, on a scale that is visible to the naked eye. While in conventional superconductors (and also in some high-temperature superconductors) the electrons in a Cooper pair have their intrinsic 'spins' pointing in opposite directions, so that the total spin of the Cooper pair is zero, in other, more exotic 'triplet' superconductors the electronic spins line up, so the Cooper pair has some intrinsic spin of its own. (*Science Daily*)

A. Electrons that form Cooper pairs act as one entity, rendering quantum-mechanical effects visible to the naked eye.

B. In conventional superconductors, the electrons form Cooper pairs so that the electronic spins form a cloud.

C. In triplet superconductors, Cooper pairs allow for quantum-mechanical effects, but they are not visible to the naked eye.

D. Conventional, high-temperature, and triplet superconductors all cannot operate above the same critical temperature.

72. Once a required stop on caravan routes that brought Asian goods west to eager Romans, Palmyra has "always been conceived as an oasis in the middle of the desert, but it's never been quite clear what it was living from," said Michal Gawlikowski, the retired head of the University of Warsaw's Polish Mission at Palmyra. And what an oasis: Among the ruins are grand avenues lined with columns, triumphal arches, and the remains of an ancient market where traders once haggled over silk, silver, spices, and dyes from India and China. The landscape around the city, it now appears, was intensively farmed and most likely included olive, fig, and pistachio groves-crops known in the region from Roman accounts and still common in Syria. Barley too was grown, according to a pollen analysis Meyer's team conducted on a mud brick from the survey area. (*National Geographic*)

A. Palmyra served not only as a caravan stop but it was most likely an agricultural centre of the region thanks to the intensive cultivation.

B. Ancient residents of Palmyra likely grew a number of different crops in the surrounding area including figs and barley.

C. Ancient residents of Palmyra likely captured the small amount of annual rainfall to water their crops and pistachio groves.

D. Palmyra once served as a caravan stop where traders bargained over silks, spices, and other goods from all over the world.

73. Several centuries ago, many practising Christians, and those of other religions, had a strong belief that the Devil could give certain people known as witches the power to harm others in return for their loyalty. A "witchcraft craze" rippled through Europe from the 1300s to the end of the 1600s. Tens of thousands of supposed witches – mostly women – were executed. Though the Salem trials came on just as the European craze was winding down, local circumstances explain their onset. The Salem witch trials occurred in colonial Massachusetts between 1692 and 1693. More than 200 people were accused of practising witchcraft – the Devil's magic – and 20 were executed. Eventually, the colony admitted the trials were a mistake and compensated the families of those convicted. Since then, the story of the trials has become synonymous with paranoia and injustice, and it continues to beguile the popular imagination more than 300 years later. (*smithsonianmag.com*)

A. The "witchcraft craze" in Europe between the 13th and 16th centuries was the gravest period in the history of witch-hunts.

B. More than 200 accused witches were executed in the Salem trials in colonial Massachusetts between 1692 and 1693.

C. Colonial Massachusetts ultimately acknowledged that the witch trials were an error and recompensed families of the convicted.

D. Practising Christians in Europe were largely responsible for stirring up paranoia about witches.

74. For the first four decades of competition, the Olympics awarded official medals for painting, sculpture, architecture, literature and music, alongside those for the athletic competitions. From 1912 to 1952, juries awarded a total of 151 medals to original works in the fine arts inspired by athletic endeavours. The story goes all the way back to the

Baron Pierre de Coubertin, the founder of the IOC and the modern Games, who saw art competitions as integral to his vision of the Olympics. "He was raised and educated classically, and he was particularly impressed with the idea of what it meant to be a true Olympian – someone who was not only athletic, but skilled in music and literature," Stanton says. "He felt that in order to recreate the events in modern times, it would be incomplete to not include some aspect of the arts." (*smithsonianmag.com*)

A. For the first four decades of the Olympics, juries awarded medals for works of fine art depicting any subject matter.

B. Between 1912 and 1952, Olympic juries awarded 151 medals to gifted artists who were also highly skilled athletes.

C. Baron Pierre de Coubertin felt that the modern Olympics would not be complete without some inclusion of the arts.

D. For the first four decades of the Olympics, the majority of art medals were awarded for paintings of the games themselves.

75. Nicolaus Copernicus was the first to demonstrate that the earth orbited the sun, upsetting the prevailing notion that the earth was the centre of the cosmos. A 30-year project, *On the Revolutions of the Heavenly Spheres* was Copernicus' response to the unwieldy mathematics used since the days of the ancient Greeks to explain the motion of the sun, moon and five known planets (Mercury, Venus, Mars, Jupiter and Saturn). Astronomers had worked from the assumption that the earth was the centre of the universe, forcing them to draw convoluted orbits for the planets, which even had to reverse directions for the theory to be consistent with their observed trajectories. Once Copernicus put the sun at the centre of the picture and adjusted the mathematics, the planetary orbits became regular, smooth and elegant. His inspiration came early, but the cautious scholar took half a lifetime to check his figures before publishing them in 1543, the year he died at age 70. (*smithsonianmag.com*)

A. Nicolaus Copernicus used convoluted mathematics and planetary orbits to demonstrate that the earth orbited the sun.

B. Copernicus delayed publishing his conclusions until he was 70 because he was cautious about his calculations and feared he would be persecuted as a heretic for his work.

C. Prior to Copernicus, astronomers used mathematics and complex planetary orbits to deduce that the earth was the centre of the universe.

D. Prior to Copernicus, astronomers had most likely explained the motions of heavenly bodies using mathematics dating to the ancient Greeks.

76. Pavegen tiles are designed to collect the kinetic energy created by the estimated 40 million pedestrians who will use that walkway in a year, generating several hundred kilowatt-hours of electricity from their footsteps. Once a Pavegen tile converts energy to electricity, 5 per cent of it is used to light the round LED-lighted logo in the centre of each tile. The other 95 per cent is either directly fed to the application or stored in a battery for later use. Pavegen is also working on a new system that will feed the power directly into a grid. The tiles are completely waterproof, so they can endure rain, snow, and ice. Pavegen's tiles are designed to have a minimal carbon footprint. All of the rubber comes from recycled truck tires, and about 80 per cent of the polymers used for the other components can be recycled. On average, one footstep generates 7 watts of electricity, though the amount varies depending on a person's weight. (*National Geographic*)

A. The amount of electricity generated by a person's single footstep depends solely on that person's weight.

B. Pavegen tiles are made with rubber from recycled tires and have a carbon footprint that is less than that of any other energy source.

C. The more recyclable components an energy source contains, the less carbon footprint it has.

D. Pavegen tiles are waterproof, have a minimal carbon footprint, and collect an average of 7 watts of electricity per footstep.

77. UC Irvine scientists have discovered intriguing differences in the brains and mental processes of an extraordinary group of people who can effortlessly recall every moment of their lives since about age 10. All had variations in nine structures of their brains compared

to those of control subjects, including more robust white matter linking the middle and front parts. Surprisingly, the people with stellar autobiographical memory did not score higher on routine laboratory memory tests or when asked to use rote memory aids. Yet when it came to public or private events that occurred after age 10½, they were remarkably better at recalling the details of their lives. The study also found statistically significant evidence of obsessive-compulsive tendencies among the group, but the authors do not yet know if or how this aids recollection. Many of the individuals have large, minutely catalogued collections of some sort, such as magazines, videos, shoes, stamps or postcards. (*Science Daily*)

A. People with remarkable autobiographical memories are more likely to have obsessive-compulsive tendencies than control subjects.

B. Obsessive-compulsive behaviours share the same neural pathways as those used to store and recall autobiographical memories.

C. The brains of people with extraordinary autobiographical memories may have larger prefrontal lobes than those of control subjects.

D. People who could remember every moment of their lives from around age 10 also scored higher when using rote memory aids.

78. Music was a key ingredient in ancient Egyptian religion. Teeter explains that it was believed to soothe the gods and encourage them to provide for their worshippers. Nehemes-Bastet was one of many priestess-musicians who performed inside the sanctuaries and in the courts of the temples. The musical instruments typically used were the menat, a multi-strand beaded necklace they would shake, and the sistrum, a handheld rattle whose sound was said to evoke wind rustling through papyrus reeds. Other musicians would have played drums, harps, and lutes during religious processions. "For years people have debated what kind of music it was," says Teeter. "But there's no musical notation left, and we're not sure how they tuned the instruments or whether they sang or chanted." The emphasis was definitely on percussion. Images often show people stamping their feet and clapping. Examples of song lyrics are recorded on temple walls. (*archaeology.org*)

A. In ancient Egypt, priestesses and musicians both sang and chanted during religious ceremonies.

B. Evidence recorded on temple walls suggests that ancient Egyptian music was like an early form of modern percussion music.

C. Music in ancient Egypt accompanied religious processions and was made using the menat and the sistrum and probably drums, lutes, and harps.

D. Musical instruments of ancient Egypt include the menat, a necklace that might have also had a decorative function.

79. The European Union has signed a fisheries agreement with Mauritania in west Africa. The total cost to the EU budget for fishing rights off the coast of the former French colony will be €70 million per year, according to the European Commission. The agreement allows EU ships to fish for demersal – a group of fish that lives or feeds near the bottom of the sea. Though the annual payment to the Mauritanian government will remain the same, access to fish has been reduced. Fish can now only be caught more than 20 miles from the shore, up from 13 miles in the previous agreement. There is also a new requirement that 2% of the catch must be given to the Mauritanian government. "The EU will pay the same amount of money but for much less fish," said Gerard van Balsfoort of the Pelagic Freezer-Trawler Association. "50–60% of the fleet was catching between 13 and 20 miles from the shore." Balsfoort said the restrictions will make the fishing rights worthless to EU fishermen. (*European Voice*)

A. Under a new fisheries agreement with Mauritania, the EU will no longer have to give 2% of its catch to Mauritania.

B. The new fisheries agreement does not allow the EU to catch fish between 13 miles and 20 miles from the shore because it is Mauritania's richest fishing area.

C. The EU will pay €70 million per year for fishing rights off the coast of Mauritania, including rights to fish for demersal.

D. Although Gerard van Balsfoort has been critical of the fishing agreement, a sizeable portion of fishermen may support it.

80. Many of the predictions we make in everyday life are vague, and many of them are wrong – like when we predict the weather – because we have incomplete information. But in quantum mechanics, the outcomes of certain experiments generally can't be predicted perfectly beforehand, even if all of the information is available. This inability to accurately predict the results of experiments in quantum physics has been the subject of a long debate, going back to Einstein and his co-workers, about whether quantum mechanics is the best way to predict outcomes. Randomness in quantum theory is one of its key features and is widely recognized, even outside the scientific community, says Tittel. "Its appeal is its fundamental nature and broad range of implications: knowing the precise configuration of the universe at the big bang would not be sufficient to predict its entire evolution, for example, in contrast to classical theory." (*Science Daily*)

A. Randomness is a central feature of quantum theory with practical applications for fields as diverse as chemistry and politics.

B. The question of whether quantum mechanics offers the best way to predict outcomes dates to Einstein and his colleagues.

C. Per quantum theory, if the universe's exact arrangement at the time of the big bang was known, its evolution could be partly predicted.

D. According to quantum mechanics, if you know all the available information at the outset, you will be able to accurately predict an outcome.

81. Consider Jan Lievens, born in Leiden in western Holland on October 24, 1607, just 15 months after the birth of Rembrandt van Rijn, another Leiden native. While the two were alive, admirers spoke of them in the same breath, and the comparisons were not always in Rembrandt's favour. After their deaths, Lievens dropped out of sight – for centuries. Though the artists took quite different paths, their biographies show many parallels. Both served apprenticeships in Amsterdam with the same master, returned to that city later in life and died there in their 60s. The work the two produced in their early 20s in Leiden was not always easy to tell apart, and as time went on, many a superior Lievens was misattributed to Rembrandt. Quality aside, it mattered that Rembrandt spent virtually his entire career in one place, cultivating a single, highly personal style, whereas Lievens moved around, absorbing many different influences. Equally important, Rembrandt lent himself to the role of the lonely genius, a figure dear to the Romantics, whose preferences would shape the tastes of generations to come. (*smithsonianmag.com*)

A. Had Lievens developed a single personal style as a painter, he would have stolen the cloak of fame from Rembrandt.

B. Although Lievens and Rembrandt produced work that is remarkably similar, critics of their time universally favoured Rembrandt.

C. Rembrandt and Lievens were both born in Leiden, apprenticed with the same master, and created some works of great similarity.

D. Lievens' life centred on continuous change, which put him out of favour with the Romantics who idolised the lonely genius.

82. Human diversity in Africa is greater than in any other place on Earth. Differing food sources, geographies, diseases and climates offered many opportunities for natural selection to force Africans to change and adapt to their local environments. The individuals who adapted best were the most likely to reproduce and pass on their genomes to the generations who followed. A recent study identifies several million previously unknown genetic mutations in humans. It finds evidence that the direct ancestors of modern humans may have interbred with members of an unknown ancestral group of hominids. It suggests that different groups evolved distinctly in order to reap nutrition from local foods and defend against infectious disease. "A message we're seeing is that even though all the individuals we sampled are hunter-gatherers, natural selection has acted differently in these different groups." (*Science Daily*)

A. Evidence indicates that ancestors of modern humans who did not interbreed with different hominid groups failed to evolve.

B. A recent study suggests that in human evolution, natural selection functioned the same in different hunter-gatherer groups.

C. A recent study suggests that humans evolved differently in order to maximise sources of nutrition and defend against diseases.

D. Early hunter-gatherers who had access to the most diverse food sources and lived in the most temperate climates were most likely to reproduce, according to one study.

83. Each new woolly mammoth carcass to emerge from the Siberian permafrost triggers a flurry of speculation about resurrecting this Ice Age giant. The two fundamental steps involved in cloning a mammoth, or any other extinct animal, are to recover its complete DNA sequence – in the case of mammoths, estimated to be more than 4.5 billion base pairs long – and to express this data in flesh and blood. The publication of the partial mammoth genome is a good start on the first problem, though the remaining 30 per cent of the genome would have to be recovered and the entire genome resequenced several more times to weed out errors. Scientists would also have to package the DNA into chromosomes – and at present they don't even know how many chromosomes the mammoth had. Yet none of these tasks appears insurmountable, especially in light of recent technical advances, such as a new generation of high-speed sequencers and a simple, inexpensive technique for recovering high-quality DNA from mammoth hair. (*National Geographic*)

A. Despite recent promising advances in technology, resurrecting a woolly mammoth in flesh and blood is not likely to happen.

B. Scientists have already sequenced part of the woolly mammoth's DNA but still have to work out how many chromosomes it had.

C. Scientists will be able to recover the 30 per cent of the mammoth genome that remains unknown from mammoth skin cells or mammoth hair.

D. Cloning a mammoth involves recovering its full DNA sequence and then recreating both male and female sex cells of the animal.

84. Harriet Menloy established the modern British field of inequality and poverty studies. She has worked on inequality and poverty for over five decades. Harriet's work is predominantly focused on income distributions and the economics of public policy for third world countries, from which an inequality measure was named after her: the Menloy index. In her recent book *"Inequality: options and strategies for reform"*, she argues that high levels of inequality are not inevitable and that policies can be designed to make our societies both more equitable and more efficient. Harriet's protégé Kingly Fisher's work is predominantly focused on macro and development economics. Much of his work concerns understanding the determinants of cross-country income differences, in particular arguing that financial underdevelopment is an important determinant of poverty and examining the effects of policies in the presence of such financial underdevelopment. His work analyses the causes and consequences of inequality within developed countries. (*eib.org*)

A. Harriet's strategies for reform have had a positive impact on society where implemented, making it both more equitable and efficient.

B. The Menloy index was named after her by Harriet Menloy's protégé Kingly Fisher.

C. Kingly's work only concerns the causes and effects of inequality in developing countries.

D. Kingly's position on the causes of poverty revolves around the consequences of financial underdevelopment.

85. The Rev. Charles Lutwidge Dodgson was a teacher of mathematics at Oxford and a deacon of the Anglican Church. Some colleagues knew him as a somewhat reclusive stammerer, but he was generally seen as a devout scholar; one dean said he was "pure in heart." To readers all over the world, he became renowned as Lewis Carroll, the author of *Alice's Adventures in Wonderland. Alice* was popular almost from the moment it was published, in 1865, and it has remained in print ever since, influencing such disparate artists as Walt Disney and Salvador Dali. Charles Dodgson was born in 1832 in Daresbury, a village in northwest

England. After enrolling at Oxford in 1850, at age 18, Dodgson became a "senior student" at the university's College of Christ Church. According to college rules, senior students had to be ordained as priests and take a vow of celibacy; Dodgson evaded the ordination rule and lived at the college unmarried, until his death in 1898, less than two weeks before his 66th birthday. (*smithsonianmag.com*)

A. Charles Lutwidge Dodgson, who used the pseudonym Lewis Carroll, was viewed as a serious scholar, a solitary man with a good heart and a stammerer.

B. Many of the characters in *Alice's Adventures in Wonderland* may have been inspired by the priests and academics that Charles Lutwidge Dodgson knew.

C. Charles Lutwidge Dodgson devoted much of his life to the craft of writing, though he did not publish much of his work.

D. Lewis Carroll's *Alice's Adventures in Wonderland* influenced Walt Disney, Salvador Dali and American filmmaker Tim Burton, among others.

86. Researchers have developed a way for security systems to combine different biometric measurements – such as eye colour, face shape or fingerprints – and create a learning system that simulates the brain in making decisions. The algorithm can learn new biometric patterns and associate data from different data sets, allowing the system to combine information, such as fingerprint, voice, gait or facial features, instead of relying on a single set of measurements. The key is in the ability to combine features from multiple sources of information, prioritise them by identifying more important/prevalent features to learn and adapt the decision-making to changing conditions. Biometric information is becoming more common in our daily lives, being incorporated in drivers' licences, passports and other forms of identification. The work is not only pioneering the intelligent decision-making methodology for human recognition but is also important for maintaining security in virtual worlds and avatar recognition. (*Science Daily*)

A. Security systems that can learn new biometric patterns and associate data from different data sets could contribute to solving crimes.

B. Security systems that can learn new biometric patterns and associate data from different data sets can make decisions better than a human.

C. While biometric information is being incorporated into passports and drivers' licences, it has no other practical applications.

D. Security systems are now capable of combining information from multiple sources and altering decision-making to shifting conditions.

87. The most popular entertainments offered by the circuses of Rome were the gladiators and chariot racing, the latter often as deadly as the former. As many as 12 four-horse teams raced one another seven times around the confines of the greatest arenas and rules were few, collisions all but inevitable, and hideous injuries to the charioteers commonplace. Ancient inscriptions record the deaths of famous racers in their early 20s, crushed against the stone *spina* that ran down the centre of the race track or dragged behind their horses after their chariots were smashed. Charioteers, who generally started out as slaves, took these risks because they could win fortunes. Successful, surviving racers could grow enormously wealthy. Spectators wagered and also won substantial sums – enough for the races to be plagued by all manner of dirty tricks; there is evidence that the fans sometimes hurled nail-studded curse tablets onto the track in an attempt to disable their rivals. (*smithsonianmag.com*)

A. Chariot racing and the gladiators were the most popular attractions at Rome's circuses, but the gladiators were always the most deadly.

B. Ancient inscriptions suggest that the majority of the charioteers in any race were killed by being dragged behind their horses.

C. Spectators could win so much money betting on chariot races that many of them lost their lives due to underhanded schemes.

D. Charioteers at Rome's circuses would have faced opposing racers, stone *spina*, and possibly curse tablets full of nails.

88. One hundred years ago, in 1912, astronomer Vesto Slipher found that the Andromeda galaxy was heading straight for us at a speed of 400,000 kilometres per hour. Scientists were unsure what this would mean for our galaxy in the long-term. Would we collide directly with Andromeda, a galaxy roughly the same size as our Milky Way? Or would we slide past it, like two ships passing in the night? Now, we know the Milky Way's ultimate fate: a galactic collision. The Milky Way and Andromeda galaxies will be slowly drawn together due to their mutual gravitational pull, colliding roughly 4 billion years from now. Subsequently, the two galaxies will orbit around each other before merging in one big galactic pile-up. The resulting supergalaxy will be different from either of the current ones: Instead of the elegant, flat, spiral-shaped disc we know and love, the new galaxy will be a three-dimensional ball of stars. Astoundingly, this massive crash won't have an enormous impact on earth or the solar system as a whole. (*smithsonianmag.com*)

A. While the Milky Way and Andromeda galaxies will collide, other galaxies in the same situation simply slide past each other.

B. The collision of the Milky Way with Andromeda will not significantly impact the earth because the process will take millions of years to complete.

C. When the Milky Way and Andromeda galaxies collide with each other, they will immediately form one big supergalaxy.

D. Scientists now predict that the Andromeda galaxy and the Milky Way galaxy will merge in several billion years to form a new galaxy.

89. Physicists at The University of Texas at Austin, in collaboration with colleagues in Taiwan and China, have developed the world's smallest semiconductor laser, a breakthrough for emerging photonic technology with applications from computing to medicine. Miniaturisation of semiconductor lasers is key for the development of faster, smaller and lower energy photon-based technologies, such as ultrafast computer chips; highly sensitive biosensors for detecting, treating and studying disease; and next-generation communication technologies. The device is constructed of a gallium nitride nanorod that is partially filled with indium gallium nitride. Both alloys are semiconductors used commonly in LEDs. The nanorod is placed on top of a thin insulating layer of silicon that in turn covers a layer of silver film that is smooth at the atomic level. (*Science Daily*)

A. The smooth arrangement of atoms in a layer of silver film inside the world's smallest semiconductor laser differentiates it from similar devices.

B. One component of the world's smallest semiconductor laser is a nanorod that is partly filled with indium gallium nitride.

C. The world's smallest semiconductor laser is composed of a thin layer of silicon that covers a gallium nitride nanorod.

D. The world's smallest semiconductor laser will soon be on the market in the form of computer chips, among other things.

90. Germany's industrial sector suffers as the eurozone slides back towards recession. The manufacturing sector in the eurozone suffered a steep decline in activity in July, according to figures recently released. It is the eurozone's worst PMI reading for three years and looks likely to contribute to the eurozone sliding back into recession. One of the sharpest falls in industrial orders came in Germany, showing that the main driver of the eurozone economy is now feeling the effects of the economic crisis. Its reading was also at a three-year low, at 43. Greece and Spain were the only two countries where the manufacturing sector contracted more rapidly. Only one country, Ireland, saw its manufacturing sector expand, with a score of 53.9. Chris Williamson said that July had been characterised by "faster rates of decline in output and new orders, leading manufacturers to cut back on head counts and inventory holdings and suggesting a fear among companies towards ongoing weakness". (*European Voice*)

A. Spain's manufacturing sector in July suffered a more severe setback than Greece, Germany, or Ireland.

B. In July, the manufacturing sectors of Germany, Greece, and Spain declined while the same sector in Ireland expanded.

C. According to Chris Williamson, July's manufacturing sector slowdown reflects a temporary and seasonally-related lapse.

D. Although Ireland's manufacturing sector expanded in July, its score of 53.9 is still the lowest it has seen in three years.

91. In the spring of 1963, Martin Luther King Jr. organised a demonstration in downtown Birmingham, Alabama. City police turned dogs and fire hoses on demonstrators. Martin Luther King was gaoled along with large numbers of his supporters, but the event drew nationwide attention. From the gaol in Birmingham, King eloquently spelled out his theory of non-violence: "Nonviolent direct action seeks to create such a crisis and foster such a tension that a community, which has constantly refused to negotiate, is forced to confront the issue." By the end of the Birmingham campaign, Martin Luther King Jr. and his supporters were making plans for a massive demonstration on the nation's capital asking for peaceful change. On August 28, 1963, the historic March on Washington drew more than 200,000 people into the shadow of the Lincoln Memorial. It was here that King made his famous "I Have a Dream" speech, emphasising his belief that someday all men could be brothers. (*biography.com*)

A. King delivered his "I Have a Dream" speech at the March on Washington just months after being gaoled in Birmingham, Alabama.

B. Without the publicity generated by the Birmingham demonstration, the March on Washington would not have drawn 200,000 people.

C. King believed that non-violence was a way to voice concerns and work toward solutions while avoiding crisis and confrontation.

D. The "I Have a Dream" speech was written to motivate and educate all Americans about the civil rights movement.

92. On May 6, 1937 the Hindenburg airship was about to complete its 35th trip across the Atlantic, having departed from Frankfurt, Germany and nearly arrived in New Jersey, U.S.A. Then, suddenly, after thousands of kilometres of uneventful travel, the great zeppelin caught fire while less than 90 metres from the ground. Within a minute of the first signs of trouble, the entire ship was incinerated, and the burning wreckage crashed to the ground. Immediately after the accident, observers disagreed about what exactly sparked the explosion and what caused the airship to burn so quickly. In the years since, scientists, engineers and others have weighed in on the debate and attempted to solve the mystery of the Hindenburg. Possible causes of the explosion include a buildup of static electricity, a bolt of lightning or a backfiring engine, but at this point it's impossible to determine what exactly caused the spark. (*smithsonianmag.com*)

A. The Hindenburg airship never reached New Jersey, as the zeppelin caught fire and crashed to the ground just metres from where it was scheduled to land.

B. In 1937, after travelling from Germany to the United States, the Hindenburg caught fire and crashed to the ground.

C. Since the Hindenburg disaster, scientists and engineers have concluded that the explosion was not caused by human error.

D. A bolt of lightning most likely caused the Hindenburg to burst into flames while less than 90 metres from the ground.

93. Despite claims in the 1890s that Mars was filled with canals teeming with water, research over the past several decades has suggested that in fact, Mars has only a tiny amount of water, mostly near its surface. During the 1970s, as part of NASA's Mariner space orbiter programme, dry river beds and canyons on Mars were discovered – the first indications that surface water may have once existed there. The Viking programme subsequently found enormous river valleys on the planet, and in 2003 it was announced that the Mars Odyssey spacecraft had actually detected minute quantities of liquid water on and just below the surface, which was later confirmed by the Phoenix lander. Now there is evidence that Mars is home to vast reservoirs of water in its interior as well. The research also provides us with an answer for how underground water may have made its way to the Martian surface: volcanic activity. (*smithsonianmag.com*)

A. The Viking programme discovered small amounts of liquid water on and just beneath the surface of Mars.

B. NASA's Mariner space orbiter programme discovered canyons and other formations on Mars during the 1970s.

C. Evidence that water exists on or near Mars' surface and in its interior suggests that the planet once possibly supported life.

D. Scientists claim that Mars has only a tiny amount of water, mostly near its surface.

94. The founding of the People's Liberation Army on 1 August 1927 is a date known to all in China. It is commemorated annually with speeches and promotions and every five years by major cultural celebrations. The events this year include operas, choral performances, photography shows and the "National Exhibition of Artistic Works in Celebration of the 85th Anniversary of the Chinese People's Liberation Army." Since the earliest days, the Communist Party and the People's Liberation Army, or P.L.A., have maximised the value of the arts as tools of propaganda. As Mao Zedong said in 1942, "To defeat the enemy we must rely primarily on the army with guns. But this army alone is not enough; we must also have a cultural army, which is absolutely indispensable for uniting our own ranks and defeating the enemy." The P.L.A. is one of the most important arts organizations in China. In Beijing, it has an arts university, opera house, opera, symphony orchestra, drama troupe and numerous bands. (*New York Times*)

A. Every year in China, the founding of the People's Liberation Army is remembered with major cultural celebrations.

B. Without the so-called cultural army, China would not be as united as it is today, nor as able to defeat its enemies.

C. In China, art is leveraged as a means of propaganda which, according to Mao Zedong, is essential for defeating the enemy.

D. China's Communist Party and P.L.A. have proven that art flourishes best when it is wedded to politics and national defence.

95. Before the Euro Cup, the International Football Association Board (IFAB) gave the green light to try goal line sensors from two of 10 competing companies: GoalRef and Hawkeye. In early July, IFAB approved both technologies, although they will remain optional. The distinction between these two technologies is that one is camera-based and one is not. And that difference could be the deciding factor. Unlike tennis, where there is almost never any thing or person obstructing the line of sight between the cameras and the ball, football presents unique challenges – especially during free kicks and corner kicks. In such situations, 10 players might be close to the goal, making it harder for cameras to unambiguously record when the ball passes the line. Not everyone is keen on goal line technology. Michel Platini, head of the UEFA, worried that introduction of this technology would begin a slippery slope toward more intrusions to the game, and he stood staunchly opposed to the technology. (*smithsoanianmag.com*)

A. The fact that the game of football presents challenges that are different from tennis is of no consequence to goal line sensor technology.

B. While the IFAB approved the optional use of two types of goal line sensors, the move was not unanimously embraced.

C. Although the IFAB has approved the use of goal line sensors, the head of UEFA is opposed and may "veto" their use.

D. Tennis most likely favours the use of GoalRef's technology because the line of sight between the ball and the cameras is rarely blocked.

96. A government investigation into insider trading in Tokyo has extended onto the trading floors of some of Wall Street's largest companies, including Goldman Sachs, UBS and Deutsche Bank. Regulators are scrutinising suspicious trading activity ahead of at least 12 public offering announcements over the last three years. The committee has been working with regulators to stiffen insider trading laws in Japan. Among the trades being investigated are those made by Goldman clients who bet against All Nippon Airways just days before the airline's stock offering last month. A company's share price typically drops when a new share issuance is announced. The commission is expected to issue an order and call for fundamental changes in

the way the company, which is based in Tokyo, handles information. The scandal has further undermined faith in Japanese stock markets, experts say, which remain some of the world's most depressed after the global financial crisis. (*New York Times*)

A. In Tokyo, a government committee investigation into insider trading involves Goldman Sachs and Deutsche Bank.

B. Of all the cases, just one company, Deutsche Bank, has clients suspected of misconduct in betting against an airway company.

C. A government investigation in Tokyo into insider trading will most likely result in more severe trading laws in Japan.

D. Suspicions of insider trading violations have caused Japanese stock markets to plunge in recent weeks.

97. Drawing on research from psychology and linguistics, the researchers seek to better understand how using different languages to discuss and express emotions in a multilingual family might play an important role in children's emotional development. They propose that the particular language parents choose to use when discussing and expressing emotion can have significant impacts on children's emotional understanding, experience, and regulation. Research from linguistics suggests that when bilingual individuals switch languages, the way they experience emotions changes as well. Bilingual parents may use a specific language to express an emotional concept because they feel that the language provides a better cultural context for expressing the emotion. Overall, the authors argue that research from psychological science and linguistics suggests that a child's emotional competence is fundamentally shaped by a multilingual environment. (*Science Daily*)

A. Research indicates that due to cultural differences native Spanish speakers experience emotions more intensely than native Finnish speakers.

B. Research suggests that growing up in a multilingual home has minor impact on a child's emotional development.

C. Children who grow up with bilingual parents are better able to express their emotions compared to their peers.

D. The perception of some bilingual parents it is that one language may provide a better means for expressing a given emotion.

98. The story about the first Penguin paperbacks may be apocryphal, but it is a good one. In 1935, Allen Lane, chairman of the eminent British publishing house Bodley Head, had a "Eureka!" moment: What if quality books were available at places like train stations and sold for reasonable prices – the price of a pack of cigarettes, say? Bodley Head did not want to finance his endeavour, so Lane used his own capital. He called his new house Penguin, apparently upon the suggestion of a secretary, and sent a young colleague to the zoo to sketch the bird. He then acquired the rights to ten reprints of serious literary titles and went knocking on non-bookstore doors. When Woolworth's placed an order for 63,500 copies, Lane first realised he had a viable financial model. Lane's paperbacks were cheap. They cost two and a half pence, the same as ten cigarettes, the publisher touted. Volume was key to profitability; Penguin had to sell 17,000 copies of each book to break even. (*smithsoanianmag.com*)

A. The key to Penguin's success was its advertising campaign comparing the price of a book to a pack of cigarettes.

B. Immediately after his "Eureka!" moment about reasonably priced books, Lane saw that his financial model would succeed.

C. If Woolworth's had not placed an early order for 63,500 books, Penguin would never have succeeded as it did.

D. After he had a "Eureka!" moment, Lane financed Penguin books and initially acquired the rights to ten reprints.

99. Born Agnes Bojaxhiu in 1910, Mother Teresa attended a convent-run primary school and then a state-run secondary school. The congregation made an annual pilgrimage to the chapel of the Madonna of Letnice atop Black Mountain in Skopje, and it was on one such trip at the age of twelve that Mother Teresa first felt

a calling to a religious life. In 1928, an 18-year-old Agnes Bojaxhiu decided to become a nun and set off for Ireland to join the Loreto Sisters of Dublin. It was there that she took the name Sister Mary Teresa after Saint Thérèse of Lisieux. A year later, she travelled on to Darjeeling, India for the novitiate period; afterward she was sent to Calcutta, where she was assigned to teach at Saint Mary's High School for Girls, a school dedicated to teaching girls from the city's poorest Bengali families. Mother Teresa had to learn to speak both Bengali and Hindi fluently as she taught geography and history and dedicated herself to alleviating the girls' poverty through education. (*biography.com*)

A. Had Agnes Bojaxhiu not joined her congregation on a pilgrimage to Skopje, she might never have felt a religious calling.

B. Agnes Bojaxhiu first took the name of Sister Mary Teresa on a trip to Darjeeling, India with the Loreto Sisters.

C. Mother Teresa taught history and geography in Bengali and Hindi at Saint Mary's High School for Girls in Calcutta.

D. After Agnes Bojaxhiu felt a religious calling, she became a nun and eventually travelled to Darjeeling and Calcutta and never left India again.

100. Prior to the 17th century, Ottoman succession had been governed by the "law of fratricide" drawn up by Mehmed II in the middle of the 15th century. Under the terms of this remarkable piece of legislation, whichever member of the ruling dynasty succeeded in seizing the throne on the death of the old sultan was not merely permitted, but enjoined, to murder all his brothers (together with any inconvenient uncles and cousins) in order to reduce the risk of subsequent rebellion and civil war. Although it was not invariably applied, Mehmed's law resulted in the deaths of at least 80 members of the House of Osman over a period of 150 years. These victims included all 19 siblings of Sultan Mehmed III – some of whom were still infants at the breast, but all of whom were strangled with silk handkerchiefs immediately after their brother's accession in 1595. (*smithsonianmag.com*)

A. Without the "law of fratricide", chaos and coups would have reigned in the Ottoman empire between the 15th and 17th centuries.

B. During the 15th century, the Ottoman Mehmed II instituted legislation that commanded a new ruler to commit fratricide.

C. The murder of the 19 siblings of Sultan Mehmed III was the most appalling incident of fratricide in the Ottoman succession between the 15th and 17th centuries.

D. Between the 15th and 17th centuries all family members of the new ruler were murdered in order to reduce the risk of subsequent rebellion and civil war.

101. Twins offer a precious opportunity to untangle the influence of genes and the environment – of nature and nurture. Because identical twins come from a single fertilised egg that splits in two, they share virtually the same genetic code. Any differences between them – one twin having younger looking skin, for example – must be due to environmental factors such as less time spent in the sun. Alternatively, by comparing the experiences of identical twins with those of fraternal twins, who come from separate eggs and share on average half their DNA, researchers can quantify the extent to which our genes affect our lives. If identical twins are more similar to each other with respect to an ailment than fraternal twins are, then vulnerability to the disease must be rooted at least in part in heredity. Lately, however, twin studies have helped lead scientists to a radical, almost heretical new conclusion: that nature and nurture are not the only elemental forces at work. (*National Geographic*)

A. Fraternal twins are more suitable than identical twins for studying how our environment impacts our lives.

B. Studies of identical and fraternal twins indicate that we are equally influenced by our genetics and our environment.

C. If one fraternal twin suffers from a disease while the other twin does not, the cause of the disease is hereditary.

D. Identical twins share nearly 100 per cent of their DNA while, on average, fraternal twins share 50 per cent of their DNA.

102. Economic growth and urbanisation go hand in hand and are critical to poverty reduction. Ultimately, cities provide both the living and working environment for most people in high-income countries, and an increasing number of middle income ones. Cities have the potential to reap major economies of scale. The United Kingdom has launched a three year programme of research funded by the World Bank and undertaken jointly by London School of Economics and Oxford University. It will look at the development of city systems – the urban hierarchy within and across countries – and at urban form – the internal organisation of particular cities, focusing on Africa. The programme of research will aim to build a credible database documenting the speed, magnitude and form of urban development in selected countries. Once completed this data will establish the facts about urbanisation. It will also predict the determinants of and consequences of differing patterns of urban growth. (*economics.ox.ac.uk*)

A. The research programme will help to anticipate the causes and effects of different types of urban growth.

B. Collaboration between academics and government officials in Africa will be required in order to collect the data on urban form.

C. Urban growth is the primary driver of poverty reduction and this study aims to document the speed, size and form of urban development.

D. Most people live outside the city in high income countries, a pattern replicated across an increasing number of middle income countries.

103. A new Internet-enabled power outlet will soon allow users to control household appliances via their smartphones and reduce their energy costs significantly. Soon there will be no need for special timers to switch lighting on and off or operate household appliances when the homeowner is absent. In the future, all of these things will be doable by means of a smartphone or PC thanks to Internet-enabled wireless power outlets that support the IPv6 Internet protocol. The wireless power outlets are a component of the HexaBus home automation system. "The HexaBus components make the smart home of the future a reality. They enable household appliances to be controlled intelligently, thus optimizing or reducing electricity consumption. For example, the householder can start the washing machine during cheap-rate off-peak hours, or run the dishwasher when the photovoltaic panels on the roof are generating sufficient power," says industrial engineer Mathias Dalheimer. (*Science Daily*)

A. Homes equipped with Internet-enabled power outlets will automatically optimise or reduce the household's use of electricity without any human control.

B. The HexaBus home automation system will soon be installed in the majority of smart homes that support the IPv6 Internet protocol.

C. Soon homeowners can start a load of laundry remotely with a smartphone or PC and Internet-enabled wireless power outlets.

D. When homeowners can control appliances and lighting from their smartphone or PC, energy consumption will drop.

104. Not only are healthy organs in short supply but donor and patient also have to be closely matched, or the patient's immune system may reject the transplant. A new kind of solution is incubating in medical labs: "bioartificial" organs grown from the patient's own cells. Thirty people have received lab-grown bladders already, and other engineered organs are in the pipeline. Researchers take healthy cells from a patient's diseased bladder, cause them to multiply profusely in petri dishes, then apply them to a balloon-shaped scaffold made partly of collagen, the protein found in cartilage. Muscle cells go on the outside, urothelial cells (which line the urinary tract) on the inside. "It's like baking a layer cake," says Atala. "You're layering the cells one layer at a time, spreading these toppings." The bladder-to-be is then incubated at body temperature until the cells form functioning tissue. The whole process takes six to eight weeks. (*National Geographic*)

A. A lab-grown bioartificial bladder is made by layering urothelial cells around muscle cells.

B. To grow a bladder in a lab, researchers must take some of the patient's healthy collagen cells.

C. A lab-grown bioartificial bladder involves petri dishes, a scaffold, cell layering, and incubation.

D. After bladder cells are transferred to the scaffold, they remain there for a period of three weeks.

105. Recent studies indicate that the brain's insular cortex may help a sprinter drive his body forward just a little more efficiently than his competitors. This region may prepare a boxer to better fend off a punch his opponent is beginning to throw as well as assist a diver as she calculates her spinning body's position so she hits the water with barely a splash. The insula does all this by anticipating an athlete's future feelings, according to a new theory. Researchers suggest that an athlete possesses a hyper-attuned insula that can generate strikingly accurate predictions of how the body will feel in the next moment. That model of the body's future condition instructs other brain areas to initiate actions that are more tailored to coming demands than those of also-rans and couch potatoes. Emerging evidence now also suggests that this brain area can be trained using a meditation technique called mindfulness – good news for Olympians and weekend warriors alike. (*smithsonianmag.com*)

A. Research shows that the brain's insular cortex can be tuned only by physically practising a given sport or skill.

B. The insular cortex may contribute to athletic excellence by anticipating how the physical body will soon feel.

C. Sprinters, boxers and divers are those athletes who benefit most from a hyper-attuned insular cortex.

D. Research indicates that, compared to boxers, athletes have larger insular cortexes.

106. The British mathematician Alan Turing probed one of computing's biggest theoretical questions: Could machines possess a mind? If so, how would we know? In 1950, he proposed an experiment: If judges in typed conversations with a person and a computer programme couldn't tell them apart, we'd come to consider the machine as "thinking." He predicted that programmes would be capable of fooling judges 30 per cent of the time by the year 2000. They came closest at the 2008 Loebner Prize competition when the top chatbot (as a human-mimicking programme is called) fooled 3 of 12 judges, or 25 per cent. Chatbots betray themselves in many ways, some subtle. They're unlikely to gracefully interrupt or be interrupted. Their responses, often cobbled together out of fragments of stored conversations, make sense at a local level but lack long-term coherence. (*smithsonianmag.com*)

A. A chatbot tricked a quarter of the judges into thinking it was human at the 2008 Loebner Prize competition.

B. The absence of sustained logical consistency most frequently alerts Turing test judges that they are talking to a chatbot.

C. Turing's prediction that computers would trick people 30 per cent of the time by the year 2000 was proven correct.

D. Within the next several years, chatbots will be able to adequately imitate how humans interrupt and are interrupted.

107. The predominant theory of sleep is that the brain demands it. But the trick is to confirm this assumption with real data. How does sleeping help the brain? The answer may depend on what kind of sleep you are talking about. Recently, researchers at Harvard tested undergraduates on various aptitude tests, allowed them to nap, then tested them again. They found that those who had engaged in REM sleep subsequently performed better in pattern recognition tasks, such as grammar, while those who slept deeply were better at memorisation. Other researchers have found that the sleeping brain appears to repeat a pattern of neuron firing that occurred while the subject was recently awake, as if in sleep the brain were trying to commit to long-term memory what it had learned that day. Yet another study showed that the sleeping brain seems to weed out redundant or unnecessary synapses or connections. So the purpose of sleep may be to help us remember what's important by letting us forget what's not. (*National Geographic*)

A. According to the study referenced, REM sleep is the most valuable in assisting memorisation.

B. The patterned neuron firing that occurs during REM sleep facilitates long-term memory.

C. Removing unneeded synapses while asleep allows us to recognise patterns while awake.

D. Some research shows that sleep may facilitate better pattern recognition and memory.

108. Bingo Friendzy, developed by the British online gambling company Gamesys, was introduced on Facebook this morning. It allows players to stake cash in 90 bingo and slot machine games. The app is marketed with cartoon graphics featuring characters that have been compared to those on Moshi Monsters, the popular children's social network. It has prompted anger from Christian groups, who called on the Advertising Standards Authority to act. Facebook has allowed the first real gambling app as it comes under unprecedented pressure to increase its revenues. Since its flotation in May the firm has reported a $157m loss and its shares have almost halved in value amid concerns about Facebook's effectiveness as an advertising medium. Facebook will take 30 per cent of revenues from Bingo Friendzy and a host of other gambling apps expected to be introduced in the coming months. (*Daily Telegraph*)

A. Christian groups angered by Bingo Friendzy believe that children should not be exposed to the sin of gambling.

B. Facebook will not benefit financially from Bingo Friendzy or any other gambling app to appear on the site.

C. Facebook shares lost half their value primarily because investors do not have faith in the company's advertising.

D. Bingo Friendzy appeared on Facebook at a time when the company was suffering from economic loss.

109. At least 10 million of the world's poorest people are set to go hungry this year because of failing crops caused by one of the strongest El Niño climatic events on record, Oxfam, the charity, has warned. The charity said several countries were already facing a "major emergency", such as Ethiopia, where 4.5 million are in need of food aid because of a prolonged scarcity of rain this year. Floods, followed by drought, have slashed Malawi's maize production by more than a quarter, farmers in central America have suffered from two years of drought and El Niño conditions have already reduced the Asian monsoon over India, potentially triggering a wider drought across the east of the continent. El Niño is a periodic climatic phenomenon where waters of the eastern tropical Pacific warm, triggering a range of potential consequences for global weather. While parts of South America are typically doused in heavy rainfall, warmer, drought-like conditions are experienced in Australia, south-east Asia and southern Africa. (*theguardian.com*)

A. El Niño is an annual event where waters of the eastern tropical Pacific warm up, causing a range of consequences in the weather.

B. The results of El Niño include floods and droughts and the effects can be observed in Malawi, India and South America, among others.

C. 4.5 million people in Ethiopia are in need of food aid because of initial floods and then a prolonged scarcity of rain, worsened by El Niño.

D. All countries effected by El Niño first experience heavy floods and then a drought.

110. Thomas, or Doubting Thomas as he is commonly known, was one of the "Twelve Apostles", disciples sent out after Christ's Crucifixion to spread the newborn faith. He was joined by Peter, Andrew, James the Greater, James the Lesser, John, Philip, Bartholomew, Matthew, Thaddaeus, Simon – and Matthias, who replaced the former disciple and alleged traitor, Judas Iscariot. In time the terms "apostle" and "apostolic" (derived from the Greek *apostolos*, or messenger) were applied to others who spread the word. In the case of Paul, he claimed the title of apostle for himself, believing he had seen the Lord and received a spiritual commission from him. Mary Magdalene is known as the apostle to the Apostles for her role of announcing the resurrection to them. Although only two of the four Evangelists – Matthew and John – were amongst the original Apostles, Mark and Luke are considered apostolic because of

the importance of their work in writing the New Testament Gospels. (*National Geographic*)

A. For at least a century following the crucifixion, the word "apostle" was only used in reference to Christ's twelve disciples.

B. Simon, Philip and Mary Magdalene are all considered apostles, a term that traces to the Greek word meaning messenger.

C. Despite their contributions to the New Testament, some conservative Christians still do not consider Mark and Luke to be apostles.

D. The twelve apostles are Thomas, Peter, Andrew, James the Greater, James the Lesser, John, Philip, Bartholomew, Matthew, Thaddaeus, Simon, and Judas Iscariot.

111. The 17th century Dutch painter Frans Hals made two great contributions. One was to combine an intense sense of realism with flamboyant brushwork – which gives his work a highly personal quality. Hals' other contribution is to fill his paintings with evident psychological intensity, the quality known as "psychological insight." His figures feel as if we could speak to them. It's surely no accident that Hals's life (1580–1666) overlapped with that of Shakespeare (1564–1616), and the way he evoked a sense of character provides interesting parallels to the characters in Shakespeare's plays who are generally two or more people in one body, engaged in internal dialogue. In that sense, Hals's portraits document the emergence of the modern self: they display a new awareness that the "self" is not a single, uniform thing, but the product of conflicting forces and disparate impulses, ruled by a consciousness filled with self-doubt. (*smithsonianmag.com*)

A. Frans Hals' use of subtle brushwork in his paintings conveyed his impression of the people he painted.

B. Frans Hals's paintings have been described as conveying a sense of realism along with psychological insight.

C. In his portraits, Frans Hals intentionally tried to impart a sense of the modern self, riddled with complexity and doubt.

D. Hals frequently attended performances of Shakespeare's plays, and the bard's influence on his painting is obvious.

112. A new genetic analysis has reconstructed the history of North Africa's Jews, showing that these populations date to biblical-era Israel and are not largely the descendants of natives who converted to Judaism. The study also shows that these Jews form two distinct groups, one of which is more closely related than the other to their European counterparts, reflecting historical migrations. The findings are the latest in a series of genetic studies, which began in the 1990s, indicating that the world's Jews share biological roots, not just cultural and religious ties. In many cases the analyses have confirmed what scholars had gleaned from archaeological finds and historical accounts. The scientists found that the Jewish populations of North Africa became genetically distinct over time, with those of each country carrying their own DNA signatures. This suggests they mostly married within their own religious and cultural group. (*Science Daily*)

A. Genetic analysis shows that the ancestors of North African Jews share biological roots with at least two other groups.

B. Forced segregation prevented the Jews of North Africa from marrying outside their culture and religion.

C. Country-specific Jewish populations in North Africa each have their own unique genetic markers.

D. Studies consistently show that while Jews are culturally and religiously similar, they are biologically dissimilar.

113. Paris has a deeper and stranger connection to its underground than almost any city, and that underground is one of the richest. The arteries and intestines of Paris, the hundreds of miles of tunnels that make up some of the oldest and densest subway and sewer networks in the world, are just the start of it. Under Paris there are spaces of all kinds: canals and reservoirs, crypts and bank vaults, wine cellars transformed into nightclubs and galleries. Most surprising of all are the *carrières* – the old limestone quarries that fan out in a deep and intricate web under many neighbourhoods, mostly in the southern part of the metropolis. Into the 19th

century those caverns and tunnels were mined for building stone. After that farmers raised mushrooms in them, at one point producing hundreds of tons a year. During World War II, French Resistance fighters – the underground – hid in some quarries; the Germans built bunkers in others. (*National Geographic*)

A. Underground limestone mining was primarily carried out under the northern part of Paris into the 19th century.

B. Today, anyone is welcome to visit the many galleries, nightclubs, and other establishments underneath Paris.

C. Underneath Paris, one can find *carrières,* bank vaults, galleries, sewers, nightclubs, tunnels, crypts, and caverns.

D. At one point in Paris' history, the tons of mushrooms produced beneath ground were most likely more than the amount produced above ground.

114. More than 200,000 individual animal species, by varying strategies, help flowers make more flowers. Flies and beetles are the original pollinators, going back to when flowering plants first appeared 130 million years ago. As for bees, scientists have identified some 20,000 distinct species so far, and about one-fifth of those pollinate flowers in the United States. Hummingbirds, butterflies, moths, wasps, and ants are also up to the task. Snails and slugs smear pollen as they slide over flower clusters. Mosquitoes carry pollen for batches of orchids, and bats, with diverse muzzles and tongues adapted to tap differently shaped blossoms, move pollen for 360 plants in the Americas alone. Flowering plants – there are more than 240,000 species of them – have evolved in step with their pollinators, using sweet scents and bright colours to lure with the promise of a meal. Flower receptacles are wonderfully varied, from tubes and gullets to flaps, brushes, and spurs. (*National Geographic*)

A. At the time plants began flowering on the planet 130 million years ago, among others flies, beetles, bees and bats spread their pollen.

B. More than 240,000 species of flowering plants are pollinated by more than 200,000 animal species, including ants and bats.

C. Hundreds of plants have evolved to match the tongue shape of some bat species that pollinate them.

D. While beetles, snails, and bees all serve to pollinate plants, only the mosquito can carry pollen for orchids.

115. Microplastics used in sewage plants could be contributing to the problem of plastic pollution in oceans, according to a new report. Dozens of UK wastewater treatment plants use tiny plastic pellets, known as Bio-Beads, to filter chemical and organic contaminants from sewage. Once the Bio-Beads are in the ocean they are hard to spot and almost impossible to remove – yet can cause significant harm to marine wildlife. Industrial pellets and small bits of plastic such as Bio-Beads are mistaken for food by birds, fish, and other marine animals. These particles can kill animals, not only by causing digestive blockages, but also as a result of the high concentrations of pollutants. Plastic pollution can also enter the food chain, which is a concern to many people. Last August, the results of a study by Plymouth University reported plastic was found in a third of UK-caught fish, including cod, haddock, mackerel and shellfish. "We are learning more all the time about the environmental impact of consumer microplastics in wastewater such as laundry fibres, cosmetic microbeads and tyre dust," said the author of the report, Claire Wallerstein. "However, it now seems that microplastics used in the wastewater plants' own processes could also be contributing to the problem." (*theguardian.com*)

A. Humans have themselves consumed Bio-Beads through eating fish such as cod, haddock and mackerel.

B. The Bio-Beads, which come from sewage plants, can poison or cause suffocation in marine wildlife.

C. Sewage plants, whether accidentally or on purpose, leak the microplastics called Bio-Beads into the ocean.

D. Most people are aware of the environmental impact of other microplastics such as laundry fibres.

116. The oldest extant play and the only surviving Greek tragedy about a contemporaneous (rather than mythological) topic, *The Persians* was written by Aeschylus in 472 BC. The play chronicles the 480 BC Battle of Salamis, one of the most significant battles in world history: As the turning point in the Persian Empire's downfall, it allowed the Greeks – and therefore the West's first experiment with democracy – to survive. Aeschylus, a veteran of the Persian Wars, also made the unusual choice of recounting the battle from the Persian perspective, creating what's generally seen as an empathetic, rather than triumphalist, narrative of their loss. Today, the play is unexpectedly trendy. It has been produced about 30 times over the last five years. Why? Consider the plot: a superpower's inexperienced, hubristic leader – who hopes to conquer a minor enemy his father tried unsuccessfully to fell a decade earlier – charges into a doomed military invasion. (*smithsonianmag.com*)

A. *The Persians* has enjoyed a renaissance in recent years because of its insight into the history of the Persian Empire.

B. In *The Persians,* Greek playwright Aeschylus tells of the Battle of Salamis from the Greek point of view.

C. *The Persians* is popular with contemporary audiences because it proves that history repeats itself.

D. Aeschylus, who fought in the Persian Wars, provides an empathetic account of how the Persians lost the Battle of Salamis in 480 BC.

117. We now know that Stonehenge was in the making for at least 400 years. The first phase, built around 3000 BC, was a simple circular earthwork enclosure similar to many "henges" (sacred enclosures typically comprising a circular bank and a ditch) found throughout the British Isles. Around 2800 BC, timber posts were erected within the enclosure. Archaeologists have long believed that Stonehenge began to take on its modern form two centuries later, when large stones were brought to the site in the third and final stage of its construction. The first to be put in place were the 80 or so bluestones, which were arranged in a double circle with an entrance facing northeast. The importance of the bluestones is underscored by the immense effort involved in moving them a long distance – some were as long as three metres and weighed four tons. Geological studies in the 1920s determined that they came from the Preseli Mountains in southwest Wales, 140 miles from Stonehenge. (*smithsonianmag.com*)

A. Stonehenge was constructed in two main stages: first it was a circle-shaped enclosure and then the large stones were added.

B. Research suggests that the bluestones of Stonehenge were moved from their source 140 miles away using only manpower.

C. According to archaeologists, the bluestones of Stonehenge were added to the structure around 2800 BC.

D. Around 2600 BC, bluestones from southwest Wales were added to the Stonehenge site in a double circle.

118. Children who think their parents are poor monitors or nag a lot tend to play videogames more than other kids, according to a study funded by the National Science Foundation. The study is one of the first to link parental behaviour to kids' videogame playing. The researchers surveyed more than 500 students from 20 middle schools and found that the more children perceived their parents' behaviour as negative (e.g., "nags a lot") and the less monitoring parents did, the more the children played videogames. The next step, said lead researcher Linda Jackson, is to find out what's fueling children's videogame behaviour – a topic Jackson and her team plan to examine. Jackson said an equally interesting question is the relationship between videogame playing and actual rather than perceived behaviour of parents. Perceptions don't always mirror reality, she said, and this may be the case in the child-parent relationship. (*Science Daily*)

A. According to a study, children play more videogames if they perceive that they have parents who closely supervise them.

B. Videogame playing causes children to interpret their parents' behaviour toward them as negative.

C. According to a study, children who think their parents pester them a lot play more videogames.

D. Research shows that children who play a lot of videogames are less likely to have parents who behave positively.

119. Walking upright on two legs is the trait that defines the hominid lineage: Bipedalism separated the first hominids from the rest of the four-legged apes. It took a while for anthropologists to realise this. At the turn of the 20th century, scientists thought that big brains made hominids unique. This was a reasonable conclusion since the only known hominid fossils were of brainy species – Neanderthals and *Homo erectus*. In more recent decades, anthropologists have determined that bipedalism has very ancient roots. The earliest hominid with the most extensive evidence for bipedalism is the 4.4-million-year-old *Ardipithecus ramidus*. Although the earliest hominids were capable of upright walking, they retained primitive features – such as long, curved fingers and toes as well as longer arms and shorter legs – that indicate they spent time in trees. It's not until the emergence of *H. erectus* 1.89 million years ago that hominids grew tall, evolved long legs and became completely terrestrial creatures. (*smithsonianmag.com*)

A. Fossils indicate that *Ardipithecus ramidus* became the first fully bipedal and terrestrial species 4.4 million years ago.

B. Fossils of Neanderthals suggest that the hominid species walked upright but was better at climbing trees.

C. Hominid species with shorter legs, longer arms, and fingers and toes that curl likely spent at least some time in trees.

D. Hominid species developed bigger brains just after they walked upright – around 4.4 million years ago.

120. In the warfare that raged in Cambodia from 1970 until 1998, all sides used land mines. There are more than 30 different types. Villagers have prosaic names for them based on their appearance: the frog, the drum, the corncob. Most were manufactured in China, Russia, or Vietnam, a few in the United States. Khmer Rouge commander Pol Pot, whose regime was responsible for the deaths of some 1.7 million Cambodians between 1975 and 1979, purportedly called land mines his "perfect soldiers." They never sleep. Although weapons of war, land mines are unlike bullets and bombs in two distinct ways. First, they are designed to maim rather than kill, because an injured soldier requires the help of two or three others, reducing the enemy's forces. Second, and most sinister, when a war ends, land mines remain in the ground, primed to explode. Only 25 per cent of land mine victims around the world are soldiers. The rest are civilians – boys gathering firewood, mothers sowing rice, girls herding goats. (*National Geographic*)

A. Land mines are different from some other weapons of war in that their intent is not to kill but to disable.

B. In Cambodia between 1975 and 1979, 75 per cent of land mine victims were civilians.

C. "Perfect soldiers" is one of many names that only Cambodian villagers use to describe land mines.

D. As weapons of war, land mines are more successful at reducing soldier forces than bullets or bombs.

121. Our working memory capacity is decidedly finite – it reflects our ability to focus and control attention and strongly influences our ability to solve problems. Converging evidence from many psychological science studies suggests that high working memory capacity is associated with better performance at mathematical problem-solving. In fact, decreased working memory capacity may be one reason why math anxiety leads to poor math performance. Overall, working memory capacity seems to help analytical problem-solvers focus their attention and resist distraction. However, these very features of working memory capacity seem to impair creative problem-solving. With creative problems, reaching a solution may require an original approach or a novel combination of diverse pieces of information. As a result, too much focus may actually impair creative problem solving. (*Science Daily*)

A. Scientific studies suggest that people who tend to be anxious are better able to solve problems creatively.

B. Scientific evidence indicates that a razor-sharp focus likely helps people to creatively solve problems.

C. A high working memory capacity is associated with the ability to focus and solve mathematical problems.

D. While our working memory capacity is limited, our ability to find creative solutions to problems is unlimited.

122. The explosion of personal devices with built in web connectivity, office applications and email can improve working practices but also comes with risks not limited to time wasting. The portability, connectivity, and storage capacity of mobile devices means they bring with them the threat of data leakage, data theft, and the introduction of viruses or other malware into workplace computing systems. Portable storage devices of every ilk whether mp3 player, tablet or mobile phone now have several ways of connecting to other devices and networks including Wi-Fi, Bluetooth, and USB. Many of these devices also now have several gigabytes of storage capacity and are often expandable and so have the ability to capture vast quantities of data, whether for legitimate work purposes or for illicit use. Many businesses and organisations are rightly concerned about the loss or disclosure of intellectual property or sensitive information about customers and employees. (*Science Daily*)

A. Businesses that issue mobile devices to employees face just two risks: data theft and potential loss of productivity.

B. Before the appearance of the mobile devices with vast storage capacity the threat of data leakage and data theft was minimal.

C. Personal technology devices like mobile phones and tablets can compromise privacy and spread viruses and malware.

D. Portable storage devices with the most storage capacity put businesses and organisations most at risk of malware attacks.

123. In northern Europe, public opinion is increasingly exasperated by what many view as an attempt by the south to rob it of its savings. A recent letter signed by 160 German economists claiming that the European Union's plan for a banking union was little more than an attempt to make Germany pay for Spanish mistakes is revealing in this respect. In turn, southern Europe is getting angry. One man saw this coming. American economist Martin Feldstein wrote in 1997 that monetary union would create conflict within Europe. Unfortunately, his insight was correct: European countries today are at loggerheads not despite the common currency but precisely because of it. History suggests that international disputes over debt and transfers are a serious danger. In the 1920s and the 1930s, representatives of European states devoted countless meetings to resolving them (at the time, mainly German reparations). Despite US goodwill, they were unable to overcome their differences. (*New York Times*)

A. Sharing a common currency is the main and only factor contributing to quarrels between northern and southern Europe.

B. Some economists in northern Europe believe their countries are being forced to pay for mistakes made by southern Europe.

C. In the 1920s and 1930s, European state representatives resolved international debt disagreements.

D. The common currency in Europe is a source of trouble because of inherent inequalities between north and south.

124. The Roman Catholic Sagrada Família has always been revered and reviled. The surrealists claimed architect Antoni Gaudí as one of their own, while George Orwell called the church "one of the most hideous buildings in the world." As idiosyncratic as Gaudí himself, it is a vision inspired by the architect's religious faith and love of nature. He understood that the natural world is rife with curved forms, not straight lines. And he noticed that natural construction tends to favour sinewy materials such as wood, muscle, and tendon. With these organic models in mind, Gaudí based his buildings on a simple premise: If nature is the work of God, and if architectural forms are derived from nature, then the best way to

honour God is to design buildings based on his work. Gaudí's faith was his own. But his belief in the beautiful efficiency of natural engineering clearly anticipated the modern science of biomimetics. (*National Geographic*)

A. The design of Antoni Gaudí's Sagrada Família is intended to bring nature into the church.

B. Antoni Gaudí's Sagrada Família directly influenced the modern field of biomimetics.

C. Antoni Gaudí's Sagrada Família incorporates wood, rounded lines, and sinewy effects.

D. Antoni Gaudí drew inspiration from his religious faith and the forms he saw in nature.

125. A bronze statue's orphaned arm. A corroded disc adorned with a bull. Preserved wooden planks. These are among the latest treasures that date back to the dawn of the Roman Empire, discovered amid the ruins of the Antikythera shipwreck, a sunken bounty off the coast of a tiny island in Greece. Marine archaeologists working on a project called Return to Antikythera announced these findings on Wednesday from this most recent excavation of the roughly 2,000-year-old wreck, which was first discovered 115 years ago. They said the haul hints at the existence of at least seven more bronze sculptures still buried beneath the seafloor. Bronze sculptures from that era are rare because they were often melted down to make swords, shields and other items. Only about 50 intact examples have survived, so if the team can salvage the submerged statues, it would be a remarkable recovery of ancient artifacts. For more than a century the wreck has yielded a trove of antiquities, from bronze and marble statues of Olympian gods and heroes to the mysterious Antikythera mechanism, a hand-held device for tracking planetary movements and predicting eclipses that is often called the "first computer." (*nytimes.com*)

A. It is highly unusual to discover bronze sculptures as humans have historically used bronze for swords and shields.

B. It is not yet known if all the bronze sculptures can be retrieved from the shipwreck.

C. This project is the first time archaeologists have been able to excavate the Antikythera shipwreck.

D. The Antikythera mechanism was among the first treasures excavated from the shipwreck.

126. The antibacterial substance triclosan, which was first developed in the 1960s to prevent bacterial infections in hospitals, has since been incorporated into everything from hand soaps to toothpastes to mouthwashes and toys. Manufacturers see it as a marketing bonus, increasing consumer confidence that a particular product kills harmful bacteria. In recent years, though, research has shed light on a number of problems with employing triclosan so widely. Studies have shown that the chemical can disrupt the endocrine systems of several different animals, binding to receptor sites in the body, which prevents the thyroid hormone from functioning normally. Additionally, triclosan penetrates the skin and enters the bloodstream more easily than previously thought, and has turned up everywhere from aquatic environments to human breast milk in troubling quantities. To this list of concerns, add one more: A new paper indicates that triclosan impairs muscle function in both animals and humans. (*smithsonianmag.com*)

A. Consumers are more confident in a product's antibacterial qualities when triclosan is listed as an ingredient.

B. People who use products that contain triclosan face a high risk of developing conditions of the endocrine system.

C. Triclosan interferes with the proper functioning of muscles and the thyroid and has been found in human breast milk.

D. The intended purpose of developing the antibacterial triclosan in the '60s was to treat infections in hospitals.

127. A pioneering technology to detect fingermarks at crime scenes is a step closer to being incorporated into traditional forensic investigations. The technology uses Matrix Assisted Laser Desorption Ionisation Mass Spectrometry Imaging (MALDI-MSI) to provide crime scene investigators with key extra details about suspects. These details, such as any

substances they might have touched, can provide crucial background information in a criminal investigation. A fingermark is made up of material from the surface of the skin and from gland secretions. Conventionally, fingermarks found at the scene of a crime are lifted, often using a powder, and are compared with prints on a police database to identify a suspect. The new technology uses MALDI-MSI for the first time to produce multiple images of fingermarks that can provide extra information on a suspect. These details can be important background information in a criminal investigation, especially if the suspect's fingermark is not on the police database. (*Science Daily*)

A. Conventional fingermark processing and MALDI-MSI both require that a suspect's prints are on the police database.

B. MALDI-MSI technology does not yield the information conventional fingermark processing does.

C. MALDI-MSI technology, which produces several images of a fingermark, may sooner or later be part of criminal investigations.

D. MALDI-MSI technology can provide the necessary details and background information to convict a criminal suspect.

128. Travel apps are increasingly popular as more people travel abroad. Over the past five years, international travel has grown 4-5% annually, exceeding 1.1 billion overnight visitors in 2014, according to the World Tourism Organisation. With competition heating up, developers are targeting niches. For PokDok – a Finnish start-up launched in early 2015 – it's "Pocket Doctor," an app that offers easy access to healthcare. PokDok offers a way around language barriers with a directory, location service and map view to help users navigate to an appropriate point of care. "People don't necessarily bring a computer with them on vacation – but everybody takes their smart phone. If something unexpected should happen, you just get your phone and immediately see where to go next," said PokDok co-founder Jussi Lipponen, who has lived in six different countries and knows first-hand the difficulty of finding good medical care in a foreign country. (*politico.eu*)

A. International travel has grown rapidly in the past 5 years, with nearly 1.1 billion overnight visitors in that period, according to the World Tourism Organisation.

B. PokDok has already helped large numbers of people to find good medical care in a foreign country since its launch in early 2015.

C. PokDok is a free app that offers easy access to healthcare and was launched in 2015.

D. The app, PokDok, helps people find appropriate medical care in a way that avoids the disadvantages of not knowing the country's language, with a directory and help with locating suitable care.

129. Burials both rich and gruesome have recently been discovered in the Pyramid of the Moon of Teotihuacan. Tunnelling deep into the 140-foot-tall stone structure, archaeologists located five burial sites. Evidence indicates that all the victims were ritually killed to consecrate successive stages of the pyramid's construction. The earliest sacrifice, from about AD 200, marked a substantial enlargement of the building. A wounded foreigner, most likely a prisoner of war, was apparently buried alive with his hands tied behind him. Animals representing mythical powers and military might surrounded him, some buried alive in cages. Finely crafted offerings included weapons of obsidian and a figurine of solid greenstone, perhaps a war goddess to whom the burial was dedicated. Each subsequent burial was different, but all had the same aim: "Human sacrifice was important to control the people," says Sugiyama, "to convince them to do what their rulers wanted." (*National Geographic*)

A. Teotihuacan's Pyramid of the Moon and the burials made there were intended to appease an honored war goddess.

B. Five burial sites, animals in cages, a greenstone figurine, and obsidian weapons were all discovered in the Pyramid of the Moon.

C. Humans were ritually sacrificed in Teotihuacan for the sole purpose of sanctifying the building of the Pyramid of the Moon.

D. Victims were buried alive in the Pyramid of the Moon so rulers could keep control of the masses.

130. Freshwater eels, of the genus *Anguilla*, are ancient fishes. They began evolving more than 50 million years ago, branching into 16 species and three subspecies. Most migratory fish, such as salmon and shad, are anadromous, spawning in fresh water and living as adults in salt water. The freshwater eel is one of the few fishes that do the opposite, spawning in the ocean and spending their adulthood in lakes, rivers, and estuaries – a life history known as catadromy. In general, female eels are found upstream in river systems, while males stay in the estuaries. Eels may spend decades in rivers before returning to the ocean to spawn, after which they die. No one has ever been able to witness freshwater eels spawning, and for eel biologists, solving this eel-reproduction mystery remains a kind of Holy Grail. Eel larvae were thought to be a separate species of fish until 1896, when two Italian biologists watched one in a tank metamorphose into an eel. (*National Geographic*)

A. Eels are catadromous, living as adults in salt water and travelling to fresh water for spawning.

B. Although biologists in 1896 saw an eel larva transform into an eel, they have not yet watched the fish spawning.

C. After spawning, eels return to lakes, rivers, and estuaries where they may remain for decades before dying.

D. That male eels mainly occupy estuaries while females occupy upstream waters is fundamental to how the fish spawn.

131. In the 19th century, coffee was a huge business in Europe with cafes flourishing across the continent. But coffee brewing was a slow process and, as is still the case today, customers often had to wait for their brew. Seeing an opportunity, inventors across Europe began to explore ways of using steam machines to reduce brewing time – this was, after all, the age of steam. Though there were surely innumerable patents and prototypes, the invention of the machine and the method that would lead to espresso is usually attributed to Angelo Moriondo of Turin, Italy, who was granted a patent in 1884 for "new steam machinery for the economic and instantaneous confection of coffee beverage." The machine consisted of a large boiler, heated to 1.5 bars of pressure, that pushed water through a large bed of coffee grounds on demand, with a second boiler producing steam that would flash the bed of coffee and complete the brew. With the exception of his patent, Moriondo has been largely lost to history. (*smithsonianmag.com*)

A. The precursor to the espresso machine invented by Angelo Moriondo used steam alone to brew coffee.

B. In the 19th century, Angelo Moriondo produced hundreds of machines that used steam to brew coffee.

C. In Europe during the 19th century, inventors sought ways to reduce the amount of time required to brew coffee.

D. Angelo Moriondo of Turin, Italy was the first to invent a machine that used steam to brew coffee.

132. Do you smile when you're frustrated? Most people think they don't, but they actually do, a new study from MIT has found. When asked to feign frustration, 90 per cent of research subjects did not smile. But when presented with a task that caused genuine frustration – filling out a detailed online form, only to then find the information deleted after pressing the "submit" button – 90 per cent of them smiled. Still images showed little difference between these frustrated smiles and the delighted smiles elicited by a video of a cute baby, but video analysis showed that the progression of the two kinds of smiles was quite different: Often, the happy smiles built up gradually, while frustrated smiles appeared quickly but faded fast. The research could pave the way for computers that better assess the emotional states of their users and respond accordingly. It could also help train those who have difficulty interpreting expressions to more accurately gauge the expressions they see. (*Science Daily*)

A. Video and still images both recorded a marked difference between frustrated and delighted smiles.

B. Computers may soon be able to provide individualised help based on the feelings of the people using them.

C. The majority of study participants who performed a frustrating task developed a smile that both appeared and disappeared quickly.

D. People who cannot easily figure out facial expressions fail to pick up on how an expression develops.

133. Double-baked biscuits with a long shelf-life were the food of choice for European voyagers starting in the 1500s. A few hundred years later, airtight and reusable biscuit tins were invented. They allowed their valuable cookie contents to travel easily, stay oven-fresh and not crumble. Credit for introducing biscuit tins goes to Huntley and Palmers, a Quaker firm in Reading, England, which, by 1900, was the largest biscuit manufacturer in the world. Huntley & Palmers' tins came in all sizes and shapes. They were elaborately decorated, from miniature replicas of vehicles to reusable tins engraved with intricate still life tableaux to street-scene designs inspired by impressionist art. Biscuits weren't a luxury item in the 1800s, but the tins served a Victorian middle class eager to show good taste. The tins became independent *objets d'art* in and of themselves. For manufacturers, branding gradually took a different tone. The tins came to represent their country, an origin, a pride, an artist's whim. (*smithsonianmag.com*)

A. While airtight tins originally kept biscuits fresh and travel-ready, they eventually became *objets d'art.*

B. Huntley & Palmers' tins came in a variety of decorations, sizes, and shapes but they all bore the same branding.

C. Beginning in the 1500s, tins provided a way to keep biscuits fresh; only later did they become *objets d'art.*

D. In the nineteenth century, the Huntley & Palmers' tins inspired by impressionist art were the most favoured by the Victorian middle class.

134. Our galaxy is far larger, brighter, and more massive than most other galaxies. From end to end, the Milky Way's starry disk, observable with the naked eye and through optical telescopes, spans 120,000 light-years. Encircling it is another disk, composed mostly of hydrogen gas, detectable by radio telescopes. And engulfing all that our telescopes can see is an enormous halo of dark matter that they can't. While it emits no light, this dark matter far outweighs the Milky Way's hundreds of billions of stars, giving the galaxy a total mass one to two trillion times that of the sun. Indeed, our galaxy is so huge that dozens of lesser galaxies scamper about it, like moons orbiting a giant planet. Because we reside within the Milky Way, we actually know less about its overall appearance than we do about distant galaxies – just as, absent a mirror, you know more about your friends' faces than your own. (*National Geographic*)

A. Scientists have learned a great deal about the Milky Way by observing galaxies that orbit it.

B. Milky Way stars weigh much less than the dark matter, which telescopes can't detect.

C. A ring of hydrogen gas surrounding a ring of stars constitutes the Milky Way galaxy.

D. Scientists know the mass of our galaxy's dark matter by calculating the mass of its stars.

135. Christopher Williams is somewhat of a revolutionary as well as a whiskey distiller. This month, led by Mr Williams, nine New York State craft distilleries — including his Coppersea Distilling — will each introduce a whiskey labelled Empire Rye.

Empire Rye — an appellation that requires, among other things, that distillers use New York State grain and age their whiskey for at least two years — represents a novel turn in American distilling. At a time when bourbon is made by small distillers in 48 of 50 states, Mr. Williams and his co-conspirators are betting that consumers will buy into the idea of a spirit distinguished by its regional pedigree, in the same way, that millions of drinkers worldwide identify Jack Daniel's as Tennessee whiskey or Château Latour as Bordeaux wine. Empire Rye is a potential answer to a problem born of craft distilling's phenomenal success: Ten years ago there were about 100 companies making spirits in the United States; today there are nearly 1,400, according to the American

Distilling Institute. "You have all these distilleries, all going the same way, so there's no touchstone," Mr Williams said. (*nytimes.com*)

A. This new whiskey can only be called Empire Rye if it meets more than two requirements.

B. This new whiskey can be called Empire Rye provided it uses grain from New York State and it is aged for at least two years.

C. Empire Rye will be made using a different method than bourbon and Tennessee whiskey.

D. Nine New York State distilleries will be introducing Empire Rye and others will follow them.

136. Bacteria are organisms that are equipped to reproduce themselves; antibiotics attack that machinery. But a virus is a parasite: It invades a host cell and co-opts the cell's own machinery to make copies of itself – thousands of copies at once, which means thousands of chances to mutate and develop drug resistance. A drug that disables a part of the human cell that helps the virus reproduce, though, could stop it with little risk of resistance. The key is finding the right target – a gene, and the protein it encodes, that the human cell doesn't need but the virus does. Human DNA contains more than 20,000 genes, but in any given cell at any given time, many are dormant; some, for instance, are only switched on during embryonic development. With the human genome now fully decoded, investigators can search for targets systematically by disabling individual genes in many cells and seeing what happens. (*National Geographic*)

A. Viruses resist drugs by changing which proteins in the host cell they use to reproduce themselves.

B. To combat viruses, researchers are looking to target a gene that is important to both the virus and the host cell.

C. Antibiotics work by scrambling the reproductive mechanism of the bacteria, causing fatal mutations.

D. Of the 20,000 genes that make up human DNA, some may be inactive and others may be used by viruses.

137. Data privacy rules are tightening in the European Union, creating a niche for start-ups that shield personal details. Even as innovators increasingly use massive sets of data from digital devices to develop products and services, security problems are increasing. The number of business data breaches worldwide rose 49 percent in 2014 from the year earlier, according to the latest annual figures from the Breach Level Index, a database run by Gemalto, a Dutch digital security firm. To protect individual privacy, companies will soon be required to protect personal details "by design or by default," under the EU's General Data Protection Regulation, adopted in 2012 and set to take effect this year. Penalties can range up to 2 percent of global turnover, capped at €100 million. The tough new law "has raised awareness about data privacy," said Jason du Preez, co-founder and CEO of London-based Privitar, a start-up that sells a "de-identification tool" that it claims can obscure personal information within large data sets while permitting a company's work on analysis. (*politico.eu*)

A. The number of business data infringements rose by almost half between 2013 and 2014.

B. Privitar's de-identification tool can help companies avoid fines of up to 2 percent of their global turnover.

C. The EU's General Data Protection Regulation has made data privacy more confusing for companies and for the general public.

D. Problems with privacy are decreasing as innovators increasingly use enormous sets of data for development purposes.

138. A 40-year retrospective study on the impact of technology in classrooms suggests that technology delivers content and supports student achievement. The research brought together data from 60,000 elementary school, high school, and post-secondary students. It compared achievement in classrooms that used computer technology versus those that used little or none. In those classrooms where computers were used to support teaching, the technology was found to have a small to moderate positive impact on both learning and attitude. "We deduce that the impact would be

even greater if observed over a student's entire educational experience," says co-author Richard Schmid. The research team found technology works best when students are encouraged to think critically and communicate effectively. "A standard PowerPoint presentation will most likely not enhance the learning experience beyond providing content or enhancing teacher-directed lectures or class discussions," says Schmid. (*Science Daily*)

A. Critical thinking skills were more developed in students whose classrooms used computer technology than in those whose classrooms did not.

B. Research shows that a student's learning is enhanced by creating and giving a PowerPoint presentation on their own.

C. Research shows that a student's attitude and ability to learn and achieve are all positively influenced by the use of computers in the classroom.

D. The extent to which technology in the classroom positively influences students' social lives correlates to the length of their exposure to it.

139. Linguistics has undergone two great revolutions in the past 60 years, on seemingly opposite ends of the discipline. In the late 1950s Noam Chomsky theorised that all languages were built on an underlying universal grammar embedded in human genes. A second shift in linguistics – an explosion of interest in small and threatened languages – has focused on the variety of linguistic experience. Field linguists are more interested in the idiosyncrasies that make each language unique and the ways that culture can influence a language's form. Some 85 per cent of languages have yet to be documented. Understanding them can only enrich our comprehension of what is universal to all languages. Different languages highlight the varieties of human experience, revealing as mutable aspects of life that we tend to think of as settled and universal, such as our experience of time, number, or colour. In Tuva, for example, the past is always spoken of as ahead of one, and the future is behind one's back. (*National Geographic*)

A. How we perceive and experience concepts like time and colour is universal and therefore not influenced by language.

B. By studying how languages relate to culture, linguists will discover a set of characteristics that all languages share.

C. While some linguists have theorised about the common foundations of language, others have chosen to investigate their differences.

D. In Tuva, it is possible to say, "I'm looking forward to getting together with you tomorrow."

140. Until recently, gene therapy has been reserved for severe diseases with few treatment options. But the recent report of its successful use to treat hemophilia B, which would offer patients a therapeutic alternative that could replace the need for regular, lifelong protein replacement infusions, has brought gene therapy to the forefront as a technology capable of competing with and disrupting traditional forms of treatment. Although gene therapy for hemophilia B is still in early-stage clinical testing, a similar approach is in development to treat hemophilia A, and together these life-threatening diseases represent a $6.5 billion market for current protein replacement therapies. The technical feasibility of gene therapy "has been established in multiple diseases and with different technology platforms," says Dr. Wilson. He predicts that "2012 will usher in an era of commercial development of gene therapy that, although likely to begin slowly, will quickly gather momentum." (*Science Daily*)

A. Gene therapy has been shown to be a technically feasible option for treating numerous diseases.

B. Dr. Wilson's prediction that gene therapy would be developed commercially in 2012 has been proven correct.

C. Gene therapy for hemophilia A and B would cost less than what is required for protein replacement therapy.

D. The technical viability of gene therapy for hemophilia B has been established through late-stage clinical trials.

141. Just six days after the Bank downgraded its inflation outlook, paving the way for more quantitative easing (QE), official

figures showed that the consumer prices index (CPI) rose from 2.4pc in June to 2.6pc in July. According to Alliance Trust, the investment company, pensioners aged 75 and over were hardest hit by the price rises as food and energy costs account for a larger proportion of their outgoings. Alliance calculated their effective inflation rate was 3pc, above June's reading of 2.9pc. "It is the over 75 year old households which continue to face the highest rate of inflation, as has now been the case since the end of last year," Alliance said. People aged between 30 and 64 had the lowest inflation rate, of 2.5pc – due largely to slower petrol inflation. The Office for National Statistics (ONS) put the surprise jump in inflation down to lower discounting by clothing and footwear retailers and an unusual spike in air fares. (*The Telegraph*)

A. Economists agree that the recent increase in inflation was driven by a sudden rise in energy and food prices.

B. People between the ages of 30 and 64 faced the lowest rate of inflation for the most part due to petrol costs.

C. Fewer discounts on clothing and footwear meant that inflation in July particularly hit poorer families.

D. Inflation has most severely affected pensioners aged 75 and over because a greater proportion of their income derives from stocks and bonds.

142. Tsunamis strike somewhere in the world almost every year, and giant ones have arguably changed history. Some archaeologists have argued, for instance, that a Mediterranean tsunami struck the north shore of Crete a bit over 3,500 years ago; the disaster, they say, sent Minoan civilisation, one of the most sophisticated of the age, into a tailspin, leading it to succumb to Mycenaean Greeks. In 1755, when an earthquake and tsunami killed tens of thousands in Lisbon, the tragedy had a lasting impact on Western thought: It helped demolish the complacent optimism of the day. In the fifth century BC the Greek historian Thucydides was the first person to document the connection between earthquakes and tsunamis. He noticed that the first sign of a tsunami is often the abrupt draining of a harbour, as the sea pulls away from the coast. "Without an earthquake I do not see how such things could happen," he wrote. (*National Geographic*)

A. Greek historian Thucydides was incorrect in his belief that earthquakes were the only cause of a tsunami.

B. Greek historian Thucydides observed that a harbour will suddenly empty out just before a tsunami strikes.

C. Had a tsunami not hit Crete 3,500 years ago, the Mycenaean culture would not have prevailed over the Minoan.

D. In the city of Lisbon in 1755, many thousands of people were tragically killed by an earthquake only.

143. Bats and toothed whales had many opportunities to evolve echolocation techniques that differ from each other, since their nearest common ancestor was incapable of echolocation. Nevertheless – as scientists have known for years – bats and toothed whales rely on the same range of ultrasonic frequencies, between 15 to 200 kilohertz, to hunt their prey. This overlap in frequencies is surprising because sound travels about five times faster in water than in air, giving toothed whales an order of magnitude more time than bats to make a choice about whether to intercept a potential meal. Bats increase the number of calls per second (what researchers call a "buzz rate") while in pursuit of prey. Whales were thought to maintain a steady rate of calls or clicks no matter how far they were from a target. But new research shows that wild whales also increase their rate of calls or clicks during a kill – and that whales' buzz rates are nearly identical to that of bats, at about 500 calls or clicks per second. (*Science Daily*)

A. Before developing the ability to increase their buzz rate while pursuing prey, toothed whales emitted a steady rate of calls.

B. Five hundred is the maximum number of calls that both bats and toothed whales can process per second.

C. Bats typically use an ultrasonic frequency range of 150 to 200 kilohertz to hunt while toothed whales use a range of 15 to 200.

D. Bats and toothed whales developed similar echolocation techniques despite their different environments.

144. The nocebo effect is the phenomenon in which inert substances or mere suggestions of substances actually bring about *negative* effects in a patient or research participant. For some, being informed of a pill or procedure's potential side effects is enough to bring on real-life symptoms. Researchers from the Technical University of Munich in Germany have published one of the most thorough reviews to date on the nocebo effect. Breaking down 31 empirical studies that involved the phenomenon, they examined the underlying biological mechanisms and the problems it causes for doctors and researchers in clinical practice. Their conclusion: although perplexing, the nocebo effect is surprisingly common and ought to be taken into consideration by medical professionals on an everyday basis. The researchers suggest that doctors reconsider conventional beliefs about pain management to avoid magnifying painful side effects. (*smithsonianmag.com*)

A. Patients always feel pain when taking a pill or undergoing a procedure if it is first mentioned as a possible side effect by a doctor.

B. After reviewing studies on the nocebo effect, researchers have concluded that the phenomenon is of little consequence.

C. A review of empirical studies of the nocebo effect indicates that the phenomenon has several identifiable biological causes.

D. If a person swallows 2 sugar pills, but is told they have swallowed pills that may cause dizziness, they could experience that side effect.

145. A painful British economic recession and rising unemployment may have driven more than 1,000 people in England to commit suicide, according to a scientific study published today. The study, a so-called time-trend analysis which compared the actual number of suicides with those expected if pre-recession trends had continued, reflects findings elsewhere in Europe where suicides are also on the rise. "This is a grim reminder after the euphoria of the Olympics of the challenges we face and those that lie ahead," said David Stuckler, a sociologist at Cambridge University who co-led the study, published in the British Medical Journal (BMJ). The analysis found that between 2008 and 2010 there were 846 more suicides among men in England than would have been expected if previous trends continued, and 155 more among women. Between 2000 and 2010 each annual 10pc increase in the number of unemployed people was associated with a 1.4pc increase in the number of male suicides, the study found. (*The Telegraph*)

A. Had it not been for the Olympic games more suicides would have occurred in England during the summer.

B. Tough economic times and high unemployment may have contributed to higher suicide rates in England between 2008 and 2010.

C. According to a time-trend analysis, the ratio of male to female suicides remained constant between 2000 and 2010.

D. Rising unemployment rates and economic decline are a direct cause of suicides in England and Europe.

146. A fall alarm. Automatic nightlight. Oven reminder. Refrigerator alarm. These are just a few of the new welfare technology solutions that may become a normal part of the lives of the elderly in the future. New technology and ways of organising activities are needed if we are to meet the challenges facing the welfare state and the enormous needs for health and care services. But technology must not replace personal care and human warmth. The aim is to enhance the quality of life of elderly people who want to live at home as long as possible. By 2050 a third of Europe's population will be over 60 years of age, and by 2035 the number of people over 80 will have doubled. The World Health Organisation estimates that the need for capacity in the health sector under the current system may increase by 130,000 person-years up until 2050 – a dramatic growth rate of 120 per cent. (*Science Daily*)

A. A third of Europe's population will be using welfare technology by 2050.

B. Welfare technology's goal is to help elderly people live on their own longer.

C. Welfare technology is an effective alternative for human care services.

D. Oven reminders and fall alarms will enhance the quality of life for all elderly people.

147. Canines were the earliest domesticated animal, a process that started somewhere between 20,000 and 15,000 years ago, most likely when grey wolves began scavenging around human settlements. Eventually the relationship became a mutual one, as we began employing dogs for hunting, guarding, and companionship. Sheltered from the survival-of-the-fittest wilderness, those semi-domesticated dogs thrived even though they harboured deleterious genetic mutations – stumpy legs, for instance – that would have been weeded out in smaller wild populations. Thousands of years later, breeders would seize on that diverse raw material when they began creating modern breeds. They tended to grab traits they desired from across multiple breeds – or tried to rapidly replicate mutations in the same one – in order to get the dog they wanted. They also favoured novelty, since the more distinct a line of dogs appeared, the more likely it was to garner official recognition as a new breed. (*National Geographic*)

A. Some early partly domesticated dogs had characteristics that would likely have threatened their survival in the wild.

B. Domesticated dogs are the evolutionary consequence of early humans' need for companionship.

C. Dog breeders usually selected for those traits that would make for the most loyal companions.

D. Semi-domesticated dogs continued to evolve according to the theory of "survival of the fittest."

148. Throughout history, periods of religious and political repression have provoked an exodus of creative and entrepreneurial talent from various countries – from 17th century Huguenots fleeing France (after the king revoked religious freedoms), to 20th century Russian writers evading the Kremlin, to Jewish intellectuals escaping Nazi Germany. Likewise, many prominent Chinese artists and intellectuals who came of age during the Cultural Revolution later left China to garner fame and fortune abroad. For sixty years, upheavals in Chinese politics have not only remade the country's economy – they have remade Chinese art. During the Mao era, Soviet-inspired "socialist realism" was the only acceptable style in the strictly controlled authoritarian society. However, in 1979 Deng Xiaoping's monumental economic reforms also paved the way for the emergence of contemporary Chinese art. Over the next decade, Chinese artists had much greater access to international news and scholarship. (*smithsonianmag.com*)

A. Under the leadership of Mao, the diversity of artistic expression in China was fostered and encouraged.

B. The Huguenots, Russian writers, Jewish intellectuals, and Chinese artists all share a common experience.

C. Deng Xiaoping's influential reforms of 1979 prevented many talented artists from leaving China.

D. History shows that artistic talents flourish best in the face of political persecution.

149. Despite their modern reputation, the original Luddites were neither opposed to technology nor inept at using it. Many were highly skilled machine operators in the textile industry. The Luddite disturbances started in circumstances at least superficially similar to our own. British working families at the start of the 19th century were enduring economic upheaval and widespread unemployment. Food was scarce and rapidly becoming more costly. On March 11, 1811, in Nottingham, a textile manufacturing centre, British troops broke up a crowd of protesters demanding more work and better wages. That night, angry workers smashed textile machinery in a nearby village. Similar attacks occurred nightly at first, then sporadically, and then in waves. Fearing a national movement, the government soon positioned thousands of soldiers to defend factories. Parliament passed a measure to make machine-breaking a capital offence. But the Luddites were neither as organised nor as dangerous as authorities believed. (*smithsonianmag.com*)

A. Although the working classes faced economic turmoil in early 19th century England, the upper classes did not.

B. The Luddite uprising of the 19th century occurred amid high levels of unemployment and high food costs.

C. Luddite protests probably ceased for the most part after the British parliament made breaking machines a capital offence.

D. Luddites in 19th century England destroyed textile machinery only to demand better wages.

150. Gian Lorenzo Bernini was said to have been only 8 when he carved a stone head that "was the marvel of everyone" who saw it, according to a contemporary biographer. He was not much older when he dazzled Pope Paul V, who reportedly declared "We hope that this youth will become the Michelangelo of his century." Prophetic words: over a long lifetime, Bernini undertook commissions for eight popes, transforming the look of 17th-century Rome as Michelangelo had helped shape Florence and Rome a century before. Much of the Baroque grandeur of the Eternal City – its churches, fountains, piazzas and monuments – can be credited to Bernini and his followers. Indeed, Bernini was a highly original thinker, not merely a consummate craftsman. In the many different arts he pursued – sculpture, architecture, painting, even playwriting – his works expressed ideas. Behind every Bernini masterpiece there lies a *concetto*, its governing concept or conceit. (*smithsonianmag.com*)

A. Without the recognition and commissions of eight popes, Bernini might have lived and died an unknown artist.

B. Bernini thoroughly explored a *concetto* through painting before translating it to a sculpture or building.

C. Bernini's paintings, sculptures, and building designs irrevocably changed the face of 17th century Florence.

D. Bernini's talent was apparent from a young age, and it is still apparent today, immortalised in the Eternal City.

151. The European Central Bank (ECB) and the Bank of England (BOE) said they are concerned about the "shrinking" market for asset backed securities, or bundles of mortgage, small business and other loans that are packaged and sold to investors. Securitization became a bad word during the financial crisis, when it was largely blamed for reckless lending decisions by banks, which were then sold to hapless investors. But the ECB has argued lately that regulation should take into account that European securitization instruments have performed far better than their U.S. counterparts. "Despite its long-term value, securitization today suffers from stigma, reflecting both its adverse reputation amongst investors and conservatism among regulators," the central banks said. ECB President Mario Draghi said at the central bank's last news conference that the ECB and BOE would present their paper at the meetings of the International Monetary Fund, currently taking place in Washington, D.C. (*online.wsj.com*)

A. The BOE and ECB maintain that securitization is worthwhile although it is not in favour at present.

B. European securitization products have not fluctuated in price as much as U.S. products.

C. The central banks believe that securitization was the major cause of the financial crisis.

D. The BOE and ECB are not worried about the size of the bundled loan market in Europe.

152. Kimbal Musk, 45, got rich working in technology alongside his older brother, Elon. Now he wants to do for food what his brother has done for electric cars and space travel. Although Mr Musk has food ventures active in Colorado, where he lives, as well as in big cities like Chicago and Los Angeles, he has become enamoured of places like Tennessee, Indiana and Ohio — parts of the country he believes are the ripest for a revolution in eating and agriculture. Mr Musk is promoting a philosophy he calls "real food," which nourishes the body, the farmer and the planet. It doesn't sound much different than what writers like Michael Pollan and everyone who has ever helped start a farmers' market or community garden have preached for years. But Mr Musk has big ideas about what the Silicon Valley crowd likes to call the food space, which is as exciting to him as the internet was in 1995. In short, he wants to create a network of business, educational and agricultural ventures big

enough to swing the nation's food system back to one based on healthy, local food grown on chemical-free farms. (*nytimes. com*).

A. A businessman living in Colorado has ambitions to change the nation's food system in the direction of "real food".

B. The Silicon Valley crowd believe Tennessee, Indiana and Ohio are ripe for a revolution in in what they call the "food space".

C. Kimbal Musk's vision for the food space will most likely be as revolutionary as the internet was in 1995.

D. Kimbal Musk's aim is to have only farms that are chemical-free in the United States

153. Mars' atmosphere was probably never thick enough to keep temperatures on the planet's surface above freezing for the long term, suggests research published today in *Nature Geoscience*. Although the planet's topography indicates that liquid water has flooded Mars in the distant past, evidence increasingly suggests that those episodes reflect occasional warm spells, not a consistently hospitable phase of the planet's history. Signs of flowing water on Mars include layered sediments presumed to have been laid down in ancient lakes, as well as rugged canyons and lowlands apparently sculpted by massive floods. These had once prompted researchers to suggest that the red planet, now frigid and dry, was warm and wet throughout its early history. But that would have required an atmosphere much thicker than today's, a prospect that now seems unlikely, says Edwin Kite, a planetary scientist at Princeton University in New Jersey. (*www.nature.com*)

A. In contrast to its cold past, Mars is currently in a relatively temperate period, researchers think.

B. The research indicates that floods on Mars occurred only intermittently rather than during a long continuous period.

C. Floods were partly responsible for the canyons and lowlands existing on Mars.

D. Mars' atmosphere has very rarely been such as to keep water above its freezing temperature.

154. Ever since the first metal workers of antiquity dug copper from a Cyprus hillside and fashioned it into tools, copper has been in high demand. So high, in fact, that researchers in February raised the prospect that international copper production could peak within a few decades. (The original Cypriot copper mine lives on in the chemical symbol Cu, drawn from the Latin name for the island's metal.) A recent discovery describes improvements to copper as a catalyst that could streamline ethanol production. A catalyst helps chemical reactions occur more efficiently. In theory, better copper catalysts could offer an efficient method to convert carbon dioxide to liquid, carbon-based fuels. The traditional copper-catalysed conversion of carbon dioxide to liquid fuel proceeds through an intermediate of carbon monoxide. Many catalysts can perform the first step, but only copper can mix the carbon monoxide with water to produce fuel. (*www.nature.com*)

A. The copper market was small before labourers began extracting the metal from Cypriot mines.

B. Copper is the sole agent that can change carbon dioxide into carbon monoxide.

C. Copper extraction will likely reach its maximum point within 25 years.

D. Improvements in the production of ethanol could result from a discovery in the use of copper as a catalyst.

155. A below-ground experiment at the South Pole discovered three of the highest-energy neutrinos ever found. These neutrinos have energies at the absurdly high scale of petaelectronvolts — roughly the energy equivalent of one million times a proton's mass. Famous physicist Albert Einstein showed in his $E = mc2$ equation that energy and mass are equivalent, and such a large amount of mass converts to an extreme level of energy. The experiment, called IceCube, reported the discovery of the first two, nicknamed Ernie and Bert last year, and announced the third, Big Bird, Monday at the American Physical Society meeting. These neutrinos are valuable because they are extremely standoffish, rarely ever interacting with other particles, and uncharged, their direction never swayed by magnetic fields. Astronomers think the neutrinos could emanate from

a variety of intense events such as large black holes accreting matter, explosions called gamma-ray bursts or galaxies forming stars at furious rates. (*www. nature.com*)

A. Ernie and Bert were identified last year by IceCube in a sub-surface test at the South Pole.

B. Ernie, Bert, and Big Bird are most probably among the highest-energy neutrinos in the universe.

C. Its aloof tendency bars a neutrino from being affected by other particles within the universe.

D. An intense process of star creation could be the source of the vigorous particles found by IceCube.

156. When planning vacation itineraries, graveyard visits may not be top of mind. But Loren Rhoads, author of the new book *199 Cemeteries to See Before You Die*, makes the case for going out of your way to see burial grounds. While it's fun to see where famous leaders and celebrities are buried, it's also instructive to see how ordinary people came to rest, too. Visiting your local cemetery can reveal the families who lent their names to the streets and neighbourhoods in your town, and looking at their groupings and ages can bring history to life. "Up until fairly recently when there were written records, the things we know about the past, for the most part, we know about because of people who've been buried — how they were buried, what they were buried with. Even the Greeks and Romans, we've learned a lot because of their tombs. And now with the move toward cremation and scattering and all that, we don't have that, and there hasn't been a replacement. So we can guess what a normal person ate in the Middle Ages, we can guess what they wore in pre-history, but we won't know that about us," Rhoads says. "Once we're gone and our ashes are scattered, there won't be any record." (*time.com*)

A. Cemeteries are one of the least popular places for tourists to visit when they are holidaying in foreign countries.

B. Our understanding of Ancient Greek culture has been significantly influenced by recent research into their places of burial.

C. Loren Rhoads believes that because of cremation a type of historical record is being lost.

D. Most streets and neighbourhoods are named after families who lived there previously.

157. The collision of a pair of neutron stars, marked by ripples through the fabric of space-time and a flash brighter than a billion suns, has been witnessed for the first time in the most intensely observed astronomical event to date. The extraordinary sequence, in which the two ultra-dense stars spiralled inwards, violently collided and, in all likelihood, immediately collapsed into a black hole, was first picked up by the Laser Interferometer Gravitational-Wave Observatory (Ligo). Albert Einstein, the German-born theoretical physicist first predicted the existence of gravitational waves a century ago, but the first experimental proof that space itself can be stretched and squeezed took until 2015 when Ligo scientists detected a collision of black holes. This time, as the stars collided, they emitted an intense beam of gamma rays and the sky was showered with heavy elements, resolving a decades-old debate about where gold and platinum come from. Neutron stars are the smallest, densest stars known to exist: about 12 miles wide, with a teaspoon of neutron star material having a mass of about a billion tons. The core is a soup of pure neutrons, while the crust is smooth, solid and 10 billion times stronger than steel. (*theguardian.com*)

A. The collision of a pair of neutron stars has attracted exceptional interest.

B. The phenomenon of stars immediately collapsing into a black hole was observed by the Laser Interferometer Gravitational-Wave Observatory.

C. Einstein predicted 100 years ago that this event would happen, but we did not know for sure until 2015 if it could happen.

D. Due to this event, we are now even closer to resolving where gold and platinum comes from.

158. Most eggshells have a barrier to repel germs but microbes that penetrate encounter an antimicrobial enzyme called lysozyme in the whites of bird eggs. Brush turkey eggs have roughly the same amount of lysozyme as chicken eggs, but their shells are 1.5 times thinner

than those of chickens. This should make them more susceptible to microbes, not less, but infections occur in only about 9% of Australian brush turkey eggs, for example. The eggs incubate in moist piles of rotting vegetation to keep them warm from the heat generated as microbes in the soil and compost decompose organic matter. Those same microbes can get through eggshells and kill the embryos, but researchers found that the shells are covered in a layer of nanometre-sized spheres of calcium phosphate, making them more water-repellent than chicken eggs and helping them to fend off bacterial attachment and penetration. The findings could one day lead to new antimicrobial coatings for plastics and other surfaces. (*www.nature.com*)

A. Diseases affect Australian brush turkey eggs less than the eggs of other related bird species.

B. Bird eggs contain chemicals within their yolks that render bacteria and other pathogens inactive.

C. Chicken eggs resist water less than those of brush turkeys but contain about equal levels of lysozyme.

D. The temperature emanating from decay in the ground negatively affects brush turkey eggs.

159. The site of the world's next generation ground-based gamma-ray detector, the Cherenkov Telescope Array (CTA), is still undecided but a panel of funders has narrowed the field slightly, following a meeting in Munich, Germany. Scientists had originally hoped to select two sites, a large one in the Southern Hemisphere and a smaller one in the North, by the end of 2013, but the selection process for the €200 million project has taken longer than originally foreseen. Representatives from 12 government ministries narrowed the potential southern sites from five to two: Aar, a site in Southern Namibia, and Armazones in Chile's Atacama desert while picking a reserve site in Argentina. The committee, a panel of representatives from Argentina, Austria, Brazil, France, Germany, Italy, Namibia, Poland, Spain, South Africa, Switzerland and the United Kingdom, decided that all four possible northern sites in Mexico, Spain and the United States needed further analysis. (*blogs.nature.com*)

A. All the potential southern hemisphere locations for the detector are in one of the 12 countries making the selection.

B. The nations financing the venture met in Germany because its economy is the largest among them.

C. The number of southern hemisphere countries with potential sites for the detector does not exceed the number of countries in the northern hemisphere with potential sites.

D. Building the southern hemisphere CTA will most likely cost more than its northern counterpart due to its greater scale.

160. The top two cement makers hope their merger isn't going to run into antitrust worries. Lafarge, based in France and Holcim, in Switzerland, plan to put $8 billion of assets around the world up for sale in a bid to secure antitrust clearance for their merger, which would create the world's largest construction-materials company with a combined market value of about $50 billion. The companies disclosed Friday that they were in advanced talks but said a deal wasn't certain. The swift progress toward completing a merger suggests the companies are confident they can overcome what are likely to be lofty antitrust hurdles. The boards of both companies approved the merger plan and Holcim executives are expected in Paris, France to announce the merger. It's not clear what production facilities or other assets the two companies will propose to part with as part of their agreement, or whether that will be enough to mollify regulators' likely concerns with the potential tie-up. (*online.wsj.com*)

A. If the organisations sell some of their assets, they will be able to combine their operations.

B. The management of one company is traveling to the national base of the other to announce their merger.

C. The companies have disclosed which resources will be disposed of in order to secure their union.

D. Government regulators are interested in the implications of the companies' combination.

161. Governments have wasted billions of dollars stockpiling antiviral drugs for use in seasonal and pandemic flu, a

non-profit group of medical experts said this week, after analysing the results of previously unpublished clinical trials. The Cochrane Collaboration, another international organisation headquartered in Oxford, UK, has been arguing its case against the efficacy of the antiviral Tamiflu, also known as oseltamivir, for more than four years, initially on the basis of a previous analysis of the limited published data available. Today, it published an analysis of more than 500 pages after a campaign with the British Medical Journal (BMJ) to access the full, unpublished, clinical-trial data on Tamiflu. But other scientists say that although scrutiny is welcome, the review has uncovered little new information and in itself does not make a strong case to stop stockpiling. (*www.nature.com*)

A. The Cochrane Collaboration launched its campaign based on access to undisclosed information while the non-profit group had to rely on widely known data.

B. The Cochrane Collaboration's evaluation produced insufficient evidence to alter antiviral policy.

C. Governments have spent more than a billion dollars on stockpiling Tamiflu.

D. The Cochrane Collaboration has argued a case based on limited published data.

162. In 1963, an inventor called Walter Munk led a team of scientists studying how swells generated by Antarctic storms travel more than 16,000km across the Pacific Ocean. The team set up stations to measure the waves as they travelled in a great circle from New Zealand to Alaska. Munk and his family spent more than a month in American Samoa for the experiment, monitoring pressure sensors mounted on the ocean floor and recording data on paper tape punched with holes. The experiment yielded a surprising discovery. The waves showed very little decay in energy on their journey across the Pacific. The biggest change was a shift in the observed period of the wave – that is, the time between passing crests. Munk's team found that the period increased as the waves moved northwards. This happens because ocean waves are dispersive, meaning that the speed of the wave depends on the period. Long-period waves move more rapidly, so they run to the front of the pack, while shorter-period waves lag behind. The phenomenon is well known to surfers, who experience this dispersive ordering as a gradual shortening of the time between sets of waves. (*time.com*)

A. The energy of the waves that Munk observed did not deplete significantly as they travelled across the Pacific Ocean.

B. The study in 1963 confirmed what a few ocean scientists had hypothesised for years, that ocean waves are dispersive.

C. We know from the passage that ocean waves speed up as they move northwards.

D. Waves travel directly in a continuous straight line northward from New Zealand to Alaska and increase in lengths of periods.

163. Chancellor Angela Merkel's government approved legislation revamping Germany's sweeping plan to generate more than 40 percent of its energy needs through renewable resources by 2025 by slowing the rapid expansion of solar and wind parks in an effort to hold down spiraling prices. Already, 25 percent of German energy comes from renewable resources, but that advance has come at a cost to consumers, who have borne the brunt of the surcharges that funded the expansion. Keeping power prices in check is a key element of the government's revised policy, even as it upholds exemptions for crucial industries that require high amounts of energy. "Restart means no longer following the illusion that the energy transformation can be achieved by expanding renewable energy as quickly as possible, but to make sure that the expansion will be safe and predictable," Sigmar Gabriel, the energy and economics minister, said in announcing the changes to the legislation, the Renewable Energy Sources Act. (*www.nytimes.com*)

A. Solar and wind power installations make up twenty-five percent of Germany's energy production.

B. Angela Merkel has stated that Germany's sweeping plan to generate more than 40 percent of its energy needs through renewable resources by 2025 was too fast.

C. Some business users pay lower charges for energy than consumers, who mostly finance Germany's shift to renewables.

D. Sigmar Gabriel thinks Germany can develop renewable energy as fast as possible without too much risk.

164. Belovezhskaya National Park houses a huge forest of old-growth evergreen, beech, oak, alder, and spruce trees. Despite its size the park protects only about 10 percent of the Białowieża Primeval Forest, which dates back some 10,000 years and stands as the sole large remnant of the ancient forests that once covered much of Europe. The park has more than a thousand trees that are 300 to 600 years old and many more in old-growth stands of 250 to 200 years old. The park is home to a number of notable ancient oak trees; some are more than 500 years old. The Białowieża Forest creates an inviting ecosystem for many other plant species, including hundreds of lichens and mosses and thousands of different fungi. Belovezhskaya borders Poland and an adjacent national park across the border, Białowieski National Park, is Poland's oldest and one of the first in Europe at its founding in 1932. (*travel.nationalgeographic.com*)

A. Belovezhskaya National Park, founded in the 1930s, contains Europe's oldest trees.

B. The country of Poland has Europe's oldest park, which is adjacent to the Belovezhskaya National Park.

C. Belovezhskaya National Park shelters a fraction of the forest having the same name as a park in Poland.

D. Woodlands in a park in a country neighbouring Poland include some trees that have existed for at least three centuries.

165. Overfishing is still the most important threat to Mediterranean underwater ecosystems, "more than pollution, invasive species, or climate change", says Enric Sala, one of the authors of the most comprehensive study made of the sea, published this week in the science journal PLoS ONE. The assessment, presented in a paper entitled Large-Scale Assessment of Mediterranean Marine Protected Areas Effects on Fish Assemblages, drew on the work of a dozen researchers. A marine ecologist and a National Geographic Explorer-in-Residence, Sala is actively engaged in exploration, research and communications to advance ocean policy and conservation. Sala believes that without radical changes to fishing practices, we're just going to reduce the Mediterranean Sea to a soup of microbes and jellyfish. (*newswatch.nationalgeographic.com*)

A. If the current rate of fishing in the Mediterranean continues, then the sea's microbe levels will increase.

B. Sala had collaborators in his research focusing on protected regions within the Mediterranean Sea.

C. Twelve researchers think that excessive fishing will do more harm to marine life than pollution.

D. Enric Sala announced the results of the research in National Geographic just this week.

166. Many avalanches are small slides of dry powdery snow that move as a formless mass and account for a tiny fraction of the death and destruction wrought by bigger, more organized avalanches. Disastrous avalanches occur when massive slabs of snow break loose from a mountainside and shatter like broken glass as they race downhill. These moving masses can reach speeds of 80 miles (130 kilometers) per hour within about five seconds and victims caught in these events seldom escape. Avalanches are most common during, and in the 24 hours right after, a storm that dumps 12 inches (30 centimeters) or more of fresh snow. The quick pileup overloads the underlying snowpack, which causes a weak layer beneath the slab to fracture. The layers are an archive of winter weather: big dumps, drought, rain, a hard freeze, more snow, and how the layers bond often determines how easily one will weaken and cause a slide. (*environment.nationalgeographic.com*)

A. Avalanches occur when strata of frozen precipitation from previous winters splinter and cause rapid movement of snow.

B. Avalanches can occur while winter storms are still happening and advance at up to eighty miles per hour.

C. Larger avalanches are less frequent than small ones but account for more damage than the latter.

D. Avalanches that do not break up as they move downhill are the most severe.

167 A ruin facing ruin, Pompeii looks to one of its doomed sister cities in its latest rescue effort. Italian officials this month unveiled details of the Great Pompeii Project, a 105-million-euro ($145 million U.S. dollar) project to restore the famed Roman town, pillaged by treasure hunters, overrun by tourists, and wracked by the elements in the four centuries since its rediscovery. A highly innovative, "maintenance-based" approach to restoration will guide the project, said Massimo Osanna, the newly appointed superintendent of the site, in a statement. Instead of piecemeal patches to individual buildings or attractions, the effort will take its cues from the conservation of the nearby buried Roman town of Herculaneum, which was a 20-million-euro ($27.7 million U.S. dollar) effort. The hope is that by putting comprehensive maintenance concerns first, more of the site can be opened to visitors. (*news.nationalgeographic.com*)

A. The previous superintendent of the Pompeii site employed a traditional piecemeal approach.

B. Both Roman towns have been ruined by weather and overwhelmed by visitors since being unearthed.

C. The new strategy for Pompeii will primarily involve piecemeal restoration of specific important structures.

D. Herculaneum's restoration cost over 20 million dollars while Pompeii's will cost under 145 million euros.

168. Lafarge and Holcim are leading players in construction materials like cement, gravel and asphalt, which are used to pave roads. Because the cement market is largely local—cement is cheap to make but expensive to transport—both companies have expanded in many of the same markets around the world. The companies' combined market share of cement-making capacity is around 60% in France, Canada and Morocco and 30% in the U.S. The two companies have combined annual sales of nearly $43 billion, dwarfing rivals such as Germany's HeidelbergCement, with $18 billion in sales, and Mexico's Cemex, with $15 billion. The European Commission has been investigating Holcim, Lafarge and six other companies for operating a suspected cartel in cement and cement-based products since December 2010. (*online.wsj.com*)

A. HeidelbergCement is being probed like Holcim and Lafarge for engaging in collusive behavior.

B. Cement producers operate only in their home countries because cement is costly to ship.

C. The profits realized by Lafarge and Holcim from non-U.S. sources are greater than those from the U.S.

D. Lafarge and Holcim make over $40 billion in annual sales combined without having half of the U.S. cement market.

169. Greece's highest mountain, Olympus, is also the legendary abode of the gods. The favor of the deities gave the mountain an honored place in Classical Greek culture and that mythical status has been passed down through the centuries across Western civilization. The mountain's highest peak, Mytikas, tops out at 9,573 feet (2,918 meters) and was called "Pantheon" by the ancients, who believed it was the meeting place of the deities. The 12 gods were believed to have lived in the alpine ravines, which Homer described as the mountain's "mysterious folds." The village of Dion, on the mountain's flanks, was a Macedonian holy city where King Archelaus (r. 414-399 B.C.) held nine days of games to honor the god Zeus and today, the Olympus Festival held in the summer there includes performances at the ancient theater. Modern-day Dion also houses a remarkable archaeological site, where work is ongoing, and an archaeological museum in which much of the region's rich Classical history is on display. (*travel.nationalgeographic.com*)

A. Greek divinities were said to have assembled on the highest mountain of the Classical world.

B. A location with antique artifacts and a theatre from antiquity still exist on the sides of Olympus.

C. Dion served as the location of a week-long event involving sports to celebrate a Macedonian royal.

D. Homer believed that Greek divinities inhabited the fissures within Greece's highest mountain.

170. The park, Snowdonia, is a Welsh landscape of mountains, valleys, forests, and lakes established in 1951 and covering 2,132 square kilometers. Snowdonia is punctuated by the park's namesake mountain peak, Snowdon - Yr Wyddfa in the local Welsh tongue - standing at 1,085 meters and the highest point in Wales and England. The Welsh name for Snowdonia is Eryri (the Highland), and nine mountain ranges cover fully half of Snowdonia with a breathtaking array of jagged peaks, gorges, and windswept uplands. King Arthur is the region's most legendary inhabitant and it is said that it was on the top of Snowdon itself that he fought an epic battle with the king-killing giant Rhita Gawr. Rhita Gawr's resting place, under summit rocks, presumably lent the mountain its ancient Welsh names Yr Wyddfa Fawr (the Great Tomb) and Carnedd y Cawr (the Cairn of the Giant). (*travel.nationalgeographic.com*)

A. A famous monarch who lived in the area of the modern-day park slayed a giant known for having killed a king.

B. The park's mountain peak has the same Welsh name as the park it is located in.

C. A series of mountain ranges spans over two thousand square kilometers within Snowdonia as well as outside its borders.

D. The mountain's ancient names, in the local language, refer to the reputed burial place of a giant who fought a legendary king.

171. Recent photos taken by NASA's Mars rover might appear to show a gleaming alien bonfire burning in the distance—at least according to some on the internet—but that's not exactly what's happening. Fact is, there still isn't any evidence for life on Mars. None. The provocative, shiny smears of light appear in two images snapped by rover Curiosity's navigation camera, one on April 2 and the other on April 3, provoking excitement among some in the UFO-spotting crowd. The photos come courtesy of the camera's right eye and show nearly vertical bright smudges emerging from a spot near the horizon. Photos of the same spot shot by the camera's left eye, meanwhile, show no such things. Rather than emanating from an underground Martian disco, the bright spots are probably caused by cosmic rays colliding with the rover's camera or by glinting rocks reflecting the Martian sunlight, according to NASA's Jet Propulsion Laboratory's Justin Maki, lead imaging scientist for the Curiosity team. (*news.nationalgeographic.com*)

A. The rover's camera was interfered with by radiation and by rubble redirecting light into its lens.

B. The right eye of Curiosity's camera failed to detect illumination found by the camera's left eye.

C. More than one snapshot has caused internet users to consider there might be extraterrestrial activity on Mars.

D. NASA says that data confirming activity by extraterrestrials on the planet Mars is lacking.

172. Most mornings at nine, the emergency responders assigned to the Seine pull on their wet suits and swim around the Île de la Cité, a teardrop-shaped island in the middle of the river in the middle of Paris. The firemen-divers scour the bottom and retrieve bikes, cutlery (which they clean and use in the nearby houseboat where they live), cell phones, old coins, crucifixes, guns, keys tossed in the water by couples hoping to affirm the eternal nature of their love, and once, a museum-grade Roman clasp. Historically, the left bank of the Seine was bohemian while its right bank was aristocratic, and as the central artery of Paris, the Seine naturally accrues the detritus of human civilization and relationships. However, through the centuries the river has also served as highway, moat, water tap, sewer, and washtub. The river's scimitar arc still slices the city, dividing it into left and right banks, but the distinctions of living on either have blurred over time. (*ngm.nationalgeographic.com*)

A. Roman money and eating utensils have been found by divers at the bottom of the river.

B. Most of the keys thrown into the river are symbols of eternal love and can't actually open anything.

C. A residence on a teardrop-shaped island in the middle of the Seine is where the firemen-divers patrolling the river live.

D. The different character of the two sides of the river is less marked than was once the case.

173. Agriculture is among the greatest contributors to global warming, emitting more greenhouse gases than all our cars, trucks, trains, and airplanes combined—largely from the methane gas released by cattle and rice farms, nitrous oxide from fertilized fields, and carbon dioxide from the cutting of rain forests to grow crops or raise livestock. Farming is the thirstiest user of our precious water supplies and a major polluter, as runoff from fertilizers and manure disrupts fragile lakes, rivers, and coastal ecosystems across the globe. Agriculture also accelerates the loss of biodiversity when areas of grassland and forest are cleared for farms, resulting in the loss of crucial habitat and making agriculture a major driver of wildlife extinction. (*www.nationalgeographic.com*)

A. Substances used to enrich the land contaminate bodies of water and partly cause the world to heat up.

B. Animal species are dying due to the increasing amounts of carbon dioxide released by deforestation.

C. Cultivating land and taking care of cattle are the principle causes of the world's temperature rising.

D. Land and air transport vehicles produce more greenhouse gases than does farming.

174. Garajonay Park is on the island of La Gomera in Spain's Canary Islands, off the northwest coast of Africa, and covered more than two-thirds by a thick laurel forest. Laurel forests are now rare in North Africa and southern Europe, where they thrived during the Tertiary, a geologic period from 66 million to 2.588 million years ago. The landscape is fed by springs, streams, and nurtured by volcanic soils, but La Gomera is the only one of the Canary Islands that has not had a volcanic eruption in the modern era.

No people live inside the park but La Gomera has an unusual cultural heritage. The island's Guanche people, possibly North African Berbers, developed a language, dubbed the silbo gomero, ideal for communicating across forested hillsides and valleys. Spain colonized the Canaries in the 15th century and the islands long served as an important stopover on sea routes from Europe to the Americas, and were Christopher Columbus's last port of call before making landfall in the Americas. (*travel.nationalgeographic.com*)

A. A Spanish explorer made a brief stop on La Gomera during his travels before continuing to America.

B. The origin of La Gomera's inhabitants may be from a region lying to the south and east of the island.

C. A type of woodland frequently found in southern Europe populates the largest proportion of the park.

D. All of the islands have experienced a volcanic event in their existence except the one with the park.

175. Montenegro houses the enormous Durmitor Massif and three breathtaking canyons, including that of the wild Tara River, which is home to Europe's deepest gorge at 1,300 meters. A massif is a demarcated portion of a planet's crust, a famous example being the massif resembling a face on Mars. Rivers also flow under Montenegro's massif with waters from Black Lake travelling below it to the upper canyon valley of the River Komarnica. A park sharing the same name as the massif was established in 1952 and spans 339 square kilometers. It is dotted with more than a dozen sparkling lakes and thickly forested with both deciduous and pine forests—including one of Europe's last virgin stands of black pine near Crna Poda. These trees are more than 400 years old and tower some 50 meters high. In the summer, many of the park's high pastures are home to grazing sheep and cattle owned by the 1,500-some people living within the park and by others in the nearby village of Zabljak. (*travel.nationalgeographic.com*)

A. A depression 1300 meters deep and 100km long has been carved out by a river in Montenegro.

B. Inhabitants of a Montenegrin community outside of Durmitor's boundaries possess foraging animals.

C. Waters from a lake travel under Durmitor's surface along with the Tara River, which makes Europe's deepest gorge.

D. An area having centuries old forest life and human inhabitants contains over twelve bodies of water.

176. The environmental challenges posed by agriculture are enormous, and they will only become more pressing as we try to meet the growing need for food worldwide. We'll likely have two billion more mouths to feed by mid-century—more than nine billion people, but sheer population growth is not the only reason we will need more food. The spread of prosperity across the world, especially in China and India, is driving an increased demand for meat, eggs, and dairy, boosting pressure to grow more corn and soybeans to feed more cattle, pigs, and chickens. If these trends continue, the double whammy of population growth and richer diets will require us to roughly double the amount of crops we grow by 2050. (*www.nationalgeographic.com*)

A. Rising demand for animal derived products is a lesser cause of overall rising food demand than other factors.

B. The food demand forecast for the century's midpoint necessitates an increase in the number of farms.

C. Growing soybean consumption by Asian people has resulted from greater wealth and living standards.

D. The trend in soybean and corn consumption by livestock results from rising global incomes.

177. It turns out that both cosmic rays and glinting rocks are pretty common on Mars and have been spotted in images sent by several of NASA's Mars rovers to Earth. NASA is the U.S. space exploration agency and cosmic rays are particles originating outside of the solar system with very high energy. A NASA scientist explained that maybe one percent of the hundreds of weekly images include cosmic ray-induced bright spots but the junked-up pixels normally don't cause much of a stir. The scientist pointed out that NASA might not see cosmic rays for two or three days in the images but certainly does at least once a week, the reason being that Mars's atmosphere is thinner and doesn't block as much cosmic radiation as Earth's does. (*news.nationalgeographic.com*)

A. Martian conditions are causing the weekly rate of luminous marks found in NASA's photographs.

B. Photographs of light-reflecting rubble are frequently beamed back by various countries' exploratory vehicles on Mars.

C. Earth's surrounding layer prevents cameras on Earth from being interfered with by energetic matter.

D. The pictures are free from irregularities for the most part and lack abnormalities in some weeks.

178. Some 80 percent of all the planet's earthquakes occur along the rim of the Pacific Ocean, called the "Ring of Fire" because of the preponderance of volcanic activity there as well. Most earthquakes occur at fault zones, where tectonic plates—giant rock slabs that make up the Earth's upper layer—collide or slide against each other. These impacts are usually gradual and unnoticeable on the surface; however, immense stress can build up between plates. When this stress is released quickly, it sends massive vibrations, called seismic waves, often hundreds of miles through the rock and up to the surface. Other quakes can occur far from fault zones when plates are stretched or squeezed. Scientists assign a magnitude rating to earthquakes based on the strength and duration of their seismic waves. A quake measuring 3 to 5 is considered minor or light; 5 to 7 is moderate to strong; 7 to 8 is major; and 8 or more is great. (*environment.nationalgeographic.com*)

A. Tremors can result far from fault zones when sections of the Earth's upper layer contract and expand but occur mostly where they meet.

B. The Atlantic, Indian, and Arctic Oceans are where twenty percent of oceanic earthquakes happen.

C. The perimeter of an ocean gets its name from the frequency of earthquakes that occur along it.

D. Grading an earthquake from magnitude three to five means that its effects are usually gradual and unnoticeable at the surface.

179. Blanketed with ash by the A.D. 79 eruption of Italy's Mount Vesuvius then rediscovered, Pompeii has seen almost three-quarters of its homes, temples, and streets exposed to the elements due to the removal of the deadly, preserving ash that once roughly buried the town. Once home to perhaps 12,000 people, Pompeii is now one of the world's great tourist sites, seeing more than two million visitors a year. Tourists, thieves, and time have made the 163-acre (66-hectare) ruin more of a ruin, with three walls suffering collapses and vandals stealing a fresco in March. Herculaneum was a nearby town buried even deeper by Vesuvius, under about 82 feet (25 meters) of ash, and is a smaller tourist site but underwent a restoration in which roofing and drains made much of the difference. (*news.nationalgeographic.com*)

A. The same eruption from the Italian volcano that covered Pompeii in ash also enveloped Herculaneum.

B. Overhead cover and better drainage could play a major role in Pompeii's restoration as they did in another city.

C. Some walls have given way but under three-quarters of Pompeii's houses, churches, and roads are vulnerable to weather damage.

D. Herculaneum's number of visitors is unknown while just under two million per year visit Pompeii.

180. In contrast to the huge surpluses that have been typical in recent years, Germany bought almost as much from its neighbors in February as it sold to them. German exports to the euro zone totaled 34.9 billion euros, or $48.2 billion, in February, a 3.7 percent increase from a year earlier. That compares with the 8.4 percent jump in imports, which were valued at €34.6 billion, according to the German Federal Statistical Office. German exports worldwide rose 4.6 percent during February to €92.4 billion. The increase in imports from the rest of Europe is mostly good news, economists say, especially for countries like Greece and Italy that suffer from very high unemployment and desperately need customers for their exports. But some analysts warn that Germany, which has Europe's largest economy, could be squandering hard-fought gains in competitiveness. (*www.nytimes.com*)

A. A rise in Germany's imports has produced more jobs in Greece and Italy.

B. Thanks to an 8.4% percent year-on-year increase, Germany's imports from the euro zone in February were less than half a billion euro lower than its exports to the euro zone.

C. Germany's worldwide exports increased under 4 percent while those just to the euro zone increased over 4 percent.

D. Greece and Italy shipped more products to Germany in February than Germany shipped to them.

ANSWERS

1. C

A. Cannot say. While this may seem a likely answer, the passage does not actually tell us why, or even if, English was chosen as the universal aviation language.

B. Cannot say. The passage does not say that English was officially adopted after the tragedy, only that it emphasized the need for a universal aviation language.

C. True. This is clearly stated in the first sentence.

D. False. It was not the pilot's inability to speak English, but a combination of a heavy accent, non-standard language and radio interference that contributed to the accident.

2. D

A. False. While it was once believed that personality patterns and behaviours persist over time, "mounting evidence is undermining that notion".

B. Cannot say. We are not told who defined the "big five" traits.

C. False. According to the passage, most people would like to change their personalities "a little", but not to have "strikingly different" personalities.

D. True. While William James believed that personalities are set by the age of 30, and "his idea stuck", new evidence strongly suggests otherwise.

3. B

A. Cannot say. It was "common practice" to use drinking establishments but we are not told if voting "usually" took place in them.

B. True. As the passage states, Edgar Allen Poe may have been caught up in a form of electoral fraud known as "cooping".

C. False. Victims of the electoral fraud method known as "cooping" were disguised so that they could vote in multiple locations because it would have otherwise been prevented.

D. False. While there is reason to believe Poe may have been made to vote on multiple occasions, there is no evidence that he actually did. Therefore, to say that it was discovered that he had done so, is an inaccurate statement.

4. C

A. Cannot say. The topic of lens price is not mentioned.

B. Cannot say. Although one might assume purple fringing is the most common colour, given that it is one of the other names for chromatic aberration, the passage does not actually state that this is the most common colour.

C. True. All that information is given in the text.

D. Cannot say. The passage states that chromatic aberration can be especially visible in high-contrast situations, but it does not say anything in regard to low-contrast situations.

5. B

A. Cannot say. This cannot be inferred from the passage as it only indicates that teams waste time on these issues, not that they fail due to conflict.

B. True. The passage tells us that both technical and leadership skills are important elements of their role.

C. Cannot say. We are told that "few take the time" to develop leadership skills but not whether this is because there are plenty of opportunities for promotion.

D. False. On the contrary, the passage indicates that the importance of leadership skills grows with seniority.

6. D

A. False. The passage merely states that "there is *no reliable evidence* that Christians were killed in the Colosseum for their faith".

B. False. The passage says that just some of the *damnati* were forced to participate in such executions.

C. Cannot say. The text addresses the midday games; what occurred at the morning games, or even if morning games were held, is not said.

D. True. Each of these facts is given in the text.

7. A

A. True. All these facts are stated in the final sentence.

B. False: "initially the robot can only babble and perceives speech as a string of sounds, not divided up into words".

C. Cannot say from the information contained in the passage, which does not address the comparative rates at which robots and humans acquire language skills.

D. Cannot say. While the passage states that, after a few minutes of "conversation" with humans, a robot will adapt its output to the most frequently heard syllables, it does not address inflections.

8. D

A. Cannot say. While the passage does state that Leonardo "hitched himself" to the theory of the microcosm, there is no information that this was "the key" to his success as an artist.

B. False. The passage clearly states that the opposite is true.

C. Cannot say. While the passage states that the idea that the human body can fit inside both a circle and a square is a metaphysical proposition to which Leonardo subscribed, based on this information alone we cannot deduce or disprove his belief in God.

D. True based on information in the text.

9. B

A. False. The passage states: "The encryption key is communicated using light signals and is received using photon detectors."

B. True. The passage states that "the encryption key is communicated using light signals" and a potential hacker can intercept and manipulate such signals.

C. Cannot say. While the passage states that quantum hacking involves light signals subverting photon detectors, whether this form of hacking is the least (or most) common is not given.

D. False. The passage states that quantum cryptography "ensures that any attempt by an eavesdropper...will lead to disturbances that can be detected by the legitimate users".

10. C

A. False. The text states: "In the past, the creation of waste in connection with production... was accepted as a necessary evil", but that this view is "increasingly being challenged". There cannot therefore be universal agreement on the matter.

B. Cannot say. There is nothing in the text to say whether member states have or have not reached such an agreement.

C. True. The passage states that: "Moving to a circular economy would alleviate... pressures", and that one of those pressures is "the inefficient use of natural resources".

D. Cannot say. While the text states that a linear economy has resulted in "over-dependency on resources from outside Europe" it does not clearly state, nor does it necessarily follow, that the move to a circular economy will decrease trade.

11. A

A. True. The passage clearly states that the Higgs boson is part of the standard model of physics and that it explains "why some particles... have mass, while others...do not".

B. False. The passage states that "if a particle interacts significantly with the Higgs field, it will have a higher mass"

C. Cannot say. The passage does not provide relevant information to determine what would happen in the absence of the Higgs field.

D. Cannot say. There is no evidence in the text as to whether the particles attach themselves in this way and so cause drag.

12. D

A. Cannot say. While the passage states that Doyle denounced his Roman Catholic faith, nothing is said about whether this was due to his father.

B. False. The passage clearly states that Doyle surprised his family by choosing to study art rather than medicine.

C. False: Sherlock Holmes' keen powers of observation were inspired by Doyle's medical school mentor, Professor Dr. Joseph Bell.

D. True. "Doyle's first paying job as a doctor took the form of a medical officer's position aboard the steamship Mayumba, travelling from Liverpool to Africa".

13. A

A. True: "birds almost certainly did not descend from theropod dinosaurs, such as tyrannosaurus".

B. Cannot say. While the passage refers to warm-blooded birds having "a unique lung structure that allows for a high rate of gas exchange," it does not indicate whether cold-blooded reptiles also have this.

C. Cannot say. The text makes no comparison of their relative efficiency in walking.

D. Cannot say. While the passage states that birds have a unique thigh complex that "helps support the lung and prevent its collapse", there is no indication as to whether or not this feature allowed them to survive what killed the dinosaurs.

14. C

A. Cannot say. The passage refers to him arguing with other painters, and "alienating those who became tired of his bickering", but does not say whether or not he had friendships with any of them.

B. Cannot say. We are told that he "was passionate, and he argued with other painters" while in Paris, but not whether he had such turbulent relationships throughout his life.

C. True: "in Paris, Van Gogh first saw impressionist art, and he was inspired by the color and light".

D. Cannot say. While the passage states that Theo "believed the painting would not be well-received" there is no information as to whether this belief proved correct.

15. A

A. True. The passage clearly states that a supermassive black hole could have formed when "a number of intermediate black holes merged in the early universe to form the supermassive black holes we see today".

B. Cannot say. While the passage states that intermediate black holes are equal to the matter of about 90,000 suns, there is no information as to whether they are instrumental in the formation of solar systems.

C. False. The passage clearly states that supermassive black holes live *exclusively* at the heart of galaxies.

D. False: "without further surveys, it's impossible to tell how common middleweight black holes are across the universe".

16. C

A. Cannot say. There is no reference to what the European Commission has asked the European Research Council to do.

B. Cannot say. Although the passage refers to a "legally binding goal" having been agreed for 2020 emissions, and EU leaders have "endorsed" a target for 2050, there is no indication as to whether the 2050 target is "legally binding".

C. True. The text describes two European Commission actions. The first is "a long-term target of cutting up to 50% of carbon emissions… by 2050". The second is "a Strategic Energy Technology Plan". The text states that the actions "originated from the Climate Action and Energy Commissioners, respectively". This means that the first action originated from the Climate Action Commissioner, and the second from the Energy Commissioner.

D. Cannot say. The text states that the EU will be "pushing for an international agreement to succeed the Kyoto Protocol aimed at achieving a 30% cut by all developed nations by 2020", but does not clearly state whether negotiations have started.

17. D

A. False. He says the opposite.

B. Cannot say. No such distinction is made in the text between those in their own homes and those in assisted care facilities.

C. Cannot say. While the passage states that "so-called 'exergames' have significant benefits for older adults by providing cognitive stimulation and a source of social interaction, exercise, and fun", whether or not elderly adults who regularly use exergames are *more mentally healthy* and *more fulfilled socially* is not said.

D. True. All these facts are stated in the text.

18. C

A. Cannot say. While the passage describes his inventiveness, whether his main passion was always invention is not stated.

B. False: "it was a clothing line that bore his name that proved to be Lacoste's greatest post-game success".

C. True. All of these aspects of Lacoste are clearly stated in the passage.

D. Cannot say. While the passage says Lacoste's clothing line "entered" the US market, it provides no information as to whether it "conquered" that market or the name and crocodile symbol became status symbols.

19. D

A. Cannot say. The text says that Caesar returned Cleopatra to the throne, but not whether she went on to rule the Mediterranean region for many years.

B. Cannot say. The passage only tells us that Pompey was *stabbed and decapitated* in 48 BC and it leaves room for us to speculate about how long Pompey was in Egypt before this occurred.

C. False. The passage states that the "twenty-one-year-old Cleopatra was at the time [48 BC] a fugitive in the Sinai on the losing side of a civil war against her brother".

D. True. "Quickly, she managed to ingratiate herself with the new master of the Roman world, Julius Caesar."

20. A

A. True. All these facts are stated in the text.

B. Cannot say. There is no information as to his preferences in this regard.

C. False. "Handel's superstar status was not the only draw; many also came to glimpse the contralto, Susannah Cibber".

D. Cannot say. While the passage states that "many also came to glimpse the contralto, Susannah Cibber, then embroiled in a scandalous divorce", whether Cibber drew crowds because of her singing or her divorce is not stated.

21. C

A. Cannot say. While research shows "a link between brain insulin resistance (diabetes) and two other key mediators of neuronal injury that help Alzheimer's disease (AD) to propagate", whether the *underlying causes* of diabetes and Alzheimer's disease are almost identical is not discussed.

B. Cannot say. The passage does not address this issue.

C. True. "There is clinical and experimental evidence that treatment with insulin… can enhance cognitive function… in AD."

D. False. The passage states that Alzheimer's disease is *one of the most* common degenerative dementias.

22. C

A. False: "the lush Tahitian masterpieces for which he is best known reflect an exotic paradise more imaginary than real".

B. Cannot say. While "the fables Gauguin spun were meant to promote himself and his art", whether Gauguin meant to promote the cause of art in general cannot be derived from the text.

C. True. The passage states that Gauguin engaged in all of the pursuits listed.

D. Cannot say. While the passage states that Gauguin's paintings sold poorly in his lifetime, whether this was because of his behaviour is not stated.

23. C

A. Cannot say. The passage makes no reference to the evolution of behaviour.

B. Cannot say. The passage does not tell us whether Felis lybica existed 10,000 years ago.

C. True. The passage tells us that we can infer cats are showing affection towards humans when they behave in ways which are known to be how they show affection to other cats.

D. False. It is lions and cheetahs which form brotherhoods, not the Felis lybica, which is a solitary animal.

24. D

A. Cannot say. The text says that Fontane was "one such fake correspondent" but does not state that he was the first.

B. Cannot say. We are told he never crossed the English Channel during the decade in question, but he may have travelled elsewhere

C. Cannot say. Fontane wrote about the Tooley Street fire, but there is no information about how much of his story was invented.

D. True. "Fake news flourished in the 19th century."

25. B

A. Cannot say from the information contained in the passage, which does not say how many attempts were needed.

B. True. The passage clearly states that "signals would be sent by the opening and closing of an electrical circuit, that the receiving apparatus would, by electromagnet, record signals as dots and dashes".

C. False. The passage clearly states that Morse quit painting before he began work on his telegraph.

D. Cannot say. The passage does not address how Morse's telegraph was received.

26. B

A. Cannot say. While the bodies showed signs of torture, there is no reference as to whether they may have been killed as part of such a ritual.

B. True. All these facts are given in the text.

C. False. The passage states that "both bog men appeared to be aristocratic dandies of their day."

D. Cannot say from the information contained in the passage, which does not address the topic of evidence of Iron Age burial modes.

27. D

A. Cannot say. There is no mention of the issue of exposure to copper before birth.

B. Cannot say. While those with Wilson's disease suffer liver damage and failure, whether liver cells die off at increasing rates without regenerating is not discussed.

C. False. It is the other way round: "too little copper can be fatal whereas too much can cause neurological impairment".

D. True. The passage states: "the body rids itself of excess copper and various other minerals by collecting them in the liver and excreting them through the liver's bile. However…when this route is impaired, there's another exit route just for copper…through urine."

28. A

A. True. This information is clearly given in the passage.

B. False. It cost $400 million.

C. Cannot say. While the new algorithm reduces the time it takes, whether it does this by utilizing the genomes of related species is not stated.

D. False. The passage states that "since 2002, the rate at which genomes can be sequenced has been *doubling every four months or so*".

29. C

A. Cannot say. While "landing strips for alien spacecraft" has been suggested as an explanation, there is no information provided in the text about the influence of popular culture.

B. False. There is only evidence "suggesting" this – so it is at this point a theory, not a proven fact.

C. True. All these interpretations are stated in the text.

D. Cannot say. While interpretations include that the lines were used for "ceremonial processions" and that they were "irrigation plans", their exact purpose and whether they had a dual purpose is not known according to the passage.

30. C

A. False. "Moody's Investors Service lowered Italy's government bond rating …citing concerns that Italy *faces higher financing costs and an increased risk of being locked out of lending markets*." No "unsuccessful efforts to escape the debt crisis" are mentioned.

B. Cannot say. The passage makes no reference to the question of Italy being too big for the euro zone to bail out.

C. True. All these facts are stated in the text.

D. Cannot say. There is no reference to whether Italy may become caught in this way.

31. D

A. Cannot say. This topic is not discussed.

B. Cannot say. While we are told that the corpus luteum "controls hormone levels during pregnancy" we are not told whether the formation of multiple corpora lutea is to maintain *steady* hormone levels.

C. False. The passage states: "one corpus luteum was derived from an egg-generating follicle, as happens in mammals such as humans, the rest of the structures formed from separate follicles…"

D. True. These facts are stated in the text.

32. A

A. True. The passage states that hard problems "take exponentially more time to solve with every additional variable that is thrown into the mix".

B. False. "With each new variable, however, it becomes tougher to find the right equation."

C. False. "Even the world's top supercomputers meet their match with a certain class of problems, known as 'hard' problems. These problems take exponentially more time to solve with every additional variable that is thrown into the mix."

D. Cannot say. The topic is not discussed.

33. C

A. Cannot say. While the passage states that Dada was an "irrational art movement", it does not indicate whether it appealed particularly to those who could not make sense of the events of the *early 20th century.*

B. False. While the passage states that Romanian artist Tristan Tzara put out the first of many Dada manifestoes, it also states that few of them "made much sense".

C. True. This information is given in the text.

D. Cannot say. While the passage states that Dada influenced abstract and conceptual art, whether the element of Dada that paved the way for abstract and conceptual art was its absurdity and irrationality is not discussed.

34. B

A. False. It plunged into Saturn's atmosphere to avoid contaminating Saturn's icy moons, in particular Enceladus.

B. True. The text states that Saturn is "some 1.4 billion km from Earth", so Cassini must have travelled more than that distance during the course of its mission, which involved reaching Saturn and touring its system for 13 years.

C. Cannot say. The text refers to "ocean-bearing Enceladus" as one of Saturn's icy moons but says nothing about whether the Cassini spacecraft discovered it.

D. False. The passage states that Saturn's icy moons are to be "left pristine for future exploration", so scientists must be open to the idea.

35. B

A. False. Mary did marry James Hepburn of Bothwell, but it was Lord Darnley with whom she had her son, the future James VI.

B. True. The passage clearly states: "While ill with smallpox, Darnley was mysteriously killed in an explosion at Kirk o' Field (1567)."

C. Cannot say from the information. While "placing herself under the protection of Queen Elizabeth, she found herself instead a prisoner for life", whether Queen Elizabeth I had Mary arrested and imprisoned because she saw her as *a serious threat to the throne* is not discussed.

D. False. The passage states that Mary "raised an army, but was defeated again by the confederate lords at Langside (1568)".

36. D

A. Cannot say. Whether or not neurosurgeons use images taken by the ultraviolet camera in making decisions or to aid surgical technique is not stated

B. False. The passage clearly states that tumor cells have irregular borders as they grow and require more energy than healthy cells.

C. Cannot say. The passage states that the use of the camera is in the pilot study stage, but not whether it will revolutionise how brain tumors and other neurological disorders are treated.

D. True. "Neurosurgeons and researchers are adapting an ultraviolet camera to possibly bring planet-exploring technology into the operating room" and "The camera employs the ultraviolet technology used in space to study planets and distant galaxies."

37. B

A. False. It was the other way round. "The team concluded that GFAJ-1 must be incorporating *arsenic* into its DNA in place of *phosphorous*".

B. True. "NASA astrobiologist Felisa Wolfe-Simon had found the organism, dubbed GFAJ-1, in arsenic-rich sediments of California's Mono Lake."

C. Cannot say. While the passage states that the discovery was "exciting" to astrobiologists who had "previously speculated that extraterrestrial life might survive in unexpected places if only such a swap were possible" it is not stated that the existence of extraterrestrial life had been confirmed.

D. Cannot say. We are told that all *known* living organisms require some phosphorous, and so does GFAJ-1, but nothing in the text either precludes or confirms that *as yet unknown* organisms might not require phosphorous.

38. B

A. Cannot say. There is no reference in the text to any relationship between his behaviour and genius.

B. True. The passage clearly states all of these facts about Morphy.

C. Cannot say. While the passage states that "for the last decade of his life he was loath to discuss the game at all", it does not say whether or not he believed that time spent playing chess was nothing more than wasted time.

D. False. "His family tried to have him committed to an asylum, but he argued his sanity so convincingly that the authorities declined to admit him."

39. C

A. Cannot say. While the passage discusses the speed of data transfer by graphene devices, there is no reference to whether they will replace existing internet cables.

B. False. A cell is made by "putting *two* closely-spaced metallic wires *on top of graphene*".

C. True. This information is all given in the text.

D. False: "the major stumbling block towards practical applications of these otherwise promising devices has been their low efficiency".

40. B

A. Cannot say. The passage states that shell shock inflicted "novel and peculiar damage to men's brains", but not whether the symptoms were similar to a concussion.

B. True. The passage says that "many soldiers arriving at the casualty clearing stations... appeared to be suffering from a remarkable state of shock" and that the term "shell shock" first appeared in *The Lancet* "only six months after the commencement of the war".

C. Cannot say. We are told only that the term "shell shock" first appeared in *The Lancet* in February 1915, but not whether it may already have been coined by military doctors in the barracks.

D. False. It was not shell shock but "Shrapnel from mortars, grenades and, above all, artillery projectile bombs, or shells" which accounted for about 60 per cent of the military fatalities.

41. B

A. Cannot say. We are told that there have been "dramatic declines of some ibex populations", but not whether the Iberian ibex is under threat of extinction.

B. True. The passage says that the "objective of the Iberian ibex stock reservoir El Toril" is to have "most of the genetic variability" of the free-ranging population of ibex.

C. Cannot say. "Overexploitation, pollution, habitat loss" have led species to extinction, but there is nothing to say whether they are responsible for the mange outbreaks among some ibex populations.

D. Cannot say. There is no reference to this topic in the text.

42. D

A. Cannot say. There is no reference in the passage to the licensing of designs.

B. Cannot say. While it may seem a plausible inference that the creation of tapestries declined after their "Golden Age", this is not explicitly stated and nor is any information given as to the relationship between the creation of tapestries and that of oil paintings.

C. False. The passage states that tapestries "had snob appeal, since only the richest of the rich could afford them."

D. True. Each of these reasons is referred to in the text.

43. B

A. Cannot say. While the passage refers to the increase in single-parent households as a factor in increasing inequality between households, whether or not children raised in such households subsequently have more difficulty moving up the income ladder is not discussed.

B. True: "though no one has suggested that it is the sole or even main driving force behind the increases in inequality, rates of single parenthood are important but sometimes overlooked."

C. False. The passage clearly states to the contrary: "changes in family structure (as opposed to wages and employment alone) have increased inequality."

D. False. The passage states that between 1970 and 2011, income inequality between the top and bottom households grew by *31 per cent* overall.

44. C

A. False. The passage tells us that it was *in 1961* that "Mandela, who was formerly committed to non-violent protest, began to believe that armed struggle was the only way to achieve change".

B. False. It was *founded* as an armed offshoot of the ANC.

C. True. The passage states: "he was arrested in 1962. He was sentenced to five years in prison for the strike, and then brought to trial again in 1963. This time, he and 10 other ANC leaders were sentenced to life imprisonment for political offences, including sabotage."

D. False. The passage states: "The African National Congress (ANC) was being challenged by the Africanists, a new breed of Black activists who believed that the pacifist method of the ANC was ineffective."

45. D

A. Cannot say. At the moment this is merely a "new theory".

B. False. The passage states that they "travelled… without the benefit of wheels, cranes, or even large animals."

C. False. The passage tells us that "*most* of them", not "*all* of them", were carved in the quarry.

D. True. This was precisely what Hunt and Lipo demonstrated.

46. A

A. True. All this information is given in the second sentence.

B. False. While the passage informs us that many Etonians have rowed in the Olympics, it also states: "For generations, Eton's crews practiced and competed on the Thames, but by the 1990s, recreational boat traffic made rowing there dangerous."

C. Cannot say. There is no reference to whether Olympic events are now held on the Thames.

D. Cannot say. We are told that British, Canadian and Dutch crews competed, but not which of them had the most success.

47. C

A. Cannot say. The text tells us that the work contains video interviews, but we don't know whether or not it is a kind of video library.

B. Cannot say. Although "Genocide" is one of the themes of the video installation, there is no reference in the text to the topic of this being perpetrated by Western societies on non-Western societies.

C. True. We are told that Kader Attia created the work and that it is an "essay on… psychiatric pathology" and "contained interviews with philosophers, ethnologists, historians, psychiatrists, psychoanalysts, musicologists, patients, healers, and fetishists".

D. Cannot say. The text states that the work uses "irrational representations" but does not say that psychiatrists are represented in an absurd way.

48. D

A. False. Researchers found the opposite; people were more likely to have good health the closer they lived to the sea.

B. Cannot say. There is no reference to this topic.

C. Cannot say. While the research shows a link between the likelihood of having good health and living close to the sea, the passage does not indicate what the reasons for that might be.

D. True. "The link between living near the coast and good health was strongest in the most economically deprived communities."

49. D

A. False. The passage tells us that Courbet vowed "to lead the life of a savage" and that "he did not mellow with age".

B. Cannot say. While the passage states that Courbet "would become one of the most innovative and influential painters of mid-19th-century France", it does not say that his rebellious spirit and corresponding vision were what made him such.

C. Cannot say. While the text states that Courbet produced "salacious canvases", it does not tell us if these *were intended to change the public's taste and way of seeing.*

D. True. The passage clearly states these facts about Courbet.

50. B

A. False. He became "the Boss of the New York City Gambino crime family" and in 1992 was convicted of 13 murders, among other crimes.

B. True. All this information is given in the text.

C. False. The passage states that Gotti "was sentenced to life in prison without parole."

D. False. His arrest record by age 21 included all those offences but he had "served little gaol time".

51. B

A. Cannot say. While the town's existence was known to his royal scribes, whether it was once visited by Charlemagne himself is not mentioned.

B. True. The passage clearly states these facts.

C. False. The passage tells us that caltrops were small, spiked iron weapons that were scattered on the ground.

D. Cannot say. While the passage states that "Arrowheads found embedded in [the long-house's] charred wall posts suggest the communal building was at some point set on fire and shot at", there is no information given as to who the attackers were.

52. D

A. Cannot say. The passage does not tell us whether this was an isolated case or a pattern of behaviour or, if the latter, whether it almost always involved young male gorillas and whether it was their role to protect the clan.

B. Cannot say. While it may seem quite likely that park employees look for and dismantle snares, and even more unlikely that young gorillas often help them with the task, the text provides no information either way on either count.

C. False. The passage clearly states that the poachers set snares for antelope and other species but that they have no interest in the gorillas.

D. True. "Adults are generally strong enough to free themselves. Youngsters aren't always so lucky."

53. D

A. False. The relevant figure is "over 35 per cent".

B. Cannot say. The passage does not tell us how the drug works.

C. Cannot say. The passage makes no reference to whether the supercomputer is used to "monitor how a drug will work at a molecular level".

D. True. The passage clearly states that for individuals with asthma and COPD, "the common cold is a serious threat to their health and could prove fatal."

54. C

A. Cannot say. In some areas the flooding is earlier and in some later, but we are not told which of these is the more usual.

B. Cannot say. While flood damage globally runs to "roughly a 100 billion dollars a year" and it would seem highly probable that Europe's share of this would be much less than "nearly 100 billion dollars", the text does not provide definite information on this topic.

C. True. We are told that "around the North Sea… the trend is towards later floods. The scientists believe this is due to changes in the North Atlantic Oscillation".

D. Cannot say. The text states that: "In… southern England, floods are now occurring 15 days earlier than they did half a century ago" and that "in… Scotland, the trend is towards later floods". But the text gives no dates as to when floods are happening, so we cannot be certain that floods in southern England take place much earlier than those in Scotland.

55. C

A. Cannot say. The text states that "the third plague pandemic functioned as a catalyst for... colonial policies [and] geopolitical struggles", but does not say that these helped spread the plague.

B. False. The third plague pandemic "lasted roughly from 1855 to 1959".

C. True. The text tells us that the pandemic "lasted roughly from 1855 to 1959" and that "incidents of this pandemic were systematically photographed and documented from beginning to end, with images from local outbreaks making newspaper headlines across the globe."

D. Cannot say. The passage tells us that "between 1898 and 1900… it struck… Portugal [and] Scotland", so we cannot be certain that the outbreaks occurred in 1898. It could have been 1898, 1899, or 1900.

56. C

A. Cannot say. The passage says that "When automation is only reliable sometimes, a person's level of trust becomes an important factor that determines *how often the aid will be used*." We are not told if it influences *how they use* the device.

B. Cannot say. While the "inclusion of an image" of a person can "significantly alter perceptions of a computerised aid", whether the overall "design" of the device will highly influence an individual's level of trust is not discussed.

C. True: "research findings have revealed that the inclusion of an image of a person can significantly alter perceptions of a computerised aid".

D. Cannot say. The passage does not discuss "reaction time".

57. C

A. False. The passage states that Francis of Assisi bore five marks but that "later stigmatics…bear only one or two wounds".

B. False. Francis of Assisi "bore five marks: two on his palms and two on his feet…and the fifth on his side".

C. True. The passage clearly states these facts about stigmata.

D. Cannot say. "This was the *first case* of stigmata…*described*". There may have been earlier cases that were *not* described.

58. C

A. False. The passage states that "the separation between modern domestic cats and big cats such as lions and tigers is also deeply rooted".

B. False. "Modern cats diverged in skull shape from their sabre-toothed ancestors early in their evolutionary history *and then followed separate evolutionary trajectories.*"

C. True. Researchers "quantified skull shape… They found an early and conspicuous divergence between the conical-toothed cats and sabre-toothed cats, with all sabre-toothed cats being more closely related to each other than they were to modern conical-toothed cats."

D. Cannot say. While the skull shapes of sabre-toothed and modern (conical-toothed) cats diverged early and they "*then* followed separate evolutionary trajectories" there is no information as to whether *the skull shapes alone* indicate that they followed different evolutionary trajectories.

59. D

A. False. The text states that "niobium-tin magnets are cooled to just 1.9 Kelvin (–271.3 °C)" in order "to reach and retain their superconductive state". A "quench" is when "superconductors fail to maintain their superconductive state".

B. Cannot say. The passage tells us that *niobium-tin* magnets are used in the Large Hadron Collider but does not state whether or not *niobium-titanium* magnets are also used.

C. Cannot say. We are told that liquid helium is used as a coolant in the Large Hadron Collider, but not whether there are any alternatives.

D. True. The text states that "above a critical temperature and above a critical magnetic field, the superconductors fail to maintain their superconductive state".

60. D

A. False. Ball's Pyramid is "another small volcanic rock island nearby".

B. Cannot say. We are told that the rock climbers found what looked like to be the extinct stick insects, but we do not know if they took samples with them.

C. Cannot say. There is no information on what kind of predators the stick insects had; we only know that the rats did not have large mammals to predate them.

D. True. The scientists used genome sequencing to compare museum specimens and the captive-bred stick insects and to officially classify them as the same species.

61. D

A. Cannot say. While the passage clearly states that *Crocodylus thorbjarnarsoni* ate our 1.2-metre tall ancestors, whether the beast likely ambushed the early humans when they went to collect water is not mentioned.

B. False. The passage states: "Other species in the wider category of crocodyliforms …are bigger".

C. Cannot say. While the passage states that *Crocodylus thorbjarnarsoni* "would have resembled a heavyset Nile crocodile", whether it is its distant ancestor is not stated.

D. True. The passage clearly states these facts.

62. C

A. Cannot say. While the passage tells us that Robert Fortune engaged in a "corporate espionage" trip to China for this purpose, whether this was the first such attempt by the British East India Company to steal the secrets is not stated.

B. False. While the passage states that "the concept of tea is simple – dry leaf infused in hot water" it also states that "the manufacture of it is not intuitive at all. Tea is a highly processed product".

C. True. The passage clearly states each of these facts.

D. Cannot say. While the passage tells us that "*few in Britain's dominions* had any firsthand or even secondhand information about the production of tea before it went into the pot", there is no reference as to whether *anyone* within the British East India Company had that information.

63. C

A. Cannot say. While the research showed that the frequent use of "language adaptations" by tween texters was reflected in lower scores in a grammar test, no information is provided as to which group of tweens are "better adapted socially".

B. False. The passage states: "there is evidence of a decline in grammar scores based on the number of adaptations in sent text messages, controlling for age and grade".

C. True. This is the main point of the passage.

D. Cannot say. While techspeak is given as *a* reason for a decline in grammar skills among tweens, there is no information that it is the *primary* reason.

64. C

A. Cannot say. The benefits and drawbacks of employing family doctors in casualty departments are discussed, but not whether this is likely to be reduced.

B. Cannot say. There is no information as to whether they disagree with each other.

C. True. Professor Taylor describes the positive effects: "patients seen by the family doctor were significantly less likely to be admitted, exceed the four-hour waiting target or leave before being seen."

D. Cannot say. We are told it "increases antibiotic prescriptions" but this is not quantified and we cannot be sure it is a "major increase".

65. A

A. True. The passage states all these facts about Giuseppe Arcimboldo.

B. Cannot say. While the passage states that Giuseppe painted sea creatures, flowers, dinner roasts, pea pods, gourds, and more, there is no information about where he learned to paint them.

C. Cannot say. Whether Arcimboldo painted Rudolf II *at the emperor's request* is not stated.

D. False. The passage refers to other elements, such as sea creatures and dinner roasts.

66. B

A. Cannot say. While the passage tells us that such a robot "can outperform humans in identifying a *wide range of natural materials* according to their textures", whether it can do this for *all* materials is not stated.

B. True. The passage clearly states these facts.

C. Cannot say. The passage refers to a robot being able to identify "natural materials", but whether it is also able to identify materials such as plastic and synthetics is not discussed.

D. False. The passage clearly states that the robot with a special tactile sensor "has no way to tell what textures people will prefer".

67. B

A. Cannot say. The passage states that "researchers could not determine if low vitamin D contributed to frailty, or whether frail people became vitamin D deficient because of health problems".

B. True. "Frail adults with low levels of vitamin D tripled their risk of death over people who were not frail and who had higher levels of vitamin D."

C. False. The passage states that older and frail adults with low vitamin D have a 30 per cent *higher* risk of dying than those with higher levels.

D. Cannot say. The passage only discusses the "new study" in which the researchers did not conclude whether frailty caused vitamin D deficiency or vice versa, while it does not discuss what the majority of studies say about the link between these two conditions.

68. D

A. Cannot say. While it was sung in "bars, back streets and brothels" there is no information as to whether they could sing it at any time or place or that this was its attraction.

B. False. The passage tells us that musicologists see fado "as an amalgam of cultures, especially African and Brazilian, stemming from Portugal's maritime and colonial past, combined with its oral poetry tradition and, possibly, some Berber-Arab influence".

C. Cannot say. While it is enjoying "increasing world appeal," there is no comparison of its current world popularity with that among the urban poor of 19th-century Lisbon.

D. True. The passage clearly states these facts.

69. C

A. Cannot say. While the passage explains that according to the study, intellectual profiles of Asperger individuals depend on which type of test is used, whether *the measure of intelligence is exactly quantifiable* is not given.

B. Cannot say. The passage tells us that Asperger individuals score much higher in Raven's Progressive Matrices than they do in other types of test, but there is no indication as to how their scores compare with those of non-Asperger individuals who take that test.

C. True. The passage explains that Asperger individuals score unevenly on Wechsler tests but higher on the Raven's Progressive Matrices test while "scores for non-Asperger individuals are much more consistent across different tests".

D. Cannot say. While the passage states that "this study reports that Asperger individuals' scores are much higher when they are evaluated by a test called Raven's Progressive Matrices, which encompasses reasoning, novel problem-solving abilities, and high-level abstraction", whether high-level abstraction and the ability to solve novel problems are considered *higher forms of intelligence* cannot be deduced from the information provided.

70. D

A. Cannot say. No such comparison is made in the text.

B. Cannot say. The passage refers to "declining bee populations and colony collapse" in reference to the honeybee but does not tell us whether they could be wiped out altogether in some areas.

C. False. The passage states that solitary bees face a *greater* threat than honeybees.

D. True. The passage states the link remains "obscure", therefore it cannot have been categorically confirmed.

71. A

A. True. All these facts are stated in the text.

B. Cannot say. The formation of a "cloud" is not referred to.

C. False. The passage refers to "quantum-mechanical effects... on a scale that is visible to the naked eye."

D. Cannot say. The topic of operating above the same critical temperature is not discussed.

72. B

A. Cannot say. While "the landscape around the city, it now appears, was intensively farmed", whether it was *most likely an agricultural centre of the region* thanks to the intensive cultivation is not given.

B. True. These facts are given in the text.

C. Cannot say. There is no reference to the capture of the small amount of rainfall.

D. Cannot say. The passage tells us goods were brought from India and China, but there is no information as to whether they came from "all over the world".

73. C

A. Cannot say. The passage tells us of the "witchcraft craze" during that period, but not whether it was "the gravest period" in the history of witch-hunts.

B. False. "More than 200 people were accused... and 20 were executed."

C. True. "Eventually, the colony admitted the trials were a mistake and compensated the families of those convicted."

D. Cannot say. While the passage states that "*many practising Christians, and those of other religions,* had a strong belief that the Devil could give certain people known as witches the power to harm others", it does not say whether practising Christians in Europe were largely responsible for stirring up paranoia about witches.

74. C

A. False. The medals were awarded for "original works in the fine arts *inspired by athletic endeavours.*"

B. Cannot say. While we are told the juries awarded 151 such medals, there is no information as to whether the artists were also highly skilled athletes.

C. True. The passage states that Baron Pierre de Coubertin "felt that in order to recreate the events in modern times, it would be incomplete to not include some aspect of the arts".

D. Cannot say. While the medals were awarded for works "inspired by athletic endeavours", whether the majority were awarded for *paintings of the games themselves* is not discussed.

75. D

A. False. "Once Copernicus put the sun at the centre of the picture...the planetary orbits became regular, smooth and elegant."

B. Cannot say. While Copernicus "took half a lifetime to check his figures before publishing them... at age 70", whether he also feared persecution is not stated.

C. False: prior to Copernicus, "astronomers *had worked from the assumption* that the earth was the centre of the universe, forcing them to draw convoluted orbits for the planets".

D. True. The passage states that Copernicus' work was a "response to the unwieldy mathematics used since the days of the ancient Greeks to explain the motion of the sun, moon and five known planets".

76. D

A. Cannot say. We are told that "on average, one footstep generates 7 watts of electricity, though the amount varies depending on a person's weight", but not whether the amount depends *solely* on a person's weight.

B. Cannot say. The tiles are made from recycled tires and have a "minimal carbon footprint" but we are not told that this is "less than that of any other energy source".

C. Cannot say. There is no information about the relationship between the proportion of recyclable components an energy source contains and the size of its carbon footprint.

D. True. The passage clearly states each of these facts.

77. A

A. True. The study "found statistically significant evidence of obsessive-compulsive tendencies" among people with remarkable autobiographical memories.

B. Cannot say. While researchers "found statistically significant evidence of obsessive-compulsive tendencies" among those with extraordinary autobiographical memories, it also states that the researchers "do not yet know if or how this aids recollection".

C. Cannot say. The size of prefrontal lobes is not discussed.

D. False. The passage states the opposite: "the people with stellar autobiographical memory *did not* score higher...when asked to use rote memory aids".

78. C

A. Cannot say: "we're not sure...whether they sang or chanted".

B. Cannot say. While "the emphasis was definitely on percussion" whether it was *like an early form of modern percussion music* is not stated.

C. True. The passage clearly states these facts.

D. Cannot say. While the passage states that instruments included "the menat, a multi-strand beaded necklace they would shake," whether it might have also had a decorative function is not said.

79. C

A. False. The requirement to give 2% of the catch is a provision of the *new* agreement.

B. Cannot say. While the passage states that "fish can now only be caught more than 20 miles from the shore, up from 13 miles in the previous agreement," whether this is because between 13 and 20 miles from the shore is Mauritania's richest fishing area is not said.

C. True. The passage states: "The total cost to the EU budget for fishing rights off the coast of the former French colony will be €70 million per year…The agreement allows EU ships to fish for demersal."

D. Cannot say. Nothing in the text refers to the level of support for the agreement among fishermen.

80. B

A. Cannot say. While the passage states that "randomness in quantum theory is one of its key features" whether it has *practical applications* for fields as diverse as chemistry and politics is not discussed.

B. True. "This inability to accurately predict the results of experiments in quantum physics has been the subject of a long debate, going back to Einstein and his co-workers, about whether quantum mechanics is the best way to predict outcomes."

C. Cannot say. While the passage states that randomness in quantum theory means that "knowing the precise configuration of the universe at the big bang would not be sufficient to predict its *entire* evolution", there is no information to indicate whether its evolution could be *partly* predicted.

D. False. The passage clearly states that "in quantum mechanics, the outcomes of certain experiments generally can't be predicted perfectly beforehand, even if all of the information is available".

81. C

A. Cannot say. The passage provides no information to make this assessment.

B. False. The passage states: "While the two were alive, admirers spoke of them in the same breath, and the comparisons were not always in Rembrandt's favour."

C. True. The passage clearly states these facts about Rembrandt and Lievens.

D. Cannot say. While "the role of the lonely genius" was "a figure dear to the Romantics" and "Lievens moved around, absorbing many different influences," whether his *life centred on continuous change* and this put him out of favour with the Romantics, is not discussed.

82. C

A. Cannot say. While "the direct ancestors of modern humans may have interbred with members of an unknown ancestral group of hominids," there is no information as to whether those who did not do so failed to evolve.

B. False: "even though all the individuals we sampled are hunter-gatherers, natural selection has acted differently in these different groups."

C. True. The study "suggests that different groups evolved distinctly in order to reap nutrition from local foods and defend against infectious disease".

D. Cannot say. While "Differing food sources, geographies, diseases and climates offered many targets for natural selection to exert powerful forces…The individuals who adapted best were the most likely to reproduce," there is no information as to the effect of having "the most diverse food sources" or living "in the most temperate climates".

83. B

A. Cannot say. While the passage states that none of the tasks involved in resurrecting a woolly mammoth "appears insurmountable" whether or not it is likely to happen is not given.

B. True. The passage clearly states that part of the mammoth genome has been published and that scientists at present "don't even know how many chromosomes the mammoth had".

C. Cannot say. While the passage states that "30 per cent of the genome would have to be recovered" and references "a simple, inexpensive technique for recovering high-quality DNA from mammoth hair," whether scientists will be able to recover the 30 per cent of the mammoth genome that remains unknown is not stated.

D. Cannot say. The text makes no reference to the issue of recreating male and female sex cells.

84. D

A. Cannot say. In her book she argues that policies can be designed to have this effect but the passage does not say whether they have been implemented anywhere.

B. Cannot say. We are told that the Menloy index was named after her but not who gave it its name.

C. False. His work includes "the causes and consequences of inequality within developed countries".

D. True. The passage states that he argues that financial underdevelopment is an important determinant of poverty.

85. A

A. True. The passage states each of these facts about Charles Lutwidge Dodgson.

B. Cannot say. There is no reference to the sources of inspiration for the characters in *Alice's Adventures in Wonderland.*

C. Cannot say. While the passage tells us he wrote *Alice's Adventures in Wonderland* it does not say what else he published or whether he devoted *much of his life* to the craft of writing.

D. Cannot say. While the passage states that *Alice's Adventures in Wonderland* influenced Walt Disney and Salvador Dali, there is no mention of Tim Burton.

86. D

A. Cannot say. The use of such security systems in solving crimes is not mentioned.

B. Cannot say. While the passage refers to researchers creating a "learning system that simulates the brain in making decisions", whether such a system can make decisions better than a human is not discussed.

C. False. The passage states that additional practical applications for biometric information include "intelligent decision-making methodology for human recognition…maintaining security in virtual worlds and avatar recognition".

D. True. "The key is the ability to combine features from multiple sources of information, prioritise them… and adapt the decision-making to changing conditions".

87. D

A. False. "The most popular entertainments offered by the circuses of Rome were the gladiators and chariot racing, *the latter often as deadly as the former.*"

B. Cannot say. While the passage says that "ancient inscriptions frequently record the deaths of famous racers… crushed against the stone *spina…* or dragged behind their horses," there is no reference to whether the *majority in any race* were killed in the latter way.

C. Cannot say. While the passage states that "spectators wagered and also won substantial sums – enough for the races to be plagued by all manner of dirty tricks", whether many of them lost their lives as a result is not mentioned.

D. True. The passage clearly states all these facts.

88. D

A. Cannot say. While the passage states that the two galaxies will collide and that scientists were initially uncertain about whether they might just pass one another "like two ships passing in the night," whether other galaxies in the same situation do in fact simply slide past each other is not given.

B. Cannot say. While the passage states that the collision between the two galaxies "won't have an enormous impact on earth or the solar system as a whole," whether this is because the process will take millions of years to complete is not stated.

C. False. When the two galaxies collide, they will first "orbit around each other before merging in one big galactic pile-up".

D. True. The passage clearly states these facts.

89. B

A. Cannot say. While the passage states that the laser includes "a layer of silver film that is smooth at the atomic level", it does not say whether this is what differentiates this laser from similar devices.

B. True. "The device is constructed of a gallium nitride nanorod that is partially filled with indium gallium nitride."

C. False. The passage clearly states that the nanorod is placed on top of the thin layer of silicon, not vice versa.

D. Cannot say. While the passage tells us that the laser "is key for the development of faster, smaller and lower energy photon-based technologies, such as ultrafast computer chips," there is no information whether the laser will *soon be on the market in the form of computer chips.*

90. B

A. Cannot say. While the passage states that in July "Greece and Spain were the only two countries where the manufacturing sector contracted more rapidly", whether Spain's contraction was greater than Greece's is not given.

B. True. The passage clearly states these facts.

C. False. Chris Williamson said that the July slowdown suggested "a fear among companies towards ongoing weakness".

D. Cannot say. While Ireland "saw its manufacturing sector expand, with a score of 53.9", there is no information as to the meaning of this score or whether this is the lowest it has seen in three years.

91. A

A. True. The passage clearly states these facts.

B. Cannot say. While the passage states that the Birmingham demonstration "drew nationwide attention," whether the March on Washington would not otherwise have drawn 200,000 people is not discussed.

C. False. The passage tells us that King believed '"nonviolent direct action seeks to create such a crisis and foster such a tension that a community, which has constantly refused to negotiate, is forced to confront the issue".

D. Cannot say. While the speech emphasised King's belief that "someday all men could be brothers," there is no reference to whether its message was written to motivate and educate all Americans about the civil rights movement.

92. B

A. Cannot say. While the passage states that "the great zeppelin caught fire while less than 90 metres from the ground," whether it crashed to the ground *just metres from where it was scheduled to land* cannot be determined from the information provided.

B. True. The passage clearly states each of these facts.

C. Cannot say. While the possible causes listed in the text do not include human error, the reason for the explosion remains a "mystery... at this point it's impossible to determine what exactly caused the spark."

D. Cannot say. While the passage states that a bolt of lightning is one realistic explanation for what caused the Hindenburg to burst into flames, it also states that "at this point it's impossible to determine what exactly caused the spark".

93. B

A. False. It was the Mars Odyssey spacecraft that detected minute quantities of liquid water on and just below the surface of Mars.

B. True. The passage clearly states these facts.

C. Cannot say. While the passage details evidence indicating that water exists on or near Mars' surface and in its interior, whether such evidence suggests that the planet once possibly supported life is not stated.

D. False. "Now there is evidence that Mars is home to vast reservoirs of water in its interior as well."

94. C

A. False. The passage states that the P.L.A. "is commemorated *annually* with speeches and promotions and *every five years* by major cultural celebrations".

B. Cannot say. While Mao Zedong said that "we must also have a cultural army, which is absolutely indispensable for uniting our own ranks and defeating the enemy", there is no reference in the text to whether, without this cultural army, China would in fact not be as united as it is today, nor as able to defeat its enemies.

C. True. The passage states: "the Communist Party and the People's Liberation Army....have maximised the value of the arts as tools of propaganda. As Mao Zedong said.... a cultural army...is absolutely indispensable for... defeating the enemy."

D. Cannot say. There is no discussion of this question in the text.

95. B

A. False. The passage states: "The distinction between these two technologies is that one is camera-based and one is not. And that difference could be the deciding factor. Unlike tennis, where there is almost never any thing or person obstructing the line of sight between the cameras and the ball, soccer presents unique challenges".

B. True. "IFAB gave the green light to try goal line sensors from… GoalRef and Hawkeye. In early July, IFAB approved both technologies…Michel Platini, head of the UEFA…stood staunchly opposed to the technology."

C. Cannot say. While the passage states that IFAB has approved the use of goal line sensors and that Platini, the head of the UEFA, is opposed, whether he has either the power or the intention to veto it is not discussed.

D. Cannot say. The text does not say which of the two technologies is favoured by tennis or whether it is GoalRef or Hawkeye where the line of sight is not an issue.

96. A

A. True. "A government investigation into insider trading in Tokyo has extended onto the trading floors of some of Wall Street's largest companies, including Goldman Sachs, UBS and Deutsche Bank."

B. False. The passage states that some of Goldman Sachs' clients are being investigated for trading misconduct involving All Nippon Airways, so it is impossible that Deutsche Bank is the only company with clients in such a situation.

C. Cannot say. While a government committee in Tokyo "has been working with regulators to stiffen insider trading laws in Japan," whether this will *most likely result* in more severe laws is not stated.

D. Cannot say. While the passage states that the insider trading scandal has "undermined faith in Japanese stock markets," there is no information that markets have plunged in recent weeks.

97. D

A. Cannot say. The differences between native Spanish and Finnish speakers are not discussed.

B. False: "research from psychological science and linguistics suggests that a child's emotional competence is fundamentally shaped by a multilingual environment".

C. Cannot say. No information is given on this topic.

D. True. "Bilingual parents may use a specific language to express an emotional concept because they feel that language provides a better cultural context for expressing the emotion."

98. D

A. Cannot say. There is no information that an advertising campaign making this comparison was "the key to Penguin's success".

B. False. "When Woolworth's placed an order for 63,500 copies, Lane first realised he had a viable financial model."

C. Cannot say. While the passage states that when Woolworth's placed an order for 63,500 books Lane realised he had a viable financial model, there is no statement that Penguin would never have succeeded without it.

D. True. The passage states each of these facts about the founding of Penguin.

99. C

A. Cannot say. While the passage tells us that "it was on one such trip…that Mother Teresa first felt a calling to a religious life," there is no information to allow us to conclude whether or not she might have felt such a calling on another occasion.

B. False. The passage states that she took the name of Sister Mary Teresa while in Ireland, a year before she travelled to Darjeeling.

C. True. The passage clearly states these facts about Mother Teresa's life.

D. Cannot say. While the passage states that Agnes Bojaxhiu felt a religious calling and then travelled to Darjeeling and Calcutta, there is no mention of whether she ever left India again.

100. B

A. Cannot say. While the passage tells us that the law of fratricide was applied "in order to reduce the risk of subsequent rebellion and civil war," there is no information as to whether *chaos and coups would have reigned* without the law.

B. True. All these facts are given in the text.

C. Cannot say. We are told that "Mehmed's law resulted in the deaths of at least 80 members of the House of Osman over a period of 150 years." While it may seem quite likely that the murder of all 19 siblings of Sultan Mehmed III, nearly one-quarter of the 150-year total, was therefore the most appalling incident, no information in the text confirms or negates that conclusion.

D. False. The passage states that the new ruler was "enjoined to murder all his *brothers*, together with any inconvenient *uncles and cousins*", i.e. not *all* family members.

101. D

A. False. The passage clearly states that it is the other way round: "identical twins…share virtually the same genetic code. Any differences between them…must be due to environmental factors".

B. Cannot say. While the passage states that "twins offer a precious opportunity to untangle the influence of genes and the environment – of nature and nurture," no information is given as to whether or not "we are *equally influenced* by our genetics and our environment".

C. Cannot say. While the passage states that "if identical twins are more similar to each other with respect to an ailment than fraternal twins are, then vulnerability to the disease must be rooted at least in part in heredity", whether the cause of a disease is necessarily hereditary if one fraternal twin suffers from it while the other twin does not is not discussed.

D. True. The passage states that "identical twins come from a single fertilised egg that splits in two, they share *virtually* the same genetic code" while fraternal twins "come from separate eggs and share *on average* half their DNA".

102. A

A. True. The passage tells us exactly that.

B. Cannot say. The passage refers to work within Africa but makes no mention of how this will be achieved.

C. Cannot say. The passage tells us that "economic growth and urbanisation go hand in hand and are critical to poverty reduction" but not whether urban growth itself is the primary driver.

D. False. Cities provide the work and living environment for most people in high income countries.

103. C

A. False. The passage clearly states that Internet-enabled power outlets do not *automatically* optimise and reduce the use of electricity, but "will soon allow users to control household appliances via their smartphones".

B. Cannot say. No information is given as to the likely take-up of the HexaBus home automation system.

C. True. All this information is in the text.

D. Cannot say. While the passage tells us that the technology will enable homeowners to reduce their energy costs, whether energy consumption will *in fact* drop is not discussed.

104. C

A. False. It is the other way round: "muscle cells go on the outside, urothelial cells (which line the urinary tract) on the inside".

B. Cannot say. Collagen cells are used, but there is no information as to where they come from.

C. True. The passage clearly states that the process involves all these elements.

D. Cannot say. We are told that the entire process of making a bioartificial bladder takes six to eight weeks, but not the length of time that the bladder cells are on the scaffold.

105. B

A. False. "Emerging evidence now also suggests that this brain area can be trained using a meditation technique called mindfulness."

B. True. The passage states: "an athlete possesses a hyper-attuned insula that can generate strikingly accurate predictions of how the body will feel in the next moment."

C. Cannot say. While sprinters, boxers and divers are mentioned in the text, it is not stated whether they will gain more benefit than other athletes.

D. Cannot say. The question of the relative size of boxers' and athletes' cortexes is not discussed.

106. A

A. True. The passage states that at the 2008 Loebner Prize competition the top chatbot fooled 3 of the 12 judges.

B. Cannot say. While the passage states that a lack of long-term coherence is one way that chatbots "betray themselves," there is no information as to whether this is the most frequent way.

C. False. The closest so far was at the 2008 Loebner Prize competition when the top chatbot fooled 3 of 12 judges.

D. Cannot say from the information contained in the passage. While they do not yet have this ability, there is no information as to whether they will in the future.

107. D

A. False. The passage states that researchers found that "those who had engaged in REM sleep subsequently performed better in pattern recognition tasks, such as grammar, while *those who slept deeply* were better at memorisation".

B. Cannot say. While the passage states that "researchers have found that the sleeping brain appears to repeat a pattern of neuron firing that occurred while the subject was recently awake, as if in sleep the brain were trying to commit to long-term memory what it had learned that day," it does not say whether such neuron firing occurs *during REM sleep.*

C. Cannot say. While the weeding out of redundant or unnecessary synapses is referred to, there is no reference to a connection with recognition of patterns.

D. True. The passage states that researchers "found that those who had engaged in REM sleep subsequently performed better in pattern recognition tasks, such as grammar, while those who slept deeply were better at memorisation".

108. D

A. Cannot say. While the passage states that Bingo Friendzy "has prompted anger from Christian groups", there is no reference to whether the groups believe that children should not be exposed to the sin of gambling.

B. False. "Facebook will take 30 per cent of revenues from Bingo Friendzy".

C. Cannot say. While the passage states that the shares "have almost halved in value amid concerns about Facebook's effectiveness as an advertising medium", whether they lost half their value *primarily* because investors do not have faith in the company as an advertising medium is not given.

D. True. All these facts are given in the text.

109. B

A. Cannot say. We are told El Niño is periodic, but not how often it happens.

B. True. All this information is given in the text.

C. Cannot say. We are told only that 4.5 million are in need of food aid in Ethiopia because of a scarcity of rain, not whether this followed floods as occurred in Malawi.

D. False. There are different consequences for different countries: South America experiences heavy rainfall, whereas drought-like conditions are experienced in Australia, south-east Asia and southern Africa.

110. B

A. Cannot say. While the passage states that "in time" the word "apostle" was applied to others besides the original 12, the exact timescale is not given.

B. True. The passage clearly states these facts.

C. Cannot say. The views of conservative Christians on this matter are not mentioned in the text.

D. False. The passage clearly states that Matthias was one of the twelve apostles, replacing the former disciple and alleged traitor, Judas Iscariot.

111. B

A. False. The passage clearly states that Hals used flamboyant brushwork and that his paintings conveyed "a sense of intense realism" rather than his impressions.

B. True. The passage states: "Hals made two great contributions. One was to combine an intense sense of realism with flamboyant brushwork... Hals' other contribution is to fill his paintings with evident psychological intensity, the quality known as 'psychological insight'."

C. Cannot say. While "Hals's portraits document the emergence of the modern self", there is no reference to whether this was intentional.

D. Cannot say. There is no information as to whether Hals attended performances of Shakespeare's plays or was influenced by them.

112. C

A. Cannot say. While the passage states that genetic analysis shows that North Africa's Jews "form two distinct groups, one of which is more closely related than the other to their European counterparts", and "the findings are the latest in a series of genetic studies... indicating that the world's Jews share biological roots", whether the ancestors of North African Jews share biological roots with at least *two other* groups is not given.

B. Cannot say. While the Jewish populations of North Africa "mostly married within their own religious and cultural group", whether this was a result of forced segregation is not mentioned.

C. True. The passage states that "the Jewish populations of North Africa became genetically distinct over time, with those of each country carrying their own DNA signatures".

D. False. "The findings are the latest in a series of genetic studies, which began in the 1990s, indicating that the world's Jews share biological roots, not just cultural and religious ties."

113. C

A. False. The quarries were "mostly in the *southern* part".

B. Cannot say. While the passage tells us that "crypts and bank vaults, wine cellars transformed into nightclubs and galleries" are located underneath Paris, whether *anyone is welcome to visit* them is not stated.

C. True. All these features are mentioned in the text.

D. Cannot say. While the passage states that farmers raised mushrooms beneath Paris, "at one point producing hundreds of tons a year", no comparison is made with the quantity produced above ground.

114. B

A. False. "*Flies and beetles* are the original pollinators, going back to when flowering plants first appeared 130 million years ago."

B. True. These facts are all stated in the text.

C. Cannot say. While the passage tells us that "bats, with diverse muzzles and tongues adapted to tap differently shaped blossoms" it also states that "flowering plants…have evolved in step with their pollinators," and whether the plants have evolved to match the bats or vice versa is not indicated.

D. Cannot say. While the passage states that mosquitos carry pollen for orchids, there is no information as to whether *only* the mosquito can do this.

115. C

A. Cannot say. The passage tells us that plastic pollution can enter the food chain, but not whether humans have consumed the Bio-Beads.

B. Cannot say. While we are told that Bio-Beads can cause digestive blockages and poison marine animals, we do not know if they suffocate as a result.

C. True. We are told that it is sewage plants that are leaking Bio-Beads into the ocean but not whether this has been deliberate or accidental, so it could be either.

D. Cannot say. There is no information in the text as to whether this is true or not.

116. D

A. Cannot say. There is no reference to the topic of providing insight into the history of the Persian Empire.

B. False. The passage clearly states that *The Persians* is told from the *Persian* perspective.

C. Cannot say. While the passage may seem to *imply* such an interpretation ("Consider the plot: a superpower's inexperienced, hubristic leader – who hopes to conquer a minor enemy his father tried unsuccessfully to fell a decade earlier – charges into a doomed military invasion"), whether the play is popular with contemporary audiences specifically *because it proves that history repeats itself* is not said.

D. True. All this information is given in the text.

117. D

A. False. The passage clearly mentions *three* phases in the construction of Stonehenge.

B. Cannot say. While the passage states that "immense effort" was involved in moving the bluestones, there is no information as to whether only manpower was used in this task.

C. False. The passage clearly states that archaeologists believe the bluestones were added two centuries after about 2800 BC.

D. True. These facts are all given in the text.

118. C

A. False. The study found the opposite: "the less monitoring parents did, the more the children played videogames."

B. Cannot say. While the study "found that the more children perceived their parents' behaviour as negative…the more the children played videogames", it is not stated which of these is *cause* and which is *effect*.

C. True. The passage clearly states that the more children perceived their parents as nagging them, the more the children played videogames.

D. Cannot say. The study shows that children who play a lot of videogames are more likely to *perceive* their parents as behaving negatively, but whether the parents are *actually* behaving negatively is not discussed.

119. C

A. False. The passage states: "It's not until the emergence of *H. erectus* 1.89 million years ago that hominids grew tall, evolved long legs and became completely terrestrial creatures."

B. Cannot say. While the passage states that "although the earliest hominids were capable of upright walking, they retained primitive features...that indicate they spent time in trees", there is no information as to whether the hominid species was *better at climbing trees* or *fossils of Neanderthals* suggest this to be the case.

C. True. The passage states: "Although the earliest hominids were capable of upright walking, they retained primitive features – such as long, curved fingers and toes as well as longer arms and shorter legs – that indicate they spent time in trees."

D. Cannot say. While the passage states that "the earliest hominid with the most extensive evidence for bipedalism is the 4.4-million-year-old *Ardipithecus ramidus*", there is no information whether hominid species developed bigger brains just after this.

120. A

A. True. The passage states: "land mines are unlike bullets and bombs in two distinct ways. First, they are designed to maim rather than kill."

B. Cannot say. While the passage tells us that "only 25 per cent of land mine victims around the world are soldiers. The rest are civilians", whether the same proportion holds true for Cambodia between 1975 and 1979 is not given.

C. False. The passage states that Pol Pot called land mines his "perfect soldiers".

D. Cannot say. There is no information given on the relative success of the different types of weapons.

121. C

A. Cannot say. While we are told that "math anxiety leads to poor math performance", there is no information on the relationship between anxiety levels and ability to solve problems creatively.

B. False: studies indicate "too much focus may actually impair creative problem solving".

C. True. The passage states that "working memory capacity seems to help analytical problem-solvers focus their attention and resist distraction."

D. Cannot say. While the passage states that "our working memory capacity is decidedly finite", there is no statement as to whether our ability to find creative solutions is unlimited.

122. C

A. False. The passage clearly states that data leakage and the introduction of viruses or other malware into workplace computing systems are among other risks faced.

B. Cannot say. While the passage tells us that "The portability, connectivity, and storage capacity of mobile devices means they bring with them the threat of data leakage, data theft...", there is no information as to whether the threat of data leakage and data theft was *minimal* before the appearance of such devices.

C. True. The passage clearly states that mobile devices "bring with them the threat of data leakage, data theft, and the introduction of viruses or other malware".

D. Cannot say. While the availability of mobile devices with large storage capacity is linked to "the ability to capture vast quantities of data, whether for legitimate work purposes or for illicit use", no link is mentioned between storage capacity and the risk of malware attacks.

123. B

A. Cannot say. While the passage states: "European countries today are at loggerheads not despite the common currency but precisely because of it", whether sharing a common currency is the *main and only factor* contributing to their quarrels cannot be concluded.

B. True. The passage states: "A recent letter signed by 160 German economists claiming that the European Union's plan for a banking union was little more than an attempt to make Germany pay for Spanish mistakes."

C. False. The representatives were "unable to overcome their differences."

D. Cannot say. While the passage highlights the economic conflict between northern and southern Europe and mentions Martin Feldstein's prediction that "monetary union would create conflict within Europe", whether the common currency in Europe is a source of trouble because of *inherent inequalities between north and south* is not said.

124. D

A. Cannot say. While the passage tells us that "Gaudí based his buildings on a simple premise: If nature is the work of God, and if architectural forms are derived from nature, then the best way to honour God is to *design buildings based on his work*", whether or not the design of the Sagrada Família is intended to *bring nature into the church* is not given.

B. Cannot say. While Gaudí's "belief in the beautiful efficiency of natural engineering clearly anticipated the modern science of biomimetics", whether his Sagrada Família directly influenced the field is not said.

C. Cannot say. While the passage states that Gaudí "understood that the natural world is rife with curved forms, not straight lines. And he noticed that natural construction tends to favour sinewy materials such as wood, muscle, and tendon", whether the Sagrada Família itself incorporates wood, rounded lines, and sinewy effects is not stated.

D. True. The passage states that Gaudí's Sagrada Família was inspired by his religious faith and mentions his "belief in the beautiful efficiency of natural engineering".

125. B

A. Cannot say. We are told that bronze sculptures from *one particular era* are rare because they were often melted down to make swords, shields and other items, but we do not know if bronze sculptures from *other eras* are highly unusual.

B. True. The passage says that "if the team can salvage the submerged statues, it would be a remarkable recovery", meaning that it isn't known if all bronze sculptures can be retrieved from the shipwreck.

C. False. The phrase "from this most recent excavation" tells us there have been other excavations.

D. Cannot say. We are not told when it was excavated.

126. C

A. Cannot say. While the passage states that "manufacturers see [triclosan] as a marketing bonus, increasing consumer confidence that a particular product kills harmful bacteria", whether consumers are more confident in a product's antibacterial qualities when triclosan is *listed as an ingredient* is not stated.

B. Cannot say. The text mentions studies showing that "the chemical can disrupt the endocrine systems of several different animals", but there is no mention of such an effect in people.

C. True. The passage clearly states each of these facts.

D. False. The passage tells us that the reason triclosan was developed in the 1960s was to help *prevent* bacterial infections in hospitals.

127. C

A. False. The passage states that MALDI-MSI technology is especially useful "if the suspect's fingermark is not on the police database".

B. Cannot say. While the passage tells us that MALDI-MSI can provide "key extra details about suspects", whether it *does not yield the information conventional fingermark processing does* is not stated.

C. True. The passage tells us that MALDI-MSI technology "is a step closer to being incorporated into traditional forensic investigations", therefore it *may* sooner or later be part of criminal investigations.

D. Cannot say. While the technology "can provide extra information on a suspect" and "important background information in a criminal investigation", whether it can provide the *necessary details and background information to convict a criminal suspect* is not stated in the text.

128. D

A. False. International travel exceeded 1.1 billion overnight visitors *in 2014 alone* according to the World Tourism Organisation.

B. Cannot say. There is nothing in the passage about how many people have made use of the app.

C. Cannot say. We are not told whether or not it is free.

D. True. All this information is in the text.

129. B

A. Cannot say. While archaeologists found "a figurine of solid greenstone, perhaps a war goddess to whom the burial was dedicated", whether the pyramid and/or the burials were in fact intended to appease a war goddess is not given.

B. True. The passage clearly states these facts about the Pyramid of the Moon.

C. False. An additional purpose was "to control the people...to convince them to do what their rulers wanted".

D. Cannot say. While a case of burial alive is mentioned and human sacrifice was used to "control the people", it is not stated whether all the victims were buried alive for that purpose.

130. B

A. False. While the passage states that eels are catadromous – or "have a life history known as catadromy" – it also explains that this means they spawn in the ocean and spend their adulthood in fresh water.

B. True. The passage clearly states these facts about eels.

C. False. "Eels may spend decades in rivers before returning to the ocean to spawn, after which they die."

D. Cannot say. While "female eels are found upstream in river systems, while males stay in the estuaries", whether this is *fundamental* to how the fish spawn is not stated.

131. C

A. False. The passage clearly states that the machine used both water and steam.

B. Cannot say. No information is provided about how many machines he produced.

C. True. The passage clearly states these facts.

D. Cannot say. While the passage tells us that Moriondo was granted a patent for a machine that used steam to brew coffee, it also says that "there were surely innumerable patents and prototypes" for such a machine, and whether his was the first is not stated.

132. C

A. False. "Still images showed little difference... but video analysis showed that the progression of the two kinds of smiles was quite different."

B. Cannot say. The passage refers to the possibility of computers "that better assess the emotional states of their users and respond accordingly" but there is no reference to the topic of computers being able to provide *individualised help*.

C. True. The passage states that "when presented with a task that caused genuine frustration...90 per cent... did smile" and that "frustrated smiles appeared quickly but faded fast".

D. Cannot say. There is no reference to this topic in the text.

133. A

A. True. All these aspects are mentioned in the text.

B. Cannot say. While we are told that Huntley & Palmers' tins came in all sizes and shapes and with a variety of decorations, there is no reference to whether their tins all bore the same branding.

C. False. The passage states that biscuit tins were not invented until a few hundred years after biscuits became "the food of choice for European voyagers starting in the 1500s".

D. Cannot say. While the elaborately decorated tins "served a Victorian middle class eager to show good taste", there is no information as to whether it was the tins inspired by impressionist art that were the *most* favoured.

134. B

A. Cannot say from the information. While the passage states that the Milky Way "is so huge that dozens of lesser galaxies scamper about it, like moons orbiting a giant planet", there is no information as to whether observation of these galaxies has helped scientists learn about the Milky Way.

B. True. The passage clearly states that the Milky Way's dark matter "far outweighs the Milky Way's hundreds of billions of stars" and that it cannot be detected by telescopes.

C. False: surrounding both stars and hydrogen is "an enormous halo of dark matter".

D. Cannot say. While the passage states that the dark matter of our galaxy "far outweighs the Milky Way's hundreds of billions of stars, giving the galaxy a total mass one to two trillion times that of the sun", whether scientists know the mass of our galaxy's dark matter by calculating the mass of its stars is not said.

135. A

A. True. The following are given as requirements for whiskey to be named Empire Rye: (1) it uses grain from New York State (2) it is aged for at least two years and (3) "other things", which means that there are in total at least 4 requirements.

B. False. The passage tells us that "other things" are also required.

C. Cannot say. We are not told whether the method of making whiskey differs between Empire Rye, bourbon and Tennessee whiskey, only that they are distinguished by their "regional pedigree".

D. Cannot say. We do not know the intentions of distilleries other than the nine referred to in the text.

136. D

A. Cannot say. While the passage states that a virus "invades a host cell and co-opts the cell's own machinery to make copies of itself – thousands of copies at once, which means thousands of chances to mutate and develop drug resistance" and that disabling this process requires "finding the right target – a gene, and the protein it encodes", we are not told whether viruses resist drugs by *switching which proteins in the host cell they use to reproduce themselves.*

B. False. Regarding the search for a drug that disables part of the human cell to destroy a virus, the passage states that "the key is finding the right target – *a gene,* and the protein it encodes, *that the human cell doesn't need but the virus does*".

C. Cannot say. While the passage states that "bacteria are organisms that are equipped to reproduce themselves; antibiotics attack that machinery", whether antibiotics work specifically by causing fatal mutations by scrambling the reproductive mechanism of the bacteria is not stated.

D. True. "Human DNA contains more than 20,000 genes, but in any given cell at any given time, many are dormant" and a virus "co-opts the cell's own machinery."

137. A

A. True. This is as stated in the text.

B. Cannot say. While we are told Privitar has developed a "de-identification tool" to obscure personal data within large data sets, we have no information as to whether this is effective in preventing data breaches that could result in fines.

C. Cannot say. According to Jason du Preez, the EU's General Data Protection Regulation had "raised awareness", but the passage does not indicate whether it has made the topic easier or more difficult to understand.

D. False. The passage states the opposite.

138. C

A. Cannot say. While "in those classrooms where computers were used to support teaching, the technology was found to have a small to moderate positive impact on both learning and attitude", no impact on "critical thinking skills" is mentioned.

B. Cannot say. Although research suggests "a standard PowerPoint presentation will most likely not enhance the learning experience beyond providing content or enhancing teacher-directed lectures or class discussions", whether a student's learning is enhanced by *creating and giving* a PowerPoint presentation *on their own* is not discussed.

C. True: "in those classrooms where computers were used to support teaching, the technology was found to have a small to moderate positive impact on both learning and attitude".

D. Cannot say. There is no reference in the text to the influence on students' social lives.

139. C

A. False. "Different languages highlight the varieties of human experience, revealing as mutable aspects of life that we tend to think of as settled and universal, such as our experience of time, number, or colour."

B. Cannot say. No information is provided either way on this topic.

C. True. The passage states that "Noam Chomsky theorised that all languages were built on an underlying universal grammar embedded in human genes," whereas "field linguists are more interested in the idiosyncrasies that make each language unique."

D. False. The passage explains that in this language "the past is always spoken of as ahead of one, and the future is behind one's back".

140. A

A. True. "The technical feasibility of gene therapy 'has been established in multiple diseases and with different technology platforms,' says Dr. Wilson."

B. Cannot say. We are given Dr. Wilson's prediction to this effect, but no information as to whether he has been proved correct.

C. Cannot say. While we are told these diseases represent a $6.5 billion market for current protein replacement therapies, whether gene therapy would cost more or less is not stated.

D. False. The passage states that "gene therapy for hemophilia B is still in early-stage clinical testing".

141. B

A. False. The passage states that "the Office for National Statistics (ONS) put the surprise jump in inflation down to lower discounting by clothing and footwear retailers and an unusual spike in air fares".

B. True. The passage states: "People aged between 30 and 64 had the lowest inflation rate, of 2.5pc – due largely to slower petrol inflation."

C. Cannot say. While we are told that "lower discounting by clothing and footwear retailers" was a factor in the increase in inflation, we are not given any information on the comparative effect of this on poorer families.

D. Cannot say. There is reference to the "outgoings" of pensioners aged 75 and over but not to their sources of income.

142. B

A. Cannot say. While the passage tells us that Thucydides "was the first person to document the connection between earthquakes and tsunamis", there is no information as to whether earthquakes are or are not the *only* cause of tsunamis.

B. True. The passage states that Thucydides "noticed that the first sign of a tsunami is often the abrupt draining of a harbour".

C. Cannot say. While a tsunami "sent Minoan civilization…into a tailspin, leading it to succumb to Mycenaean Greeks", whether or not this might have happened anyway cannot be concluded from the text.

D. False. The passage clearly states that in 1755 an earthquake *and tsunami* killed many thousands of people in Lisbon.

143. D

A. Cannot say. There is no information on what toothed whales did before developing this ability.

B. Cannot say. The passage states that "whales' buzz rates are nearly identical to that of bats, at about 500 calls or clicks per second", but also that both whales and bats have variable click rates, which increase while hunting – so whether 500 is the *maximum* number they can process cannot be concluded.

C. False. The passage states that bats and toothed whales both rely on the same range of ultrasonic frequencies, between 15 to 200 kilohertz, to hunt.

D. True. These facts are clearly stated in the passage.

144. D

A. False. "*For some*, being informed of a pill or procedure's potential side effects is enough to bring on real-life symptoms."

B. False: researchers concluded it "ought to be taken into consideration by medical professionals on an everyday basis."

C. Cannot say. The review "examined the underlying biological mechanisms" but whether it indicates that the phenomenon has *several identifiable biological causes* is not stated.

D. True. The passage explains: "The nocebo effect is the phenomenon in which inert substances or mere suggestions of substances actually bring about *negative* effects in a patient or research participant."

145. B

A. Cannot say. While the passage refers to the study being "a grim reminder after the euphoria of the Olympics of the challenges we face and those that lie ahead", no connection is discussed between the staging of the Olympics and the number of suicides.

B. True. "A painful British economic recession and rising unemployment may have driven more than 1,000 people in England to commit suicide…between 2008 and 2010 there were 846 more suicides among men in England than would have been expected if previous trends continued, and 155 more among women."

C. Cannot say. There is no information on the ratio of male to female suicides.

D. Cannot say. While the passage states that "a painful British economic recession and rising unemployment *may* have driven more than 1,000 people in England to commit suicide" and that the trend "reflects findings elsewhere in Europe where suicides are also on the rise", there is no information to conclude whether rising unemployment rates and economic decline are a *direct* cause of suicides.

146. B

A. Cannot say. While the passage states that "by 2050 a third of Europe's population will be over 60 years of age", there is no statement of what proportion of Europe's population will be using welfare technology.

B. True. "The aim [of welfare technology] is to enhance the quality of life of elderly people who want to live at home as long as possible."

C. False. The passage clearly states that "technology must not replace personal care and human warmth".

D. Cannot say. While oven reminders and fall alarms are cited as examples of technology "to enhance the quality of life of elderly people who want to live at home as long as possible", whether they will enhance the quality of life for *all* elderly people is not discussed.

147. A

A. True. This information is clearly given in the text.

B. Cannot say. While "companionship" is mentioned as one of the reasons why humans began to employ dogs, there is no information as to whether domesticated dogs are the *evolutionary consequence* of a human need for companionship.

C. False: breeders "favoured novelty, since the more distinct a line of dogs appeared, the more likely it was to garner official recognition as a new breed".

D. False. "Sheltered from the survival-of-the-fittest wilderness, those semi-domesticated dogs thrived…"

148. B

A. False. "During the Mao era, Soviet-inspired 'socialist realism' was the only acceptable style in the strictly controlled authoritarian society."

B. True. All these groups are referred to in the text as examples of how "periods of religious and political repression have provoked an exodus of creative and entrepreneurial talent".

C. Cannot say. There is reference to the impact of Deng Xiaoping's economic reforms on Chinese art and access of Chinese artists to international news and scholarship, but no information as to whether his reforms prevented many talented artists from leaving China.

D. Cannot say. The topic is not discussed in the text.

149. B

A. Cannot say. We are told that "British working families at the start of the 19th century were enduring economic upheaval," but there is no reference to the circumstances of the upper classes.

B. True. All this information is given in the text.

C. Cannot say. While the passage states that "Parliament passed a measure to make machine-breaking a capital offence", there is no information as to whether the protests *ceased for the most part.*

D. False. "British troops broke up a crowd of protesters demanding *more work and better wages.* That night, angry workers smashed textile machinery in a nearby village."

150. D

A. Cannot say. While Bernini "undertook commissions for eight popes", there is nothing in the text to suggest whether he might or might not have otherwise died an unknown artist.

B. Cannot say. While the passage tells us that "Behind every Bernini masterpiece there lies a *concetto*, its governing concept or conceit", nothing is said about whether Bernini thoroughly explored a *concetto* through *painting* before translating it to a sculpture or building.

C. False. The passage clearly states that Bernini's work transformed the look of 17th century Rome, not Florence.

D. True. "Bernini was said to have been only 8 when he carved a stone head that 'was the marvel of everyone' who saw it" and "much of the Baroque grandeur of the Eternal City – its churches, fountains, piazzas and monuments – can be credited to Bernini and his followers".

151. A

A. True. "'Despite its *long-term value*, securitization today *suffers from stigma*, reflecting both its adverse reputation amongst investors and conservatism among regulators,' the central banks said."

B. Cannot say. The passage only says that the ECB has argued that regulation should take into account European securitization instruments performing better than their U.S. counterparts. We cannot say what "performing better" means or if this has anything to do with fluctuations in price.

C. Cannot say. The passage states that securitization became a "bad word" during the financial crisis, when it was largely blamed for reckless lending decisions by banks. We cannot say for certain, however, that securitization was the *major cause* of the financial crisis given the information in the passage, nor that this is the belief of the central banks.

D. False. On the contrary, the text tells us that "The European Central Bank (ECB) and the Bank of England (BOE) said they are concerned about the 'shrinking' market for asset backed securities, which are bundles of loans that are packaged and sold to investors."

152. A

A. True. This information is all in the text.

B. Cannot say. We know that Kimbal Musk believes this but there is no indication of what the Silicon Valley crowd believe.

C. Cannot say. The text says that the food space is as "exciting" to Kimbal Musk as the internet was in 1995, but we don't know if it will "most likely be as revolutionary".

D. Cannot say. We are told that he would like the US to be a country based on healthy, local food grown on chemical-free farms, but not that his aim is having only farms that are chemical-free.

153. B

A. False. The passage says the opposite: Mars is now "frigid and dry" but in the past had been "warm and wet".

B. True. The passage states that floods have occurred on Mars because of "occasional warm spells" and not because of a "consistently hospitable phase".

C. Cannot say. The text says that signs of flowing water on Mars include rugged canyons and lowlands "apparently" sculpted by massive floods but this is not given as a certain fact.

D. Cannot say. The passage tells us only that "Mars' atmosphere was *probably* never thick enough to keep temperatures on the planet's surface above freezing for the long term", but that is not given as a certainty, and we are not told how frequent any above-freezing periods may have been.

154. D

A. Cannot say. The passage tells us that *ever since* the first metal workers dug copper from a Cyprus hillside and fashioned it into tools, copper has been in high demand. It does not refer to whether there was a copper market *before* that point and what its scale was: it is possible there was a market for copper for purposes other than making tools – we are not told.

B. False. It is true according to the passage that copper is the only catalyst that can mix carbon monoxide with water to produce fuel. However, the passage also states that the traditional copper-catalysed conversion of carbon dioxide to liquid fuel proceeds through an intermediate of carbon monoxide and that many catalysts can perform this first step, the opposite of the statement.

C. Cannot say. Researchers raised the prospect that international copper production could "peak within a few decades" but the timescale for that is indefinite and could be more or less than 25 years.

D. True. "A recent discovery describes improvements to copper as a catalyst that could streamline ethanol production."

155. D

A. Cannot say. The passage states that IceCube *reported* the discovery of Ernie and Bert last year but not when they were actually discovered.

B. Cannot say. The passage only tells us that Ernie, Bert, and Big Bird are "three of the highest-energy neutrinos ever found", but makes no reference to their likely ranking in the universe as a whole.

C. False. The passage states that neutrinos "rarely ever" – as opposed to *never* – interact with other particles because they are "extremely standoffish".

D. True. The passage asserts that neutrinos could emanate from "galaxies forming stars at furious rates" and the particles found by IceCube were neutrinos.

156. C

A. Cannot say. We are told only that cemeteries may not be "top of mind" for tourists, not that they are "one of the least popular places for tourists to visit".

B. Cannot say. Loren Rhoads has said that "we've learned a lot" about the Greeks from their tombs, but we do not know whether our understanding has been "significantly influenced by recent research".

C. True. Loren Rhoads says exactly that.

D. Cannot say. The passage says that visiting your local cemetery can reveal the families who lent their names to the streets and neighbourhoods in your town, but we are not told if *most* streets and neighbourhoods are named this way.

157. A

A. True. It has been "the most intensely observed astronomical event to date".

B. Cannot say. The collision of the neutron stars was observed by the Laser Interferometer Gravitational-Wave Observatory; the stars "in all likelihood" collapsed into a black hole, so we cannot be certain this was observeD.

C. Cannot say. Einstein first predicted the existence of gravitational waves a century ago, but we do not know if he predicted the event of the collision of a pair of neutron stars.

D. False. The passage says that this event has resolved a decades-old debate about where gold and platinum come from, meaning not that we are "now even closer" to finding out, but that we definitely know.

158. C

A. Cannot say. The passage tells us that infections occur in about 9% of Australian brush turkey eggs, but it does not say whether this percentage is more or less than for other related bird species.

B. Cannot say. We are told that egg whites have an enzyme called lysozyme that is antimicrobial but there is no reference to chemicals in the yolks.

C. True. All this information is in the text.

D. False. The passage states that the heat generated as microbes in the soil decompose organic matter is actually helpful for the eggs, keeping them warm for incubation.

159. C

A. False. One of the potential southern hemisphere locations is in Chile, which is not included on the 12-member selection committee.

B. Cannot say. The passage does not refer to the size of the economies of the countries on the panel nor does it say why the members met in Germany.

C. True. There are two potential southern hemisphere sites, in Namibia and Chile, with a reserve in Argentina, making three countries, whereas there are four potential northern hemisphere sites, in Mexico, Spain and the United States, i.e. also three countries.

D. Cannot say. The text tells us that the site for the southern hemisphere detector will be larger than the northern one but it does not say how the project's money will be allocated between the two sites. Other factors than the size of the sites could affect the costs.

160. B

A. Cannot say. The passage tells us that Lafarge and Holcim "plan to put $8 billion of assets around the world up for sale in a bid to secure antitrust clearance for their merger", but we cannot say for sure whether their plan will work. Their merger may not be cleared even if they sell $8 billion of assets.

B. True. Holcim is based in Switzerland and Holcim executives are expected in Paris, France to announce the merger. Lafarge, the company Holcim is merging with, is based in France.

C. False. The text tells us that "it's not clear what production facilities or other assets the two companies will propose to part with as part of their agreement".

D. Cannot say. The actions the companies are taking are in response to the "likely" regulatory hurdles facing their merger. However, the passage does not explicitly say that any regulators are actually interested in the merger.

161. D

A. False. "The Cochrane Collaboration ... has been arguing its case... *initially* on the basis of a previous analysis of the *limited published data available*", whereas the non-profit group reported "after analysing the results of *previously unpublished clinical trials*" – the exact opposite of the statement.

B. Cannot say. It is only the opinion of some other scientists that the review by the Cochrane Collaboration did not make a strong case to stop stockpiling. We cannot say for certain that the group's evaluation produced insufficient evidence to alter antiviral policy.

C. Cannot say. We are told that governments have spent billions of dollars stockpiling antiviral drugs, but not how much of that was spent on Tamiflu.

D. True. It is stated that the Cochrane Collaboration "has been arguing its case against the efficacy of the antiviral Tamiflu ... for more than four years, initially on the basis of a previous analysis of the limited published data available."

162. A

A. True. The passage clearly states that the waves showed very little decay in energy on their journey across the Pacific

B. Cannot say. The text states that the experiment yielded a "surprising discovery", but we do not know whether it had been hypothesised previously.

C. False. The opposite is true: long-period waves move quickly, short-period waves move slowly. As the passage tells us that the period increases as waves move northwards, it can be inferred that ocean waves slow down as they move northwards.

D. False. Waves travel in a great circle from New Zealand to Alaska, not in a continuous straight line.

163. C

A. Cannot say. We are told that 25 percent of German energy is derived from renewable sources but not whether there are other renewable sources than solar and wind power.

B. Cannot say. The passage makes no mention of a statement by Angela Merkel on this subject.

C. True. The passage gives all this information.

D. False. Sigmar Gabriel says that it is an "illusion" that "energy transformation can be achieved by expanding renewable energy as quickly as possible"; instead, he says that Germany should make sure that the expansion is "safe and predictable".

164. D

A. Cannot say. Although the text tells us that Belovezhskaya National Park contains ancient trees, including some that are 600 years old, it does not say whether they are the oldest trees in Europe. Furthermore, it is *Białowieski* National Park which was founded in 1932, while the date of founding of *Belovezhskay*a National Park is not given.

B. Cannot say. The passage tells us that Białowieski National Park is Poland's oldest and *"one of the first* in Europe" but not whether it was *the* first.

C. False. It is true that Belovezhskaya National Park protects only about 10 percent of the Białowieża Primeval Forest, but that forest's name is not the same as Poland's park, Białowieski National Park.

D. True. All this information is given in the text.

165. B

A. Cannot say. While Enric Sala "believes" that the Mediterranean Sea will be reduced to "a soup of microbes and jellyfish" without radical changes to fishing practices, we cannot say for certain that this will be the outcome given the information in the passage.

B. True. The passage states that Sala was only one of the authors of the study, which was itself called "Large-Scale Assessment of *Mediterranean Marine Protected Areas* Effects on Fish Assemblages".

C. Cannot say. The study drew on the work of a dozen researchers but we cannot say for certain whether they all share Sala's opinion that overfishing is the most important threat to

Mediterranean marine ecosystems, more than pollution, invasive species, or climate change.

D. False. Sala published the results of his study this week but in the science journal PLoS ONE.

166. B

A. Cannot say. The passage tells us that avalanches occur when a weak layer in the snowpack fractures under pressure from pileups of snow but not when these layers were formed. They could have originated in the current or previous winters.

B. True. The passage tells us that avalanches are most common "*during*, and in the 24 hours right after, a storm" and "can reach speeds of 80 miles (130 kilometers) per hour within about five seconds".

C. Cannot say. While the passage tells us that bigger avalanches cause more death and destruction than small ones, it does not discuss their comparative frequency.

D. False. The text says that disastrous avalanches occur when massive slabs of snow break loose from a mountainside and shatter like broken glass as they race downhill.

167. D

A. Cannot say. The passage does not discuss the approach adopted by the previous superintendent of the site, or indeed whether there was a superintendent before Massimo Osanna.

B. Cannot say. While we are told that Pompeii has been "overrun by tourists, and wracked by the elements in the four centuries since its rediscovery", we are not given such information about Herculaneum.

C. False. There will be "comprehensive maintenance" rather than "piecemeal patches to individual buildings or attractions".

D. True. The passage gives the dollar and euro values for each restoration. Herculaneum was a 20-million-euro ($27.7 million U.S. dollar) effort while the Great Pompeii Project will be a 105-million-euro ($145 million U.S. dollar) project.

168. D

A. Cannot say. Holcim and Lafarge along with six other companies are being investigated by the European Commission but we do not know who the other six are. The passage does not mention HeidelbergCement as being among the group being investigated.

B. False. The passage says that the cement market is "largely" local and that cement is expensive to transport but it also says that Holcim and Lafarge "have expanded in many of the same markets around the world", not just in their home countries.

C. Cannot say. The passage only refers to their *market shares* in the U.S. and in some other countries. There is no reference to the relative contribution to profits.

D. True. This information is clearly stated in the passage.

169. B

A. Cannot say. While we are told that Olympus was believed to the "meeting place of the deities" and that it is Greece's highest mountain, there is no reference to whether the territory of the "Classical world" corresponds to modern Greece or what other mountains there may have been in that territory.

B. True. The passage includes all this information.

C. False. In Dion King Archelaus held nine days, not seven days (a week) of games and these were "to honor the god Zeus", not a Macedonian royal.

D. Cannot say. The passage only tells us that "12 gods were believed to have lived in the alpine ravines", which Homer described as the mountain's "mysterious folds." It does not explicitly state that Homer himself believed the gods resided there.

170. D

A. Cannot say. It is only given as conjecture ("it is said") and not fact that King Arthur fought an epic battle with the king-killing giant Rhita Gawr. Further, the passage never says that Arthur slayed the giant; it only says that he battled with him.

B. False. Snowdonia's highest peak, Snowdon, is known as Yr Wyddfa in Welsh, whereas the park, Snowdonia, is known as Eryri.

C. Cannot say. The passage only says that Snowdonia covers 2,132 square kilometers with nine mountain ranges covering half of the park. These ranges may be fully contained within the park or spread outside its borders, and in total cover over or under 2000 square kilometers.

D. True. We are told that Welsh is the local tongue and that the mountain has two ancient Welsh names, Yr Wyddfa Fawr (the Great Tomb) and Carnedd y Cawr (the Cairn of the Giant), derived from Rhita Gawr's resting place. Rhita Gawr was a "king-killing giant" that fought an epic battle with King Arthur, who is Snowdonia's most legendary inhabitant.

171. C

A. Cannot say. NASA scientist Justin Maki says that "the bright spots are *probably* caused by cosmic rays colliding with the rover's camera or by glinting rocks reflecting the Martian sunlight" – so this is a hypothesis not a definite fact.

B. False. The statement is the opposite of what happened. The camera on Curiosity showed nearly vertical bright smudges emerging from a spot near the horizon in its *right* eye but these did not show up in the camera's left eye.

C. True. All this information is given in the text.

D. Cannot say. Although the passage says that no evidence exists for life on Mars, it does not explicitly state what NASA's stance is on this subject. The text only refers to a NASA scientist's analysis of Curiosity's photos.

172. D

A. Cannot say. The passage only says that divers once found a museum-grade Roman clasp. Although they have found old coins and cutlery, the text does not tell us whether these were Roman in origin.

B. Cannot say. Although there are "keys tossed in the water by couples hoping to affirm the eternal nature of their love", there is no information as to whether most of these keys can open anything.

C. False. The text states that they live on a houseboat.

D. True. This is clearly stated in the passage.

173. A

A. True. All this information is given in the text.

B. Cannot say. The text tells us that agriculture is "a major driver of wildlife extinction" but this is in the context of loss of habitat when land is cleared for farming; it also says that agriculture, through deforestation, is leading to increased levels of carbon dioxide, but it does *not* refer to whether those increased levels are resulting in the death of animal species.

C. Cannot say. The passage only says that agriculture is "among" the greatest contributors, not that it is the greatest contributor, to global warming.

D. False. The statement is the opposite of what is in the text. The passage says that agriculture emits "more greenhouse gases than all our cars, trucks, trains, and airplanes combined".

174. B

A. Cannot say. The passage does not refer to a "Spanish explorer".

B. True. The passage says that La Gomera's Guanche people were possibly North African Berbers. It also tells us that the island of La Gomera is off the northwest coast of Africa; therefore it follows that North Africa lies to the south and east of the island.

C. False. The type of thick laurel forest covering over two-thirds of the park is "now rare in … southern Europe".

D. False. We know from the passage that La Gomera is the only one of the Canary Islands that has not had a volcanic eruption *in the modern era*. However, we can also deduce from the passage that it has experienced volcanic activity at some point in its history as we are told that the landscape is "nurtured by volcanic soils".

175. D

A. Cannot say. The canyon of the Tara River in Montenegro is "home to Europe's deepest gorge at 1,300 meters", but its length is not given.

B. Cannot say. The passage says that people in the nearby village of Zabljak own grazing sheep and cattle that roam the park in the summer, but it does not say if the village is Montenegrin.

C. Cannot say. Although the passage states that waters from the Black Lake travel below the Durmitor massif, and that the Tara River is home to Europe's deepest gorge, it only says that *rivers* flow under the massif, and not whether this includes the Tara.

D. True. All this information can be found in the passage.

176. D

A. Cannot say. Although the passage states that the spread of prosperity across the world is increasing demand for animal derived products, it does not measure the extent of this demand (as less or more) in comparison to other factors responsible for the overall rising food demand, such as population increase.

B. Cannot say. The passage only gives a hypothesis that if trends continue we will have to roughly double the amount of crops we grow, not necessarily double the number of farms, by 2050.

C. Cannot say. The text says only that there is pressure to grow more soybeans to feed cattle, pigs, and chickens – not necessarily humans.

D. True. "The spread of prosperity across the world … is driving an increased demand for meat … boosting pressure to grow more corn and soybeans to feed more cattle… ".

177. A

A. True. The passage says that NASA sees cosmic rays in the images at least once a week because Mars's atmosphere is thinner and doesn't block as much cosmic radiation as Earth's does. The cosmic rays are responsible for creating bright spots in the images.

B. Cannot say. Although "glinting rocks are pretty common on Mars and have been spotted in images sent by several of NASA's Mars rovers to Earth", we are not told if this phenomenon has been observed by other countries' rovers or even if other countries have rovers on Mars.

C. Cannot say. We only know that Mars's atmosphere is thinner and doesn't block as much cosmic radiation as Earth's does. We are not told if Earth's atmosphere blocks cosmic radiation to the extent that it thereby prevents interference with terrestrial cameras.

D. False. Although the scientist says that maybe one percent of the hundreds of weekly images include cosmic ray-induced bright spots, he follows that by saying that they are certainly found once a week.

178. A

A. True. "Most earthquakes occur at fault zones, where tectonic plates—giant rock slabs that make up the Earth's upper layer—collide or slide against each other … Other quakes can occur far from fault zones when plates are stretched or squeezed."

B. Cannot say. The passage says that 80 percent of all the planet's earthquakes occur along the rim of the Pacific Ocean, but there is no reference to where 20 percent of oceanic earthquakes occur.

C. False. The Pacific Ocean's rim gets its name, "Ring of Fire," from all of the volcanic activity that occurs along it, not the frequency of earthquakes.

D. Cannot say. A magnitude rating of 3 to 5 "is considered minor or light", but the passage doesn't explain what "minor" or "light" equates to for this type of event. It says that most earthquakes occur at fault zones and their impacts are "usually gradual and unnoticeable on the surface" – but we are not told whether such earthquakes are less or more than magnitude 3.

179. C

A. Cannot say. The passage never explicitly states that the events in Pompeii and Herculaneum occurred at the same date, only that both towns were buried by Vesuvius in ash.

B. Cannot say. Although "roofing and drains made much of the difference" in Herculaneum's restoration, we cannot conclude that they would do the same in a restoration of Pompeii. Pompeii may have its own unique circumstances and some are given in the passage.

C. True. According to the text three walls have collapsed at Pompeii and *almost* three-quarters of its homes, temples, and streets are exposed to the elements.

D. False. The number of visitors to Herculaneum is not given but the passage explicitly states that Pompeii sees *more than*, not under, two million visitors a year.

180. B

A. Cannot say. While we are told that the increase in imports by Germany "is mostly good news, economists say, especially for countries like Greece and Italy that suffer from very high unemployment", there is no information in the text as to whether the increase has actually produced more jobs in those two countries.

B. True. All these facts are given in the passage.

C. False. The statement is the reverse of the truth. German exports worldwide rose 4.6 percent while German exports to the euro zone increased 3.7 percent.

D. Cannot say. We are not given any figures for Germany's trade with Greece and Italy.

6. Succeeding in Numerical Reasoning Tests

Introduction

It is often said that the difficulty in taking numerical reasoning tests lies not in finding the actual answer to the question but doing it within the limited time available. This observation is correct inasmuch as these tests do not require complex mathematical calculations but rather the ability to:

- **identify data** relevant to answering the question from a larger set of information
- **identify the quickest way** to extract the answer from the relevant data
- discover one or several **possible shortcuts** that will allow us to arrive at the answer quickly
- determine the **level of accuracy** required to select the correct answer, and
- make **quick mental calculations**

In order to be prepared for the above, there are certain aspects of numerical reasoning tests that we must be aware of.

First of all, the "alternative reality" of a numerical reasoning test is different from what we are used to in everyday life – relevant data is not provided in a clean format but is rather hidden among other pieces of information that we may call "noise". Our first task is to always identify what we will need to work with from the information provided and avoid getting bogged down in wondering why other data might also be present.

Secondly, such tests have a surprising tendency to reach back to basic mathematical skills that may in fact come naturally to a secondary school student but are often lost during later academic stages and at the workplace. It is useful to refresh our basic calculus (see for instance www.calculus.org or www.sosmath.com and the "math refresher" Webinar on Online EU Training).

Also, many candidates dread the numerical reasoning test simply because it is based on mathematics and they have always considered this discipline their weakness. What we must realize here is that the "mathematical" aspect of numerical reasoning tests is rather basic – addition, subtraction, multiplication, division, ratios and percentages and simple equations will always be sufficient to perform the necessary calculations. As we will see, in some cases even such calculations are unnecessary and arriving at the correct answer is rather based on an intuitive insight or the realization of a relationship between figures that is in fact right in front of our eyes – we just need to learn to see it.

It is also useful to note here that, just like in the case of verbal reasoning, the broad term "numerical reasoning" may be used to designate various test types related to the handling of numbers, calculations and data, such as:

- **Computation tests** are basic tests that measure the speed at which the test-taker is able to make basic mental calculations such as addition, subtraction, multiplication and division (e.g. "how much is (15+65) / 2 ?").

- **Applied reasoning tests** represent a higher level where the focus is not on the actual ability to make calculations but rather the insight required to find out which calculations need to be performed to arrive at the answer. In other words, *applied reasoning* is tested. These tests are usually text-based in which a certain scenario involving numbers is described – it is this situation that the test-taker is expected to interpret in mathematical terms. To take an example of such a scenario: "There are 60 children at a camp site. Each child either wants to play hide and seek or go to the movies. Twice as many children want to play hide and seek. How many children want to go to the movies?"
- **Data interpretation tests** are similar to the above but instead of using a text, a "scenario" or story as the input, the basis of the exercise is a data set presented in the form of a table, a chart, or any combination of these (e.g. "Based on the data in the chart, by what percentage did the proportion of English-speaking people in cities change in France between 2000 and 2010?").
- **Estimation tests** resemble computation tests in that the calculations to be made are very similar, but the numbers with which you have to work may be greater. The point of the test is not to measure ability to perform the actual calculation but rather the speed and accuracy at which candidates can approximate the result of the calculation. The aim is to select an answer option that will be close to what the result would be if the actual calculation was performed (e.g. 3.98 times 997 is approximately 4000).

EPSO's numerical reasoning tests use elements of these four test types. Yet it is easy to see how each test type builds on skills and routines used in the other types. Quick estimations can only be made if we can make quick calculations as well. When you are faced with text-based numerical reasoning tests and you need to find a way to arrive at the answer, once you have done that, you must actually perform the required calculations or estimations to end up with the correct figure. When it comes to data interpretation based on tables and charts, the task is very similar to those in a text-based numerical reasoning test, with the added twist of having the data presented in a tabular or graphical format.

Let's now turn our attention to a real numerical reasoning test item and see how the above skills come into play.

High-Definition Television Sets in Various Countries (thousands)

	2000	2005	2010
Belgium	345	612	880
Slovakia	230	462	510
Netherlands	702	950	1002
Spain	810	1230	1600

Q. Approximately what percentage of total high-definition television sets across the four countries shown were in Belgium in 2010?

A. 10% B. 15% C. 22% D. 30% E. 35%

Using this sample test item, we can demonstrate how the above-described skills (data interpretation, applied numerical reasoning, estimation and computation) can be used to quickly and efficiently solve EPSO's numerical reasoning tests.

The first step is to interpret the data that we need to work with.

In the present case, the first step is to determine which figures from the table we actually need. The question concerns the number of high-definition television sets in 2010, so we can concentrate on the 2010 column in the table knowing that all the other figures are irrelevant to the task.

Next, we need to figure out what calculations we actually need to perform – in other words, we apply our numerical reasoning skills to the task at hand. Since the question is about Belgium's share of the total number of television sets in the four countries shown in the table, we need to calculate the total (by adding up the individual figures for the four countries), and then calculate Belgium's share in it (by dividing Belgium's number by the total). Finally, we need to convert the result of this division into a percentage figure (multiplying it by 100).

The next question we have to decide is whether we actually need to perform the exact above calculations at all. We can decide this by considering if there is any possibility of estimating certain results. Let's look at the four numbers we need to add up from this perspective:

880

510

1002

1600

Whenever making a decision about the use of estimation, we must take into account the answer options first. In our case, these are percentages which are quite far apart from one another: 10%, 15%, 22%, 30% and 35% – this will tell us that the level of accuracy required to answer the question is not too high and you can feel free to "guesstimate".

Looking at the numbers, we can see that they lend themselves quite nicely to rounding up and down. By doing this, we can arrive at some more "convenient" numbers:

900 (rounded up)

500 (rounded down)

1000 (rounded down)

1600 (stays the same)

Now that the numbers are easy to work with, we can perform some actual computation. Since all numbers end in 00, we can disregard those two digits and work with one and two-digit numbers as their relative proportions (percentages) will remain the same. Add up these four numbers to get to the total number of subscriptions:

9+5+10+16 = 40

Remember that we are looking for a percentage. This means that we do not need to add back the two zeroes – that would only be needed if we had to arrive at an actual value. Instead, we can just compare our total (40) with Belgium's number: 9. (The methodology for this calculation is under Ratios below.)

9 / 40 = 0.225

To convert this to a percentage, simply multiply the number by 100:

0.225 x 100 = 22.5%

Remember at this point that we rounded all the numbers up and down a bit – this explains why our result is not exactly the same as any of the answer options provided. It is, however, overwhelmingly clear that it is closest to Answer C (22%), which will be the correct answer.

Let's take stock of what we did in solving this test problem:

1. We interpreted the data in the table.
2. We applied our reasoning to determine what calculations we needed to perform.
3. We made estimations to simplify our calculations.
4. Finally, we performed the actual calculations.

Hopefully, this example demonstrates how the various skills required for succeeding in numerical reasoning depend on one another. If you keep these simple principles in mind and follow the steps laid out above, you will gain a systematic approach to solving all numerical reasoning tests successfully. There are, of course, lots of other things to look out for in test items, traps to avoid and tactics to use and become accustomed to and these are explored in the practice questions in Chapters 7 and 8.

Based on the required skills and the aspects introduced above, we will now provide an overview of the following:

- Mental calculus
- Ratio calculation
- Percentages and percentage points
- Per capita calculations
- Order of magnitude
- Calculations around speed, time and distance
- Estimation
- Equations
- Tables and charts

After reviewing these various methods and aspects, we will discuss how to approach numerical reasoning tests, what to focus on in each exercise and how to practice for the exam.

Mental Calculus

If you read through the information made available to candidates, it will be stated that a physical calculator will be available for you to use at the exam centre. In light of this, you might be doubtful as to why it is so important to be able to perform quick mental calculations. There are a few important reasons for this:

- There are some calculations that it is faster to perform in your head
- Overreliance on a calculator may make you less intuitive and prevent you from realizing whether certain calculations are really required to answer the question
- You will be able to make any necessary reality checks for every step of the solution, which can be useful, for example, when you are not finding a plausible answer (e.g. because of wrongly inserting numbers into the calculator)

Wherever possible, therefore, it is strongly advised to practise without using a calculator, saving the calculator for problems where its use is essential.

Fractions

As mentioned above, certain types of calculations can quite simply be performed more efficiently without any "technical assistance". One such example is the handling of fractions (as in the illustration below).

Consider the following scenario. We are looking for the proportion of households living in one-bedroom apartments with access to a garden from all households in the United Kingdom. Based on the data provided, let's say that you realize that approximately one in six households in the United Kingdom live in a one-bedroom apartment and among those, two out of three have access to a garden. One way of approaching this calculation would be to use the calculator to do the following:

Numerator

$$\frac{1}{6} \text{ X } \frac{2}{3}$$

Denominator

1 ÷ 6 = 0.1667 (proportion of UK households living in one-bedroom apartments)

2 ÷ 3 = 0.6667 (proportion of these that have access to a garden)

0.6667 * 0.16667 = 0.1111 (proportion of UK households living in one-bedroom apartments with access to a garden)

If we also have the total number of households, say 19,540,000, we then perform one additional calculation:

0.1111 * 19,540,000 = 2,170,894

Now, let's see how this calculation would go without the use of a calculator, by using fractions:

$$\frac{1}{6} \text{ X } \frac{2}{3} = \frac{2}{18} \quad \frac{\text{Numerator}}{\text{Denominator}}$$

How did we do this calculation? Fractions are multiplied by multiplying the first numerator by the second numerator and the first denominator by the second denominator.

We can then simplify the fraction by finding a number that both the numerator and the denominator can be divided by – in our case, this is the number 2:

$$\frac{2}{18} = \frac{1}{9}$$

It is easy to see that the above two calculations can be performed very quickly by mental arithmetic. Also, the final figure we arrive at is extremely convenient – now we know that one in nine UK households are one-bedroom apartments with garden access. If we consider that there are 19,540,000 households, the remaining calculation will also be very simple:

19,540,000 / 9 = 2,171,111

You can see that the number we get this way is slightly different from the number we get using the first method. We can be sure that the latter is more accurate because we did not have to do any rounding in the interim calculation stages.

There are two observations to make here:

- We arrived at the required figure by making extremely simple calculations with easy, round numbers
- Using fractions is actually more accurate than the calculator, because during the first method, we "truncated" many of the figures.

Calculations with Fractions

Multiplication:

$$\frac{3}{5} \times \frac{4}{6} = \frac{12}{30}$$

Division:

$$\frac{4}{7} \div \frac{2}{3} = \frac{4}{7} \times \frac{3}{2} = \frac{12}{14}$$

Addition and subtraction:

Lowest Common Multiple

$$\frac{2}{3} + \frac{3}{7} = \frac{14}{21} + \frac{9}{21} = \frac{23}{21}$$

Multiplication

Method

If we need to multiply two fractions, we first multiply the two numerators (the numbers at the top) and then the two denominators (the numbers at the bottom).

Example of Application

Imagine that you are given a table showing IBM's 2013 revenues in billions. You are also given the following two pieces of information in the question text itself:

- 30% of revenue was made from selling datacenter components
- Of the datacenter revenue, 40% was generated in China

Your task could be to calculate either how much or what percentage of revenue was generated from datacenter components in China. A quick answer to this question can be found using fractions.

30% can be transcribed as a fraction, 3/10 and 40% as 4/10. Based on this, the calculation would go as follows:

$$\frac{3}{10} \text{X} \frac{4}{10} = \frac{12}{100}$$

If the question was "what percentage", we are extremely lucky because the fraction we arrived at after the multiplication is already "per hundred", so the answer is 12%. If the question was "how much", we simply calculate the 12% of the total revenue by multiplying it by 0.12.

Division

Method

If we need to divide a fraction by another fraction, our first task is to turn the operation into multiplication. We do this by "inverting" the numerator and the denominator in one of the fractions. This way, $^2/_3$ would become $^3/_2$, and so on.

Next, we multiply the two numerators and then the two denominators in the same way as we do when multiplying fractions.

Example of Application

Q. 20% of France's annual wine production is equal to half of England's annual consumption. If all of the wine consumed in England were French, what percentage of France's production would be imported into England?

We can transcribe the above information with fractions as follows.

$$20\% = \frac{1}{5} \qquad half = \frac{1}{2}$$

We are looking for England's total consumption in terms of France's total production. We have the following information:

$$\frac{1}{5} \times Production_{France} = \frac{1}{2}\ Consumption_{England}$$

We want only England's total consumption on one side of the equation, so we need to divide both sides of the equation by one half:

$$\frac{1}{5} \div \frac{1}{2} \times Production_{France} = Consumption_{England}$$

We can now invert the numerator and the denominator (say, in the second fraction) and then perform the multiplication as described above:

$$\frac{1}{5} \times \frac{2}{1} \times Production_{France} = Consumption_{England}$$

$$\frac{1}{5} \times 2 \times Production_{France} = Consumption_{England}$$

$$\frac{2}{5} \times Production_{France} = Consumption_{England}$$

With a little practice, we can readily see that two-fifths is equal to four-tenths, or, in more familiar terms, 40%.

In the above very simple example, we could have calculated this even more easily by simply saying that if 50% of England's consumption is equal to 20% of France's production, then the full consumption (which is twice as much), will represent twice as much of France's production, or 40%. In other situations, however, things are not as self-evident and fractions can serve a very useful purpose.

Addition and Subtraction

Method

When adding or subtracting fractions, we need to make sure first that the denominators are the same in both fractions. We can do this by finding the smallest number that can be divided by both denominators. If our two denominators are 3 and 7, as in the illustration at the start of this section on Calculation with fractions, that number will be 21. Once we have done that, we need to multiply the numerators by the same number as the one with which we had to multiply the denominator in the same fraction. In the illustration, the numerator in the left fraction needs to be multiplied by 7 and the numerator in the right fraction needs to be multiplied by 3.

The last step is to simply add up the two numerators.

Example of Application

Imagine that you have the following three pieces of information:

- 30% of Italians believe that the minimum wage must be increased
- three in five Italians believe that the minimum wage must remain unchanged
- the rest believe it should be eliminated to increase competitiveness

Based on the wording of the above, we can be sure that there is no overlap between the groups – one group believes in an increase, the other in maintaining the current level, the third in eliminating it.

We have to answer the following question:

Q. What percentage of Italians believe that the minimum wage must remain unchanged or increase?

To answer the above question with fractions, we need to express "30%" and "three in five" in the form of fractions and then add up the two.

"30%" = 3 / 10

"three in five" = 3 / 5

The proportion we are looking for, then, is as follows:

3/10 + 3/5

You will notice that in this particular case, only the second fraction will need to be "converted". If we multiply both the numerator and the denominator of that fraction by 2, the two denominators will be identical and we can perform the addition.

3/10 + 6/10 = 9/10

By using fractions, we can answer the question by saying that 90% of Italians believe the minimum wage needs to be retained or increased, and 10% believe it should be eliminated. When solving numerical reasoning tests, it is always worth considering for a second whether we can take advantage of fractions – they are an extremely powerful tool in reducing seemingly complex relationships into the simplest of calculations.

Calculating Ratios

The two major mathematical concepts used during the exam are ratio and percentage calculations.

What, then, is a ratio? Let's take the following example:

Q. There are 120 people working in a company of whom 24 are Hungarian. What is the percentage of Hungarians in the company?

In such calculations there are three elements: the total (in this case the 120 employees), the subgroup we are looking at (here the 24 Hungarians), and the ratio, which is the relationship between the other two elements. In the exam you will be given two of these elements and have to find the third.

Scenario 1: Calculating the Ratio

The formula for this is:

Ratio = Subgroup divided by the Total Group.

If, again using our example, you divide the subgroup (24) by the total group (120) with your calculator you will get 0.2. This is the ratio expressed as an absolute number; to turn it into a percentage you simply multiply it by 100, so 20%.

Scenario 2: Calculating the subgroup

This is a common type of question. A typical question would be:

Q. In a company with 150 employees, 12% are Norwegians. What is the number of Norwegians?

Here the formula becomes:

Total x Ratio = Subgroup

In other words, 150 x 12% = 18 Norwegians (or 150 x 0.12 if we use the ratio as an absolute number)

Scenario 3: Calculating the Total

Perhaps the least common type of question is where we are asked to find the total. In this case Total = Subgroup divided by the ratio.

Here is a typical question of this type:

Q. In a company, 20 people are Irish, and they represent 5% of the company's workforce. How many people work for the company?

The calculation is 20 / 5% = 400, or put another way: 20 / 0.05

Scenario 4: Dividing a group into subgroups in a certain proportion to each other

Let us consider the following question:

Q. In a class of 32 children there are 5 boys to every 11 girls. How many boys and how many girls are there in the class?

This sort of problem is much more straightforward than it can sound. Think of the class as our group. To make one complete subgroup of boys and girls we need 5 boys and 11 girls, i.e. 16 children. We know there are 32 children in the class. If we divide 32 by 16, the size of our subgroup, we get 2, which is the number of subgroups in the class. To get the number of boys in total in the class we therefore simply multiply 2 x 5 and to get the number of girls we do 2 x 11. Therefore, there are 10 boys and 22 girls in the class.

This method also works when we are dealing with 3 or more subgroups. Let's say we have to divide 50 people into 3 subgroups that have a proportion to each other of 2 to 3 to 5. We first total 2 + 3 + 5 = 10, and then divide 50 by 10, giving us 5. We then multiply back with every number, to get 5 x 2 = 10, 3 x 5 = 15 and 5 x 5 = 25. In other words there will be 3 subgroups, one of 10 people, one of 15 people and one of 25.

Percentages

Consider the following example:

Q. Profits in a company were 80,000 euro in June. They increased by 50% between June and July and then decreased by 50% between July and August. What were the profits in August?

Previously we were looking at ratios in static situations but here we have a dynamic situation where we need to calculate more than one value to get to the answer – in this case, we need to find out what the profits were in July before we can get to the figure for August.

June	July	August
80,000 EUR		

Here we start with the known value (80,000 euro) to which we add the relevant percentage change: 80,000 + (80,000 x 50%) = 80,000 + 40,000 = 120,000.

Let's name all the elements in this equation: our starting value will be called Basis, the percentage change called Change and the resulting value the New Value. Using these, our formula is therefore like this:

Basis + Basis x Change = New Value

We can notice that Basis is part of both elements on the left side, therefore, we can group these elements. By pulling out Basis, we get the following formula:

Basis x (1 + Change) = New Value

This formula can be our starting point for any calculation. As mentioned above, we will always be asked to calculate one of the three elements of this formula.

Scenario 1: Calculating the New Value (both increase and decrease)

As shown above, the first half of the problem can be solved like this:

80,000 x (1 + 0.5) = 80,000 x 1.5 = 120,000

Continuing from here, we can use the formula again for the second half to calculate August, but this time applying a minus for the 50% because profits decreased:

120,000 x (1 – 0.5) = 60,000.

Scenario 2: Calculating the Change

<u>Calculating the Change in the case of an Increase</u>

Remember our formula: Basis x (1 + Change) = New Value

To calculate Change we have to rearrange the formula:

1 + Change = New Value / Basis

Let's return to our previous example, but assume we instead know the profits for June and July and have to calculate the percentage increase:

June	July	August
80,000 EUR	120,000 EUR	

1 + Change = 120,000 / 80,000

Change = (120,000 / 80,000) – 1

Change = 1.5 – 1

Change = 0.5 = 50%

A more challenging case is where the increase is bigger than 100%, but the formula can handle this as well:

June	July	August
40,000 EUR	180,000 EUR	

In this case 1 + Change = (180,000 / 40,000)

Change = (180,000 / 40,000) – 1

Change = 4.5 – 1

Change = 3.5 = 350%

A word of warning here: you might easily think that 350% is wrong because 180,000 is four-and-a-half times as much as 40,000. However, it is the correct answer. Think of 350% this way: to get to the 180,000 figure for July profits you add 40 to the initial 40 (our initial 100%) three times, plus an additional 20, which is 50%. In total, we have: 40 + (3 x 40) + 20 = 180, which is the correct amount for July profits.

<u>Calculating the Change in the case of a Decrease</u>

June	July	August
180,000 EUR	135,000 EUR	

In our example here the profit has dropped from 180,000 euro in June to 135,000 euro in July, but the formula works the same way.

Change = (135,000 /180,000) – 1

Change = 0.75 – 1

Change = –0.25 = –25%

In other words, profits decreased by 25%.

Scenario 3: Calculating Basis

A typical question here would look like the following:

Q. The value of profits in July was 144,000 EUR which was 20% higher than in June. What was the value in June?

June	July	August
	144,000 EUR	

Remember again our formula: Basis x (1 + Change) = New Value

We can rearrange this as follows: Basis = New Value / (1 + Change)

So in the case of our sample question:

Basis = 144,000 / (1 + 20%)

Basis = 144,000 / 1.2

Basis = 120,000

Therefore profits in June were 120,000 euro.

Be careful with this sort of question. You can't simply deduct 20% from the July figure. In that case you would calculate 144,000 x 0.8 which is 115,200. This sort of pitfall can often appear in a numerical reasoning test and there are lots of examples with full explanations in the questions later in this book.

Percentages and Percentage points

Mixing up these two concepts (percentage change and percentage point change) is a common source of error for candidates taking a numerical reasoning test.

Let us consider the following example (some lines are blocked out):

Bus Companies in the United States, 2013

Company	Profit (in million USD)	Number of Passengers (in millions)	Number of vehicles	Average vehicle utilization (%)
[redacted]				
Greyhound	*46*	*289*	*4560*	*73*

In many numerical reasoning tests, you will be faced with data where calculation of the correct answer will require working with percentages. A straightforward case is where one figure (for example the number of cars in Italy) is an amount, and the other figure (for example the proportion of foreign-made cars) is a percentage. In such cases, the calculation is obvious:

No. of cars in Italy * % of foreign-made cars = No. of foreign made cars in Italy

Let us, however, consider another example. There are cases when *both* figures are proportions or percentages. What happens when the first piece of data (in the table, the average utilization of Greyhound buses) and the second piece of data (the % change in average utilization, for example) are both percentages?

Suppose that the question based on the above table is the following:

Q. What was the average vehicle utilization of Greyhound in 2012 if its vehicle utilization was 22% worse than in 2013?

In this example, where average utilization in 2013 is 73%, and it was 22% worse in 2012, our natural instinct might well be to perform the following calculation:

73% - 22% = 51%, therefore the average utilization in 2012 was 51%.

However, this would not be the correct answer. For comparison, keep in mind how we would calculate a 22% decrease of a regular amount, for example 1200:

1200 * (100% – 22%) = 1200 * 78% = 1200 * 0.78 = 936

Now apply the above logic to capacity utilization:

73% * (100% – 22%) = 73% * 78% = 73% * 0.78 = 56.94%

We can see that the correct calculation yields a significantly different result from what our initial instinct suggested.

When it comes to percentage changes in values that are themselves percentages, what many people think of as a 22 per cent change (for example 62% to 40%) is in fact a 22 percentage point change.

Through an intuitive example, we will be able to appreciate the fundamental difference between the two concepts.

Suppose that a bank in Switzerland pays 10% interest on deposits (we wish!). Now let's take a look at possible changes to this interest rate:

- If the interest rate drops by 5 percentage points, the new interest rate will be 5%
- If the interest rate drops by 5 percent, the new interest rate will be 9.5%
- A 10% interest rate can decrease by a maximum of 10 percentage points, but it can decrease by as much as 100 per cent – both resulting in a 0% interest rate

Per Capita Calculations

Per capita calculations are quite often needed, so it is important to be confident about them.

Let's imagine a country with the following parameters:

Population:	12 million people
Area:	60,000 km^2
Production of apples:	15 million

Let's now answer the following two questions:

Question 1: what is the population per km^2?

Question 2: what is the production per capita?

These calculations are always asking for the creation of an average, meaning that we need to find how many of a certain thing we have for one unit of another thing. A simple way to think of this is to always divide with what comes after the word per. Following this principle, we can answer both questions:

Q1: 12 million people / 60,000 km^2 = 200 people per km^2

Q2: 15 million apples / 12 million people = 1.25 apples per person

Order of Magnitude

Apple Production in Various European Countries

	Population in 2000 (thousands)	*Apple Production (thousands of tonnes)* 1990	2000	2010
Slovakia	4 895	31	25	35
Croatia	4 290	103	98	112
Bulgaria	8 930	120	90	134
Austria	10 354	546	490	560

Note: 1 tonne=1000kg

Q. What was the production of apples per person in Croatia in 2000?

A.0.23 kg B. 2.29 kg C. 22.84 kg D. 228.4 kg E. 2.28 tonnes

An order of magnitude is a scale of amounts where each amount is in a fixed ratio to the amount preceding it. The most common ratio is 1:10, which means that the next amount in a scale can be calculated by multiplying the previous figure by 10.

For example: 1, 10, 100, 1000, 10000 …and so on…

If we look at the above answer options, we can see that that is exactly the situation we have here:

0.23, 2.29, 22.84, 228.4, 2.28 tonnes, (which is 2280 kg) – with some small variations from exact multiples of ten which slightly disguise the relationship.

When we are faced with a set of numbers like the ones above, it gives us an important hint that the actual calculation of the figure may not really be necessary – all we need to figure out is the order of magnitude of the correct answer.

Let us consider the above sample test from the perspective of whether we can take advantage of this observation.

We have the following information:

- The amount of apples produced in Croatia in 2000 in thousands of tonnes – 98
- The population of Croatia in thousands – 4290

Since the answer options only differ in their order of magnitude, we can be quite flexible in rounding our numbers up or down to simplify our calculations.

Let us round 98 up to 100 and 4290 down to 4000. You can disregard the exact number of digits for a second. What is the relationship between the numbers 100 and 4000? If you think about that for a second, you will realize that 100 and 4000 are in a relationship to each other that is similar to that between 1 and 4 – that is, to one quarter. Expressed in decimal terms, this is 0.25. Our answer options are close to this (this is especially apparent in option A – the difference of 0.23 versus 0.25 is caused by having rounded down the numbers). Remember – we do not need to be particularly accurate in this case, all that we are looking for is the number of digits in the correct answer. Now turn your attention to those zeroes we disregarded so far.

Apple Production: 98 thousand tonnes – we will add 6 zeroes here to make it kilogrammes: 98 000 000 kg

Population: 4 290 thousand – we will need to add three zeroes here: 4 290 000

If we turn back to our simplified figures, our calculation would look like this:

100 million divided by 4 million

We could use a calculator to obtain the result here, but let us recall what we said earlier – this is very close to one quarter of 100, which is 25.

25 is closest to Option C and that is the correct answer.

Calculations with Speed, Time and Distance

Questions involving the calculation of speed, time and distance can be expected at the exam. Let's have a look first at the three elements and how they interact with each other.

Speed = distance / time

From this, we can deduce the other two formulas.

Distance = speed x time
Time = distance / speed

You can also remember them by thinking of real-life situations, e.g. driving for 3 hours at 100 km/h will take us a distance of 3 x 100 = 300 kms.

A major pitfall with these questions can be converting between different units, as in the following example: Let's assume that we drove 180 kilometers and it took us 2 hours and 15 minutes. What was our average speed?

To answer this, it might be tempting to divide 180 kilometers by 2.15 hours. However 2 hours and 15 minutes is not 2.15 hours, because there are 60 minutes in an hour not 100. Therefore, we need to find what part of an hour is represented by 15 minutes. This we can get as a simple ratio calculation, dividing 15 minutes / 60 minutes, which is 0.25 hours. Here we don't need to further convert this into a percentage, we simply add it to the number of hours, giving us 2.25 hours. Our calculation becomes 180 kilometers / 2.25 hours, resulting in 80 km/h

Estimation

In a previous section, when calculating the per-capita apple production of Croatia, we applied a sort of estimation to get to the correct answer. In that case, the estimation took the form of concentrating only on the number of digits in the correct answer. There are cases, however, where we need to be a little more precise than that

Let's go back to our table and ask a different question:

Bus Companies in the United States, 2013

Company	Profit (in million USD)	Number of Passengers (in millions)	Number of vehicles	Average vehicle utilization (%)
[redacted]				
Greyhound	46	289	4560	73

Q. How many passengers would Greyhound carry in 2014 if its average vehicle utilization improves by 10% and its number of vehicles doesn't change?

a) 317.9 million

b) 356.6 million

c) 232.07 million

d) 260.1 million

Again, let us first consider the less innovative (and therefore more time-consuming) way of calculating the correct answer.

The data we will work with are:

- Number of passengers in millions in 2013: 289
- Average vehicle utilization in 2013: 73%
- The fact that average vehicle utilization in 2014 is forecast to increase by 10%

The first thing we would do is calculate the new utilization. An important point to remember here is the difference between percentage change and percentage point change, as discussed above.

New capacity utilization = 73% * (100% + 10%) = 73% * 110% = 73% * 1.1 = 80.3%

One mistake we could make here is equating the 2014 figure for passengers carried with the following (i.e. confusing the Basis and New Value discussed earlier):

289 million * 80.3% = 289 million * 0.803 = 232.07 million (note that this is one of the answer options)

Why is the above calculation incorrect? We must bear in mind that the number 289 million is actually equal to 73% of the total vehicle capacity of Greyhound, since its average utilization according to the table was 73%.

We also know the new capacity utilization figure (80.3%), but we must also calculate total capacity, the Basis (X). We know the following:

X * 0.73 = 289 million (73% of the total capacity is 289 million passengers)

Let's solve the equation for X:

X = 289 million / 0.73 = 395.9 million

We can now calculate the number of passengers transported at 80.3% capacity utilization:

395.9 * 0.803 = 317.9 million

Answer A is in fact the correct answer.

While the above series of calculations were all correct, we must always be suspicious when so many raw calculations are required to get to the correct answer. Do not forget that numerical reasoning in EPSO exams is not primarily a mathematical exercise, so this might be a hint that an easier solution may exist.

We need to make two observations here:

- Some of the data is irrelevant
- The "distance" between the values in the answer options allows for estimation

Let's go back to the problem. As the question referred to average vehicle utilization, we immediately started to work with that number. However, we should reconsider the meaning of this term. If average vehicle utilization increases by 10%, and the number of vehicles does not change, is this not just another way of saying that Greyhound carried 10% more passengers? This immediately simplifies our calculation:

289 million + 10% = 289 million * 110% = 289 million * 1.1

Now let us look at the answer options again:

a) 317.9 million

b) 356.6 million

c) 232.07 million

d) 260.1 million

Answers C and D can be immediately ruled out because those numbers are smaller than the 289 million in the table, which is impossible when the utilization increases.

Answer B has a greater number than in the table, but if we estimate 10% of 289 million (about 30 million, or exactly 28.9 million) we will immediately see that Answer B's 356.6 million is simply too large an amount, which leaves only Answer A as a feasible option.

The correctness of Answer A can also be verified very quickly, with a simple subtraction:

317.9 million – 28.9 million = 317.9 million – (17.9 million + 11 million) = 300 million – 11 million = 289 million

The above calculation also shows an example of how to make subtractions easier. In this example, we reformulated 28.9 million as 17.9 million + 11 million so it became much easier to first subtract 17.9 million from 317.9 million (leaving the round number of 300 million), and then deal with the rest.

Equations

Equations might sound too mathematical, yet they are a brilliantly inventive way of dealing with problems where multiple calculations must be made. Consider this:

Q. There are 13 600 customers in a café in a month. Out of them, 45% order coffee; of these, 30% opt for coffee with milk, of whom 200 ask for soy milk. Of the other customers, 25% ask for espresso macchiato, for which 60 millilitres of regular milk is used per customer. How much regular milk is used in a month for espresso macchiatos?

A. 245.4 litres

B. 245.4 millilitres

C. 24.54 litres

D. 29.54 litres

One way of approaching the problem would be to perform a series of individual calculations. First, we would calculate 45% of 13 600 customers to get 6120, then 30% of 6120 to get 1836, then we would subtract 200 from that to get 1636, then we would calculate 25% of this to get 409. Finally, we would multiply 409 by the amount of milk (60 ml, or 0.06 litres) and get the correct result, which is answer C. This is all perfectly reasonable.

However, by denoting the amount of milk used for macchiatos (which is the answer we are looking for) by X, we can create an equation which will make the calculation faster:

X = (13 600 * 0.45 * 0.3 – 200) * 0.25 * 60 (where 0.45 equals 45%, 0.3 equals 30%, and 0.25 equals 25%)

We can further simplify the equation:

X = (13 600 * 0.135 – 200) / 4 * 60

X = (1836 – 200) / 4 * 60

X = 1636 / 4 * 60

X = 409 * 60

X = 24 540

The final thing we need to remember is that this is in millilitres. Since this doesn't match any of the available answer options, let's convert it into litres:

24 540 / 1 000 = 24.54 litres

This matches Answer C. By denoting the figure we are looking for as X and then using the data to find X, we can work systematically with all levels of difficulty in the figures and reduce the risk of "getting lost" in a jumble of numbers.

Tables and Charts

Bus Companies in the United States, 2013

Company	Profit (in million USD)	Number of Passengers (in millions)	Number of vehicles	Average vehicle utilization (%)
Trailways	12	123	2140	71
National	14	150	2400	69
Roger's	7	65	1300	75
Greyhound	46	289	4560	73

Q. How many passengers would Greyhound carry in 2014 if its average vehicle utilization improves by 10% and its number of vehicles doesn't change?

A. 317.9 million B. 356.6 million C. 232.07 million D. 260.1 million

The above table may seem familiar. This is because we previously used a version of this table with some rows "blacked out" for demonstrating certain methods. In real numerical tests, however, the table always contains lots of superfluous data that you will not need for your calculations – this is what we referred to as "noise" in the introduction. When starting to solve a numerical reasoning question, it is always important to first decide exactly what data is necessary for the calculation because the superfluous information will just confuse you and can take valuable time if you become distracted.

For this reason, it is good advice to mentally "black out" that data from the table which you will not need. In this instance, the first thing we will realize is that we don't need any of the data about the other three bus companies (Trailways, National, Roger's). So let's black out the data for the other companies.

Bus Companies in the United States, 2013

Company	Profit (in million USD)	Number of Passengers (in millions)	Number of vehicles	Average vehicle utilization (%)
[redacted]	[redacted]	[redacted]	[redacted]	[redacted]
Greyhound	46	289	4560	73

Since the question refers to the number of passengers carried, we will certainly not need profit data to answer the question, so let's black out that data:

Bus Companies in the United States, 2013

Company	Profit (in million USD)	Number of Passengers (in millions)	Number of vehicles	Average vehicle utilization (%)
[redacted]	[redacted]	[redacted]	[redacted]	[redacted]
Greyhound	[redacted]	289	4560	73

Based on our reasoning in the section on Estimation, we will also realize that the number of vehicles is a superfluous figure, as is average vehicle utilization, so let's black those out too:

Bus Companies in the United States, 2013

Company	Profit (in million USD)	Number of Passengers (in millions)	Number of vehicles	Average vehicle utilization (%)
[redacted]	[redacted]	[redacted]	[redacted]	[redacted]
Greyhound	[redacted]	289	[redacted]	[redacted]

If we systematically exclude all superfluous data, the task will seem significantly less complicated. As it turns out, in our example, the table's only purpose is to tell us that Greyhound carried 289 million passengers in 2013!

How to Approach Numerical Reasoning Tests

This chapter demonstrated the number of factors we must consider in order to efficiently solve the problems posed in numerical reasoning tests. Consider aspects such as the required level of accuracy, the relevance of data or the possibility of estimation, then decide the approach to take – whether to perform raw calculations, apply estimates, draw up an equation, or simply read a relationship or a trend off a chart.

As is true in the case of verbal and abstract reasoning tests, a systematic approach will make your test-taking experience much more efficient. Below, you will find a a summary of the recommended approach:

1. Read the question and the answer options first as carefully as possible.
2. The question will help you identify which data sets will be relevant and necessary for answering the question and know what to ignore.
3. Looking at the answer options will help you decide the level of accuracy required. If, for example, the values in the answer options are very far apart, you may consider estimation.
4. Based on the question, determine the relevant information and mentally "black out" the unnecessary data.
5. Having looked at the answer options and the data in the table, you can now make a final decision about whether to go for an exact figure or make an estimate, whether to use an equation, and so on. Before you start, think through your calculation methodology step by step.
6. Make sure you exclude all unrealistic answer options (for example numbers representing an increase when the question refers to a decrease).
7. Once you have performed your calculations, you can match the result against the remaining answer options. If you estimated, look for the answer option closest to your estimated result. If the result is significantly closer to one answer option than to all others, you were probably on the right track.

Practice Methods

Finally, a few suggestions for how to practice for the numerical reasoning test:

- Start your practice by identifying your weaknesses. Percentages? Subtraction? Estimation? Equations? Calculus in general? Or is it instead deciding what data is relevant when there is a great deal of irrelevant "noise" in the tables and charts?
- Once you have identified your weaknesses, you should particularly practice these operations, all of which are tested in the next two chapters
- Make sure you check how many questions you will face in the actual exam and how much time you will have to answer them
- Start decreasing the time needed to answer the questions so it gets closer to the time available at the exam
- Ideally, by the time of the exam, you should be able to answer more questions in the time available than required at the exam, because you cannot account for stress and other outside factors are impossible to recreate at home
- The EPSO test will be administered on a computer, which will make it much more challenging (and stranger) to take than a paper-based test where you can scribble on the paper and make quick calculations, write down equations, underline key concepts and so on – so if you have access to such services, try to practice online

7. Targeted Numerical Reasoning Practice

Before starting on the mixed questions full numerical reasoning test in the next chapter, where different types of questions are mixed at random, we recommend you first practise specific operations in this "warm-up" exercise. The operations in sequence are (A) Order of Magnitude, (B) Per capita/Percentage Calculations, (C) Speed, Time and Distance, (D) Equations, (E) Ratios, with a final section (F) on Estimating techniques.

As this is a warm-up exercise rather than a test, we have kept the answer explanations immediately under the questions.

A. ORDER OF MAGNITUDE QUESTIONS

Set A1 (Order of magnitude)

Total Population (millions)			
Country	2009	2012	2015
Belgium	10.75	11.08	11.24
Denmark	5.51	5.58	5.66
Norway	4.80	4.99	5.17
Spain	46.24	46.82	46.45
United Kingdom	62.04	63.50	64.88

Foreign-born Population (thousands)			
Country	2009	2012	2015
Belgium	1444	1678	1783
Denmark	486	532	596
Norway	489	615	746
Spain	6226	6295	5891
United Kingdom	6862	7762	8412

Q1. Which country had the second-highest percentage of foreign-born population in 2012?

A. Belgium
B. Denmark
C. Norway
D. Spain
E. United Kingdom

Correct Answer: D

Data Interpretation

From the tables we need:

- The 2012 total population figures for all countries
- The 2012 foreign-born population figures for all countries

Reasoning

We have to calculate the foreign-born population as a percentage of the total population for each of the 5 countries in 2012 and then select the second-highest.

Calculation

To get the foreign-born population percentage for each country, we need to divide its foreign-born population in 2012 by its total population in 2012.

The total population figures are provided in millions and the foreign-born population figures are in thousands. To get a comparable ratio for each country there is no need to use the figures with all the zeroes added, we can just use the figures as given. The result will not be the actual foreign-born percentage but since we only need to compare the numbers between countries, it will suffice.

Belgium:

1 678 / 11.08 = 151.444

Denmark:

532 / 5.58 = 95.341

Norway:

615 / 4.99 = 123.246

Spain:

6 295 / 46.82 = 134.451

United Kingdom:

7 762 / 63.50 = 122.236

If we arrange the above results in descending order (highest to lowest), we get:

1st Belgium (151.444)

2nd Spain (134.451)

We do not need to go further as we now have the second-highest result, Spain.

Potential Shortcuts / Pitfalls

There is no need to calculate the exact foreign-born population percentages as we are only looking for the comparable ratios for each country, which are easy to calculate. If you add the zeroes for the millions and the thousands into your calculation, it will both take more time and make it more likely you will make a mistake.

There's also no need to waste time on writing down the resulting numbers with too many decimal places. The numbers before the decimal point are all different anyway and are relatively easy to compare.

Be careful to avoid reading the population figures of 2009 or 2015 from the tables or mixing up figures of different countries. It's easy to make that sort of mistake when rushing.

Q2. Given that the EU's total population in 2009 was 502.09 million and that Spain's non foreign-born population was 8% of the EU's total population in 2015, by how many millions did the EU's total population increase between 2009 and 2015?

A. 0.4898
B 4.898
C. 4.285
D. 40.285
E. 48.98

Correct Answer: B

Data Interpretation

From the table we need:

- The 2009 foreign-born population figure for Spain
- The 2009 total population figure for Spain

From the question text we need:

- EU's total population figure for 2009
- Spain's non foreign-born population as a percentage (8%) of EU's total population in 2015

Reasoning

We need to find the EU's total population in 2015 to determine the increase between 2009 and 2015. We can calculate the EU's total population for 2015 by using Spain's 2015 non foreign-born population percentage.

Calculation

To calculate the EU's total population for 2015 by using Spain's 2015 non foreign-born population percentage (which is provided), we must first find Spain's 2015 non foreign-born population. For that we must subtract Spain's 2015 foreign-born population (given in thousands) from Spain's 2015 total population (given in millions). We must however convert both figures to either thousands or millions before our calculations (remember, 1 million = 1 000 thousand). We are going to work with millions.

Spain's 2015 non foreign-born population (millions):

(46.45) – (5891 / 1 000) = 46.45 – 5.891 = 40.559

40.559 million people were equivalent to 8% of the EU's total population of 2015, therefore we can reverse-calculate the EU's total population in 2015 (in millions):

40.559 / 8% = 40.559 / 0.08 = 506.9875

We already know the EU's total population for 2009, which is 502.09 million. By subtracting the EU's total population in 2009 from the EU's total population in 2015, we will get the increase (millions):

506.9875 – 502.09 = 4.8975

Potential Shortcuts / Pitfalls

There are two major pitfalls to avoid in answering this question.

Firstly, you must read the question very carefully. The question refers to the "non foreign-born population" whereas the table has figures only for the foreign-born and total populations. If you miss the key word "non" you will go wrong from the very outset.

Secondly, the foreign-born population (given in thousands) has to be subtracted from the respective total population (given in millions). You cannot simply subtract a figure in thousands from a figure in millions; therefore you need to do all the calculations in either thousands or millions. We could have also opted to perform our calculations by converting all figures to units, but this complicates matters unnecessarily.

By simply looking at the answer options, using common sense, you might intuitively realise that the answer is likely to be either B or C. However these answers are too close together to risk guessing which is right – unless, of course, you are completely out of time and need to take a 50/50 gamble.

Q3. Which of the following is the best estimate of Spain's foreign-born population in 2014 assuming that it changed by an even annual amount between 2012 and 2015?

A. 6.026
B. 6 341
C. 6 026
D. 6 341 000
E. 6 026 000

Correct Answer: E

Data Interpretation

From the table we need:

- The 2012 foreign-born population figure for Spain
- The 2015 foreign-born population figure for Spain
- From the question, the information that the foreign-born population changed by an even annual amount between 2012 and 2015

Reasoning

We can use the trend in Spain's foreign-born population between the years 2012 and 2015 to estimate its foreign-born population in 2014.

Calculation

We know Spain's foreign-born populations for the years 2015 and 2012. We can find the change between these two years (in thousands) by deducting the 2012 figure from the 2015 figure:

5 891 – 6 295 = -404

Thus Spain's foreign-born population decreased by 404 thousand during the 3 years between 2012 and 2015. Therefore, the approximate yearly change (in thousands) was:

-404 / 3 = -134.667

Spain's foreign-born population decreased by approximately 134.667 thousand every year after 2012. Based on this statistic, we can estimate the approximate change that took place in the two years from 2012 to 2014 (in thousands):

-134.667 * 2 = -269.334

If we add this approximate change to Spain's actual foreign-born population in 2012, we will get an estimate for Spain's foreign-born population in 2014 (in thousands):

6 295 + (-269.334) = 6 295 – 269.334

= 6 025.666

The question simply asks for the best estimate (and does not mention whether it should be in thousands or millions which means that it has to be in units). Therefore:

6 025.666 * 1 000 = 6 025 666

The result 6 025 666 can be rounded off to 6 026 000.

Potential Shortcuts / Pitfalls

The key to this question is the statement that the population "changed by an even annual amount between 2012 and 2015". Without this information it would be impossible to answer the question. Consider this example: someone earns 10,000 euro in Year 1 and 30,000 euro in Year 3. If you know their earnings increased by an even annual amount, it is obvious that in Year 2 they earned 20,000 euro. But if you don't have that information it is impossible to say what their earnings were in Year 2 – they might, for instance, have carried on earning 10,000 euro, or they might alternatively have gone straight to 30,000 or indeed any other figure.

The foreign-born population figures in the table are given in thousands, so it is simplest to keep the calculations in thousands too. However, you must be careful to provide the final answer in units, as required in the question, and not in millions or thousands. You would end up choosing Answer A if you were thinking in millions or C if you were thinking in thousands.

Set A2 (Order of Magnitude)

Fishing Catch (1000 tonnes)

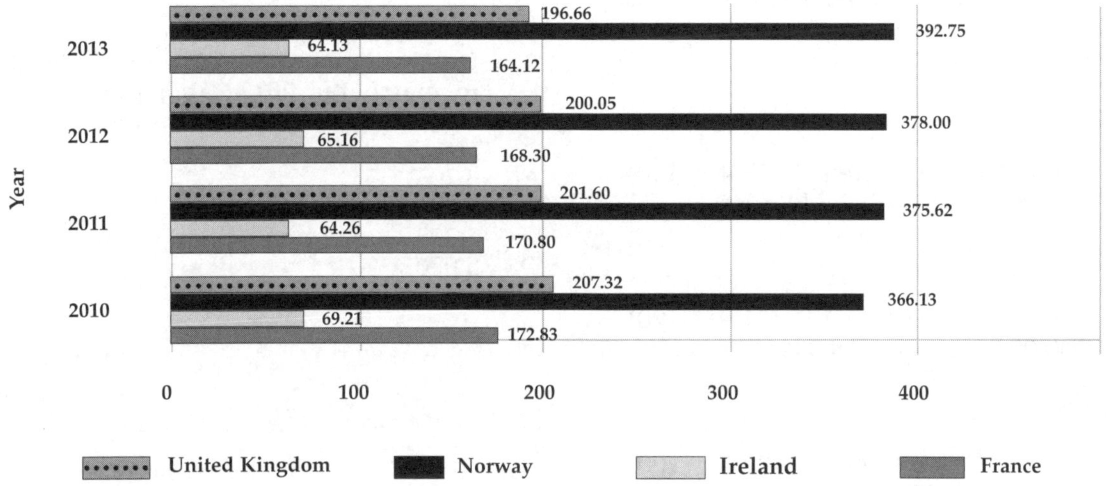

Fishing Fleet (Number of Vessels, hundreds)	2010	2011	2012	2013
France	72.2	72.1	71.4	71.2
Ireland	21.4	21.9	22.5	21.9
Norway	63.1	62.5	62.1	61.3
United Kingdom	64.6	63.9	63.6	63.0

Q1. In which year(s) did Ireland's fishing catch exceed 30 000 kgs per vessel?

A. 2010 only
B. 2011 and 2013 only
C. 2013 only
D. 2010, 2011, 2012 and 2013
E. None of these years

Correct Answer: A

Data Interpretation

From the table and chart we need:

- The fishing catch of Ireland for all four years
- The size of the fishing fleet of Ireland for all four years

From the question text we need:

- The benchmark with which to compare Ireland's fishing catch per vessel

Reasoning

We must compute Ireland's fishing catch per vessel figures for all four years and compare them to the 30 000 kgs per vessel benchmark.

Calculation

To calculate the catch per vessel (in kgs per vessel), we must divide the total fishing catch (in kgs) by the number of vessels (in units) for each year. To convert the total fishing catch from 1 000 tonnes to kgs, we must multiply by 1 000 (as the figures are given in thousands) and then again multiply by 1 000 (1 tonne =1 000 kgs). To convert the number of vessels from hundreds to units, we must multiply by 100. The catch per vessel (in kgs per vessel) is as follows:

2010:

(69.21 * 1 000 * 1 000) / (21.4 * 100) = 69 210 000 / 2 140 = **32 340**

2011:

(64.26 * 1 000 * 1 000) / (21.9 * 100) = 64 260 000 / 2 190 = **29 342**

2012:

(65.16 * 1 000 * 1 000) / (22.5 * 100) = 65 160 000 / 2 250 = **28 960**

2013:

(64.13 * 1 000 * 1 000) / (21.9 * 100) = 64 130 000 / 2 190 = **29 283**

Thus the calculations show that Ireland exceeded the 30 000 kgs per vessel mark in 2010 only.

Potential Shortcuts / Pitfalls

Not confusing the units in which the data is provided is key to this problem. As we saw above, we must first convert the units of the fishing catch from 1 000 tonnes to kgs and the number of vessels from hundreds to units. An order of magnitude error could lead to the selection of options D or E.

Flicking between chart and table can be tricky at speed, so beware of using another country's data instead of Ireland's.

There is a useful shortcut which you might spot if you read the answer options carefully. Once we have worked out the 2010 figure, we know that the correct answer cannot be options B, C or E. At this point, D could still be right. However, once we have worked out the 2011 figure that also eliminates answer D. In other words, *we don't actually need to calculate the 2012 or 2013 figures at all.*

Q2. How many more tonnes would Ireland need to have caught in 2012 to match the 2013 catch per vessel figure of the United Kingdom?

A. 3.203
B. 5.076
C. 3 203
D. 5 076
E. 50 760

Correct Answer: D

Data Interpretation

From the table and chart we need:

- The 2013 fishing catch of United Kingdom
- The 2013 fishing fleet of United Kingdom
- The 2012 fishing catch of Ireland
- The 2012 fishing fleet of Ireland

Reasoning

We need to calculate the United Kingdom's catch per vessel figure for 2013 and use it to find the additional catch Ireland would have needed to achieve this level in 2012.

Calculation

The formula for catch per vessel is:

$$\text{Catch per vessel} = \frac{\text{Total catch}}{\text{Number of vessels}}$$

In 2013, the United Kingdom's catch per vessel (in tonnes per vessel) was:

(196.66 * 1 000) / (63.0 * 100) = 196 660 / 6 300 = 31.2159

Using the formula for catch per vessel we can write:

Total catch = Catch per vessel * Number of vessels

By using Ireland's number of vessels in 2012 we can calculate the catch Ireland needed in 2012 to match the United Kingdom's 2013 catch per vessel figure:

(31.2159) * (22.5 * 100) = 70 235.8

Therefore, the additional catch (in tonnes) Ireland needed was the required catch minus the actual catch:

(70 235.8) – (65.16 * 1 000) =
70 235.8 – 65 160 = **5 076**

Q3. Which of the following is the best estimate for Norway's average monthly fishing catch between July 2010 and June 2012?

A. 20.769 tonnes
B. 31.154 tonnes
C. Impossible to say
D. 31 104 tonnes
E. 31 154 tonnes

Correct Answer: C

Reasoning

You have to think carefully about this question because a vital piece of information is missing. If you don't spot this, you will end up doing a large number of complicated calculations and most likely end up choosing Answer E.

Remember question 3 in the previous set. In that case we could make a similar sort of estimate because we knew what the trend was in the data. But in this case we don't have any information of that type (for example that that the monthly fishing catch was more or less balanced over this period). If the yearly fishing catch was spread out evenly across the 12 months of a year, we could make a calculation, but we don't know that to be the case. Suppose that most of the catch in 2010 was in the *first* 6 months of the year and most of the catch in 2012 was in the *last* 6 months. That would result in a much lower average monthly catch for the period July 2010 to June 2012 than if most of the catch in 2010 was in the *last* 6 months of the year and most of the catch in 2012 was in the *first* 6 months.

"Impossible to say" type questions can occur in EPSO exams so you need to be alert to this.

B. PER CAPITA/PERCENTAGES CALCULATIONS

Set B1 (Per Capita / Percentages)

Netherlands Butter and Cheese Production

(Thousands of tonnes)

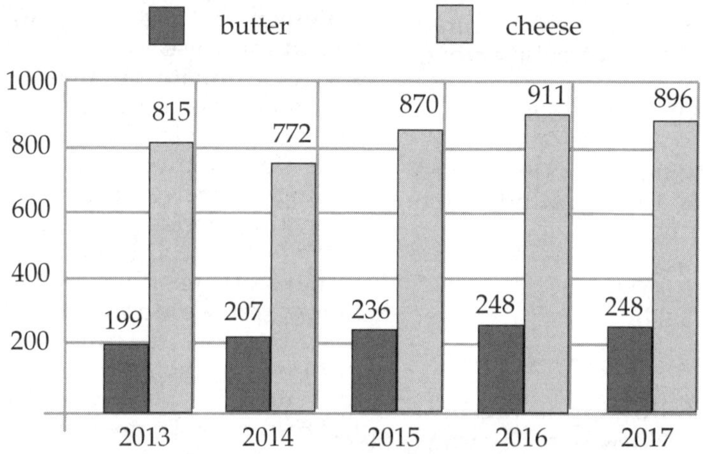

Netherlands Total Population (millions)	
2013	16.78
2014	16.83
2015	16.90
2016	16.98
2017	17.08

Q1. If the average price of butter in 2016 was €3.25 per kg, what was Netherlands' per capita turnover for butter in 2016?

A. €14.61
B. €47.47
C. €53.65
D. €806
E. €14 605

Correct Answer: B

Data Interpretation

From the table and chart we need:

- The 2016 butter production figure for Netherlands
- The 2016 total population figure for Netherlands

From the question text we need:

- The average price of butter in 2016

Reasoning

We must calculate the per capita production of butter in 2016, in kilograms, and multiply it by the average price to get the per capita turnover of butter.

Calculation

To calculate the 2016 per capita production of butter, we need to divide the total production of butter in 2016 by the population of the Netherlands in 2016.

The population figures are provided in millions (which has six zeroes), whereas the butter production is given in 1 000 tonnes. Since 1 tonne = 1 000 kgs the production figure also has six zeroes when converted to kgs. Therefore, to get the per capita production of butter in kgs we can simply divide the butter production figure by the population figure.

248 / 16.98 ≈ 14.605

So, in 2016 Netherlands produced 14.605 kgs of butter per capita (per person). To convert this into per capita turnover, we must multiply the per capita production by the average price:

14.605 * 3.25 ≈ 47.47

Therefore Netherlands produced butter worth €47.47 per person in 2016.

Potential Shortcuts / Pitfalls

It is easy to end up using the wrong year's production figure or the figure for cheese instead of butter. You need to be careful in this regard when working at speed.

As indicated earlier, it isn't necessary to convert the production quantity of butter to kgs and the population from millions to units before calculation. The same order of magnitude (six zeroes) in each figure cancels out. You will waste precious time as well as risk making a mistake if you don't spot this.

Another typical mistake would be to consider the per capita production of butter in kilograms as the final answer. It is the per capita *turnover* and not the per capita *production* that is being asked for.

Q2. The total production of butter and cheese in Netherlands declined from 2013 to 2014. What percentage increase in the total production in 2014 would have been required for the per capita production of butter and cheese to have been the same as in 2013?

A. 0.3%
B. 3.6%
C. 3.7%
D. 3.9%
E. 5.5%

Correct Answer: A

Data Interpretation

From the table and chart we need:

- The 2013 total population figure for Netherlands
- The 2014 total population figure for Netherlands

Reasoning

We must work out the percentage increase in the combined production of butter and cheese that would offset the increase in population from 2013 to 2014, such that the combined per capita production of butter and cheese remains constant.

Calculation

There is a simple solution to this problem for which we need to understand how the per capita production is calculated. It is the ratio of the combined production of butter and cheese and the corresponding total population:

$$\text{Per capita combined production in 2013} = \frac{\text{Combined production in 2013}}{\text{Total population in 2013}}$$

We know that we want the per capita value for 2014 to be the same as in 2013. We also know that the population changed from 16.78 million to 16.83 million between 2013 and 2014, a percentage change of:

([16.83 – 16.78] / 16.78) * 100% = 0.3%

To offset a 0.3% increase in the denominator (population), the numerator (production) should also have increased by the same percentage. Therefore, the total production should have increased by 0.3% for the per capita combined production to remain constant from 2013 to 2014.

$$\text{Per capita combined production in 2013} = \frac{\text{Total production in 2013 * 100.3\%}}{\text{Total population in 2014}}$$

Potential Shortcuts / Pitfalls

The major pitfall to this question is thinking it is a lot more complicated than it is. Because the question starts with the information that "the total production of butter and cheese in Netherlands declined from 2013 to 2014" it is natural to assume that we should be doing a lot of calculations with butter and cheese, whereas this is not necessary. As we have seen, all we actually needed was the population figures.

A more obvious but far longer method involves calculating the per capita combined production of butter and cheese in 2013 and then using the population of 2014 to find the necessary level of combined production in 2014. The required percentage change in production from 2013 to 2014 would be found by subtracting the two values and calculating the percentage. As we have seen, a bit of smart numerical reasoning can save us a lot of unnecessary calculations.

It is also important to realise that the 6 zeroes from production (1 000 tonnes) and population (millions) can be ignored to simplify calculations or you will make more work for yourself.

Q3. Which of the following hypothetical situations will definitely result in an increased per capita production of butter in Netherlands?

A. Decrease in production of butter and decline in population.
B. Decrease in production of butter and an increase in population.
C. Increase in production of butter and decline in population.
D. Increase in production of butter and an increase in population.
E. No change in production of butter and an increase in population.

Correct Answer: C

Data Interpretation

The answer is found by straight numerical reasoning; we do not require any specific information from the table or the question.

Reasoning

We must consider each option separately to ascertain the situation in which the per capita production of butter will definitely increase.

Calculation

The per capita production of butter is calculated by dividing the production of butter by the total population.

$$\text{Per capita production of butter} = \frac{\text{(Production of butter)}}{\text{(Total population)}}$$

Option A: Decrease in production of butter and decline in population.

The numerator and denominator of our ratio are both decreasing. The resulting per capita production can decrease or increase depending upon the percentage decrease in production and population. Only specific numbers can tell us what will actually happen. Therefore, this option will not definitely result in an increase in per capita production of butter.

Option B: Decrease in production of butter and an increase in population.

The numerator is decreasing while the denominator is increasing. This will result in a definite decrease in per capita production.

Option C: Increase in production of butter and decline in population.

The numerator is increasing while the denominator is decreasing. Both of these changes cause the per capita production to increase. Therefore, this situation will definitely lead to an increase.

Option D: Increase in production of butter and an increase in population.

As with option A, the per capita production can increase or decrease depending on the percentage increase in production and population. Only specific numbers can tell us the exact outcome. Therefore no definite predictions can be made.

Option E: No change in production of butter and an increase in population.

The numerator stays constant while the denominator increases. This will lead to a definite decrease in the per capita production.

Potential Shortcuts / Pitfalls

The qualitative nature of this question (i.e. no specific numbers involved) should not prevent us from believing that there can be a definite answer to this problem.

Options A and D can possibly result in an increase in the per capita production but since the problem asks us to be definite in our assessment we must reject these two options.

Finally, if you look at the options in sequence (A, B, C...) you will get to the correct answer as soon as you reach C. As there can only be one correct answer in this test, you would be wasting your time to go any further.

Set B2 (Per Capita / Percentages)

Artificial land cover (million square metres)	2009	2012	2015
European Union	160 770	166 733	173 295
Finland	5 134	5 326	5 531
France	27 847	28 574	29 415
Italy	19 815	20 346	20 837
Slovakia	1 272	1 361	1 461

Artificial land cover (square metres per capita)	2009	2012	2015
European Union	347.3	357.0	367.2
Finland	966.6	983.8	1 009.4
France	444.7	449.7	456.2
Italy	335.3	341.7	343.1
Slovakia	236.2	251.7	269.4

Q1. What was the difference in the populations of Finland and Slovakia in 2015?

A. 56 330
B. 168 092
C. 5 189 398
D. 5 423 163
E. 56 330 000

Correct Answer: A

Data Interpretation

From the tables we need:

- The 2015 artificial land cover of Finland
- The 2015 artificial land cover per capita of Finland
- The 2015 artificial land cover of Slovakia
- The 2015 artificial land cover per capita of Slovakia

Reasoning

We need to calculate the populations of Finland and Slovakia in 2015 by using the respective artificial land cover areas and per capita figures. We can then calculate the difference in population.

Calculation

$$\text{Artificial land cover per capita} = \frac{\text{Artifical land cover}}{\text{Total population}}$$

Hence

$$\text{Total population} = \frac{\text{Artifical land cover}}{\text{Artificial land cover per capita}}$$

Substituting the data from the table, the total population (in millions) of Finland in 2015 was:

5 531 / 1 009.4 5.47949

Since the artificial land cover area was provided in million square metres, the total population we calculated is also in millions.

The total population (in millions) of Slovakia in 2015 was:

1 461 / 269.4 5.42316

Therefore the difference (in millions) in the populations of Finland and Slovakia in 2015 was:

5.47949 – 5.42316 = 0.05633

We need to convert our answer to units by multiplying by 1 million:

0.05633 * 1 000 000 = 56 330

Potential Shortcuts / Pitfalls

We need to be careful in applying the per capita formula. If we multiply the per capita figure with the area, our answer will be incorrect.

The artificial land cover area is provided in million square metres. We must account for this in our calculations. We can solve our problem in millions but the answer choices are provided in units. We must therefore convert the final population figure from millions to units.

Q2. What was the European Union's artificial land cover per capita (in square metres per capita) in 2009 excluding France?

A. 322.8
B. 332.1
C. 342.4
D. 347.3
E. 353.1

Correct Answer: B

Data Interpretation

From the tables we need:

- The 2009 artificial land cover for the EU
- The 2009 artificial land cover for France
- The 2009 artificial land cover per capita for the EU
- The 2009 artificial land cover per capita for France

Reasoning

We need to calculate the EU's artificial land cover and population, excluding France, in 2009, and use those figures to calculate the EU's per capita artificial land cover in 2009.

Calculation

The EU's artificial land cover excluding France in 2009 was (in million square metres):

160 770 – 27 847 = 132 923

The EU's population in 2009 (in millions):

160 770 / 347.3 ≈ 462.91391

France's population in 2009 (in millions):

27 847 / 444.7 ≈ 62.61974

Therefore the EU's population excluding that of France in 2009 was (in millions):

462.91391 – 62.61974 = 400.29417

Now we know the EU's artificial land cover excluding France in 2009 as well as the EU's population excluding France in 2009.

We use the formula:

$$\text{Artificial land cover per capita} = \frac{\text{Artifical land cover}}{\text{Total population}}$$

The EU's artificial land cover per capita (in square metres per capita) in 2009 excluding France was:

132 923 / 400.29417 ≈ 332.1

Potential Shortcuts / Pitfalls

It is vital to realise that you cannot simply subtract the per capita land cover of France from that of the European Union. You must first find the two components, area and population, separately and then use them to find the new per capita value.

Remember that since we calculated all the population figures in millions and the areas we used were also in million square metres, the effect of both sets of zeroes cancels each other out in the per capita formula.

Q3. The population of Italy was approximately 340 000 larger in 2016 than in 2015. If the artificial land cover per capita remained unchanged from 2015, what was the percentage change in the artificial land cover in 2016 from 2015?

A. Increase of 0.15%
B. Increase of 0.56%
C. Increase of 5.60%
D. Decrease of 0.56%
E. Decrease of 5.60%

Correct Answer: B

Data Interpretation

From the tables we need:

- The 2015 artificial land cover of Italy
- The 2015 artificial land cover per capita of Italy

From the question text we need:

- The increase in population of Italy from 2015 to 2016
- The change (none) in artificial land cover per capita of Italy from 2015 to 2016

Reasoning

We need to calculate the population of Italy in 2016 and use the per capita figure for 2015 to estimate the artificial land cover in 2016. The percentage change in artificial land cover area can then be calculated using the figures for 2015 and 2016.

Calculation

Population of Italy in 2015 (in millions):

20 837 / 343.1 ≈ 60.731565

The population of Italy in 2016 was equal to the population in 2015 plus the increase in 2016:

60.731565 + (340 000 / 1 000 000)

≈ 61.071565 million

Italy's artificial land cover per capita in 2016 was the same as that in 2015.

Artificial land cover = Artificial land cover per capita * Total population

Italy's artificial land cover in 2016 was (in million square meters):

343.1 * 61.071565 ≈ 20 954

The percentage change in Italy's artificial land cover from 2015 to 2016 will be:

([20 954 – 20 837] / 20 837) * 100%

≈ 0.56%

Potential Shortcuts / Pitfalls

It is convenient to solve this problem by keeping the population figures in millions. The population growth for 2016 has, however, been provided in units. Therefore, we must convert this figure to millions before adding it to the population of 2015.

There is also a quicker way of solving this problem. Since the per capita figure does not change from 2015 to 2016, we know that the percentage change in the population (denominator) will be equal to the percentage change in the artificial land cover (numerator).

The percentage change in the population of Italy from 2015 to 2016 was:

(340 000 / [60.731565 * 1 000 000]) * 100%

≈ 0.56%

Therefore, the percentage change in the artificial land cover must also have been 0.56% for the per capita figure to have remained unchanged.

C. SPEED, TIME AND DISTANCE QUESTIONS

Set C1 (Speed, Time and Distance)

Distance-Time Chart

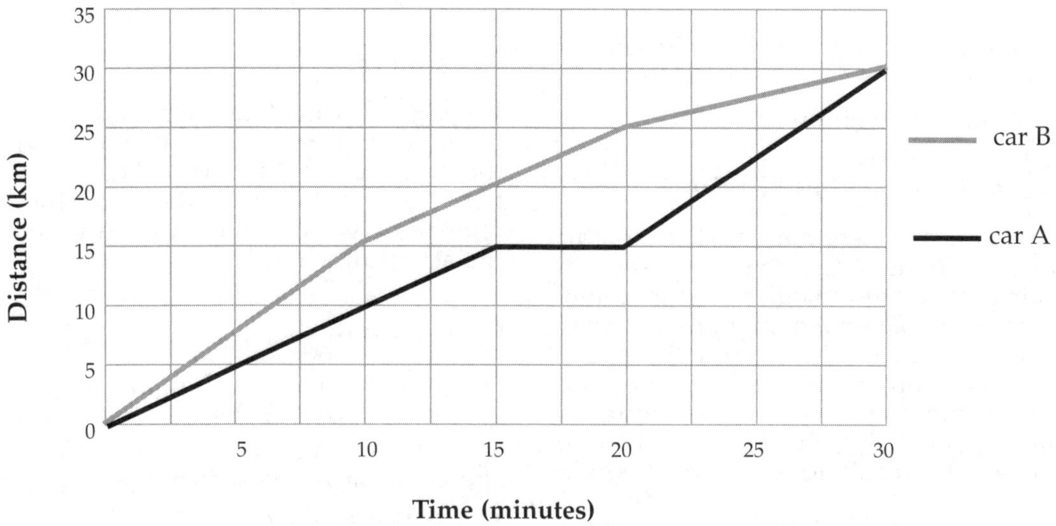

Q1. What was the average speed of Car B between minutes 10 and 20?

A. 1 km/h
B. 30 km/h
C. 60 km/h
D. 75 km/h
E. 90 km/h

Correct Answer: C

Data Interpretation

From the chart we need:

- The distance travelled by Car B at time = 10 minutes
- The distance travelled by Car B at time = 20 minutes

From the question text we need:

- The time interval for which the speed needs to be calculated

Reasoning

We must calculate the speed by dividing the distance Car B travels, during the specified time interval, by the duration of the time interval.

Calculation

At time 10 minutes, the total distance travelled by Car B was 15 km while at time 20 minutes the total distance travelled was 25 km. Therefore, the distance travelled between 10 and 20 minutes was:

25 – 15 = 10 km

We now have to divide this distance (10 km) by the time taken, which is:

20 – 10 = 10 minutes

Since the required answer is in km/h, we need to convert the time taken into hours by dividing by the number of minutes in an hour.

10 / 60 = 0.16667 hours

Recall the formula from chapter 6:

$$\text{Speed} = \frac{\text{Distance}}{\text{Time}}$$

The speed of Car B between 10 and 20 minutes was:

10 / 0.16667 ≈ 60 km/h

Potential Shortcuts / Pitfalls

There is a very simple shortcut to this problem. Remember what was said in looking at methodologies about sometimes being able to use fractions as a way that is both quicker (you can do it in your head) and more accurate? That's the case here. 10 minutes is 1/6 of an hour, so simply multiplying the distance (10 km) by 6 would result in the correct km/h value.

As for the pitfalls, it is easy to overlook the units and divide the distance travelled (10 km) by the time taken (10 minutes) and choose the incorrect answer of 1 km/h, which is given as answer option A. Always be careful about the units. It is also possible to misunderstand the problem and subtract the average speed for the first 10 minutes from the average speed during the first 20 minutes.

Q2. Had Car A not stopped during the journey but instead continued at its initial speed for the entire journey, how many minutes earlier would it have reached its destination?

A. 0 minutes
B. 5 minutes
C. 10 minutes
D. 25 minutes
E. 30 minutes

Correct Answer: A

Data Interpretation

From the chart we need:

- The distance travelled by Car A at time = 15 minutes
- The total distance for the entire journey of Car A

Reasoning

We need to calculate the speed of Car A before it stopped and use this to calculate the time it would have taken for it to travel 30 km. We must then find the difference between this calculated time and the actual time taken.

Calculation

Car A stopped when the time was 15 minutes (or 15/60 = 0.25 hours). It had travelled 15 km at this time. Therefore the speed of Car A before it stopped was:

15 / 0.25 = 60 km/h

We can use this speed to calculate the time it would have taken Car A to travel 30 km without stopping. Since:

$$\text{Speed} = \frac{\text{Distance}}{\text{Time}}$$

Then:

$$\text{Time} = \frac{\text{Distance}}{\text{Speed}}$$

Therefore:

30 / 60 = 0.5 hours

The time taken without stopping would have been 0.5 hours (or 0.5 * 60 = 30 minutes) which is exactly equal to the actual time taken by Car A with the stop. Therefore, Car A would not have arrived any earlier. This is of course because the speed of the car after it stopped and then resumed its journey was greater than the initial speed.

Potential Shortcuts / Pitfalls

You have to be careful with the units involved. To calculate the speed in km/h you must convert all times to hours. The calculated time will be in hours and that has to be converted back to minutes.

There is an easy visual shortcut to this problem. If you look at the graph you can see that Car A travels 15 km (3 gridlines vertically) in 15 minutes (6 gridlines horizontally) during the first half of the journey. Extend this straight line upwards and to the right, up to the 30 km mark on the vertical axis (length of the journey). You will see that the line meets with the original graph at time equals 30 minutes.

Q3. If both cars continue their journey for an extra 10 minutes, at the same speed they are travelling at time = 30 minutes, what would be the ratio between Car A to Car B of the total distance travelled over the whole journey?

A. 1 : 1
B. 2 : 1
C. 9 : 7
D. 5 : 3
E. 3 : 1

Correct Answer: C

Data Interpretation

From the table we need:

- The distance travelled by Car A at time = 20 minutes
- The distance travelled by Car A at time = 30 minutes
- The distance travelled by Car B at time = 20 minutes
- The distance travelled by Car B at time = 30 minutes
- The total distance travelled in the first 30 minutes

From the question text we need:

- The additional time for the journey (10 minutes)

Reasoning

Both cars travelled 30 km during the first 30 minutes. We must therefore calculate the additional distances both cars will travel in the next 10 minutes and then find the ratio of the total distances travelled.

Calculation

Car A's speed at 30 minutes can be calculated from the time interval 20 to 30 minutes. The distance travelled during these 10 minutes (0.16667 hours) was:

30 – 15 = 15 km

We could then calculate the speed as:

15 / 0.16667 ≈ 90 km/h

In the additional 10 minutes (0.16667 hours), Car A will travel:

90 * 0.16667 ≈ 15 km

Similarly, Car B's speed after 30 minutes can be calculated from the time interval 20 to 30 minutes. The distance travelled during these 10 minutes (0.16667 hours) was:

30 – 25 = 5 km

Therefore its speed was:

5 / 0.16667 ≈ 30 km/h

In the additional 10 minutes (0.16667 hours), Car B will travel:

30 * 0.16667 ≈ 5 km

We can now calculate the total distance travelled by Car A in 40 minutes as:

30 + 15 = 45 km

And for Car B:

30 + 5 = 35 km

The ratio of these total distances is:

45:35

This can be simplified to:

9:7

Potential Shortcuts / Pitfalls

The ≈ signs in the calculations above tell you that the figures are approximations, even if they are very close approximations. It's actually easier (and totally accurate) in this case to use fractions, like in question 1: instead of considering 10 minutes as 0.16667 of an hour you can simply say it is 1/6 of an hour. All the calculations can then be done very rapidly in your head.

You can also work out the answer just by using your eyes. By looking at the graph you can see see that Car A travelled 15 km (3 gridlines vertically) in the last 10 minutes. Therefore it will travel another 15 km in the additional 10 minutes bringing the total distance to 45 km. Similarly, Car B travelled only 5 km (1 gridline vertically) in the last 10 minutes, therefore it will travel another 5 km in the additional time. Car B's total distance travelled will be 35 km. In this case using the graph can help avoid time consuming calculations.

Set C2 (Speed, Time and Distance)

London Underground Metropolitan line timetable	
Time	*Station*
06:56	Aldgate
07:01	Barbican
07:10	Great Portland Street
07:27	Wembley Park
07:39	North Harrow
07:49	Moor Park
07:56	Watford

Q1. If the average speed of trains on the Metropolitan line is 34 km/h, what is the approximate distance from Aldgate to Moor Park?

A. 28 km
B. 30 km
C. 34 km
D. 49 km
E. 53 km

Correct Answer: B

Data Interpretation

From the table we need:

- The clock time at Aldgate
- The clock time at Moor Park

From the question text we need:

- The average speed on the Metropolitan line

Reasoning

We need to calculate the time taken to travel from Aldgate to Moor Park and use it in the speed formula, along with the average speed, to give us the approximate distance between the two stations.

Calculation

The train travels between Aldgate and Moor Park from 06:56 to 07:49. It took:

4 minutes between 6:56 and 7:00

49 minutes between 7:00 and 7:49

4 + 49 = 53 minutes

Convert the time to hours, since the average speed is given in km/h:

53 / 60 ≈ 0.88333 hours

Recall the speed formula:

$$\text{Speed} = \frac{\text{Distance}}{\text{Time}}$$

Multiply both sides by Time to get a formula for the distance:

Distance = Speed × Time

Substitute the values to calculate the approximate distance between Aldgate and Moor Park:

34 * 0.88333 ≈ 30.03 km

Potential Shortcuts / Pitfalls

You have to read the question carefully; it asks for the distance between the first and the *second last* stations and not for the length of the whole route.

The time difference is calculated in minutes which must be converted to hours since the average speed for the journey has been provided in km/h.

You can also eliminate answer options C, D and E straight away. If the journey had taken one complete hour, the train would have travelled 34 km. Since the time taken was less than an hour, it means that the train must have travelled less than 34 km. You still have to do the calculations to be sure of getting the right answer because answer options A and B are so close together. However, if you spot this and have no time left at all for calculations, it means you have a 50/50 chance if you just guess either A or B.

Q2. The distance from Barbican to Watford is 30.94 km. The train was delayed for 3 minutes due to a technical problem at Wembley Park. If the train continued the rest of the journey at the usual time intervals, what was the average speed of the train between Barbican and Watford?

A. 32 km/h
B. 33.75 km/h
C. 36 km/h
D. 44 km/h
E. 58 km/h

Correct Answer: A

Data Interpretation

From the table we need:

- The clock time at Barbican station
- The clock time at Watford station

From the question text we need:

- The distance from Barbican to Watford
- The time delay at Wembley Park

Reasoning

We must calculate the total time taken for the journey, including the delay, and use it along with the distance provided to find the average speed of the journey.

Calculation

Had there been no delay, the train would have travelled from 07:01 till 07:56, i.e. for 55 minutes. However with the delay, the total time taken was:

55 + 3 = 58 minutes

We have to convert this time to hours:

58 / 60 ≈ 0.96667 hours

The total distance travelled was 30.94 km. Therefore, by using the speed formula, the average speed of this trip including the delay was:

30.94 / 0.96667 ≈ 32 km/h

Potential Shortcuts / Pitfalls

You must remember that the time interval has to be converted to hours before using it in the speed formula as the speed has been given in km/h.

Q3. If the management decides to operate the trains at 20% higher average speed, what percentage of time will be saved between Great Portland Street and North Harrow?

A. 10.00%
B. 16.67%
C. 20.00%
D. 33.34%
E. 83.33%

Correct Answer: B

Data Interpretation

From the question text we need:

- The change in average speed of the train

Reasoning

Since the distances remain the same, we must find the percentage change in time taken based on the percentage change in speed. We will use the percentage change in time to find the time saving.

Calculation

Recall the speed formula:

$$\text{Speed} = \frac{\text{Distance}}{\text{Time}}$$

Or:

$$\text{Time} = \frac{\text{Distance}}{\text{Speed}}$$

This can be re-written as follows:

New Time as a percentage of old Time = (New Distance as a percentage of old Distance)/(New Speed as a percentage of old Speed)

Therefore, our new journey time based on the 20% higher speed will be as follows:

100% / (100% + 20%) = 100% / 120%

≈ 0.8333 or 83.33%

This means that on average, all distances on the Metropolitan line will now be covered in 83.33% of the original time. Hence the time saving will be:

100% – 83.33% = 16.67%

Potential Shortcuts / Pitfalls

We could very easily have wasted time by taking a long route to solve this problem. We could have calculated the time taken to travel between Great Portland Street and North Harrow at the old speed and then used it to compute the distance between the two stations. We would then have used the distance and the new speed to calculate the time for the quicker journey. Finally, we would have used the old and the new times to find the percentage time saving.

In contrast, in the method we used in the calculation section above, we realised that since the speeds have been increased throughout the Metropolitan line, the specific stations involved do not matter; the percentage time savings will be the same all along the line irrespective of the stations of departure and arrival.

D. EQUATIONS

Set D1 (Equations)

GDP of Germany by sector
(total GDP = $3 700 billion)

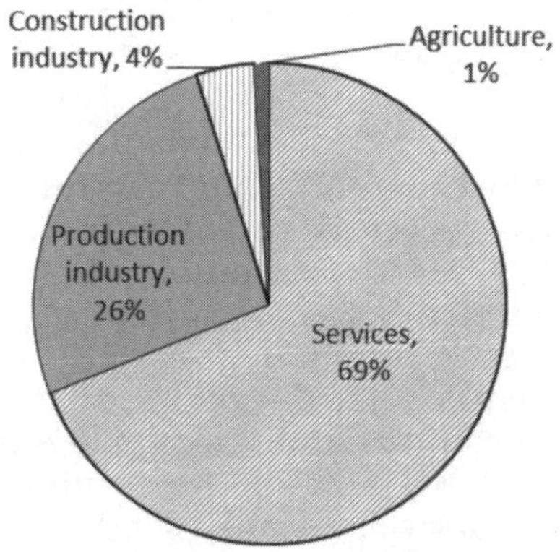

Turnover of Services Sector in Germany

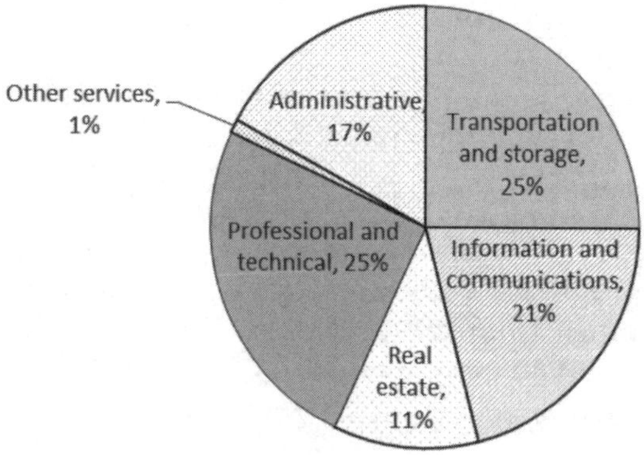

Turnover of Transportation Sector and Storage Sector

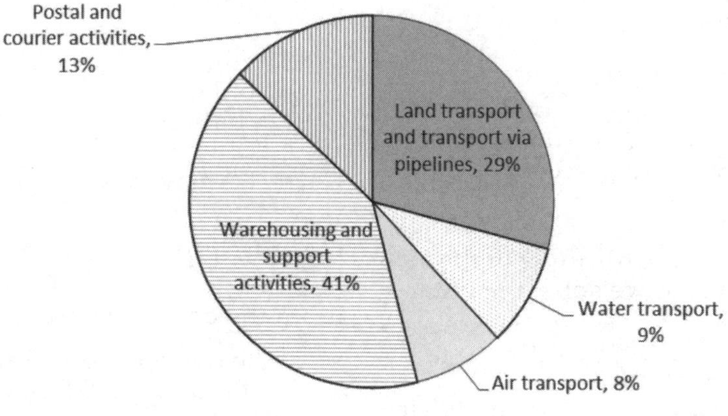

Q1. What is the turnover of the air transport sector in Germany?

A. $51 billion
B. $83 billion
C. $185 billion
D. $638 billion
E. $2 553 billion

Correct Answer: A

Data Interpretation

From the charts we need:

- The percentage share of services in Germany's GDP
- The percentage share of the transportation and storage sector in the turnover of Germany's services sector
- The percentage share of the air transport sector in the turnover of the transportation and storage sector

Reasoning

We need to form an equation to calculate the turnover of the air transport sub-sector (2 levels down) using Germany's GDP.

Calculation

Let X be the turnover of the air transport sector, in billions $.

From the three pie charts, we know that 69% of Germany's GDP is based on services, of which 25% is based on the transportation and storage sector, of which 8% comes from air transport. We can write this in an equation as follows:

X = ([{3 700 * 0.69} * 0.25] * 0.08)

Note that 0.69 equals 69%, 0.25 equals 25% and 0.08 equals 8%. When we solve the inner-most parentheses, we get the turnover of the services sector of Germany as follows:

X = ([{**2 553**} * 0.25] * 0.08)

The number inside the second set of parentheses gives us the turnover of the transportation and storage sector:

X = ([**638.25**] * 0.08)

Finally, we can find the turnover of the air transport sector when we solve the outermost parentheses:

X = 51.06

Therefore, the turnover of Germany's air transport sector is approximately $51 billion.

Potential Shortcuts / Pitfalls

The calculation above was done in full, working out the actual turnover at each stage. However, that full calculation is not really necessary here. You can get to the answer much faster simply by multiplying the percentage of the services sector in the GDP with the percentage of the transportation and storage services in the services sector and then multiplying with the percentage of air transport in the transportation and storage services.

(0.69 * 0.25 * 0.08) = 0.0138

This can then be multiplied by the total GDP to find the answer:

0.0138 * 3 700 = 51.06 (billion)

Much quicker!

Q2. The transportation and storage service sector is forecast to contribute 30% of the turnover of the entire service sector after 2 years. Assuming that growth is uniform across all sub-sectors of the transportation and storage sector and that the size of the services sector remains the same, what will be the increase in turnover of the air transport sector after 2 years?

A. $10 billion
B. $15 billion
C. $51 billion
D. $61 billion
E. $128 billion

Correct Answer: A

Data Interpretation

From the charts we need:

- The percentage share of services in Germany's GDP
- The percentage share of the air transport sector in the turnover of the transportation and storage sector
- The current turnover of the air transport sector (solution to the last question)

From the question text we need:

- The new percentage share of the transportation and storage sector in the turnover of Germany's services sector

Reasoning

We need to form an equation to work out the increase in turnover by subtracting the forecast turnover from the current turnover of the air transport sector.

Calculation

Let Y be the increase in the turnover of the air transport sector, in billions $.

We know that the size of the services sector is 69% of Germany's GDP, which is:

(3 700 * 0.69)

We also know that after 2 years 30% of this is forecast to come from the transportation and storage sector. Since growth will be uniform across all the subsectors, the air transport sector will still be 8% of the transportation and storage sector. This will let us work out the forecast turnover of the air transport sector. To find the increase we must then subtract the current turnover of the air transport sector ($51 billion, the solution to question 1 above) from the forecast figure. We can write this in an equation as follows:

Y = ([{3 700 * 0.69} * 0.30] * 0.08) – 51

Note that 0.69 equals 69%, 0.30 equals 30% and 0.08 equals 8%.

Y = 61.272 – 51

Y = 10.272

Solving the above equation gives the increase in turnover of Germany's air transport sector as approximately $10 billion.

Potential Shortcuts / Pitfalls

A quicker, though slightly complicated, way to solve this problem is to find the percentage change in the total turnover of the transportation and storage sector and use it directly to calculate the increase in turnover of the air transport sector. The percentage change in the turnover of the transportation and storage sector is:

([0.30 – 0.25] / 0.25) * 100% = 20% or 0.20

Therefore the increase in turnover of the air transport sector is:

0.20 * 51 = 10.20

To put both of the above steps into one equation:

Y = ([0.30 – 0.25] / 0.25) * 51 = 10.20

Note that since the GDP is provided in billions $ and the solution required is also in billions $, we should keep our figures in billions $ to simplify the calculation and to avoid any mistakes.

Q3. The information and communications sector can be subdivided into telecommunications and "other information services". If the other information services sector contributes three times as much as the telecommunications sector, what is the turnover generated by the other information services sector?

A. $134 billion
B. $179 billion
C. $357 billion
D. $402 billion
E. $536 billion

Correct Answer: D

Data Interpretation

From the charts we need:

- The percentage share of services in Germany's GDP
- The percentage share of the information and communications sector in the turnover of Germany's services sector

From the question text we need:

- The relationship between the share of the other information services sector and the telecommunications sector (i.e. three times as large)

Reasoning

We need to form an equation to calculate the turnover of the other information services sector by using Germany's GDP and sector percentages and relationships.

Calculation

Let Z be the turnover of the telecommunications sector, in billions $. The turnover of the other information services sector is then 3Z. The combined GDP of these two subsectors is equal to the GDP of the information and communication services sector. The information and communications services sector is 21% of the services sector, which is 69% of Germany's GDP. We can write this as:

$Z + 3Z = 0.69 * 0.21 * 3700$

$4Z = 536.13$

$Z \approx 134$

Solving the equation gives the value of Z as 134 billon. The other information services sector is, however, 3Z. Multiply 134 billion by 3 to get the answer:

$134 * 3 = 402$

The turnover of Germany's other information services sector is approximately $402 billion.

Potential Shortcuts / Pitfalls

You need to read this question particularly carefully because of the multiple layers so you do not end up calculating the wrong thing.

There is also a very simple shortcut. Based on the information in the question, the information and communications sector can be subdivided into telecommunications (25%) and other information services (75%). This can be written as:

$3700 * 0.69 * 0.21 * 0.75 = 402.1$

D2 (Equations)

Number of shares			
Company	**Alex**	**Bob**	**Charles**
Xancom	1000	0	250
Yayvo	0	1500	70
Zem	800	0	1200

Current unit share prices (Price of 1 share)	
Company	**Unit share price**
Xancom	$86.00
Yayvo	?
Zem	$22.00

Q1. Charles's total investment in Xancom and Yayvo is equal in value to his investment in Zem. What is the current unit share price of Yayvo?

A. $4.08
B. $19.60
C. $54.00
D. $70.00
E. $108.00

Correct Answer: D

Data Interpretation

From the tables we need:

- The number of Charles's shares in all three companies
- Current unit share price of Xancom
- Current unit share price of Zem

From the question text we need:

- The relationship between Charles's investments in Xancom, Yayvo and Zem

Reasoning

We must equate Charles's investment in Xancom and Yayvo with his investment in Zem to work out the current unit share price of Yayvo.

Calculation

We first form an equation as follows:

Charles's investment in Xancom + Charles's investment in Yayvo = Charles's investment in Zem

Then:

(Charles's shares in Xancom * Current unit share price of Xancom) + (Charles's shares in Yayvo * Current unit share price of Yayvo) = (Charles's shares in Zem * Current unit share price of Zem)

Let y be the variable for the current unit share price of Yayvo. When we substitute figures in the equation we get:

(250 * \$86.00) + (70 * y) = (1 200 * \$22.00)

(**\$21 500**) + (70 y) = (1 200 * \$22.00)

(\$21 500) + (70 y) = (**\$26 400**)

70 y = \$26 400 - \$21 500

70 y = **\$4 900**

y = \$4 900 / 70

y = **\$70.00**

Therefore, the current unit share price of Yayvo is \$70.00.

Potential Shortcuts / Pitfalls

You have to be careful with the equation to make sure you do not mix up the companies and the share prices. This can easily happen in switching from one table to the other.

Q2. After one year, the value of Alex's total investment grew by 26% but the unit share price of Zem fell to \$19.36. Assuming Alex did not purchase or sell any shares during the year, what was the new unit share price of Xancom?

A. \$190.19
B. \$115.05
C. \$108.36
D. \$86.00
E. \$26.00

Correct Answer: B

Data Interpretation

From the tables we need:

- Number of Alex's shares in all three companies
- Current unit share price of Xancom
- Current unit share price of Zem

From the question text we need:

- Alex's total investment percentage change
- New unit share price of Zem

Reasoning

To work out the new unit share price of Xancom we must create an equation where we set the increased total of investments as equal to the sum of the new investment amounts in each company.

Calculation

The new value of Alex's total investment is made up of (a) his 800 shares in Zem, which we know fell in unit value from \$22 to \$19.36, and (b), his 1000 shares in Xancom, whose unit price was \$86 and whose new unit price we are trying to calculate. We also know that the value of his total investment increased by 26%, so it can be expressed as 1.26.

Let us designate the new unit share price of Xancom as x.

By substituting values we get:

(1.26 * [{1 000 * \$86} + {800 * \$22}])

= (1 000 * x) + (800 * \$19.36)

Where 1.26 is equivalent to 126%

We have to simplify this equation:

(1.26 * [{**\$86 000**} + {**\$17 600**}])

= (1 000 * x) + (800 * \$19.36)

\$130 536 = (1 000 * x) + (800 * \$19.36)

\$130 536 = (1 000 * x) + (**\$15 488**)

\$130 536 = (**1 000x**) + (\$15 488)

1 000x = \$130 536 - \$15 488

1 000x = **\$115 048**

x = \$115 048 / 1 000

x = \$115.048 ≈ **\$115.05**

Potential Shortcuts / Pitfalls

You have to do these rather complex calculations to be sure of getting the right answer. However, if you need to take a guess, notice that since the total investment amount *increased* and the new unit share price of Zem *decreased*, the unit share price of Xancom must have increased as Alex only has these two types of shares. This immediately eliminates options D & E without any calculations.

You can also eliminate Option C with one simple calculation because it only increases the unit share price of Xancom by 26% whereas we know the total value of his investment increased by 26% and the value of his other shares fell.

Q3. Alex plans to purchase some Yayvo shares from Charles so that the total value of his investment becomes equal to Bob's total investment. How many Yayvo shares should Alex purchase from Charles if the current unit share price of Yayvo is $70?

A. 0
B. 20
C. 22
D. 70
E. 1500

Correct Answer: B

Data Interpretation

From the tables we need:

- Number of Alex's shares in all three companies
- Number of Bob's shares in all three companies
- Current unit share price of all three companies

From the question text we need:

- The new relationship between the total investments of Alex and Bob

Reasoning

We need to formulate an equation based on the new relationship between the total investments of Alex and Bob to find the number of Yayvo shares Alex should purchase from Charles.

Calculation

The new relationship can be written in the form of an equation:

Alex's new total investment = Bob's existing total investement

Let z be the variable for the number of Yayvo shares Alex purchased from Charles.

Substituting values into the equation:

(1 000 * $86) + (z * $70) + (800 * $22) = (1 500 * $70)

(**$86 000**) + (z * $70) + (**$17 600**) = (1 500 * $70)

($86 000) + (z * $70) + ($17 600) = (**$105 000**)

z * $70 = $105 000 – $86 000 – $17 600

z * $70 = **$1 400**

z = $1 400 / $70

z = 20

Therefore, Alex needs to purchase 20 Yayvo shares from Charles in order for his total investment to equal Bob's total investment.

Potential Shortcuts / Pitfalls

Note that Bob's investment remains unaffected from the sale of shares; hence his total investment stays constant. Also remember that Alex is purchasing Yayvo shares from Charles but his total investment is being compared to Bob's. Comparing Alex's new investment to Charles's new investment by mistake will lead to the wrong answer.

E. RATIOS

Set E1 (Ratios)

Statistics for 2017	GDP: Gross Domestic Product (billions €)	Tax Revenue (billions €)	Public Debt to GDP Ratio
Croatia	49.0	22.44	0.784
Greece	180.2	86.68	1.819
Iceland	21.7	9.22	0.409
Norway	354.3	194.87	0.367
Portugal	194.6	83.09	1.256

(The Public Debt to GDP ratio is the ratio of a country's public debt to its GDP and the Tax-to-GDP ratio is the ratio of a country's tax revenue to its gross domestic product)

Q1. What is the difference in the Tax-to-GDP ratios of Norway and Iceland?

A. 0.125
B. 0.425
C. 0.550
D. 0.558
E. 0.773

Correct Answer: A

Data Interpretation

From the table we need:

- The 2017 tax revenue of Norway
- The 2017 tax revenue of Iceland
- The 2017 GDP of Norway
- The 2017 GDP of Iceland

Reasoning

We need to work out the Tax-to-GDP ratios of the two countries separately and then find the difference.

Calculation

The information at the foot of the table tells us that the Tax-to-GDP ratio is the ratio of a country's tax revenue to its gross domestic product (GDP).

Since all currency values are in billions €, we do not need to convert them to €.

Norway's Tax-to-GDP ratio is:

194.87 / 354.3 ≈ 0.55

Similarly, Iceland's Tax-to-GDP ratio is:

9.22 / 21.7 ≈ 0.425

Subtract the Tax-to-GDP ratio of Iceland from that of Norway:

0.55 – 0.425 = 0.125

Potential Shortcuts / Pitfalls

Since the GDPs and the tax revenues are provided in billions $ and you need to divide one by the other (the zeroes will cancel each other out), you should keep your calculation in billions $ to keep things simple and to avoid any mistakes.

You must find the two Tax-to-GDP ratios separately. If you try to find the ratio of the difference in tax Revenues and the difference in the GDPs, your solution will be incorrect.

Since you need to calculate the *Tax-to-GDP* ratio you must remember to divide the tax revenue by the GDP instead of the other way around.

Q2 By how much does the public debt of Greece exceed that of Croatia?

A. €36.6 billion
B. €38.4 billion
C. €135.8 billion
D. €289.4 billion
E. €327.8 billion

Correct Answer: D

Data Interpretation

From the table we need:

- The 2017 Public Debt to GDP ratio of Greece
- The 2017 Public Debt to GDP ratio of Croatia
- The 2017 GDP of Greece
- The 2017 GDP of Croatia

Reasoning

We must calculate the public debts for Greece and Croatia separately using the Public Debt to GDP ratios and the GDPs of the two countries, and then find the difference.

Calculation

The Public Debt to GDP ratio is the ratio of a country's public debt to its GDP:

$$\text{Public Debt to GDP Ratio} = \frac{\text{Public Debt}}{\text{GDP}}$$

To find the public debt using the Public Debt to GDP ratio and the GDP, we can rearrange the above formula as follows:

$$\text{Public Debt} = \frac{\text{Public Debt to GDP Ratio}}{\text{GDP}}$$

Greece's public debt (billions €) is:

1.819 * 180.2 ≈ 327.78

Croatia's public debt, in billions €, is:

0.784 * 49 ≈ 38.42

Greece's public debt exceeds Croatia's public debt by:

327.78 – 38.42 = 289.36

Which is rounded to 289.4

Potential Shortcuts / Pitfalls

The public debts of both countries must first be calculated separately and then subtracted. If you subtract the two Public debt to GDP ratios and the two GDPs, your answer will be incorrect. Also, make sure you use the GDP in the calculation and not the tax revenue by mistake.

Q3. If Portugal's Tax-to-GDP ratio increases by 10% to approximately 0.4697, its tax revenue increases by 5% to €87.2445 billion, and its Public Debt to GDP ratio remains constant, what will be the percentage change in its public debt?

A. Decreases by 4.6%
B. Increases by 4.6%
C. Increases by 4.8%
D. Increases by 7.5%
E. Increases by 95.5%

Correct Answer: A

Data Interpretation

From the table we need:

- The 2017 Public Debt to GDP Ratio of Portugal
- The 2017 GDP of Portugal

From the question text we need:

- Portugal's new Tax-to-GDP ratio (0.4697)
- Portugal's new tax revenue (€87.2445 billion)

Reasoning

We need to calculate the new GDP using the new Tax-to-GDP ratio and the new tax revenue and then use it to find the percentage change in public debt using the Public Debt to GDP ratio.

Calculation

Recall that:

$$\text{Tax to GDP Ratio} = \frac{\text{Tax Revenue}}{\text{GDP}}$$

Hence:

$$\text{GDP} = \frac{\text{Tax Revenue}}{\text{Tax to GDP Ratio}}$$

Portugal's new GDP is:

87.2445 / 0.4697 ≈ 185.745

Now, we can use the public debt formula:

Public debt = Public Debt to GDP ratio * GDP

Since Portugal's Public debt to GDP ratio remains constant, Portugal's new public debt is:

1.256 * 185.75 ≈ 233.296

Portugal's original public debt was:

1.256 * 194.6 ≈ 244.418

The percentage change in Portugal's public debt is:

([233.296 – 244.418] / 244.418) * 100% ≈ –4.6%

The negative percentage change tells us that Portugal's public debt has *decreased* by 4.6%.

Potential Shortcuts / Pitfalls

Another, slightly quicker, way of solving this problem is to evaluate all unknowns in terms of percentage changes. First, we can find the new GDP as a percent of the original GDP:

1.05 / 1.10 = 0.9545

Note: 1.05 equals 105%, 1.10 equals 110% and 0.9545 equals 95.45%.

Now we can find the new public debt as a percentage of the original public debt value:

Public debt = Public Debt to GDP ratio * GDP

Since the Public Debt to GDP ratio remains constant, we get:

1.00 * 0.9545 = 0.9545

Note: 1.00 equals 100% and 0.9545 equals 95.45%.

Therefore, we know that the Public debt has decreased by:

1.00 – 0.9545 = 0.0455 ≈ 4.6 (%)

Set E2 (Ratios)

Average Exchange rates versus various currencies (1 Euro =)			
Year	2011	2014	2017
US Dollar	1.39200	1.32850	1.12970
Pound Sterling	0.86788	0.80612	0.87667
Swiss Franc	1.23260	1.21460	1.11170
Russian Rouble	40.88460	50.95180	65.93830

Q1. How many more (or less) Swiss Francs would we get in exchange for 100 Pounds Sterling in 2017 as compared to 2014?

A. 15.21 more Swiss Francs
B. 23.86 more Swiss Francs
C. 10.29 fewer Swiss Francs
D. 15.21 fewer Swiss Francs
E. 23.86 fewer Swiss Francs

Correct Answer: E

Data Interpretation

From the table we need:

- The 2014 exchange rate for Pounds Sterling
- The 2017 exchange rate for Pounds Sterling
- The 2014 exchange rate for Swiss Francs
- The 2017 exchange rate for Swiss Francs

From the question text we need:

- The amount of Pounds Sterling to convert

Reasoning

We must calculate the Swiss Francs equivalent to 100 Pounds Sterling in 2014 and compare it with the amount of Swiss Francs that could be exchanged for 100 Pounds Sterling in 2017.

Calculation

To convert from Pounds Sterling to Swiss Francs we must use the Euro exchange rates.

In 2014:

0.80612 Pounds Sterling = 1 Euro = 1.21460 Swiss Francs

Hence:

0.80612 Pounds Sterling = 1.21460 Swiss Francs

Therefore:

1 Pound Sterling = (1.21460 / 0.80612) Swiss Francs

1 Pound Sterling ≈ 1.50672 Swiss Francs

100 Pounds Sterling = 100 * 1.50672 Swiss Francs

100 Pounds Sterling = 150.672 Swiss Francs

Similarly, in 2017:

0.87667 Pounds Sterling = 1 Euro = 1.11170 Swiss Francs

1 Pound Sterling = (1.11170 / 0.87667) Swiss Francs

1 Pound Sterling ≈ 1.26809 Swiss Francs

100 Pounds Sterling = 100 * 1.26809 Swiss Francs

100 Pounds Sterling = 126.809 Swiss Francs

The change in the number of Swiss Francs that 100 Pounds Sterling would get in 2017 as compared to 2014 is therefore:

126.809 – 150.672

= –23.863

The negative sign signifies that the number of Swiss Francs we get in 2017 will be less than in 2014.

Potential Shortcuts / Pitfalls

A typical error in rushing would be to use the exchange rates for the wrong years or the wrong currencies. Another potential pitfall is to convert the 100 Pounds Sterling to Euros in both the given years, calculate the difference and then convert the amount back to Swiss Francs from Euros at the 2017 rate.

You can clearly see from the currency table that, from 2014 to 2017, the Pound Sterling has depreciated (got weaker) against the Euro while the Swiss Franc has appreciated (got stronger). This can only mean that the Pound Sterling will be able to buy fewer Swiss Francs. Hence, answer options A & B can be easily ruled out. If you can't do any calculations and have to guess the answer, this at least improves your odds to 1 in 3 from 1 in 5.

Q2. In 2011, the sum of 50 US Dollars and 249 Russian Roubles was closest in value to which of the following?

A. 36 Euros + 10 Pounds Sterling
B. 48 Swiss Francs + 125 Roubles
C. 101 Pounds Sterling
D. 50 US Dollars + 199 Russian Roubles
E. 42 Euros + 32 Swiss Francs

Correct Answer: B

Data Interpretation

From the table we need:

- The 2011 exchange rates for all currencies

From the question text we need:

- The original amounts in US Dollars and Russian Roubles to compare
- All amounts provided in each option

Reasoning

Since Euros is the common currency in the table, we need to calculate the Euro equivalent of the sum of currencies in the question and then evaluate all options, one at a time, to find a similar Euro value.

Calculation

The 2011 equivalent Euro value of 50 US Dollars and 249 Russian Roubles was:

(50 / 1.39200) + (249 / 40.88460)

≈ 35.92 + 6.09

≈ 42.00

If we examine the available options, we can eliminate options C, D and E for various reasons.

Option C is 101 Pounds Sterling. We already know that 1 Pound Sterling was more valuable than 1 Euro. Therefore, 101 Pounds Sterling would have a much greater value than 42 Euros.

Option D has exactly the same amount of US Dollars but a different amount of Roubles as compared to the amounts mentioned in the question. Hence this option cannot result in an amount equivalent to 42 Euros.

Option E has 42 Euros (exactly the target amount) plus some Swiss Francs. This sum will definitely be greater than 42 Euros.

We are left with options A & B, which we will now evaluate.

Option A (36 Euros + 10 Pounds Sterling):

36 + (10 / 0.86788)

= 36 + 11.522

= 47.522

Option B (48 Swiss Francs + 125 Roubles):

(48 / 1.23260) + (125 / 40.88460)

≈ (38.942) + (3.057)

≈ 41.999

Option B was therefore closest in value to 50 US Dollars and 249 Russian Roubles in 2011.

Potential Shortcuts / Pitfalls

As explained in the calculations section, we can avoid unnecessary calculations for options C, D & E if we use pure numerical reasoning to eliminate the unlikely options.

Beware of multiplying with the exchange rate when you need to divide and vice versa during conversions.

Q3. In 2011, a businessman converted 1000 Euros into Russian Roubles and invested them into Russian bonds. His investment had grown by 50% in value after 6 years. In 2017, he withdrew all his Roubles and converted them back to Euros. How many Euros more or less did he have in 2017 as compared to 2011?

A. He had 500 more Euros in 2017
B. He had 930 more Euros in 2017
C. He had 70 fewer Euros in 2017
D. He had 930 fewer Euros in 2017
E. He had the same amount of Euros in 2017

Correct Answer: C

Data Interpretation

From the table we need:

- The 2011 exchange rate for Russian Roubles
- The 2017 exchange rate for Russian Roubles

From the question text we need:

- The original amount of Euros
- The investment return for 6 years

Reasoning

We need to calculate the equivalent in Roubles in 2011 and then add the increment after 6 years. We will then convert the total amount back to Euros as per the exchange rate in 2017 and compare.

Calculation

1 000 Euros converted to Roubles in 2011:

1 Euro = 40.88460 Russian Roubles

1 000 Euros = 1 000 * 40.88460 = 40 884.60 Russian Roubles

After six years, the Russian Roubles grew by 50%. The total amount of Russian Roubles in 2017 was:

40 884.60 + (40 884.60 * 50%)

= 40 884.60 + 20 442.30

= 61 326.90 Russian Roubles

In 2017 the businessman withdrew all the Roubles and converted them back to Euros:

1 Euro = 65.93830 Russian Roubles

61 326.90 Russian Roubles = 61 326.90 / 65.93830 Euros

61 326.90 Russian Roubles ≈ 930.06 Euros

We must subtract the amount of Euros in 2017 from the amount of Euros in 2011 to find the overall change:

930.06 Euros – 1 000 Euros

= -69.94 Euros ≈ –70 Euros

The negative sign indicates a decrease of 70 Euros.

Potential Shortcuts / Pitfalls

The major pitfalls to avoid in this problem are the use of incorrect exchange rates. Exchange rates for 2011 must be used for the start and 2017 exchange rates must be used for the end of the 6 year period.

The significant fall in the value of Russian Rouble as compared to the Euro over six years led to an overall loss on investment despite an increase in the amount of Roubles.

Be careful, the question asks for the *difference* in Euros from 2011 to 2017, not the *amount* of Euros in 2017.

F. ESTIMATING AND MENTAL ARITHMETIC

The practice questions in this section involve extensive use of estimating and sums you can do in your head, without using a calculator. In numerical reasoning tests you can sometimes solve what might appear quite tricky problems in these ways, but it means you need to apply reasoning to work out what the question is actually asking and how to use the information you are provided with.

SET 1

Employee Satisfaction Survey Results, ABC Company
Share of employees in the 'satisfied' category

	2016			2017		
	Marketing	Sales	Engineering	Marketing	Sales	Engineering
Pay	65%	68%	79%	78%	75%	49%
Facilities	49%	51%	50%	51%	52%	49%
Morale	80%	70%	75%	88%	76%	90%
CEO	66%	79%	78%	48%	50%	52%

Departmental Headcount

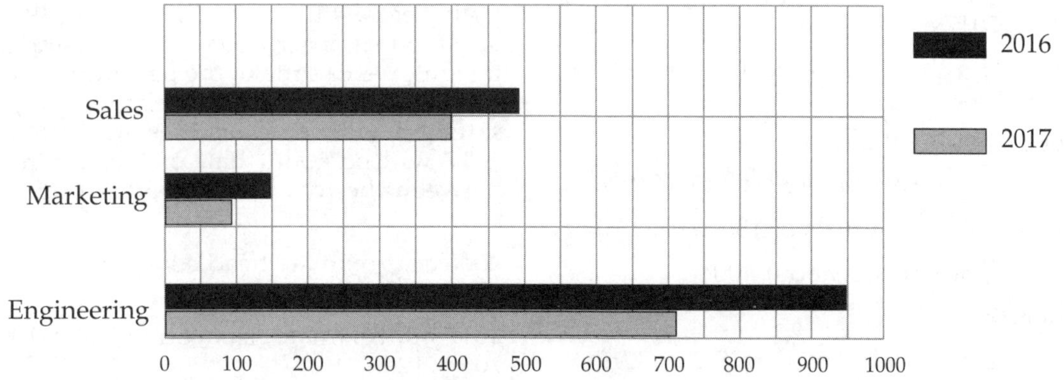

Q1. What was the difference between the number of marketing and sales employees satisfied with the CEO in 2016 and 2017?

A. 44
B. 79
C. 205
D. 243
E. 437

Correct Answer: D

Explanation

While the CEO satisfaction rates across various departments are given as exact percentages, the head count in each department is given in the form of a bar chart without exact figures. This is always a strong indication that we are encouraged to estimate the result.

If we look at the CEO satisfaction rates, we can observe the following:

Marketing: about two-thirds are satisfied in 2016 and about a half in 2017

Sales: about 4/5th are satisfied in 2016, and about half in 2017

Turning to the head counts:

Marketing: about 150 in 2016, less than 100 in 2017

Sales: less than 500 in 2016, about 400 in 2017

Let's combine the two.

Employees satisfied with the CEO in 2016:

Marketing: two-thirds of 150, about 100

Sales: 4/5th of 500, about 400

Total: 500

Employees satisfied with the CEO in 2017:

Marketing: half of 100, about 50

Sales: half of 400, about 200

Total: 250

The question was about the difference between the 2016 and 2017 numbers, so the estimated answer is 500 – 250 = 250.

The closest answer to this is 243 (option D), and all the other answer options are too far from our estimate.

It is important not to confuse which departments and which satisfaction metric we are calculating with as some of the other answer options match results that you would arrive at if you did so.

Q2. What was the change in the total number of employees satisfied with the facilities from 2016 to 2017?

A. Increased by 198
B. Increased by 393
C. Decreased by 198
D. Decreased by 393
E. Decreased by 98

Correct Answer: C

Explanation

As in the previous problem, we need to rely on the departmental head count bar chart, hinting at a relatively low level of required accuracy and telling us that we can estimate.

Another important thing to notice is that the facilities satisfaction rates were very similar in all departments and across both years: 49, 51, 50, 51, 52 and 49, i.e. about one half across the board. Using this insight, we can make the assumption that the total difference between employees satisfied with the facilities in 2016 and 2017 will be about half of the difference between the total head counts in the two years.

2016 approximate head count: 500 + 150 + 950 = 1600

2017 approximate headcount: 400 + 100 + 700 = 1200

Difference: 400

The correct answer is approximately half of this, about 200, and a decrease, which is option C.

It is important to keep in mind the direction of change and that only half of the difference is to be counted, as both of these mistakes are represented by incorrect answer options.

Q3. If we assume that everyone who was dissatisfied with their pay in 2017 leaves the company within the same year, and nothing else changes, how many employees will the company have at the beginning of 2018?

A. 482
B. 592
C. 512
D. 719
E. 981

Correct Answer; D

Explanation

We already know that the departmental head count figures from the bar chart can only be estimated, so we will continue to do so.

Turning to those who are dissatisfied with their pay in 2017, we must first remember that the figures given represent the *satisfaction* rate, so to get the number of those who are *dissatisfied*, we need to subtract these percentages from 100:

Marketing: 100 – 78 = 22%, less than one quarter

Sales: 100 – 75 = 25%, one quarter

Engineering: 100 – 49 = 51%, about half

If all these people leave, that means:

Marketing: (less than) one quarter of (less than) 100 = less than 25

Sales: one quarter of about 400 = about a 100

Engineering: about half of (more than) 700 = 350

Total: about 475

We know from the previous problem that the approximate number of employees in 2017 was 1200. If 475 of them leave, about 725 remain, and answer option D is the closest to this.

We could save even more time by calculating instead the number of employees who are satisfied with their pay and will consequently stay at the company. The percentages for this category are directly available from the table. We can calculate the total and subtract that from overall headcount, saving us a bit more time.

SET 2

Government digital transformation Government services accessed through digital and non-digital channels						
	2005			2015		
	Digital	Non-digital		Digital	Non-digital	
		Phone	Post		Phone	Post
Passport applications	33%	39%	28%	80%	5%	15%
Tax returns	20%	21%	59%	67%	16%	17%

Number of transactions (thousands)

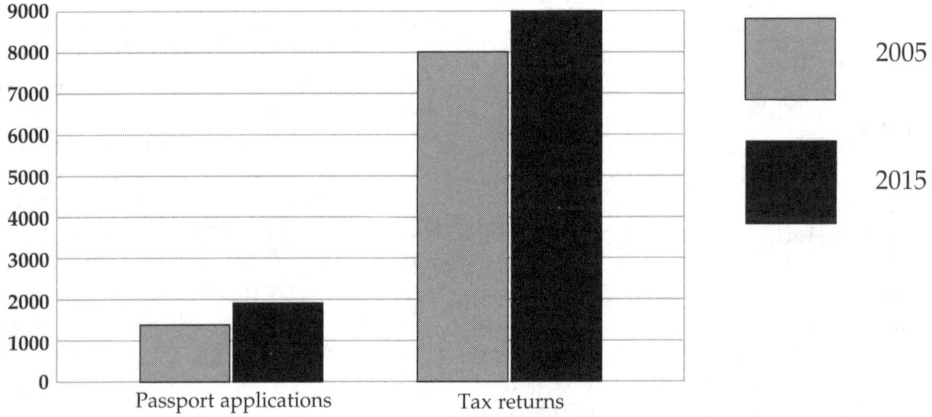

Q1. Digitally submitted tax returns cost 25% as much to process for the government as it does to process those returned in the post, and half as much as those submitted on the phone. If each digital tax return costs the government 1 euro, how much did they spend on processing tax returns in 2015?

A. 11 897 euros
B. 14 962 euros
C. 11.897 million euros
D. 14.962 million euros
E. 17.846 million euros

Correct Answer: D

Explanation

Here again we are faced with a problem where some of the figures we need can only be approximated as they appear in a chart, so estimation is required.

We know that processing each digitally submitted tax return costs the government 1 euro, so let's start there.

We can estimate the number of digitally submitted tax returns to be:

9 million x 67% (about two thirds) = about 6 million

We can apply a shortcut at this point. We know that the number of tax returns using the other two methods must then be 9 – 6 = about 3 million.

If we look at the percentages for phone and post, we see that they are 16% and

17%, i.e. approximately the same, so to simplify things, we will assume that there were 1.5 million phone and 1.5 million postal tax returns.

We know that a digital tax return (1 euro) costs half as much as a phone tax return, so that must be 2 euros; and it costs 25% (one quarter) as much as a postal return, so that must be 4 euros.

We can now calculate the cost of the other two methods:

1.5 million x 2 euros = 3 million euros

1.5 million x 4 euros = 6 million euros

And altogether:

6 + 3 + 6 million = 15 million euros, which means that option D is correct.

Q2. If the cost of digitally submitted passport applications is 61% higher than the cost of digitally submitted tax returns (which stands at 1 euro), what is the difference between the amount spent on each in 2005?

A. 793 729 euros
B. 988 529 euros
C. 1 103 530 euros
D. 1 215 040 euros
E. 1 611 400 euros

Correct Answer: A

Explanation

The approximate number of passport applications submitted digitally in 2005 was:

1.5 million x 33% (about one third) = 0.5 million

Since they cost 61% more than digitally submitted tax returns (which are 1 euro each), the cost of processing these passport applications must be:

0.5 x 1.61 = about 0.8 million euros

The approximate number of digitally submitted tax returns in 2005 was 8 million x 20% = 1.6 million, and since each of those costs 1 euro, this represents a 1.6 million euro cost.

The difference is about 1.6 – 0.8 = 0.8 million, or 800 000 euros, which is closest by far to option A.

Q3. How many fewer people used the phone to submit a tax return or apply for a passport in 2015 than in 2005?

A. 158 790
B. 503 610
C. 753 500
D. 1 628 810
E. 2 291 210

Correct Answer: C

Explanation

This problem can be approached in either of two ways. It is perfectly reasonable to *calculate* the correct answer accurately, but this requires 4 multiplications (to calculate the number of people who used the phone channel for each service and for each year), two subtractions (to subtract the 2015 number from the 2005 number for each service) and one addition (to calculate the difference for the two services combined).

The other option is to *estimate*. Although this requires practice and the ability to make quick mental calculations, it is still faster than the calculation method.

Here is what this method looks like.

Around 40% of about 1.5 million users used the phone channel in 2005, which is about 600 000, and 5% of about 2 million, about 100 000, did so in 2015, giving a difference of around 500 000.

For tax returns, this was 21% of about 8 million. We need to recognise here that the 1% from the 21% figure cannot be disregarded because of the high number (8 million) of transactions. 20% of 8 million is 1.6 million, 1% is 80 000, so this gives us 1.68 million.

In 2015, the total was about 9 million,

and 16% used the phone channel. Similarly to the above, we cannot round 16% down to 15% because of the high number of transactions. What we do is estimate that 15% of 9 million is about 1.35 million, and 1% is about 90 thousand, leaving the total at 1.44 million.

The approximate difference is then about 240 000.

Adding up the two "difference" figures (which are both decreases) gives us about 740 000 as the estimated result, which is clearly closest to option C.

SET 3

CO_2 emissions of various production methods kg / unit of production		
Product / Production Method	Method A	Method B
Dishwasher	101	50
Washing Machine	95	47
Fridge-freezer	197	98

Carbon tax rates USD/ton of CO_2 emissions per company		
	2010-2014	2015 onwards
First 1000 tonnes	2	3
For each additional tonne	3	5

Production volumes in 2015, ABC Company (units)

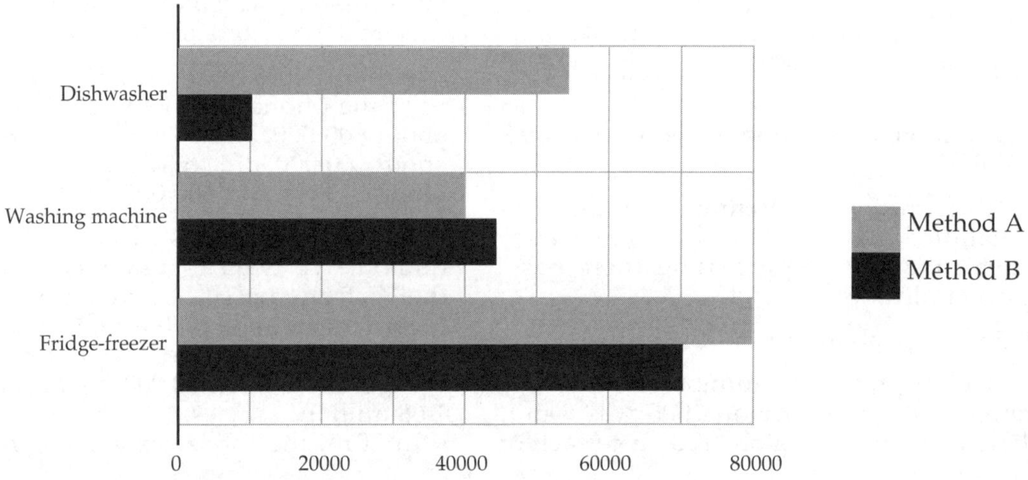

Q1. XYZ company produces 10 000 dishwashers, 10 000 washing machines and 5 000 fridge-freezers a year using production method A exclusively. How much higher/lower will their carbon tax bill be in 2015 than in 2014 if they switch exclusively to production method B?

A. 2535 USD
B. 4455 USD
C. 5300 USD
D. 7835 USD
E. 8125 USD

Correct Answer: A

Explanation

It is key in this problem to notice that the tables are generic, i.e. not specific to one company, and that the chart is about ABC company's production volume whereas the question talks about another company, XYZ. By using approximate figures we can get to the answer doing any calculations in our head, without using a calculator.

To answer the question effectively, we should notice that the carbon emission of production method A is roughly twice as much as that of production method B. Also, production method A has carbon emissions at around 0.1 t (around 100 kg) per unit for dishwashers and washing machines and around 0.2t (around 200 kg) per unit for fridge-freezers.

First, we should calculate the total carbon emissions for 2014:

10 000 dishwashers x about 0.1tonnes = 1000 t

10 000 washing machines x about 0.1 t = 1000 t

5000 fridge-freezers x about 0.2t = 1000 t

That adds up to about 3000 tonnes. In 2014, this is taxed at:

2 USD/t for the first 1000 tonnes = 2000

3 USD/t for the remaining 2000 tonnes = 6000

Total = 8000

If they switch exclusively to production method B in 2015, their emissions will be about half, i.e. 1500 tonnes, and new tax rates will apply. This will add up to:

3 USD/tonne for the first 100 tonnes = 3000

5 USD/tonne for the remaining 500 tonnes = 2500

Total = 5500

The difference is 2500 USD, which is an estimate, but it is clearly closest to option A.

We must take care not to forget about the tax changes and the fact that half as many fridge-freezers are produced as dishwashers and washing machines, as there are answer options matching the results of these mistakes.

Q2. What was ABC company's carbon tax bill in 2015 on its production of dishwashers and washing machines?

A. 11 970.3
B. 34 910.9
C. 35 912.7
D. 59 851.5
E. 71 834.5

Correct Answer: D

Explanation

This question is about ABC company, which is a clue that information from the chart now has to be used. As the chart is purely visual, without providing exact figures, we will be using approximate figures to get to the closest estimate we can.

The approximate production volumes of dishwashers for ABC company for each production method are:

Production method A: 55 000
Production method B: 10 000

For washing machines:

Production method A: 40 000
Production method B: 45 000

Looking at the carbon emissions of the two methods for the two products, we can make the simplification that each method has the same emissions for both products, 0.1t/unit for method A and 0.05t/unit for method B.

With this, we can calculate the total emissions:

Method A: (55 000 + 40 000) x 0.1 = 9500 tonnes

Method B: (10 000 + 45 000) x 0.05 = 2 750 tonnes

Total = 12 250 tonnes

Using the 2015 tax rates, this adds up to:

3000 USD for the first 1000 tonnes

5 USD/tonne for the remaining 11 250 tonnes = 56250

Total = 59 250 USD

The answer option closest to this estimate is D.

It is essential in this question to use the correct tax rates, kg/tonne conversions and the correct products because there are incorrect answer options exploiting these mistakes.

Q3. In 2016, ABC company increased its production volumes by 10% compared to 2015 levels across all of its products and switched its entire operation to production method B. What percentage of the total number of units produced did dishwashers represent in 2016?

A. 19.76%
B. 21.74%
C. 25.78%
D. 28.36%
E. 52.13%

Correct Answer: B

Explanation

For this problem, we must first notice that the information in the question about the company switching its entire operation to method B is a distractor – we do not actually need this to answer the question. We can get to the answer just by using mental arithmetic if we use a little bit of approximating in the final step.

Since the production method doesn't matter, we can add up all of the 2015 production volume figures from the chart to calculate the total volume and the total dishwasher volume. Once we have increased both of these figures by 10%, we can easily calculate what percentage dishwashers represent in the total number of units produced by the company in that year.

Total production in 2015:

Dishwashers: 65 000 units
Washing machines: 85 000 units
Fridge-freezers: 150 000 units
Total: 300 000 units

The 10% increase (for both dishwashers separately and for the total volume) account for:

Dishwashers: 65 000 + 10% = 71 500 units
Total: 300 000 + 10% = 330 000 units

The final calculation will give us what percentage 71500 represents of 330 000:

71 500/330 000 = 21.67%

We would need to use a calculator to give us this exact percentage figure, but we can get our answer even faster without a calculator by using a little bit of rounding and fractions. Simplify 71 500/330 000 to 7/33. Then, given that 33 is about one-third of 100, we only a have to multiply the 7 by 3 to get 21, which is close enough to give us the correct answer.

There is also one more trick we can use to save even more time: calculating the 10% increase is actually superfluous. The question is about the *percentage* one product represents of total production, and this is not affected if both the numerator and denominator are increased by the same percentage.

We can demonstrate this as follows:

$(X \times 1.1) \div (Y \times 1.1) = X \div Y$

Since the 10% increase (represented by the multiplication by 1.1) is on both sides of the fraction, they cancel each other out, resulting in the same percentage as using the original 2015 figures.

Regardless of whether we use this shortcut or not, we can see that while some of the answer options were quite close, this estimate is clearly closest to option B.

SET 4

Cost and speed of various shipping methods			
	Cost / haul (€)	*Speed*	*Haul (units)*
Rail	200	17	500
Road	8	11	10
Boat	1000	50	5000
Speed is defined as the number of hours needed to travel 1000 kilometers			

Order details for Company X				
	Unit price	*Number sold*	*Delivery distance*	*Priority bonus*
Order A	200 USD	20 000	3 000 km	0.5%
Order B	500 USD	30 000	8 000 km	5%
Priority bonus is paid to the supplier if delivery is made within 2 days. It is a percentage of the total price paid. *Revenue = sales price minus delivery costs plus priority bonus (if applicable)*				

Q1. Company X has to deliver Order A to the customer. What is the maximum revenue it can generate from this order?

A. 3.984 million USD
B. 3.992 million USD
C. 3.996 million USD
D. 4.004 million USD
E. 4.012 million USD

Correct Answer: D

Explanation

To solve this problem, we need to carefully consider all the information available in the tables and in the question. The first thing to establish is that the question is about maximum revenue. This is a prompt for us to look at the definition of revenue in the second table. This tells us that revenue includes any priority bonus we can earn by delivering the items quickly, which in turn will prompt us to consider the speed as well as the price of each delivery method. With a little bit of confidence, the calculations can be done without a calculator.

We can start by calculating the sales price of the items in Order A. This is:

200 USD/item x 20 000 items = 4 000 000 USD

Next, we need to consider the cheapest delivery option, taking into account the priority bonus (0.5%) we might earn if we deliver within 2 days. Looking at the delivery distance, only road delivery would allow the company to earn the priority bonus. If we disregard the priority bonus, the cheapest delivery option is by boat, so these are the two methods we should compare.

Boat: 4 hauls of 5 000 items each (total 20 000 items) would cost 4 x 1 000 USD = 4 000 USD.

Road: 2 000 hauls of 10 items each would cost 2000 x 8 USD = 16 000 USD.

However, if the delivery is made by road, the priority bonus is applied, earning the company:

4 000 000 USD x 0.5% = 20 000 USD

After evaluating the two methods, we find:

Revenue with transport by boat: 4 000 000 – 4000 USD = 3.996 million USD

Revenue with transport by road: 4 000 000 – 16 000 + 20 000 = 4.004 million USD

The correct answer, then, is option D.

In this question it is essential to take account of the speed of delivery, as the train would be a cheaper option than by road, but that is just outside the priority bonus timeframe.

Q2. What is the minimum cost of delivering both orders to the customer, irrespective of speed?

A. 4 000 USD
B. 8 000 USD
C. 10 000 USD
D. 20 000 USD
E. 400 000 USD

Correct Answer: C

Explanation

In this problem, the hint is the statement in the question text that we should only consider the cost of delivery *and nothing else.* A second important observation is that the two deliveries must be considered separately as the two different distances for the two orders indicate that they do not go to the same location.

This problem can now be solved with some simple mental arithmetic.

As speed does not matter, we should look for the cheapest delivery option, and that is by boat.

Order A has 20 000 units, which takes up 4 hauls by boat. Order B has 30 000 units, accounting for 6 hauls.

A total of 10 hauls by boat costs 10 000 USD, so option C is the correct answer.

Q3. If order A has to be delivered on land and both orders must be delivered within 5 days, what is the minimum cost of delivery?

A. 10 000 USD
B. 20 000 USD
C. 32 000 USD
D. 40 000 USD
E. 42 000 USD

Correct Answer: C

Explanation

The actual calculations involved in this problem are quite easy and can be done by mental arithmetic. This problem is all about carefully weighing all the constraints set in the question itself:

Both orders must be delivered in less than 5 days

Order A can only be delivered by land (i.e. excluding the boat option)

Based on these constraints, we can consider the cost and speed of rail and road transport options. We should look at speed first, focusing on whether both modes can make the delivery in 5 days (or 120 hours)

Order A (3000 km), by rail: 17 x 3 = 51 hours

Rail can deliver within 5 days and it is

cheaper than by road, so we should use this for Order A. This will cost:

20 000 units / 500 = 40 hauls
40 x 200 USD = 8000 USD

Order B's delivery destination is 8000 km away, so we must again consider the delivery speeds:

Rail: 17 x 8 = 136 hours (this takes too long)

This leaves us with the road delivery option. Order B contains 30 000 units, so the delivery cost is:

30 000 units / 10 = 3 000 hauls
3 000 x 8 USD = 24 000 USD

The total, then, is 32 000 USD, making option C the correct answer option.

SET 5

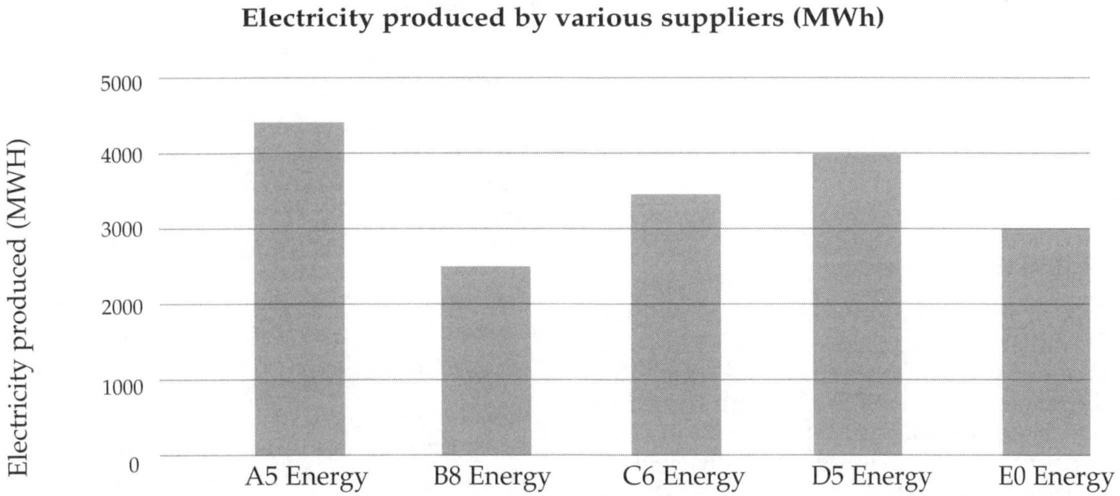

Q1. 15% of the electricity produced by A5 Energy is from renewables, 5% from B8 Energy, 10% from C6 Energy, 15% from D5 Energy, and 20% from E0 Energy. Which supplier produces the most electricity from renewable sources?

A. A5 Energy
B. B8 Energy
C. C6 Energy
D. D5 Energy
E. E0 Energy

Correct Answer: A

Explanation

If we look carefully at the chart and the percentages in the question, it is clear that by using estimation we can eliminate answer options one by one:

- B8 Energy has the lowest total electricity produced and the lowest renewable share as well – it can't be the correct answer
- D5 Energy has the same renewable share as A5 Energy, but a lower total, so it can't be the correct answer either
- C6 Energy has a lower share and a lower total than the already eliminated D5 Energy, so we can eliminate it as well
- While E0 Energy has a higher share of renewables than A5 Energy, this does

not fully compensate for the lower total, so it can't be the correct answer

This leaves A5 Energy as the only remaining possibility.

Q2. If B8 Energy increased the share of renewable energy in its electricity production by a factor of five, where would it rank among the five suppliers in terms of the share of renewable energy in electricity production?

A. First
B. Second
C. Third
D. Fourth
E. Fifth

Correct Answer: A

Explanation

This problem requires only the simplest mental arithmetic, but it is possible to go wrong by misinterpreting the question. The question asks us to rank the suppliers in a hypothetical scenario based on their *share* of renewable energy in their electricity production. It is important to distinguish this from a ranking based on the *amount* of electricity produced from renewable sources as this would result in a different answer being selected.

B8 Energy's current share of renewables is 5%. If they increased this share by a factor of 5, this would take their share to 25%, which is the highest among the 5 suppliers, making option A the correct answer.

If, however, we misinterpret the question and calculate the amount of electricity produced from renewable sources, we would get:

2500 x 25% = 625 MWh

This would place B8 Energy ahead of C6, D5 and E0 Energy, but it would still be behind A5 Energy, whose corresponding figure is 4500 x 15% = 675 MWh

This misinterpretation would lead us to pick option B, which would be incorrect.

Q3. What is the total amount of electricity produced by the five suppliers from non-renewable energy sources?

A. 2 350 MWh
B. 3 150 MWh
C. 14 350 MWh
D. 15 150 MWh
E. 17 500 MWh

Corrrect Answer: D

Explanation

The total amount of electricity produced by the 5 suppliers can be easily read off the chart. We also know the share of renewable energy for each supplier, expressed as percentages. One way to calculate the share of non-renewable energy is to calculate the remaining percentage. For example, for A5 Energy, this would be:

100% – 15% = 85%

Some may find this method unnecessarily time-consuming. As an alternative, we can instead calculate the total amount of electricity produced by the 5 suppliers from renewable sources, and subtract this from the grand total.

Grand total for all suppliers: 4 500 + 2 500 + 3 500 + 4 000 + 3 000 = 17 500

Then, we can calculate the total from renewable sources, summing up as we go:

15% x 4 500 = 675
5% x 2 500 = 125 (800)
10% x 3 500 = 350 (1150)
15% x 4 000 = 600 (1750)
20% x 3 000 = 600 (2350)

The correct answer will be the difference between 17500 and 2350 = 15150, i.e. option D.

It is essential not to forget about this last step, as the interim calculation steps are among the answer options.

8. Numerical Reasoning Mixed Questions Test

40 Sets – Total 120 Questions
ANSWERS follow Set 40

This test consists of mixed question types, testing all the operations and techniques we practised in the previous chapter.

You should aim to eventually be able to answer these questions at a rate of 10 in 20 minutes, which is a typical EPSO scenario. However you will most likely struggle to achieve these speeds at first. Read the answer explanations carefully and focus on the range of strategies they give for speeding up your calculations until they become second nature to you.

Remember, too, to check the exact rules of your competition for the number of questions, time allowed and pass mark and use those for your practice.

Note: the symbols × and * are both used for multiplication.

Set 1

Intra-EU air traffic at country level, top-5 country pairs						
Rank	*Country pairs*		*2015*		*2016*	
			Passengers carried (in 1000)	*Share in total intra-EU (%)*	*Passengers carried (in 1000)*	*Share in total intra-EU (%)*
1	United Kingdom	Spain	35922.6	9.10	41637.8	9.60
2	Spain	Germany	25063.9	6.35	27581.6	6.36
3	United Kingdom	Germany	13302.7	3.37	13877	3.20
4	United Kingdom	Italy	12711.3	3.20	14123.5	3.24
5	Italy	Germany	12427.1	3.15	13296	3.07

Q1. What was the increase in total intra-EU traffic between 2015 and 2016 (*rounded to the nearest million*)?

A. 11 million
B. 39 million
C. 13 million
D. 73 million
E. 4 million

Q2. What was the percentage increase in traffic for the three top destinations from the United Kingdom between 2015 and 2016 (*rounded to one decimal place*)?

A. 0.9%
B. 8.9%
C. 11.2%
D. 12.4%
E. 0.4%

Q3. In 2015 the average cost of a Spain-Germany flight was €147.60, and it increased by 2.1% in 2016. What was the increase in the total amount spent by Spain-Germany passengers between 2015 and 2016 (*rounded to the nearest thousand euros*)?

A. €457 thousand
B. €364 thousand
C. €457115 thousand
D. €2108 thousand
E. €364091 thousand

Set 2

Trips, nights spent and expenditure of EU residents, EU-28, 2016			
	All trips (Thousand)	*Domestic trips (Thousand)*	*Outbound trips (Thousand)*
Trips	1 206 953	898 331	308 622
Nights	6 126 026	3 530 916	2 595 110
Expenditure in million €	428 198	192 949	235 249

Top 5 destinations for outbound trips made by EU residents outside the EU, in terms of number of trips, EU-28 2016 (%)

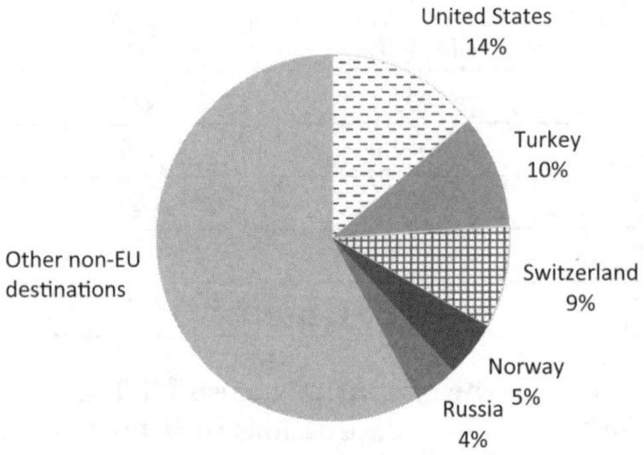

Q1. What was the difference between the numbers of outbound trips made by EU residents in 2016 to the U.S. and to Switzerland (*to the nearest million*)?

A. 60 million
B. 39 million
C. 15 million
D. 15431 million
E. 18934 million

Q2. The number of outbound trips made by EU residents to Turkey decreased by 0.6% between 2016 and 2017, and the total number of outbound trips increased by 1.8% during the same period. What was the share of outbound trips made by EU residents to Turkey in 2017 (*rounded to one decimal place*)?

A. 9.2%
B. 9.4%
C. 10.2%
D. 9.8%
E. 10.8%

Q3. The share in the expenditure of outbound trips made by EU residents to Norway in 2016 was 1.4 times larger than the share of Norway in the number of outbound trips, and the share in the expenditure of outbound trips made by EU residents to Russia in 2016 was by 25% less than the share of Russia in the number of outbound trips. What was the ratio between the expenditures of outbound trips made by EU residents to Norway and to Russia in 2016?

A. 4 : 5
B. 7 : 5
C. 5 : 4
D. 3 : 7
E. 7 : 3

Set 3

Health care expenditure, top-5 EU member states, 2015		
	Million EUR	*EUR per inhabitant*
France	241 366	3 623
Germany	338 207	4 140
Italy	148 029	2 437
Spain	98 586	2 123
United Kingdom	254 827	3 913

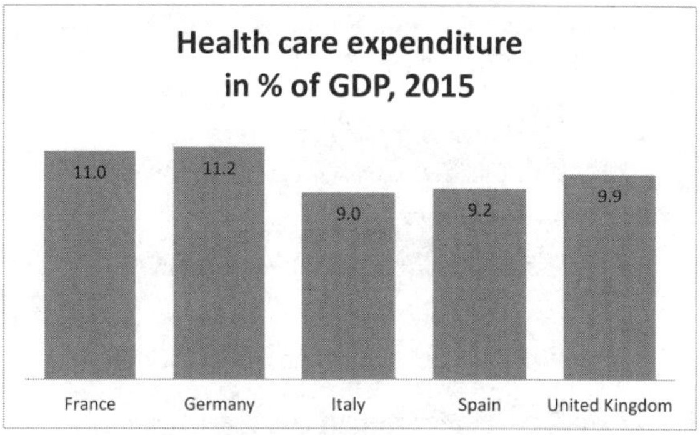

(*GDP = Gross domestic product*)

Q1. The average health care expenditure of the top-5 EU members increased by 4.5% between 2015 and 2017. What was the average expenditure of the top-5 EU members in 2017 (*rounded to the nearest billion euros*)?

A. 226 billion
B. 39 billion
C. 216 billion
D. 236708 billion
E. 225932 billion

Q2. What was the difference between the GDP of the United Kingdom and France in 2015 (*rounded to the nearest billion euros*)?

A. €13461 billion
B. €380 billion
C. €415561 billion
D. €379774 billion
E. €13 billion

Q3. The population of Spain increased by 3.1% in 2016, and by 3.4% in 2017. What was the population of Spain by the end of 2017 (*rounded to the nearest million*)?

A. 49 million
B. 49505 million
C. 50 million
D. 49501 million
E. 46 million

Set 4

Dataset: Generation of waste by sector							
Variable	*01-03: Agriculture, forestry and fishing*						
Unit	*Tonnes, Thousands*						
Year	*2004*	*2005*	*2006*	*2007*	*2008*	*2009*	*2010*
Country							
Austria	469	..	513	..	459	..	550
Belgium	1 187	..	361	..	288	..	231
Chile	1 515	1 393	1 367	1 470	1 435	1562	..
Hungary	4 000	..	1 998	..	337	..	488
Ireland	9	..	0	..	19	..	101
Italy	710	..	554	..	341	..	302
Japan	89 300	87 584	87 945	87 837	87 992	88 446	85 109
Korea	..	..	..	..	..	..	152
Latvia	208	..	96	..	75	..	68
Netherlands	2 393	..	2 659	..	3 468	..	4 978
Sweden	314	..	314	..	314	..	309
United Kingdom	719	..	666	..	681	..	495
Data extracted on 11 Oct 2018 15:40 UTC (GMT) from OECD.Stat							

Q1. If the generation of waste in the agriculture, forestry and fishing sector in Chile had been 500,000 tonnes less in both 2005 and 2007, what percentage would this decrease have represented in the total waste generated in this sector in Chile in the period from 2004 to 2007?

A. 11.4%
B. 17.4%
C. 18.9%
D. 21.1%
E. 174%

Q2. In which country did the generation of waste in this sector decrease at the greatest rate between 2006 and 2008, Austria, Belgium or Italy?

A. Austria
B. Belgium
C. Italy
D. Belgium and Italy (the difference between them is negligible)
E. The difference between all three is negligible

Q3. In which year did Japan's waste generation in this sector deviate the most from the average amount of waste it generated in the 2004–2010 period?

A. 2004
B. 2006
C. 2008
D. 2009
E. 2010

Set 5

Distribution of people aged 25–64 by knowledge of foreign languages, 2011 and 2016								
(%)	*No foreign language*		*One foreign language*		*Two foreign languages*		*Three or more foreign languages*	
	2011	2016	2011	2016	2011	2016	2011	2016
Czech Republic	30.9	21.0	39.6	44.7	22.4	26.9	7.1	7.4
Poland	38.1	32.9	38.7	45.0	19.2	19.2	4.0	2.8
Slovakia	14.7	11.8	30.2	24.5	33.5	35.7	21.6	28.0
Slovenia	7.6	20.0	15.0	17.6	32.6	24.7	44.9	37.7

People aged 25–64 reporting they knew one or more foreign languages, by educational attainment level, 2016, %

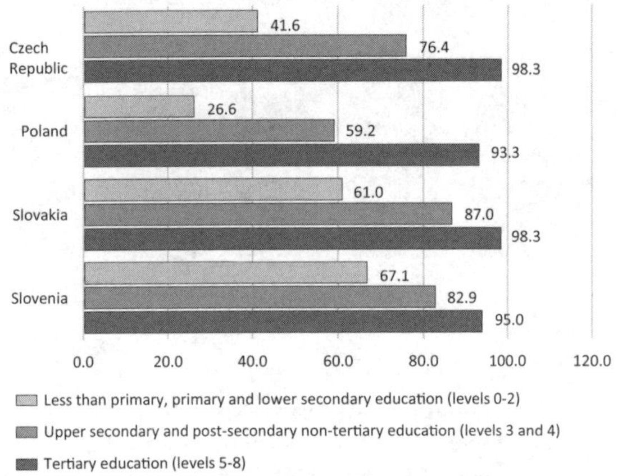

Q1. What was the average percentage change between 2011 and 2016 of people aged 25–64 reporting they knew three or more foreign languages across the four countries shown (*rounded to three decimal places*)?

A. –0.48%
B. –0.425%
C. 0.425%
D. 0.48%
E. 0.34%

Q2. What was the ratio of the share of Slovenian people aged 25-64 and having tertiary education reporting that they knew one or more foreign languages, to the share of all Slovenian people of this age reporting that they knew one or more foreign languages in 2016?

A. 15 : 13
B. 10 : 9
C. 4 : 19
D. 19 : 4
E. 19 : 16

Q3. The population of Poland aged 25-64 changed from 31.2 million to 30.7 million between 2011 and 2016. What was the difference between the number of Polish people aged 25–64 reporting they knew just one foreign language in 2016 and in 2011 (*rounded to one thousand*)?

A. 2 thousand
B. 174 thousand
C. –1741 thousand
D. 1741 thousand
E. –174 thousand

Set 6

Marathon Results 2010 (42.2 km)	
Runner	*Time (h:mm:ss)*
Anderson	2:12:14
Benoit	2:12:38
Canard	2:13:31
Dennis	2:14:12
Ekimov	2:14:20

Q1. Canard passed the halfway marker at 1:07:50. What was his average speed for the second half of the race?

A. 15.20 km/h
B. 17.38 km/h
C. 18.63 km/h
D. 19.27 km/h
E. 20.31 km/h

Q2. Dennis and Ekimov passed the "1km to go" marker at exactly the same time, 2:11:00. How much faster than Ekimov did Dennis run in the last kilometre?

A. 1%
B. 4.2%
C. 6.6%
D. 8%
E. 12.5%

Q3. Benoit ran the last 150m at a speed 5% faster than his overall average for the race. How far was Benoit from the finishing line when Anderson finished?

A. 84m
B. 92m
C. 100m
D. 133m
E. 149m

Set 7

Tobacco Use Amongst High School Students in 2017			
Tobacco Product	*Overall*	*Females*	*Males*
Any tobacco product	19.6%	17.5%	21.6%
Electronic cigarettes	11.7%	9.9%	13.3%
Cigarettes	7.6%	7.5%	7.6%
Cigars	7.7%	6.3%	9.0%
Smokeless tobacco	5.5%	3.0%	7.7%
Hookahs	3.3%	3.2%	3.3%
Pipe tobacco	0.8%	0.5%	1.0%
Bidis	0.7%	0.6%	0.7%

Q1. If 60 male students in a high school use any kind of tobacco product, how many female students does the school have?

A. Fewer than 250
B. Around 260
C. Around 280
D. Around 290
E. More than 320

Q2. In a high school with 300 male students, of whom 20 use both electronic and regular cigarettes, how many male students use only one of them?

A. 15
B. 63
C. 20
D. 23
E. 43

Q3. If there are 100 students using any kind of tobacco product in a school where the number of male students is twice the number of female students, how many of the school's female students are using electronic cigarettes?

A. 7
B. 34
C. 12
D. 17
E. 39

Set 8

Meat consumption *Beef and veal / Pork meat / Poultry meat / Sheep meat, Kilograms/capita 2017*			*Source: OECD-FAO Agricultural Outlook (Edition 2017)*	
Location	*Beef and veal*	*Pork*	*Poultry*	*Lamb*
Algeria	3.9	0.1	6.3	7.1
Argentina	41.2	8.8	37.5	1.2
Australia	20.9	20.7	44.5	8.5
Bangladesh	0.9	0.0	1.2	1.2
Brazil	26.5	11.8	39.9	0.4
BRICS	4.5	15.5	10.8	1.7
Canada	18.4	15.9	34.9	0.9
Chile	18.1	18.6	34.8	0.4
China (People's Republic of)	4.1	30.8	12.3	3.1
Colombia	11.7	4.7	27.3	0.2
Egypt	9.3	0.2	9.2	1.3
Ethiopia	2.4	0.0	0.5	1.2

Q1. The carcass weight to retail weight conversion rate for beef and veal is 0.7. Assuming that Argentina had a population of 44.27 million people in 2017, what was the weight of bovine carcasses necessary to meet the beef and veal consumption?

A. 2.6 million kg
B. 2.6 million tonnes
C. 1.8 million kg
D. 1.8 million tonnes
E. None of the above

Q2. Assuming that Brazil has a population of 209.3 million people, what would be the overall rate of decrease of meat consumption in that country if both beef and veal, and poultry consumption decreased by 20%?

A. 15.3%
B. 16.9%
C. 18.7%
D. 20.3%
E. 22.2%

Q3. Australia's population is 24.6 million. Assuming that the weight of carcasses required to meet the country's pork consumption is 652.85 million kg, what is the carcass weight to retail weight ratio for pork?

A. 1 to 0.62
B. 1 to 0.72
C. 1 to 0.78
D. 1 to 0.88
E. None of the above

Set 9

Acme Closing Share Prices (€)		
	Buy	*Sell*
Monday	2.37	2.32
Tuesday	2.41	2.37
Wednesday	2.39	2.34
Thursday	2.28	2.25
Friday	2.34	2.29

Q1. You buy 2000 shares on Tuesday at 1.4% below the previous day's closing price. There is a €15.95 dealing charge. How much does it cost you?

A. €4673.64
B. €4689.59
C. €4734.37
D. €4761.47
E. €4768.47

Q2. You sell 2000 shares on Friday which incurs a €15.95 dealing charge. Your total proceeds amount to €4664.05. By what percentage had the price risen since yesterday's close?

A. 2%
B. 3%
C. 4%
D. 5%
E. 6%

Q3. The difference between the buying price and the selling price on a given day is known as 'the spread'. If the percentage spread is calculated as a percentage of the higher value, which day has the largest percentage spread?

A. Monday
B. Tuesday
C. Wednesday
D. Thursday
E. Friday

Set 10

Costs of Introducing New Accounting Software				
	Accounts Pro 10	*BSheet 12*	*BSheet Lite*	*BookKeeper Standard*
Licence fee (€)	4500 / year	3500 / year	8000 / year	9000 one-time fee
Installation fee (€)	130	150	200	550
*Staff needed to operate**	4	4	3	5
Working hours needed to operate / person (monthly)	20	20	25	15
* The hourly wage of staff operating the accounting software is 20 (€)				

Q1. Which of the accounting software shown in the table is projected to cost the least to acquire and operate over a two-year period?

A. Accounts Pro 10
B. BSheet 12
C. BSheet Lite
D. BookKeeper Standard
E. BSheet 12 and BookKeeper Standard

Q2. If the company manages to negotiate a 15% discount on the licence fees and the installation is done free of charge, how much would it cost to introduce and operate the BSheet 12 software for 5 years?

A. 16 475 €
B. 19 100 €
C. 110 875 €
D. 113 500 €
E. 111 025 €

Q3. How much money will the company save or lose over 3 years if it introduces BookKeeper Standard instead of Accounts Pro 10?

A. 2 605 € in savings
B. 6 840 € in savings
C. 7 680 € in savings
D. 10 320 € in losses
E. 13 820 € in losses

Set 11

Crop Production in France (thousands of tonnes)			
	2005	*2010*	*2015*
Corn	12 107	12 211	12 409
Rapeseed	4 541	5 472	5 801
Sugar	2 814	2 920	2 702
Sunflowers	18 442	19 194	21 199
Wheat	7 422	7 719	7 792

Q1. If the table were ordered by percentage increase in production between 2010 and 2015, which crop would be in the middle of the table?

A. Corn
B. Rapeseed
C. Sugar
D. Sunflowers
E. Wheat

Q2. How many more tonnes of sugar would France have needed to produce in 2010 for its percentage increase from 2005 (to the nearest whole percentage point) to be the same as the corresponding increase for wheat?

A. 245.6
B. 6560
C. 191
D. 224.7
E. 2926.6

Q3. The yield (tonnes produced per hectare) of rapeseed is 3.1 tonnes per hectare in 2005. This improves by 6% by 2015. What is the percentage increase in land usage for rapeseed production between 2005 and 2015?

A. 27.7%
B. 13.7%
C. 35.4%
D. 26.2%
E. 20.5%

Set 12

Top-5 total production of fishery products, 2008 and 2015			
	(1 000 tonnes live weight)		*Share of EU-28, %*
	2008	*2015*	*2015*
Denmark	728	905	14.1
Spain	1,106	1,195	18.7
France	728	661	10.3
Netherlands	422	427	6.7
United Kingdom	768	913	14.3

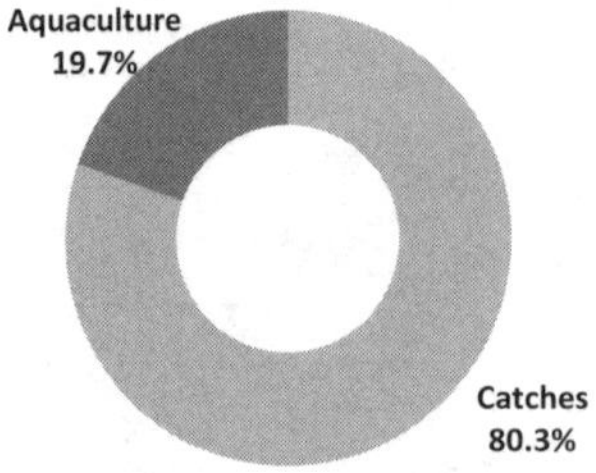

Aquaculture production and fish catches, EU-28, 2015
(% of total fisheries production)

Q1. What was the total EU-28 aquaculture production in 2015 (*in million tonnes, rounded to one decimal place*)?

A. 1.3 million tonnes
B. 5.1 million tonnes
C. 1264.4 million tonnes
D. 1189.3 million tonnes
E. 0.8 million tonnes

Q2. The French fish catch was 271 thousand tonnes greater than its aquaculture production in 2015. What was the share of French aquaculture production in the total EU-28 production of fishery products (*rounded to the nearest whole percent*)?

A. 6%
B. 4%
C. 7%
D. 3%
E. 1%

Q3. By what percentage was the increase in the total production of fishery products in the United Kingdom from 2008 to 2015 greater than that in Spain in the same period (*rounded to one decimal place*)?

A. 86.1%
B. 71.2%
C. 18.0%
D. 56.0%
E. 10.8%

Set 13

Percentage of Total Power Generated in the UK				
Source	2000	2005	2010	2015
Fossil Fuel	85.2	78.8	66.4	53.0
Wind	1.7	3.7	9.8	15.4
Solar	0.3	0.9	7.8	12.3
Tide/Wave	0.1	1.3	1.8	3.3
Nuclear	10.9	12.4	10.4	9.8
Other	1.8	2.9	3.8	6.2

Q1. The total power generated in the UK increased by 7.25% between 2000 and 2005. What was the percentage increase in nuclear power generation over the same period?

A. 14.8%
B. 22%
C. 19.3%
D. 13.8%
E. 96%

Q2. Which form of power generation shows the greatest percentage increase in the percentage of total power generated between 2010 and 2015?

A. Fossil fuel
B. Wind
C. Solar
D. Tide/Wave
E. Nuclear
F. Other

Q3. In 2005, 20% of the 'Other' power was generated by biomass. By 2010 this amount had increased by 50%. If the total power generated in the UK had increased by 10% over the same period, what percentage of 'Other' power was generated by biomass in 2010?

A. 30%
B. 63.6%
C. 22.9%
D. 48.6%
E. 20.8%

Set 14

The Natural Disasters That Inflict The Most Economic Damage Economic damage by disaster type and region from 1995 to 2005

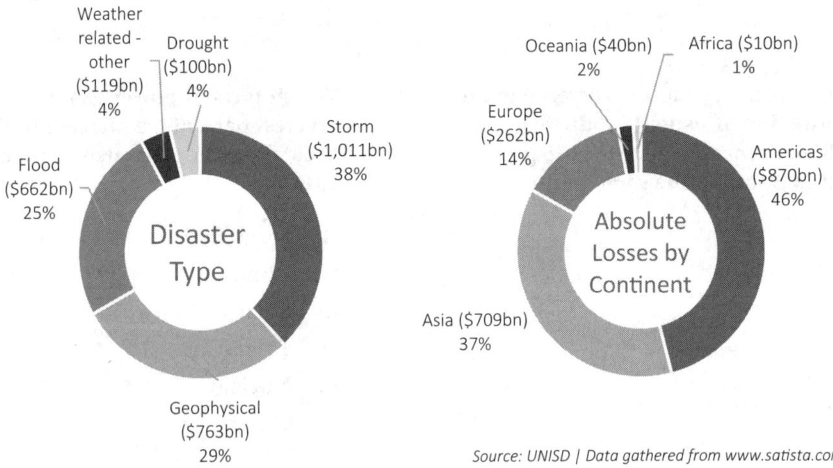

Source: UNISD | Data gathered from www.satista.com

Q1. If the economic damage caused by storms had doubled, what percentage of the total economic damage would have been caused by storms?

A. 55.2%
B. 62%
C. 71.8%
D. 76%
E. 83.7%

Q2. If the total cost of economic damage had stayed the same, but Asia had suffered 45% of it, what would have been the absolute loss of Asia?

A. Approximately 820 to 835 bn USD
B. Approximately 835 to 850 bn USD
C. Approximately 850 to 865 bn USD
D. Approximately 865 to 880 bn USD
E. Approximately 880 to 895 bn USD

Q3. What was the cost of economic damage caused by storms in the Americas?

A. $292 billion
B. $314 billion
C. $387 billion
D. $455 billion
E. There is not enough information

Set 15

100m Men's Final	
Runner	*Time (s)*
Adams	9.95
Best	9.98
Carter	10.03
Davies	10.07

Q1. Davies ran the last 10m at a speed 8% faster than his overall average speed. By what distance, to the nearest centimetre, did he miss out on the bronze medal (3rd place)?

A. 43
B. 37
C. 32
D. 26
E. 18

Q2. How much faster did Adams run than Best on average?

A. 0.1%
B. 0.3%
C. 0.7%
D. 1.0%
E. 1.2%

Q3. Carter ran the final 1.3% faster than he ran in the semi-final which was 1.8% faster than his performance in the heat (the race before the semi-final). He won his heat by 3 hundredths of a second. What was the finishing time of the runner who came second in Carter's heat?

A. 10.09
B. 10.18
C. 10.29
D. 10.34
E. 10.37

Set 16

Sold production and trade of chemical products, EU-28, 2017				
	EUR billion			
	Sold production	*Extra-EU-28*		*Intra-EU-28*
		Exports	*Import*	*Exports*
Total Chemicals	674	333	195	527
51-Organic chemicals	102	44	45	81
52-Inorganic chemicals	32	10	12	17
53-Dyeing,tanning&colouring materials	41	12	5	23
54-Medical and pharmaceutical products	168	156	77	171
55-Essential oils, resinoids and perfume materials	57	32	10	48
56-Fertilizers (other than those of group 272)	14	3	4	7
57-Plastics in primary forms	93	27	17	76
58-Plastics in non-primary forms	68	15	9	39
59-Chemical materials and products	98	34	16	66

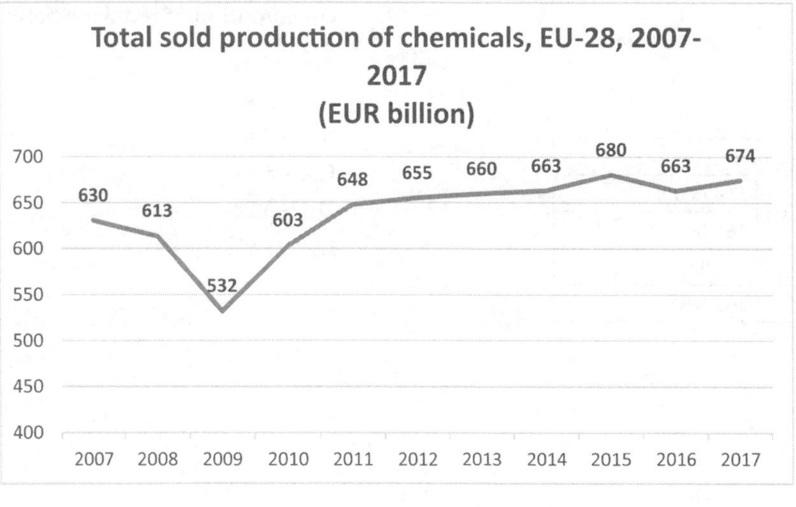

Q1. What was the ratio of the percentage change of the total EU sold production of chemicals between 2016 and 2017 to the percentage change between 2014 and 2015?

A. 674 : 663
B. 11 : 17
C. 17 : 11
D. 2 : 5
E. 16 : 17

Q2. The amount sold of medical and pharmaceutical products increased by 5.2% between 2016 and 2017. What was the share of medical and pharmaceutical products in total sold production of chemicals in 2016 (*rounded to one decimal place*)?

A. 23.8%
B. 24.4%
C. 26.7%
D. 25.6%
E. 24.1%

Q3. What was the difference between the organic and inorganic shares in intra-EU-28 exports of chemicals in 2017 (*rounded to one decimal place*)?

A. 12.1%
B. 18.6%
C. 64.0%
D. 29.5%
E. 63.6%

Set 17

Netherlands Population	
Year	*Pop ('000)*
2005	16 316
2010	16 492
2015	16 714

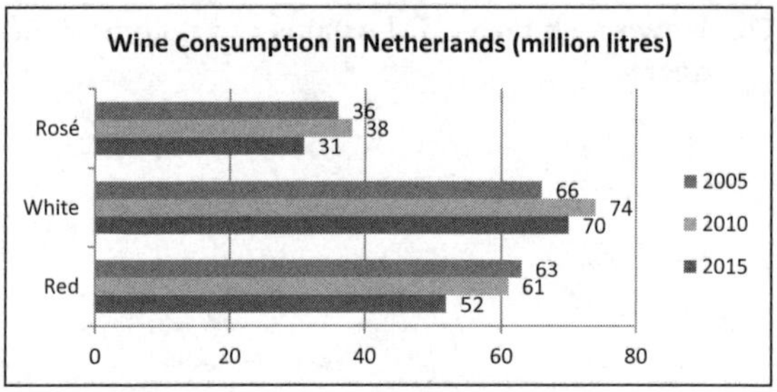

Q1. If the average cost of a 75cl bottle of red wine in the Netherlands was €6.63 in 2015, what was the per capita spending on red wine in 2015?

A. €18.15
B. €27.87
C. €20.62
D. €27.50
E. €37.02

Q2. If the change in consumption of white wine between 2010 and 2015 had been the same as the change for rosé wine over the same period, what would the consumption figure for white wine have been in 2015?

A. 56
B. 60
C. 67
D. 14
E. 66

Q3. What was the percentage change in per capita consumption of red wine between 2005 and 2010?

A. −4.2%
B. −4.4%
C. −5.1%
D. −3.2%
E. −3.9%

Set 18

Participation rates of young people in education, 2015				
(%)	15-29 years	15-19 years	20-24 years	25-29 years
EU-28	45.0	86.4	41.4	13.3
Germany	50.2	88.4	49.3	20.8
Spain	48.4	87.1	49.1	16.1
France	42.8	85.2	35.6	6.8
Italy	41.1	83.9	33.8	10.6
United Kingdom	40.2	84.3	32.0	10.0

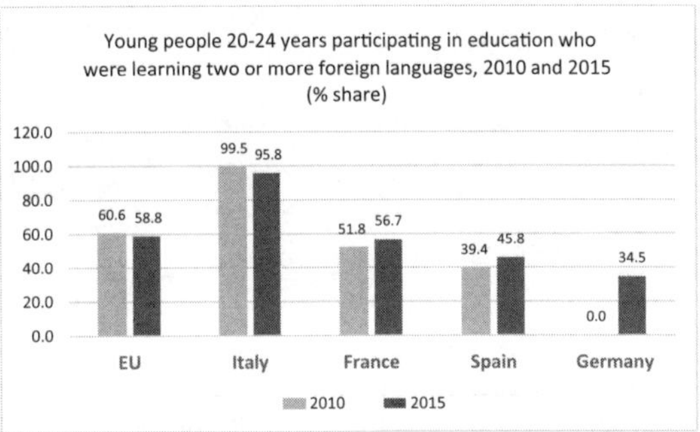

Q1. What was the ratio of the share of Italian young people aged 20-24 years participating in education and learning two or more foreign languages in 2015 to the share for the EU-28? Choose the closest option.

A. 8 : 5
B. 17 : 10
C. 4 : 3
D. 3 : 2
E. 96 : 59

Q2. The number of French young people aged 20-24 years participating in education was 1.365 million in 2010, and it increased by 3.6% between 2010 and 2015. Find the increase between 2010 and 2015 of French young people aged 20-24 years who were participating in education and learning two or more foreign languages (*in thousands*).

A. 95 thousand
B. 67 thousand
C. 94747 thousand
D. 56 thousand
E. 765 thousand

Q3. The German population aged 15-29 years in 2015 was 23% greater than that of Italy. By what percentage was the number of German young people aged 15-29 years participating in education in 2015 larger than that in Italy (*rounded to one decimal place*)?

A. 9.1%
B. 50.2%
C. 64.2%
D. 29.5%
E. 12.2%

Set 19

U.S. energy consumption by energy source, 2017

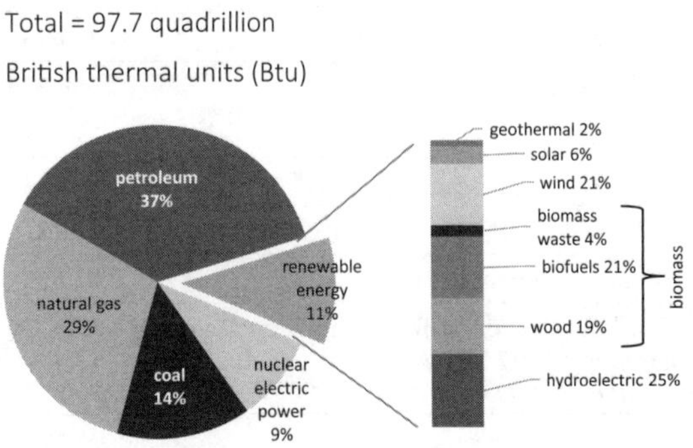

Note: Sum of components may not equal 100% because of independent rounding.

Q1. What percentage of biomass energy did bio fuels account for in 2017 in the US?

A. Around 21%
B. Around 36%
C. Around 48%
D. Around 54%
E. There's not enough information

Q2. If all the percentage values had stayed the same and the amount of hydroelectric energy produced had been 2 quadrillion Btu, what would have been the total amount of energy produced in 2017 in the US?

A. 18.2 quadrillion Btu
B. 33.4 quadrillion Btu
C. 57.6 quadrillion Btu
D. 72.7 quadrillion Btu
E. 91.9 quadrillion Btu

Q3. If the amount of petroleum based energy had decreased by 10%, and energy from the other sources had increased by equal amounts so that the total amount of energy produced stayed the same, what would have been the amount of energy produced from coal?

A. 13.2 quadrillion Btu
B. 14.2 quadrillion Btu
C. 14.6 quadrillion Btu
D. 16.1 quadrillion Btu
E. 17.3 quadrillion Btu

Set 20

Number of books in the subcategories of Teen and young adult books	
Annuals, Anthologies & Poetry	10 096
Education	390 686
Fiction	371 140
Non-fiction	310 547
Reference	15 387
Society & Social Issues	81 664
Total number of books in the Teen & young adult category: 1 017 540 *(Each book may belong to one or two subcategories)*	

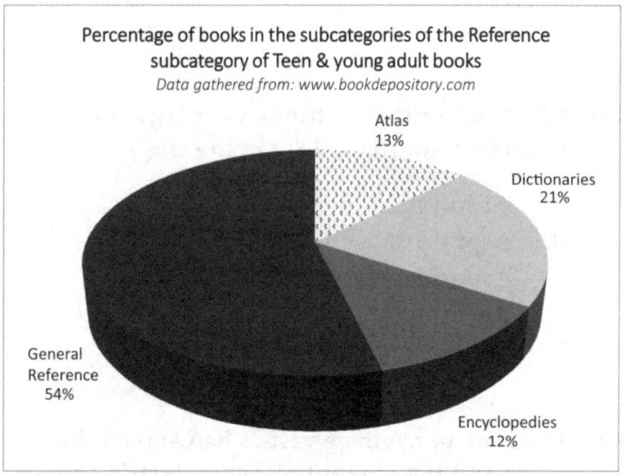

Q1. What percentage of Teen & young adult books belong to more than one subcategory?

A. 12.3%
B. 15.9%
C. 17.2%
D. 20.4%
E. 22.8%

Q2. What percentage of Teen & young adult books belong to the general reference subcategory?

A. 0.45%
B. 0.7%
C. 0.82%
D. 1.51%
E. 1.12%

Q3. What percentage of the reference subcategory would dictionaries represent if we added another 1000 atlases?

A. 15.67%
B. 16.8%
C. 18.21%
D. 19.72%
E. 25.82%

Set 21

European Rail Travel – normal journey times		
Brussels to …	*Distance (km)*	*Time (hours:mins)*
Amsterdam	210	1:24
Berlin	770	5:20
Luxembourg	220	1:35
Paris	320	2:40
Strasbourg	435	3:45

Q1. You travel from Brussels to Strasbourg, departing and arriving on time. The cruising speed of your train is 15% faster than its overall average speed. What is its cruising speed to the nearest kilometre per hour?

A. 100
B. 116
C. 125
D. 133
E. 150

Q2. You are travelling from Brussels to Luxembourg but due to adverse conditions the train travels 10% slower than normal. How late do you arrive in Luxembourg?

A. 5m 35s
B. 9m 30s
C. 10m 31s
D. 12m 45s
E. 15m 10s

Q3. Trains leave Brussels for Berlin every 2 hours starting at 0600 and similarly from Berlin starting at 0500. If you depart Brussels at 0800, how many Brussels-bound trains do you pass on your journey to Berlin?

A. 4
B. 5
C. 6
D. 7
E. 8

Set 22

	Pop 2015 ('000)	*Workforce (% of Pop)*	
		2010	*2015*
Croatia	4887	41.9	42.1
Hungary	11086	46.1	46.7
Ireland	4606	48.7	48.5
Portugal	11602	41.8	42.1
Ukraine	51629	46.1	47.6

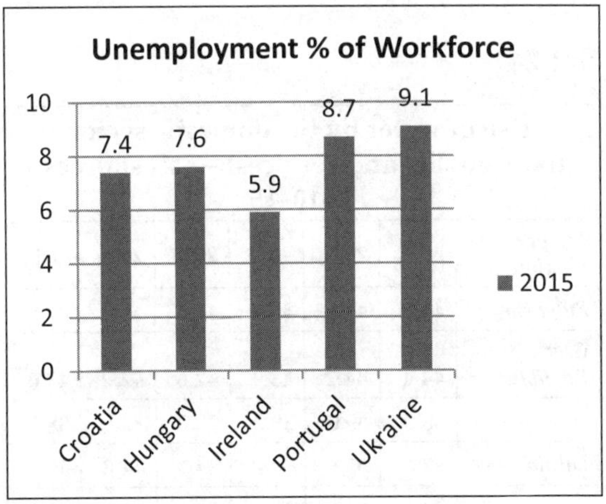

Q1. In 2015 the number of unemployed in Ireland was 10000 more than in 2010 and the percentage of the workforce unemployed was 0.1 percentage points less in 2010 than 2015. What was the percentage change in population in Ireland between 2010 and 2015?

A. −0.5%
B. 0%
C. 5.7%
D. 6.8%
E. −3.8%

Q2. What percentage of the number of unemployed people in Portugal is the number of unemployed in Hungary in 2015?

A. 87.4%
B. 92.6%
C. 96.9%
D. 96.6%
E. 103%

Q3. The percentage of the workforce unemployed in Croatia rose by 5% between 2010 and 2015 and the population rose by 3.3% over the same period. What was the rise in the number of unemployed in Croatia between 2010 and 2015?

A. 5715
B. 18912
C. 7939
D. 104680
E. 12542

Set 23

Population in Hungary in the years 2007–2017

Year	*Population*
2007	10 023 887
2008	9 991 201
2009	9 958 942
2010	9 927 840
2011	9 898 204
2012	9 869 684
2013	9 841 697
2014	9 813 335
2015	9 783 925
2016	9 753 281
2017	9 721 559

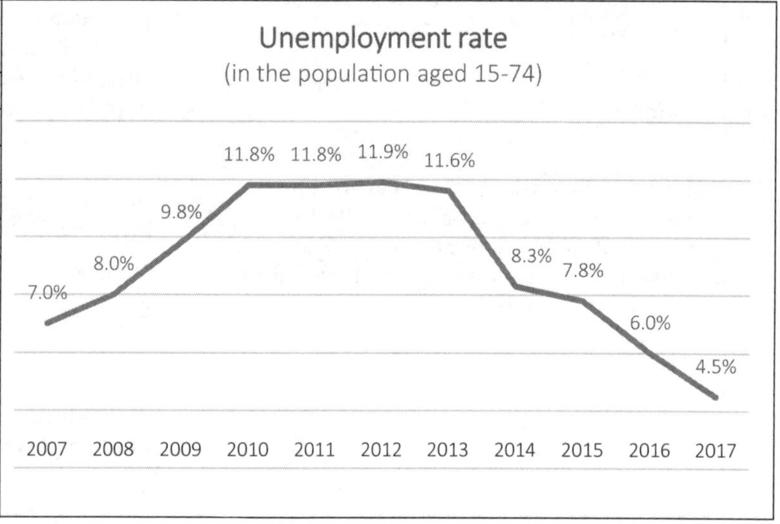

Q1. Assuming that 66% of the population is of working age, in what year in the 2007-2011 period was the number of unemployed people of working age at its peak?

A. 2007
B. 2008
C. 2009
D. 2010
E. 2011

Q2. Assuming that 66% of the population is of working age from 15 to 74, and that every age group is equally represented in the unemployed working age population, how many of those unemployed people who are of working age in 2017 will be older than 74 years in 2020?

A. Less then 14000
B. Around 14500
C. Around 15000
D. Around 15500
E. More then 16000

Q3. At what rate did the number of people (of any age) who were not working change from 2007 to 2017, assuming that 66% of the population is of working age, and that nobody outside the 15-74 age group has a job?

A. Around a 7% increase
B. Around a 38% increase
C. It stayed roughly the same
D. Around a 38 % decrease
E. Around a 7% decrease

Set 24

Use of water by the domestic sector (households and services) — all sources, 2010–15

(m³ per inhabitant)	2010	2011	2012	2013	2014	2015
Bulgaria	44.7	45.1	45.9	46.7	45.4	47.1
Czech Republic	44.4	44.2	43.9	42.6	42.2	43.0
Hungary	38.9	39.0	39.2	38.0	37.5	38.9
Latvia	57.4	93.6	64.8	44.1	44.8	56.8
Lithuania	34.5	35.5	35.0	37.8	40.6	50.9

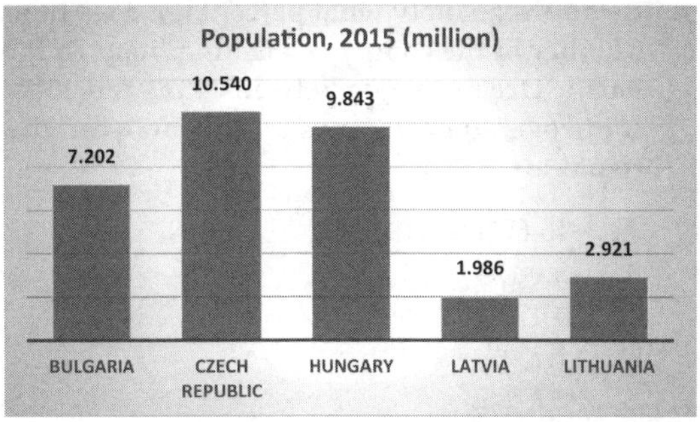

Q1. What was the total water usage of the domestic sector in Latvia in 2015 as a percentage of that of Lithuania (*rounded to one decimal place*)?

A. 68.0%
B. 75.9%
C. 87.4%
D. 111.6%
E. 115.1%

Q2. What was the difference in the average per capita water usage of each of the five countries in 2015 and 2010 (*in m³, rounded to one decimal place*)?

A. 3.4 m^3
B. 17.4 m^3
C. 13.2 m^3
D. 16.8 m^3
E. 5.9 m^3

Q3. Total water usage by the domestic sector in Lithuania increased by 40.3 million m^3 between 2011 and 2015. What was the population of Lithuania in 2011 (*in millions, rounded to one decimal place*)?

A. 4.2 million
B. 2.9 million
C. 2.4 million
D. 2.7 million
E. 3.1 million

Set 25

Populations	
	2005 ('000)
Croatia	4 443
Denmark	5 417
Portugal	10 547
Sweden	9 293

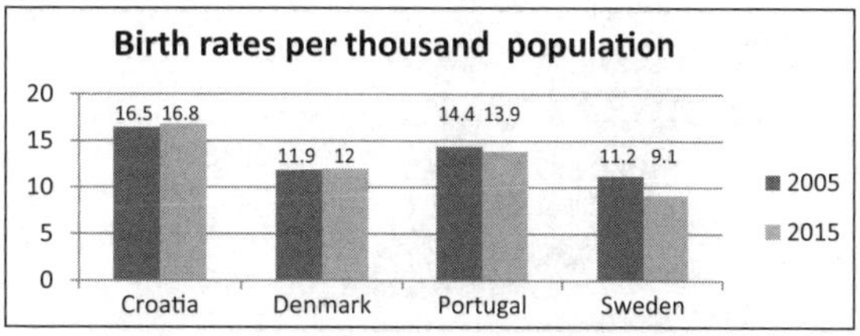

Q1. The population of Croatia increased by 7.5% between 2005 and 2015. How many more births were there in Croatia in 2015 than in 2005 (*rounded to the nearest whole number*)?

A. 6931
B. 1433
C. 1333
D. 73310
E. 80241

Q2. What is the average number of births across all four countries shown in 2005 (*rounded to the nearest whole number*)?

A. 92704
B. 102314
C. 98433
D. 96154
E. 100238

Q3. In Portugal there were 4 more births in 2015 than there were in 2005. What was the percentage change in population of Portugal over this time?

A. 5%
B. −5%
C. 0.1%
D. −0.1%
E. 3.6%
F. −3.6%

Set 26

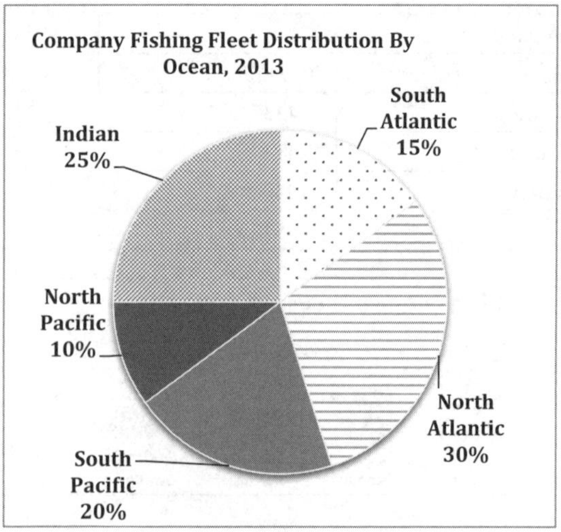

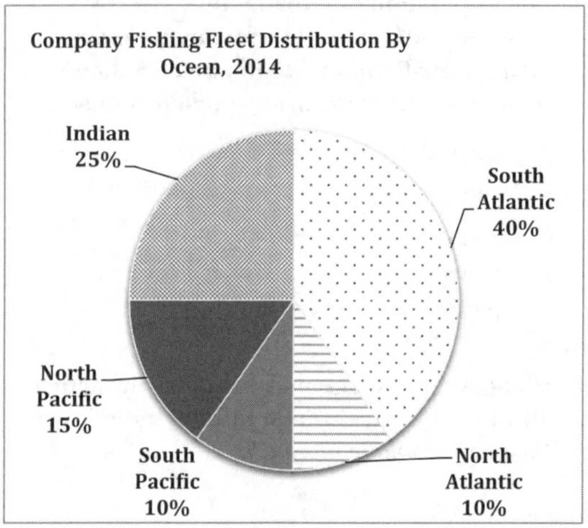

* *The Indian Ocean is not considered part of the Pacific Ocean.*

Q1. The company is realigning its fishing fleet distribution according to changing catch expectations. If, in 2013, the company had 42 fishing boats in the South Atlantic and the company increases its total fleet size by 15% in 2014, how many fishing boats will it have overall in the Atlantic Ocean in 2014, rounded to the nearest whole boat?

A. 105
B. 112
C. 129
D. 140
E. 161

Q2. By approximately what percentage does the number of the company's fishing boats in the Pacific Ocean change between 2013 and 2014 if the overall fleet grows by 15% between the two years?

A. -16.67%
B. -5.00%
C. -4.17%
D. -1.25%
E. +27.78%

Q3. If the Pacific Ocean is 2.3 times as large as the Indian Ocean, by what percentage is the company's number of boats per square kilometer in the Indian Ocean greater than in the Pacific Ocean in 2014?

A. 30%
B. 92%
C. 130%
D. 230%
E. Impossible to tell

Set 27

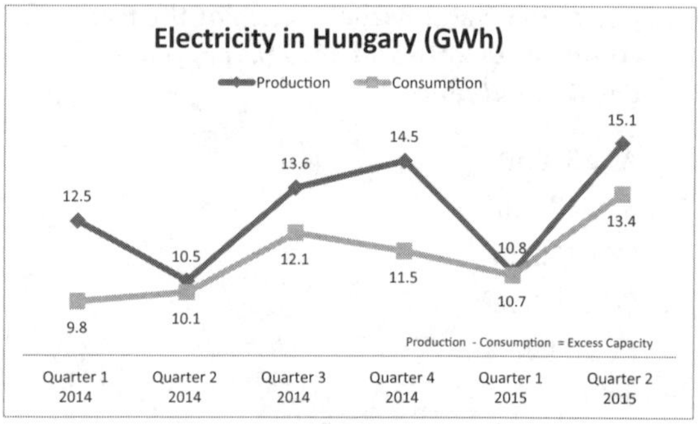

Q1. If 5% of production in Quarter 1 2014 came from 50 wind farms and the same percentage of Quarter 2 2014 production was also contributed by wind farms, how many wind farms produced electricity in that quarter? You should assume that all operational wind farms produce identical amounts of electricity as each other and in each quarter.

A. 42
B. 48
C. 52
D. 55
E. Cannot say

Q2. In 2014, Hungary exported 79% of its excess capacity. How many GWh of excess electricity does Hungary still need to generate in the rest of 2015 to achieve the same export volume in 2015 if in the first half of 2015 it exported 50% of its excess capacity?

A. 4.2 GWh
B. 5.1 GWh
C. 5.8 GWh
D. 6.7 GWh
E. It cannot achieve the same export volume

Q3. The Paks nuclear power plant in Hungary produces 14.8 GWh annually and its rate of production is constant. In how many of the quarters shown was Paks's production more than 30% of total production?

A. In none of them
B. 1
C. 2
D. 4
E. In all of them

Set 28

Private households by household composition, 2007-2017 (number of households in 1 000 and % of household types)

	Total (thousand)		*Couple with children (%)*		*Couple without children (%)*	
	2007	*2017*	*2007*	*2017*	*2007*	*2017*
EU-28	200 974.5	221 326.2	21.2	20.0	24.1	24.9
Germany	39 290.5	40 722.6	16.5	15.7	28.1	28.4
Spain	16 643.0	18 512.5	22.3	23.1	20.3	21.8
France	26 456.5	29 314.4	23.7	21.2	27.5	26.2
Italy	23 710.7	25 864.7	23.5	20.9	20.4	20.7

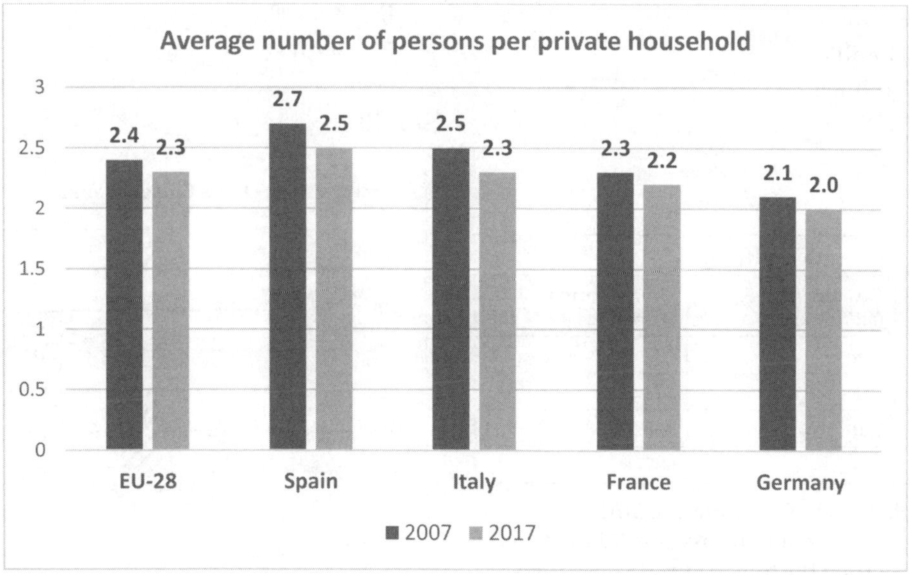

Q1. What was the difference between 2017 and 2007 in the total number of persons living in French private households (*in millions, rounded to one decimal place*)?

A. 2.9 million
B. 3.6 million
C. 9.2 million
D. 6.3 million
E. 8.0 million

Q2. What was the percentage change between 2007 and 2017 in the number of couples with children living in private households in Italy (*rounded to two decimal places*)?

A. 3.40%
B. 9.08%
C. –2.98%
D. –2.60%
E. 5.91%

Q3. The total number of EU-28 private households increased by 0.65% in 2018, and the share of couples without children didn't change. What was the EU-28 total number of persons without children in 2018 (*rounded to the nearest million*)?

A. 110 million
B. 55 million
C. 111 million
D. 27 million
E. 1 million

Set 29

The Planets		
Planet	*Distance from Sun (million km)*	*Orbital Period (Earth Days)*
Mercury	58	88
Venus	101	224.7
Earth	150	365.25
Mars	228	687

Q1. As a planet travels around the Sun (orbital period), the distance it covers is 6.3 times its distance from the Sun. At what speed does the Earth travel around the Sun in km/sec?

A. 0.03
B. 0.3
C. 3
D. 30
E. 300

Q2. How much faster than Venus is Mercury travelling? The distance travelled by a planet around the Sun is the distance of the planet from the Sun multiplied by 6.3.

A. 24%
B. 47%
C. 67%
D. 85%
E. 125%

Q3. A future astronaut on Mars has to wait at least 8m 40s to get a response from Earth to his messages. This minimum delay occurs when the distance of Mars from Earth is the distance of Mars from the Sun minus Earth's distance from the Sun. At what speed do his messages travel (in km/sec)?

A. 120,000
B. 150,000
C. 210,000
D. 270,000
E. 300,000

Set 30

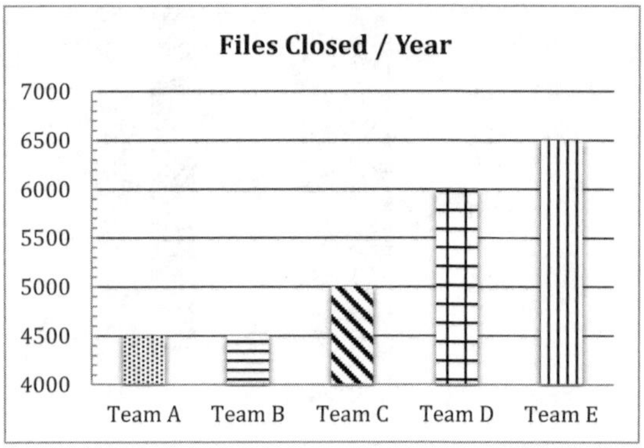

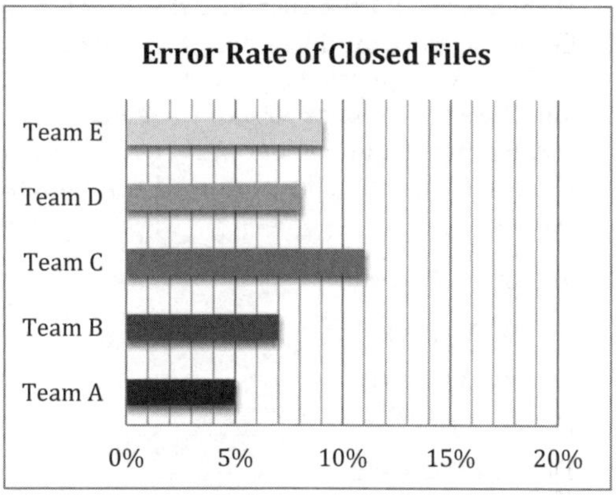

Q1. Five teams work on closing financial audit files and each team sometimes makes errors. Which team closes the lowest number of files per year without errors?

A. Team A

B. Team B

C. Team C

D. Team D

E. Team E

Q2. If Team C's error rate deteriorated to 17% and Team B's improved to 2%, how many fewer files would Team C be able to close without errors than Team B?

A. 35

B. 250

C. 260

D. 350

E. 500

Q3. If teams progress through files at a constant rate from month to month, how many files will the five teams close by the end of September?

A. 16525

B. 17667

C. 18258

D. 19875

E. 22083

Set 31

Tax Systems		
SYSTEM 1 Tax free allowance: 10000 10001–30000: 15% 30001–50000: 25% 50001+: 31% Insurance tax: 100 per month	**SYSTEM 2** Tax free allowance: Nil 0–30000: 15% 30001+: 21% Insurance tax: 50 per month	**SYSTEM 3** Tax free allowance: 15000 15001–30000: 17% 30001–60000: 22% 60001+: 28% Insurance tax: 200 per month
All amounts are in euro and are annual except where otherwise indicated. Tax rates are marginal (the percentage indicated is levied only on that part of the income falling in the given range). *Effective tax rate (%) = tax / income × 100*		

Q1. A country is considering the adoption of a new tax system. Under which system does a person earning 55 000 € / year owe the least in taxes?

A. System 1

B. System 2

C. System 3

D. Systems 1 and 2 are the same

E. All Systems are the same

Q2. What is the effective tax rate of a person earning 62 000 € annually under System 3?

A. 15.66%

B. 15.98%

C. 19.53%

D. 19.77%

E. 23.65%

Q3. A person earns 75 000 € a year. By what percentage is their after-tax income greater or smaller under System1 than under System 3?

A. Approximately 1% smaller

B. Approximately 2% smaller

C. Approximately 2% greater

D. Approximately 3.9% smaller

E. Approximately 3.9% greater

Set 32

Power Station	Country	Annual Electricity Production (TWh)
Itaipu Dam	Brazil	98.30
Three Gorges Dam	China	98.50
Krasnoyarsk	Russia	20.40
Grand Coulee	USA	20.00
Guri	Venezuela	53.41

Country Annual Electricity Consumption Statistics (MWh)	
Brazil	455 700 000
China	5 322 300 000
Russia	1 016 500 000
USA	3 886 400 000
Venezuela	85 850 000
1 TWh = 1 000 000 MWh	

Q1. If they are ranked by the percentage that a power station generates of the total electricity consumption of the given country, which station would be in the middle?

A. Three Gorges Dam
B. Itaipu Dam
C. Guri
D. Grand Coulee
E. Krasnoyarsk

Q2. Venezuela plans to build another power station of the same production capacity as that of Guri. If existing power stations produce 78% of the electricity consumed in Venezuela, how much electricity will Venezuela have available for export after completion of the new power station?

A. 20.97 TWh
B. 34.523 MWh
C. 34 523 MWh
D. 20 970 000 MWh
E. 34 523 000 MWh

Q3. If the electricity produced by the Three Gorges Dam would be enough to cover 3.24% of the electricity consumed in the EU, and the EU produces 30% of the electricity it consumes from nuclear power, how much electricity in the EU is produced from nuclear power?

A. 912.04 MWh
B. 91.20 TWh
C. 912.00 TWh
D. 912.04 TWh
E. 3040.12 TWh

Set 33

Energy Ratings of Selected Household Appliances, 2014					
Appliance	*A+ / A*	*B*	*C*	*D*	*Total units*
Air conditioners	10%	45%	20%	25%	3 400
Washing machines	45%	35%	10%	10%	5 500
Dryers	25%	10%	50%	15%	2 000
Refrigerators	40%	25%	25%	10%	9 000
Appliances with A+, A and B energy ratings are considered energy-efficient.					

Distribution of Household Appliances

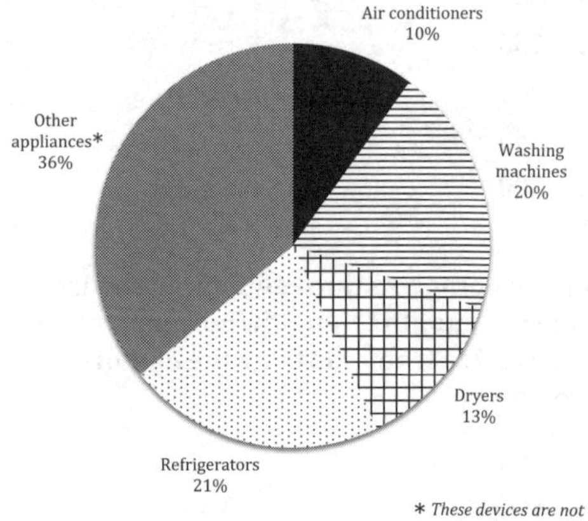

* *These devices are not considered energy-efficeient.*

Q1. What percentage of all household appliances are energy-efficient washing machines?

A. 9%
B. 13%
C. 16%
D. 20%
E. 80%

Q2. If the share of energy-efficient units among refrigerators and air conditioners rose by 20%, how many energy-efficient refrigerators and air conditioners would there be?

A. 4 728
B. 6 024
C. 6 420
D. 9 264
E. 10 200

Q3. If D-rated household appliances are ranked by the number of such units in a highest-to-lowest list, which one would be at the top of the list?

A. Air conditioners
B. Washing machines
C. Dryers
D. Refrigerators
E. Impossible to tell

Set 34

Population age structure by age groups, 2007 and 2017						
	(% of the total population)					
	0–14 years old		*15–64 years old*		*65 years old or over*	
	2007	*2017*	*2007*	*2017*	*2007*	*2017*
Denmark	18.6	16.6	66.1	64.3	15.3	19.1
Finland	17.1	16.3	66.5	62.8	16.5	20.9
Iceland	21.3	19.7	67.1	66.2	11.6	14.0
Norway	19.4	17.8	66.0	65.5	14.6	16.6
Sweden	17.0	17.6	65.6	62.6	17.4	19.8

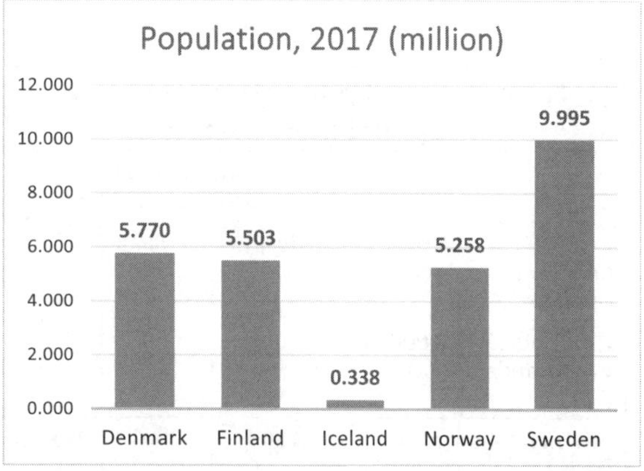

Q1. The population of Norway increased by 577 thousand between 2007 and 2017. By how much did the number of persons aged 0-14 in Norway change between these years (*rounded to the nearest thousand*)?

A. –39 thousand
B. –84 thousand
C. 28 thousand
D. 103 thousand
E. 112 thousand

Q2. By what percentage was the number of persons 15 years old or over in Denmark in 2017 larger than the number of persons belonging to the same age group in Finland (*rounded to two decimal places*)?

A. 3.52%
B. 4.48%
C. 7.36%
D. 2.61%
E. –0.30%

Q3. What was the average change per country in the 5 countries in the share of persons aged 15-64 between 2007 and 2017?

A. –1.98%
B. –9.90%
C. –2.99%
D. –4.60%
E. –1.14%

Set 35

Factory annual production and wood supplier figures, tonnes				
		Utilisation of forestry production volume for:		
Forestry (number of employees)	*Production Volume*	*Roofing*	*Outdoor Furniture*	*Indoor Furniture*
Craybourne Woodlands (50)	8 000	2 000	4 000	850
Stirling Forest (80)	14 000	3 800	5 900	2450
Woodcombe Hills Woods (30)	3 000	1 600	1 200	0
Hampton Forest (30)	3 000	1 600	1 300	55
Frasier Green (40)	8 000	4 000	2 800	1 045

Q1. Which forestry has the most productive employees?

A. Craybourne Woodlands
B. Stirling Forest
C. Woodcombe Hills Woods
D. Hampton Forest
E. Frasier Green

Q2. If 50 tonnes of wood are needed for each outdoor furniture shipment, how many shipments could have been manufactured in total relying on all forestries if 10% of the wood used for roofing had been shifted to outdoor furniture?

A. 26
B. 88
C. 114
D. 304
E. 330

Q3. Based on the average of all five forestries, how much roofing wood is supplied by each forestry employee?

A. 56.52 tonnes
B. 66.09 tonnes
C. 156.52 tonnes
D. 565.2 tonnes
E. 156.2 tonnes

Set 36

Restaurant Wine List		
	Glass (€)	*Bottle (€)*
Chablis	8.95	31.95
Chardonnay	7.50	28.50
Margaux	7.15	27.00
Sancerre	9.20	34.80
Tavel	7.95	29.50

Q1. Assuming a glass is a fifth of a bottle, which wine provides the most extra profit in euro terms when sold by the glass?

A. Chablis
B. Chardonnay
C. Margaux
D. Sancerre
E. Tavel

Q2. The restaurant makes 220% profit on all bottles of wine. In one evening they make €287.10 profit on Sancerre alone. How many bottles of Sancerre did they sell?

A. 6
B. 10
C. 12
D. 15
E. 18

Q3. If a glass is 187.5ml and a bottle is 750ml, what is the percentage increase in revenue on a bottle of Tavel when sold by the glass?

A. 5.9%
B. 7.8%
C. 8.3%
D. 9.4%
E. 11.1%

Set 37

Results for Swimming Championships (m:ss.ss) *In medley races, the swimmers swim equal distances in four different styles: butterfly, backstroke, breaststroke, freestyle.*				
	100m Freestyle	*200m Backstroke*	*400m Medley*	*100m Breast-stroke*
Gold	50.91	1:58.31	3:48.7	1:03.41
Silver	50.99	1:59.72	3:49.6	1:04.06
Bronze	51.31	1:59.88	3:53.2	1:04.92

Q1. In the medley, the winner spent 26.2% of the time on the butterfly section of the race. What was his average speed during that leg of the race?

A. 1.67 m/s
B. 1.75 m/s
C. 1.8 m/s
D. 2.0 m/s
E. 2.25 m/s

Q2. How much faster was the gold medal winner than the bronze medal winner in the 200m backstroke event?

A. 0.1%
B. 1.0%
C. 1.3%
D. 1.5%
E. 2.0%

Q3. From the moment that the gold medallist finished until he himself finished, the freestyle silver medal winner swam 10% faster than his overall average. To the nearest centimetre, by what distance did the gold medallist beat the silver medallist?

A. 14
B. 17
C. 25
D. 36
E. 51

Set 38

Country	Export *(2014,% of production)*	Export Volume *(2014, million t)*	Change from 2013 *(volume)*
China	34%	279.5	+ 3%
USA	27%	23.8	+ 5%
Japan	19%	21	– 2 %
EU	34%	55.9	–
Rest of World	62%	285.4	+ 9%

Domestic consumption = Production – Export + Import

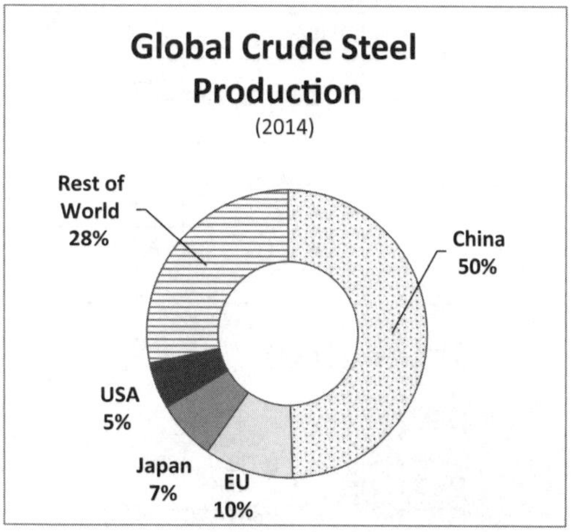

Q1. If China exported 30% of its steel production to the United States in 2014, how much steel did the US use in that year?

A. 143.85 million tonnes
B. 166.05 million tonnes
C. 310.97 million tonnes
D. 328.82 million tonnes
E. Cannot say

Q2. How much more steel did the EU export in 2013 than Japan?

A. 66.2% more
B. 71.6% more
C. 161% more
D. 166.2% more
E. 171.6% more

Q3. Approximately what percentage of global steel production did 2013 exports make up if production in every region was the same in 2013 as in 2014?

A. Around 6%
B. Around 14%
C. Around 38%
D. Around 50%
E. Around 70%

Set 39

Electricity Generation in the Netherlands (%)		
	2005	*2010*
Fossil Fuel	81.1	76.4
Wind	6.8	8.1
Solar	3.4	5.2
Nuclear	3.9	3.8
Other	4.8	6.5

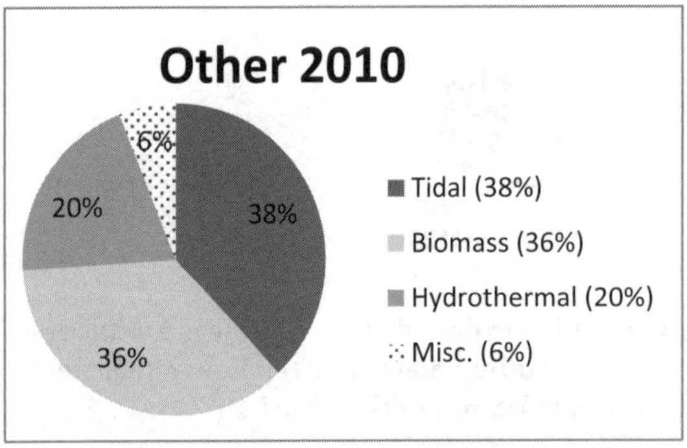

Q1. Generation of electricity rose by 10% between 2005 and 2010. Tidal power generation doubled over that period. What percentage of the electricity was generated by tidal power in 2005?

A. 1.12%
B. 1.36%
C. 1.59%
D. 1.73%
E. 1.94%

Q2. In 2010, 2.4 million kWh of electricity was generated from biomass. How much was generated from solar power (in millions of kWh)?

A. 5.3
B. 5.9
C. 6.2
D. 6.8
E. 7.3

Q3. If total electricity generation rose by 10% between 2005 and 2010, what was the percentage change in fossil fuel generated electricity over that time?

A. +3.6%
B. +1.8%
C. No change
D. -1.8%
E. -3.6%

Set 40

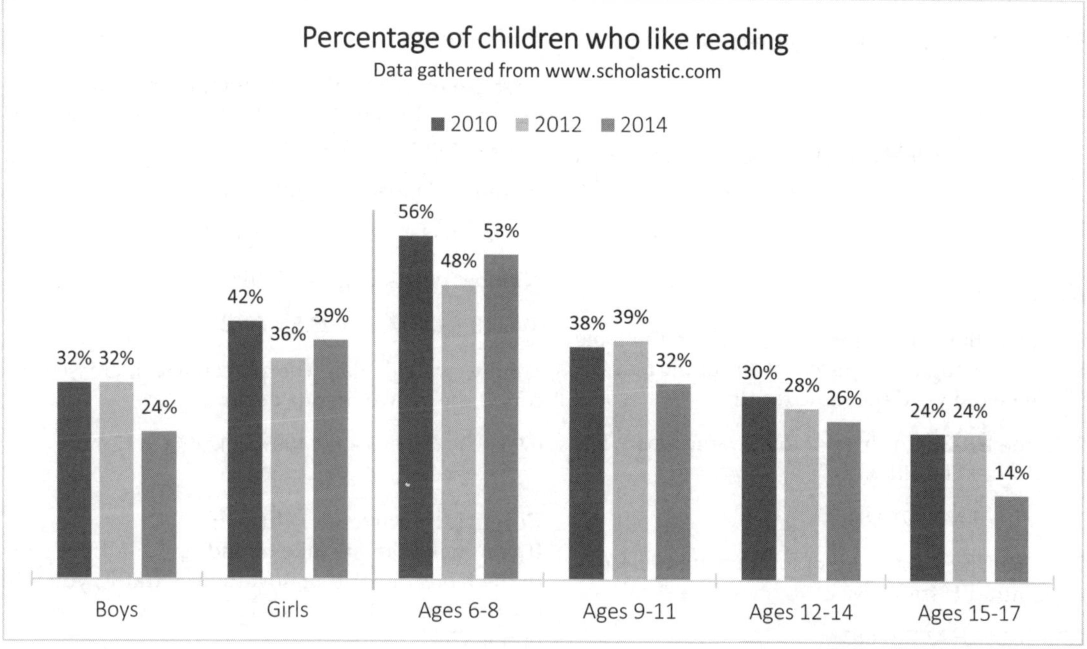

Q1. Assuming a sample size of 1000 children, where each gender is represented equally, by what percentage did the number of boys who like reading decrease from 2010 to 2014?

A. 8%
B. 12%
C. 17%
D. 21%
E. 25%

Q2. What was the sample size if in 2012 the number of boys and girls who liked reading were both 150?

A. 792
B. 823
C. 833
D. 886
E. 938

Q3. Assuming an overall sample size of 1000 children where the four different age groups are equally represented, and in each age group the genders are also equally represented, what was the number of boys aged 9 to 11 who liked reading in 2010?

A. 41
B. 48
C. 58
D. 64
E. There's not enough information

ANSWERS

SET 1, Q1. Correct Answer: B

Reasoning

We need to calculate the total intra-EU traffic in both 2015 and 2016, and then the difference between the two figures.

Calculation

We will use the data from the first pair in the table (UK-Spain), though the figures for *any* of the pairs in the table would yield the same result.

In 2015 the UK-Spain share of total traffic was 9.1%, so total intra-EU traffic was:

35922.6 / 0.091 = 394753.846

In 2016 the UK-Spain share of total traffic was 9.6%, so total intra-EU traffic was:

41637.8 / 0.096 = 433727.083

Finally, we calculate the difference, and round it to the nearest million.

Total intra-EU traffic increase:

433727.083 – 394753.846 = 38973.237 thousand ≈ 39 million

Potential Shortcuts / Pitfalls

Don't make the mistake of simply adding up the top-5 pairs in the table, instead of calculating the total intra-EU traffic. This would give the incorrect figure of 11 million, which is option A.

SET 1, Q2. Correct Answer: D

Reasoning

We need to calculate the total number of passengers carried from the UK in 2015 and 2016 using the 3 relevant pairs in the table. We then calculate the percentage increase by dividing those numbers, subtracting 1, and multiplying the result by 100%.

Calculation

First, we must calculate the total number of passengers carried from the UK to the three top destinations in both 2015 and 2016.

Number of passengers in 2015:

35922.6 + 13302.7 + 12711.3 = 61936.6

Number of passengers in 2016:

41637.8 + 13877 + 14123.5 = 69638.3

Finally, we calculate the percentage increase, and round the answer to one decimal place:

(69638.3 / 61936.6 – 1) * 100% = 12.43% = 12.4%

Potential Shortcuts / Pitfalls

If you make the mistake of adding up all the pairs in the table, rather than just the UK traffic, you will get the incorrect figure of 11.2%, which is given as option C.

Another, and more common error, would be to add up the *percentage shares* rather than the *actual number* of passengers. In other words, to add 9.10 + 3.37 + 3.20 to get 15.67, and 9.60 + 3.20 +3.24 to get 16.04. This would give you a difference of 16.04 minus 15.67, which is 0.37. Rounded to one decimal space, as the question asks, this would give you 0.4% – which is answer option E. To understand why this is wrong, take a simple example. 50% of 100 is 50 and 20% of 50 is 10. However 50 + 10 is not 70% of 150, it is 40%.

SET 1, Q3. Correct Answer: C

Reasoning

First, we need to calculate the average 2016 cost of a Spain-Germany flight using the 2015 average cost and percentage increase for 2016. Then we have to work out the total amount spent by passengers on Spain-Germany flights in 2015 and in 2016. Finally, we calculate the increase as the difference between the amounts spent in 2016 and in 2015.

Calculation

The average cost of a Spain-Germany flight in 2016:

147.60 * 1.021 ≈ €150.70

The amount spent by passengers for the flights between Spain and Germany in 2015 (in thousand euros):

25063.9 * 147.60 ≈ €3699432

Note that the number of passengers is given in the table in thousands, so we don't need to multiply it by 1000.

Amount spent in 2016:

27581.6 * 150.70 ≈ €4156547

Finally, we need to calculate the difference:

4156547 – 3699432 ≈ €457115 thousand

Potential Shortcuts / Pitfalls

You can go wrong if you miss that the numbers of passengers are given in the table in thousands. If you make this mistake, you would get the incorrect figure of 457 thousand (answer option A).

A possible shortcut is to combine all the steps shown above by factorizing: 1000 * 147.60 * (27581.6 * 1.021–25063.9), which would reduce the number of keystrokes and multiplications. This would, because of rounding errors, give only the approximately correct figure of 457104. However this would not be a problem in this case as the answer options are all sufficiently far apart.

SET 2, Q1. Correct Answer: C

Reasoning

We need to work out the numbers of outbound trips made by EU residents in 2016 to the U.S. and to Switzerland, and then calculate the difference. The number of outbound trips is the total number of outbound trips by EU residents multiplied by the respective percentages.

Calculation

First, we must calculate the number of outbound trips made by EU residents in 2016 to the U.S. given the total number of trips and the U.S. share of 14% (in thousands of trips):

308622 * 0.14 = 43207.08 thousand

Second, we calculate in the same way the number of outbound trips made by EU residents in 2016 to Switzerland:

308622 * 0.09 = 27775.98 thousand

Finally, we calculate the difference, and round it to the nearest million:

43207.08 – 27775.98 = 15431.1 thousand ≈ 15 million

Potential Shortcuts / Pitfalls

If you miss that the numbers of passengers are presented in the table in thousands you will get the incorrect answer of 15431 million, which is given as answer option D. And If you use the total number of trips made by EU residents in 2016 instead of the number of outbound trips only, you will get 60 million (option A).

A shortcut is to combine all the steps shown above by factoring out the total number of outbound trips:

308622 (0.14 – 0.09) = 308622 * 0.05 = 15431.10 (thousands)

This would significantly reduce the number of keystrokes and arithmetical operations.

SET 2, Q2. Correct Answer: D

Reasoning

We need to calculate the total number of outbound trips made by EU residents in 2017, then the number of outbound trips to Turkey in 2016 and 2017, and then the Turkey percentage share. The number of outbound trips to Turkey in 2016 is the total number of outbound trips multiplied by the Turkey share in 2016, and the number of outbound trips to Turkey in 2017 is the number of outbound trips to Turkey in 2016 adjusted by the percentage decrease.

Calculation

First, we calculate the total number of outbound trips made by EU residents in 2017 (in thousands of trips), using the number in 2016 and the percentage increase between 2016 and 2017:

308622 * 1.018 = 314177.196 thousand

Second, we calculate the number of outbound trips made by EU residents in 2016 to Turkey:

308622 * 0.1 = 30862.2 thousand

Third, the number of outbound trips made by EU residents in 2017 to Turkey using the number of trips in 2016 and the percentage of decrease of 0.6%:

30862.2 * (1 – 0.006) = 30677.0268 thousand

Finally, we calculate the Turkey share in 2017, and round it to one decimal place:

30677.0268 / 314177.196 ≈ 0.09764 ≈ 9.8%

Potential Shortcuts / Pitfalls

If you make a calculator mistake and decrease the number of trips to Turkey by 6% instead of 0.6% you would get the incorrect figure of 9.2% (option A). Another possible error would be to calculate Turkey's share as 10% – 0.6% = 9.4% (option B), ignoring the increase in the total number of trips made by EU residents between 2016 and 2017.

It is possible to do the calculation faster by combining all the steps shown above by using the expression 308622 * 0.1 * (1 – 0.006) / 308622 / (1 + 0.018), and, after cancelling the total number of outbound trips, 0.1 * 0.994 / 1.018, which would significantly reduce the number of keystrokes and arithmetical operations.

SET 2, Q3. Correct Answer: E

Reasoning

We need to work out the percentage shares in the expenditure made by EU residents in 2016 for Norway and Russia, then calculate their ratio. The percentage share of the expenditure is the share in the number of outbound trips to Norway and Russia, multiplied or divided by the respective scale factor.

Calculation

First, we must calculate the percentage share of the expenditure made by EU residents in 2016 for Norway:

5% * 1.4 = 7%

Second, the percentage share of the expenditure made by EU residents in 2016 for Russia:

4% * = 4% * 0.75 = 3%

Finally, we need to calculate the ratio between Norway and Russia shares in 2016:

7% : 3% = 7 : 3

Potential Shortcuts / Pitfalls

The length of this question can make it seem a lot more complicated than it really is. You just have to take it step by step and, as we have seen, it actually requires only a few calculations.

A possible mistake would be to swap the places of Norway and Russia in the ratio. This would give the incorrect ratio of 3 : 7, and as this is given as answer option D you would not realise the error. Another potential error would be to calculate the ratio between Norway and Russia using their respective shares in the number of trips instead of expenditure. This would give the incorrect ratio of 5 : 4 (option C).

SET 3, Q1. Correct Answer: A

Reasoning

We need to calculate the average health care expenditure of the top-5 EU members in 2015, and then increase it by the given percentage. The average health care expenditure of the top-5 EU members is the sum of their expenditures divided by five.

Calculation

First, we must calculate the sum of the top-5 EU members' health care expenditures in 2015 (in million euros):

241366 + 338207 + 148029 + 98586 + 254827 = 1081015 (million euros)

Second, we calculate the average health care expenditure of the top-5 EU members in 2015:

1081015 / 5 = 216203 (million euros)

Finally, we calculate the average health care expenditure of the top-5 EU members in 2017, rounded to the nearest billion euros:

216203 * (1 + 0.045) = €225932.135 million ≈ €226 billion

Potential Shortcuts / Pitfalls

If you miss that the average expenditure is required to be given in billion euros, instead of millions, you would get the incorrect figure of 225932 (option E). Likewise, if you ignore the fact that average expenditure increased between 2015 and 2017 you would get the incorrect figure of 216 billion (option C).

SET 3, Q2. Correct Answer: B

Reasoning

We need to calculate the GDP of the United Kingdom and France in 2015, and then calculate the difference. The GDP of a country is its health care expenditure divided by its health care expenditure percentage share in GDP.

Calculation

First, we must calculate the GDP of the United Kingdom given the health care expenditure and the respective share in GDP of 9.9% (in million euros):

254827 / 0.099 ≈ €2574010 million

Then we calculate the GDP of France in the same way:

241366 / 0.11 ≈ €2194236 million

Finally, we calculate the difference, and round it to the nearest billion:

2574010 – 2194236 = €379774 million ≈ €380 billion

Potential Shortcuts / Pitfalls

If you miss that the health care expenditures are presented in the table in million euros you would get the incorrect figure of 379774 (option D). If you calculate the difference in health care expenditures instead of the GDP (i.e. 254827 – 241366 = 13461), you would get either answer option E (after rounding to the nearest billion) or, if you forget the figures in the table are in millions not billions, option A.

SET 3, Q3. Correct Answer: C

Reasoning

We need to calculate the population of Spain in 2015, and then in 2016 and 2017 using the percentage increases for each year. The population of Spain in 2015 is the health care expenditure divided by the health care expenditure per inhabitant.

Calculation

First, we must calculate the population of Spain in 2015:

98586 / 2123 ≈ 46.437 (million)

Note that the health care expenditure is presented in the table in million euros, and the health care expenditure per inhabitant is presented in euros, so we don't need to scale the resulting number.

Second, we calculate the population of Spain by the end of 2016 given the population increase of 3.1%:

46.437 * (1 + 0.031) ≈ 47.877 (million)

Finally, we calculate the population of Spain by the end of 2017 given the population increase of 3.4%, and round it to the nearest million:

47.877 * (1 + 0.034) ≈ 49.505 million ≈ 50 million

Potential Shortcuts / Pitfalls

If you simply add the annual percentage population increases together, i.e. 3.1% + 3.4% = 6.5%, and then use 6.5% to calculate the population of Spain in 2017 directly from 2015, you would get 49.455 million, which you would then round down to 49 million. This is given as option A and also looks a very plausible answer, given that it is very close to the correct answer.

SET 4, Q1. Correct Answer: B

Reasoning

We need to calculate the total waste generated in Chile in the agriculture, forestry and fishing sector by adding together the figures for each year of the 2004-2007 period. Then we have to divide the hypothetical decrease in generated waste by our total, and multiply by 100 to get the percentage.

Calculation

First, we add together the annual figures:

1515 + 1393 + 1367 +1470 = 5745 (thousand tonnes)

The total hypothetical decrease is 500 + 500 = 1000 (thousand tonnes)

The percentage decrease is then: (1000 / 5745) * 100 ≈ 17.4%

Potential Shortcuts / Pitfalls

This question is very straightforward provided you are careful in reading the data off the table. For instance, if you add up ALL the figures in the Chile row rather than just 2004 to 2007, you would end up with answer option A.

SET 4, Q2. Correct Answer: C

Reasoning

We need to calculate the amount of decrease from 2006 to 2008 in each country, and then what percentage this amount is of the generated waste in 2006.

Calculation

For Austria the decrease from 2006 to 2008 is: 513 – 459 = 54

Let us call the percentage change X

As 54 is X% of 513, that means that 513 * (X / 100) = 54
X = (54 / 513) * 100
X ≈ 10.53%

We can in the same way calculate the decrease in Belgium ([73 / 361] * 100) and in Italy ([213 / 554] * 100) as around 20.2% and 38.45% respectively. From this we can see that the greatest rate of decrease, 38.45%, was in Italy, answer C.

Potential Shortcuts / Pitfalls

Since the initial (2006) amount of waste was *larger* in Italy than in Austria, and the final (2008) amount of waste was *smaller* in Italy than in Austria, we know without any calculation that the rate of decrease must be higher in Italy. We don't know the exact difference, but looking at the numbers, we can estimate that it's not negligible. This means that we only have to compare Belgium and Italy.

SET 4, Q3. Correct Answer: E

Reasoning

We need first to calculate the average amount of waste generated in each year, by dividing the total waste by the number of years, and then calculate the difference for each year.

Calculation

The total amount of waste generated is:

89300 + 87584 + 87945 + 87837 + 87992 + 88446 + 85109 = 614213

We then divide by the number of years, 7, to get our average amount, which is 87745 (thousand tonnes). Therefore the deviation from the average amount in the first year of the series, 2004, was 89300 – 87745 = 1555

We *could* now calculate the *exact* deviation for each year in turn and then compare all the resulting figures one by one. But do we really need to do all those calculations? In fact we can get to the answer very rapidly just with a bit of rounding and simple mental arithmetic.

We know that to beat our 2004 figure the deviation for any other year has to be more than 1555. Simplify the average amount to 87.7 and the 2004 deviation to 1.5 (it is slightly larger).

You can instantly see that the 2004 figure can only be beaten either by an amount more than 1.5 *smaller* than 87.7, i.e. less than 86.2, or *bigger* than the 89.3 for 2004. It is immediately apparent that the answer has to be 85.1, the figure for the year 2010.

SET 5, Q1. Correct Answer: B

Reasoning

We need to calculate the percentage change between 2011 and 2016 of people aged 25–64 reporting they knew three or more foreign languages for each country, and then calculate their average.

Calculation

Percentage change in Czech Republic = 7.4 – 7.1 = 0.3%
Percentage change in Poland = 2.8 – 4.0 = –1.2%
Percentage change in Slovakia = 28 – 21.6 = 6.4%
Percentage change in Slovenia = 37.7 – 44.9 = –7.2%

Now we calculate the average of the percentages above:

Average = (0.3 – 1.2 + 6.4 – 7.2) / 4 = –0.425%

Potential Shortcuts / Pitfalls

This is a simple enough question as long as you remember you have a percentage decrease at the end and not an increase, which would give you answer option C.

SET 5, Q2. Correct Answer: E

Reasoning

We need to calculate the total share of Slovenian people aged 25-64 reporting they knew one or more foreign languages in 2016, which is the sum of the shares for one, two, and three or more foreign languages, and then find the ratio to the share of such people having tertiary education.

Calculation

We first calculate the share of ALL Slovenian people aged 25-64 reporting they knew one or more foreign languages in 2016:

17.6 + 24.7 + 37.7 = 80%

The bar chart tells us that 95% of those aged 25 to 64 *with tertiary education* reported they knew one or more foreign language. Therefore the ratio to all people of that age reporting one or more language is 95 : 80. This ratio can be simplified since both sides of it are multiples of 5. By dividing each side by 5, we will reduce the ratio to the lowest terms, i.e. to 19 : 16.

Potential Shortcuts / Pitfalls

The most likely mistake would be to use the figure for those knowing *exactly* one foreign language (17.6) instead of all those knowing *one or more*. This would lead you to the incorrect ratios of either 19 : 4 (option D) or 4 : 19 (option C).

There is an easy shortcut. The table tells us that 20% don't know ANY foreign language, therefore those who know 1 or more must be 100% less this 20%. Our calculation then becomes 95 / (100 – 20). You can most likely do this straight away in your head without any need for a calculator.

SET 5, Q3. Correct Answer: D

Reasoning

We need to calculate the number of Polish people aged 25–64 reporting that they knew just one foreign language, for both 2016 and 2011. This is the total population of that age multiplied by the respective percentage share. We then work out the difference between the two years.

Calculation

First, we must calculate the number of Polish people aged 25–64 reporting they knew just one foreign language in 2016 (in thousands):

30700 * 0.45 = 13815 thousand

Note that the Polish population is given in millions in the question, so we needed to multiply the number given us by 1000 to convert it to thousands.

Second, we do the same for 2011:

31200 * 0.387 = 12074.4 thousand

Finally, we calculate the difference, and round it to the nearest thousand:

13815 – 12074.4 = 1740.6 ≈ 1741 thousand

Potential Shortcuts / Pitfalls

You have to be careful not to get the population figures for 2011 and 2016 the wrong way round. If you do, you would get the negative figure of (option C). And if you don't convert the Polish population figure from millions to thousands, you would get the incorrect figure of 2 thousand (option A).

SET 6, Q1. Correct Answer: D

Reasoning

We need to calculate the average speed of the runner, which is the distance divided by the time taken. We also need to figure out a way to convert the time given in hours, minutes and seconds into decimals.

Calculation

The distance run in the second half of the race is simply half the total distance:

42.2 / 2 = 21.1

The time taken to run this is the total time taken less the time taken to run the first half of the race:

2:13:31 – 1:07:50 = 1:05:41

The calculation of distance / time is simple enough but here, the time is not in an easily usable form so we must first convert it. To do this, take the seconds and divide by 60 (seconds per minute) to convert it to minutes and then add in the minutes. Now divide the minutes by 60 (minutes per hour) and add in the hours:

41 / 60 = 0.683
0.683 + 5 = 5.683
5.683 / 60 = 0.0947
0.0947 + 1 = 1.0947

Now calculate the average speed:

21.1 / 1.0947 = 19.27 km/h.

SET 6, Q2. Correct Answer: B

Reasoning

We need to calculate the average speed for each of the runners, which is distance / time. We then need to calculate the percentage difference.

Calculation

We first need to calculate the time taken by each of the runners for the last kilometre. For Dennis it was:

2:14:12 – 2:11:00 = 3:12 minutes
3:12 minutes = 3 × 60 seconds + 12 seconds = 192s

For Ekimov it was:

2:14:20 – 2:11:00 = 3:20
3:20 = 3 × 60 + 20 = 200s

Their speeds can now be calculated as distance (1000m) divided by the time taken. For Dennis:

1000 / 192 = 5.21m/s

Note that the calculated speed is in metres per second. If we had written 1 km as 1 km rather than 1000 metres, the unit would have been kilometres per second and the number would have been 0.00521 km / s. These are unusual units but we don't even have to write them out. Since we are going to calculate only the *percentage difference between them,* we can just take note of the number itself.

And for Ekimov:

1000 / 200 = 5m/s

The percentage difference is the difference divided by the slower speed and then multiplied by 100:

100 × (5.21 – 5) / 5 = 4.2%

Potential Shortcuts / Pitfalls

Because both runners are covering the same distance (1km) then their percentage difference in *speed* is actually the same as their percentage difference in *time.*

Why is this important? The reason is that *it is not necessary to calculate the two runners' speeds at all.* Once we know the time they took to cover the last kilometre (and this was the first calculation we performed), we can directly proceed to the difference in time, which is 200-192 = 8 seconds and so the percentage difference is:

100 × (8 / 192) = 4.2%

SET 6, Q3. Correct Answer: D

Reasoning

First, we need to work out Benoit's overall average speed. Then we calculate his speed in the last 150 metres. Once we have done this, we can calculate how far he was from the finishing line when Anderson finished.

Calculation

Benoit's overall average speed is distance divided by time but the time first needs converting to decimal form to make it easier to use. As above, divide the seconds by 60, add in the minutes and divide by 60 again and add in the hours:

38 / 60 = 0.633
0.633 + 12 = 12.633
12.633 / 60 = 0.211
0.211 + 2 = 2.211

Benoit's overall average speed is therefore:

42.1 / 2.211 = 19.04 km/h

He ran the final 150m of the race at a speed 5% faster than this, which is:

19.04 × 1.05 = 20 km/h

The time gap between Anderson and Benoit was:

2:12:38 – 2:12:14 = 24 seconds

The distance by which Anderson beat Benoit is then *the distance run by Benoit in 24 seconds at 20km/h.* We have a mismatch of units here, because the speed is given in kilometres / hour and the time difference in seconds, so we can *either* convert the time difference to hours by dividing by 3600 (60 minutes × 60 seconds) *or* convert Benoit's speed to metres/second by multiplying by 1000 (metres in a kilometre) and dividing by 3600 (seconds in an hour). Let's do the latter.

Why is this the way to convert km/m to m/s, you might ask? Let's see.

20 km / h = 20 000 m / hour

But we want to establish how many metres the runner can cover in *one second* (because the unit we are looking for is metres / second, not metres / hour). 1 hour is 60 × 60 seconds. 60 × 60 is 3600, so the speed is:

20 000 m / 3600 seconds

There is one last step to take, because we are interested in how many metres are covered in 1 second, so we divide by 3600:

5.56 m / second

Benoit ran for 24 seconds at this speed from the moment Anderson finished until the moment he himself crossed the finishing line.
The distance is then:

5.56 m * 24 = 133m

SET 7, Q1. Correct Answer: B

Reasoning

We need to form an equation with only one variable. To do this, let X be the number of male and Y be the number of female students in the school. The overall number of smokers is 19.6% of all students, i.e.19.6% of X + Y. It is also 21.6% of all male students (X) plus 17.5% of all female students (Y). Since the two are equal, we can formulate an equation. After substituting the number of male students and the number of male smokers, we are left with an equation that contains only one variable (Y). We solve this to get the result.

Calculation

The starting equation looks like this:

(X + Y) * 0.196 = X * 0.216 + Y * 0.175

We know that X * 0.216 = 60 (from the question) and from this we can easily deduce that X ≈ 278

Substituting these values we get:

(278 + Y) * 0.196 = 60 + Y * 0.175

If we move every term that contains Y onto the left side, and the rest onto the right we get:

Y * (0.196 – 0.175) = 60 – 278* 0.196
Y* 0.021 = 5.512

The solution for this equation is Y ≈ 262, which corresponds to answer B as being around 260.

Possible Shortcuts / Pitfalls
If by mistake you calculate the number of males instead of females, you would get 278 (option C, around 280). Or if you calculate the number of females directly as 60 / 17.5%, you get 343 (option E, more than 320).

There is a shortcut if you calculate the number of male students as 60 / 0.216 = 278, and then compose the equation for only one variable, Y = number of female students. This gives the equation 0.196 (Y + 278) = 0.175Y + 60, which would significantly reduce the time taken.

SET 7, Q2. Correct Answer: D

Reasoning

To calculate the number of male students who use ONLY electronic cigarettes, we must first calculate the *total* number of male students who use electronic cigarettes, and then subtract the number of male students who use *both* types of cigarette. Then we do the same calculations with regular cigarettes and add the results together.

Calculation

Using the percentage from the table, male students using electronic cigarettes: 300 * 0.133 ≈ 40

We know from the question that 20 use both electronic and regular cigarettes, therefore the number using ONLY electronic cigarettes is 40 – 20 = 20.

Male students using regular cigarettes: 300 * 0.076 ≈ 23. Again, as the question tells us that 20 use both types, the number using *only* regular cigarettes is 23 – 20 = 3.

The number of male students using only one type is therefore 20 for electronic and 3 for regular, total 23.

Potential Shortcuts / Pitfalls
The calculations here are fairly straightforward provided you do not get confused by the data. For

example, if you calculate the total number of male students using *either* type, forgetting that the number of students using *both* types must be subtracted, you would get 63 (option B).

SET 7, Q3. Correct Answer: D

Reasoning

We can calculate the number of students based on the number and percentage of students using any kind of tobacco product. Since there are twice as many males as females in the school, this means that one-third of the students are female, of whom 9.9% use electronic cigarettes.

Calculation

The table tells us that 19.6% of students use some kind of tobacco product. Therefore the total number of students in the school is 100 /0.196 ≈ 510

There are then 510 / 3 = 170 female students, of whom 170 * 0.099 ≈ 17 use electronic cigarettes.

Potential Shortcuts / Pitfalls
If you reverse the ratio between the male and female students, you would get the incorrect figure of 34 (option B). If you take 100 as the total number of students in school, instead of the students using any kind of tobacco product, you would get the incorrect figure of 7 students (option A).

SET 8, Q1. Correct Answer: B

Reasoning

We must calculate the total weight of beef and veal consumed in Argentina. To do this we multiply the population by the amount of meat consumed per capita in 2017. Since this only gives us the retail weight, we also have to divide the result by 0.7 to get the carcass weight required to meet the consumption.

Calculation

Total amount of beef and veal consumed in Argentina in 2017:

44.27 million * 41.2 =1823.924 million kg.

The carcass weight required to produce this amount of meat:

1823.924 /0.7 ≈ 2605.606 million kg, which is roughly 2.6 million tonnes.

Potential Shortcuts / Pitfalls
If you forget to convert the calculated result from kilograms to tonnes you would get 2.6 million kg (option A). And if you fail to divide the total amount of beef and veal consumed by 0.7, you would get 1.8 million tonnes (option D), or 1.8 million kg (option C) if you also forget to convert the result into tonnes.

SET 8, Q2. Correct Answer: B

Reasoning

Total meat consumption would decrease by the same percentage as total meat consumption *per capita*, so we don't need to bother with the former. The total meat consumption per capita is the sum of all the data in Brazil's row of the table. We can then calculate the amount that meat consumption would decrease, and determine what percentage this change would represent.

Calculation

The total per capita meat consumption is 26.5 + 11.8 + 39.9 +0.4 = 78.6 kg

The decrease is (26.5 + 39.9) * 0.2 = 13.28

If 13.28 is X% of 78.6 then 78.6 * (X / 100) =13.28

X = (13.28 / 78.6) * 100
X ≈ 16.9%

Potential Shortcuts / Pitfalls
With this problem you need to avoid being distracted by the data into making unnecessary calculations. EPSO numerical reasoning tests will make use of *distractors* which can overload you with data and make the problem seem more confusing than it really is. As mentioned, in this question there is no need to calculate the actual total Brazilian meat consumption. And the reference in the question to the population of Brazil being 209.3 million is a red herring as you do not need to know it.

You can go wrong if you try to calculate the rate of decrease by dividing the initial consumption by the decreased consumption. This would lead to 78.6 / (78.6 – 13.28) –1 = 20.3% (option D).

SET 8, Q3. Correct Answer: C

Reasoning

The total amount of pork consumed in the country in 2017 is the population times the pork consumed per capita. We need to convert this total to a percentage of the carcass weight required in order to get to the conversion ratio for pork.

Calculation

The total amount of pork consumed: 24.6 million * 20.7 kg = 509.22 million kg.

This number is (509.22 / 652.85) * 100 ≈ 78% of the total carcass weight, which means a 1 to 0.78 ratio.

Potential Shortcuts / Pitfalls
If you incorrectly calculate the ratio by dividing the carcass weight by the retail weight, thus doing 1– (652.85/509.22–1) ≈ 0.72, you would get 1 to 0.72 (option B).

SET 9, Q1. Correct Answer: B

Reasoning

We need to calculate the price at which we purchased 1 share, work out the total for 2000 shares and then add the dealing charge.

Calculation

Monday's closing price is given as 2.37 and we purchase at 1.4% below this so we have to multiply by (1-0.014) or 0.986. This is so because, remember, 100% is 1, so 1.4% must be 0.014. If the price is 1.4% below another value, another way of saying that is that the price was 98.6% of that:

2.37 × 0.986 = 2.33682

The total cost is then the number of shares multiplied by the price:

2000 × 2.33682 = 4673.64

We also have to pay the dealing charge:

4673.64 + 15.95 = 4689.59

Potential Shortcuts / Pitfalls
The actual price is 1.4% below yesterday's price. This means that we needed to multiply yesterday's closing price by 1 – 0.014. If the actual price had been 1.4% *above* yesterday's closing price, we would have multiplied by 1 + 0.014 – this is an important difference not to mix up.

SET 9, Q2. Correct Answer: C

Reasoning

We need to calculate the price at which we sold the shares and hence the rise since yesterday's close. In order to calculate the selling price, we must add the dealing charge to our proceeds.

Calculation

We are told how much we got from the sale of the shares, but we must remember that that amount was already reduced by the dealing charge of 15.95. This means that the actual selling price was 15.95 *higher* than the figure given in the question text:

4664.05 + 15.95 = 4680

This was the amount we got for selling 2000 shares so the amount per share was:

4680 / 2000 = 2.34

Yesterday, the closing selling price was 2.25 and so the percentage rise is the difference divided by the starting value and then multiplied by 100:

2.34 – 2.25 = 0.09
100 × (0.09 / 2.25) = 4%

Potential Shortcuts / Pitfalls
First of all, there are a couple of small but important issues to notice:

The question again talks about Friday but we need to compare our selling price to that of Thursday

There is a temptation to say that in order to calculate the price increase, we simply compare the Thursday selling price to the Friday selling price. This would be wrong because we did not sell at Friday's *closing* price but at an another price that we must calculate from our total proceeds

These were the pitfalls. There's also a shortcut. *You should be able to do this question without a calculator at all.* When dividing by 2000, be aware that this is basically division by 2 and then by 1000. Division by 2 simply means halving the number. Division by 1000 is moving the decimal point 3 places to the left.

When calculating the percentage, note that 2.25 is 2¼ which is the same as 9/4 (2 = 8/4). Remember that when we divide by a fraction it is the same as multiplying by the inverted version of that fraction, so when we divide 0.09 by 9/4 this is the same as multiplying by 4/9:

$(100 \times 0.09 \times 4) / 9$

When you multiply by 100 you can just move the decimal point 2 places to the right so 0.09 becomes 9 and now the 9s cancel out, leaving just 4:

$$\frac{9 \times 4}{9} = 4$$

SET 9, Q3. Correct Answer: E

Reasoning

We need to calculate the spread for each day as a percentage of the buy price.

Calculation

This is in essence a very easy problem because all the numbers are very similar. We can readily see the difference between the buy and sell price just by mentally subtracting the sell from the buy to get 0.05, 0.04, 0.05, 0.03 and 0.05 respectively. We can then calculate the percentage of the buy price by dividing the spread by the buy price and multiplying by 100:

Monday: $100 \times 0.05 / 2.37 = 2.11\%$
Tuesday: $100 \times 0.04 / 2.41 = 1.66\%$
Wednesday: $100 \times 0.05 / 2.39 = 2.09\%$
Thursday: $100 \times 0.03 / 2.28 = 1.32\%$
Friday: $100 \times 0.05 / 2.34 = 2.14\%$

From this we can clearly see that Friday has the largest percentage spread.

Potential Shortcuts / Pitfalls

Because we only want to know which is the largest spread we don't need to concern ourselves with the actual value, just whether it is larger or smaller than the others. Consequently, there is *no need to do all the '100 x' operations* which are common to all the calculations. Furthermore, as all the numbers are very similar, then the largest result is going to come from the largest numerator, that is, the largest spread value. There are three which are equal at 0.05 and so only these need to be considered. Secondly, the largest result will come from the smallest denominator. Why is that?

Let's say you have some apples, you eat 5 of them and you want to work out what that 5 represents as a percentage of the total number of apples. If you had 10 apples in total, you ate half (50%) of the apples. If you had 100 apples, you ate 5% of the apples. This illustrates that the smaller the total (here 10 instead of 100), the higher the percentage a fixed number of apples represent.

On the same principle, since Friday's Buy price was the lowest, the fixed spread (0.5) will represent a higher percentage of that than of any other day's Buy price.

This can be determined without a single keystroke of the calculator!

SET 10, Q1. Correct Answer: E

Reasoning

First, we must determine how to work out the total cost of acquiring and operating the software and then calculate this amount for all of the software options. The total cost is calculated by adding up the licence fee for the given period, the one-off installation fee and the total working hours spent operating the software multiplied by the hourly wage of the operating staff.

Calculation

We can start by writing out the formula for calculating the total cost for each of the options.

Total cost = Installation Fee + Licence Fee (Year 1) + Licence Fee (Year 2) + (Staff Number × Working Hours × Number of Months × Hourly Wage)

Let's now calculate this for each of the options.

Accounts Pro 10:

$130 + 4\,500 + 4\,500 + (4 \times 20 \times 24 \times 20) = 47\,530$

BSheet 12:

$150 + 3\,500 + 3\,500 + (4 \times 20 \times 24 \times 20) = 45\,550$

BSheet Lite:

200 + 8 000 + 8 000 + (3 × 25 × 24 × 20) = 52 200

BookKeeper Standard (remember that this software has a one-off licence fee only to be counted once):

550 + 9 000 + (5 × 15 × 24 × 20) = 45 550

We can now pick BSheet 12 and BookKeeper Standard as the two options that represent the lowest cost.

Potential Shortcuts / Pitfalls
One obvious pitfall to avoid is calculating BookKeeper Standard's one-off fee twice (once for each year). Also, there are a few opportunities where we can save time.

If you use a calculator, it is much better to start by calculating the total cost of the operating staff and only then adding the licence fees and the installation fee. Why? Because of the order of precedence between the various operations. The staff cost is the only factor which involves multiplication. Since multiplication is "higher priority" in a calculator than addition, we would either run into an error or would have to take note of an interim result – both of which make us lose time.

Let's take the BookKeeper Standard calculation to illustrate this. We started by adding up the licence fee and the installation fee:

550 + 9000

We then have to stop, memorize or write down this result, clear the calculator, calculate the staff costs and then add the above result in at the end. So what happens if we don't do that, and just continue with the calculations?

550 + 9000 + 5

A simple calculator will not wait to see which operation comes next, nor does it support the use of parentheses – it would simply add 5 to 550 + 9000, and then perform the multiplications, which would result in an obviously wrong answer.

SET 10, Q2. Correct Answer: C

Reasoning

We must first calculate the total licence fees for 5 years and then subtract the discount. We will then calculate the total cost of staff for 5 years and add up these two figures.

Calculation

Let's calculate the discounted licence fees for 5 years first. We do this by multiplying the yearly licence fee by the number of years and then calculating the discounted figure. A 15% discount can be expressed by saying that the new price is 85% of the original:

3 500 × 5 × 85% = 3 500 × 5 × 0.85 = 14 875

We now calculate the total staff cost, which is the number of staff needed multiplied by the monthly working hours and the number of months (5 × 12 = 60), multiplied by the hourly wage:

4 × 20 × 60 × 20 = 96 000

The total cost is the sum of the above two figures:

96 000 + 14875 = 110 875 EUR

Potential Shortcuts / Pitfalls
Important to avoid:

- do not forget about the 15% reduction in licensing costs (if you do, you get option D)
- do not forget that the installation fee was waived (if you do, you get option E)
- do not forget about multiplying the staff costs by the number of months (if you do, you get option A or B, depending on whether you perhaps also forget about the licence fee discount)

SET 10, Q3. Correct Answer: C

Reasoning

We need to work out the total cost of introducing and operating each of the two software options for three years and then calculate the difference.

Calculation

The total cost of operating either software option for three years is as follows:

(Staff needed to operate × Working hours × Number of Months × Hourly Wage) + Licence fees + Installation fee

For BookKeeper Standard, this is:

(5 × 15 × 36 × 20) + 9 000 + 550 = 63 550

For Accounts Pro 10, this is:

(4 × 20 × 36 × 20) + (4500 × 3) + 130 = 71 230

Since the question was about the savings or losses if the company introduces BookKeeper Standard *instead of* Accounts Pro 10, we should subtract the costs of BookKeeper Standard from Accounts Pro 10, not the other way around:

71 230 – 63 550 = 7 680

Since the total cost of BookKeeper Standard is lower (the result of the above subtraction is positive), this represents a net saving, so option C is the correct answer.

SET 11, Q1. Correct Answer: A

Reasoning

The percentage increase in production for each crop is calculated by taking the difference in production between the two given years and then dividing this by the starting (2010) value and finally multiplying the answer by 100 to make it a percentage.

Calculation

Corn: (12409 – 12211) / 12211 x 100 = 1.62%
Rapeseed: (5801 – 5472) / 5472 x 100 = 6.01%
Sugar: (2702 – 2920) / 2920 x 100 = -7.47%
Sunflowers: (21199 – 19194) / 19194 x 100 = 10.45%
Wheat: (7792 – 7719) / 7719 x 100 = 0.95%

The correct answer is therefore Corn (A)

Potential Shortcuts / Pitfalls

If you perform all the calculations above with a calculator you will use well over 100 keystrokes. This can be shortened considerably and even eliminated completely just by taking a few moments to think about the data.

The question asks for the middle crop so we don't actually need an exact figure, just a relative figure compared to the other crops. A quick look at the data shows that sugar production has actually fallen and so without any calculation we know that this will be at the bottom of the new table. Next, try rounding all the figures to the nearest hundred. Now we can see that corn goes up 2 from 122, rapeseed goes up 3 from 55, sunflowers go up 20 from 192, and wheat goes up 1 from 77. From this we can see that sunflowers have risen enormously compared to the others and will be at the top of the table, with rapeseed close behind. The remaining two are a little bit closer, and you could use your calculator if you are unsure, but given that the rounding would overestimate the wheat growth then corn is clearly going to be higher. This will make corn the third highest and hence in the middle of the table.

SET 11, Q2. Correct Answer: B

Reasoning

The percentage increase in production for wheat is calculated by taking the difference in production between the two given years and then dividing this by the starting (2005) value, finally multiplying the answer by 100 to make it a percentage. We can then reverse this process for sugar to calculate what value we should use for the 2010 production to get this same figure. Finally we need to subtract the actual amount produced to get the difference.

Calculation

Wheat: (7719 – 7422) / 7422 x 100 ≈ 4.0016%

This can be called 4% to the nearest percentage point

Let the 2010 figure for sugar be X, then:

(X – 2814) / 2814 x 100 = 4.0%
X / 2814 – 2814 / 2814 = 4.0% / 100
X / 2814 – 1 = 0.04
X = (1 + 0.04) x 2814 = 2926.56

Now subtract the actual production value to obtain the difference or increase as mentioned in the question.

2926.56 – 2920 ≈ 6.56 which is in thousands of tonnes.

Potential Shortcuts / Pitfalls

This problem can be simplified considerably by initially setting the two calculations to be equal to each other:

(X -2814) / 2814 = (7719 – 7422) / 7422

We can simplify this further because when you expand the bracketed parts of the equation we get 2814/2814 and 7422/7422; these are both equal to one and since they appear on each side of the equation then they just disappear.

Now we have:

X / 2814 = 7719 / 7422

And so:

X = 7719 x 2814 / 7422 = 2926.605

You will note that this is not the same as the answer given because this method has effectively used an exact figure for the percentage increase (7719/7422). To circumvent this, do that part of the calculation first and then only use the first two decimal places of the answer to continue with the rest of the calculation.

Don't forget to subtract the actual production figure to get the difference and remember that the figure is in thousands of tonnes.

SET 11, Q3. Correct Answer: E

Reasoning

The amount of land used for rapeseed production is the number of tonnes produced divided by the yield. We need to calculate this for 2005 and then can increase the yield by 6% and use this figure to calculate the land usage in 2015. We can then calculate the percentage increase by taking the difference and dividing by the 2005 figure.

Calculation

First, calculate the amount of land given over to rapeseed production. This is 4541 (thousand) tonnes divided by 3.1 tonnes per hectare:

4541 / 3.1 ≈ 1464.84

Increase the yield by 6%:

3.1 x 6% = 3.1 x 1.06 = 3.286

Now use this yield to calculate the land usage in 2015:

5801 / 3.286 = 1765.37

As a percentage of the 2005 rapeseed land use this is:

(1765.37 – 1464.84) / 1464.84 x 100 ≈ 20.5%

Potential Shortcuts / Pitfalls

Some things leap out as obvious and some things are really quite well hidden. If we write out the whole procedure above as one equation it looks quite messy…

((5801 / (3.1 x 1.06)) – (4541 / 3.1)) / (4531 / 3.1)

However, there are effectively three terms in the equation (B – A) / A, and you can see that all of them have the yield (3.1) as a common term as a divisor. As a result, this cancels out and can be eliminated from the equation entirely. *So, in a question that, at first, seems to focus on the crop yield, it turns out that it is not even required.*

SET 12, Q1. Correct Answer: A

Reasoning

We need to calculate the EU-28 total production of fishery products in 2015, and then the aquaculture production using its share of the total. The EU-28 total production of fishery products can be calculated using *any* country's production divided by its share.

Calculation

First, we must calculate the EU-28 total production of fishery products in 2015. We can use any country to do this, so let's use Denmark and its share of 14.1%:

905 / 0.141 ≈ 6418 thousand tonnes

Second, we must calculate the EU-28 aquaculture production in 2015, in millions, and round it to one decimal place:

6418 / 1000 * 0.197 ≈ 1.3 million tonnes

Note that since the EU-28 total production is represented in *thousand* tonnes, we needed to divide it by 1000 to convert to *million* tonnes.

Potential Shortcuts / Pitfalls

If you miss that fishery production is given in the table in thousand tonnes, and don't convert to millions, you would get 1264.4 million tonnes (option C). If you simply added up the production figures for the 5 countries in the table, without calculating the entire EU-28 production, you would get 0.8 million tonnes (option E).

SET 12, Q2. Correct Answer: D

Reasoning

We need to calculate French aquaculture production in 2015, and then find what percentage of all EU-28 fishery production this represented.

Calculation

We must first calculate the aquaculture production of France in 2015.

We know from the table that fishery products totaled 661 (thousand tonnes). There are two elements to this total, aquaculture and fish catches. The question text tells us that the fish catch of France was 271 thousand tonnes greater than its aquaculture production.

Therefore total production of fishery products in 2015 was:

(aquaculture) + (aquaculture + 271)

Hence, aquaculture = (total – 271) / 2

= (661 – 271) / 2 = 195 thousand tonnes

Now we must calculate the aquaculture production share of total EU-28 production, using the information given in the table that the total French production of 661 thousand tonnes represents a 10.3% share of the EU-28 total.

Aquaculture production share = 195 / 661 * 10.3 ≈ 3%

Potential Shortcuts / Pitfalls
You have to be careful in this question to realise that in the first calculation you must use the 271 thousand figure twice. Also, if you incorrectly calculate the amount of French aquaculture production, swapping it with catches, you would get 7% (option C).

SET 12, Q3. Correct Answer: E

Reasoning

We need to calculate the percentage increase from 2008 to 2015 in the total production of fishery products for both the United Kingdom and Spain, and then calculate the difference.

Calculation

First, we must calculate the percentage increase from 2008 to 2015 in total production of fishery products for the United Kingdom:

(913 / 768 – 1) * 100% ≈ 18.88%

Now the equivalent calculation for Spain:

(1195 / 1106 – 1) * 100% ≈ 8.05%

Finally, we find the difference and round it to one decimal place:

Difference = 18.88 – 8.05 ≈ 10.8%

Potential Shortcuts / Pitfalls
You can go wrong with this question if you confuse the *percentage* of increase with the *amount* of increase. If you use the amount you will calculate the UK as 913 – 768 = 145 and Spain as 1195 – 1106 = 89, resulting in 145 – 189 = 56. This is answer option D.

A shortcut lies in combining all the steps shown above, and doing (913 / 768 – 1195 / 1106) * 100%, which would significantly reduce the number of keystrokes and arithmetical operations.

SET 13, Q1. Correct Answer: B

Reasoning

The percentage increase in nuclear power generation is calculated by taking the difference in generation figures between the two given years and then dividing this by the starting (2000) value and finally multiplying the answer by 100 to make it a percentage. However we first need to increase the 2005 figure by 7.25% to take account of the increase in the total amount of energy being generated.

Calculation

First, calculate the total amount of electricity generated in 2005. This is 7.25% higher than in 2000. Let us assume that the total in 2000 was X. Then:

2005: Total = X * 1.0725

So the increase is:

(X * 1.0725 * 12.4 – X * 10.9) / X * 10.9

As there is a common term (X) in every element of the calculation both above and below the dividing line we can cancel it out, leaving:

(1.0725 * 12.4 – 10.9) / 10.9 = 0.22

Multiply this by 100 to make it a percentage:

0.22 * 100 = 22%

Potential Shortcuts / Pitfalls
This question is far more straightforward than it first looks. The main problem is what to do with the 7.25% increase given that there is no total power generation figure to use. However, provided there is a common base figure (the 2000 total power generation) that is being worked from, then it is always going to cancel out and need not even be considered.

Make sure you apply the increase to the 2005 figure before you calculate the difference for the increase rather than applying it to the increase itself.

SET 13, Q2. Correct Answer: D

Reasoning

The percentage increase in generation for each form of energy generation is calculated by taking the difference in percentage generated between the two given years and then dividing this by the starting (2010) value and finally multiplying the answer by 100 to make it a percentage.

Calculation

First, calculate the percentage change in percentage of total energy generated for each of the forms.

Fossil: (53.0 – 66.4) / 66.4 * 100 = 20.2%
Wind: (15.4 – 9.8) / 9.8 * 100 = 57.1%
Solar: (12.3 – 7.8) / 7.8 * 100 = 57.7%
Tide: (3.3 – 1.8) / 1.8 * 100 = 83.3%
Nuclear: (9.8 – 10.4) / 10.4 * 100 = -5.8%
Other: (6.2 – 3.8) / 3.8 * 100 = 63.2%

The correct answer is Tide/Wave (D)

Potential Shortcuts / Pitfalls

Virtually all the calculations can be made redundant just by taking a moment to examine the data and do a little bit of estimation and approximation. First and foremost, the question asks for the *largest increase* and so we can immediately eliminate Fossil and Nuclear because they have actually fallen.

The others are a little closer but other work that need not be done is the multiplication by 100 to make percentages. You only want the *relative* values of these figures and so any identical operation is going to do the same thing to all of them and make no difference to their relative values.

Take Wind: it starts at about 10% and increases to about 16% which is an increase of about 60%. Solar increases 4.5 from a starting value of about 8. This is clearly more than 50% but less than 2/3. Tide and wave power increases by 1.5 from a base of 1.8 which is 5/6 – which leaves the previous 2 way behind. Finally, 'Other' increases 2.4 from a base of 3.8 which is less than ¾, so Tide/Wave is left as the clear winner.

SET 13, Q3. Correct Answer: E

Reasoning

We need to calculate the percentage of the total power generated by biomass in 2005 and increase this by 50%. We then need to calculate the amount generated by 'Other' in 2010 and work out the proportion of this generated by biomass.

Calculation

First, calculate the percentage of total power generated by biomass in 2005. If we say the total amount generated is X, then the amount generated by 'Other' is:

X * 2.9% = 0.029X

The amount generated by biomass is:

0.029X * 20% = 0.029X * 0.2 = 0.0058X

This increases in 2010 to:

0.0058 * 150% = 0.0058 * 1.5 = 0.0087X

In 2010 the total power is 10% higher than 2005, which is:

X * 110% = 1.1X

So, in 2010 the percentage of total power generated by 'Other' is:

1.1X * 3.8% = 1.1X * 0.038 = 0.0418X

The percentage of this generated by biomass is:

(0.0087X / 0.0418X) * 100 = 20.8%

Potential Shortcuts / Pitfalls

As you can see from the calculation, the total power generated in 2005 (X) is unspecified and cancels out so needn't be considered at all. It is used primarily to explain the process. However, we can shorten this calculation considerably if we stop and think about the data in question and what we are trying to achieve.

In 2010 'Other' accounts for 3.8% of the total generation, which increases by 10% to about 4.2 when applied to the 2005 base (X). So 'Other' rises from 2.9 to 4.2.This is very close to 50%, which is the same rise that has applied to biomass and so they pretty much cancel each other out.

SET 14, Q1. Correct Answer: A

Reasoning

Only the data in the left-side diagram is needed. We must first add together the economic damage costs for all the disaster types, counting the damage dealt by storms twice to get our new total. We can than work out what the doubled amount caused by storms is as a percentage of this new total.

Calculation

The cost of the total damage would have been:

763 + 662 + 119 +100 + (2 * 1011) = $3666 billion

The damage caused by storms would have been 2 * 1011 = $2022 billion

2022 is (2022 / 3666) * 100 ≈ 55.2 percent of 3666

Potential Shortcuts / Pitfalls
If you simply double the percentage damage caused by storms, 38%, you would get 76% (option D).

SET 14, Q2. Correct Answer: C

Reasoning

For this question we only need information from the right-side diagram. First we calculate the total cost of economic damage, then what 45% of this number is. Another method is to calculate what 1% of the total economic damage is, and multiply it by 45.

Calculation

The total cost of economic damage:

709 + 262 + 40 + 10 + 870 = $1891 billion
45% of this is 1891 * 0.45 ≈ $851 billion

The alternative solution: If 709 billion dollars is 37 percent of the total economic damage, then 1% is 709 / 37 ≈ 19.16 billion dollars. The absolute loss of Asia would have been 19.16 * 45 = 862 billion dollars.

Notice how the two different methods lead to different results, although both produce answer option C. This is because the percentages and the dollar values are individually rounded. This is anticipated in the answer options which refer to approximate ranges rather than specific numbers.

SET 14, Q3. Correct Answer: E

Reasoning

We cannot do this calculation as there is not enough information. Although we have a figure for total global storm damage in the left-side diagram ($1.011 bn), and a figure for all types of damage in the Americas ($870 bn), there is no information as to *what proportion* of the damage in the Americas was caused by storms. It could have been all the damage or none at all, or anything in between.

Possible Shortcuts / Pitfalls
The danger with this question is that you assume a calculation can actually be made and waste time on trying to find a way to do it. If you make the mistake of using the fact that globally $1011 bn of damage was done by storms, and apply the same proportion to the Americas, you would calculate 1101 * 0.45 = $455 billion and choose the incorrect answer option D.

SET 15, Q1. Correct Answer: A

Reasoning

We need to calculate the speed of the runner and then the distance he would cover at that speed over the time difference between the two runners. We also need to remember when calculating the speed that Davies ran the last 10 metres (when the fate of the bronze medal was decided) 8% faster than his overall average.

Calculation

First, we calculate Davies' overall average speed, which is the distance covered divided by the time taken:

100 m / 10.07 s = 9.93m/s

In the closing 10 metres, he was actually running 8% faster than this, which is:

9.93 × 1.08 = 10.72m/s

He finished 4th, just 0.04s behind the 3rd placed runner. In those 0.04 seconds he ran the following distance:

10.72 * 0.04 = 0.43m

which is 43cm.

Potential Shortcuts / Pitfalls
A risk in this question is that of confusing speeds and times because they are very similar in value. A runner covering 100m in 10s is travelling at 10m/s. As the times chosen are very close to 10 then so are the speeds, so care must be taken to ensure you keep track of each step.

Another thing to be careful about is the fact that we need to work with the 8% increased speed to calculate the distance covered in the last 0.04 seconds as this was the speed Davies ran at in the final 10 metres.

SET 15, Q2. Correct Answer: B

Reasoning

We need to calculate the speed of each runner and then the percentage difference between these speeds.

Calculation

The speed of the runner is calculated by dividing the distance run by the time taken. For Adams this is:

100 / 9.95 = 10.05 m/s

And for Best it is:

100 / 9.98 = 10.02 m/s

The percentage difference is the difference divided by the slower speed and then multiplied by 100 to make it a percentage:

100 × (10.05 – 10.02) / 10.02 = 0.3%

Potential Shortcuts / Pitfalls
If you try and do this in one step then you would get:

$$\frac{100 / 9.95}{100 / 9.98}$$

When we divide by a fraction (we have a fraction in the denominator as well) we invert it and then multiply instead:

$$\frac{100}{9.95} \times \frac{9.98}{100}$$

Now we can see that the 100s cancel out and we are simply left with:

9.98 / 9.95 = 1.003

Remember that this is not the percentage increase of one speed compared to other but rather how much faster the first place finisher was than the second. To get the percentage, you subtract 1 and multiply by 100. This way, you get the same answer of 0.3%.

SET 15, Q3. Correct Answer: E

Reasoning

We need to calculate the speed of the runner in the final, and from that calculate his speed in the previous races. Then we calculate his time in the heat (the first race) and hence the time of the unnamed runner-up in that heat. To calculate this last step, we use the information from the question text.

Calculation

First we need to calculate Carter's speed in the final. This is the distance run divided by the time taken:

100 / 10.03 = 9.97m/s

This was 1.3% faster than in the semi-final. The easiest way to calculate the semi-final speed from this is by imagining what we would have done if we had been provided the semi-final speed instead. If we knew the semi-final speed and the fact that Carter became 1.3% faster in the final, we would calculate his speed in the final as follows:

Semi-final speed × 1.013 = Final speed

Since we already have the final speed and we actually need to calculate the semi-final speed, we can work backwards:

Final speed / 1.013 = semi-final speed

With actual numbers:

9.97 / 1.013 = 9.84m/s

Similarly, this is 1.8% faster than in the heat which was:

9.84 / 1.018 = 9.67m/s

So he ran the heat at 9.67m/s. This would take:

100 / 9.67 = 10.34s

Don't forget that he beat the runner-up by 0.03 seconds:

10.34 + 0.03 = 10.37s.

SET 16, Q1. Correct Answer: B

Reasoning

We need to find the percentage change in the total EU sold production of chemicals between 2016 and 2017, then the change between 2014 and 2015, and then calculate the ratio.

Calculation

This problem can be solved very easily if you notice that the total EU sold production of chemicals is the same in both 2014 and 2016, i.e. 663, so this provides a common denominator. We therefore only need to subtract the denominator from the nominator.

The change in the total EU sold production of chemicals between 2016 and 2017:

674 – 663 = 11

And for 2014 and 2015:

680 – 663 = 17

The denominator, 663, is the same in both cases so the ratio is simply 11 : 17.

Potential Shortcuts / Pitfalls
You have to be careful here not get the ratio the wrong way round. If you do that then you will get answer C, 17 : 11.

SET 16, Q2. Correct Answer: E

Reasoning

We need to calculate the amount sold of medical and pharmaceutical products in 2016, and then calculate its share in the total sold production of chemicals in 2016. The amount sold of medical and pharmaceutical products in 2016 is the respective amount in 2017 adjusted by the percentage change between the two years.

Calculation

First, we must calculate the amount of medical and pharmaceutical products sold in 2016 using the amount sold in 2017 and the increase of 5.2% between 2016 and 2017 (in billion euros):

168 / (1 + 0.052) ≈ €159.7 billion

Second, we must calculate the share of medical and pharmaceutical products in total sold production of chemicals in 2016, and round it to one decimal: place:

159.7 / 663 * 100% ≈ 24.1%

Potential Shortcuts / Pitfalls
If you mistakenly assume that the total sold production of chemicals between 2016 and 2017 increased by the same amount as the medical and pharmaceutical products you would get the incorrect figure of 24.9% (option B). If you calculate the amount of medical and pharmaceutical products sold in 2016 as the respective amount in 2017 divided by (1 – 0.052) instead of (1 + 0.052), thus mixing the percentages of increase and decrease, you would get the incorrect figure of 26.7% (option C).

SET 16, Q3. Correct Answer: A

Reasoning

We need to calculate the shares of organic and inorganic chemicals in intra-EU-28 exports in the total intra-EU-28 exports of chemicals in 2017, and then calculate their difference. The percentage shares of organic and inorganic chemicals are their respective intra-EU-28 export amounts divided by the total intra-EU-28 exports of chemicals in 2017.

Calculation

First, we must calculate the share of *organic* chemicals in intra-EU-28 exports in the total intra-EU-28 exports of chemicals:

81 / 527 * 100% ≈ 15.37%

Second, the equivalent share of *inorganic* chemicals:

17 / 527 * 100% ≈ 3.23%

Finally, we need to calculate the difference between organic and inorganic shares, and round it to one decimal place:

15.37% – 3.23% ≈ 12.1%

Potential Shortcuts / Pitfalls
If you calculate the difference between organic and inorganic chemicals in intra-EU-28 exports, instead of their respective shares you would get the incorrect answer of 64.0% (option C).

You can do the whole calculation even faster by factoring out the division by the total intra-EU-28 exports of chemicals, thus: (81 – 17) / 527 * 100%

SET 17, Q1. Correct Answer: D

Reasoning

We need to calculate the number of bottles of red wine consumed in 2015, which is the total consumption divided by the size of a bottle. From this we can work out the total spending on red wine, which is the number of bottles multiplied by the cost. Finally we can calculate the per capita spending, which is the total spending divided by the population.

Calculation

First, let's calculate the total number of bottles consumed (and as wine consumption is in litres, we need to convert 75cl into litres, which is 0.75):

52 / 0.75 = 69.333

Remember that this figure is in millions of bottles.

Therefore the total spending on red wine in 2015 is:

69.333 * 6.63 = 459.678

This figure is millions of euros.

Now calculate the per capita spending:

459.678 / 16714 = 0.0275

Now we need to think about the order of magnitude. The total spending was in millions and the population is in thousands, so we need to multiply the answer by 1000 to get a per capita value:

0.0275 * 1000 = 27.50

Potential Shortcuts / Pitfalls
This problem can seem a bit more complicated than it really is. You just need to be methodical in following each step, converting litres to bottles, to money, etc. and you also need to be careful to keep an eye on the different magnitudes of the data items.

SET 17, Q2. Correct Answer: B

Reasoning

We need to calculate the percentage change in consumption of rosé wine between 2010 and 2015 and then apply this change to the white wine to calculate what the consumption would have been with the same percentage change.

Calculation

First, calculate the change in consumption of rosé wine between 2010 and 2015. This is the difference in consumption divided by the starting value (2010 figure) and then multiplied by 100:

(31 – 38) / 38 * 100 = –18.42%

Now we apply this change to the white wine figure:

74 * –18.42% = 74 * –0.1842 = –13.63

Now add this to the original 2010 figure for white wine:

74 + –13.63 = 60.37

Given that all the answer options are in millions then this can be rounded to 60.

Potential Shortcuts / Pitfalls
This question gives you the opportunity to make a quick estimation of the answer. If you look at the data you can see that the 2010 starting value for white wine (74) is very close to twice that of rosé wine (38). So, given that rosé wine reduced by 7 (million litres), then white wine will decline by pretty much double that, i.e. 14 (million litres), from 74 to 60.

SET 17, Q3. Correct Answer: A

Reasoning

We need to calculate the per capita consumption of red wine in 2005 and 2010. Then we can calculate the percentage change, which is the difference between the two figures divided by the starting value and multiplied by 100.

Calculation

First, calculate the per capita consumption in 2005:

63 (million) / 16316 (thousand) = 3.8612

The 2010 per capita consumption is:

61 (million) / 16492 (thousand) = 3.6988

Now calculate the percentage change in consumption:

(3.6988 – 3.8612) / 3.8612 * 100 = –4.2%

Potential Shortcuts / Pitfalls

Although it's often necessary to be aware of the difference in magnitude of the different data items, it is not actually necessary in this particular case as they cancel out.

However, we do have the little difficulty of keeping track of enough significant digits in each of the intermediate answers to ensure enough accuracy in the final answer. If you aren't accurate enough you can arrive at answers between 4.0% and 5.1% even using the correct procedure, leaving 3 of the answer options as possibly right. To get around this difficulty, you can do the calculation slightly differently. When calculating the percentage change you can use (final value / starting value) – 1 and multiply this by 100. This method is less intuitive but it has the advantage that you can do the whole calculation in one go. Remember when you divide by a fraction then you invert the divisor and multiply instead. This leads to:

61 / 16492 * 16316 / 63 * 100 = 95.8

This eliminates the need to record partial answers and gives full accuracy.

SET 18, Q1. Correct Answer: C

Reasoning

We need to calculate, for both Italy and the EU-28, the share of young people aged 20-24 years who were participating in education and learning two or more foreign languages in 2015, and then calculate the ratio. The share is the product of two percentage shares, i.e. of young people participating in education, and of young people learning two or more foreign languages.

Calculation

First, we must calculate the percentage share of Italian young people aged 20-24 years who were participating in education and learning two or more foreign languages in 2015:

0.338 * 0.958 = 0.323804

The same way, the percentage share for the E-28:

0.414 * 0.588 = 0.243432

Finally, we calculate the ratio, and simplify it to the lowest terms:

0.323804 : 0.243432 ≈ 32 : 24 = 4 : 3

Notice that although the initial ratio is 32 : 24, it can be simplified since both sides of it are multiples of 8. By dividing each term of the initial ratio, 32 : 24, by 8, we reduce the ratio to the lowest terms, i.e. to 4 : 3.

Potential Shortcuts / Pitfalls

A risk here is of trying to calculate the ratio using only the values from the bar chart, i.e. 95.8 and 58.8. If you do you would end up choosing either 8 : 5 (answer option A) or 96 : 59 (option E).

As always in using data from tables and bar charts, you have to be careful in flicking between the two that you do not by mistake take data from the wrong table row or column or the wrong bar. This is an easy mistake to make when working at speed.

SET 18, Q2. Correct Answer: A

Reasoning

We need to calculate the number of French young people aged 20-24 years who were learning two or more foreign languages in 2010 and 2015, and then calculate the difference.

Calculation

First, we must calculate the number of French young people aged 20-24 years who were learning two or more foreign languages in 2010 (in thousands):

1.365 * 1000 * 0.518 = 707.07 thousand.

Note that the number of young people is given in the question in millions, so we needed to multiply it by 1000 to work in thousands.

Second, we calculate the number of French young people aged 20-24 years participating in education in 2015 (in thousands):

1.365 * 1000 * (1 + 0.036) = 1414.14 thousand

Third, we calculate the number of French young people aged 20-24 years who were learning two or more foreign languages in 2015 (in thousands):

1414.14 * 0.567 = 801.81738 thousand

Finally, we calculate the difference between 2015 and 2010, and round it to thousands:

801.81738 – 707.07 ≈ 95 thousand

Potential Shortcuts / Pitfalls

If you ignore the increase in the number of young people participating in education between 2010 and 2015, thus using the same number of 1.365 million for both years, you would get the incorrect figure of 67 thousand, which is given as option B.

If you forget that the number in the question is presented in millions, you would get the incorrect figure of 94747 thousand (option C). Common sense would normally tell you that answer must be wrong as 94747 thousand is more than the entire population of France, but when you are rushing in a numerical reasoning test you can end up blindly following your calculations and not step back and think if the answer makes sense.

SET 18, Q3. Correct Answer: B

Reasoning

We need to use the ratio between the German and Italian populations of people aged 15-29 years in 2015, to calculate the shares of German and Italian young people aged 15-29 years participating in education in 2015. We then convert the ratio to the percentage of increase.

Calculation

The question text tells us that the German population of young people aged 15-29 years in 2015 was 23% greater than that of Italy: Therefore the ratio was 1.23 : 1.

We must now multiply the sides of the ratio by the respective shares of German and Italian young people aged 15-29 years who were participating in education in 2015:

1.23 * 0.502 : 1 * 0.411 = 0.61746 : 0.411

Finally, we need to convert the ratio to the percentage, and round it to one decimal place:

(0.61746 / 0.411 – 1) * 100% ≈ 50.2%

Potential Shortcuts / Pitfalls

If you ignore the fact that the German population aged 15-29 is larger than that of Italy, and only calculate the difference between young people participating in education, you would get the incorrect figure of 9.1% (option A).

SET 19, Q1. Correct Answer: C

Reasoning

We need to use the biomass waste to bio fuels to wood ratio as these are the energy sources that count to biomass energy. Using this ratio we can then calculate the bio fuels share as a percentage.

Calculation

The diagram tells us that the biomass waste to bio fuels to wood ratio is 4 to 21 to 19. This means that out of every 4 + 21 + 19 = 44 quadrillion Btu of biomass energy, 21 quadrillion Btu was supplied by bio fuels.

By calculating what percentage 21 is of 44, we get what percentage of biomass energy was supplied by bio fuels. 21 expressed as a percentage of 44 is:

(21 / 44) * 100 = 47.72 ≈ 48%, which gives us answer C.

Potential Shortcuts / Pitfalls

If you simply use the biofuel energy percentage of renewable energy straight from the diagram as the answer you would get 21% (option A).

SET 19, Q2. Correct Answer: D

Reasoning

First we calculate what would have been the amount of *renewable energy* by dividing 2 (quadrillion Btu), the amount given in the question, by the percentage of renewable energy that is produced by hydroelectric (25%). Then we determine the *total amount of all energy* by dividing the total of renewable energy by the percentage (11%) coming from renewable energy.

Calculation

The amount of *renewable energy* produced would have been 2 / 0.25 = 8 quadrillion Btu

The total amount of *all energy* produced would have been 8 / 0.11 ≈ 72.7 quadrillion Btu

Therefore the correct answer is D.

Potential Shortcuts / Pitfalls
Be careful not to skip the first step of the calculation. If you do, you would calculate 2 / 0.11 = 18.2 quadrillion Btu (option A).

SET 19, Q3. Correct Answer: C

Reasoning

We must calculate what amount of energy was actually produced from petroleum by multiplying the total for all energy types by the petroleum share of 37%. We then reduce this amount by 10%. In order for the total amount of energy produced to stay the same, we have to make up for this decrease by increasing the other 4 sources by equal amounts, so we divide the previous result by 4 to get what those amounts are. We then have to add this number to the original amount of energy produced via coal, which we can calculate by multiplying the total amount by 0.14.

Calculation

The amount of energy produced from petroleum originally: 97.7 * 0.3 7 ≈ 36.15

The amount of decrease is then 10% of this number which is 36.15 * 0.1 ≈ 3.62

That means that energy from other sources must increase by 3.62 / 4 ≈ 0.9 each

The amount of energy produced from coal originally is 97.7 * 0.14 ≈ 13.68

The answer to the question is therefore 13.68 + 0.9 = 14.58 quadrillion Btu

Potential Shortcuts / Pitfalls
This question can seem rather complex and needs to be read carefully. The phrase "energy from the other sources had increased by equal amounts" means that energy from all the other sources increased by a *combined* total of 3.62 and therefore *each* source increased by 3.62 / 4 ≈ 0.9. If you mistakenly calculate at 3.62 each you would get a total increase of 4 * 3.62, leading to 97.7 * 0.14 – 3.62 = 17.3 quadrillion Btu (option E).

A further risk is that you interpret the question in such a way as to increase the energy produced from each source by an equal *percentage* instead of an equal *amount*. This would give the incorrect figure of (97.7 + 3.62) * 0.14 = 14.2 quadrillion Btu (option B).

SET 20, Q1. Correct Answer: B

Reasoning

The number of books belonging to two subcategories is the sum of the books in each subcategory minus the total number of books in the Teen & young adult category. Once we have this figure, we can determine the percentage.

Calculation

The number of books belonging to two subcategories is:

10096 + 390686 + 371140 + 310547 +15387 + 81644 = 1179500

Now we deduct the figure for the total number of books in the Teen & young adult category:

1179500 –1017540 = 161960

If X is the percentage that this number represents, then

1017540 * (X / 100) = 161960
X = (161960 / 1017540) * 100

Solving the equation we get that X ≈ 15.9%, which is answer B.

SET 20, Q2. Correct Answer: C

Reasoning

We need to calculate the number of general reference books, using data from both the table and the pie chart. We can then convert this number to a percentage of the total number of Teen & young adult books.

Calculation

There are 15387 reference books, of which 54% belong to the general reference subcategory. So the number of books in the general reference subcategory is:

15387 * 0.54 ≈ 8309

If 8309 is X percent of 1017540 (the total number of books in the Teen & young adult category) then the equation is:

1017540 * (X / 100) = 8309
X = (8309 / 1017540) * 100

Solving for X we get that X ≈ 0.82%, giving us answer option C.

Potential Shortcuts / Pitfalls
Although the actual calculation here is not too difficult, it is very easy to get confused between the different categories and subcategories and end up calculating with the wrong values. If you use the sum of the books in each subcategory, 1179500, instead of the total number of Teen & young adult books, 1017540, you would end up with 0.7% (option B). Or if you use the number of books in the *reference* subcategory, 15387, instead of the number of books in the *general reference* subcategory (one level further down), you would get 1.51% (option D).

SET 20, Q3. Correct Answer: D

Reasoning

We must first calculate the number of dictionaries and then the percentage of reference books this represents after the addition of 1000 atlases.

Calculation

The number of dictionaries is 15387 * 0.21 ≈ 3231

The number of reference books after the addition of 1000 atlases:

15387 + 1000 = 16387

The percentage the dictionaries represent after the addition:

(3231 / 16387) * 100 ≈ 19.72%

Potential Shortcuts / Pitfalls
Again, you can go wrong by confusing the data. For instance, if you increased by 1000 the number of dictionaries, instead of atlases, you would end up with 25.82% (option E).

SET 21, Q1. Correct Answer: D

Reasoning

We need to calculate the overall average speed of the train. Speed is distance divided by time. Once we have the average speed, we can easily calculate the cruising speed by adding 15% to this value.

Calculation

The calculation of speed (distance / time) is quite straightforward, but here the time is not in an easily usable form. The hour component of the journey time is simple enough: 3 hours. The problem is with the minutes, as we do not express time in the decimal system. This means that 45 minutes is not equal to 0.45 hours, so we must first convert the minutes to a decimal value.

To do this, take the minutes, divide by 60 (minutes per hour) and then add the hours:

45 / 60 = 0.75
0.75 + 3 = 3.75

Now calculate the average speed:

435 / 3.75 = 116

The cruising speed is actually 15% faster than this. Remember how we convert a 15% increase to 1.15:

116 × 1.15 = 133.4

Which, to the nearest whole number, is 133 km/h.

Potential Shortcuts / Pitfalls
The first part of this problem can be done more quickly without a calculator.

The time taken is 3:45, which is 3 whole hours and 3 quarters of an hour. This is a total of 15 quarter hours (3 × 4 = 12, plus 3 quarters), so when we calculate the average speed we can use:

435 / (15 / 4)

But remember, if we are dividing by a fraction then we *invert* it and *multiply* instead:

435 × (4 / 15)

This next step is difficult to spot but if you do, it can save a lot of time. 45 is 3x15 and so 450 is 30x15. So what? Well, notice that 435 is just 15 less than 450. Since 450 is 30x15, then 435 must be 29x15. Our division then looks like this:

(29 × 15 × 4) / 15

Notice how the 15 is both in the numerator and in the denominator – this means that they will cancel each other out, reducing the calculation to:

29 × 4 = 116

There is one last thing we should not forget about in dealing with minutes. 45 minutes is three quarters of an hour. We are trying to convert this into the decimal system, so what is three quarters of one hundred? The answer is of course 75, with or without using a calculator.

SET 21, Q2. Correct Answer: C

Reasoning

We need to calculate the normal average speed for the train. Once we have this, we can calculate the actual average speed of the train and then the delay caused by the slowdown.

Calculation

We first need to convert the time into a usable format. To do this, take the minutes, divide by 60 and add the hours back in:

35 / 60 = 0.583
0.583 + 1 = 1.583

Now calculate the normal average speed:

220 / 1.583 = 138.98

Because of adverse conditions, our *actual* average was only 90% of this (which is just another way of saying that it was 10% slower):

138.98 × 0.9 = 125.1

So, if we travelled all 220km at this speed it would take:

220 / 125.1 = 1.7586

This answer is in the decimal format, which we need to convert back to hours and minutes. Subtract the whole hours and then multiply the decimal part by 60:

0.7586 × 60 = 45.516

This is what we know so far: the journey took 1 hour and 45.516 minutes. This is still not good enough, as now it is the minutes that is in the decimal format. Now subtract the minutes and repeat the above step to get the seconds:

0.516 × 60 = 30.96s

This is 1:45:31 which is 10m 31s late.

Potential Shortcuts / Pitfalls

There may be a temptation to take the time of 1 hour and 35 minutes and convert it to minutes. This would be 95 minutes. Some candidates would then take 10% of this and add it to the original 95 minutes to calculate the delay. This would give an answer of 9m30s delay, which is wrong. What this actually calculates is *how far you would be from your destination at the normal arrival time*, if you continued your journey at the normal average speed.

A shortcut we can take is *checking the level of accuracy needed* to answer the question. We initially calculated that the new journey time would be 1 hour and 45.516 minutes. We can see from the data in the table that 1 hour and 45.516 minutes is 10 minutes and × seconds longer than the normal journey time. As it turns out, this level of accuracy is more than enough, as option C is the only one which starts with 10 minutes – so we do not actually need to convert 0.516 of a minute into seconds.

SET 21, Q3. Correct Answer: B

Reasoning

We need to work out the number of trains we will pass. The easiest way to do this is to make note of when we depart and arrive and then calculate how many trains either (1) arrive after our departure time or (2) depart before our arrival time.

Calculation

To calculate our arrival time:

08:00 + 5:20 = 13:20

The first train leaving Berlin set off at 05:00 and so it will arrive at:

05:00 + 5:20 = 10:20

So, the first train of the day from Berlin to Brussels will still be en route when we set off. This means that we will pass every train leaving after 05:00 and before 13:20, when we arrive in Berlin.

Since trains leave from Berlin every two hours, this will add up to 5 trains:

05:00, 07:00, 09:00, 11:00 and 13:00, 5 in total.

Potential Shortcuts / Pitfalls
There may be a temptation to say that the journey is 5 hour and 20 minutes long and the trains set off every two hours, so we must pass only two trains (one after 2 hours, the second after 4 hours). This would only be true if we simply sat in a stationary train for 5 hours and 20 minutes! This incorrect approach disregards the fact that our train is also moving in the opposite direction.

SET 22, Q1. Correct Answer: D

Reasoning

The number of unemployed is the population multiplied by the size of the workforce as a percentage of the population, multiplied by the percentage of the workforce that is unemployed. We need to calculate this for 2015, subtract 10000 from it, adjust the percentages by the given values and calculate the population of Ireland in 2010. We can then calculate the percentage change in the population.

Calculation

First, calculate the number of unemployed in 2015:

4606 * 0.485 * 0.059 = 131.8

This number is in thousands because the population is given in thousands. Therefore before we subtract 10000 from it we need to convert it to the same units. You can either multiply the above answer by 1000 or divide the change in unemployed figure by 1000:

131.8 – 10000 / 1000 = 121.8

The percentage of the workforce that is unemployed rose by 0.1 percentage points (*not* 0.1%) and so in 2010 it would have been:

5.9 – 0.1 = 5.8

So, the population that would have this level of unemployed people is:

121.8 / (0.058 * 0.487) = 4312.12

This means that the percentage rise in population is therefore:

(4606 – 4312.12) / 4312.12 * 100 = 6.8%

Potential Shortcuts / Pitfalls
This is relatively straightforward but there are a lot of steps to it. Also, there are a few units that don't match up very easily. When you have calculated the number of unemployed in 2015, you cannot simply multiply in a percentage change because the change in the number of unemployed is given as an *absolute figure* rather than a percentage change. Also the change in the percentage of the workforce unemployed is given as a change in the figure rather than as a percentage change even though the data item itself is a percentage. This sort of thing is often a source of confusion.

SET 22, Q2. Correct Answer: B

Reasoning

The number of unemployed is the population multiplied by the size of the workforce as a percentage of the population, multiplied by the percentage of the workforce that is unemployed. We need to do this calculation for both Hungary and Portugal and then work out the percentage that the former is of the latter.

Calculation

First, calculate the number of unemployed in Hungary:

11086 * 0.467 * 0.076 = 393.5

Now do the same for Portugal:

11602 * 0.421 * 0.087 = 425

Now calculate the percentage Hungary is of Portugal:

393.5 / 425 * 100 = 92.6%

Potential Shortcuts / Pitfalls
Just be careful to get the fraction for the final percentage the correct way round and that you don't use the wrong year for the percentage of population figure.

SET 22, Q3. Correct Answer: E

Reasoning

The number of unemployed is the population multiplied by the size of the workforce as a percentage of the population, multiplied by the percentage of the workforce that is unemployed. We need to work this out for Croatia in 2015, then modify the figures for the population and the percentage of the workforce unemployed as indicated and calculate the number of unemployed in 2010. Finally, we can calculate the difference between the two.

Calculation

First, calculate the number of unemployed in Croatia in 2015:

4887 * 0.421 * 0.074 = 152.25

The percentage of the workforce who are unemployed rose by 5% from 2010 to 2015, so the 2010 figure would be:

0.074 / 1.05 = 0.0705 or 7.048%

The population of Croatia rose by 3.3% and so the population in 2010 would have been:

4887 / 1.033 = 4730.88

The number of unemployed in 2010 was:

4730.88 * 0.419 * 0.07048 = 139.708

The difference in numbers of people unemployed is then:

152.25 – 139.708 = 12.542

This is in thousands and so the answer is 12542.

Potential Shortcuts / Pitfalls

Try and avoid too many intermediate results as these can rounding errors if too few significant digits are used. Also note that although the percentage of the workforce unemployed is a percentage (7.4%), when this changes by a percentage then you must treat the figure if it were any other piece of data and multiply or divide as appropriate. The fact that it is a percentage is irrelevant. Do not just add or subtract 5 percentage points.

SET 23, Q1: Correct Answer: D

Reasoning

For each year we have to find the number of unemployed people of working age. We calculate the number of working age people for a given year by multiplying the population by the percentage of working age people. Then we multiply the result by that year's unemployment rate to get the number of unemployed people of working age.

Calculation

We can combine the steps of the calculation as follows:

For 2007: 10023887 *0.66 * 0.07 ≈ 463104
For 2008: 9991201 *0.66 * 0.08 ≈ 527535
For 2009: 9958942 *0.66 * 0.098 ≈ 644144
For 2010: 9927840 *0.66 *0.118 ≈ 773180

We do not need to do any calculation for 2011. Since the unemployment rate was the same in 2010 as in 2011, the year with the higher population will automatically have more unemployed people. The chart tells us that the population was higher in 2010 than in 2011, therefore the correct answer is 2010.

Potential Shortcuts / Pitfalls

Remember that we are not looking for an absolute number but to find which is the largest number in a range. As we are told that 66% of the population are of working age in every year, we do not actually need to use this 66% figure at all in the calculation, because its proportional effect will be the same in every year.

SET 23, Q2. Correct Answer: B

Reasoning

The people who are older than 74 years in 2020 are those who are aged 74, 73 or 72 in 2017. Since every age group is equally represented, the number of unemployed people for any given age group is one-sixtieth of the number of unemployed working age people in 2017. To calculate the latter figure we have to multiply the population by the percentage of working age people and the percentage of unemployed people of working age.

Calculation

The number of unemployed working age people in 2017:

9721559 * 0.66 * 0.045 ≈ 288730.3

The number of unemployed people at any given age between 15 and 74:

288730.3 / 60 ≈ 4812.2

The number of unemployed people at the age of 74, 73 or 72:

3 * 4812.2 = 14436.6

The answer options don't ask for exact figures, so 14436.6 corresponds to answer option B, around 14500.

Potential Shortcuts / Pitfalls
If you don't apply the scale factor of 0.66, you would end up with the incorrect figure of 21900 (option E).

You can also combine all of the calculations above, using the fact that 3 years out of 60 (i.e. those aged 15 to 74) is exactly one twentieth of the respective population:

9721559 * 0.66 * 0.045 / 20 = 14436.6

SET 23, Q3. Correct Answer: E

Reasoning

To calculate the number of people of any age who were not working in 2007 we need to calculate the number of unemployed working age people, and the number of people not of working age, and add them together. We will have to do the same for 2017. To calculate the rate of change, we must divide the number of people not working in 2017 by the number of people not working in 2007.

Calculation

The number of unemployed working age people in 2007:

10023887 * 0.66 * 0.07 ≈ 463104

The number of people not of working age in 2007:

10023887 * (1 – 0.66) ≈ 3408122

Now the number of people not working in 2007:

463104 + 3408122 = 3871226

With a similar calculation, we get the number of not working people in 2017:

9721559 * 0.66 * 0.045 ≈ 288730
9721559 * (1 – 0.66) ≈ 3305331
288730 + 3305331 = 3594061

If 3594061 is X% of 3871226, then 3871226 * (X / 100) = 3594060

X = (3594060 / 3871226) * 100
X = 92.84%, which means a (100 –92.84) = 7.16% decrease.

Potential Shortcuts / Pitfalls
If you calculate the rate of change of unemployed people aged 15-74 years, instead of using the total number of not working people, you would calculate a decrease of approximately 38% (option D).

The last steps of the calculation can also be shortened to:

3871226 – 3594061 = 277165
277165 / 3871226 = 7.16%, which is the rate of decrease

SET 24, Q1. Correct Answer: B

Reasoning

We need to calculate the total water usage of the domestic sector in both Latvia and Lithuania in 2015, and then the percentage difference between the two countries. The total water usage by the domestic sector in each country is the water usage per inhabitant multiplied by the population in 2015.

Calculation

First, we must calculate the total water usage by the domestic sector in Latvia in 2015:

56.8 * 1.986 = 112.8048

Note that since we only need to calculate a *percentage* difference between two numbers using the same unit of measurement, we don't need to determine the *actual units.*

Now we do the same calculation for Lithuania in 2015:

50.9 * 2.921 ≈ 148.6789

Finally, we need to calculate the percentage, and round it to the one decimal place:

112.8048 / 148.6789 * 100% ≈ 75.9%

Potential Shortcuts / Pitfalls
If you mistakenly calculate the percentage difference between the water usage *per inhabitant* by the domestic sectors in Latvia and Lithuania in 2015, instead of the *total* water usage, you would get the incorrect percentage of 111.6% (option D).

If you calculate the percentage difference between the populations of Latvia and Lithuania in 2015, instead of the total water usage you would get 68.0% (option A).

SET 24, Q2. Correct Answer: A

Reasoning

We need to calculate the average water usage per inhabitant for each of the five countries in both 2015 and 2010, and then calculate their difference. The average water usage per inhabitant per country is the sum of the average water usages per inhabitant in each of the 5 countries divided by 5.

Calculation

First, we must calculate the average water usage per inhabitant in each of the five countries in 2015 (in m^3):

(47.1 + 43.0 + 38.9 + 56.8 + 50.9) / 5 = 47.34 m^3

The same for 2010:

(44.7 + 44.4 + 38.9 + 57.4 + 34.5) / 5 = 43.98 m^3

Finally, we need to calculate the difference between 2015 and 2010, and round it to one decimal place:

47.34 – 43.98 ≈ 3.4 thousand m^3

Potential Shortcuts / Pitfalls

If you calculate the difference between the *totals* of water usage instead of *averages* you would get 16.8 m^3 (option D).

A small shortcut lies in combining all the water usages per inhabitant, and only then dividing the difference by 5:

(47.1 + 43.0 + 38.9 + 56.8 + 50.9 – 44.7 – 44.4 – 38.9 – 57.4 – 34.5) / 5

SET 24, Q3. Correct Answer: E

Reasoning

We need to calculate the total water usage in Lithuania in 2011, then divide it by the water usage per inhabitant to get the population in 2011. To find the total water usage in Lithuania in 2011 we need to calculate the amount in 2015 by multiplying the water usage per inhabitant by the population, and then decrease it by the amount given in the question.

Calculation

First, we must calculate the total water usage by the domestic sector in Lithuania in 2015:

50.9 * 2.921 = 148.6789 million m^3

Note that the population of Lithuania is represented in millions in the figure, so we don't need to scale the resulting amount.

Now we calculate the equivalent figure for 2011:

148.6789 – 40.3 = 108.3789 million m^3

Finally, we need to calculate the population of Lithuania in 2011, in millions, and round it to one decimal place:

108.3789 / 35.5 ≈ 3.1 million

Potential Shortcuts / Pitfalls

If you ignore the increase of the total water usage in Lithuania, and just scale its population to the total water usage in 2015, you would get the incorrect figure of 4.2 million (option A).

SET 25, Q1. Correct Answer: A

Reasoning

We need to work out the number of births in Croatia in 2005 and 2015 and then calculate the difference. The number of births is simply the population multiplied by the birth rate. However, before we can calculate the number of births in 2015 we must first calculate the population given the population has increased since 2005.

Calculation

First, calculate the population in 2015 given the increase from 2005 is 7.5%:

Population = 4443 * 1.075 = 4776.225

Now calculate the number of births in 2015:

4776.225 * 16.8 = 80241

Note that the population is in thousands and the birth rate is per thousand and so these cancel each other out. Also we can round to an exact number as this is a number of births and you cannot have a fractional birth.

Now calculate the number of births in 2005:

4443 * 16.5 = 73310

The difference is:

80241 – 73310 = 6931

Potential Shortcuts / Pitfalls
You must remember to take into account the scale of the units in the data tables. On this occasion they cancel each other out but this is not always the case.

Also, you can combine all the steps above by doing (16.8 * 1.075 – 16.5) * 4443. This is not quite as intuitive but it reduces the number of keystrokes and also saves the need to store partial results, which can lead to errors.

SET 25, Q2. Correct Answer: C

Reasoning

We need to calculate the total number of births for each country, add them together and then divide by 4, which is the number of countries.

Calculation

First, calculate the number of births for each country (rounding *each number of births to the nearest whole number*):

Croatia:	4443 * 16.5 = 73310
Denmark:	5417 * 11.9 = 64462
Portugal:	10547 * 14.4 = 151877
Sweden:	9293 * 11.2 = 104082

Now add all these together:

73310 + 64462 + 151877 + 104082 = 393731

And then divide this by the number of countries to get the average:

393731 / 4 = 98433

Potential Shortcuts / Pitfalls
It is important to understand that the average number of something is the total number of things divided by the number of data items. In this case it is births and countries. This is not the same as adding up all the populations and dividing by 4 (the average population) and multiplying this by the total of all the birth rates divided by 4 (the average birth rate). This would give the incorrect figure of 100238, and as this is given as one of the answer options you might easily think you had got the calculation right.

SET 25, Q3. Correct Answer: E

Reasoning

We need to calculate the number of births in Portugal in 2005 then add in the increase in births for 2015. From this we can calculate the population of Portugal in 2015 and hence the increase in population from 2005.

Calculation

First, calculate the total number of births in 2005:

10547 * 14.4 = 151877

Therefore the total number of births in 2015 is:

151877 + 4 = 151881

Now calculate the population in 2015 that would give rise to this number of births:

Population * 13.9 = 151881
Population = 151881 / 13.9 = 10927

Now calculate the percentage change in population:

Change = (10927 – 10547) / 10547 *100 = 3.6%

Potential Shortcuts / Pitfalls
The increase in the number of births is obviously tiny (4 extra births out of a total of some 150,000). However, this small increase comes despite the birth rate having fallen between 2005 and 2015, and this means that the population must have grown. Therefore *you can immediately dismiss 3 of the possible answers,* because they have the population falling. Furthermore, as the growth in births is virtually nothing you can deduce that the fall in birth rate is basically equal to the rise in population. So, by simply calculating the fall in birth rate (13.9 – 14.4) / 14.4 = –3.6% we know that the population increased by this much.

SET 26, Q1. Correct Answer: E

Reasoning

We need to use the figures for the number of boats in the South Atlantic and the share this represents of the total to work out the total fleet size in 2013. Once we have done that, we calculate the increased fleet size in 2014 and, from that, the number of boats stationed in the Atlantic Ocean in that year.

Calculation

We know from the question that in 2013 the company had 42 fishing boats in the South Atlantic, and from the chart that this was equal to 15% of its total fleet.

Let us call the total 2013 fleet size F:

$42 = 0.15 \times F$

We now need F to be alone on one side of the equation, and everything else on the other side. We achieve this by performing the same operations on both sides of the equation. In this case, if we divide both sides by 0.15, we get there in one step:

$F = 42 / 0.15 = 280$

Now we can calculate the 2014 fleet size by increasing the 2013 size by 15%:

$280 \times 1.15 = 322$

We know that 40% of the fleet is in the South Atlantic in 2014 and 10% is in the North Atlantic, so a total of 50% of the fleet is in the Atlantic Ocean:

$322 \times 0.5 = 161$

Potential Shortcuts / Pitfalls

A couple of things to look out for:

- make sure you read off the correct data from the pie chart, as it is easier to confuse things here than in a table
- do not forget about the 15% fleet increase: disregarding this results in picking Option D

SET 26, Q2. Correct Answer: C

Reasoning

The chart does not tell us the number of fishing boats the company operates in 2013, only the proportions in each ocean. However we do not need to know the *actual 2013 fleet size* to answer the question. We simply take the 2013 *proportion* of the fleet that is in the Pacific Ocean (10% North Pacific + 20% South Pacific = 30%) and compare that to the share it has in 2014 in a 15% increased overall fishing fleet.

Calculation

Even with an unknown 2013 fleet size, we can express how many boats the company had in the Pacific Ocean in that year:

$30\% \times \text{Fleet} = 0.3 \times \text{Fleet}$

Now for 2014. We know that the fleet size increased by 15%:

$\text{Fleet in 2014} = 1.15 \times \text{Fleet}$

We also know that the Pacific Ocean share of this total is 25%:

$25\% \times 1.15\ \text{Fleet} = 0.25 \times 1.15 \times \text{Fleet} = 0.2875 \times \text{Fleet}$

We therefore have values of 0.3 Fleet in 2013 and 0.2875 Fleet in 2014. We can calculate the difference in the usual way, by taking the difference between the two values and dividing by the originating (2013) value:

$$\frac{0.2875\ \textit{Fleet} - 0.3\ \textit{Fleet}}{0.3\ \textit{Fleet}} = \frac{-0.0125\ \textit{Fleet}}{0.3\ \textit{Fleet}}$$

Notice that the unknown Fleet size is present in both the numerator and the denominator. This means that they cancel out, leaving us with a simpler calculation:

$-0.0125 / 0.3 = -0.0417$ (rounded)

Multiply this by a 100 to get a percentage:

$-0.0417 \times 100 = -4.17\%$

Potential Shortcuts / Pitfalls

The major pitfall here is the possibility of getting bogged down in the issue of how to frame the calculation when you do not have any figures for the number of boats, only proportions.

One other mistake not to make is to confuse a percentage change and a percentage point change. If you calculate the difference between 30% and 28.75% by simply subtracting one from the other, it would result in 1.25%, which is wrong – but since it is one of the answer options, it is easy to think you have got it right.

SET 26, Q3. Correct Answer: C

Reasoning

Since both oceans are home to 25% of the fishing fleet in 2014 and therefore have the same number of boats, the difference in the number of boats per square kilometre is the same as the difference in ocean size.

Calculation

To calculate the difference in ocean size, we simply subtract the size of the smaller ocean (the Indian Ocean) from the size of the larger ocean (the Pacific) and divide by the size of the smaller ocean.

Since we do not know the actual size of either ocean, only that the Pacific is 2.3 times as large as the Indian Ocean, we can think of the size of the latter as being 1. The advantage of this is that the size of the Pacific will then simply be 2.3.

Based on this, the calculation is as follows:

$(2.3 - 1) / 1 = 1.3$

To convert this to a percentage, we simply multiply by 100:

$1.3 \times 100 = 130\%$

Potential Shortcuts / Pitfalls

In this case it is essential to realize that you can in fact do the calculation just with the ocean sizes, without knowing the actual number of boats. If that is not immediately obvious, you might be tempted by answer option E, "impossible to tell".

A further key thing to bear in mind is that the question text states that the Pacific Ocean is 2.3 times as large as the Indian Ocean (i.e. 2.3 times larger) – this is not the same as saying that the Pacific Ocean is 230% larger than the Indian Ocean.

This distinction is nicely illuminated by using the alternative method of calculating a percentage increase. In the calculation section of chapter 6, we took the difference in size and divided by the smaller area. When it comes to percentage differences, we can also use the formula where we simply divide the larger value by the smaller value, in our case:

$2.3 / 1 = 2.3$

If we multiply this by 100, we get a percentage. In this case, however, we must remember that this merely gives us the *ratio* of the two values. To get the *percentage difference*, we must subtract the originating value, which is the size of the Indian Ocean in this case, which we denoted by 1 – or, in other words, by 100%:

$230 - 100 = 130\%$

Even when the values are different, using the above calculation and then subtracting 1 or 100% works, and some people will prefer this method.

SET 27, Q1. Correct Answer: A

Reasoning

First, we must calculate 5% of the total electricity production in Q1 2014, and then work out the production per wind farm. We then calculate the total wind farm production in Q2 2014 and from that, the number of operational wind farms in that quarter.

Calculation

5% of the total Q1 2014 production gives us the production from wind farms:

$12.5 \times 0.05 = 0.625$ GWh

There were 50 wind farms operating in this quarter, so the production of one wind farm is:

$0.625 / 50 = 0.0125$ GWh

Now let's calculate the total wind farm production in Q2 2014:

$10.5 \times 0.05 = 0.525$ GWh

We now know the total wind energy production in this quarter and the production value for 1 wind farm, so we can calculate the number of wind farms that were operating in this quarter:

$0.525 / 0.0125 = 42$

Potential Shortcuts / Pitfalls

First, it is important to make sure to use the production figures from the chart, not the consumption figures.

Secondly, a moment's reflection will show that no real calculations are required at all in this case. We are told in the question text that that all operational wind farms produce identical amounts of electricity as each other and in each quarter. This means we can immediately rule out Answer E, as we have all the data we need to answer the question. We also know from the chart that production fell between the two quarters, which means therefore that the total number of operational wind farms must also have fallen – which rules out Answers C and D. The scale of the drop, from 12.5 to 10.5 GWh, is also clearly bigger than that from 50 to 48 (answer B), leaving answer A as the only possible option.

SET 27, Q2. Correct Answer: B

Reasoning

The definition of excess capacity as production minus consumption is given in the chart. Using this, we must first calculate the excess capacity for 2014, and from that calculate the amount exported.

We then calculate the excess capacity in the first half of 2015 and from that the amount exported.

Finally, we calculate the difference between the two export amounts to see how much more electricity Hungary needs to export in the second half of 2015 to match the 2014 export amount.

Calculation

The total excess capacity for 2014 is the sum of the excess capacities for the 4 quarters:

12.5 – 9.8 + 10.5 – 10.1 + 13.6 – 12.1 + 14.5 – 11.5 = 7.6 GWh

The exported amount is 79% of this:

7.6 x 0.79 = 6.004 GWh

The excess capacity in the first half of 2015 was:

10.8 – 10.7 + 15.1 – 13.4 = 1.8 GWh

50% of this was exported:

1.8 x 0.5 = 0.9 GWh

In order for the country to export as much as it did in 2014, it needs to export a total of 6.004 GWh. To achieve this, it still needs to generate the following excess capacity:

6.004 – 0.9 = 5.104 GWh

Which is Answer B (rounded).

Potential Shortcuts / Pitfalls

This question is basically straightforward but it involves a sequence of calculations which you have to do systematically to avoid getting lost: excess capacity first, then the export amount, then the difference between the two years, and so on. The incorrect answer options are deliberately designed so that if you forget any of these steps, your incorrect result might match one of the incorrect answer options.

SET 27, Q3. Correct Answer: C

Reasoning

First we must calculate the quarterly production figure for Paks. Then we calculate 30% of each quarterly production value and count the number of quarters in which the Pak production figure was higher.

Calculation

The quarterly production figure for Paks is:

14.8 / 4 = 3.7 GWh

We now calculate 30% of the total quarterly production figures:

Q1 2014: 12.5 x 0.3 = 3.75 GWh
Q2 2014: 10.5 x 0.3 = 3.15 GWh
Q3 2014: 13.6 x 0.3 = 4.08 GWh
Q4 2014: 14.5 x 0.3 = 4.35 GWh
Q1 2015: 10.8 x 0.3 = 3.24 GWh
Q2 2015: 15.1 x 0.3 = 4.53 GWh

We can see that the Paks production figure of 3.7 GWh is greater than 30% in the case of two of the quarterly production figures.

Potential Shortcuts / Pitfalls

There is no real need to calculate 30% of each quarterly production figure. We know that Paks always produces 3.7 GWh per quarter. Therefore it will produce more than 30% of the total in any quarter in which total production is less than 3.7 / (100 / 30) = 12.33 GWh. A glance at the chart shows that this is the case in two quarters. We have replaced six calculations with one.

SET 28, Q1. Correct Answer: B

Reasoning

We need to calculate the total number of persons in French private households in both 2007 and 2017, and then the difference between the two figures. The total number of persons is the number of households multiplied by the average number of persons per household for each year.

Calculation

First, we must calculate the total number of persons in French private households in 2017 (in thousands):

29314.4 * 2.2 = 64491.68 thousand

Now we do the same calculation for 2007:

26456.5 * 2.3 = 60849.95 thousand

Finally, we need to calculate the difference, in millions, and round it to one decimal place:

64491.68 – 60849.95 ≈ 3.6 million

Potential Shortcuts / Pitfalls
If you calculate only the difference between the number of French households in 2017 and 2007, forgetting the difference in the number of persons per household, you would get 2.9 million (option A). If you used the 2017 number of persons per household, 2.2, and then didn't adjust for the 2007 figure, you would get 6.3 million (option D). Finally, if you have the number of persons per household in 2017 and 2007 the wrong way round, you would get 9.2 million (option C).

SET 28, Q2. Correct Answer: C

Reasoning

We need to calculate the number of Italian couples with children in 2007 and 2017, and then the percentage of change between 2007 and 2017. The number of Italian couples with children for a particular year is the total number of private households in that year multiplied by the percentage of couples with children.

Calculation

First, we must calculate the number of Italian couples with children in 2017 given its share of 20.9%:

25864.7 * 0.209 = 5405.7223 thousand

Then the number of Italian couples with children in 2007 given its share of 23.5%:

23710.7 * 0.235 = 5572.0145 thousand

Finally, we calculate the percentage of change between 2007 and 2017, and round it to two decimal places:

([5405.7223 – 5572.0145] / 5572.0145) * 100 ≈ –2.98%

Potential Shortcuts / Pitfalls
If you calculate the percentage increase between the total number of households instead of the couples with children you would get 9.08% (option B). If you simply calculate the percentage of decrease as the difference between the shares in 2017 and 2007, ignoring the change in the total number of households, you would get 2.60% (option D).

SET 28, Q3. Correct Answer: C

Reasoning

We need to calculate the total number of EU-28 private households in 2018, and then multiply it by the doubled percentage share of the couples without children. The total number of EU-28 private households in 2018 can be calculated using the 2017 number and the percentage of increase.

Calculation

First, we must calculate the total number of EU-28 private households in 2018:

221326.2 * (1 + 0.0065) = 222764.820 thousand:

Second, we must calculate the number of EU-28 couples without children in 2018, then multiply it by 2 to get the number of persons, and round the answer to the nearest million:

Total number of persons without children in 2018:

222764.820 * 0.249 * 2 = 110.936880 thousand ≈ 111 million

Remember that we must multiply the number of couples by 2 if we want to get the number of persons, since obviously a couple is two persons.

Potential Shortcuts / Pitfalls
The most likely mistake in this question would be to fail to multiply the number of couples by two, forgetting that each couple consists of two persons. This would give the incorrect figure of 55 million (option B).

If you ignore the percentage of increase between 2017 and 2018, you would get the incorrect figure of 110 million (option A).

SET 29, Q1. Correct Answer: D

Reasoning

The speed is the distance travelled divided by the time it takes. When coming to the final result, we need to take into account the order of magnitude of the distance and the unit of time given in the table.

Calculation

The Earth is 150 million km from the Sun and the question tells us that the distance round its orbit is 6.3 times this, which is:

150 m × 6.3 = 945m km

The speed is then calculated as distance divided by time:

945m / 365.25 = 2.587 m km/day

This is how far the Earth travels in 1 day. For the purpose of calculating the speed per hour, then minutes, then seconds, let's add in the zeroes representing the million:

2,587,000 km/day

Divide this by 24 to calculate its speed per hour:

2,587,000 / 24 = 107,791.67 km/day

Next divide this by the number of seconds in an hour (60 minutes × 60 seconds = 3600):

107,791.67 / 3600 = 29.94 km/sec

Which is about 30 km/sec.

SET 29, Q2. Correct Answer: B

Reasoning

We need to calculate the speed of each planet, which is the distance travelled divided by the time taken. We then need to do the percentage calculation of the difference.

Calculation

The speed is distance travelled divided by time taken. The distance travelled is the distance of the planet from the Sun multiplied by 6.3.

Mercury = 365.4 million
Venus = 636.3 million

The time it takes to make these journeys is the orbital period. From this, we can calculate the speeds of both planets.

Speed of Mercury = 365.4 million / 88 days = 4.152 m km / day
Speed of Venus = 636.3 million / 224.7 days = 2.832 m km / day

Since we are going to calculate the percentage difference between these two speeds, we don't really care about what unit they are in, so we can leave them in the unusual million km / day format.

The question is how much faster Mercury is than Venus, so the percentage difference will be the difference in speeds divided by Venus's speed, multiplied by 100:

(4.152 – 2.832) / 2.832 × 100 = 46.61 %, or cca. 47%.

Potential Shortcuts / Pitfalls

The above calculation is a perfectly good way of arriving at the correct answer, but we in fact performed a couple of completely unnecessary calculations. Let's write out all the calculations we performed in one formula to see what I mean.

Mercury speed calculation: 58 × 6.3 / 88
Venus speed calculation: 101 × 6.3 / 224.7

What do we notice? The × 6.3 is present in both calculations. Since we are going to use the results of these calculations in a division, we can completely omit the × 6.3 from our process. Let's observe:

$$\frac{58 \times \cancel{6.3} / 88}{101 \times \cancel{6.3} / 224.7}$$

What does this mean? It means that *we do not need to waste our time calculating the actual speeds* when all we need for a percentage difference is their *relative* speeds in the same units.

The relative speed of Mercury is: 58 / 88 = 0.66
The relative speed of Venus is: 101 / 224.7 = 0.45

Now we can calculate the percentage difference by calculating the actual difference:

0.66 – 0.45 = 0.21

The percentage rise is this difference divided by the starting point and multiplied by 100:

100 × 0.21 / 0.45 = 47%

SET 29, Q3. Correct Answer: E

Reasoning

We need to calculate the distance between Mars and Earth and then the speed of the messages travelling between them.

Calculation

We are told that the delay in response is a minimum of 8m 40s and that this occurs when their distance is at a minimum. We are also told how to calculate this minimum distance, namely by subtracting the Earth – Sun distance from the Mars – Sun distance. This is simply:

228m – 150m = 78 million km

So, each message has to travel 78m km from Mars to Earth. But remember, the question is not about how much time it takes for the message to travel from Mars to Earth but how much time it takes to get a response. If we assume that Earth begins to reply immediately, that response still needs to travel the same distance as well, so the total distance travelled is twice as much as the Earth – Mars distance:

78m × 2 = 156m km

It takes a total of 8m 40s to do this journey. We need first to convert this into seconds which is:

8 × 60 seconds + 40 seconds = 520 seconds

So the speed is now calculated as distance divided by time:

156 million / 520 = 300,000 km/sec

Of course if you remember from school, you'll know that this is the speed of light.

Potential Shortcuts / Pitfalls

You might already know that radio signals travel at the speed of light and what the speed of light is – you should NOT, however, mark that as the correct answer without doing the calculations since the test designer is under no obligation to use realistic data (even though this is *mostly* the case).

SET 30, Q1. Correct Answer: B

Reasoning

The lowest number of error-free files is calculated by subtracting the erroneous files from the total number of files closed for each team and picking the lowest number.

Calculation

The error rate denotes the percentage of files that were closed with errors, so in order to calculate the number of error-free files, we must subtract this percentage from 100% and calculate with those figures.

The number of error-free files for the five teams are as follows.

Team A:

4 500 × (100% - 5%) = 4 500 × 95% = 4 500 × 0.95 = 4275

Team B:

4 500 × (100% - 7%) = 4 500 × 93% = 4 500 × 0.93 = 4 185

Team C:

5 000 × (100% - 11%) = 5 000 × 89% = 5 000 × 0.89 = 4450

Team D:

6000 × (100% - 8%) = 6 000 × 92% = 6 000 × 0.92 = 5 520

Team E:

6 500 × (100% - 9%) = 6 500 × 91% = 6 500 × 0.91 = 5 915

We can clearly see that Team B closed the smallest number of files without errors.

Potential Shortcuts / Pitfalls

If you take a moment to consider the two charts, you can easily figure out the correct answer without performing any calculations. The first thing to notice is that Teams A and B closed the smallest number of files (with or without errors). The only way one of those two didn't close the smallest number of error-free files is if their error rate was very low and the other three teams' error rates were disproportionately higher. This doesn't seem to be the case.

Teams D and E closed many more files and their error rates are only slightly higher, so we can safely disregard them. Team C closed only slightly more files and its error rate is much higher, so it is worth looking at it.

Team C closed 500 more files than either Team A or Team B, and its error rate is 11% compared to 5% for Team A and 7% for Team B. The only way Team C can be worse than A or B is if the difference in the error rates accounts for more files than the difference in the total number of files – this, again, doesn't seem to be the case.

The maximum difference in erroneous files is between Team A (7% of 4 500) and Team C (11% of 5 000). That is 4 percentage points, and 4 percentage points of 5 000 is never going to make up for the 500-file difference between Teams A and B on the one hand, and Team C on the other.

This leaves us with Teams A and B. Since they closed the same number of files, the correct answer is the team which has the higher error rate, namely Team B.

SET 30, Q2. Correct Answer: C

Reasoning

We need first to calculate the number of error-free closed files for Team B and Team C, and then the difference between the two values.

Calculation

The number of error-free files closed by Team B:

4 500 × (100% - 2%) = 4 500 × 98% = 4 500 × 0.98 = 4 410

The number of error-free files closed by Team C:

5 000 × (100% - 17%) = 5 000 × 83% = 5 000 × 0.83 = 4 150

The difference between the two figures is:

4 410 – 4 150 = 260

Option C is the correct answer.

Potential Shortcuts / Pitfalls

Since the answer options are quite close to each other, there isn't much leeway for shortcuts and estimations in this exercise. On the other hand, you must be careful when interpreting the changes in the error rates: contrary to how a lot of EPSO numerical reasoning questions are worded, it is not the *change* in error rates that is given, but the *actual* new error rates – and this saves you a set of calculations which you don't have to perform.

SET 30, Q3. Correct Answer: D

Reasoning

We must first calculate the total number of files closed by the five teams throughout the year, and then what proportion of this total was closed by the end of September.

Calculation

The total number of files closed is simply the sum of the number of files closed by each team:

Total = 4 500 + 4 500 + 5 000 + 6 000 + 6 500 = 26 500

Since teams progress through files at a constant rate from month to month, we can calculate how many files they close in one month:

26 500 / 12 = 2 208.33

Since September is the 9th month of the year, we can multiply the above value by 9 to get the number of files closed by the end of that month:

2 208.33 × 9 = 19 875 (rounded up)

Potential Shortcuts / Pitfalls

There is an alternative way of calculating this which might be quicker and could yield an even more accurate result.

If we think of September as the 9th month in a 12-month year, we can say that the teams closed 9/12th of the files. We can then use this fraction in our calculations:

26 500 × 9 / 12 = 19875

As it turns out, this method yields exactly 19 875 and there was no need for it to be rounded to match option D.

SET 31, Q1. Correct Answer: B

Reasoning

We work out the total tax owed on 55 000 EUR of income by calculating the tax owed in each tax bracket and then adding on the total insurance tax for 12 months.

Calculation

First, let's calculate the tax owed on 55 000 EUR in each of the three systems.

System 1

First 10 000 EUR: tax free

10 001 – 30 000 EUR: The tax is the amount of income falling within this range multiplied by the percentage. Since the person's income is more than 30 000 EUR, we need to calculate the tax for the full range. This is done by subtracting the top of the previous range from the top of the current range:

$30\,000 - 10\,000 = 20\,000$

The tax is then:

$20\,000 \times 15\% = 20\,000 \times 0.15 = 3000$

30 001 – 50 000 EUR:

Using the same formula as above, the tax is:

$20\,000 \times 0.25 = 5000$

We still have 5 000 EUR left to account for. This falls into the 50 001+ range.

50 001+ EUR:

$5\,000 \times 0.31 = 1550$

We must also not forget about the insurance tax, which is a flat fee of 100 EUR / month:

$100 \times 12 = 1200$

The total tax owed is then:

$3000 + 5000 + 1550 + 1200 = 10\,750$ EUR

We now have to do the calculations for the other two systems as well.

System 2

System 2 has no tax free allowance.

0 – 30 000 EUR: 4500 EUR tax

30 001+ EUR: 5250 EUR tax

Insurance tax: 600 EUR

Total: 10 350 EUR

System 3

System 3 has a tax free allowance of 15 000 EUR.

15 001 – 30 000 EUR: 2 550 EUR tax

30 001+ EUR: 5 500 EUR tax

Insurance tax: 2400 EUR

Total: 10 450 EUR

From the above, we can see that the person owes the smallest amount in taxes under System 2.

Potential Shortcuts / Pitfalls

Unfortunately there aren't really any shortcuts you can use for this question. However there are some potential pitfalls to watch out for. You must make sure to check whether there is a tax free allowance in the system, and it is crucially important to read and understand the description of marginal tax rate – namely that only the amount falling within the range must be taxed at the given rate.

If, for example, you look at the table for System 3 and conclude that 62 000 EUR must be taxed at 28%, and you calculate the tax at 28% for the entire amount, you will get an incorrect result.

SET 31, Q2. Correct Answer: C

Reasoning

First we must calculate the total tax owed on 62 000 EUR, and then we will divide that amount by the income and multiply by 100 to get a percentage.

Calculation

For the general logic of how to work with tax brackets, see the previous explanation.

Let's calculate the tax owed in each bracket.

0 – 15 000 EUR: no tax

15 001 – 30 000 EUR: 2 550 EUR

30 001 – 60 000 EUR: 6 600 EUR

60 001+ EUR:

There are 2 000 EUR left to tax at this rate, so the tax is:

$2\,000 \text{ EUR} \times 28\% = 2\,000 \times 0.28 = 560$

We must also not forget about the insurance tax, which is 200 EUR / month, so:

200 × 12 = 2400 EUR / year

The total tax is then:

2 550 + 6 600 + 560 + 2400 = 12 110 EUR

Now to the effective tax rate, which is calculated by dividing the above value by the person's income and multiplied by 100:

12 110 / 62 000 × 100 = 19.53%

Potential Shortcuts / Pitfalls
One error that people sometimes make is to try to calculate the effective tax rate by adding up the rates of tax in the various tax brackets and then dividing the total by the number of tax brackets: this is obviously wrong because of the different weights of the ranges.

SET 31, Q3. Correct Answer: B

Reasoning

We must first calculate the tax owed under each of the two systems using the already familiar method. We can then calculate the difference in after-tax income under the two systems and divide that difference by the value under System 3.

Calculation

Let's first calculate the tax owed under System 1.

System 1

0 – 10 000 EUR: no tax

10 001 – 30 000 EUR: 3 000 EUR tax

30 001 – 50 000 EUR: 5 000 EUR tax

50 001+ EUR: 7 750 EUR tax

Insurance tax: 1200 EUR

Total tax:

3 000 + 5 000 + 7 750 + 1 200 = 16 950 EUR

The after-tax income is then:

75 000 – 16 950 = 58 050 EUR

And now under System 3.

System 3

0 – 15 000 EUR: no tax

15 001 – 30 000 EUR: 2 550 EUR

30 001 – 60 000 EUR: 6 600 EUR

60 001+ EUR: 4 200 EUR

Insurance tax: 2 400 EUR

Total tax:

2 550 + 6 600 + 4 200 + 2 400 = 15 750 EUR

The after tax income is:

75 000 – 15 750 = 59 250 EUR

Here we must be careful to get our figures the right way round. The question asks "by what percentage is their after-tax income greater or smaller under System 1 than under System 3". If you look at the figures for Systems 1 and 3, this will tell you that the after-tax income is smaller under System 1 so we are dealing with a negative figure:

58 050 (System 1) - 59 250 (System 3) = -1 200 EUR

We must now divide this by the after-tax income for System 3, since the question compares System 1 to System 3, and multiply that by 100 to get a percentage:

-1 200 / 59 250 = -2% (rounded)

This corresponds to answer option B.

Potential Shortcuts / Pitfalls
The risk here is that if you get the comparison the wrong way round, you will calculate:

1 200 / 59 250 = 2% (rounded)

This will "look right" because it is indeed one of the answer options, C.

SET 32, Q1. Correct Answer: E

Reasoning

We must calculate the percentage each power plant's electricity production represents of the total for that country and then see which one is in the middle.

Calculation

To calculate the proportion the production of a power plant represents in the total consumption of that country, we simply divide its production by the country's consumption.

Since all of the operations we will perform are divisions, and there are five zeroes at the end of almost all consumption figures, we can simply disregard those. In the case of Venezuela, this means that we will divide by 858.5.

Itaipu Dam / Brazil:

98.3 / 4 557 = 0.02157121

Three Gorges Dam / China:

98.5 / 53 223 = 0.001850704

Krasnoyarsk / Russia:

20.4 / 10 165 = 0.002006886

Grand Coulee / USA:

20 / 38 864 = 0.0005146151

Guri / Venezuela

53.41 / 858.5 = 0.06221316

The numbers above are a little hard to compare because they are so small, but with a bit of care it is possible. We can see that Grand Coulee is the only one with 3 zeroes after the decimal point, so that will be the smallest proportion. Also, Guri and Itaipu Dam only have one zero after the decimal point, and the next number is greater (6 versus 2) in the case of Guri, so that will be the largest proportion, followed by Itaipu Dam.

This is what we have so far, from smallest to largest proportion:

Grand Coulee / USA
?
?
Itaipu Dam / Brazil
Guri / Venezuela

We are now left with Three Gorges Dam / China and Krasnoyarsk / Russia – one of them will be in the middle. Both of them have two zeroes after the decimal point, but the next number is greater in the case of Russia (2 versus 1), so we have our final order:

Grand Coulee / USA
Three Gorges Dam / China
Krasnoyarsk / Russia
Itaipu Dam / Brazil
Guri / Venezuela

Krasnoyarsk is clearly in the middle.

Potential Shortcuts / Pitfalls
There is a great opportunity to estimate here.

We can quite easily see that Guri tops the list for generating the highest proportion of its country's electricity. The Guri power plant generates more than half the electricity of either the Brazilian or Chinese power stations, but Venezuela's consumption is far smaller than that of Brazil or China.

The next smallest consumption figure belongs to Brazil, yet Itaipu Dam has the second largest production, so it must come second (while Itaipu Dam produces almost twice as much electricity as Venezuela's Guri, Brazil's consumption is about 5 times as large as Venezuela's).

If we compare the USA's consumption to China's, we see that they are fairly comparable (3.9 to 5.3) but the Grand Coulee generates only a fifth of the electricity generated by the Three Gorges Dam, so it must be in the last position.

We are now again left with Russia and China, but without having performed any calculations. The way to compare the Russian and Chinese power stations is to look at the relationship between their production and their national consumptions.

Krasnoyarsk to Three Gorges is 1 to slightly less than 5.

Russia to China, however, is 1 to slightly more than 5.

This means that the Three Gorges percentage will be lower, so it will be the fourth in the list, leaving Krasnoyarsk in the middle.

SET 32, Q2. Correct Answer: E

Reasoning

We must first calculate how much electricity is currently produced in Venezuela from the total consumption and the percentage which current production contributes to this. We will then add the capacity of the new power station to this total and subtract Venezuela's total consumption to see how much is left for export.

Calculation

To find the current total production, we calculate 78% of the total consumption of Venezuela. To keep things consistent, we should decide whether we are going to perform all calculations in TWh or MWh. We will use TWh on this occasion.

The electricity consumption of Venezuela is then:

85 850 000 MWh / 1 000 000 = 85.85 TWh

78% of this is produced by the existing power stations:

85.85 × 78% = 85.85 × 0.78 = 66.963 TWh

After the completion of the new power station (which has the same capacity as that of Guri), the new total production will be:

66.963 TWh + 53.41 TWh = 120.373 TWh

If we subtract the current total consumption from the above figure, we get the amount available for export:

120.23 TWh – 85.85 TWh = 34.523 TWh

Since this is not among the answer options, we must also convert this into MWh and check if that is correct:

34.523 TWh × 1 000 000 = 34 523 000 MWh

which is answer option E.

Potential Shortcuts / Pitfalls

There are two major issues to be careful with here.

First, we must notice and then not get confused by the different orders of magnitude represented by the two different units of measurement, as defined in a footnote to the table. In situations like this, it is advisable to make a decision about which one you will use and then consistently convert all values to that unit before performing the actual calculations.

Also, it is tempting to simply double the capacity of the Guri power station (since the new one has the same capacity) and compare that to the consumption of Venezuela. That, however, would disregard the information given in the question text, namely that current production represents 78% of the total consumption (which means there must be other power stations in the country).

SET 32, Q3. Correct Answer: D

Reasoning

The electricity consumption of the EU is unknown at the beginning of this exercise, but we know that the capacity of the Three Gorges Dam is equal to 3.24% of this, from which we can calculate the total (100%). Once we have that, we simply take 30% of this total to get the amount generated from nuclear power.

Calculation

Since the total electricity consumption of the EU is unknown, let's call it X. We do know that 3.24% of this is equal to the capacity of the Three Gorges Dam, and this capacity is a known value:

3.24% × X = 98.5 TWh

Let's convert 3.24% to a decimal:

0.0324 × X = 98.5 TWh

Our aim is to find the total consumption of the EU, or X. Remember, in equations like this, we want 1 X to be alone on one side, and we achieve that by performing the same operations on both sides. Here, all we have to do is divide by 0.0324:

X = 98.5 / 0.0324 = 3 040.12346 TWh

This is the total consumption of the EU, 30% of which is produced from nuclear power:

3 040.12346 × 30% = 3 040.12346 × 0.3 = 912.04 TWh (rounded)

Potential Shortcuts / Pitfalls

There are several things to watch out for in this question.

- do not stop after having solved the equation – that is the *total* consumption of the EU, not the share of nuclear power
- do not round prematurely: if you round the total consumption to the nearest whole number and you calculate 30% of that, you would erroneously mark option C as the correct answer
- watch out for the units of measurement: all throughout the calculations, we only worked with TWh, so be careful with the answer options expressed in MWh

SET 33, Q1. Correct Answer: C

Reasoning

We need to calculate what percentage of all washing machines are energy-efficient, and then what percentage this represents of all household appliances.

Calculation

To find the percentage of washing machines that are energy-efficient, we simply add up the percentages of A+/A and B-rated washing machines:

45% + 35% = 80%

We know that washing machines (energy-efficient and non-efficient together) represent 20% of the total of all household appliances, and 80% of these are energy-efficient:

80% × 20% = 0.8 × 0.2 = 0.16 = 16%

SET 33, Q2. Correct Answer: D

Reasoning

We need to work out the current number of refrigerators and air conditioners that are energy-efficient from their percentage share of all refrigerators and air conditioners, and then increase this number by 20%.

Calculation

The current share of energy-efficient refrigerators:

40% + 25% = 65%

And that of air conditioners:

10% + 45% = 55%

We can now calculate the number of energy-efficient units.

Refrigerators:

9 000 × 65% = 9 000 × 0.65 = 5 850

Air conditioners:

3 400 × 55% = 3 400 × 0.55 = 1 870

The current total of energy-efficient units is:

5 850 + 1 870 = 7 720

If this increases by 20%, we get:

7 720 + 20% = 7 720 × 120% = 7 720 × 1.2 = 9 264

Potential Shortcuts / Pitfalls

The key issue here is not to confuse what the question is asking and end up calculating a 20 percentage point increase rather than a 20% increase. Remember: if your share of a cake is one-half and your share increases by 20%, you will have 60% of the cake, not 70%.

If you make this mistake you will calculate as follows:

Refrigerators:

9 000 × 85% = 9 000 × 0.85 = 7 650

Air conditioners:

3 400 × 75% = 3 400 × 0.75 = 2 550

This will give you a combined total (7650 + 2550) of 10200, and as this is one of the answer options you will think you have got the question right.

SET 33, Q3. Correct Answer: D

Reasoning

We need to calculate the number of D-rated units for each of the four appliances, and then see which number is the largest.

Calculation

The number of D-rated units is the total of appliances multiplied by the percentage share that are D-rated.

Air conditioners:

25% × 3 400 = 0.25 × 3 400 = 850

Washing machines:

10% × 5 500 = 550

Dryers:

15% × 2 000 = 300

Refrigerators:

10% × 9000 = 900

From the above, we can see that D-rated refrigerators would be at the top of this list.

Potential Shortcuts / Pitfalls

It is easy to solve this question without using a calculator at all – let's see how.

10%

There are two values where 10% needs to be calculated – we can do this by simply taking away a 0 from the end of the figure.

15%

First we calculate 10%. Then we take half of that value and add it to the 10%. 15% of 2 000 then becomes 200 + 100 = 300.

25%

Calculating 25% of 3 400 seems to be the hardest of the four to calculate, but if you think of 25% as one quarter, it becomes much simpler. But how much is one quarter of 3 400? Again, if you think of 3 400 as 3 200 + 200, then you can take one quarter of both and add these two numbers up.

One quarter of 3 200 is the same as one quarter of 32 (plus the zeroes). Since 32 is 8 × 4, this is 800. One quarter of 200 is 50, so the result here is 850.

SET 34, Q1. Correct Answer: C

Reasoning

We need to calculate the number of persons in Norway aged 0-14 in 2007 and in 2017, and then work out the difference. The number of persons aged 0-14 is the total of the Norwegian population multiplied by the share who are 0-14. The population of Norway in 2007 can be calculated using the population in 2017 and the amount of increase between 2007 and 2017.

Calculation

First, we must calculate the number of persons in Norway aged 0-14 in 2017 (in thousands):

5.258 * 1000 * 0.178 = 935.924 thousand

Note that since the population of Norway is represented in millions in the diagram, we needed to multiply it by 1000 to get our results into thousands.

Second, we calculate the population of Norway in 2007:

5.258 * 1000 – 577 = 4681 thousand

Third, the number of persons in Norway aged 0-14 in 2007:

4681 * 0.194 = 908.114 thousand

Finally, we need to calculate the difference, and round it to the nearest thousand:

935.924 – 908.114 ≈ 28 thousand

Potential Shortcuts / Pitfalls

If you calculate the difference between the numbers aged 0-14 in the two years, ignoring the change in share from 19.4% in 2007 to 17.8% in 2017, you would get the incorrect figure of 103 thousand (using the 2017 share, option D), or 112 thousand (using the 2007 share, option E). If you calculate the difference while ignoring the increase in the total Norwegian population referred to in the question text, you would get –84 thousand (option B).

A shortcut lies in combining all the steps shown above, and factoring out the population of Norway in 2017:

577 * 0.194 – 5258 * (0.194 – 0.178)

This would reduce the number of keystrokes and arithmetical operations.

SET 34, Q2. Correct Answer: B

Reasoning

We need to calculate the number who are 15 years old or over in both Denmark and Finland in 2017, and then the percentage difference between these numbers. The number who are 15 years old or over is the total population multiplied by the sum of the shares of two age groups, 15-64 years old, and 65 years old or older.

Calculation

First, we must calculate the number who are 15 years old or over in Denmark in 2017 (in millions):

5.77 * (0.643 + 0.191) = 4.81218 million

Now the equivalent figure for Finland:

5.503 * (0.628 + 0.209) = 4.606011 million

Finally, we calculate the percentage difference between Denmark and Finland, and round it to two decimal places:

(4.81218 / 4.606011 – 1) * 100% ≈ 4.48%

Potential Shortcuts / Pitfalls

A likely mistake would be to use just the figure for those aged 15-64, rather than adding in the 65+ age group. This would give you 7.36% (option C).

If you did your calculations by treating the percentage change just as the difference between the respective shares of the major groups, ignoring the population of the countries, you would get –0.30% (option E).

SET 34, Q3. Correct Answer: A

Reasoning

We need to calculate the change in the share of persons aged 15-64 years for each of the five countries shown in the table, and then calculate the average as the sum divided by five. The change of share for a country is the difference between the respective shares in 2017 and 2007.

Calculation

First, we must calculate the change of the share of persons aged 15-64 years for each of the five countries shown in the table (in percent):

Denmark = 64.3 – 66.1 = –1.8
Finland = 62.8 – 66.5 = –3.7
Iceland = 66.2 – 67.1 = –0.9
Norway = 65.5 – 66.0 = –0.5
Sweden = 62.6 – 65.6 = –3.0

Second, we must calculate the average of the values calculated in the previous steps:

Average = (–1.8 – 3.7 – 0.9 – 0.5 – 3.0) / 5 = –1.98

Potential Shortcuts / Pitfalls

If you simply add up the different percentage changes and forget to average them, you would get the incorrect figure of –9.90 (option B).

You can combine all the steps shown above to reduce the number of keystrokes:

(64.3 – 66.1 + 62.8 – 66.5 + 66.2 – 67.1 + 65.5 – 66.0 + 62.6 – 65.6) / 5

SET 35, Q1. Correct Answer: E

Reasoning

The productivity of the employees is calculated by dividing the production volume by the number of employees.

Calculation

Craybourne Woodlands: 8 000 / 50 = 160 tonnes
Stirling Forest: 14 000 / 80 = 175 tonnes
Woodcombe Hills Woods: 3000 / 30 = 100 tonnes
Hampton Forest: 3000 / 30 = 100 tonnes
Frasier Green: 8000 / 40 = 200 tonnes

The correct answer is therefore Frasier Green (E).

Potential Shortcuts / Pitfalls

The above calculations are straightforward enough but we can reduce the number of calculations further. Just by looking at the ratio of production to employees, we can see straight away that Hampton Forest and Woodcombe Hills Woods employees each contribute half as much as those of Frasier Green (30:3 versus 80:4). Also, Craybourne Woodlands' employees clearly produce less than those of Frasier Green as the total production is the same but the number of employees is greater.

Be careful here to perform the calculations on production volume, not the volume actually utilised / sold.

SET 35, Q2. Correct Answer: E

Reasoning

First, we calculate the number of outdoor furniture shipments that were actually produced. Then, we calculate the total production volume for roofing, take 10% of it, and calculate how many outdoor furniture shipments that would have made up. We get the total by adding up the two numbers.

Calculation

The total volume used for outdoor furniture:

4 000 + 5 900 + 1 200 + 1 300 + 2 800 = 15 200

The total volume used for roofing:

2000 + 3800 + 1600 + 1600 + 4000 = 13 000

10% of the roofing figure is:

13 000 / 10 = 1300

The new total volume to be utilised for outdoor furniture:

15200 + 1300 = 16 500

With 50 tonnes per shipment, this adds up to:

16 500 / 50 = 330 shipments, which is Answer E.

Potential Shortcuts / Pitfalls
Notice how we saved time by only calculating the number of shipments (dividing by 50 tonnes) using the grand total, i.e. not twice, once for the original volume and once for the overall volume.

SET 35, Q3. Correct Answer: A

Reasoning

Similarly to how we calculated productivity, we need to divide the total production utilised for roofing by the total number of employees across all forestries.

Calculation

The total production utilised for roofing is:

2 000 + 3 800 + 1 600 + 1 600 + 4 000 = 13 000

The total number of employees is:

50 + 80 + 30 + 30 + 40 = 230

The roofing production of one employee, on average, is then:

13 000 / 230 = 56.52 tonnes (rounded)

Potential Shortcuts / Pitfalls
An important thing to notice is that we calculated the average by adding up all the production volumes and we divided it by the total number of employees.

A typical mistake would be to divide each production volume by the corresponding number of employees. This is incorrect because it does not take into account the relative weight of each forestry in the average. For example, Frasier Green produces twice as much roofing wood as Craybourne Woodlands but with fewer employees.

SET 36, Q1. Correct Answer: A

Reasoning

We need to calculate the difference in revenue between 5 glasses of wine and a whole bottle.

Calculation

Calculate the price of 5 glasses of each wine and subtract the price of the whole bottle:

Chablis – 5 × 8.95 – 31.95 = 12.80
Chardonnay – 5 × 7.50 – 28.50 = 9.00
Margaux – 5 × 7.15 – 27.00 = 8.75
Sancerre – 5 × 9.20 – 34.80 = 11.20
Tavel – 5 × 7.95 – 29.50 = 10.25

From this we can see that Chablis is clearly the highest.

Potential Shortcuts / Pitfalls
Unlike with many questions of this type, you *cannot* omit the '5 x' that appears on each line because it is not applied to the bottle price as well. If the bottle price was multiplied or divided by the glass price (for example if the question had been about the highest *percentage* of extra profit) then the '5 x' would be common to all terms and could be omitted.

SET 36, Q2. Correct Answer: C

Reasoning

We need to calculate the profit on 1 bottle of Sancerre and then work out the number of bottles sold by dividing the total profit by the profit on one bottle.

Calculation

The first thing to do is to figure out what the unknown is in the question. We can set this to be *either* the profit on one bottle *or* the price of a bottle before profit. Whichever we choose, we will end up being able to determine the profit on one bottle of Sancerre.

If the cost of a bottle of Sancerre before profit is B then:

B + Profit = 34.80

We know that the profit rate is 220%. What does this mean? It means that the profit is 2.2 times as much as the cost of a bottle before profit, so:

B + 2.2 × B = 34.80

We can now perform various operations to get 1 B (price of a bottle before profit) on one side:

3.2 × B = 34.8
B = 34.80 / 3.2 = 10.875

This is the cost of a bottle before profit, and so the profit on each bottle is the selling price minus this cost price:

34.8 – 10.875 = 23.925

If the profit on one bottle is 23.925 then the number of bottles needed to produce 287.10 profit is:

287.1 / 23.925 = 12

Potential Shortcuts / Pitfalls
This question may appear more difficult than it really is simply because the profit is more than 100%. Treat it in the same way as any other profit margin. The crucial juncture at which you could go down the wrong path is how you define the price of the bottle before profit: if you say that it is the selling price divided by 2.2, that is incorrect: it would only be correct if the profit rate was 120%.

SET 36, Q3. Correct Answer: B

Reasoning

We need to calculate the revenue from one bottle of wine when sold by the glass and then calculate the percentage difference from the point of view of the revenue when sold by the bottle.

Calculation

We first need to calculate the number of glasses in one bottle:

750 / 187.5 = 4

The revenue from 4 glasses will be:

4 × 7.95 = 31.80

The percentage increase in revenue is the difference in revenue when sold by the glass compared with when sold by the bottle, divided by the revenue when sold by the bottle and multiplied by 100:

100 × (31.80 – 29.50) / 29.50 = 7.8%

Potential Shortcuts / Pitfalls
Most of this could be done by mental arithmetic for speed. Let's see how this can be accomplished.

750 / 187.5 – this seems to be quite close to 800 / 200, which is 4 – so let's assume this is 4 as well.

4 × 7.95 – this is almost the same as 4 × 8, so let's work with that – the result is 32. We only need to subtract 4 × 0.05 to get the accurate result, which is 31.8.

The revenue from a bottle is 29.50. The difference in revenue would then be 2.30 and the percentage difference can then be calculated using a calculator.

With some practice and confidence, this method can be significantly faster than typing everything in.

SET 37, Q1. Correct Answer: A

Reasoning

Speed is calculated as distance divided by time. Since the answer options are in metres / second, and the distance is already given in metres, the easiest thing to do is convert the winning time into seconds.

Calculation

The total time taken for the medley was 3 minutes and 48.7 seconds, which we need to convert to seconds before we can use it. To do this, multiply the minutes by 60 and add in the seconds:

(3 × 60) + 48.7 = 228.7

The winner spent 26.2% of the total time doing the butterfly leg of the race, which is:

228.7 × 0.262 = 59.92s

So, he travelled 100m (one fourth of the total distance of 400 metres) in 59.92 seconds, which gives an average speed of:

100m / 59.92s = 1.67 m/s

SET 37, Q2. Correct Answer: C

Reasoning

The speed is calculated by dividing the distance covered by the time taken. The percentage difference is then the difference divided by the *slower* speed (since the question was how much faster the gold medallist was) and then multiplied by 100.

Calculation

Before we can calculate the speeds we must first convert the times into seconds. This is done by multiplying the minutes by 60 and then adding in the seconds:

1m 58.31s = 60 + 58.31 = 118.31
1m 59.88s = 60 + 59.88 = 119.88

The winner's speed is then:

200 / 118.31 = 1.6905 m/s

And the bronze medal winner's speed is:

200 / 119.88 = 1.6683 m/s

The percentage difference is:

100 × (1.6905 – 1.6683) / 1.6683 = 1.3%

Potential Shortcuts / Pitfalls

Because the men are racing over the same distance (200 metres), we do not actually need to calculate their speeds – the percentage difference in the *times* it took to swim the distance will be the same as the percentage difference between their *speeds* would be.

Following this logic, we can simply our calculation to:

$$\left(\frac{119.88\ 0\ 118.31}{119.88}\right) * 100 = 1.3\%$$

Note that we divided the difference by the higher number. Why? The higher number represents the time of the slower swimmer (the bronze medallist). Since the question asked how much faster the gold medallist was than the bronze medallist, we need to calculate the percentage increase on the basis of the slower swimmer's time.

SET 37, Q3. Correct Answer: B

Reasoning

The calculation for speed is distance divided by time and the calculation for distance is speed multiplied by time. We will use the first to calculate the silver medallist's speed in the last segment of the race, and the latter to calculate the distance he covered after the gold medallist completed the race.

Calculation

The overall average speed of the silver medal winner is calculated by dividing the distance by the time taken:

100m / 50.99s = 1.96 m/s

In the last few metres of the race he was travelling 10% faster than this:

1.96 × 1.1 = 2.16 m/s

The difference in time between the gold and silver medallists is:

50.99 – 50.91 = 0.08s

So, he was swimming at 2.16 m/s for 0.08 seconds; therefore in that time he travelled:

2.16m/s × 0.08s = 0.173m

which to the nearest centimetre is 17.

SET 38, Q1. Correct Answer: E

Reasoning

Domestic consumption is defined in the note to the table as production minus exports plus imports so we need to establish how much of its own production the US used itself and how much was added to this by imports.

From the table we know what 27% of US production amounts to, so we can calculate the quantity that the US does not export, which will be 100% - 27% = 73% of its production:

23.8 / 27 x 73 = 64.35 million tonnes

We can also establish the amount of imports to the USA from China. The Chinese export quantity, 279.5 million tonnes, is known, and we also know that this represents 34% of Chinese production. Further, we are told in the question text that 30% of Chinese production is exported to the US:

279.5 / 34 x 30 = 246.62 million tonnes

We now have a total of 64.35 + 246.62

= 310.97 million tonnes

At this point, however, we hit a problem because we do not have any data on the proportion of exports from any of the other regions that went to the USA. Without this information we cannot complete the calculation and so must choose Answer option E, "Cannot say".

Calculation

Following the reasoning above, we cannot do this calculation.

Potential Shortcuts / Pitfalls
The risk with this question is that you assume it must be possible to determine the quantity and waste valuable time in trying to make the data do this.

A particular danger is that you successfully calculate the amount of US production used domestically and the quantity of imports from China, as above, but forget about the lack of data for imports from other regions. If you do this you will choose Answer C, which is 310.97 million tonnes.

SET 38, Q2. Correct Answer: C

Reasoning

We must calculate the 2013 export volume for both Japan and EU by using the % change between 2013 and 2014 shown in the table.

Calculation

The 2013 export volume for the EU is identical to the 2014 export volume: 55.9 million tonnes.

To calculate the 2013 export volume for Japan, we need to consider the % change from 2013 to 2014. If we think of the 2013 export volume as X, we can write the following equation:

2013 export volume (X) – 2% = 2014 export volume = 21 million tonnes

In more usable terms:

98% of 2013 export volume = 21 million tonnes

From this, it is easy to calculate the 2013 export volume by dividing by 98 and multiplying by 100:

21 / 98 x 100 = 21.43 million tonnes (rounded)

We can now calculate the difference between the EU and Japanese export volumes:

55.9 – 21.43 = 34.47

And from this, the percentage difference:

34.47 / 21.43 = 1.6085 x 100 = 160.85%

Rounded, this is 161%.

Potential Shortcuts / Pitfalls
Be careful with data expressed as a percentage change between two years. Imagine we know a value for 2014 is 50 and that it is 20% higher than the figure for 2013. The temptation is to simply deduct 20% from the 2014 value to get the 2013 value. If we do that we get a 2013 value of 40, which is incorrect. Think of the problem in terms of having an unknown number (X = the 2013 value) that increases by 20% to result in the known value (50). Thus we calculate X + 20% = 50, which becomes 50/120 x 100, giving us 41.66 (rounded). If you approach the problem this way, you can ensure that you will perform the correct calculation.

SET 38, Q3. Correct Answer: C

Reasoning

Using data from both the chart and the table, and the statement in the question that production in every region was the same in 2013 as in 2014, we need to calculate the 2013 share of exports from the production of the various regions in 2013 and then what percentage total exports make up of total global production.

Calculation

To calculate the 2013 share of exports in the various regions, we need to take into account the percentage changes. To do this, the easiest thing to do is to think of the 2013 export percentages as unknown values (X) and see how they compare to the 2014 percentages. In the case of China, this would be:

X + 3% of X = 34%
1.03X = 34%

The 2013 export share in China is then:

X = 34 / 1.03 = 33%

For the other regions:

USA: X = 27/1.05 = 25.7% (rounded)
Japan: X = 19 / 0.98 = 19.4% (rounded)
EU: X = 34% (as there was no change between 2013 and 2014)
Rest of World: X = 62 / 1.09 = 56.9% (rounded)

Next, we can calculate what share of global production each of the above export shares makes up by multiplying the share of each region's production from the global total by the export share. For example, for China, this is:

50% x 33% = 50% x 0.33 = 16.5%

For the other regions the figures are:

USA: 5% x 0.257 = 1.285%
Japan: 7% x 0.194 =1.358%
EU: 10% x 0.34 = 3.4%
Rest of World: 28% x 0.569 = 15.9% (rounded)

To get the total export share, we simply add up the above percentages:

16.5 + 1.285 + 1.358 + 3.4 + 15.9 = 38.443%

This is roughly 38%, so the correct answer is C.

Potential Shortcuts / Pitfalls

The calculations described above would be very time-consuming to perform, which you should take as a hint that they might not actually be necessary.

The key words in this question are "approximately" in the question text and "around" in the answer options. This should tell you that you can estimate the correct answer without calculating it to a high degree of accuracy. The level of accuracy you need to achieve depends on how much the answer options differ from each other so you need to make an initial judgement on this.

Let's look at the shortcuts.

1. We can see from the 4th column of the table that the export share of production while rising a bit didn't change radically from 2013 to 2014 overall. So we can try using the 2014 figures to aim for an approximate result, saving a lot of calculations. Very importantly, the answer options – 6%, 14%, 38%, 50%, 70% – are far apart, which suggests we can be fairly generous with our approximating.
2. The 3rd column of the table tells us that China and Rest of the World were overwhelmingly the dominant factors in exports so we can put aside the other regions unless we can't get a clear result from the China and Rest of the World data.
3. The 2nd column of the table tells us that in 2014 China exported 34% of its production and the Rest of the World 62%. Although the 2013 shares for each were lower, they are still in the same ballpark relative to the spread in the answer options. We can immediately tell therefore that answers A (6%) and B (14%) are far too low and E (70%) is far too high. That leaves us with just C (38%) and D (50%) to decide between.
4. At this point we can't avoid doing some calculations, but we can do some serious rounding:

Export % of Rest of World = ca. 60%
Global production share of Rest of World = ca. 30%
Share of exports from global production = ca. 60 x 0.3 = 20%
Export % of China = ca. 30%
Global production share of China = 50%
Share of exports from global production = ca. 30 x 0.5 = 15%
Total: 20% + 15% = 35%

The net result of all of this is very approximate, but it's close enough for our purposes to choose answer option C, 38%. We can get closer by calculating more of the variables but in this case it's unnecessary as the only alternative answer we were left with, 50%, is too far away.

SET 39, Q1. Correct Answer: B

Reasoning

We need to calculate the proportion of total electricity generated by tidal power and then determine that as a percentage of the 2005 total.

Calculation

We need to calculate the proportion of electricity generated by tidal power. Clearly, the big unknown in this exercise is the *total* electricity generated: we aren't told this number, so let us assume that the total power generated in 2005 was E. The question states that this rose by 10% in 2010 to:

$E \times 1.1 = 1.1E$

From the *table* we can see that 6.5% of this was generated by 'Other' means in 2010:

$1.1E \times 0.065 = 0.0715E$

The *pie chart* tells us that 38% of this was due to tidal power:

$0.0715E \times 0.38 = 0.02717E$

The *question* tells us that this doubled over the 5 years so in 2005 it was:

$0.02717E / 2 = 0.013585E$

To calculate this as a percentage of the total power generated in 2005, we need to divide by that total and then multiply by 100. We assumed that total was E at the beginning, so it is quite easy from this point on:

$(0.01358E / E) \times 100 = 1.3585\%$

which is rounded to 1.36%.

SET 39, Q2. Correct Answer: A

Reasoning

We need to calculate the total amount of electricity generated from 'other', and then calculate the solar power production.

Calculation

First, we need to calculate the total electricity generated from 'other'. The question tells us that 2.4 million kWh is the total generated from biomass, and the pie chart tells us this is 36% of 'other' generation. We can use this to calculate the total 'other' generation using the familiar 'reverse' method.

Other × 36% = 2.4
Other × 0.36 = 2.4
Other = 2.4 / 0.36 = 6.67

The table tells us that 'other' generation is, in turn, just 6.5% of the total generated which using the same method is:

6.67 / 0.065 = 102.62

5.2% of this total is generated by solar power, which is:

102.62 × 0.052 = 5.3mKwh

Potential Shortcuts / Pitfalls
It is usually good advice that you should *estimate whenever possible* to avoid the use of the clumsy calculator. This instance demonstrates that this advice has its limits. Let's say you decide to estimate the answer in this question. Quite quickly you would run into the problem that it is very hard to round up or down while also preserving at least a modest level of accuracy and therefore a chance to pick the correct answer at the end. This is made even more difficult by the fact that the answer options are quite close to each other.

Always consider these factors before deciding which method to use in calculating the answer.

SET 39, Q3. Correct Answer: A

Reasoning

We need to calculate the percentage change in fossil fuel generation.

Calculation

To calculate the total generated by fossil fuel, we need to know the overall total, which isn't given, so we can substitute the 2005 total with E. Then, the total generated by fossil fuel is:

E × 0.811 = 0.811E

In 2010, the overall total rose by 10% to:

E × 1.1 = 1.1E

So, in 2010, fossil fuel generation was:

1.1E × 0.764 = 0.8404E

This is a difference of:

0.8404E – 0.811E = 0.0294E

As a percentage of the 2005 generation this is:

100 × 0.0294E / 0.811E = 3.6%

Potential Shortcuts / Pitfalls
Once again, the *actual total figure is not required* as it cancels out in the last step.

There are, however, several pitfalls you can fall into along the way:

1. At first glance, you might look at the two fossil fuel percentages and say that the change is actually 81.1 – 76.4 = 4.7 %. This would be wrong on many fronts; for example it doesn't take into account the 10% rise in total generation or the fact that this would be a *percentage point* change.

2. You could also calculate the above by dividing the difference (4.7%) by the starting value (81.1), but again, this would not take into account the rise in total production.

SET 40, Q1. Correct Answer: E

Reasoning

Since the genders are represented equally, we know that there are 500 boys in the sample. The chart tells us that the percentage of boys who like reading was 32% in 2010 and 24% in 2014, so we have to turn those percentage shares into actual numbers. We then convert the 2014 number to a percentage of the 2010 number.

Calculation

The number of boys who like reading in 2010:

500 * 0.32 = 160

The equivalent number in 2014:

500 * 0.24 = 120

If 120 is X percent of 160 then 160 * (X / 100) = 120

X = (120 / 160) * 100, X = 75%

If the number in 2014 is 75% of the number in 2010, that means a 25% decrease, which is answer E.

Potential Shortcuts / Pitfalls
If you just subtract the 2014 percentage value, 24%, from the value for 2010, 32%, you would get the incorrect answer of 8% (option A).

There are two shortcuts.

Once you have done the first two calculations you can forget the calculator and do the rest in your head. The number of boys who like reading decreased from 160 to 120, i.e. by 40. You can see straight away that the decrease is one-quarter of the value in 2010. In other words, it is a 25% decrease.

Even better is simply to calculate the percentage decrease between the two given percentage values, 32% and 24%, using the formula (32 – 24) / 32 = 25%. Doing it this way we don't actually need the sample size and indeed the calculation is instantly done with a bit of mental arithmetic.

SET 40, Q2. Correct Answer: D

Reasoning

To find the number of boys in the sample, we have to calculate the number of which 150 is 32% (the percentage of boys who like reading in 2012, according to the chart); then we do an analogous calculation for the girls. We then add the results together to get the full sample size.

Calculation

Let the number of boys in the sample be X:

X * 0.32 = 150.
X ≈ 469

Now let Y be the number of of girls in the sample:

Y * 0.36 = 150, so Y ≈ 417

Therefore the total sample size is 469 + 417 = 886

Potential Shortcuts / Pitfalls
You can combinine all of the calculations above as 150 / 0.32 + 150 / 0.36, or, after factorizing, as 150 (1 / 0.32 + 1 / 0.36), which would reduce the number of operations.

SET 40, Q3. Correct Answer: E

Reasoning

We don't have enough information to answer this question.

Since all four age groups are equally represented in the sample of 1000 children, we know that there were 250 children in each age group. And since in each age group the genders were equally represented, we also know that there were 125 boys and 125 girls in each age group.

We know from the chart that in the 9-11 age group 38% of children like reading, so we can work out that there were 250 * 0.38 = 95 children who liked reading in that age group. However, we have no information about *how many of those were boys*. Likewise, while we know that there were 500 boys altogether in the sample, of whom 500 * 0.32 =160 liked reading, we have no information as to *which age group* they belonged.

Potential Shortcuts / Pitfalls
If you use the given percentage of 38% for the 9-11 age group in 2010 you would get 125 * 0.38 = 48 boys. As this is answer option B you would assume that you had been able to solve the problem.

9. Succeeding in Abstract Reasoning Tests

In an EPSO abstract reasoning test you are presented with a series of figures in a sequence which follows some rules you are not told. You are also given a second set of figures (A, B, C, D, E) as answer options, from which you must choose the correct one to answer the question "Which of the following figures comes next in the series?" (or similar).

It can certainly be a daunting experience to face such a test for the first time. Your eyes will tend to scan the shapes of the figures in a haphazard fashion. You finally get an idea about the possible rules, and then look at the figures in the answer options to see which one fits. And then you realise that the figure you carefully selected would only fit the series pattern if just one thing was a little bit different. So now you must start all over again...

But, just as in the case of verbal and numerical reasoning tests, understanding the principles involved and a systematic approach to applying them can produce results much more reliably and quickly.

As part of such a systematic approach, let us therefore first review the various abstract reasoning test types, which are based on:

- the use or avoidance of colours
- the logical relationship between the various figures, whether they are part of a series, a grid, or if there is one figure which is the odd-one-out
- the number of dimensions in the test (two- or three-dimensional tests both exist)

Fortunately, it is now known that EPSO have chosen a type of abstract reasoning test that is very well defined:

- only black-and-white images are used (possibly with various shades of grey)

A typical abstract question: *Which figure is next in the series?*

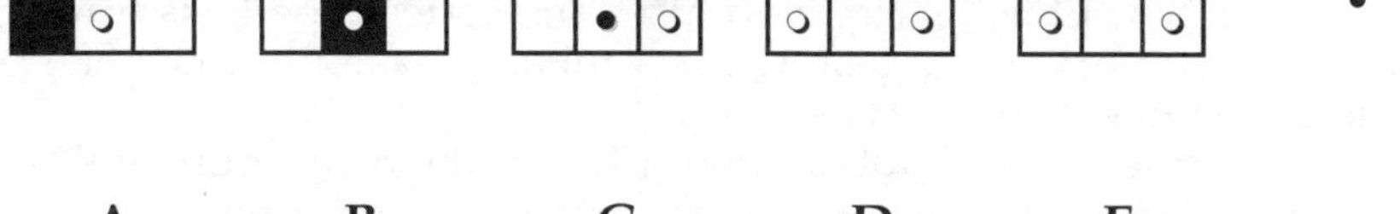

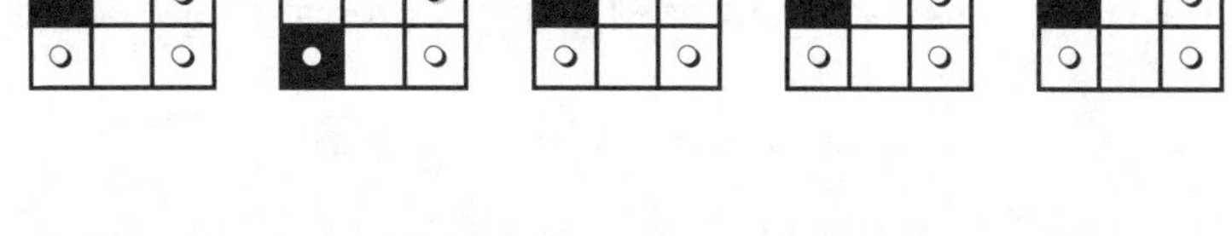

- only two-dimensional tests are given
- only series-type questions are used
- five items of the series are shown, and the candidate must select the next, sixth item
- there are usually five answer options (though EPSO may vary this).

In abstract reasoning tests, the most important skill is learning to identify the components. Let us look at these one-by one:

- Building blocks: the building blocks of abstract reasoning tests are the following:
  - **Shapes and patterns** are the actual visual objects that are used to construct the figures in the test: triangles, squares, circles and other geometric shapes, as well as the physical properties of these objects: striped, dotted or solid fill patterns
  - **Operations** are various visual changes that these objects can undergo, such as colour inversion, multiplication, rotation, change of position, and countless others
  - **Rules** are text-based descriptions of the relationship between the various shapes/patterns and the operations affecting them

In this chapter, we will:

- Introduce how abstract reasoning tests are designed: insight into the thought process that is behind the creation of abstract reasoning tests will be very valuable when you are on the other side, that is, when taking such tests
- Introduce the various building blocks, typical shapes, patterns and operations that you will encounter in abstract reasoning tests
- Discuss how to approach abstract reasoning tests
- Provide tips on how to prepare for them

By identifying the building blocks of a test item and systematically looking for the above patterns and operations, you will quickly be able to identify the rules that the question author invented to create the figures and the answer options.

Consequently, you will be able to "generate" or "anticipate" the correct figure in your mind without even looking at the answer options. This method is highly reliable since you will not select one of the answer options as the correct answer just because it seems the best or most suitable option: you will also have independent confirmation – the figure you came up with yourself based on the rule(s) you have figured out.

How Are Abstract Reasoning Tests Designed?

In this section, we will provide a look into the "workshop" of abstract reasoning test designers and, through a real test example, introduce how abstract reasoning exercises are designed.

As mentioned earlier, EPSO exclusively uses the series type tests in its competitions. In this type of abstract reasoning test, the test taker is asked to find the figure that correctly completes a series.

If we identify the rule, we will not only be able to tell which figure will be the sixth one (as in the example above), but also the ninth or the sixteenth one.

When designing an abstract reasoning test, the designer has specific steps to take:

1. The designer decides what shapes and patterns will be used in the tests. Based on the sample test above, let's say we will use basic geometric shapes (circles and squares).

2. Next, the designer has to decide on the difficulty level of the test. The importance of this lies in the fact that the number of rules (generally) correlates with the difficulty of the test.
3. Once the rules and the shapes/operations are identified and drawn, the designer needs to come up with one correct and several incorrect answer options. The trick to keep in mind here is that the incorrect answer options are not random – they all follow the rules of the test item up to a point, then deliberately err in one or more respects, thus making them *almost* correct.

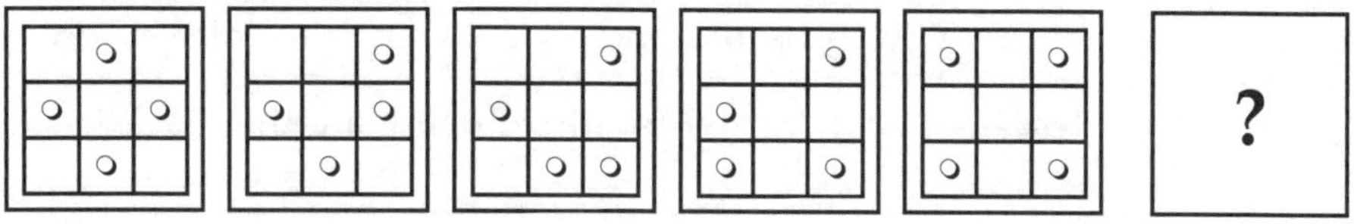

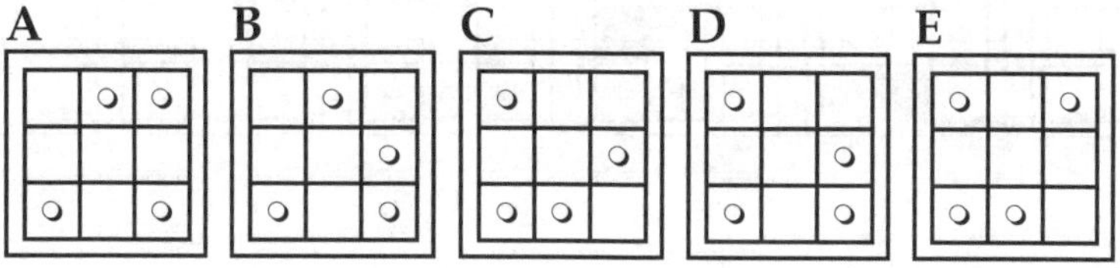

Consider the sample item above. We can identify the following building blocks:

- unshaded **circles**
- **squares** forming 3x3 areas.

  The first rule you may notice is the movement of the circles. We might describe this as follows:

Rule #1: *One by one, the circles move in a clockwise direction.*

Based on this rule we can quickly find the correct answer – which is **option D.**

Let's see how we could make this test item a bit harder.

If you look at the sample item below, you will immediately realize that a new building block was introduced: **shaded squares**.

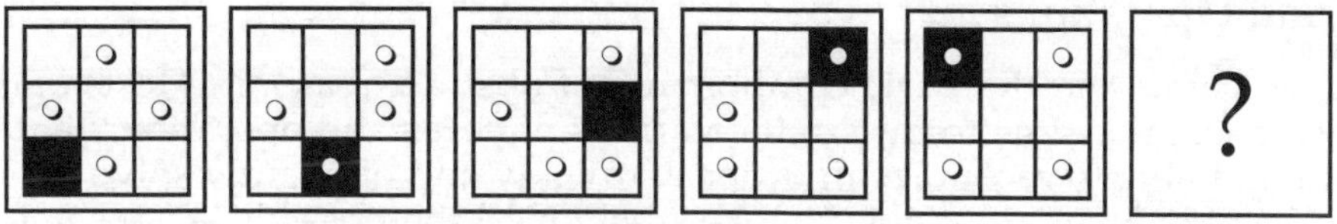

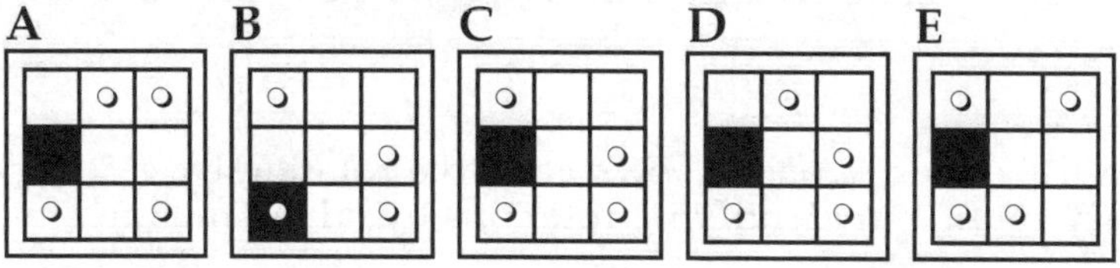

Before we try to find the rule governing the shading of certain squares, notice that the rule we came up with above still holds:

***Rule #1**: One by one, the circles move in a clockwise direction.*

This rule, however, does not explain the appearance of shaded squares, as any number of different images could be correct from the answer options. We need to identify the second rule:

***Rule #2**: The shading alternatingly takes one and two steps in an anticlockwise direction.*

The only answer option that matches both of these rules is **option C**.

Note how close option B is to be the correct answer, but deliberately misusing the second rule.

We can make the test item even harder by introducing another additional component:

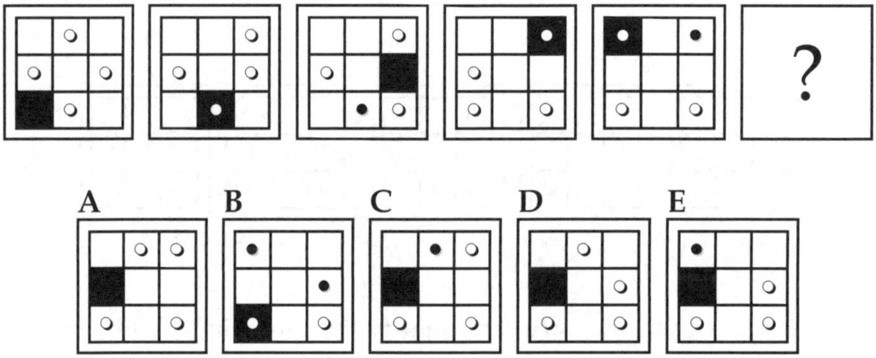

Notice that, again, a new building block and rule must have been introduced governing the appearance of the **shaded circle**. We can describe this regularity as follows:

***Rule #3**: Circles that stood on a shaded square will become shaded themselves for a turn.*

The only answer option matching all three rules is **option E**.

As a summary, let us overview what techniques we can use to understand the thought process of the designer of the test items better:

- Determining what building blocks to use (unshaded/shaded squares and circles) and the number of rules governing their change
- Eliminating answer options based on each rule we have identified

Patterns and Operations

Now that we have seen the basic components of abstract reasoning tests and the way they are designed, it is time to turn to the various patterns and operations that you must be aware of and able to recognize in order to quickly and efficiently solve these tests.

It would be of course impossible to take stock of all the possible shapes and patterns, but we will try to give a comprehensive overview in the next section.

Rotation

Figs. 1 and 2 on the opposite page shows a simple rotation by 45° clockwise. You can gain the necessary routine in identifying rotations by taking the time to sit down with a piece of paper and a pencil, draw various shapes and then redraw them after rotating them various degrees in either direction, clockwise or counter-clockwise.

The example below shows a different kind of rotation. In strict geometrical terms, the relationship between the two figures is not rotation at all, yet for convenience's sake, we will discuss it in this section.

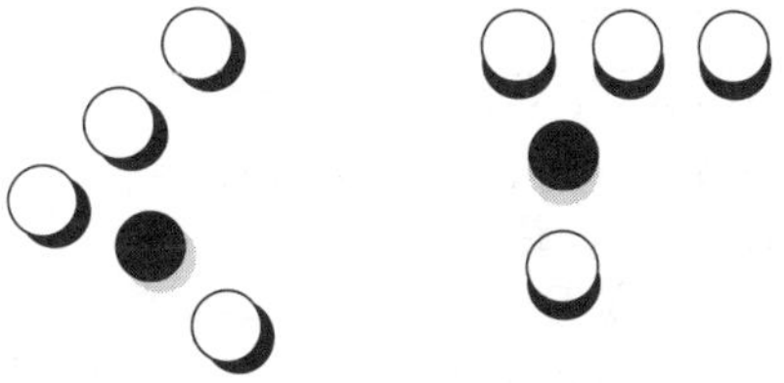

Fig. 1 Fig. 2

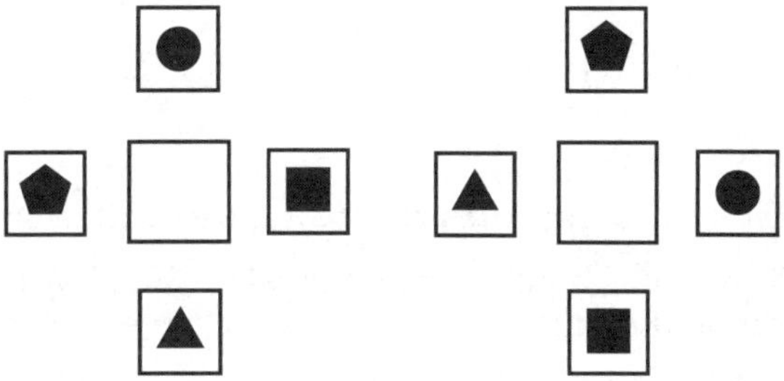

In the two figures, the small icons in the small squares around the larger one in the middle swap places with their neighbours in a clockwise direction. In a sense we can say that the icons "rotate" along an imaginary circle around the larger square.

Axial Reflection

The two examples on the right show the geometrical operation called "axial reflection". The thin lines between the two figures in each of the two sets represent an imaginary mirror. In the first set, the figure on the right is the reflection of the figure on the left in the "mirror" in the middle and vice versa. This is an example of a horizontal reflection.

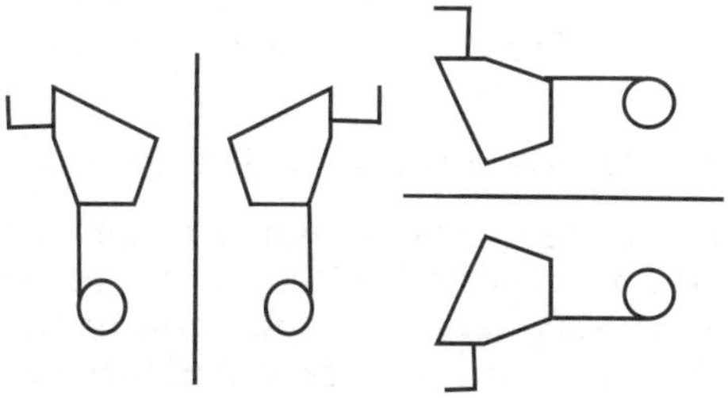

Horizontal reflection ***Vertical reflection***

The second set represents a so-called vertical reflection. While for demonstration's sake the examples show the horizontal reflection side by side and the vertical reflection with one figure below the other, in real tests this may not always be the case.

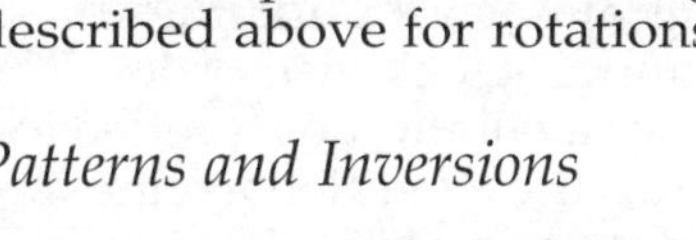

Vertical reflection

In the example on the left, the figure on the right is still the vertical "reflection" of the figure on the left, but the placement of the second figure does not correspond with where it would actually be in a strictly geometrical sense, that is, below the first image – this makes it harder to consider the relationship between the two figures as a reflection.

You can practice the recognition of this operation in the same cost-effective way as described above for rotations – all you need is paper, a pencil and loads of patience.

Patterns and Inversions

"Which of the following figures completes the series?"

In the example on the top right, a new building block component is introduced – patterns. The example features three of the next page shapes:

- Stars

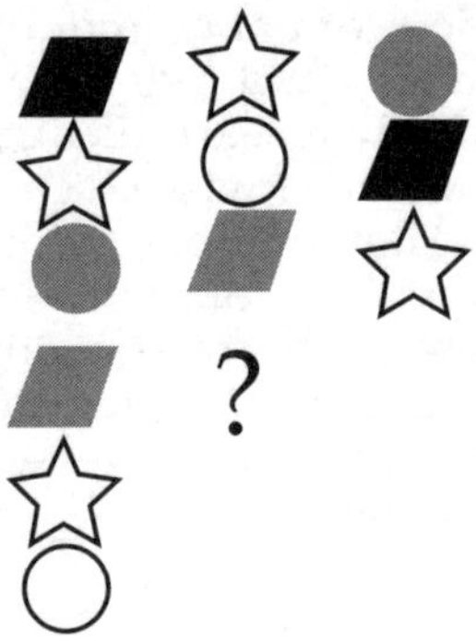

- Circles
- Rhombuses

... and three distinct patterns or "fills":

- No fill (or solid white fill)
- Solid black fill
- Solid Grey fill

Looking at the sample test, we notice that two "operations" take place:

- The shapes in each figure change places according to some rule
- The patterns (or fill) of the rhombuses and the circle also change according to some rule
- The pattern (or fill) of the star never changes

After further observation, we can establish the following rules regarding the patterns:

Rule #1a: If a rhombus has a grey fill, change it to solid black in the next step. If it has a solid black fill, change it to a grey pattern in the next step.

Rule #1b: If a circle has a grey pattern, change it to solid white in the next step. If it has a solid white fill, change it to a grey pattern in the next step.

Rule #1c: Always leave the star's pattern unchanged.

There are of course many other combinations possible, involving more types of patterns and different relationships between them. Another typical case is so-called inversion. In such tests, the solid colour fill (usually black or white) of each shape and object turns into its exact opposite. Every shape with black fill becomes white, and vice versa.

The other component of our rule for the above example has to do with the positions of the shapes in relation to each other. We will discuss this in the next section.

Translation

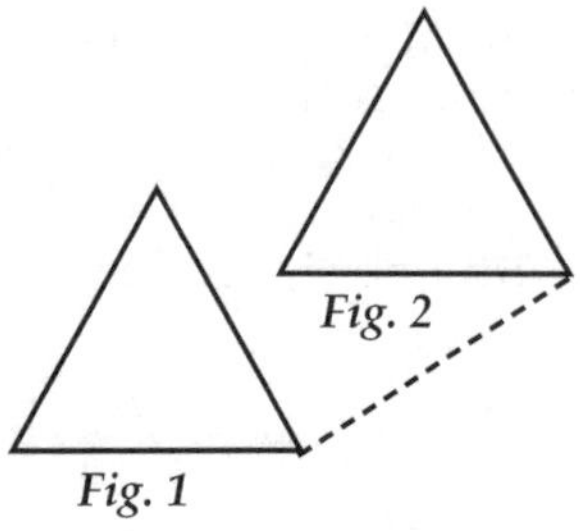

In geometry, translation is an operation where each and every point of a shape is moved to a specified distance in a specified direction. In the example on the right, each point of the triangle is moved (or "translated") to the same distance and in the same direction, as indicated by the dotted line or "vector" connecting the two shapes. The vector is only shown here for demonstration purposes and would not be visible in a real exercise. We must also keep in mind that the movement sometimes occurs along an actual shape that is part of the figure:

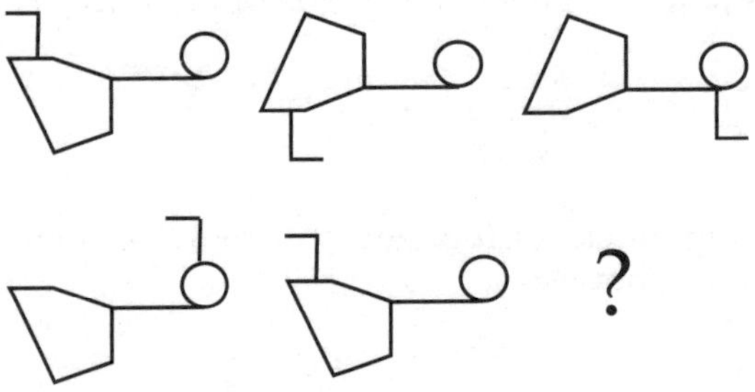

In the example on the left, the handlebar line "migrates" around the other shapes in a counter-clockwise order. The movement is not a rotation or a reflection – the points of the handlebar line are simply moved at a certain distance in a certain direction in each step of the series.

Therefore the correct answer is a shape that is the same as the middle one in the top row.

Similarly to rotation, there is also a geometrically less accurate meaning of the term "translation". Looking at the sample question with the star, the circle and the rhombus, we may notice the following rule governing the placement of the three shapes in the figures of the series:

Rule #2: Move each of the three shapes one position up. If the shape is already in the top position, it will now occupy the bottom position in the figure.

In the example, the six answer options were intentionally deleted. Based on the method described earlier in this chapter, we can mentally generate the correct figure based on the rules we have established for the series (repeated below for convenience).

Rule #1: "If a rhombus has a grey fill, change it to solid black in the next step. If it has a solid black fill, change it to a grey pattern in the next step. If a circle has a grey pattern, change it to solid white in the next step. If it has a solid white fill, change it to a grey pattern in the next step. Always leave the star's pattern unchanged."

In the fifth item in the series (the figure that will take the place of the question mark), then, the circle will become grey and the rhombus will become solid black. The star will remain white.

Rule #2: "Move each of the three shapes one position up. If the shape is already in the top position, it will now occupy the bottom position in the figure."

In the figure we are looking for, the now black rhombus will take the bottom position, the now grey circle will go to the middle, and the still white star will move to the top position.

Angles

In geometry, an angle is defined as a figure formed by two lines extending from the same point. In simple geometry, angles are usually given as being any number that is larger than zero and smaller than 360°.

When it comes to abstract reasoning tests, we need to be aware of angles for various reasons. In the case of identifying rotations, the rotation is usually done at a certain angle: 45°, 90° (also called a "right angle"), 180°, or 270°. Of course, rotation at any angle is possible, but due to the difficulty in identifying "custom" angles (say, 67°), such rotations are not likely to appear in EPSO's abstract reasoning tests.

When establishing the "rule" for a test question, we must always think about angles as well.

Consider the example below:

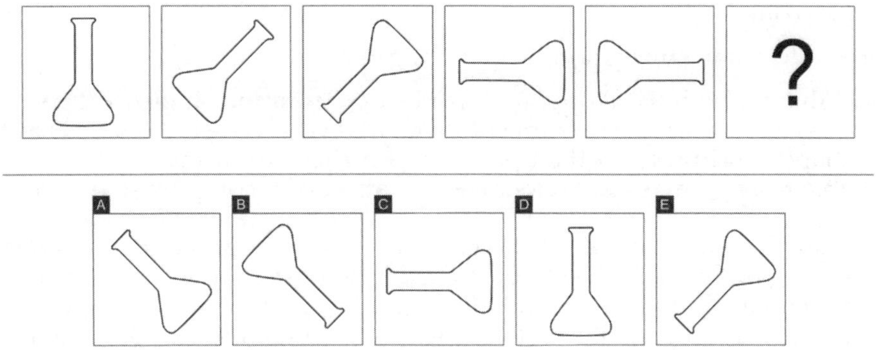

If we look at the images in the sample test above, we see a flask in various positions. After some further observation, we will notice that the flasks in the second, third and further figures are rotated at certain angles when compared to the flask in the first figure. We might describe this regularity based on angles as follows:

Rule #1: The flask is rotated around a fixed point 45 then 180 degrees, and then the cycle repeats.

Visual Arithmetic

The last typical abstract reasoning component we discuss here is sometimes referred to as visual arithmetic.

If we look at the figure extracted from a real abstract reasoning test, we see a large outer square with seven smaller squares along its sides. The top left square is black, and there are various shapes in the other squares (the fact that not all squares contain shapes is not relevant for our purposes now). What is the rule that could govern which kind of shape appears in each of the small squares? One tactic we can follow in items similar to this is to first count the number of sides the shapes have. Obviously, the triangle has three sides, the pentagon has five and the hexagon has six. How many sides should we "allocate" to the circle? Let's worry about that a bit later.

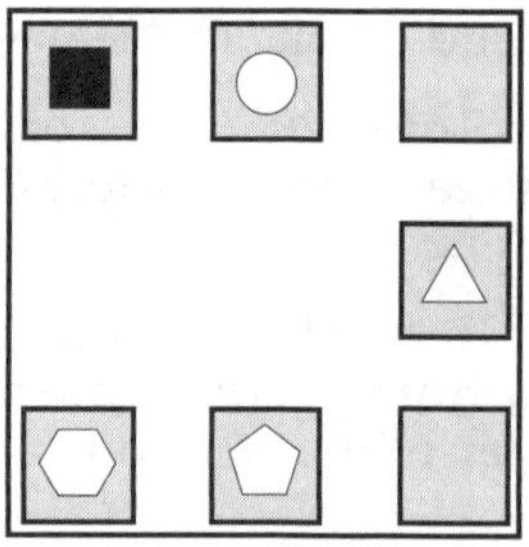

The other question is what determines why a certain shape is placed in a certain position in the figure. Counting can again help us out. If we count the distance (defined as the number of squares) between the shapes and the black square in a clockwise direction, we will notice that the position with the triangle, for example, is three steps away, the position with the pentagon is five shapes away, and so on.

We can now identify a rule:

Rule #1: The distance of a shape in any given square is governed by the number of sides the shape has.

It is important to bear in mind that EPSO's abstract reasoning tests, similarly to all such well-designed tests, attempt to measure the candidate's intuition and intelligence both visually (identification of shapes, patterns, and so on) and logically (e.g. identifying relationships and numerical regularities).

Summary and Approaches to Practice

In this chapter, we have overviewed various aspects of abstract reasoning tests:

- Test design, difficulty, rules and distractors
- Building blocks: operations, rules and patterns (rotation, reflection, angles, visual arithmetic, and so on)

Let us now add some suggestions on how to practice.

- If you feel that a geometrical operation (reflection, rotation, angles, etc.) is one of your weak points, do not shy away from sitting down with some paper and a pencil. Draw various shapes and perform the operations on them until they become routine and you are able to recognize a 90° clockwise rotation of a complex shape in a couple of seconds
- Once you are familiar with all of the typical rules and operations as detailed above, start practicing on the actual test questions in the next chapter of this book
- Since abstract reasoning tests are all about shapes, it is especially important to try to model the infrastructure of the exam while practicing – the EPSO test will be admin-

istered on a computer, which will make it harder (and stranger) to take than a paper-based test where you can scribble on the paper (even though you will be given scrap paper in the exam centre). If you have access to such services, try also to practice online

It is also important to develop a systematic approach when tackling abstract reasoning tests. One recommended approach is summarized below:

1. Quickly glance through the set of figures. Do not spend time looking at the answer options at this stage.
2. Run through all the rules, operations and patterns you familiarised yourself with during practice and try to apply them to the set of figures. Start with the one that, based on glancing at the figures, intuitively seems the most promising lead.
3. If you believe you have found the rule or rules governing the exercise, try to "generate" the correct answer figure in your mind or draw a sketch on a bit of scrap paper.
4. Look at the answer options provided and match them against the one you came up with yourself. If a test item is based on multiple rules, you may still be able to exclude one or two of the answer options based on only the first rule. If you are able to do that, you can continue looking for the second rule with a smaller set of answer options to work with – thereby speeding up the process one rule at a time.
5. If you have found a match (and only one), you can mark that as the correct answer. If there are no matches, or multiple matches to your rule(s), they probably have a flaw. Apply your rule to all the figures in the test – this will most likely reveal the flaw, which you can then correct and generate a new, hopefully correct, answer figure in your mind,
6. While practicing, you may consider writing every idea and step down for each exercise to make sure you are aware of the logic and rules at play.

In the following chapter, you will find a complete set of abstract reasoning questions that you can use to build up your your speed and accuracy.

10. Abstract Reasoning Test

160 Questions – Answers follow on from Question 160

In each question you must choose which of the figures in the bottom line - A, B, C, D or E - completes the series in the top line.

For practice purposes, you should try to complete 10 questions in 10 minutes. If you can't identify the rules for a particular question within 1 minute, move straight on to the next question rather than wasting time. For the actual number of questions, time allowed and pass mark in your exam, always check the Notice of Competition.

Comparatively harder and easier questions are mixed at random through the test, but if you want to specially concentrate on hard questions the final 40 (i.e. questions 121 to 160) are mainly of that type.

1 Which figure completes the series below?

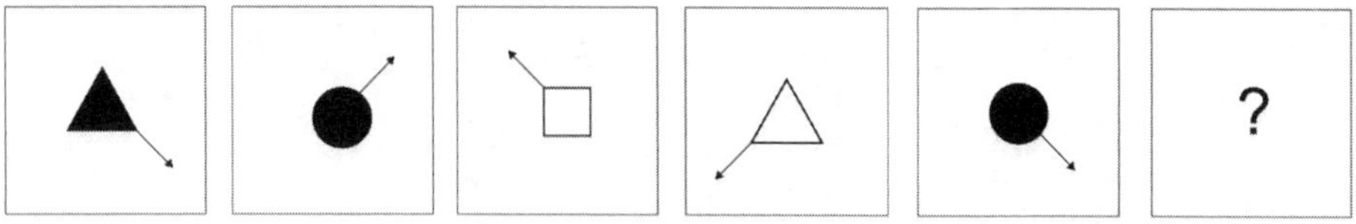

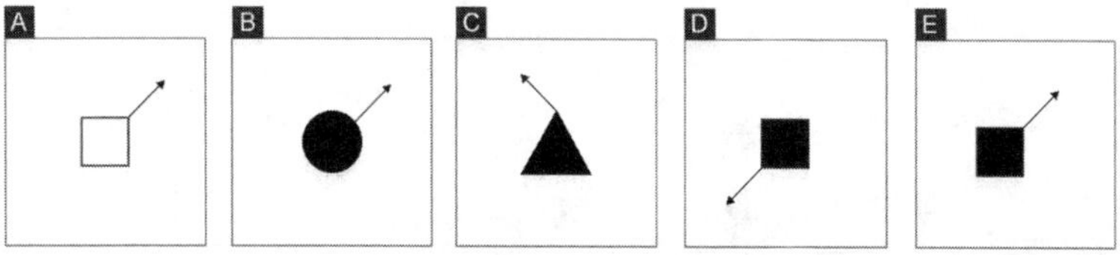

2 Which figure completes the series below?

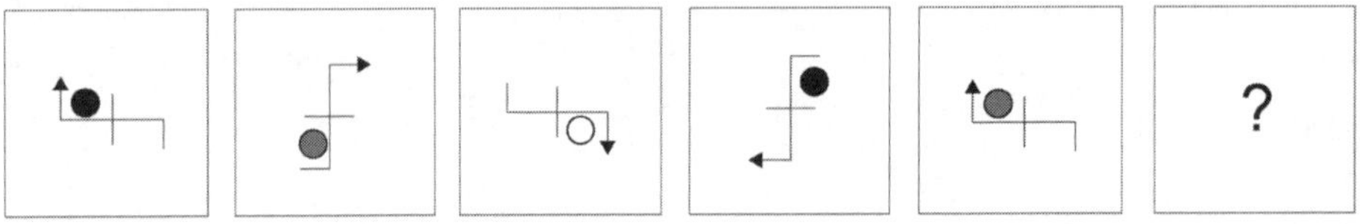

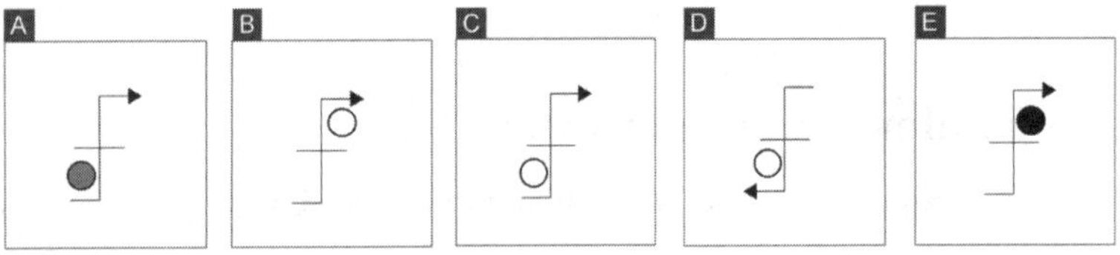

3 Which figure completes the series below?

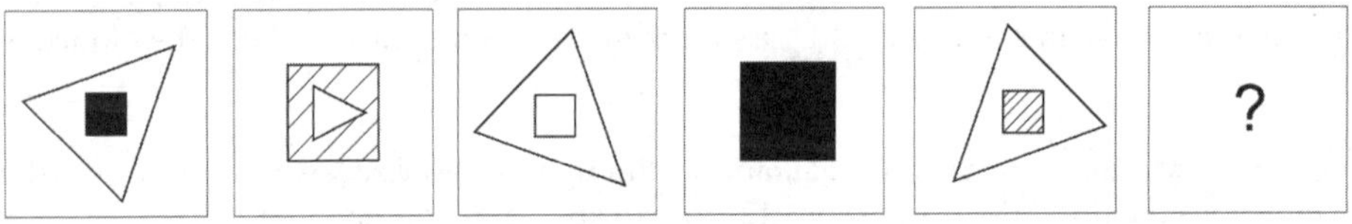

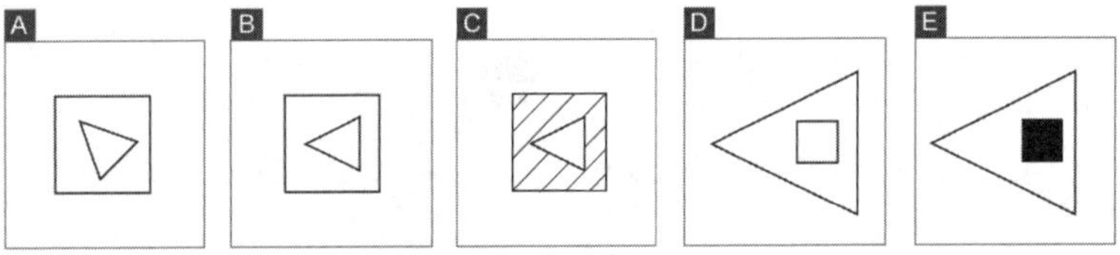

4 Which figure completes the series below?

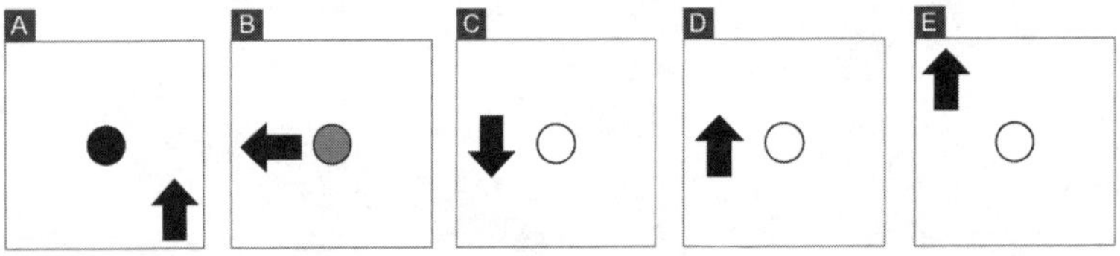

5 Which figure completes the series below?

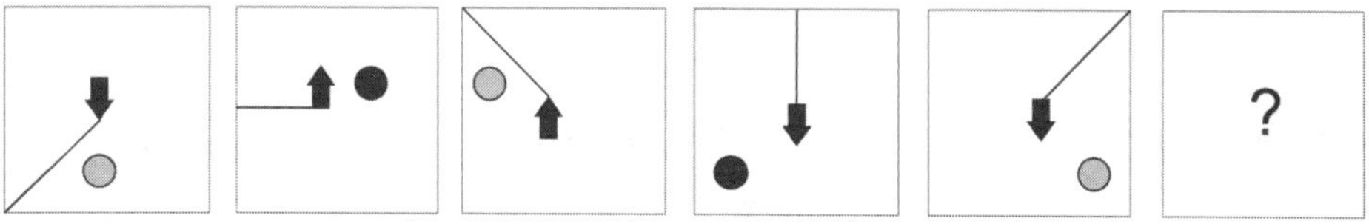

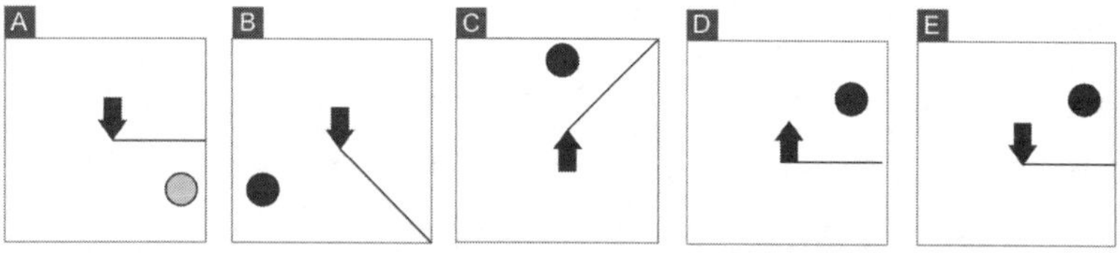

6 Which figure completes the series below?

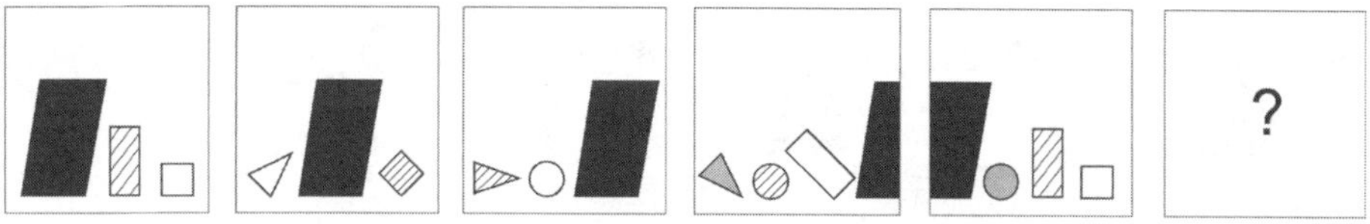

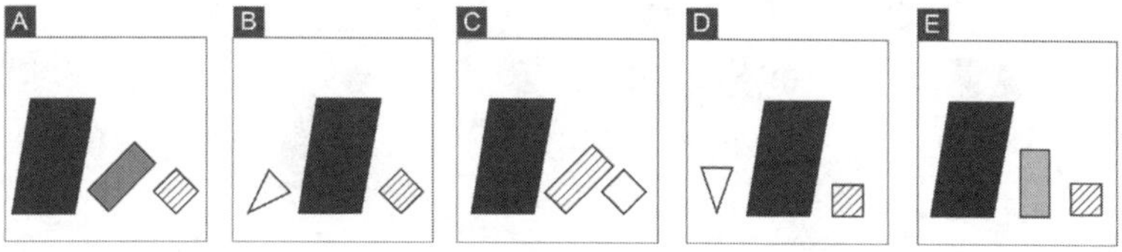

7 Which figure completes the series below?

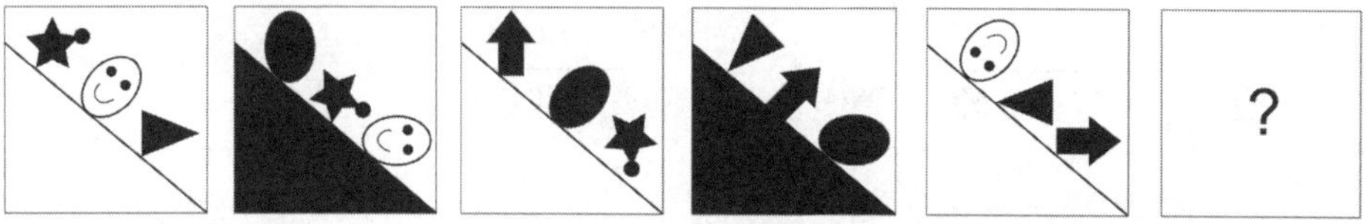

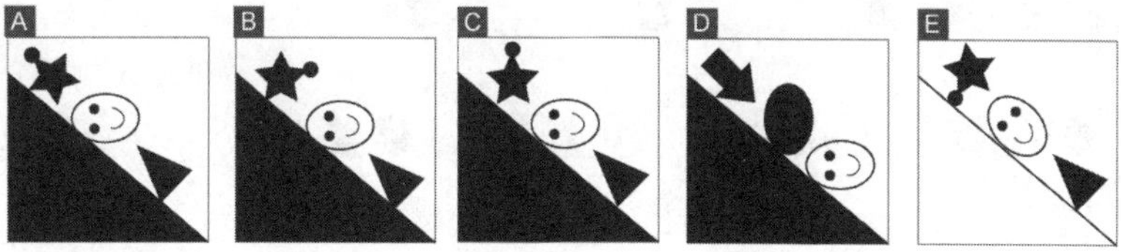

8 Which figure completes the series below?

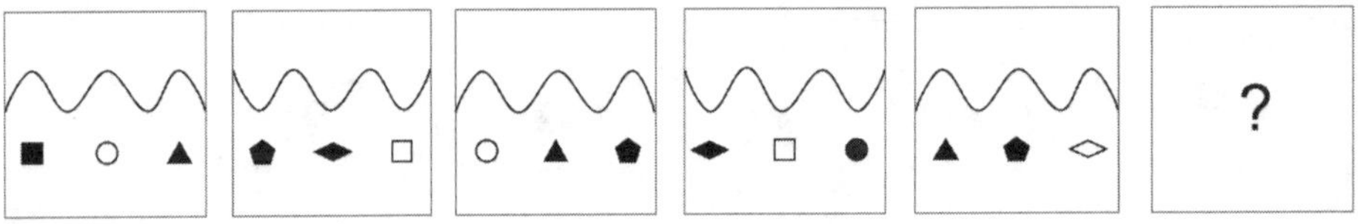

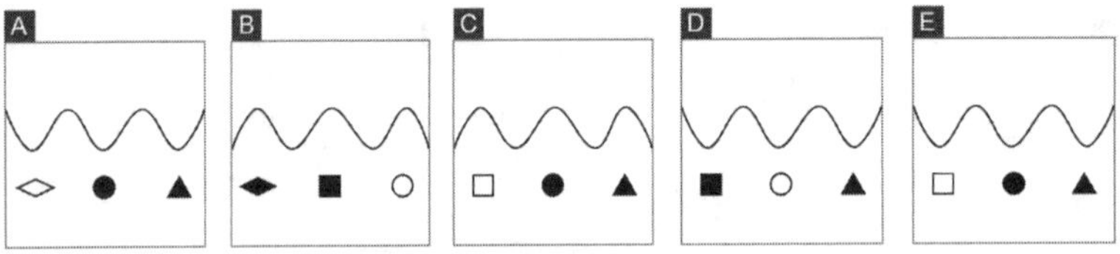

9 Which figure completes the series below?

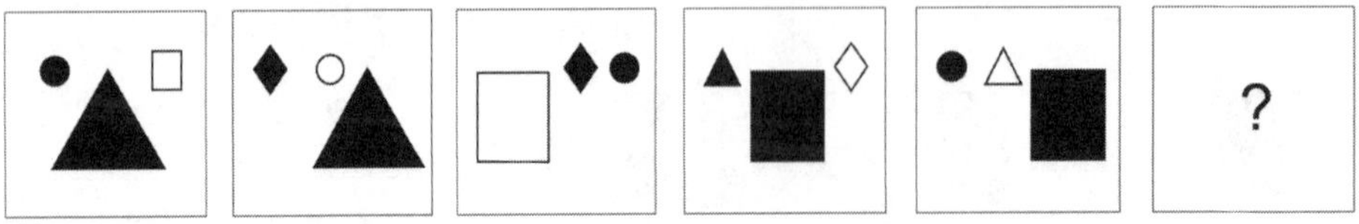

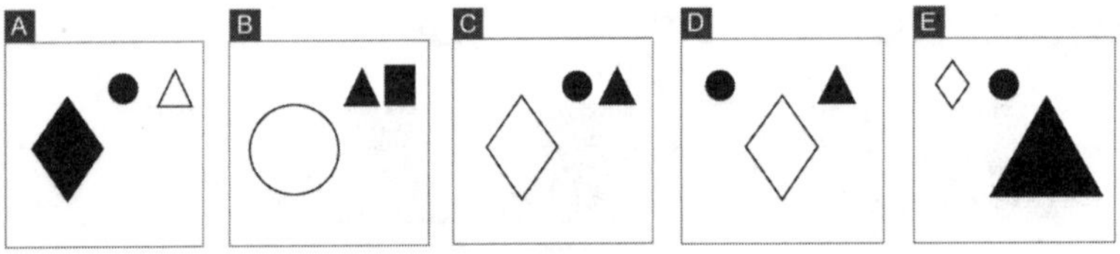

10 Which figure completes the series below?

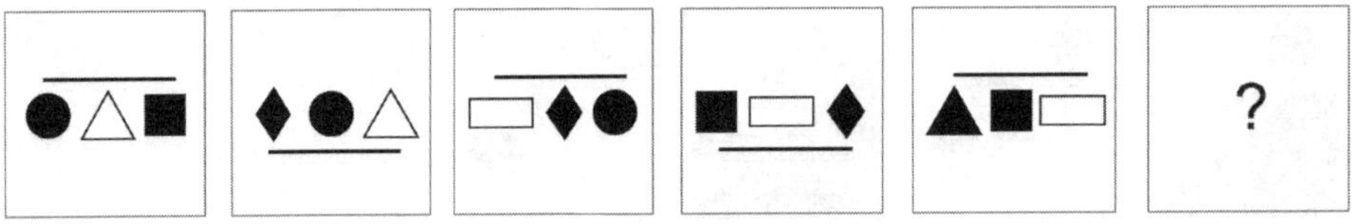

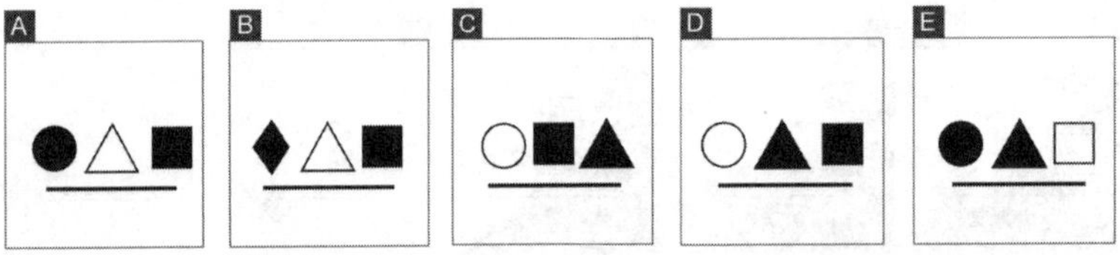

11 Which figure completes the series below?

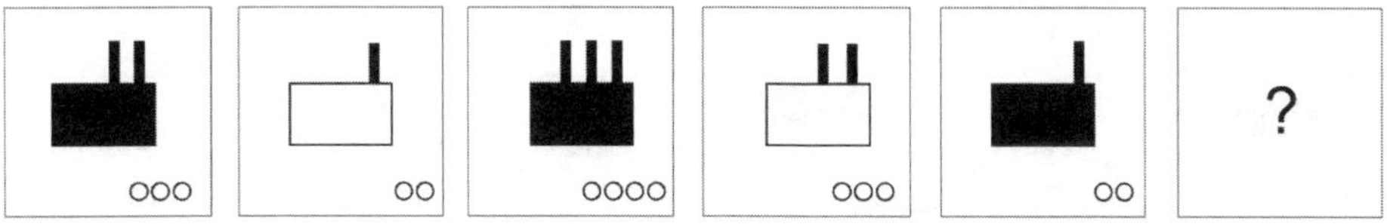

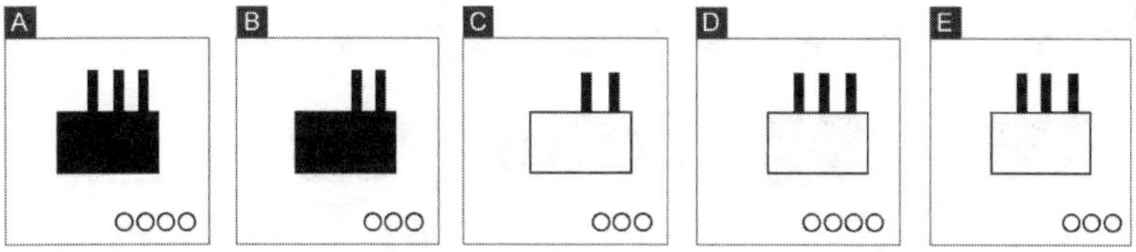

12 Which figure completes the series below?

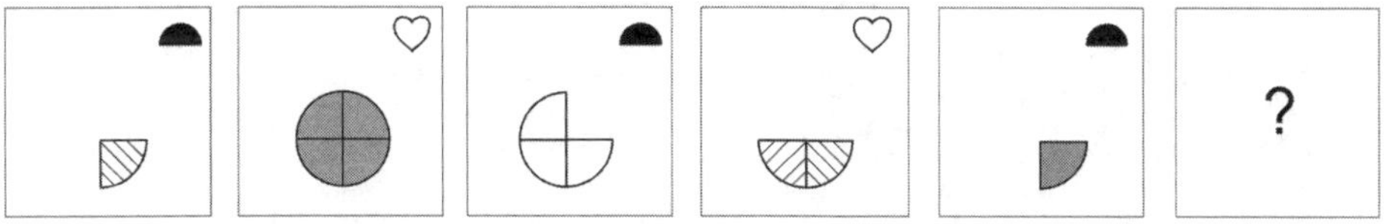

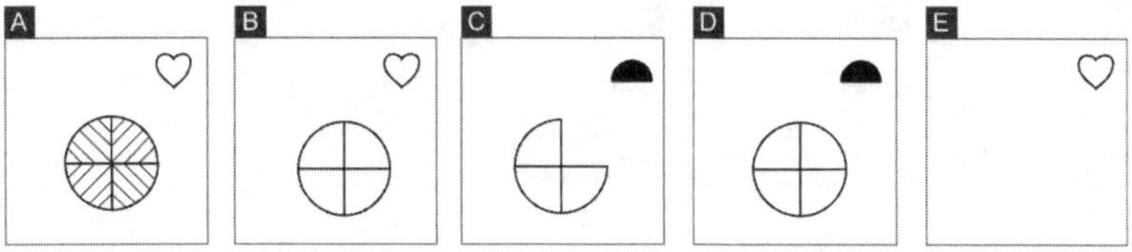

13 Which figure completes the series below?

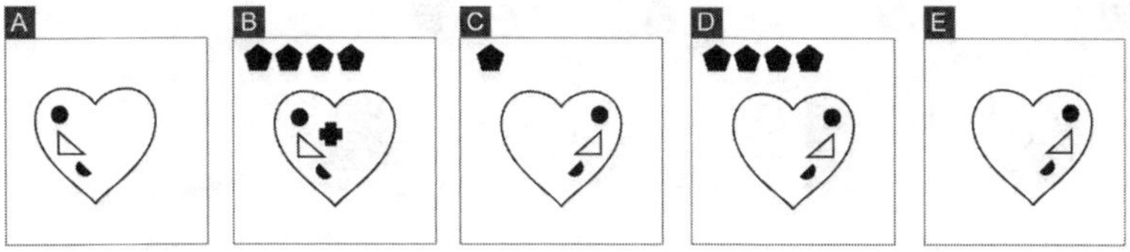

14 Which figure completes the series below?

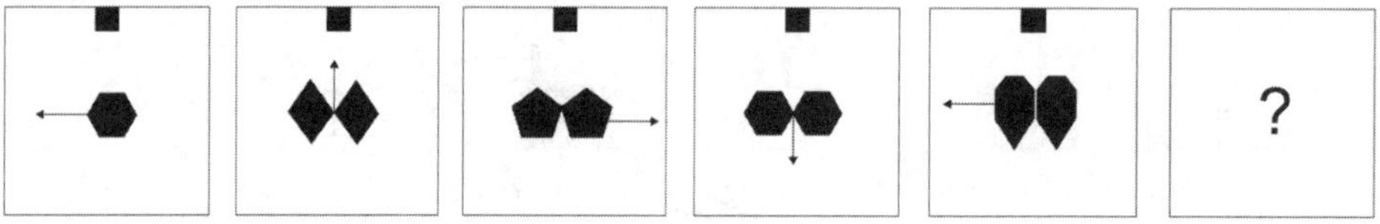

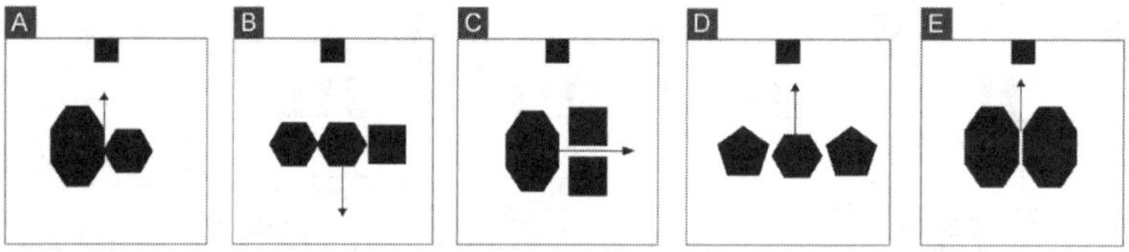

15 Which figure completes the series below?

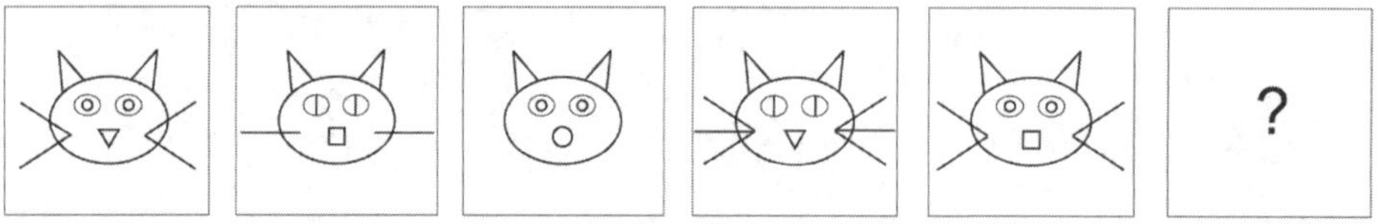

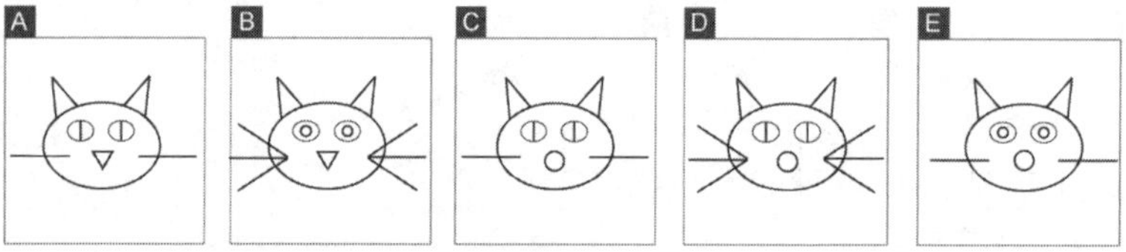

16 Which figure completes the series below?

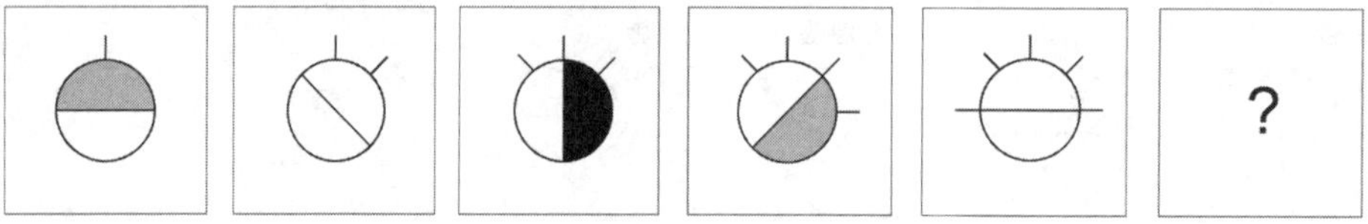

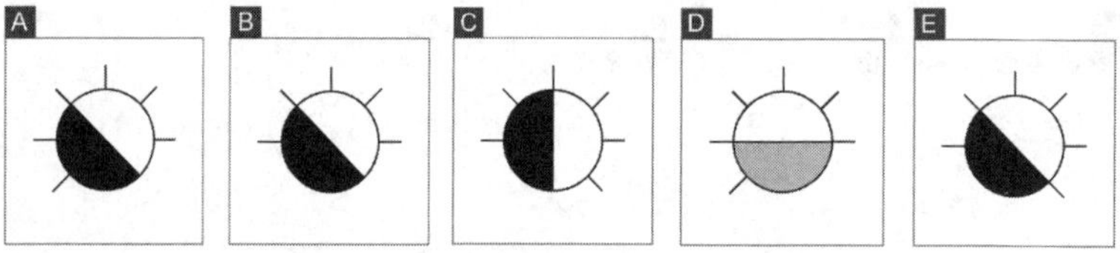

17 Which figure completes the series below?

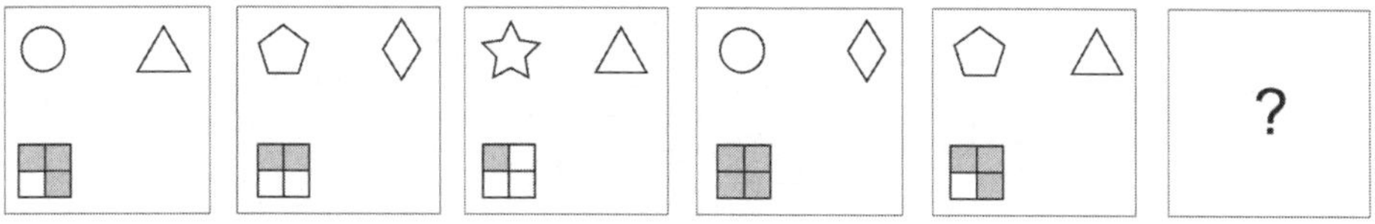

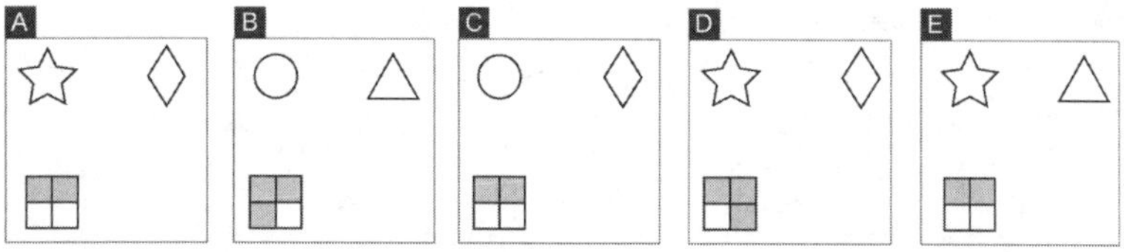

18 Which figure completes the series below?

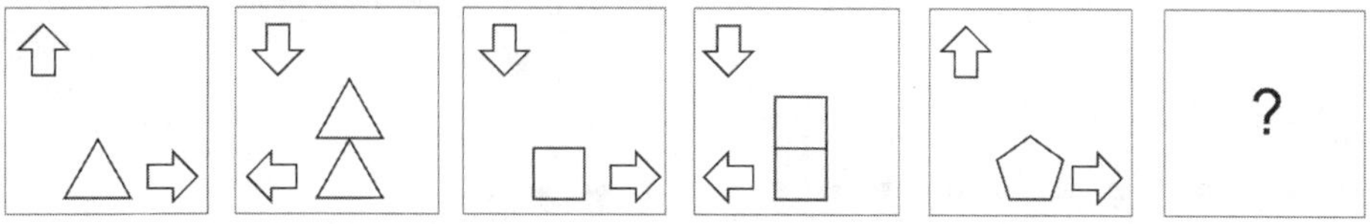

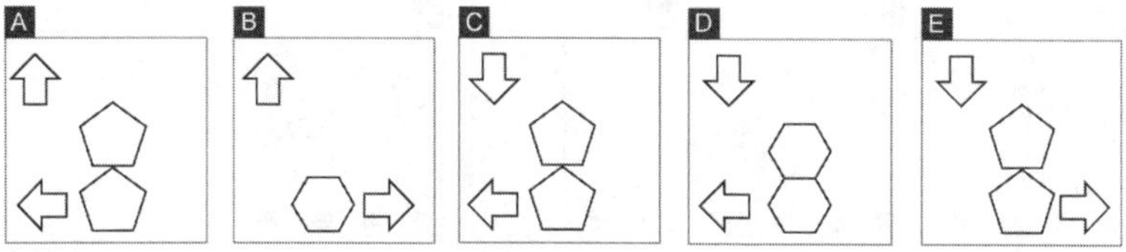

19 Which figure completes the series below?

20 Which figure completes the series below?

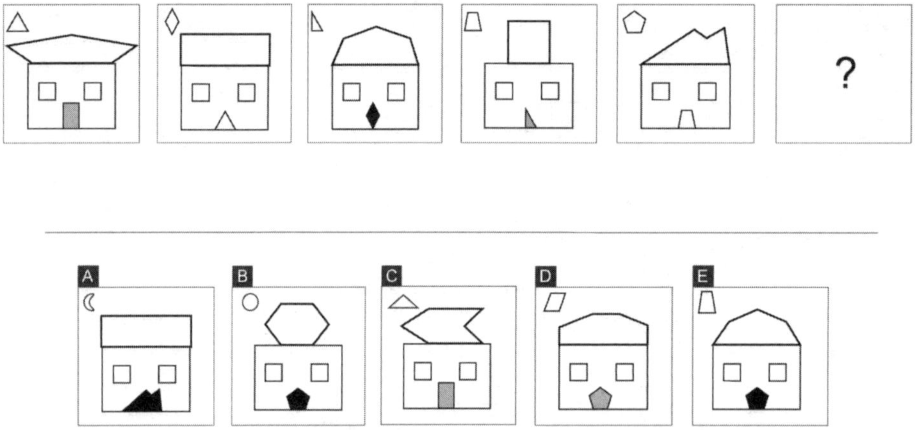

21 Which figure completes the series below?

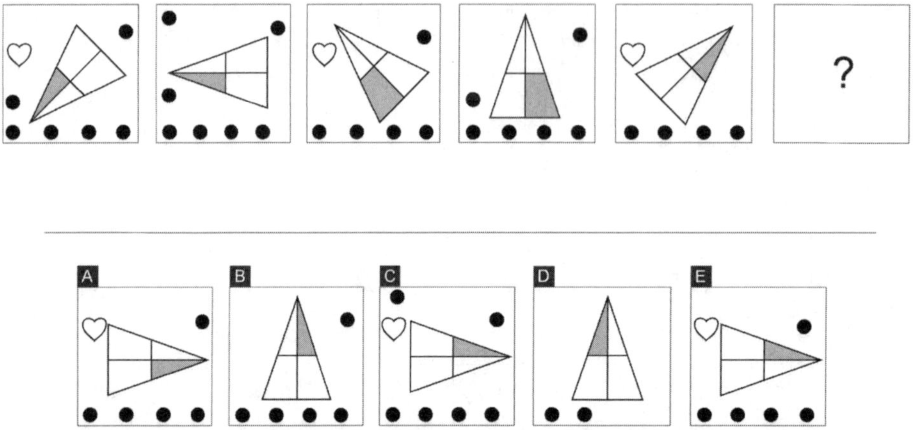

22 Which figure completes the series below?

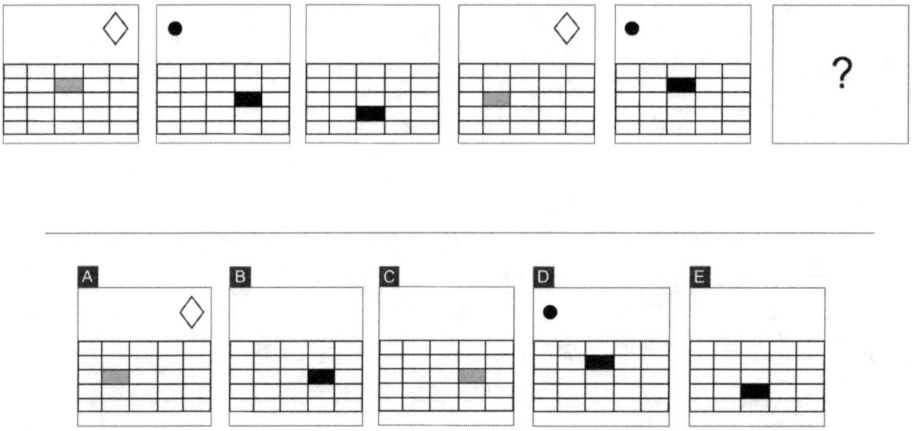

23 Which figure completes the series below?

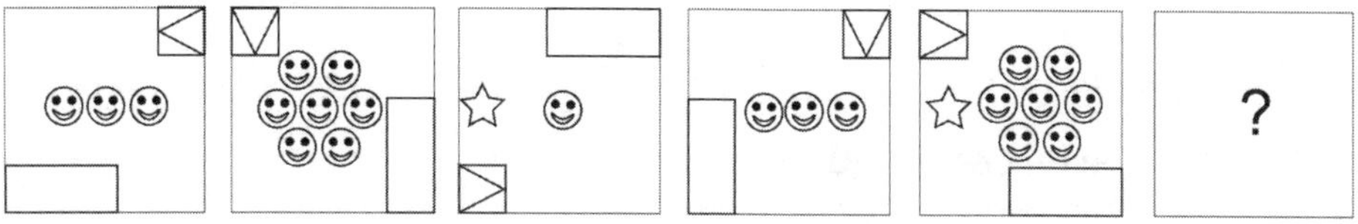

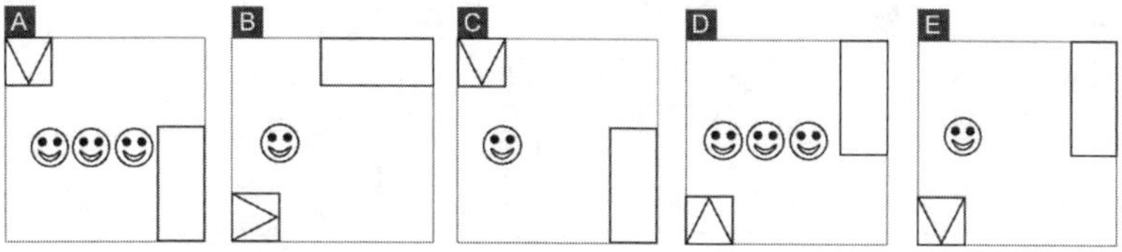

24 Which figure completes the series below?

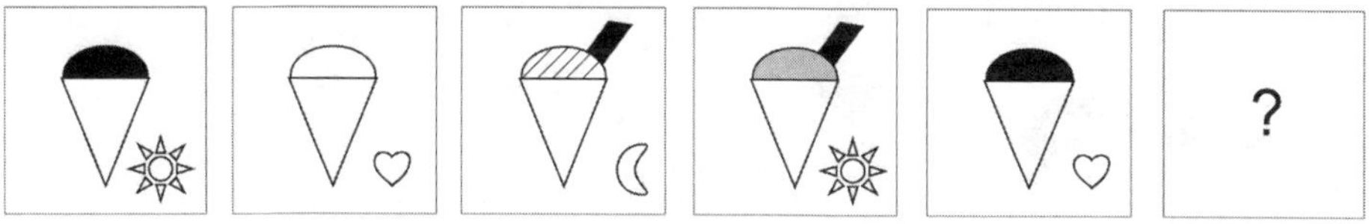

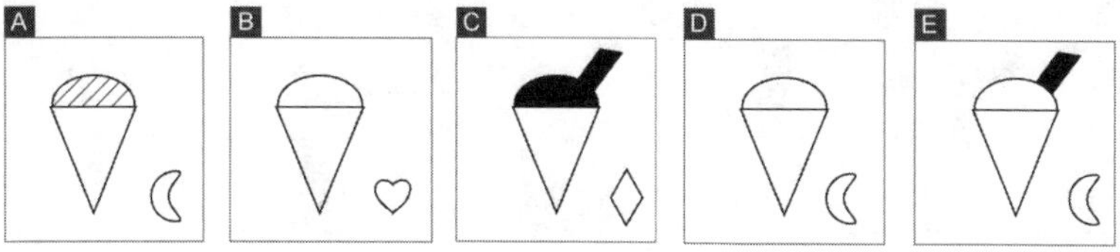

25 Which figure completes the series below?

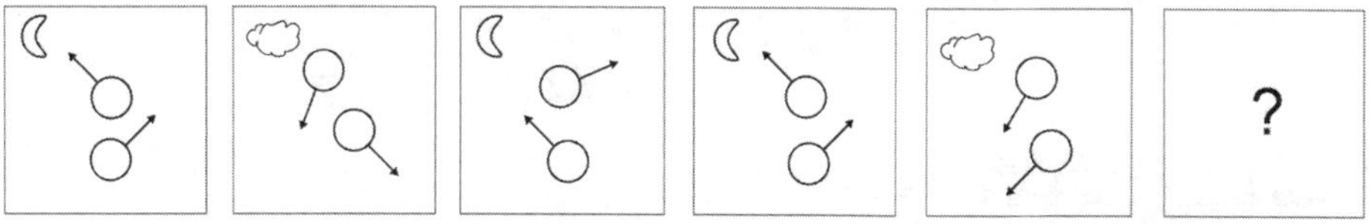

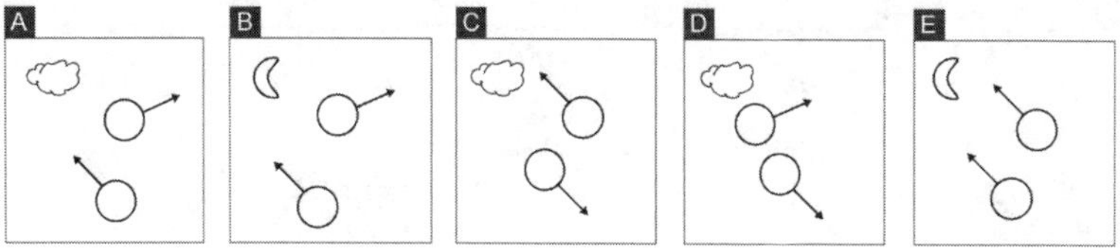

26 Which figure completes the series below?

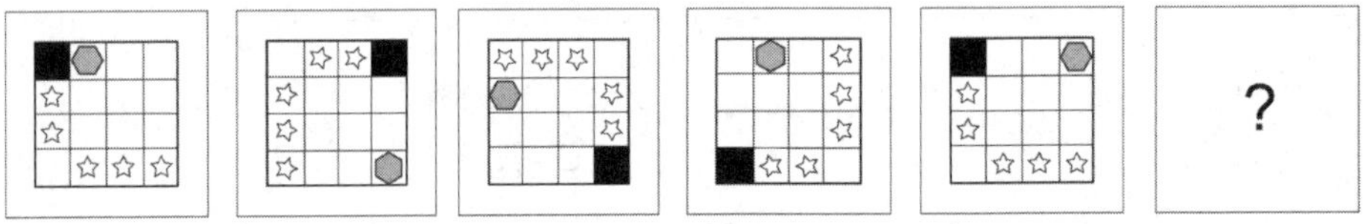

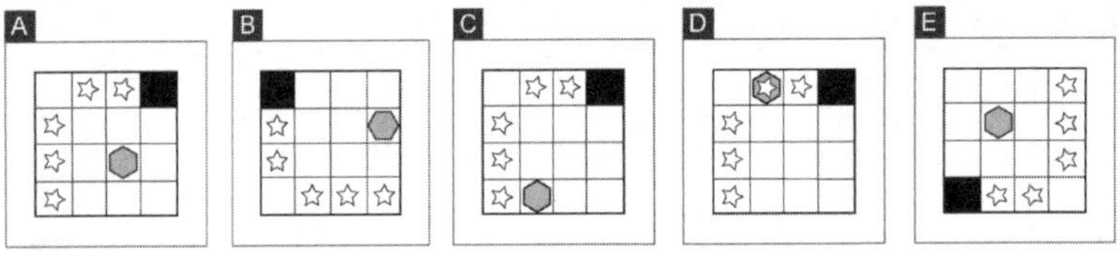

27 Which figure completes the series below?

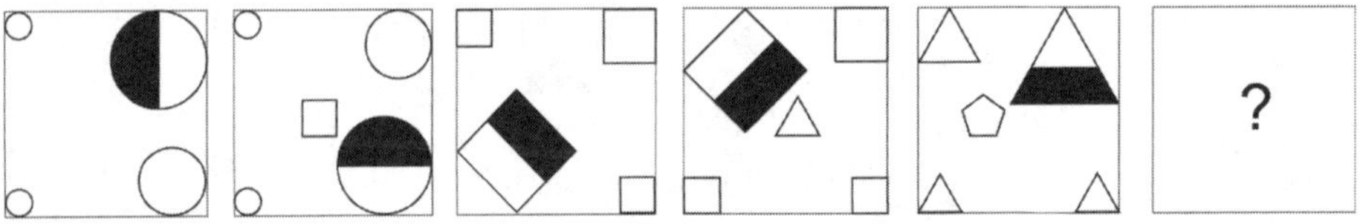

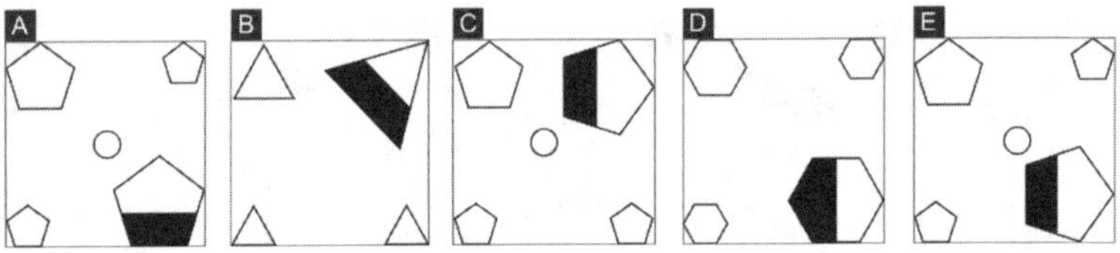

28 Which figure completes the series below?

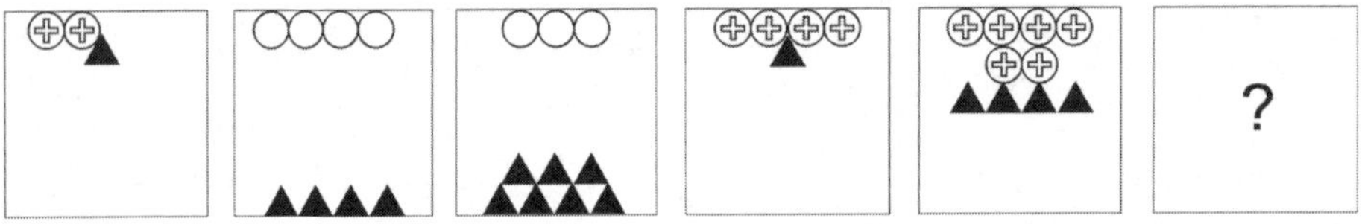

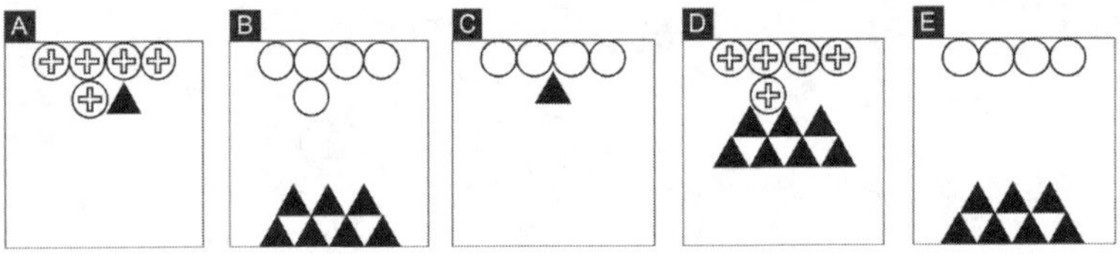

29 Which figure completes the series below?

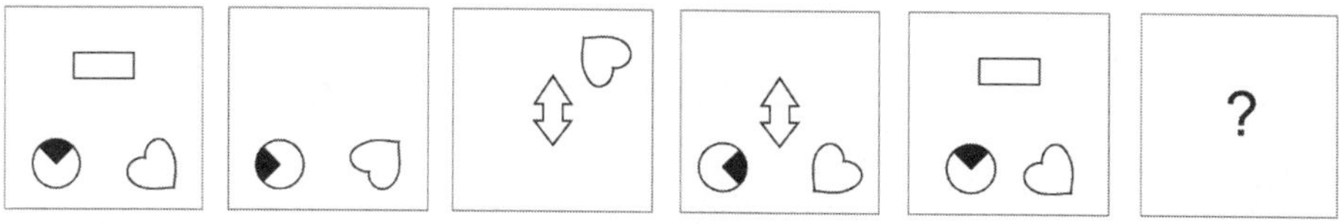

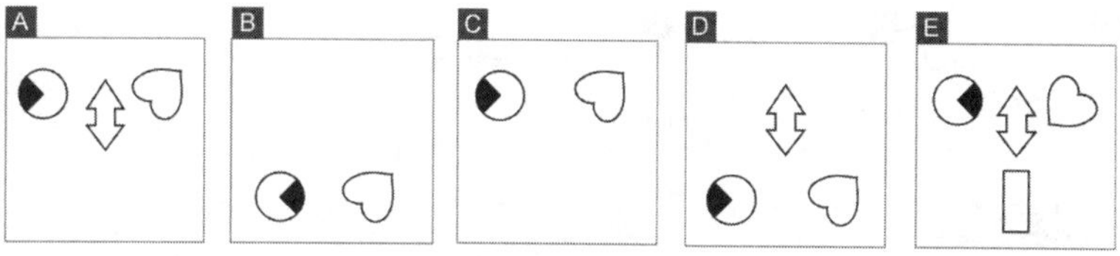

30 Which figure completes the series below?

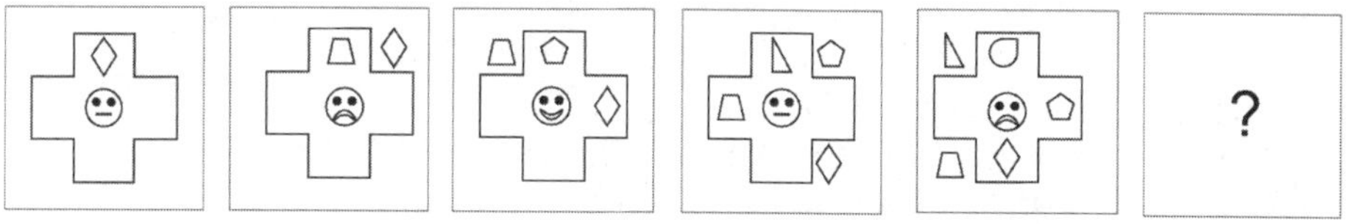

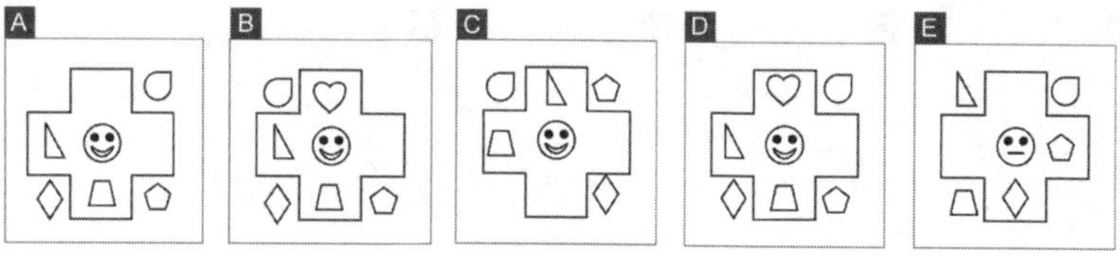

31 Which figure completes the series below?

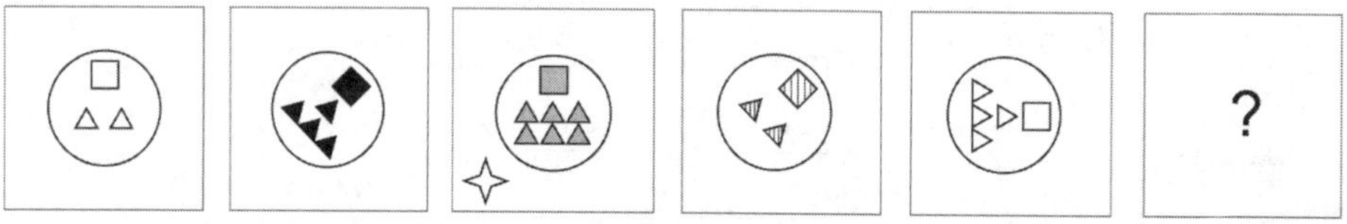

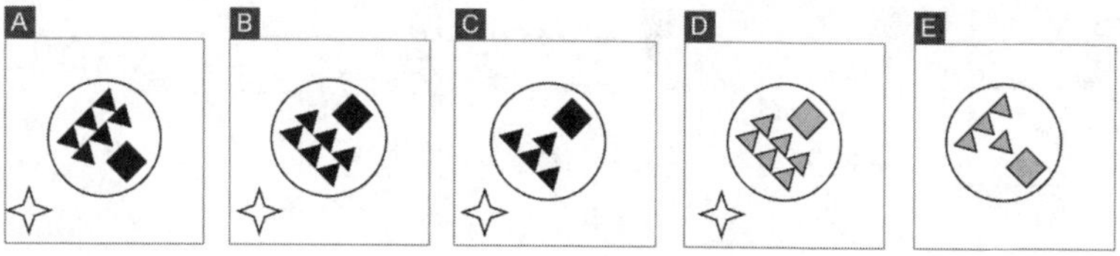

32 Which figure completes the series below?

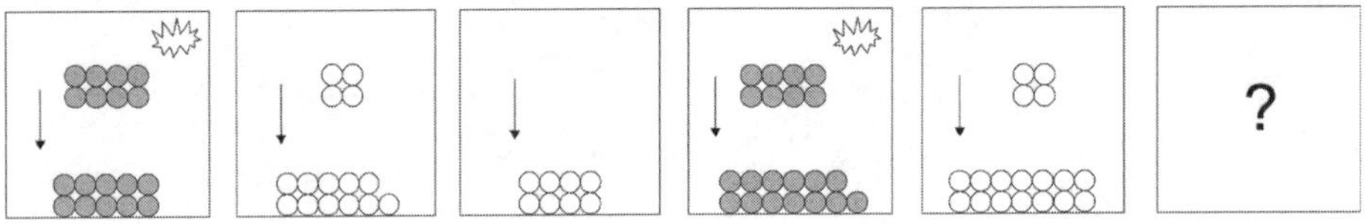

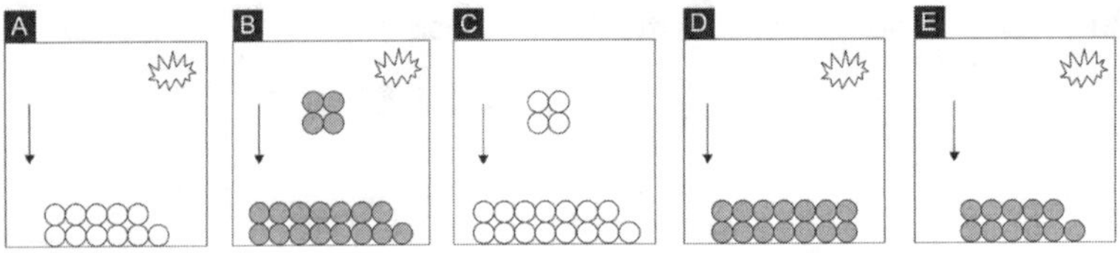

33 Which figure completes the series below?

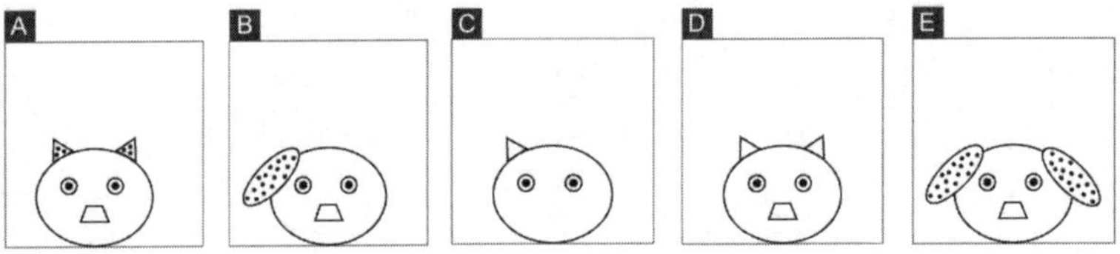

34 Which figure completes the series below?

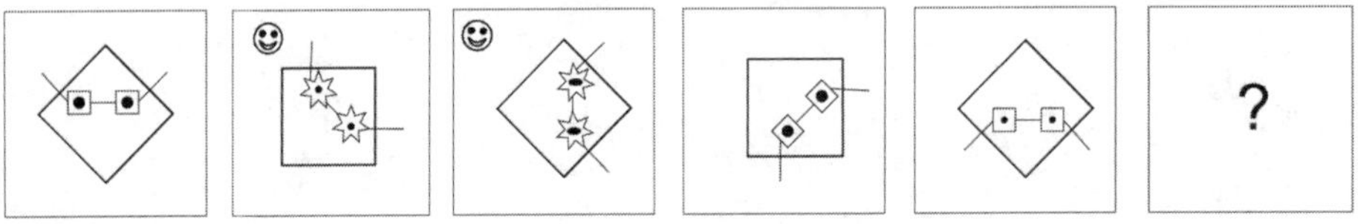

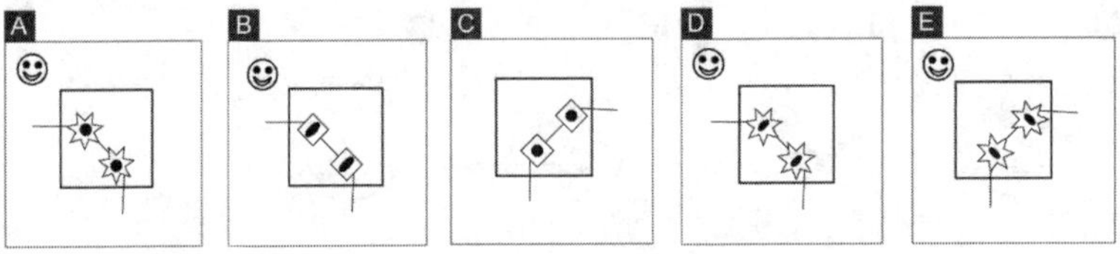

35 Which figure completes the series below?

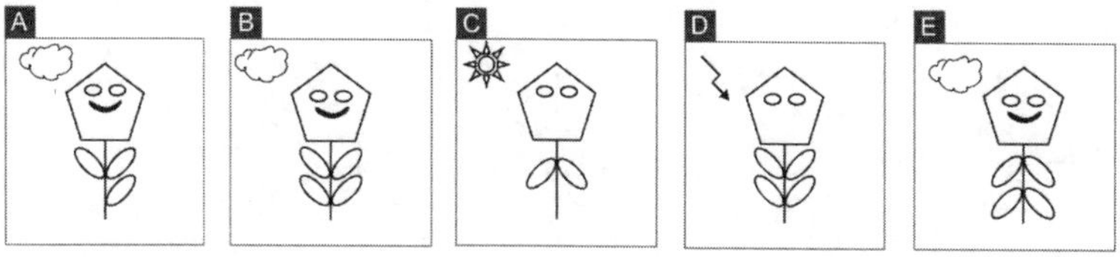

36 Which figure completes the series below?

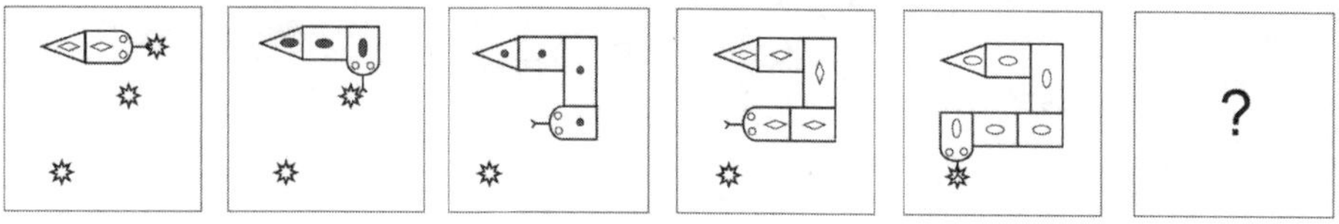

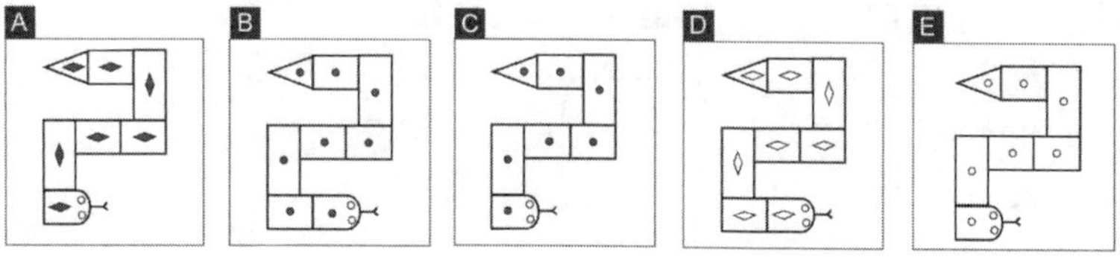

37 Which figure completes the series below?

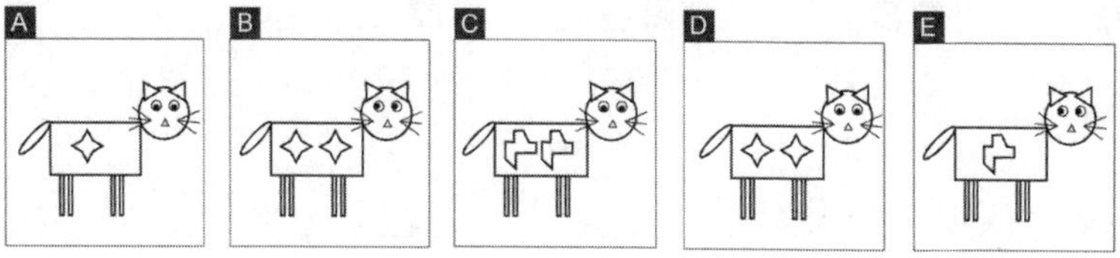

38 Which figure completes the series below?

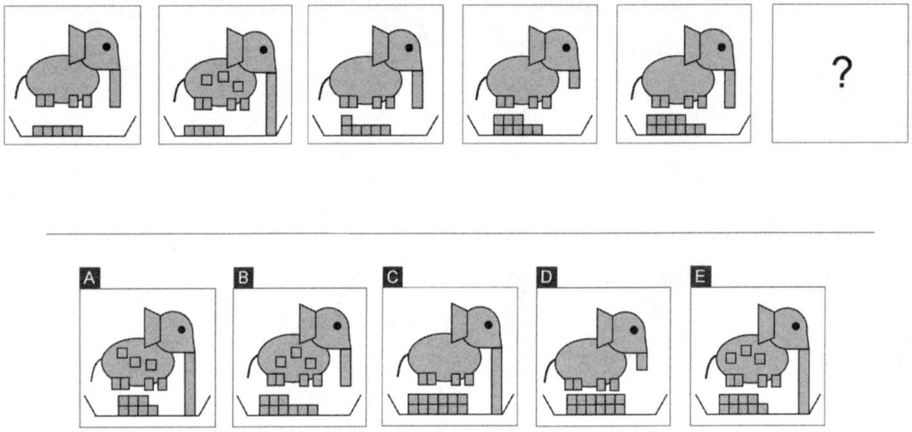

39 Which figure completes the series below?

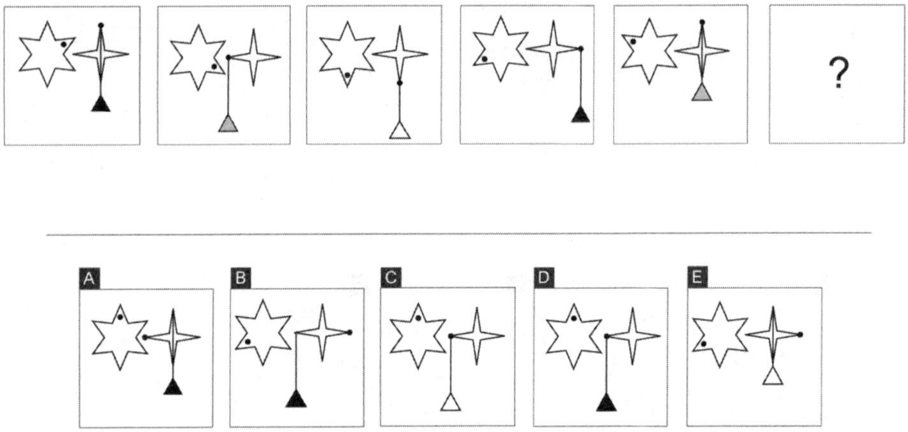

40 Which figure completes the series below?

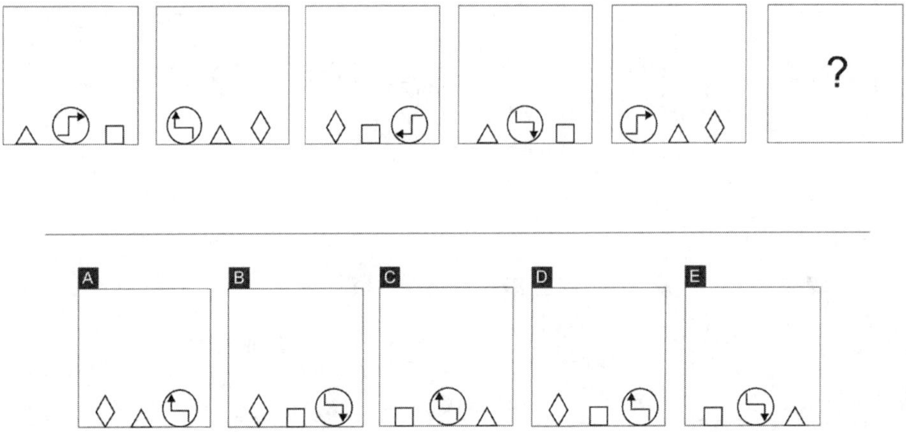

41 Which figure completes the series below?

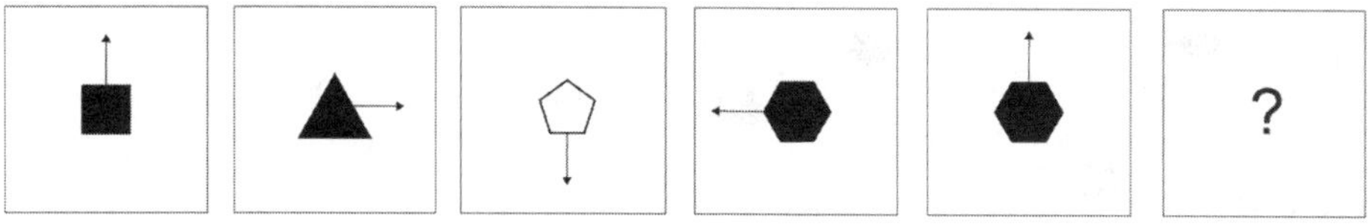

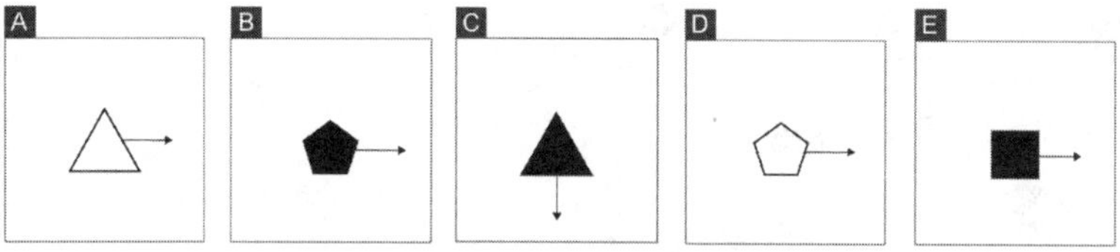

42 Which figure completes the series below?

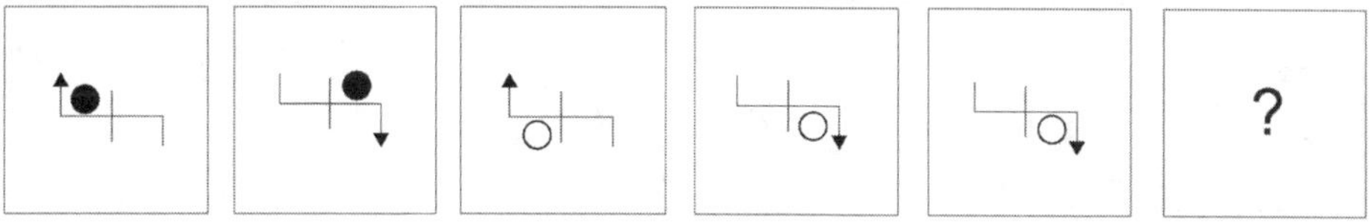

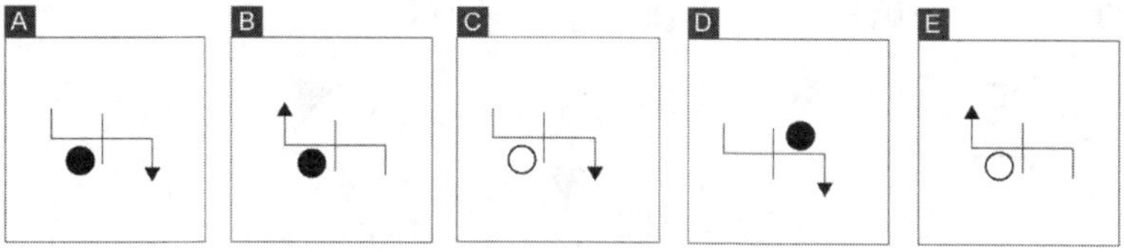

43 Which figure completes the series below?

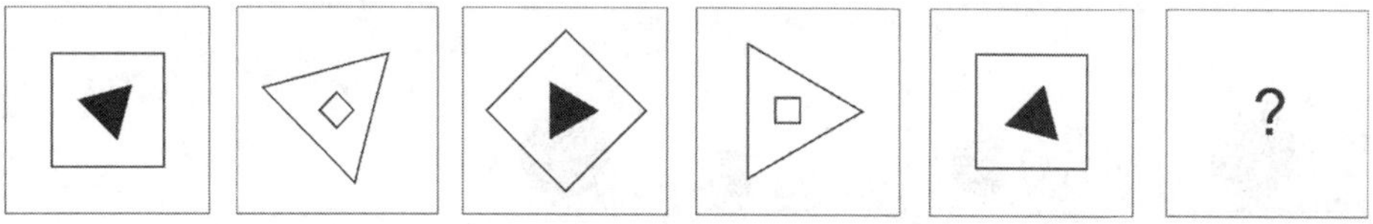

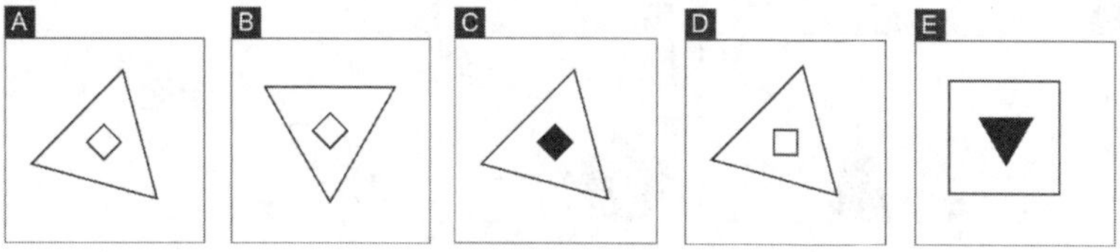

44 Which figure completes the series below?

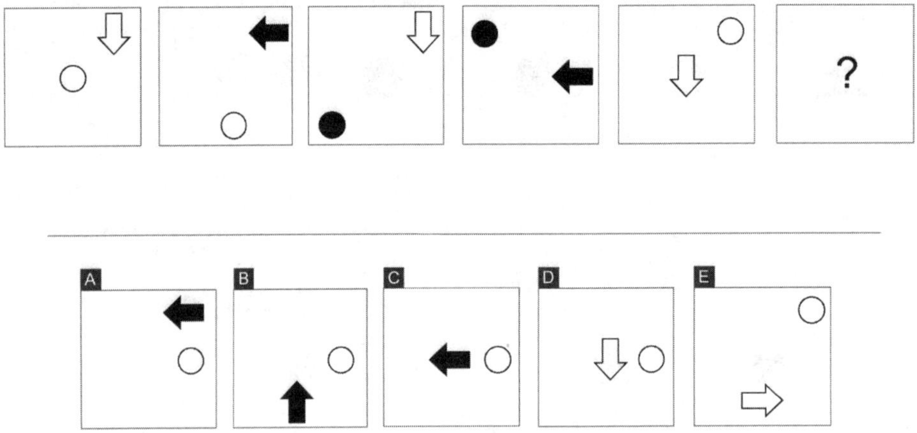

45 Which figure completes the series below?

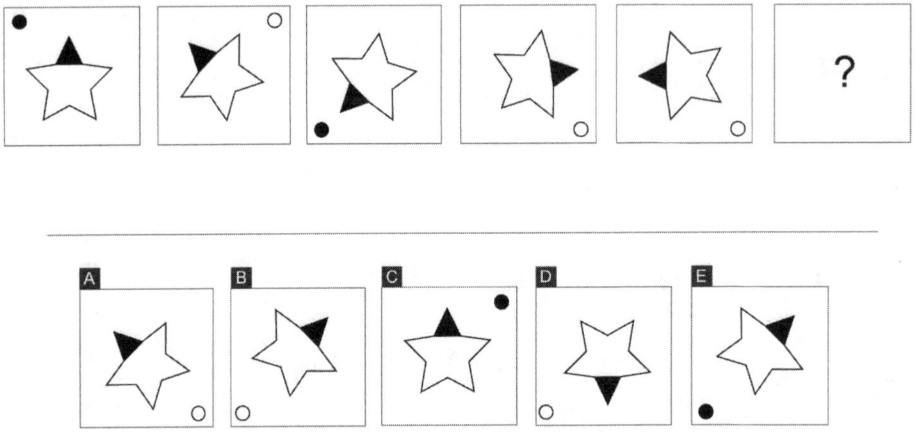

46 Which figure completes the series below?

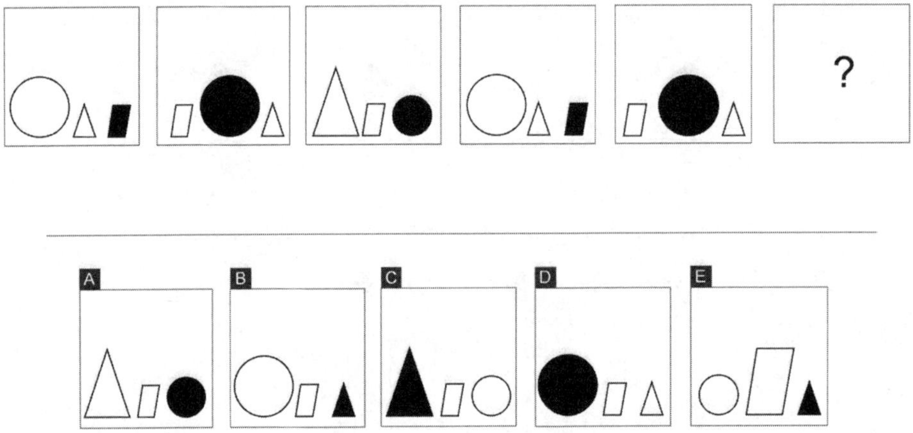

47 Which figure completes the series below?

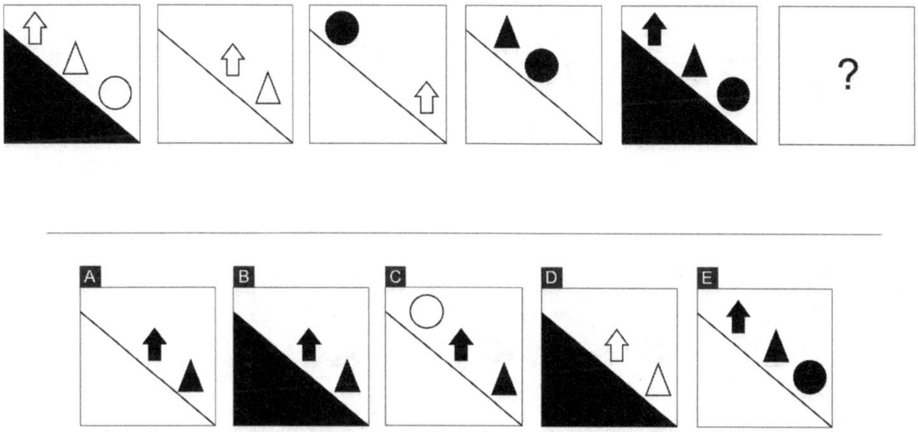

48 Which figure completes the series below?

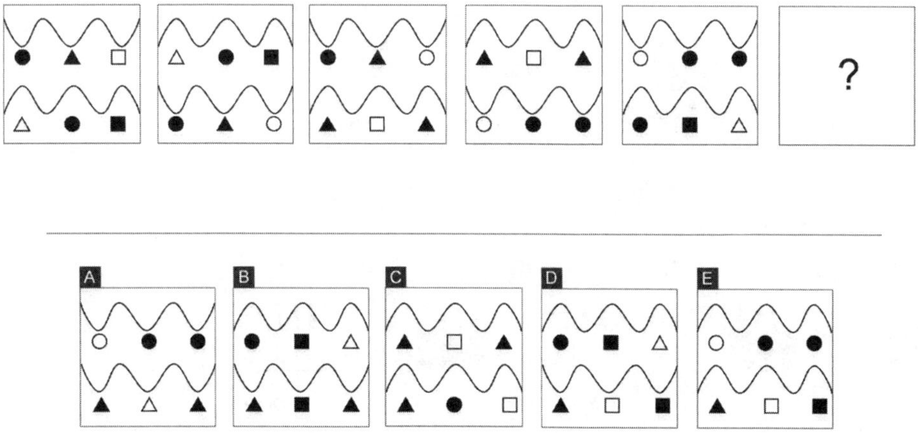

49 Which figure completes the series below?

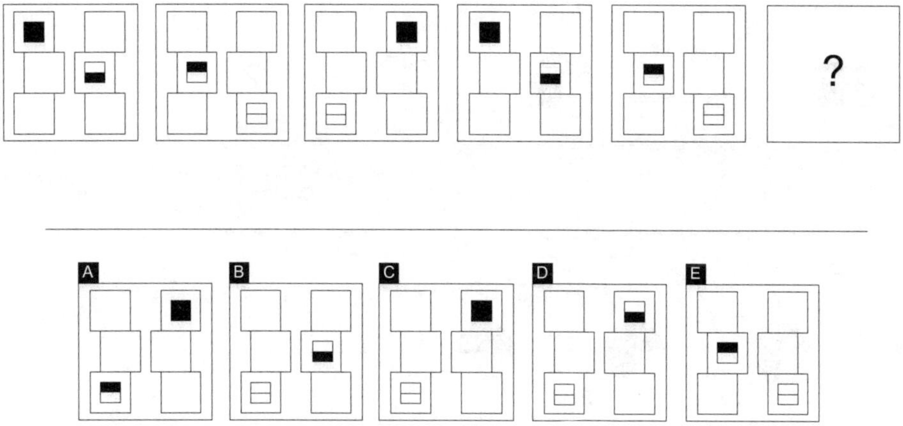

50 Which figure completes the series below?

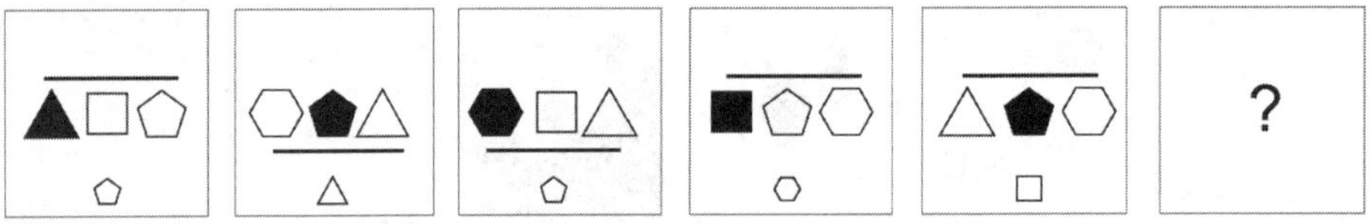

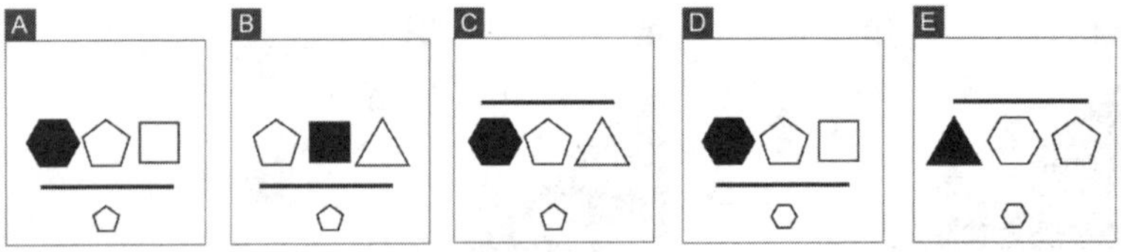

51 Which figure completes the series below?

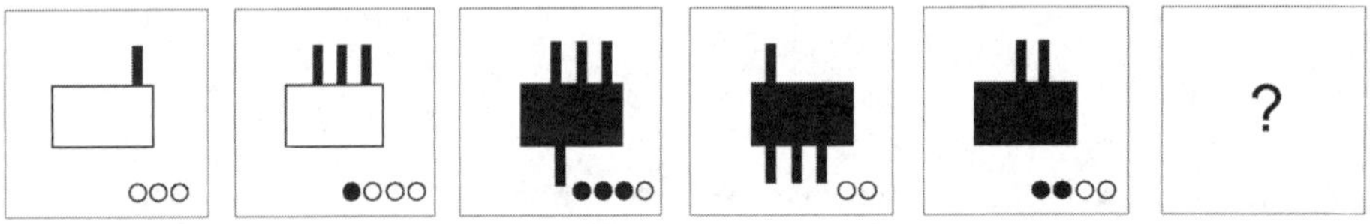

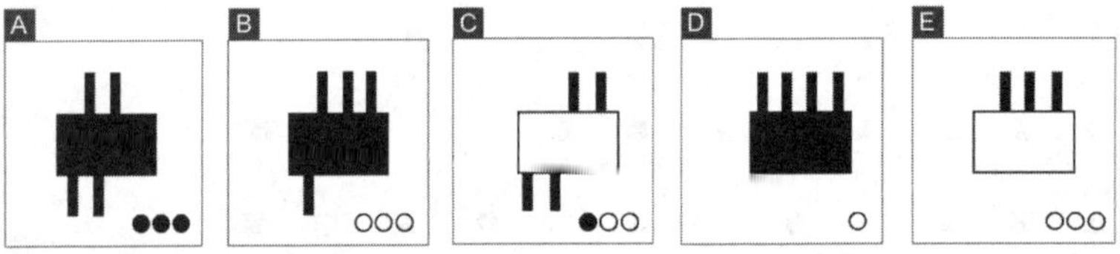

52 Which figure completes the series below?

53 Which figure completes the series below?

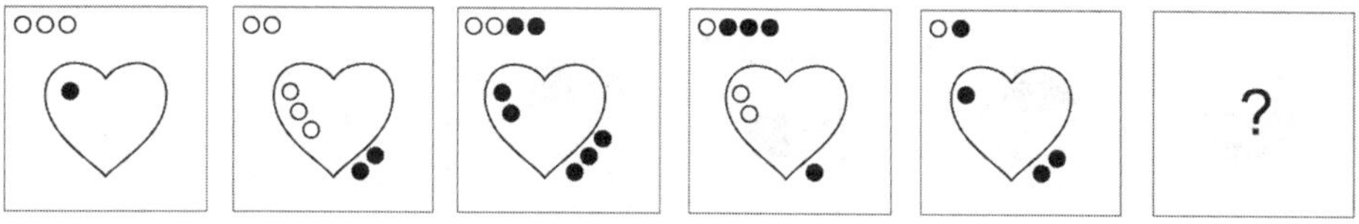

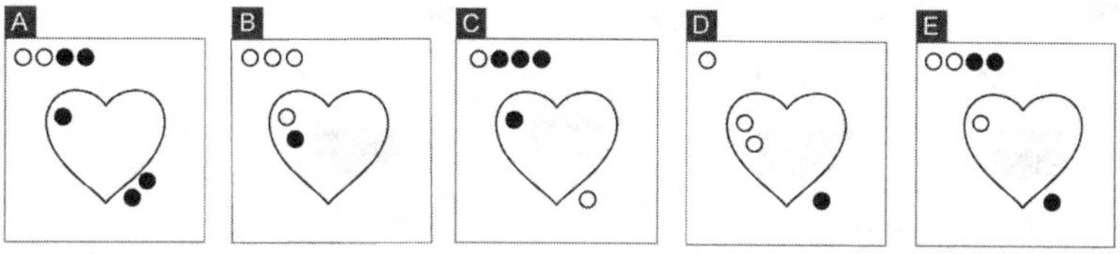

54 Which figure completes the series below?

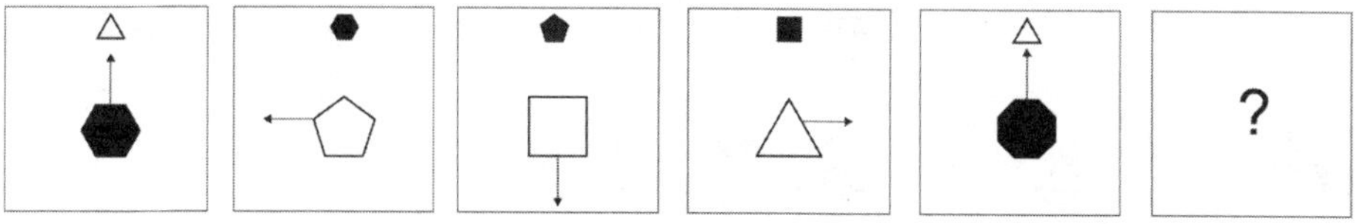

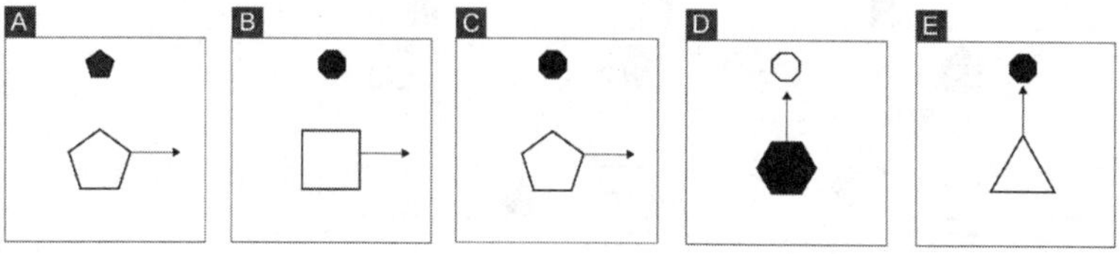

55 Which figure completes the series below?

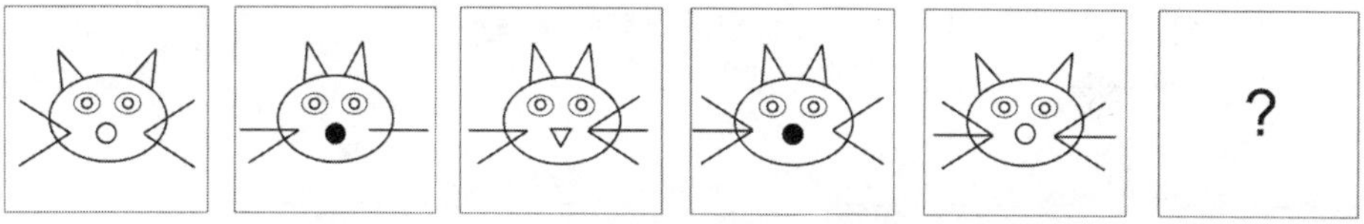

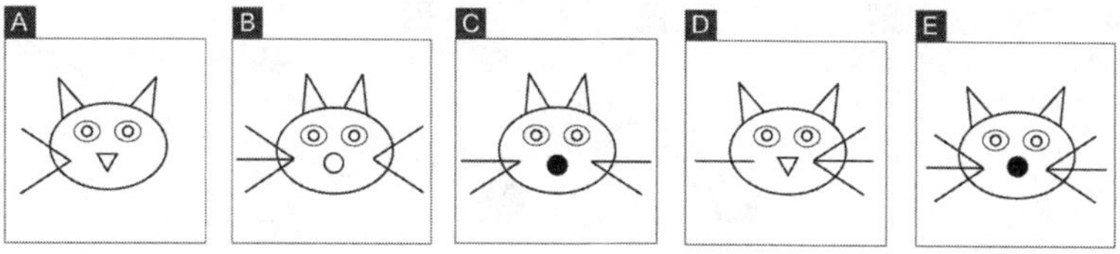

56 Which figure completes the series below?

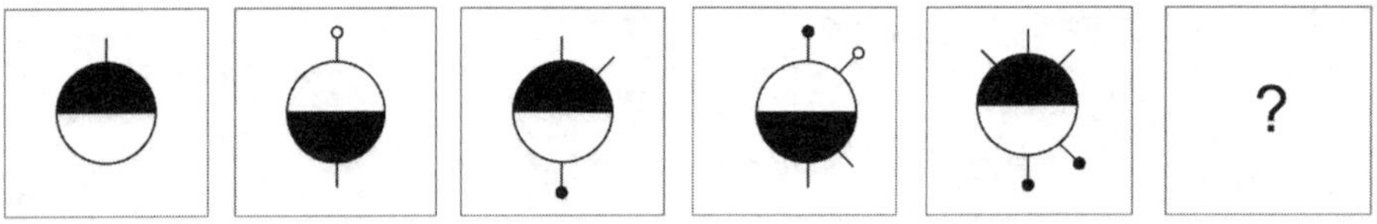

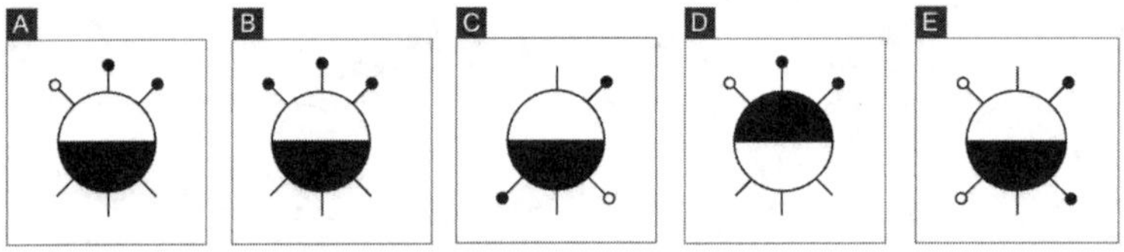

57 Which figure completes the series below?

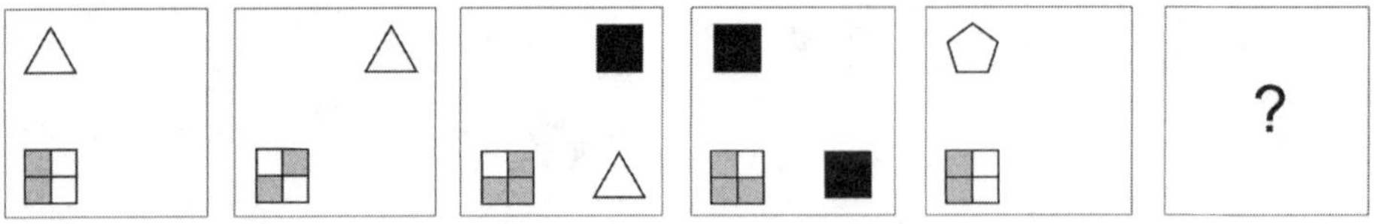

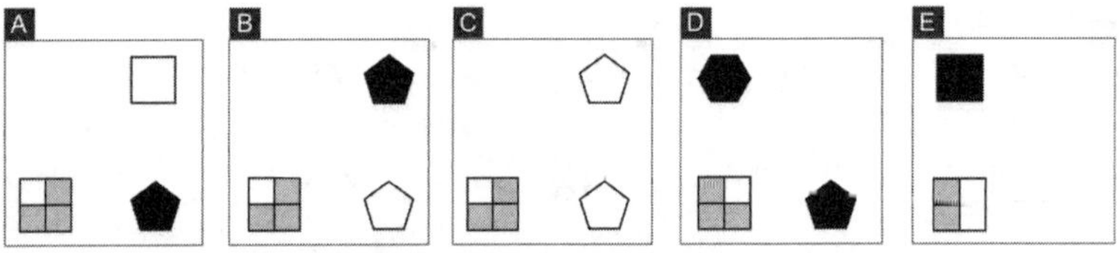

58 Which figure completes the series below?

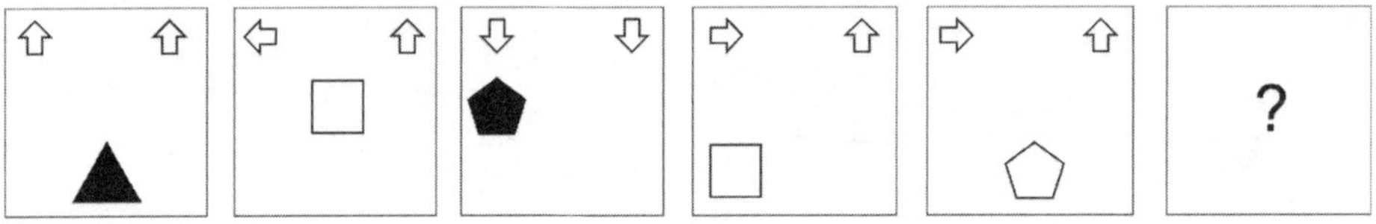

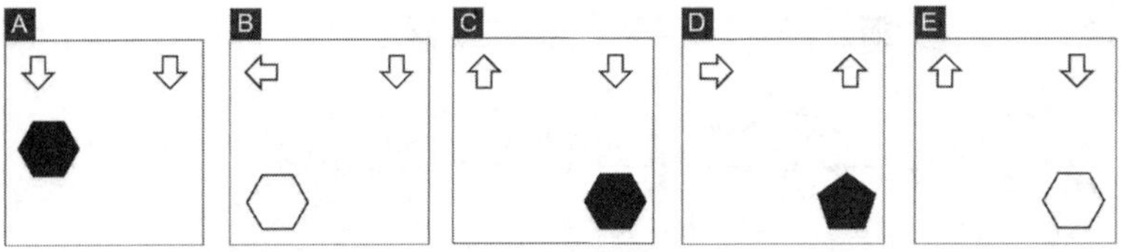

59 Which figure completes the series below?

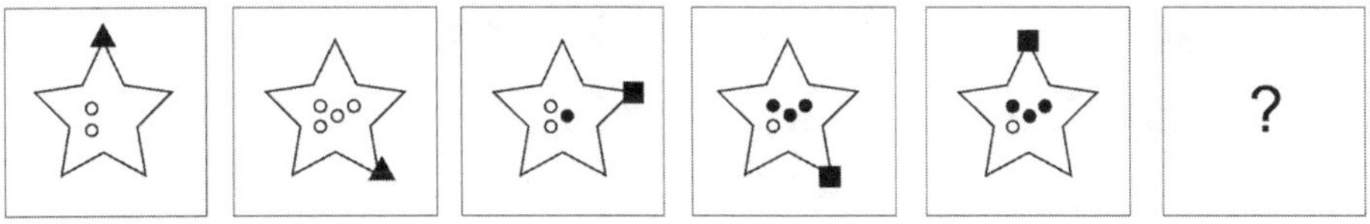

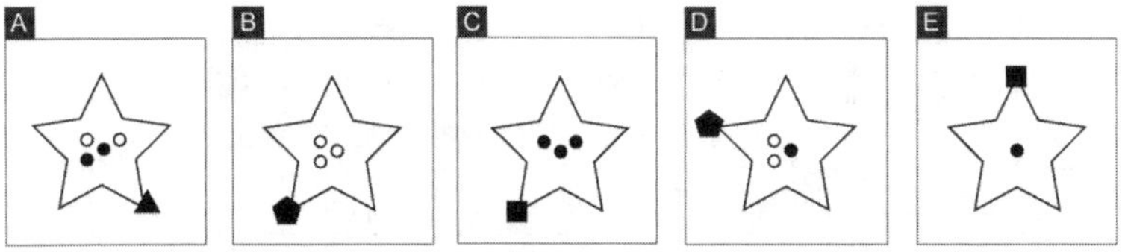

60 Which figure completes the series below?

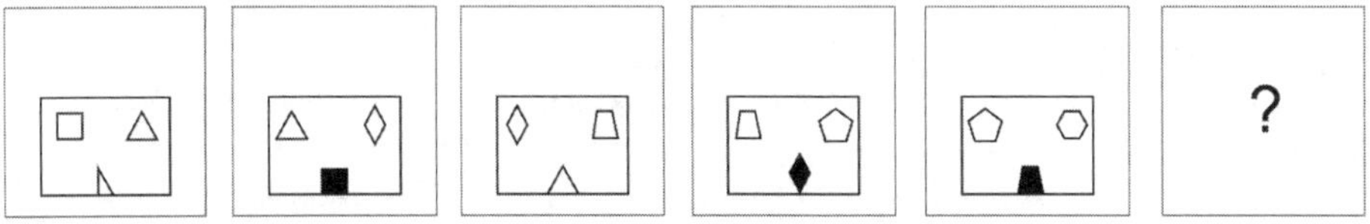

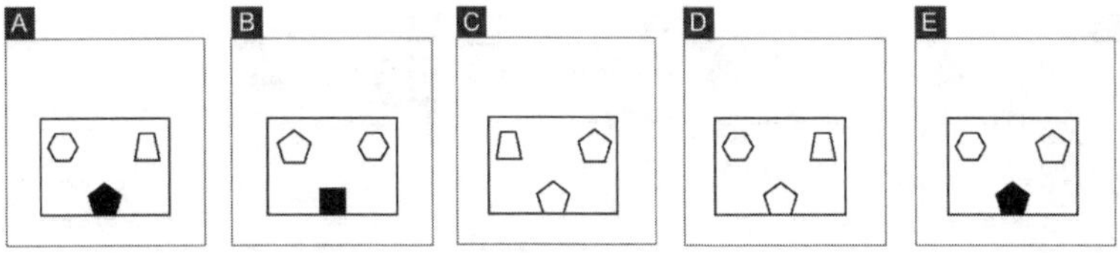

61 Which figure completes the series below?

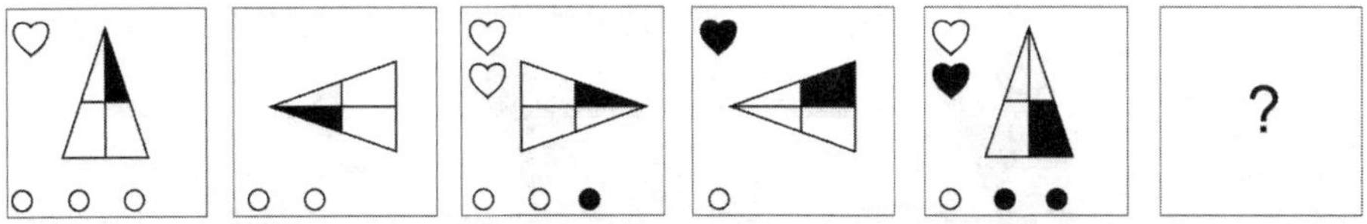

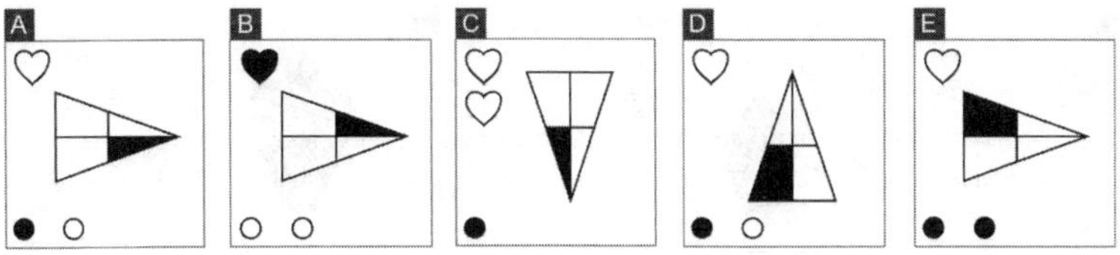

62 Which figure completes the series below?

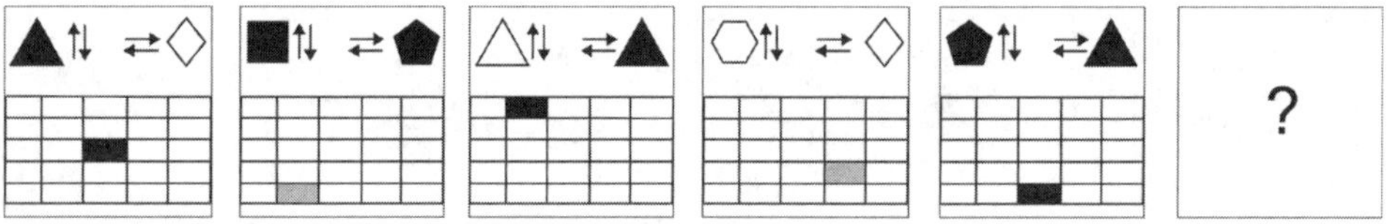

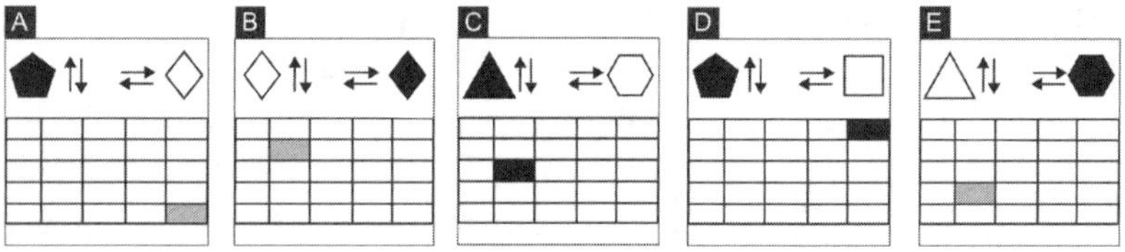

63 Which figure completes the series below?

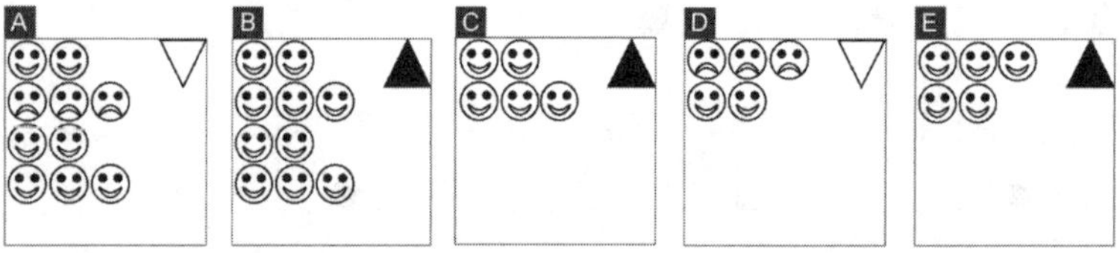

64 Which figure completes the series below?

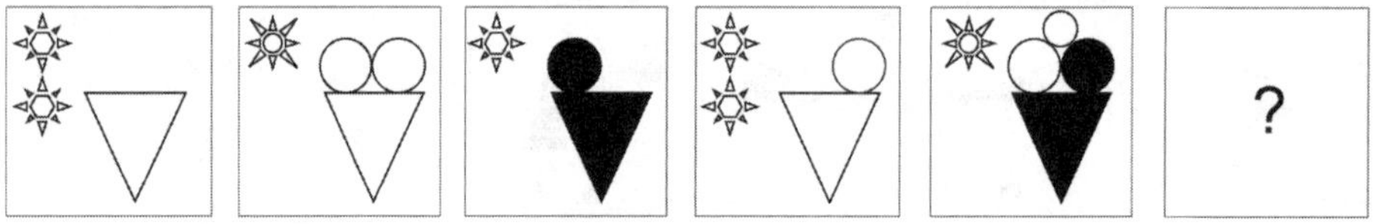

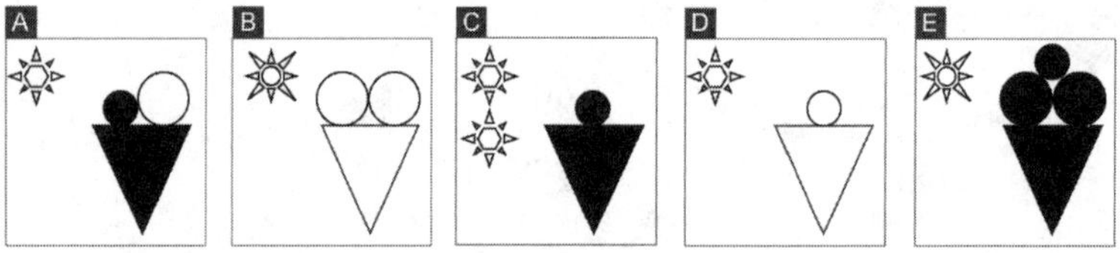

65 Which figure completes the series below?

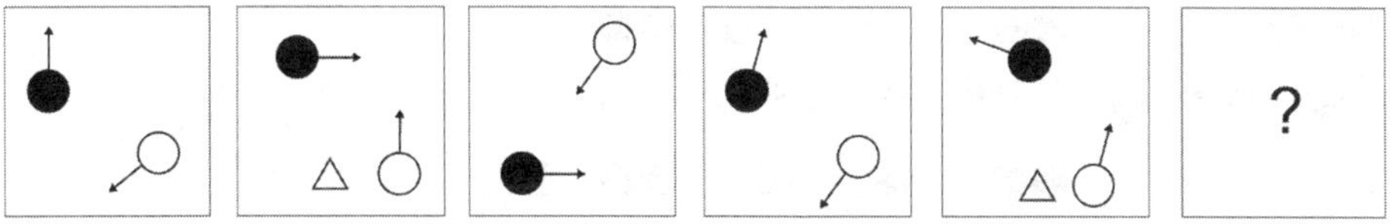

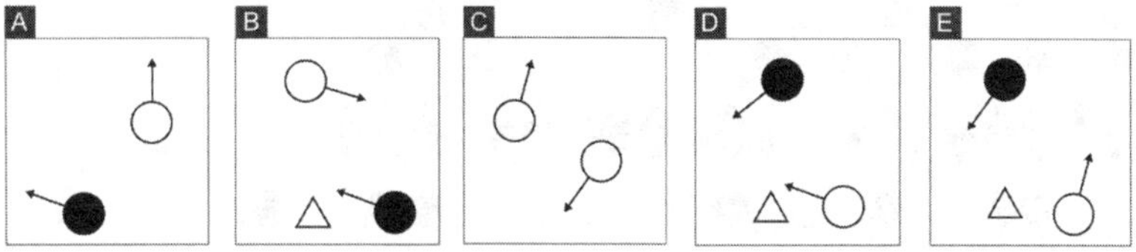

66 Which figure completes the series below?

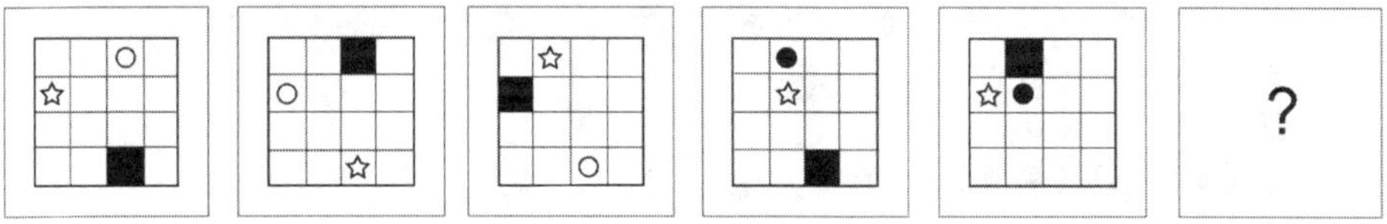

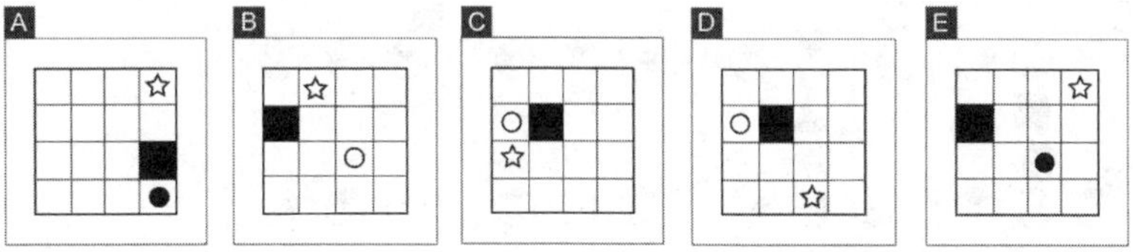

67 Which figure completes the series below?

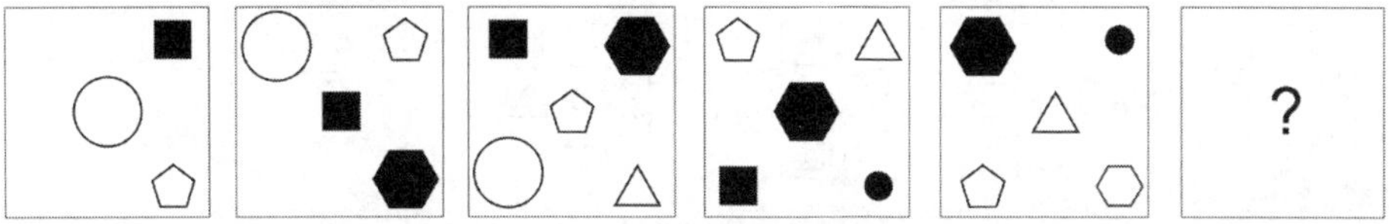

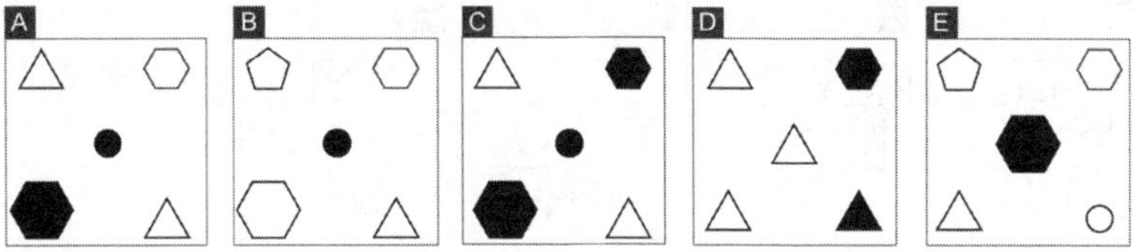

68 Which figure completes the series below?

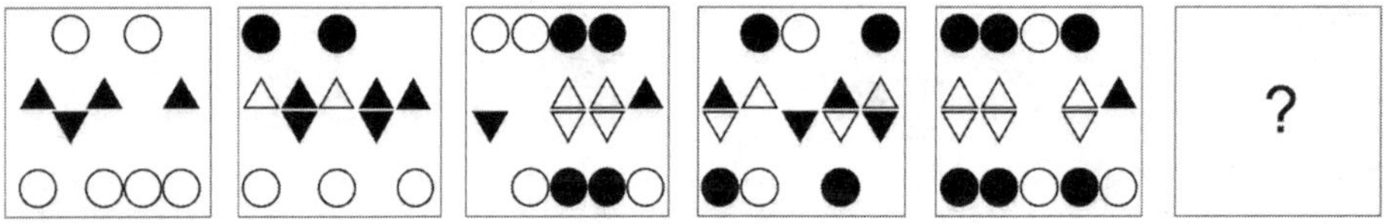

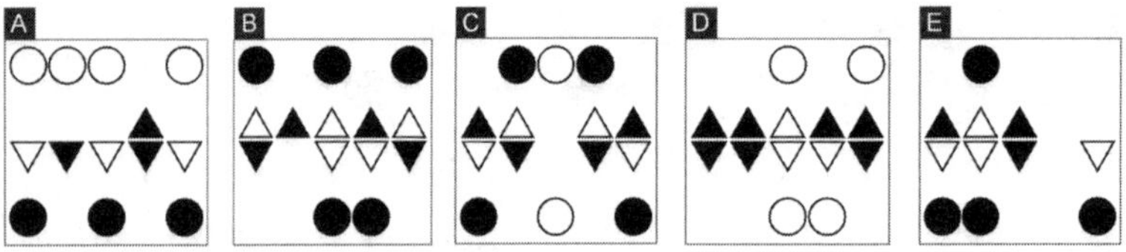

69 Which figure completes the series below?

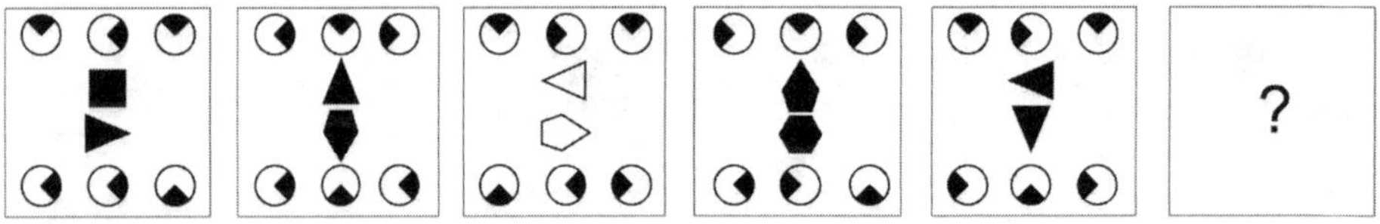

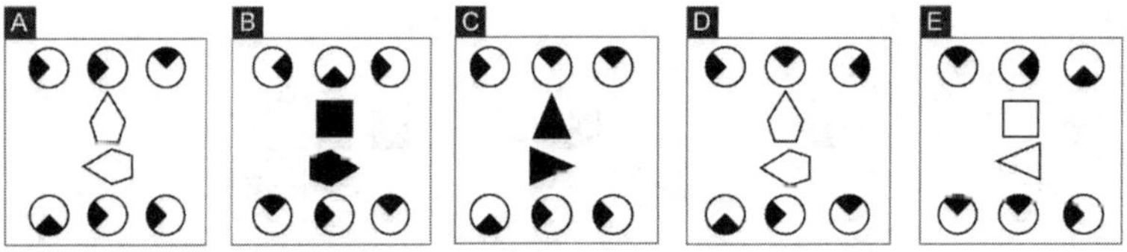

70 Which figure completes the series below?

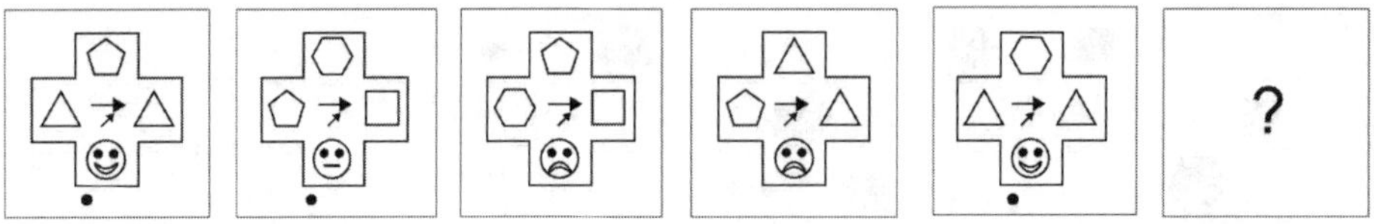

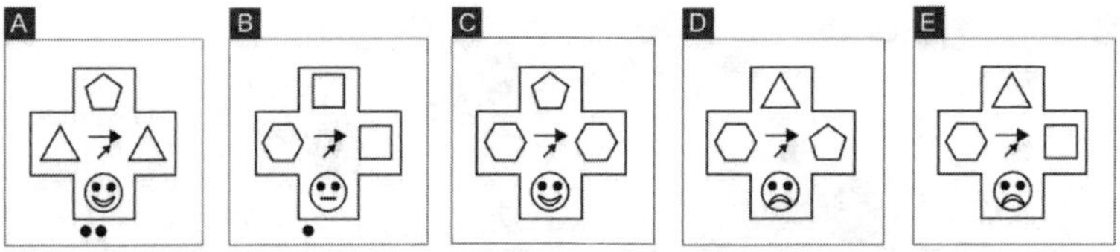

71 Which figure completes the series below?

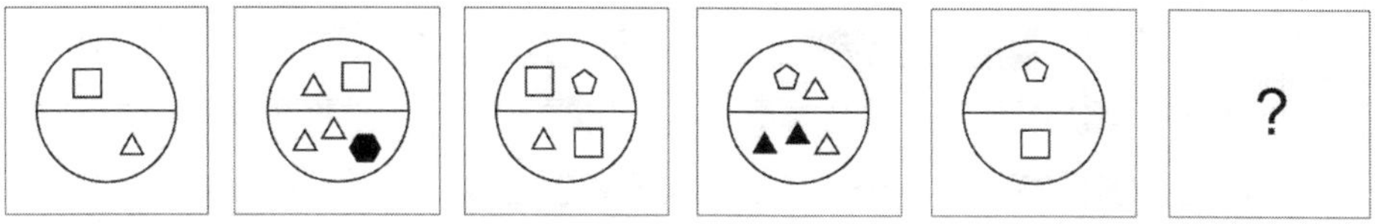

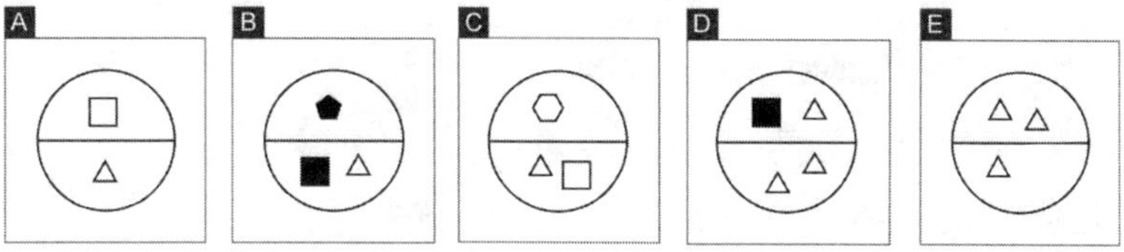

72 Which figure completes the series below?

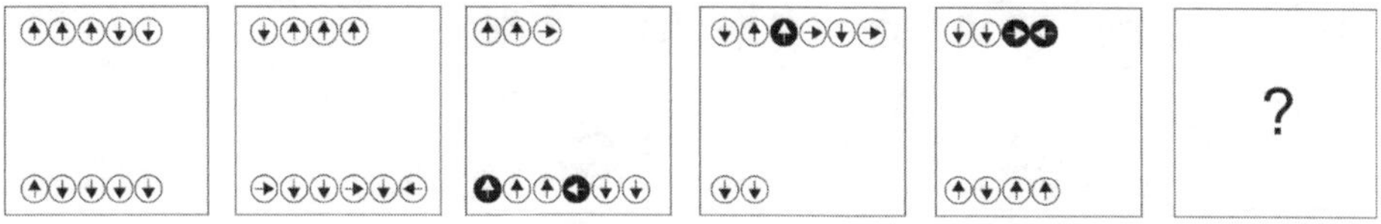

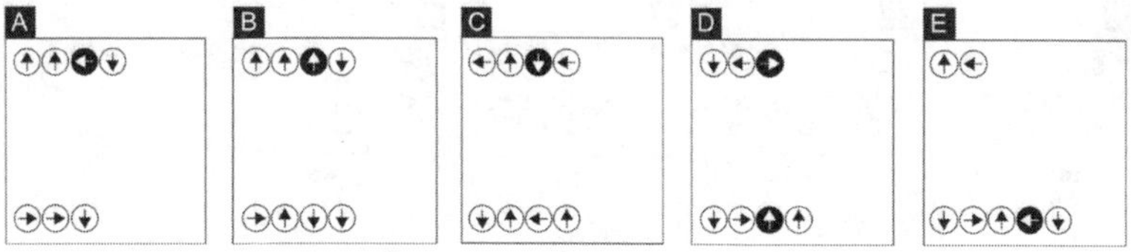

73 Which figure completes the series below?

74 Which figure completes the series below?

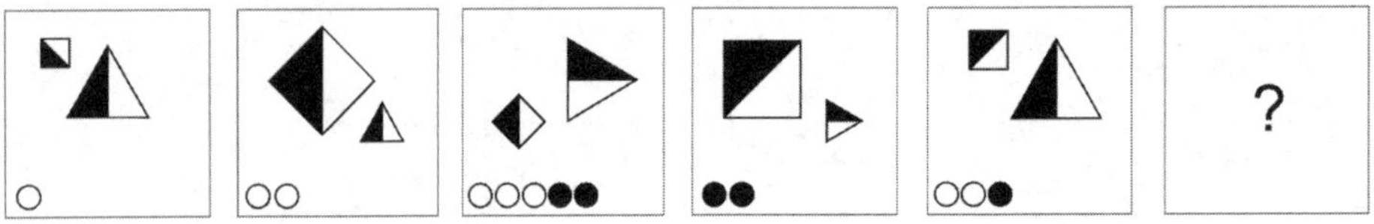

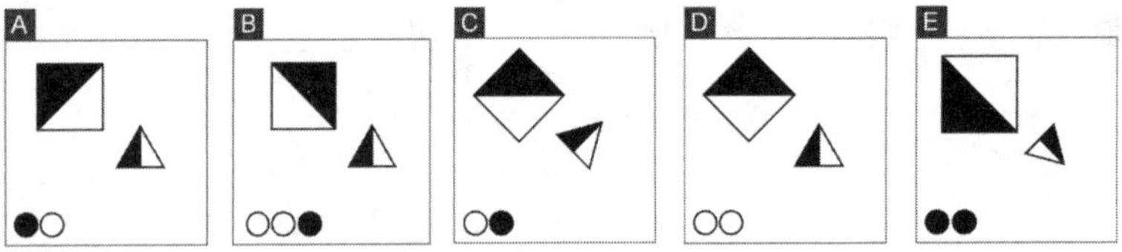

75 Which figure completes the series below?

76 Which figure completes the series below?

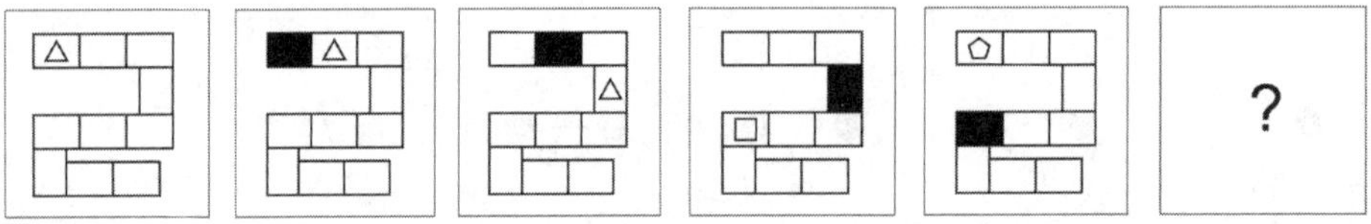

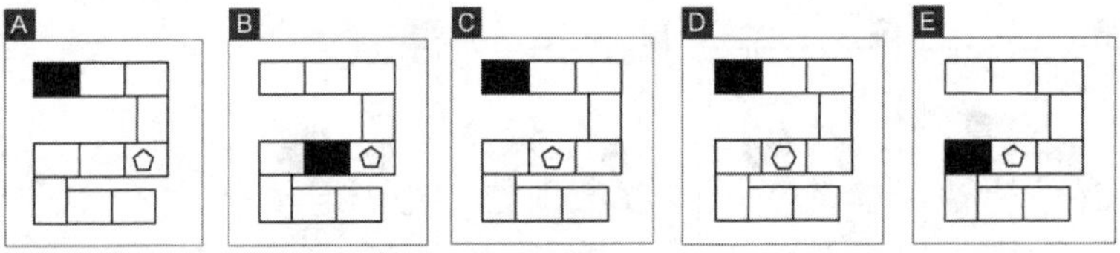

77 Which figure completes the series below?

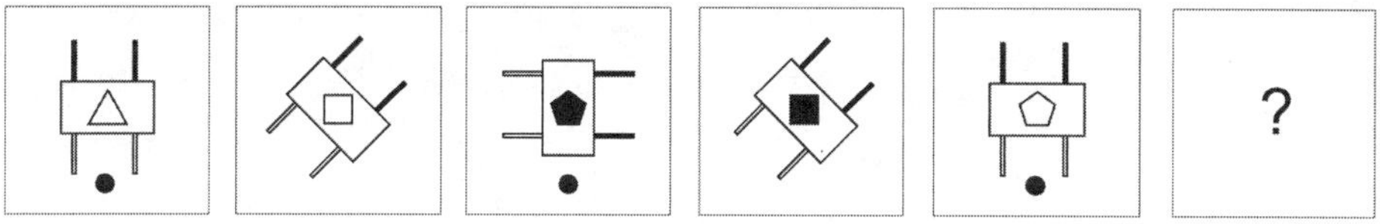

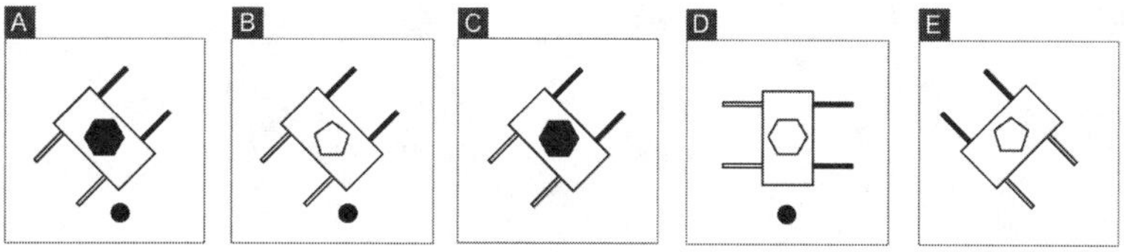

78 Which figure completes the series below?

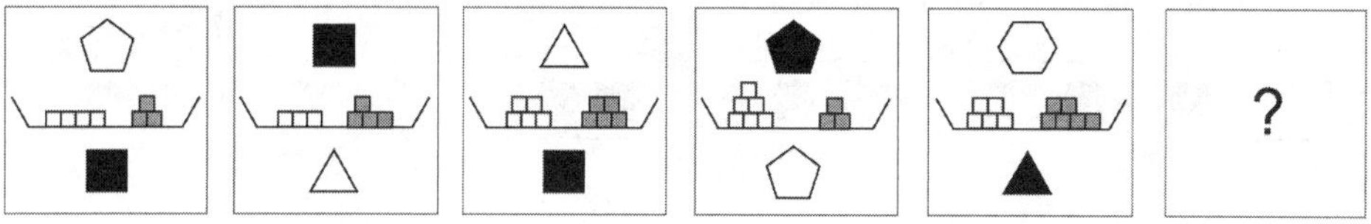

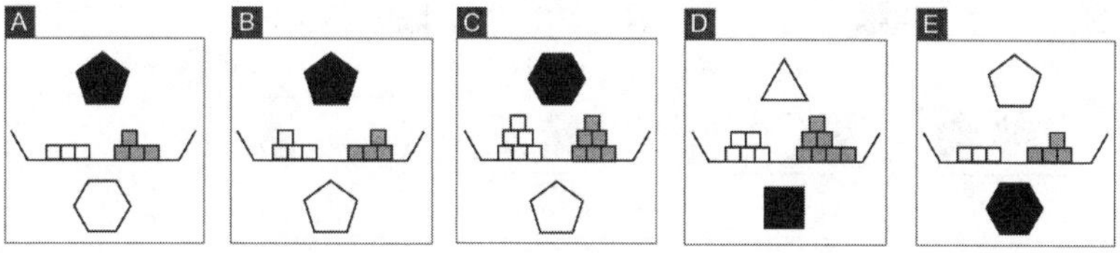

79 Which figure completes the series below?

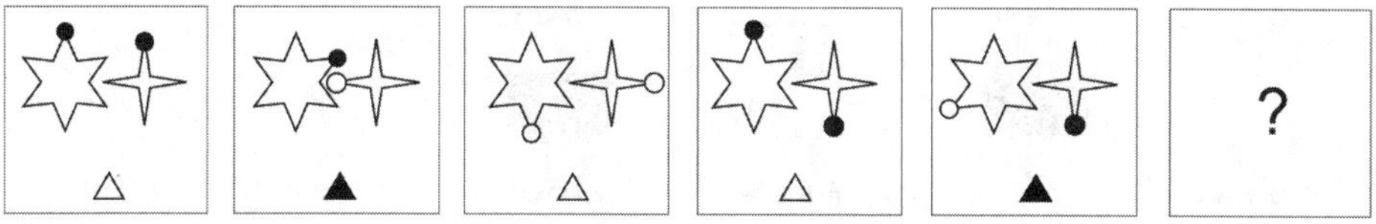

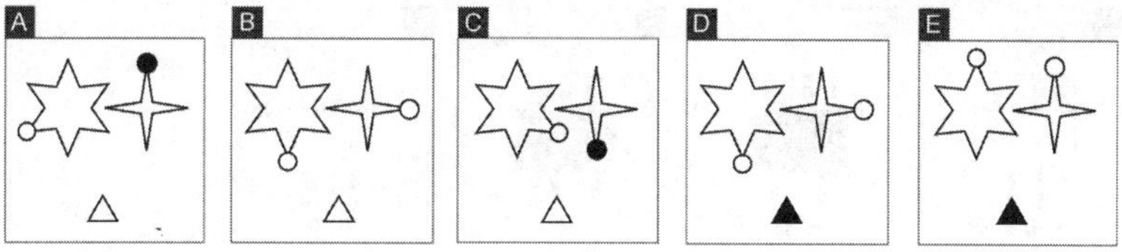

80 Which figure completes the series below?

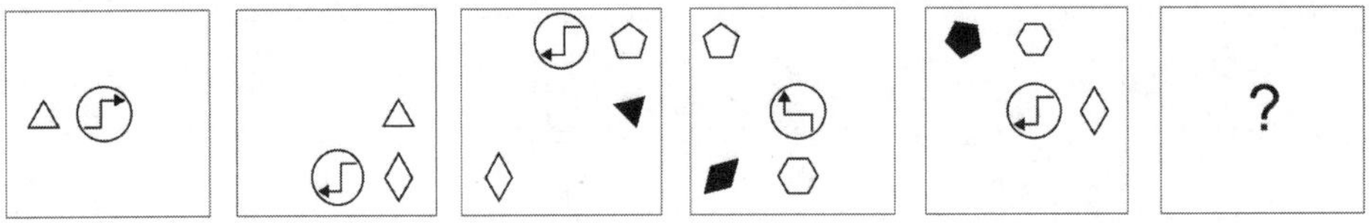

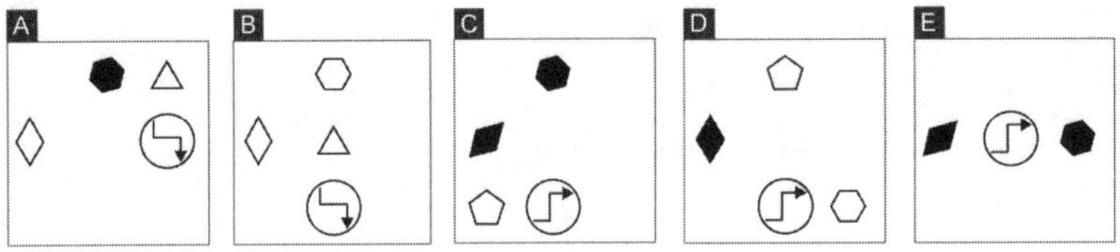

81 Which figure completes the series below?

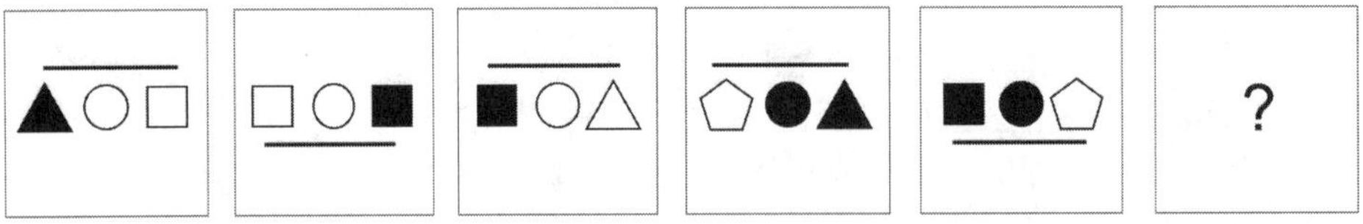

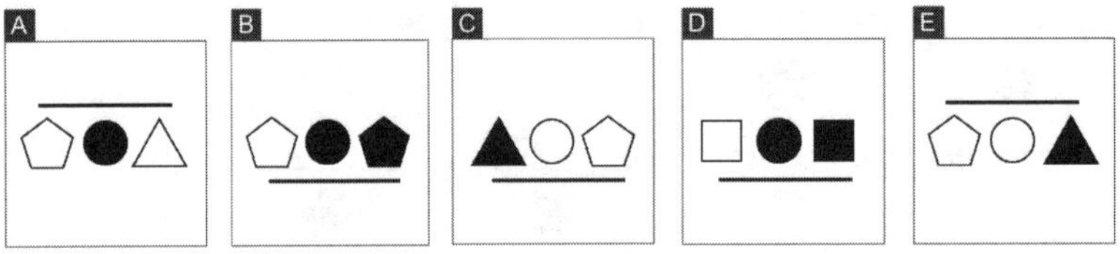

82 Which figure completes the series below?

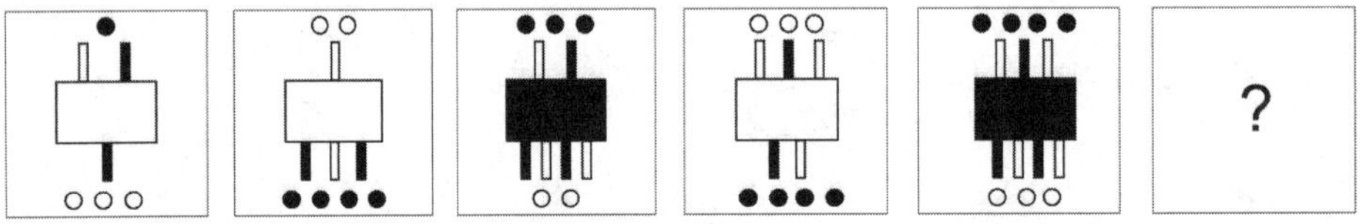

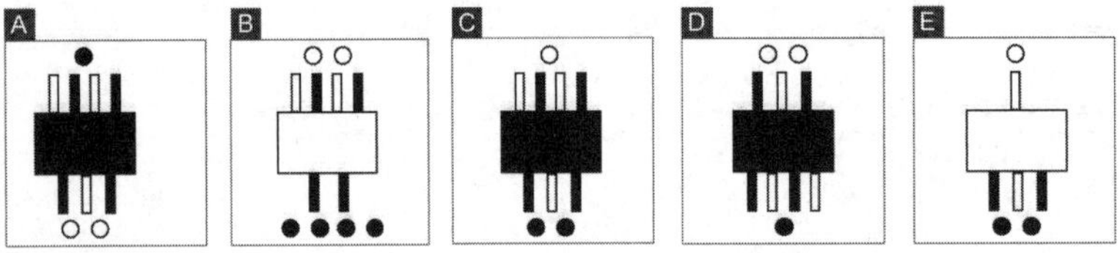

83 Which figure completes the series below?

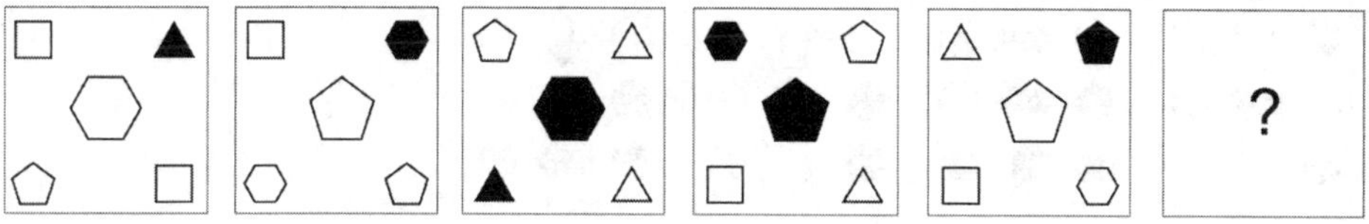

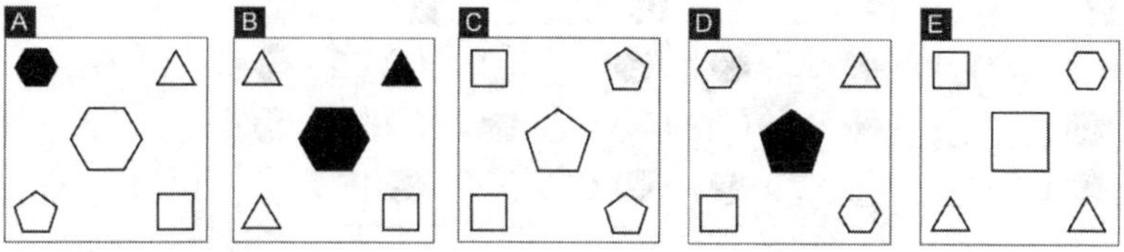

84 Which figure completes the series below?

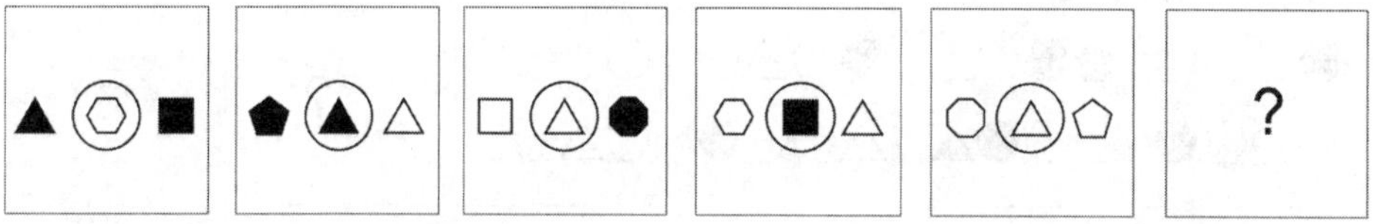

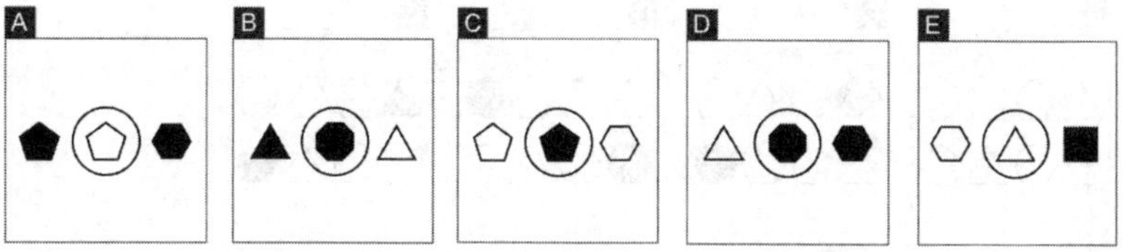

85 Which figure completes the series below?

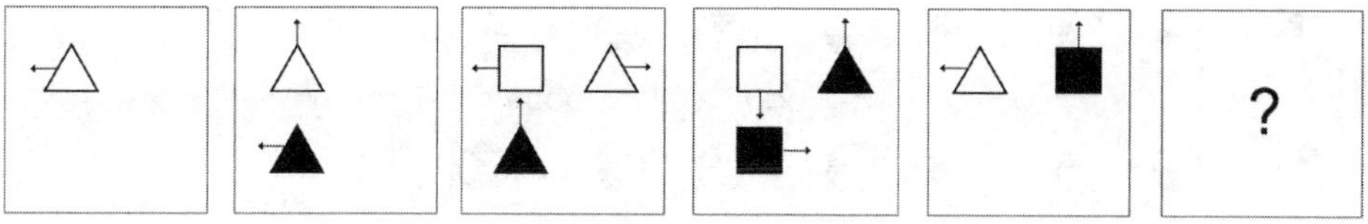

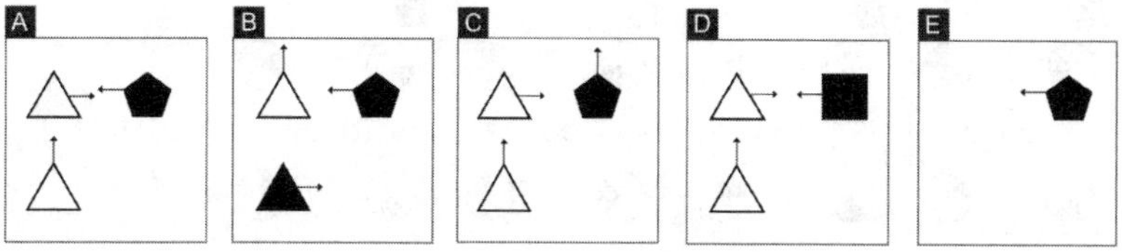

86 Which figure completes the series below?

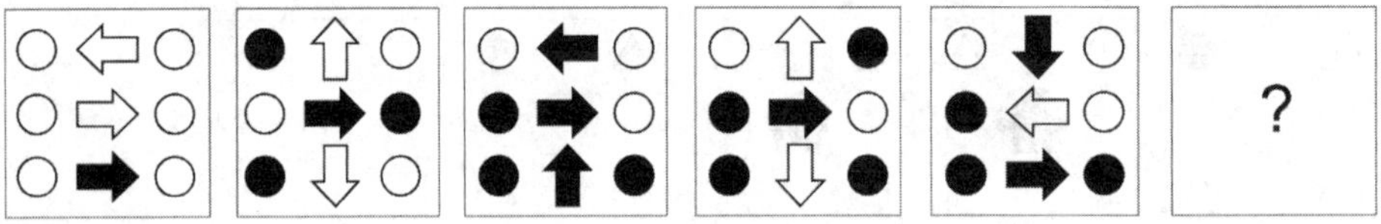

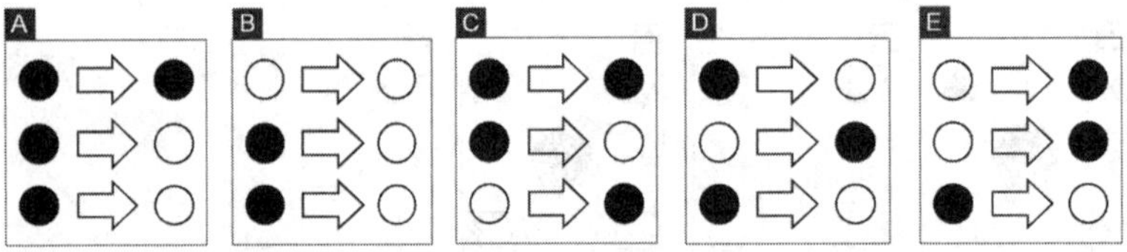

87 Which figure completes the series below?

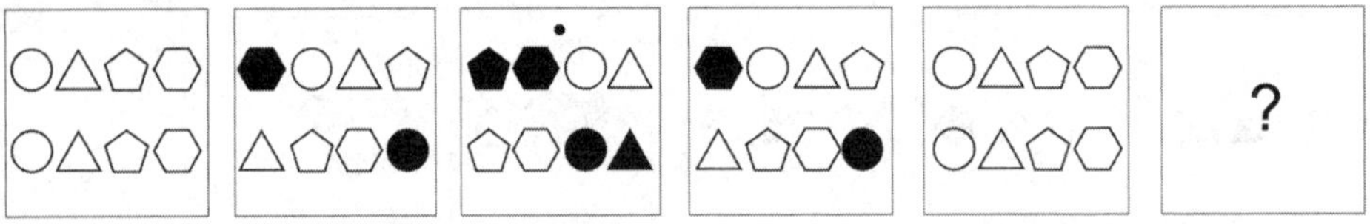

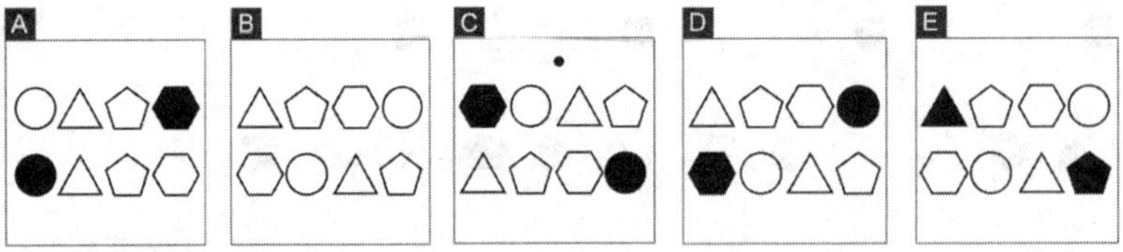

88 Which figure completes the series below?

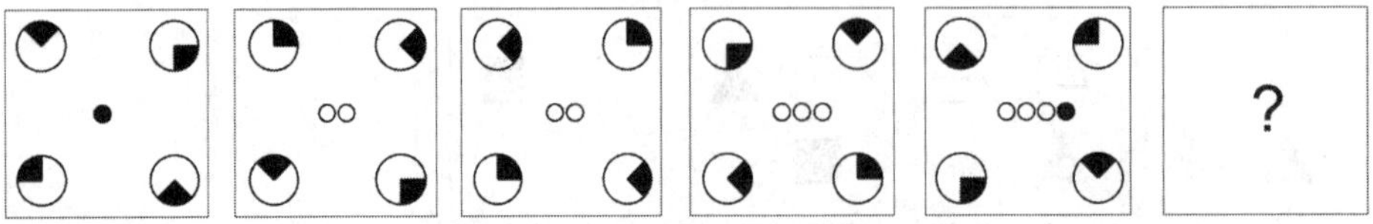

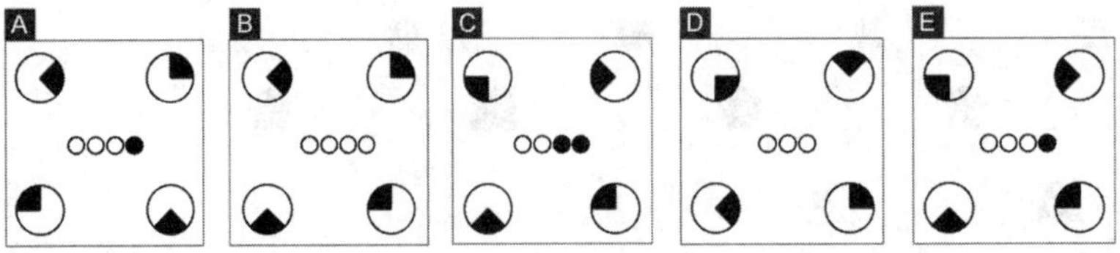

89 Which figure completes the series below?

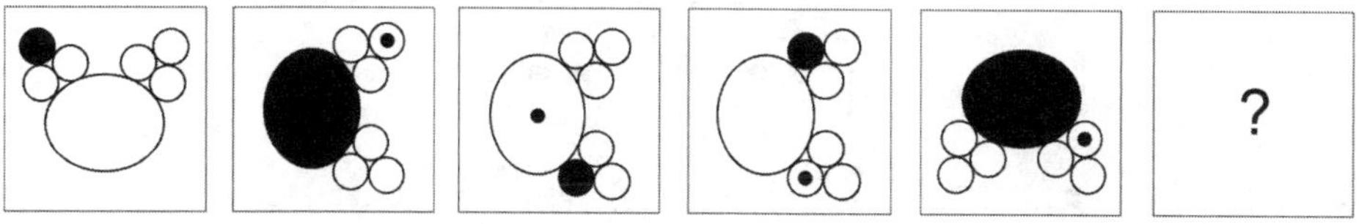

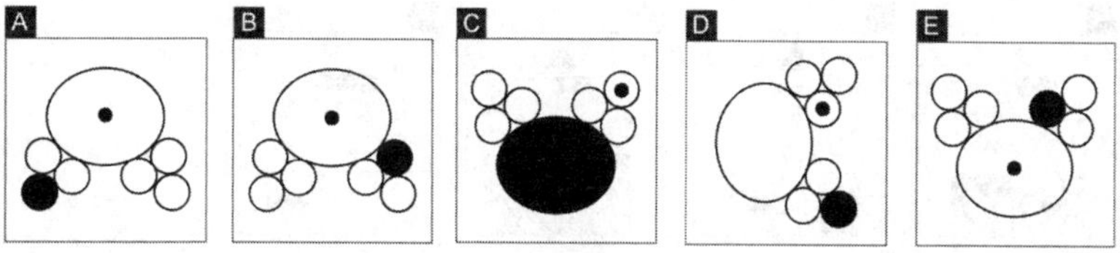

90 Which figure completes the series below?

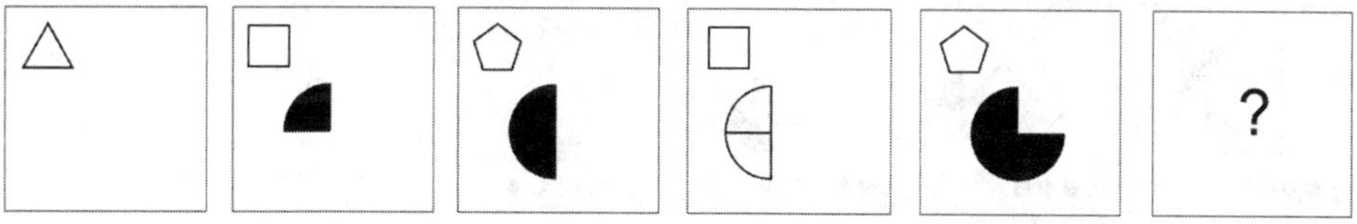

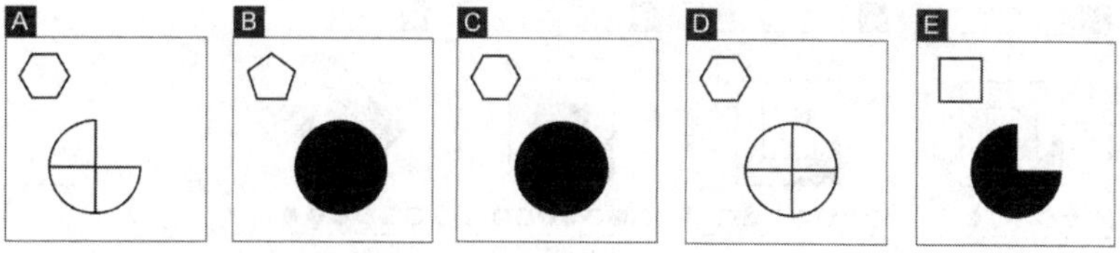

91 Which figure completes the series below?

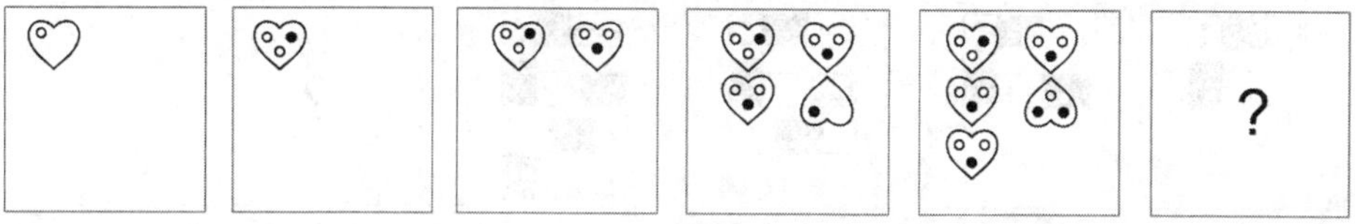

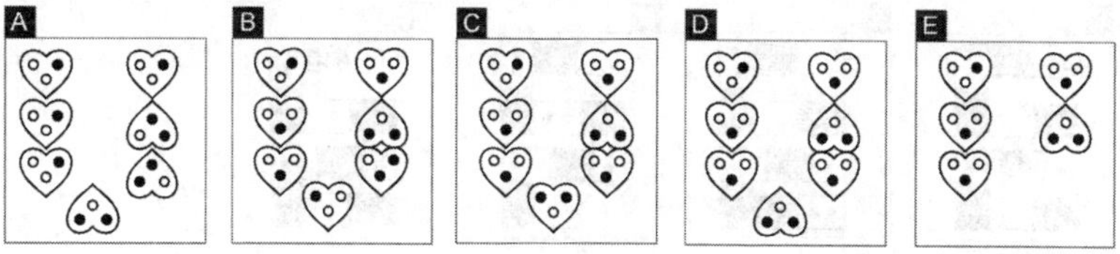

92 Which figure completes the series below?

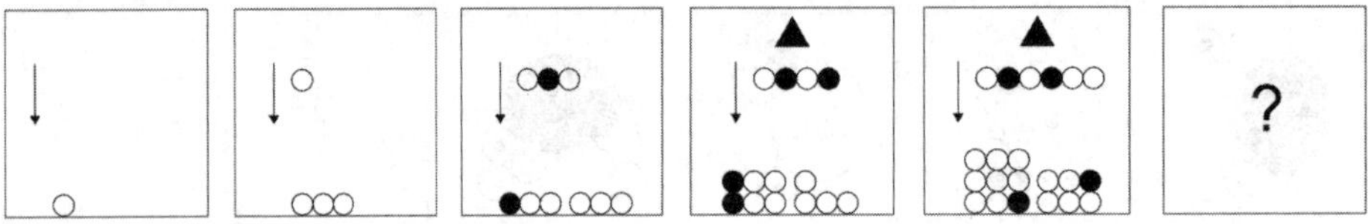

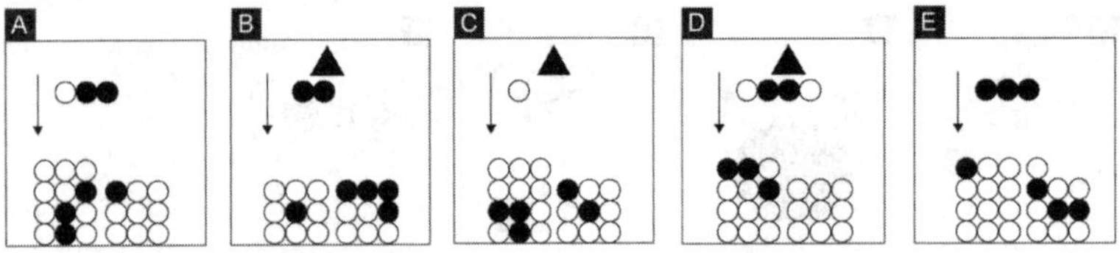

93 Which figure completes the series below?

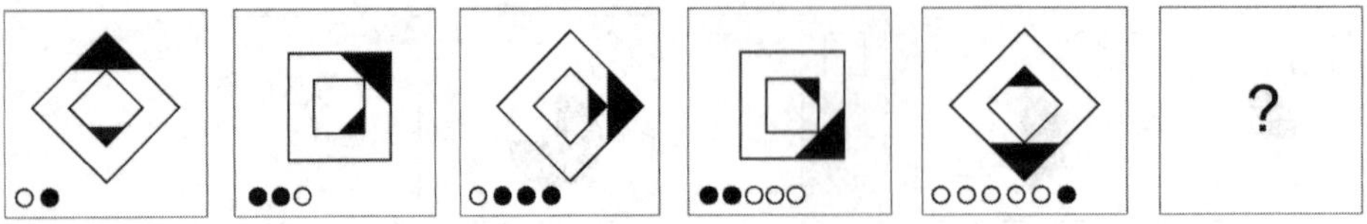

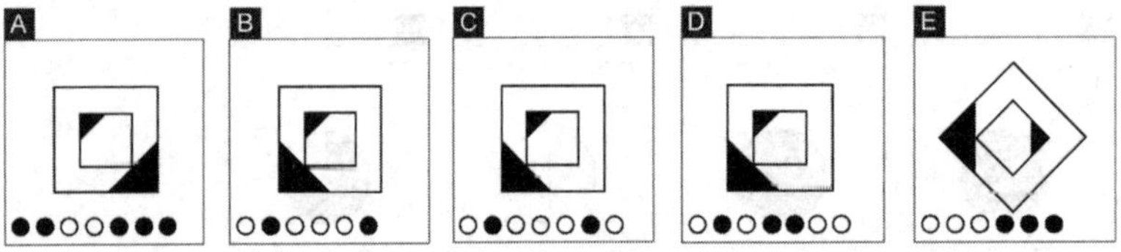

94 Which figure completes the series below?

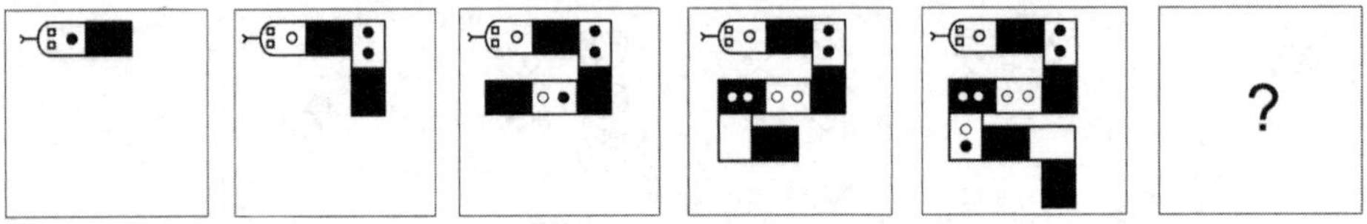

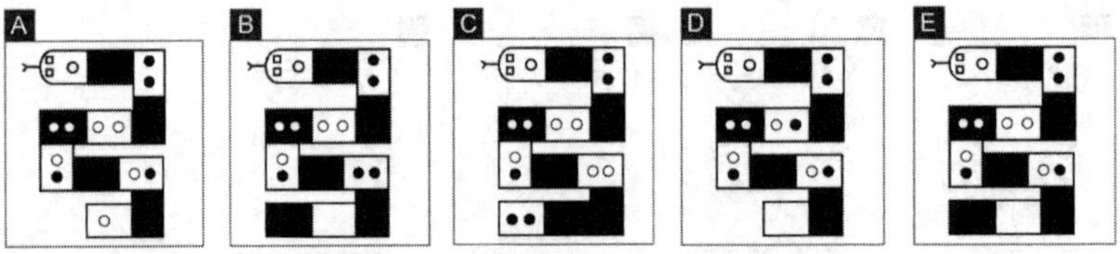

95 Which figure completes the series below?

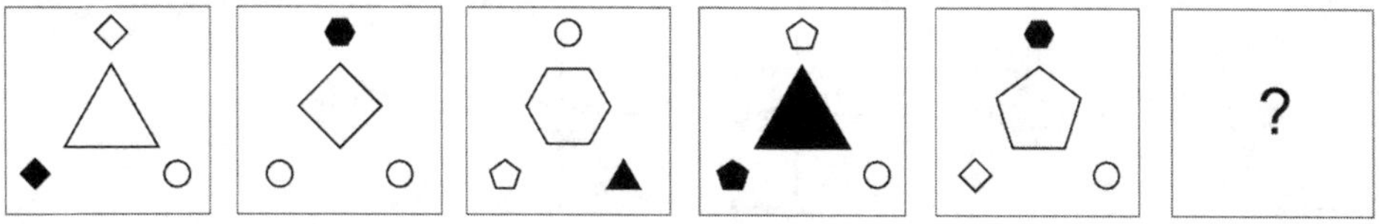

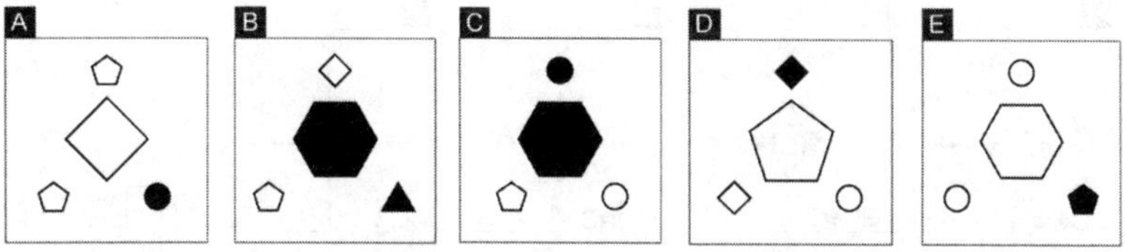

96 Which figure completes the series below?

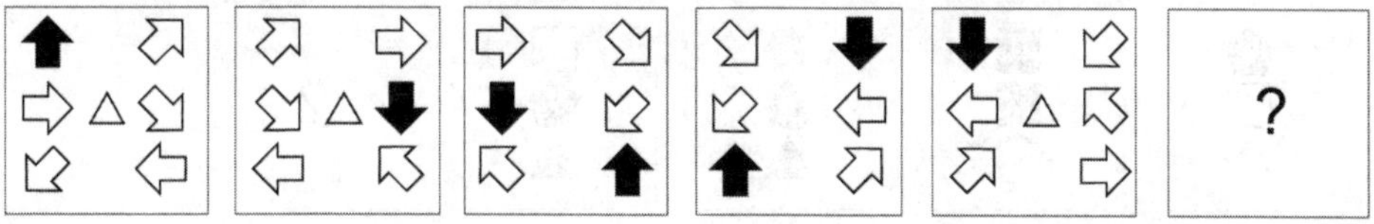

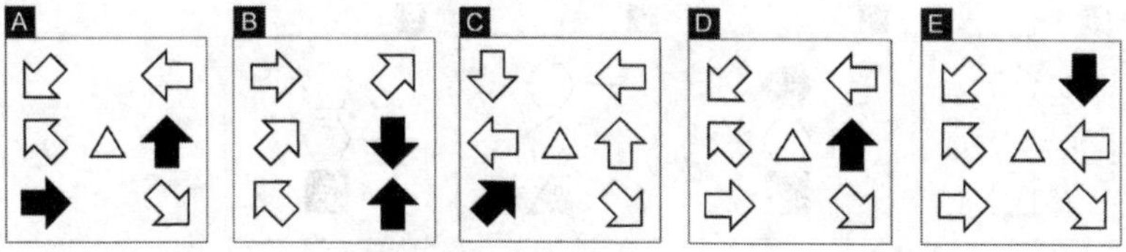

97 Which figure completes the series below?

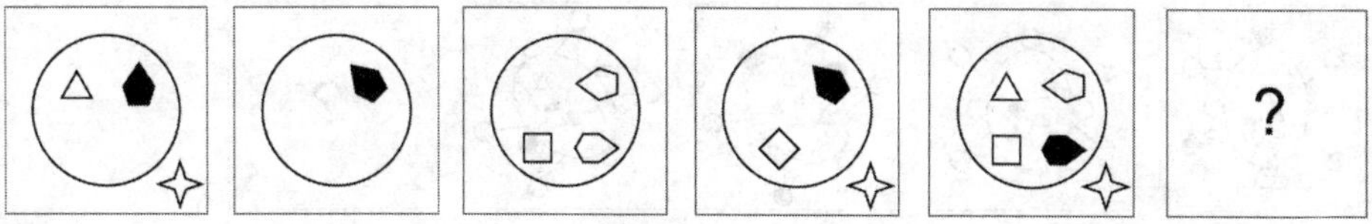

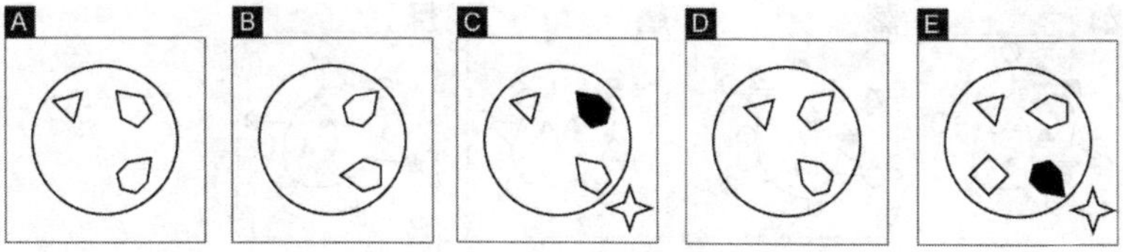

98 Which figure completes the series below?

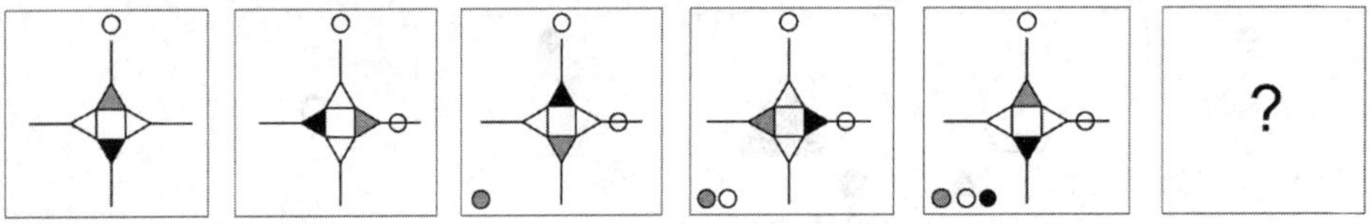

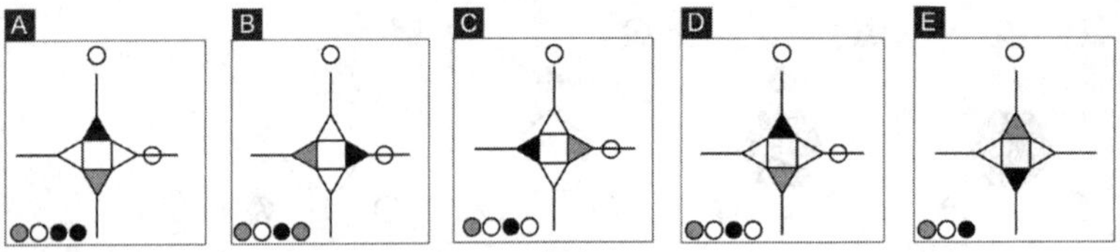

99 Which figure completes the series below?

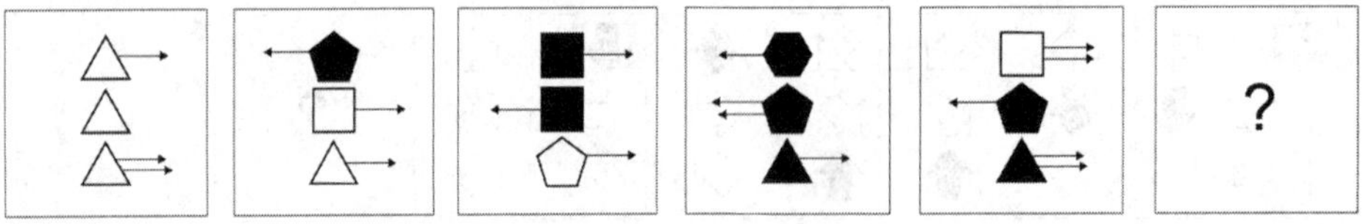

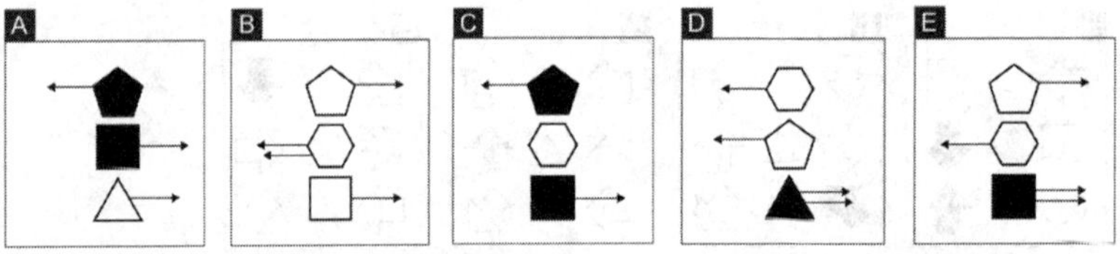

100 Which figure completes the series below?

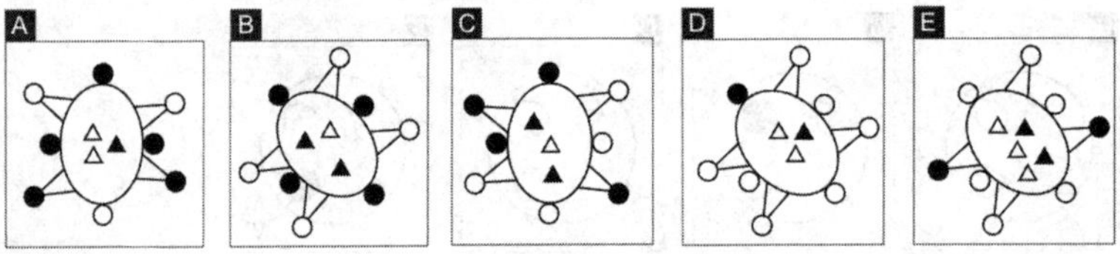

101 Which figure completes the series below?

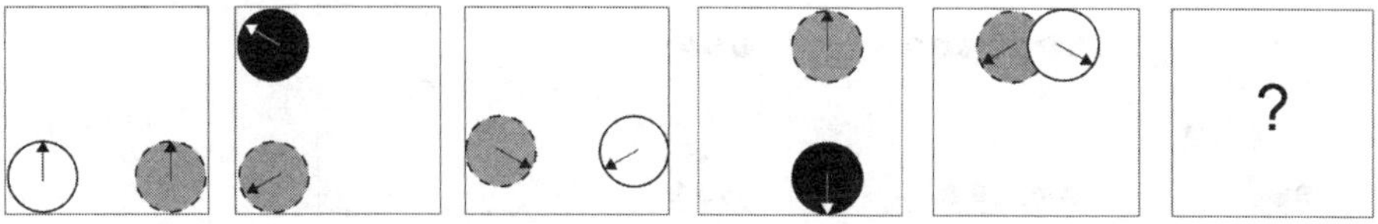

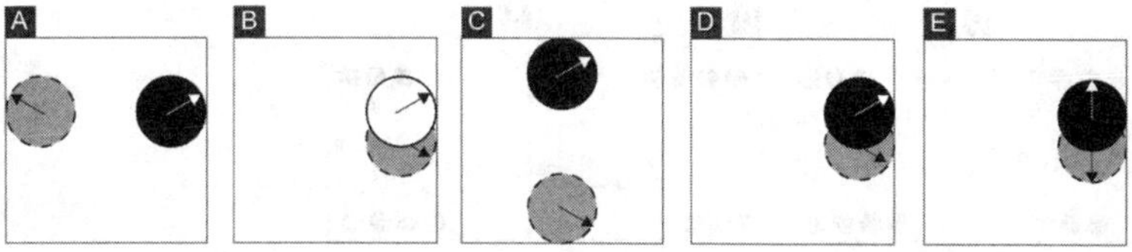

102 Which figure completes the series below?

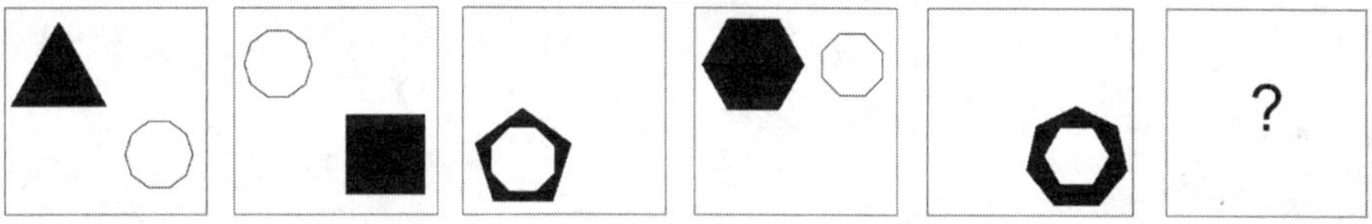

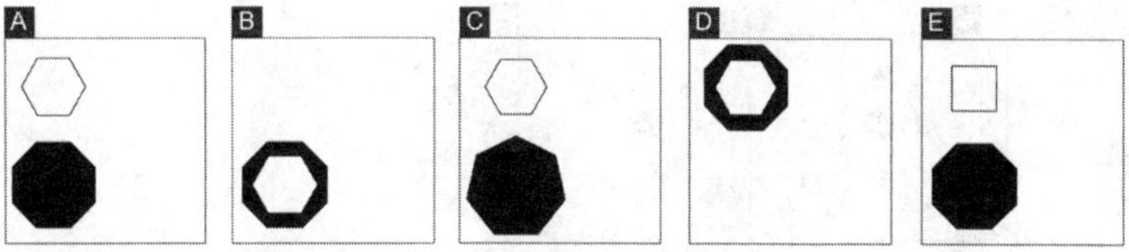

103 Which figure completes the series below?

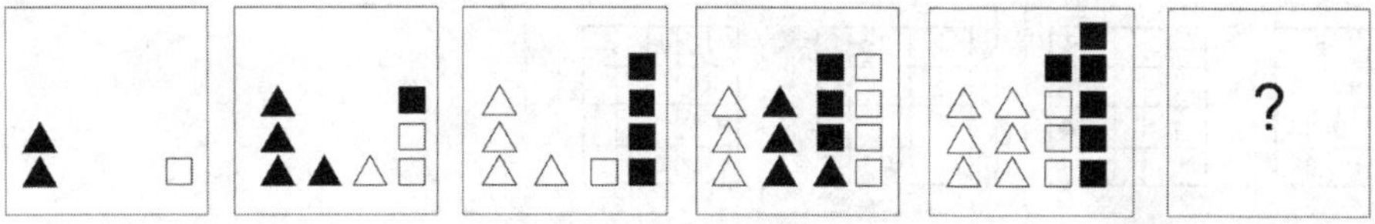

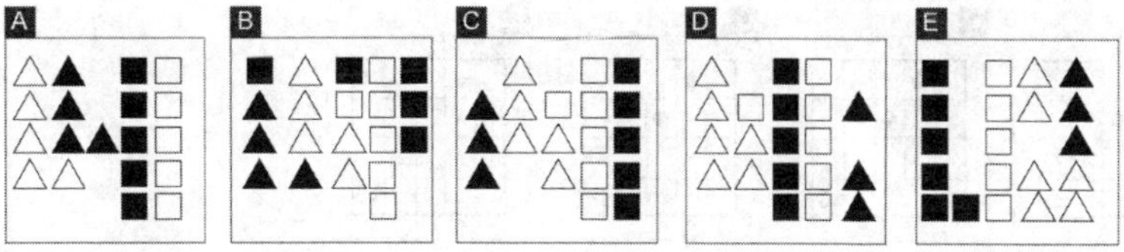

104 Which figure completes the series below?

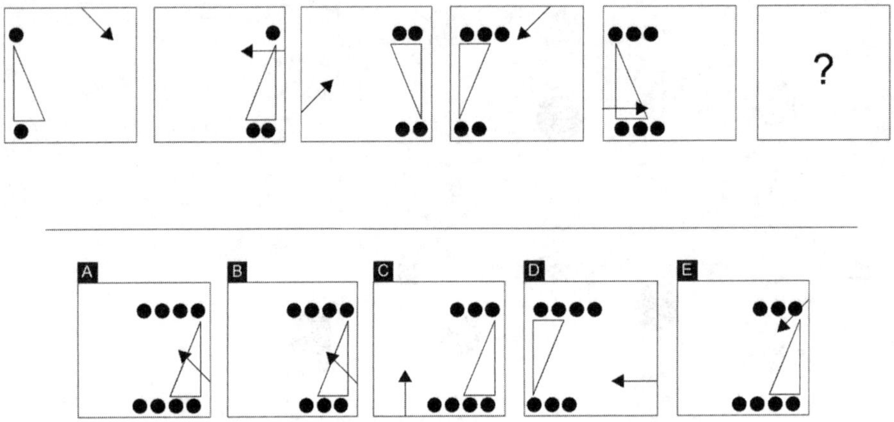

105 Which figure completes the series below?

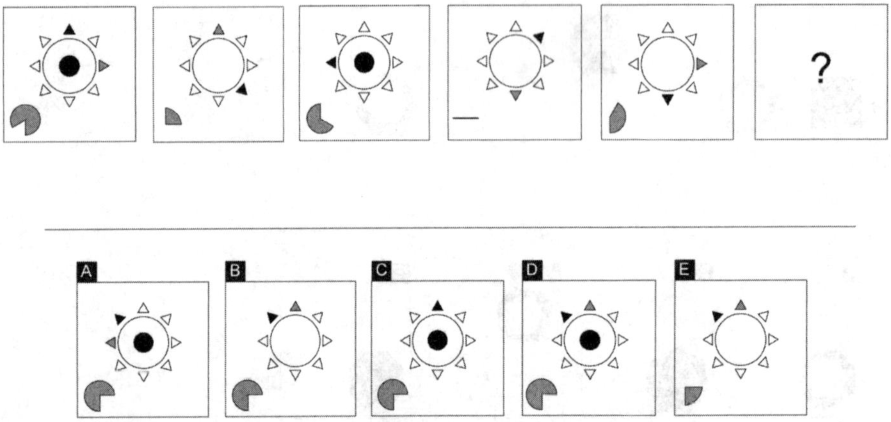

106 Which figure completes the series below?

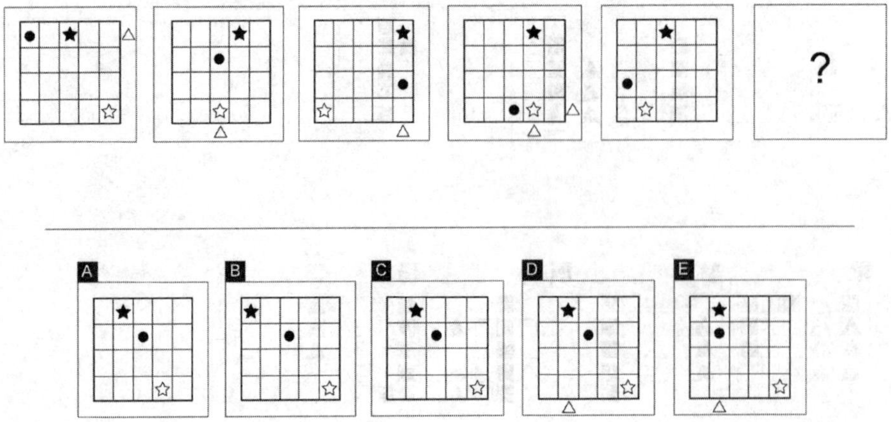

107 Which figure completes the series below?

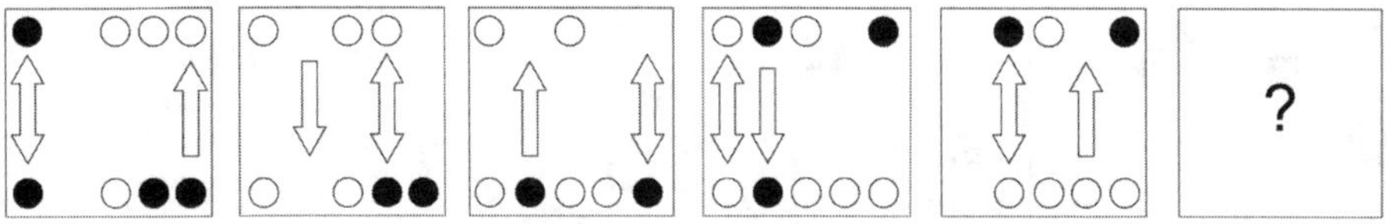

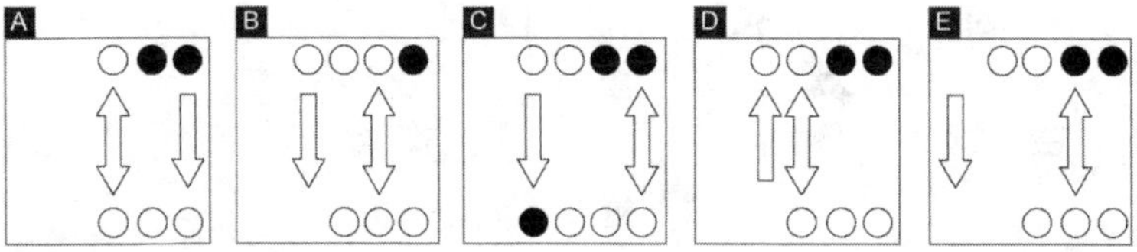

108 Which figure completes the series below?

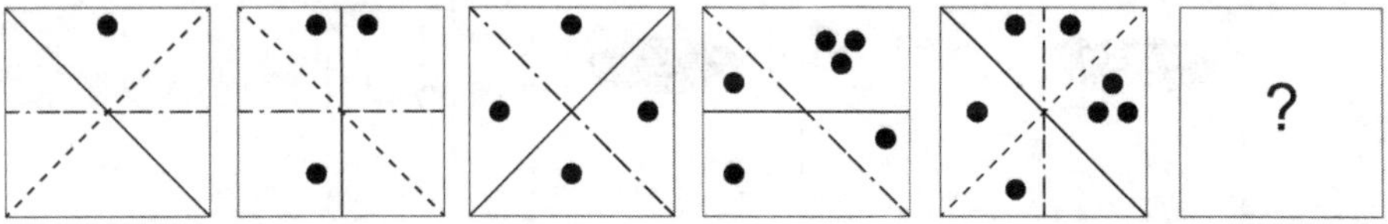

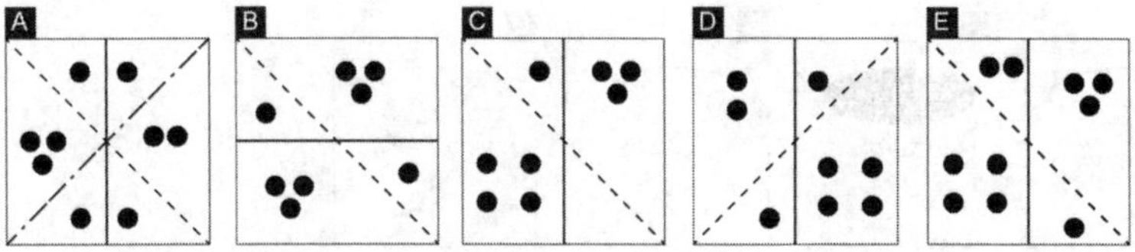

109 Which figure completes the series below?

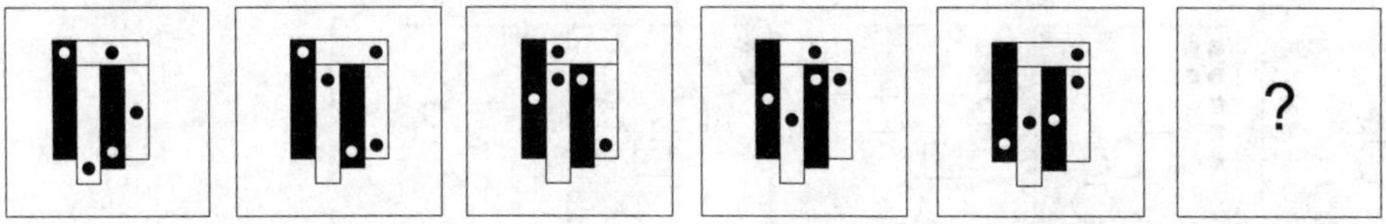

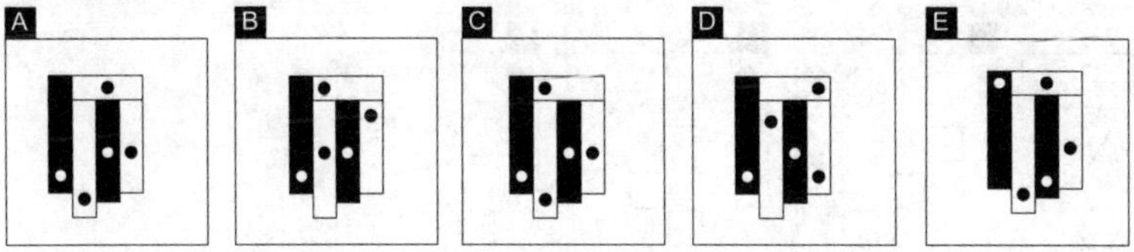

110 Which figure completes the series below?

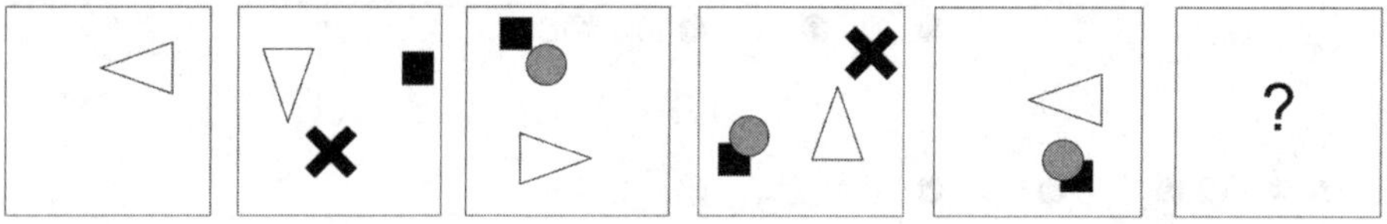

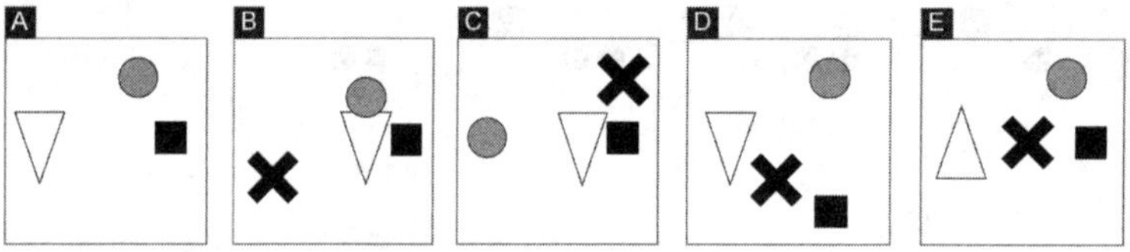

111 Which figure completes the series below?

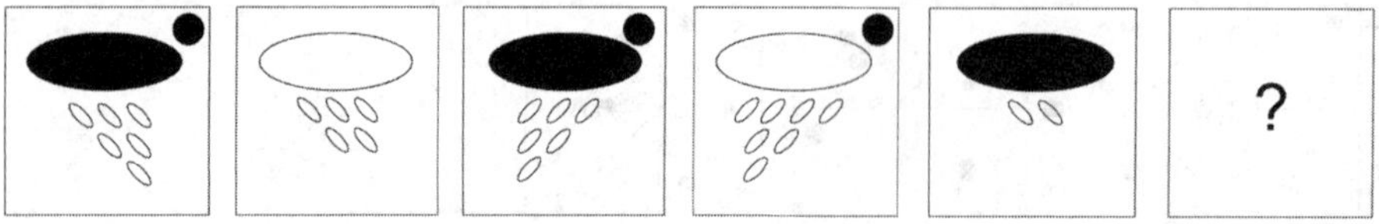

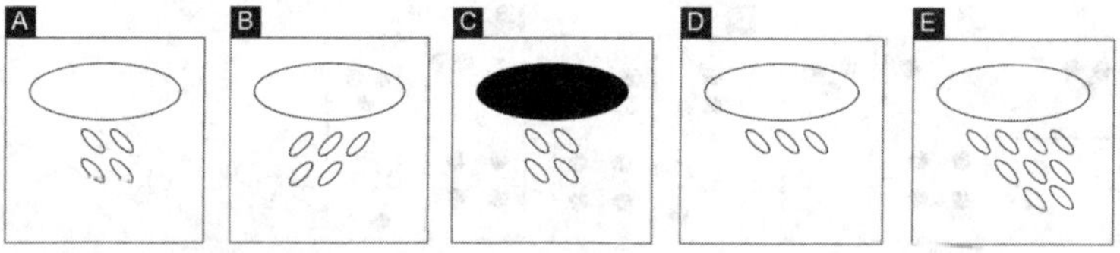

112 Which figure completes the series below?

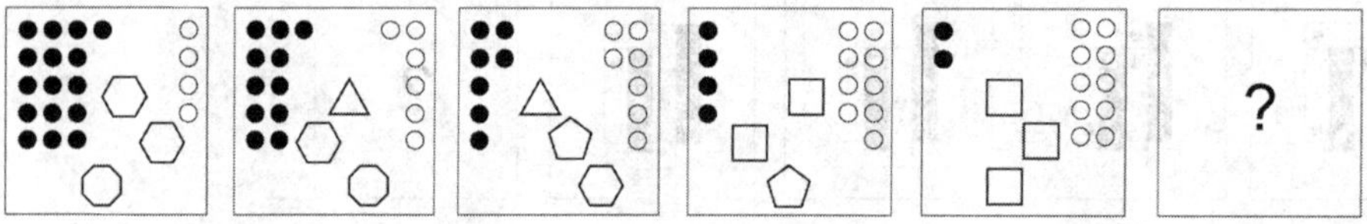

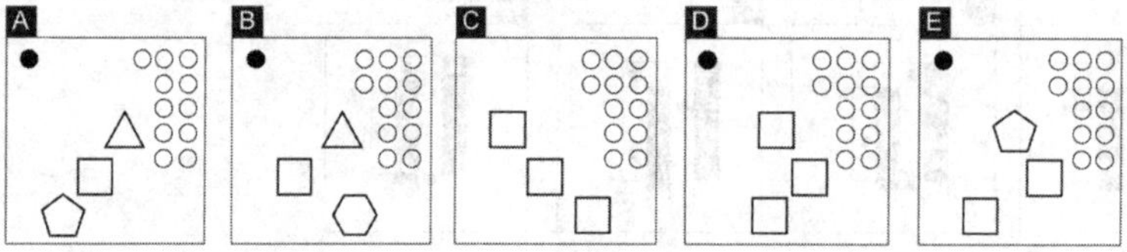

113 Which figure completes the series below?

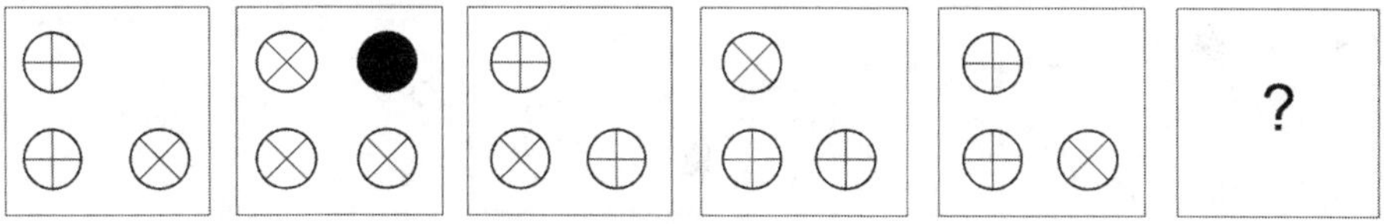

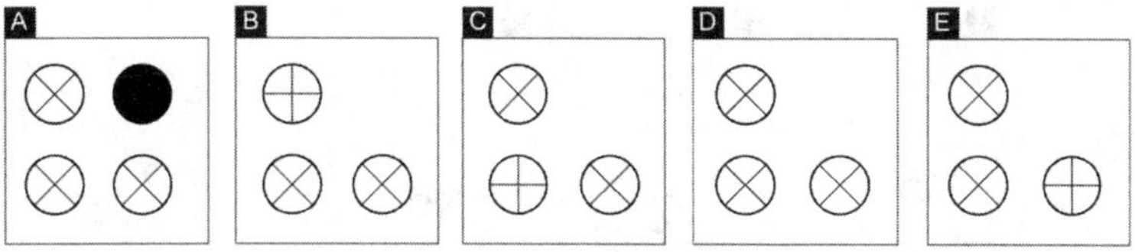

114 Which figure completes the series below?

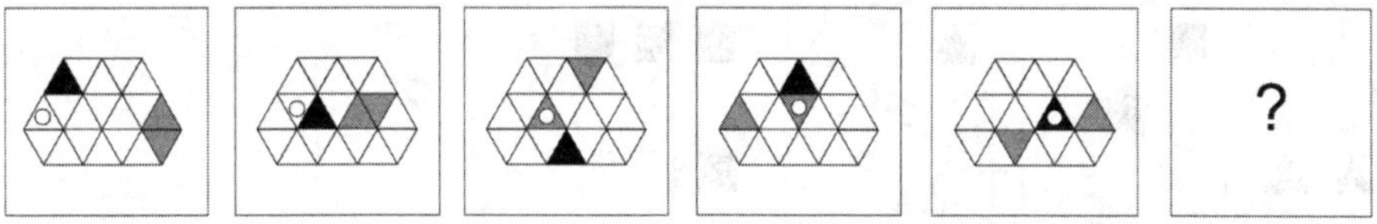

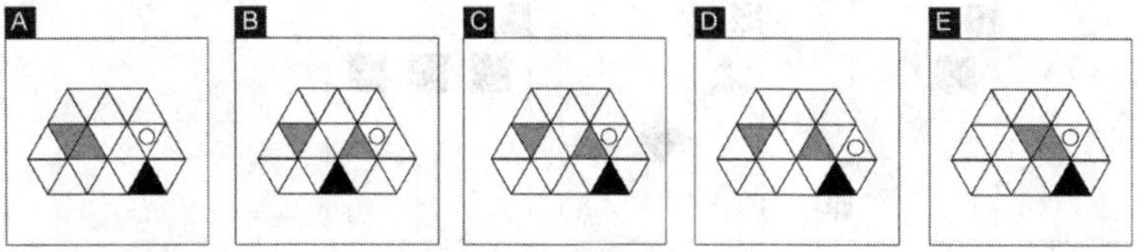

115 Which figure completes the series below?

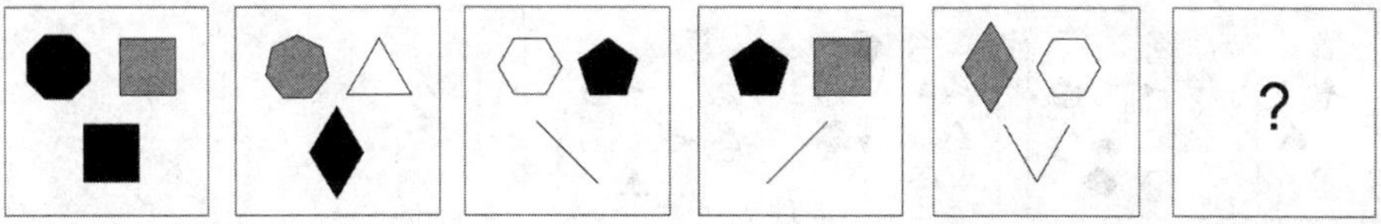

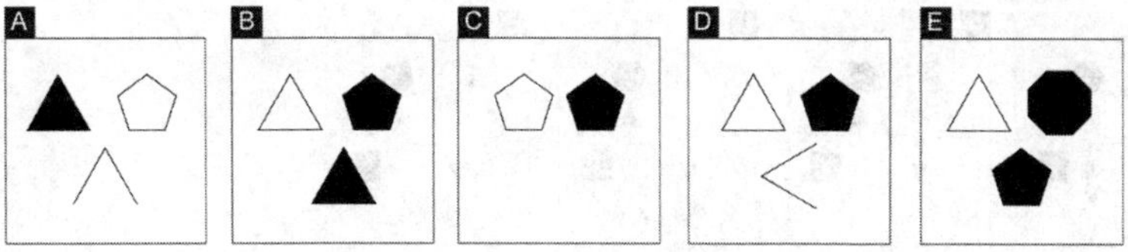

116 Which figure completes the series below?

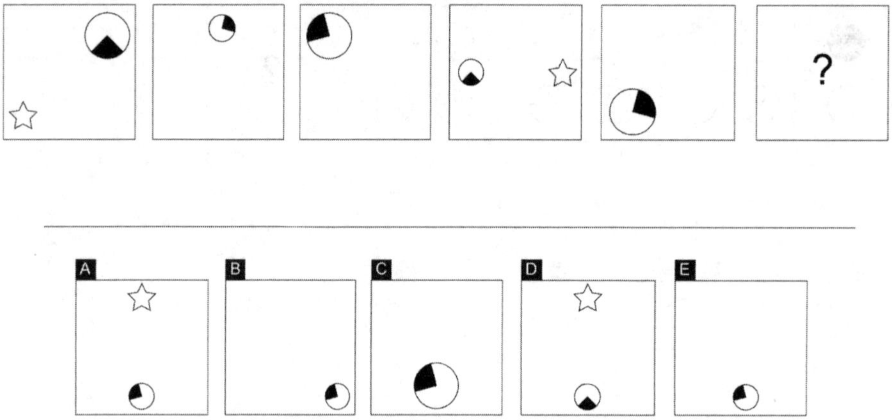

117 Which figure completes the series below?

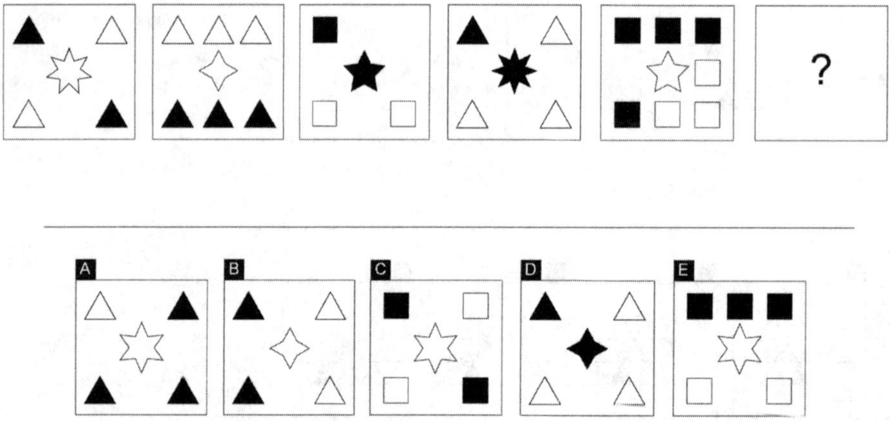

118 Which figure completes the series below?

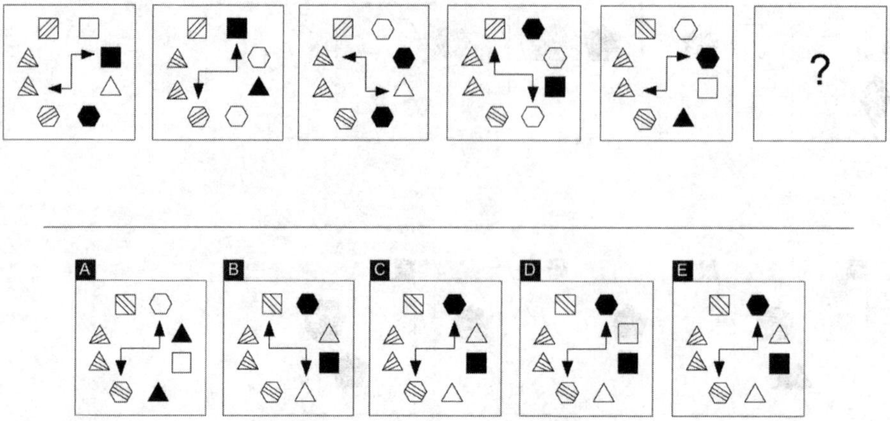

119 Which figure completes the series below?

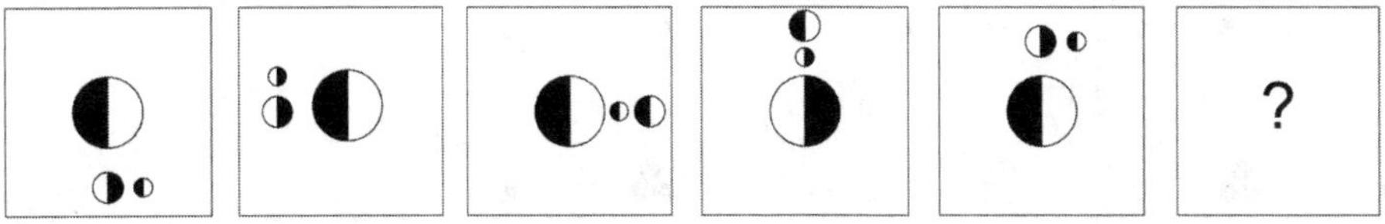

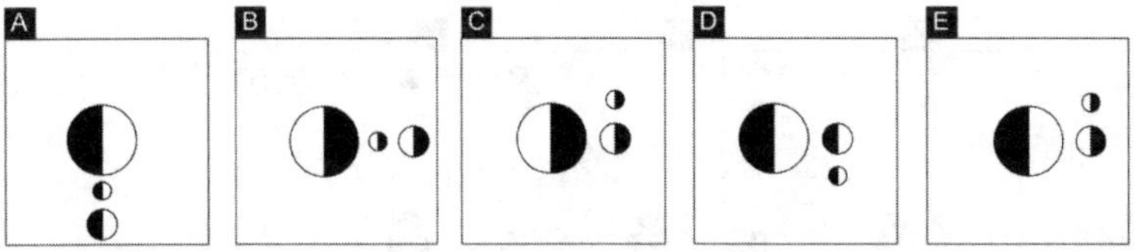

120 Which figure completes the series below?

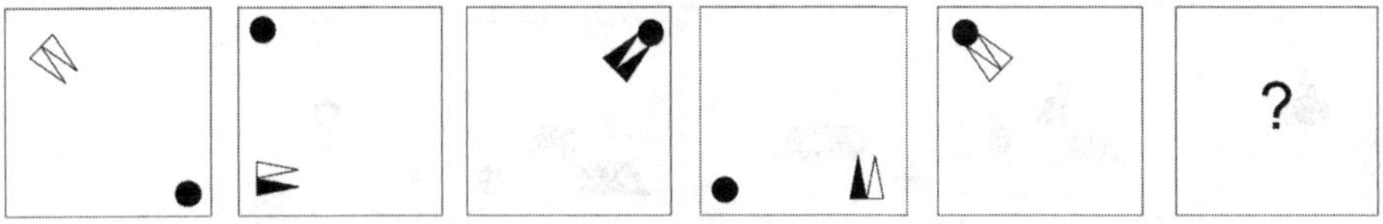

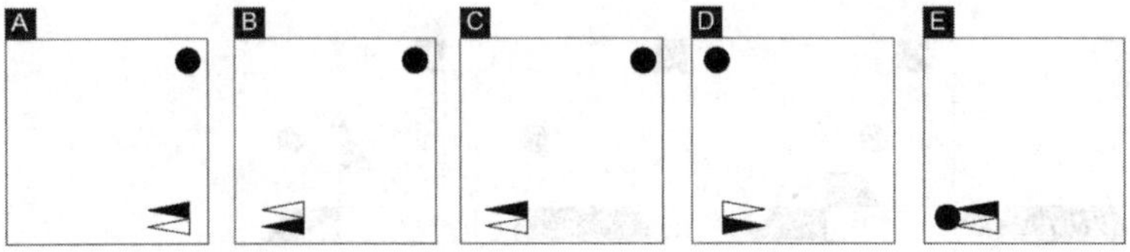

121 Which figure completes the series below?

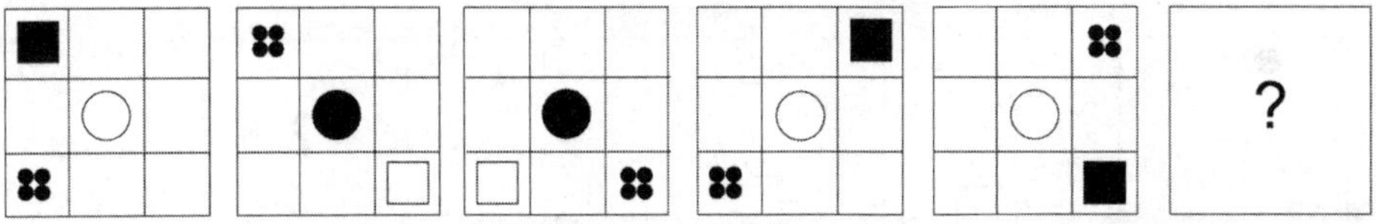

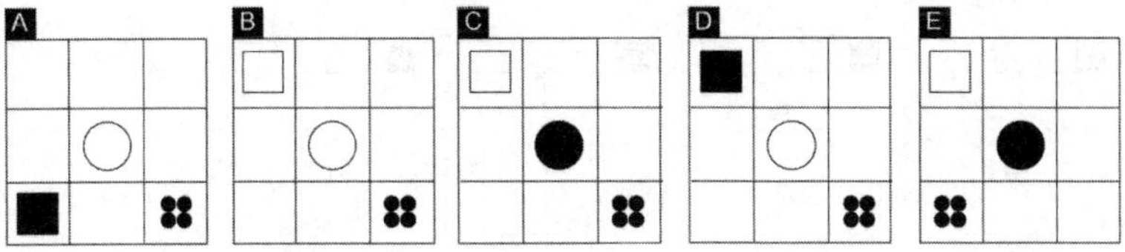

122 Which figure completes the series below?

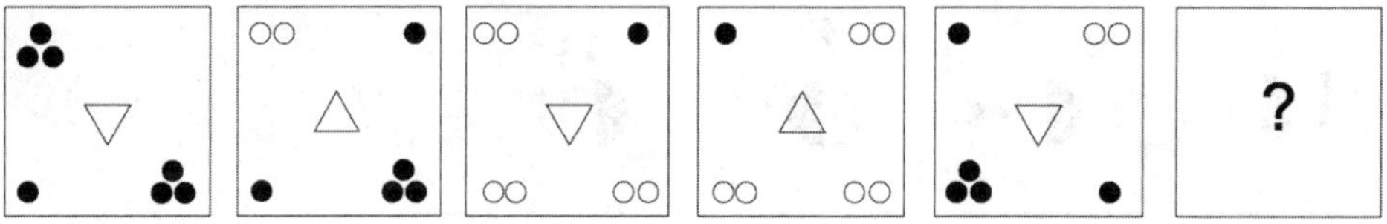

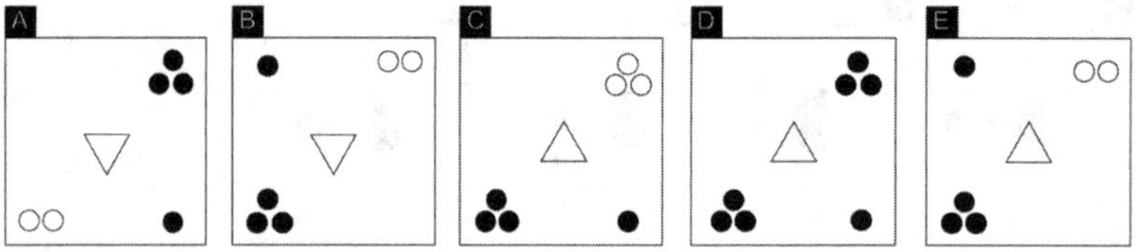

123 Which figure completes the series below?

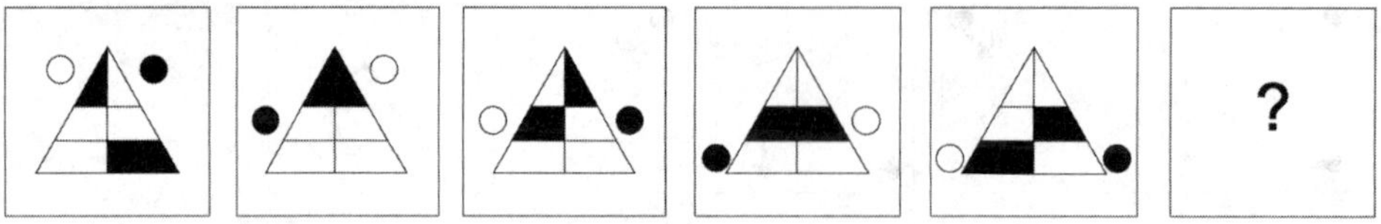

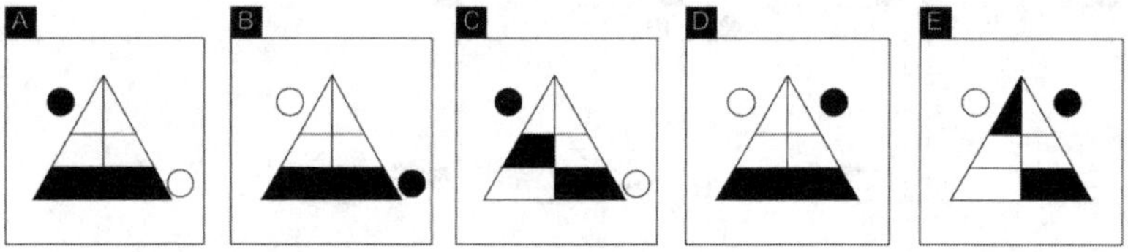

124 Which figure completes the series below?

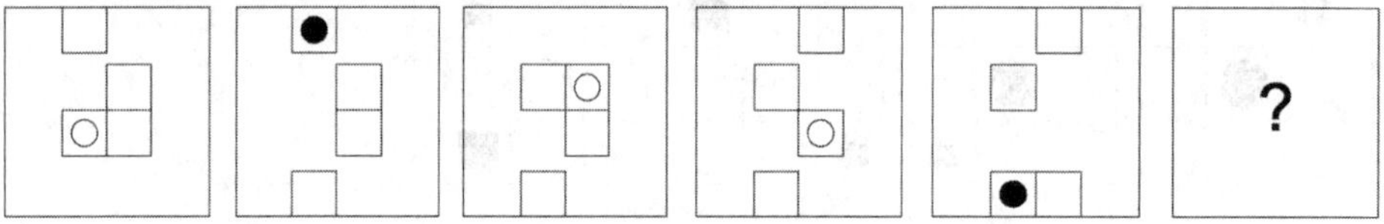

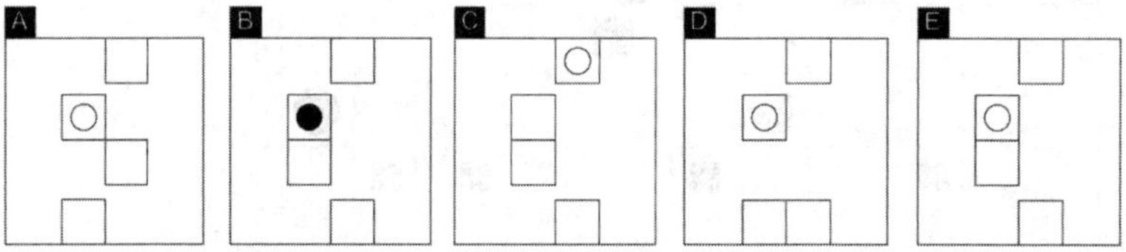

125 Which figure completes the series below?

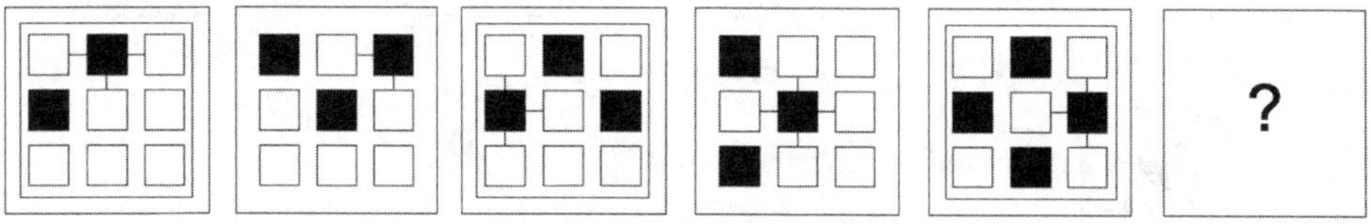

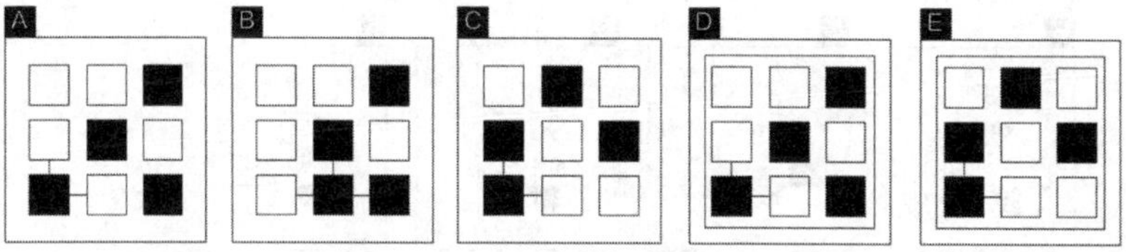

126 Which figure completes the series below?

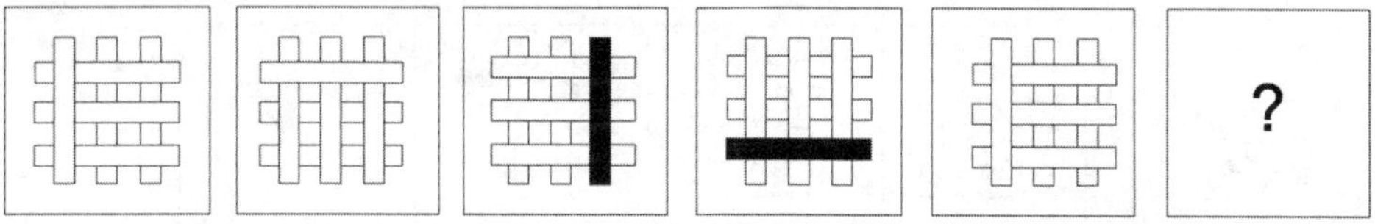

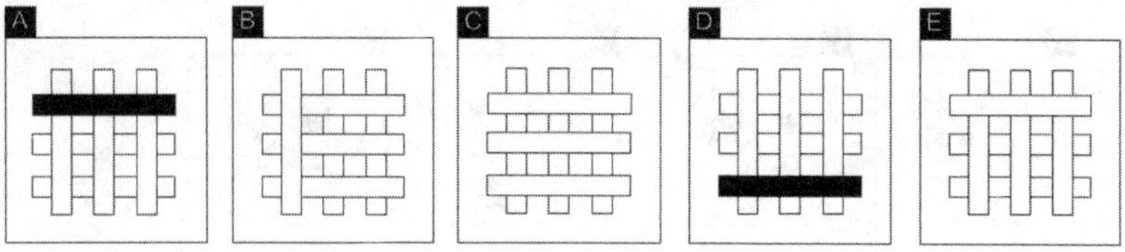

127 Which figure completes the series below?

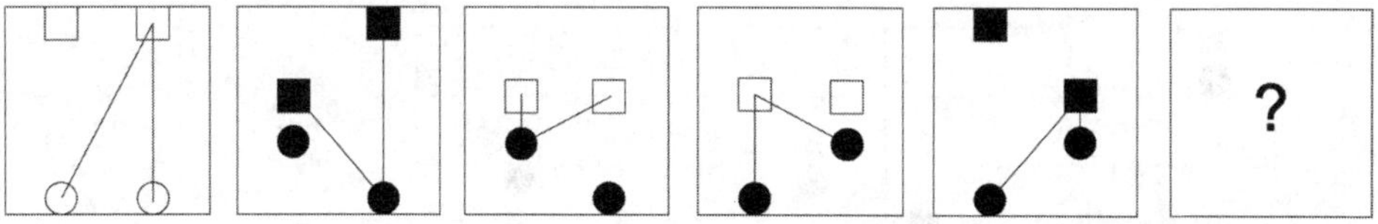

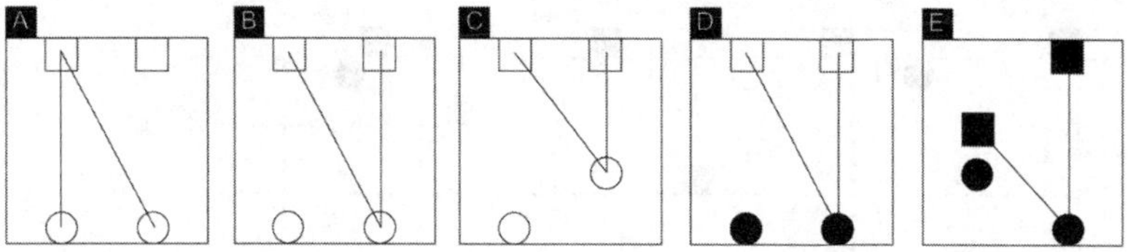

128 Which figure completes the series below?

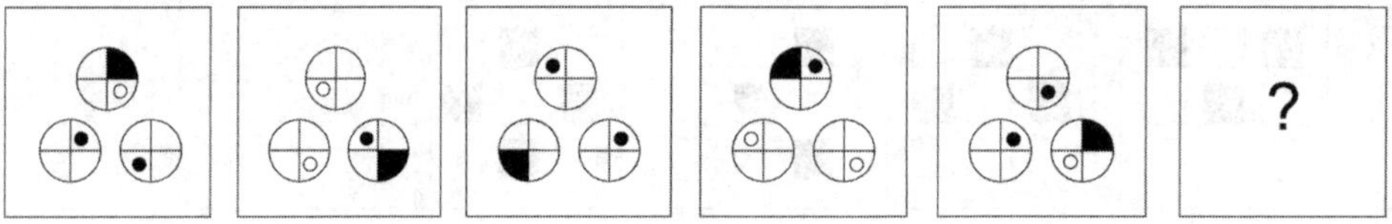

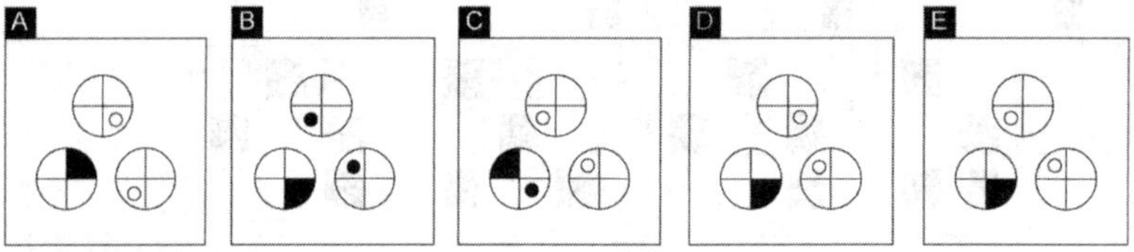

129 Which figure completes the series below?

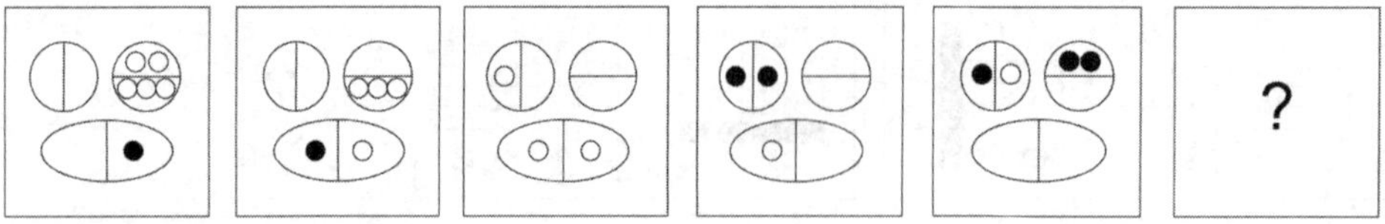

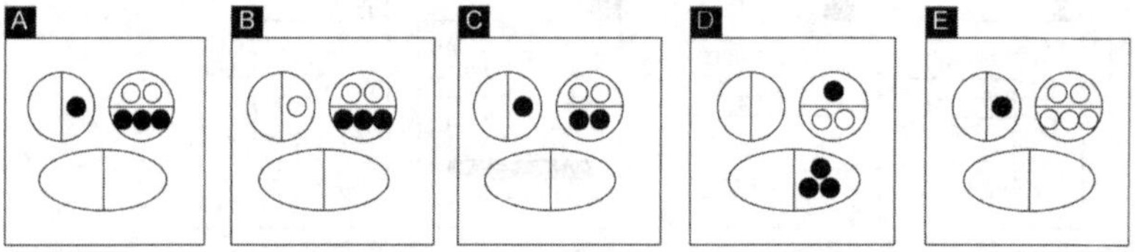

130 Which figure completes the series below?

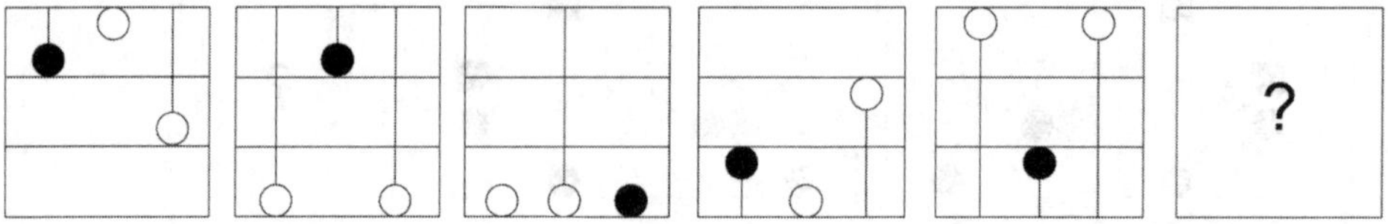

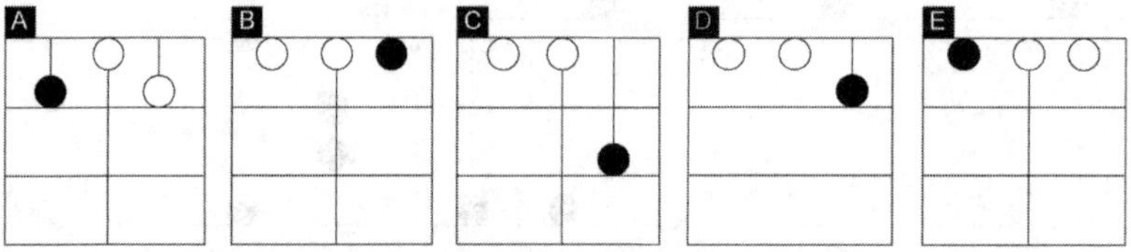

131 Which figure completes the series below?

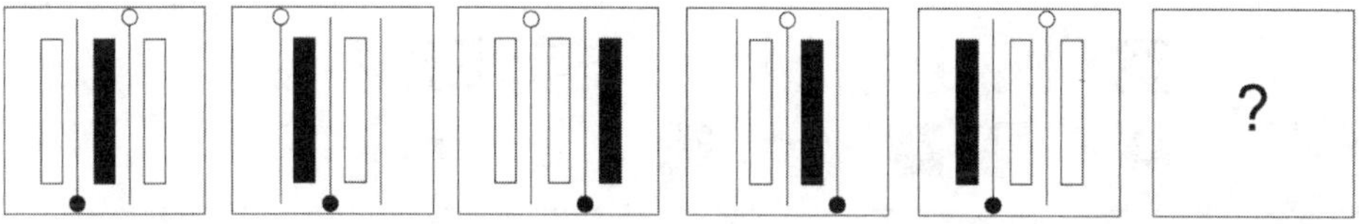

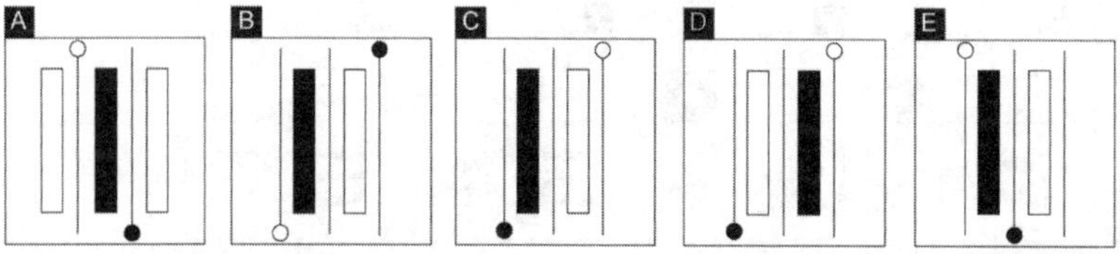

132 Which figure completes the series below?

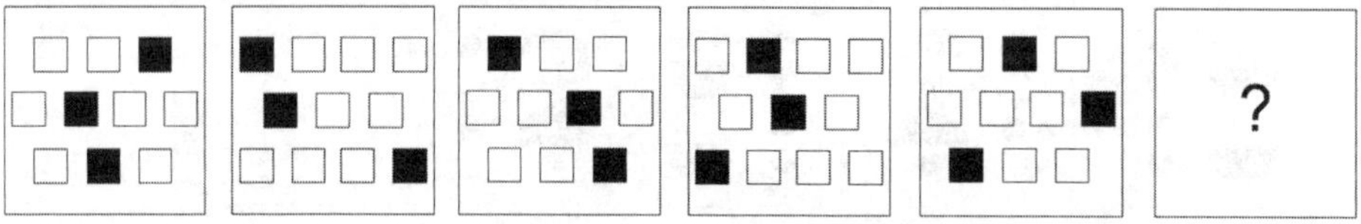

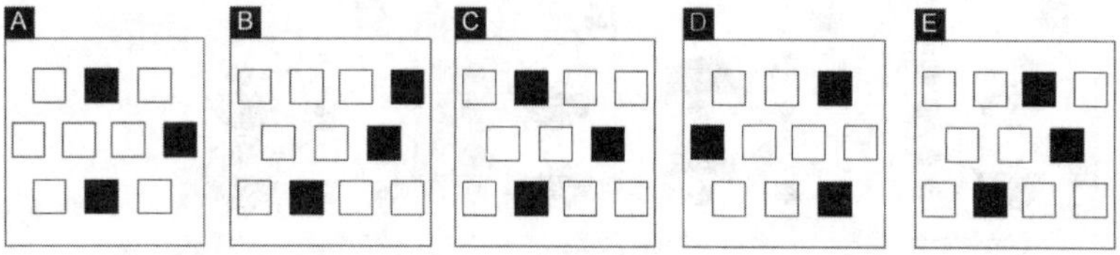

133 Which figure completes the series below?

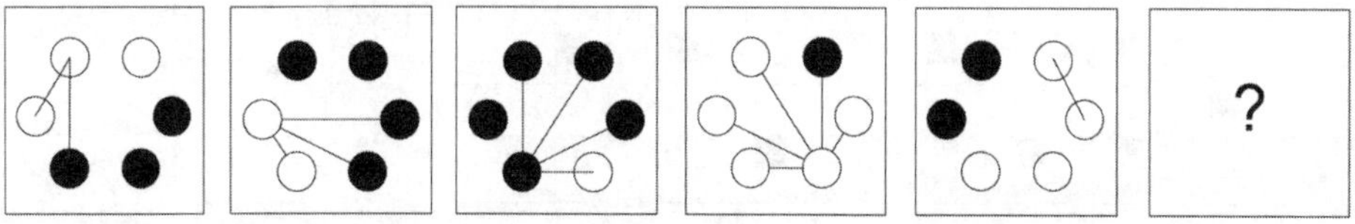

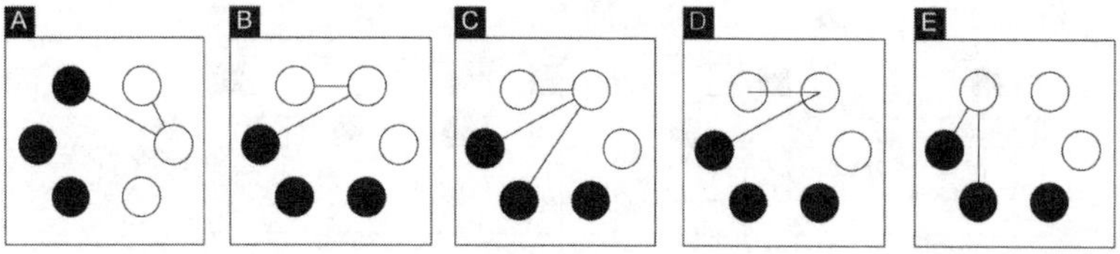

134 Which figure completes the series below?

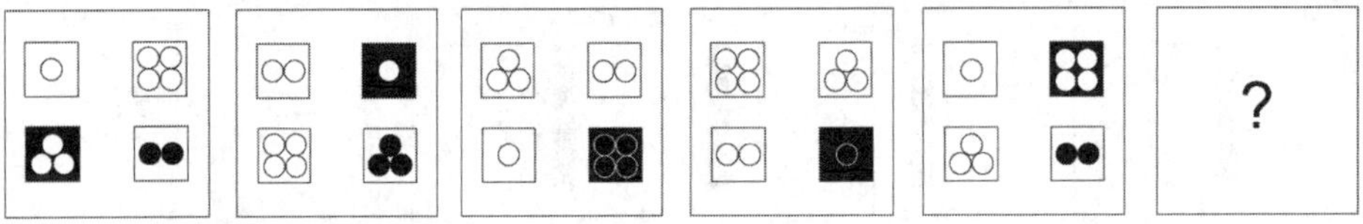

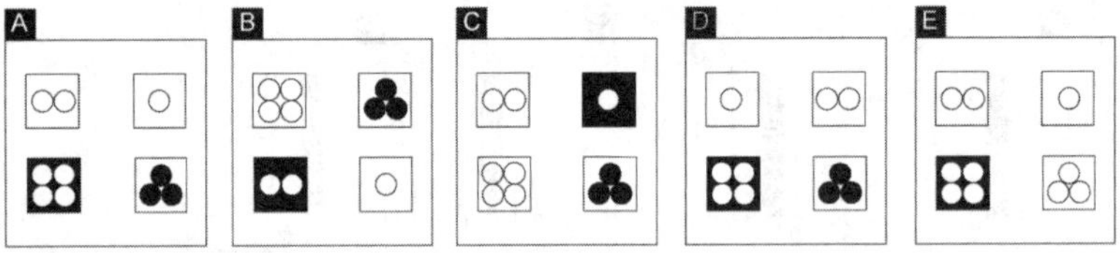

135 Which figure completes the series below?

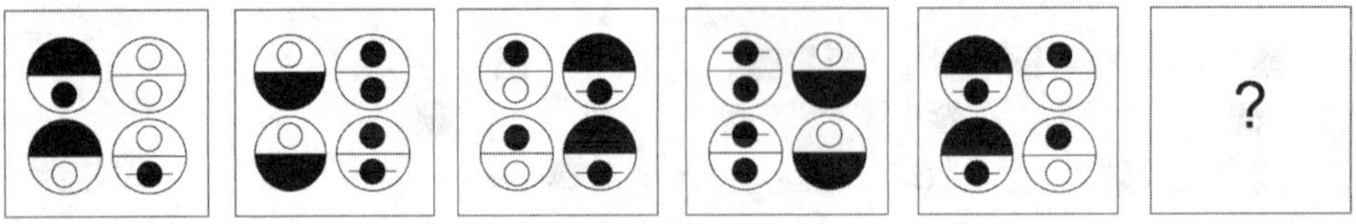

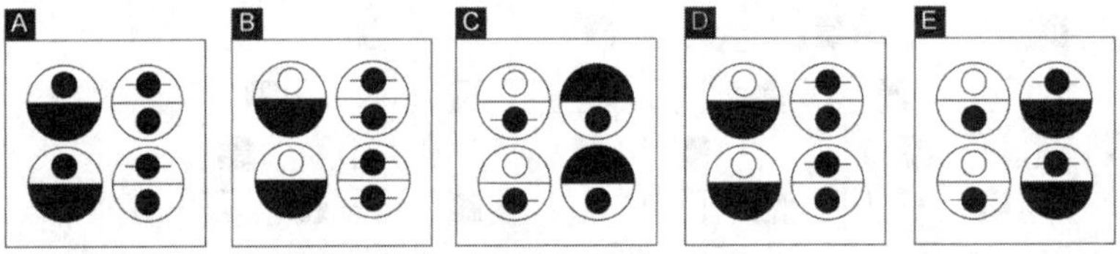

136 Which figure completes the series below?

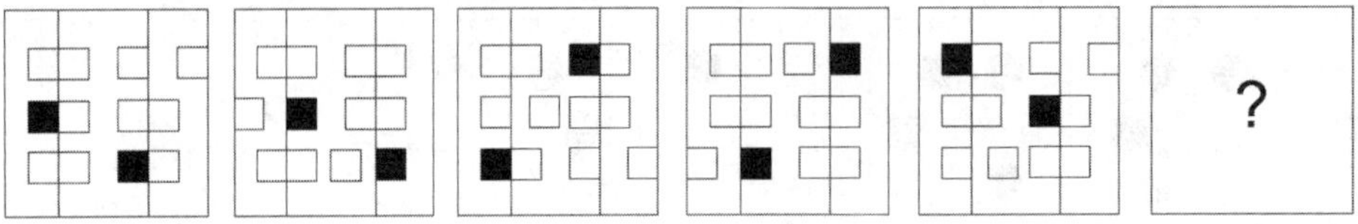

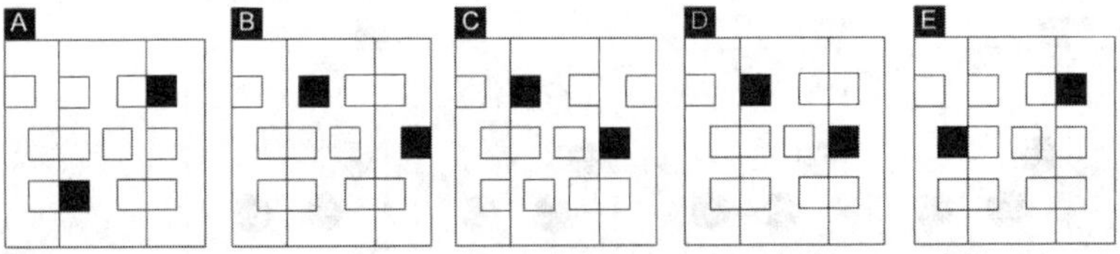

137 Which figure completes the series below?

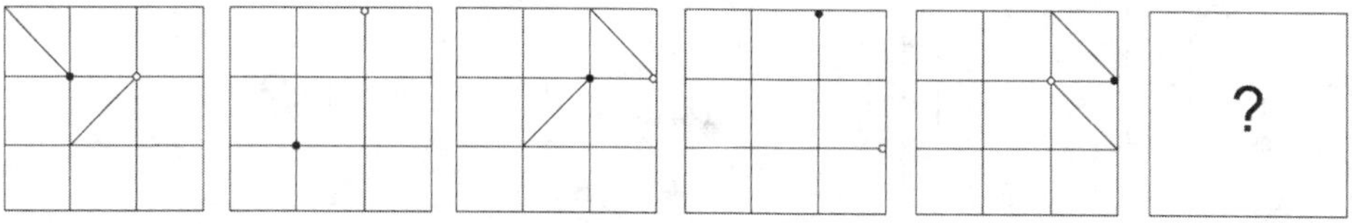

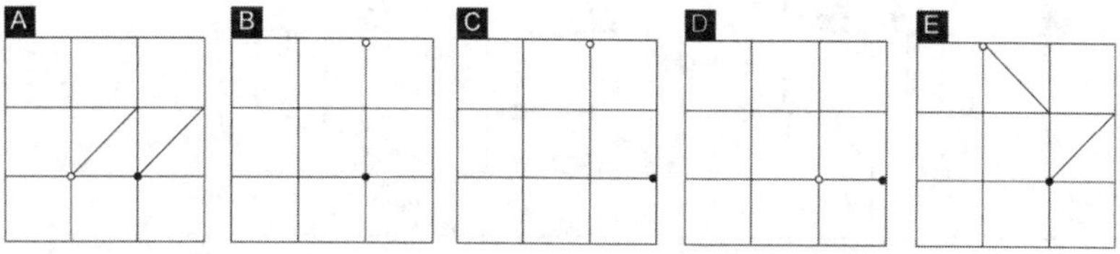

138 Which figure completes the series below?

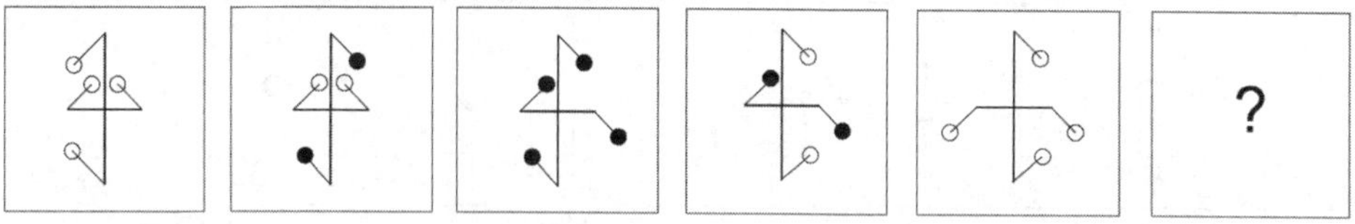

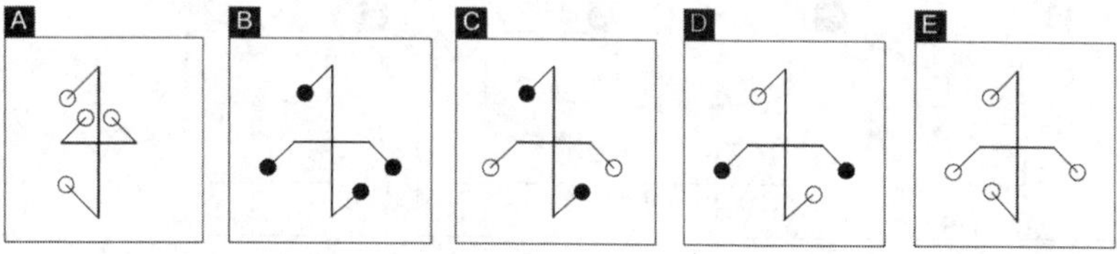

139 Which figure completes the series below?

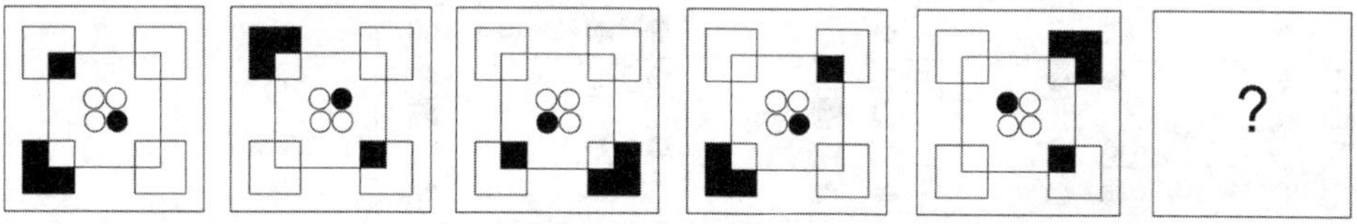

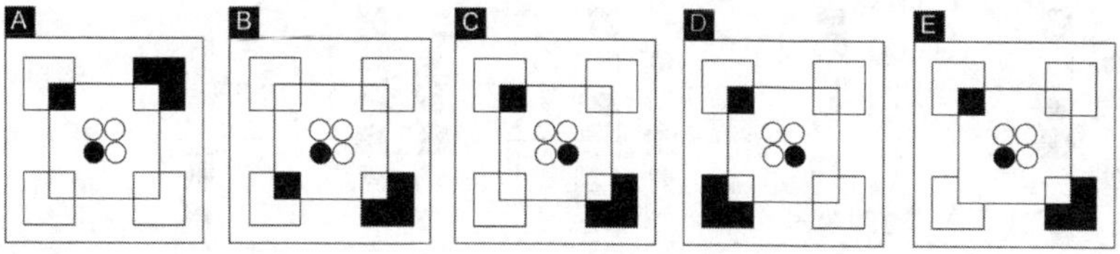

140 Which figure completes the series below?

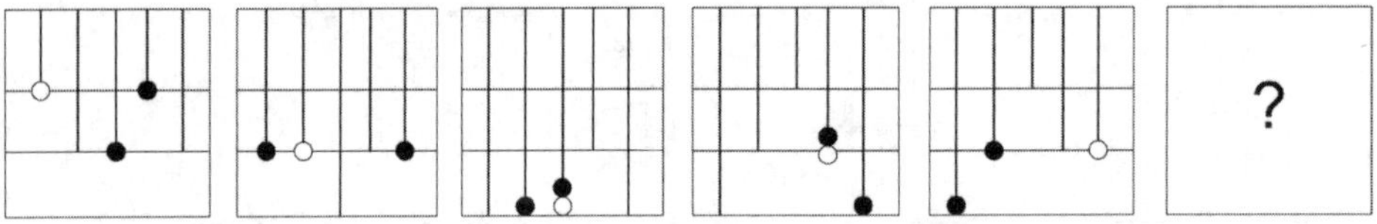

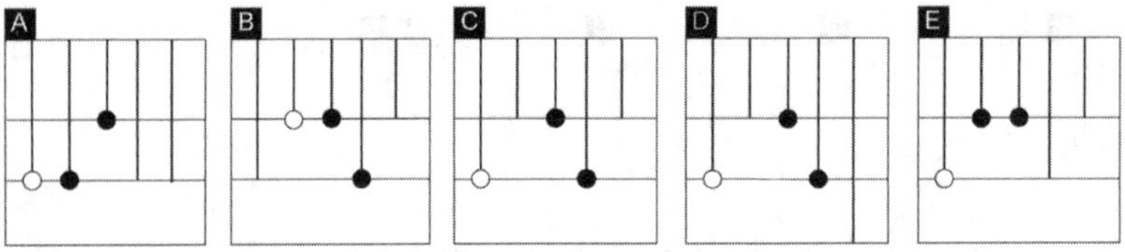

141 Which figure completes the series below?

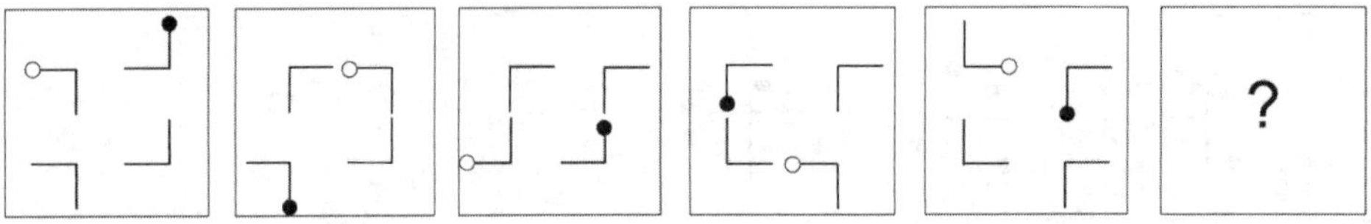

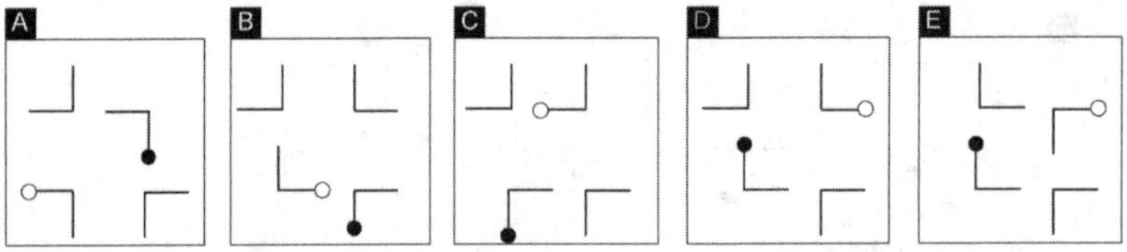

142 Which figure completes the series below?

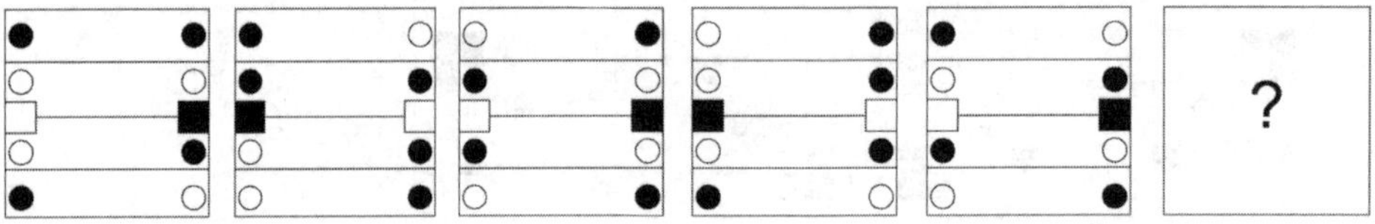

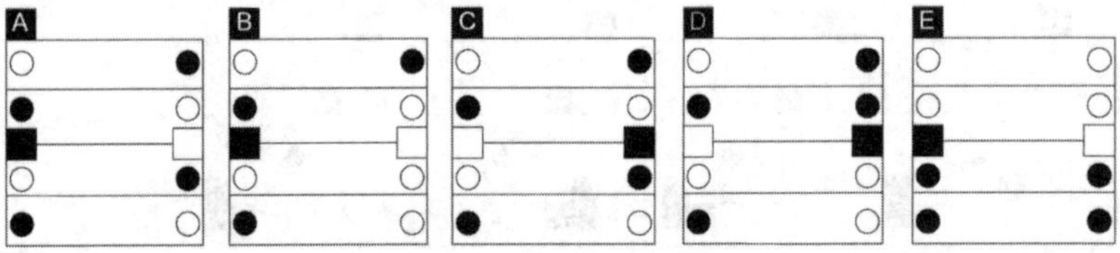

143 Which figure completes the series below?

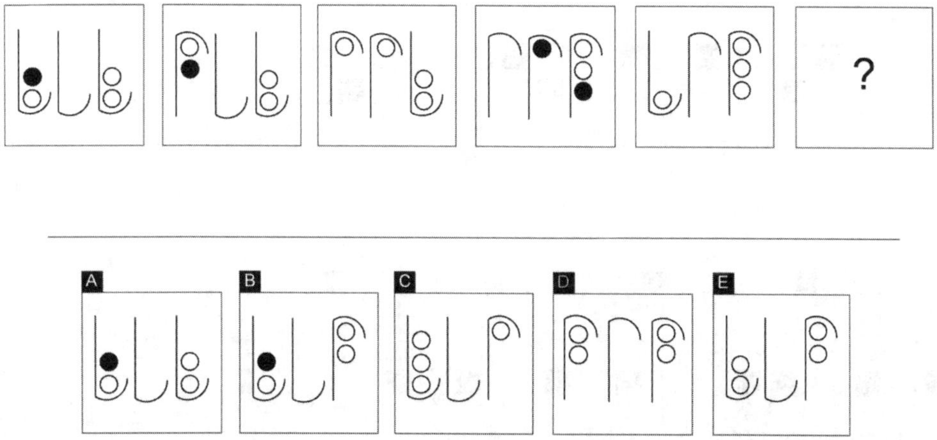

144 Which figure completes the series below?

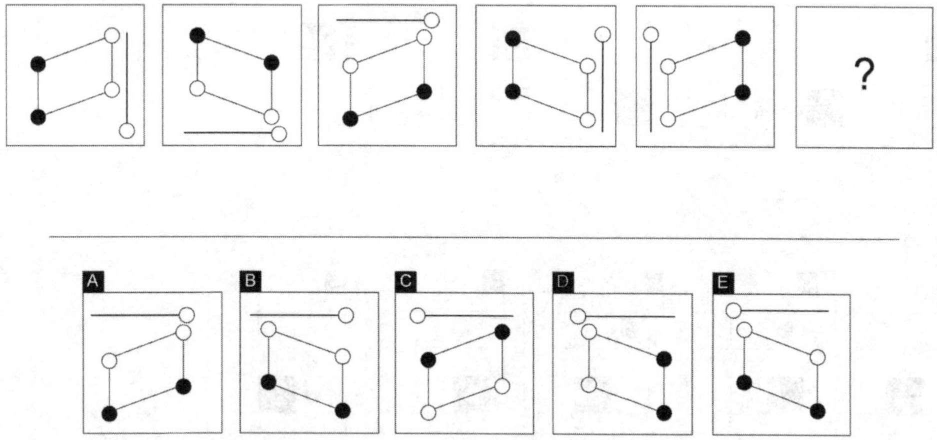

145 Which figure completes the series below?

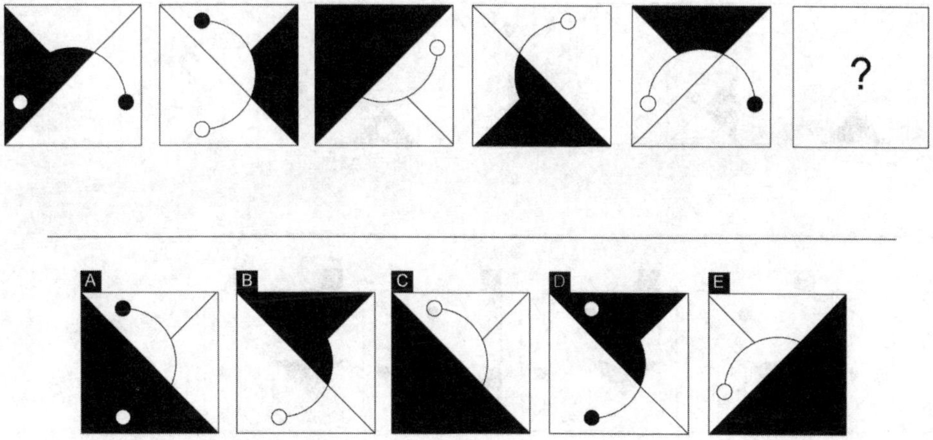

146 Which figure completes the series below?

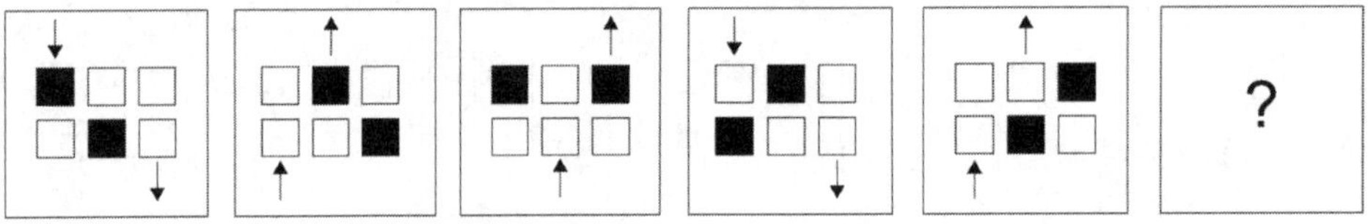

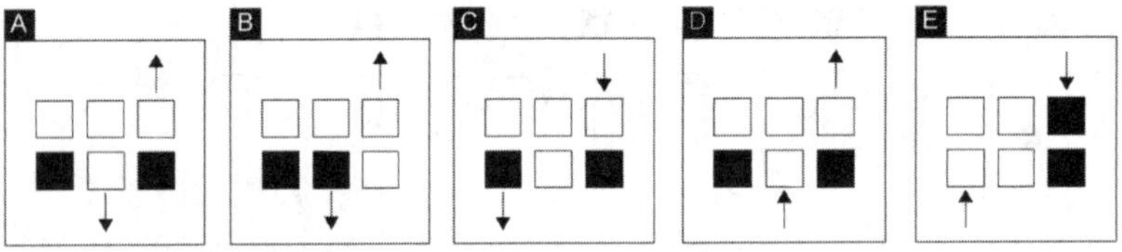

147 Which figure completes the series below?

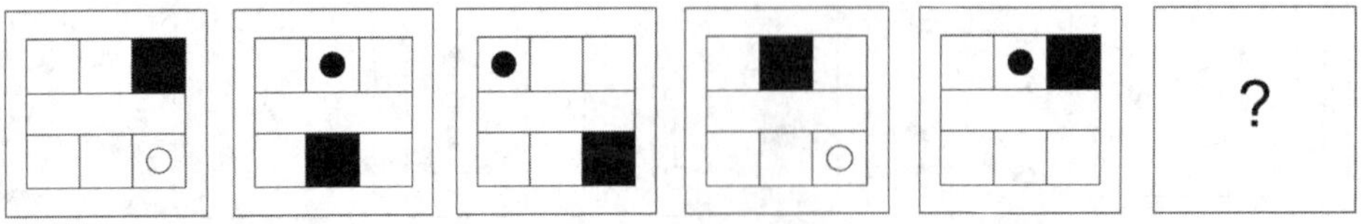

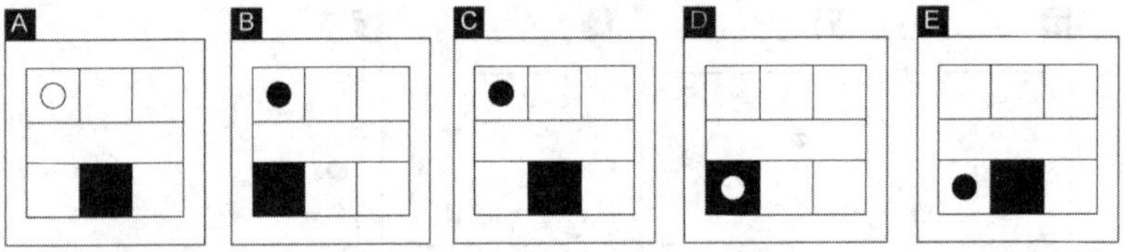

148 Which figure completes the series below?

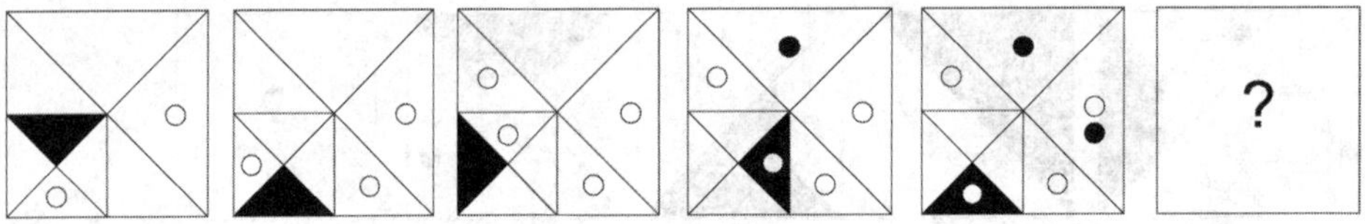

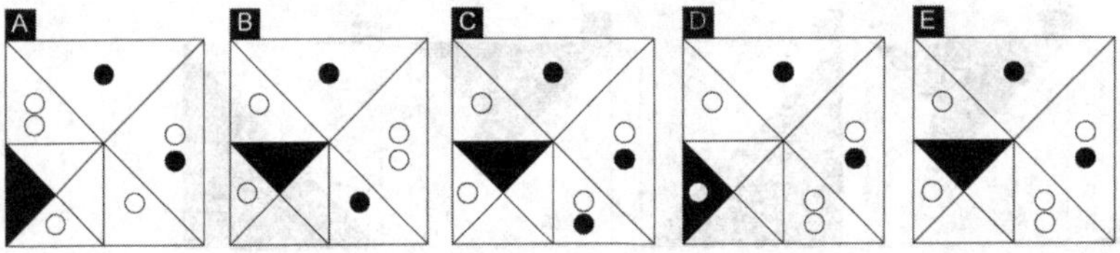

149 Which figure completes the series below?

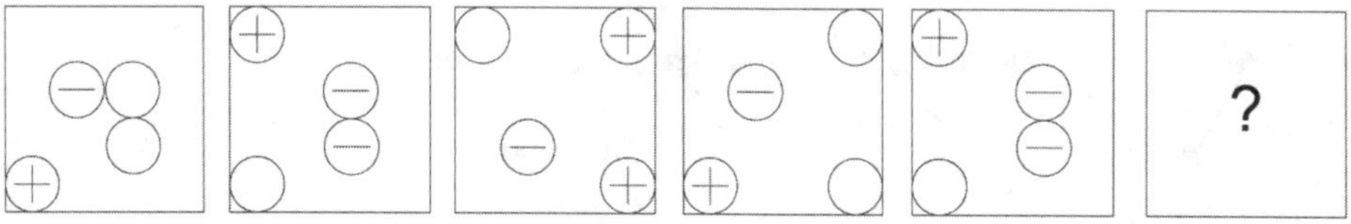

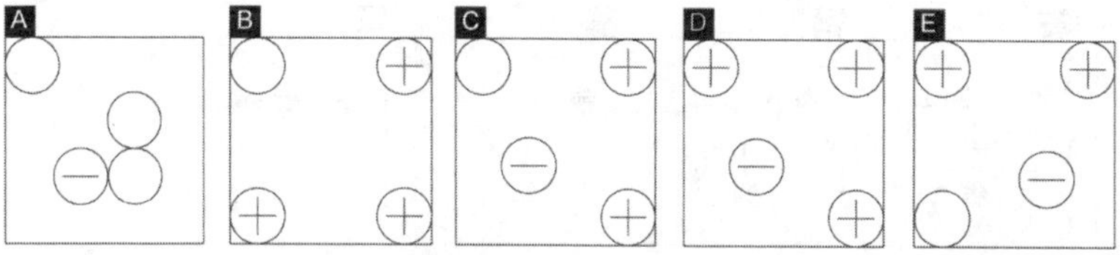

150 Which figure completes the series below?

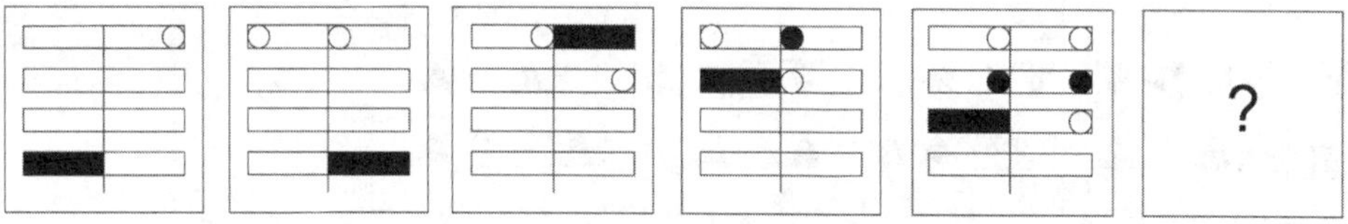

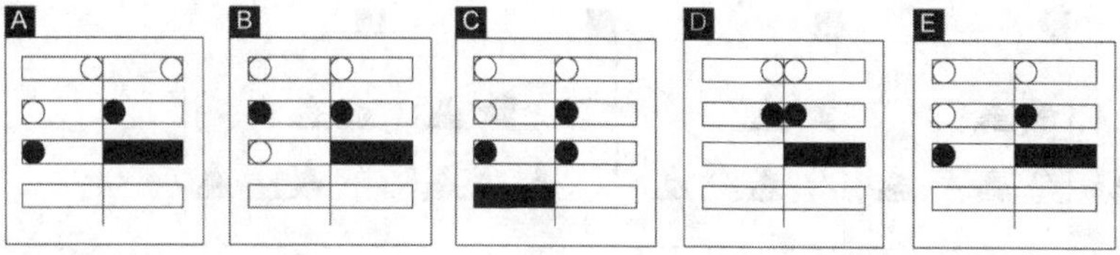

151 Which figure completes the series below?

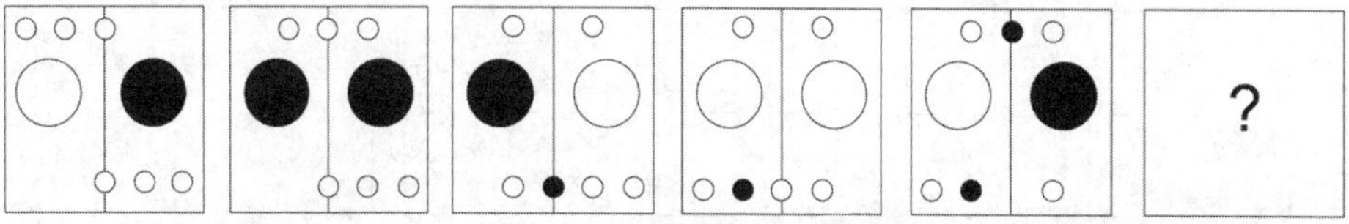

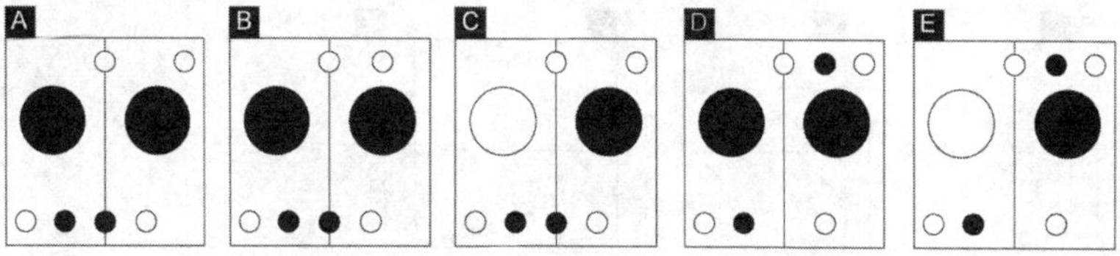

152 Which figure completes the series below?

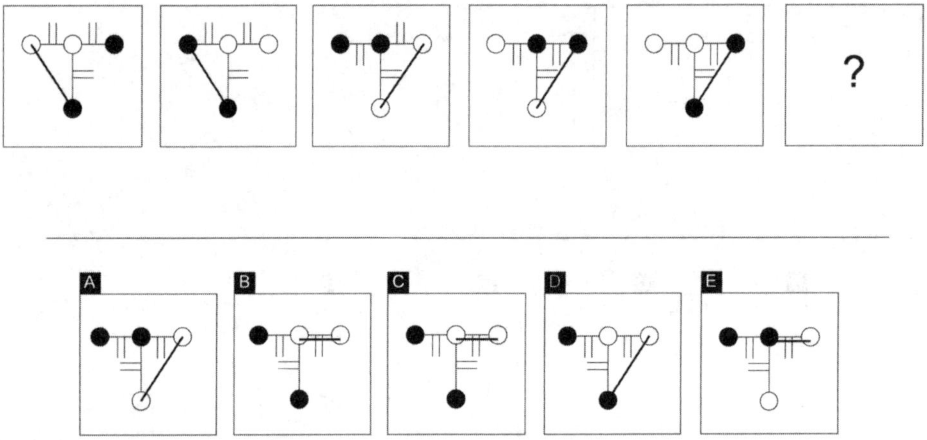

153 Which figure completes the series below?

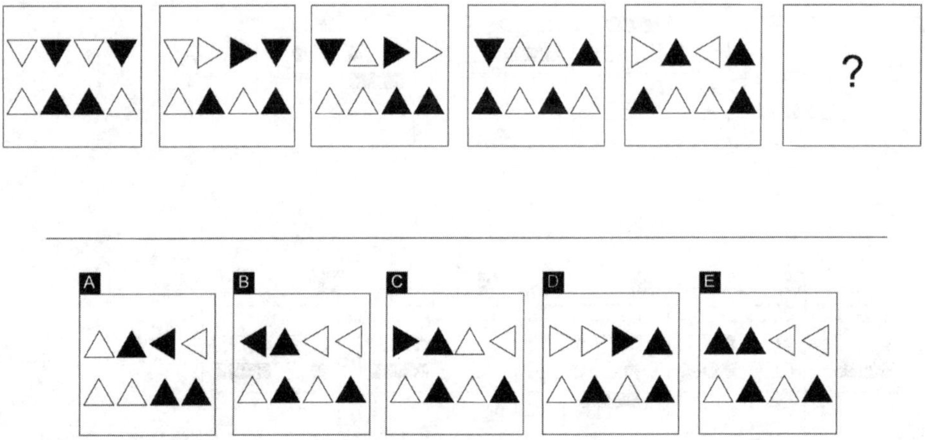

154 Which figure completes the series below?

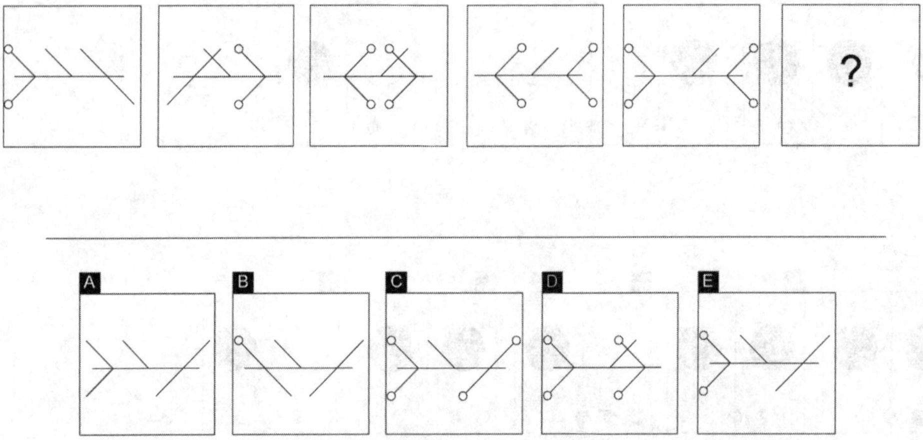

155 Which figure completes the series below?

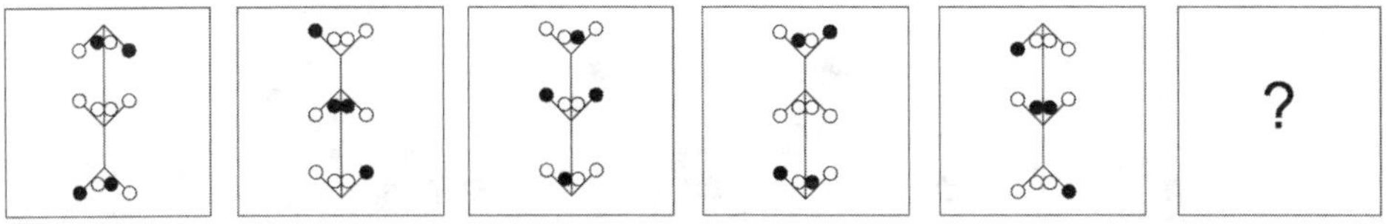

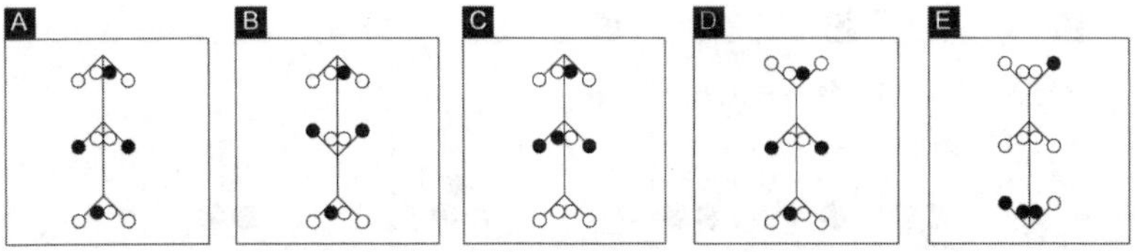

156 Which figure completes the series below?

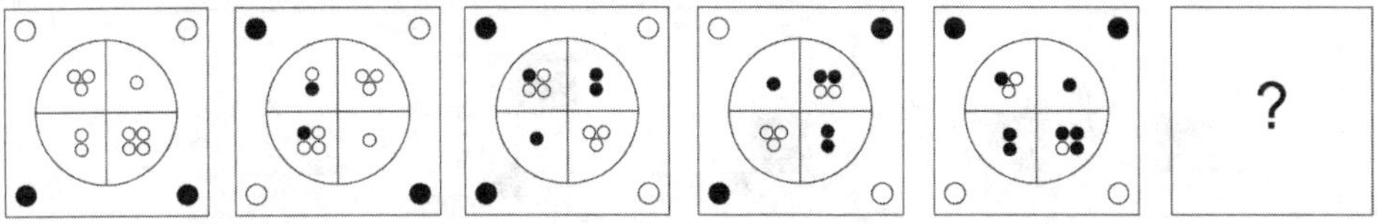

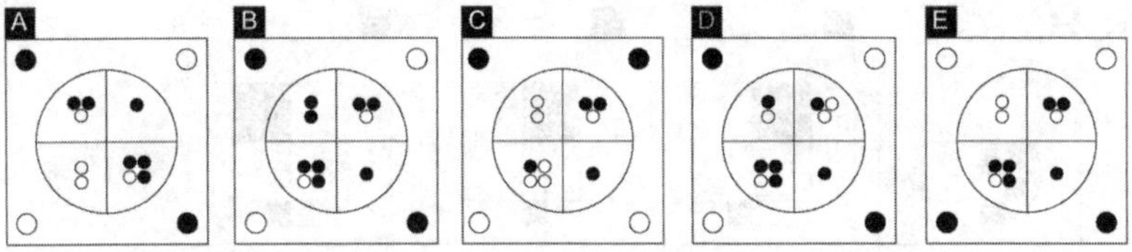

157 Which figure completes the series below?

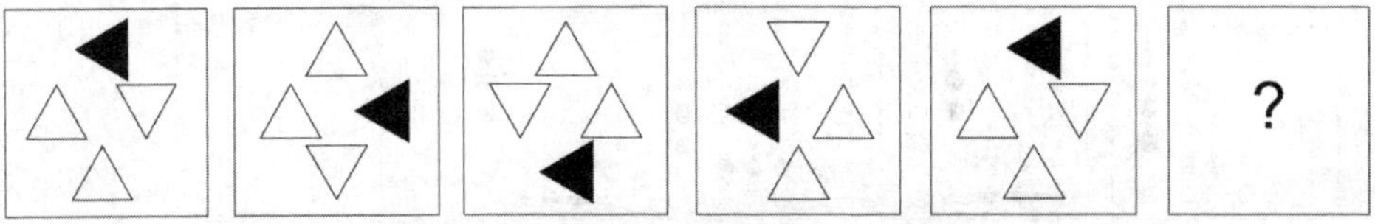

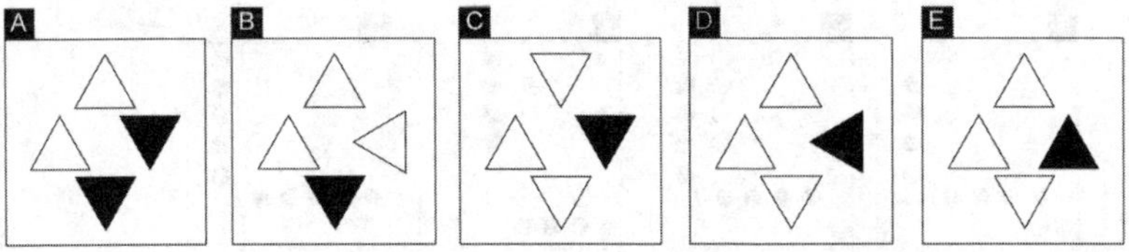

158 Which figure completes the series below?

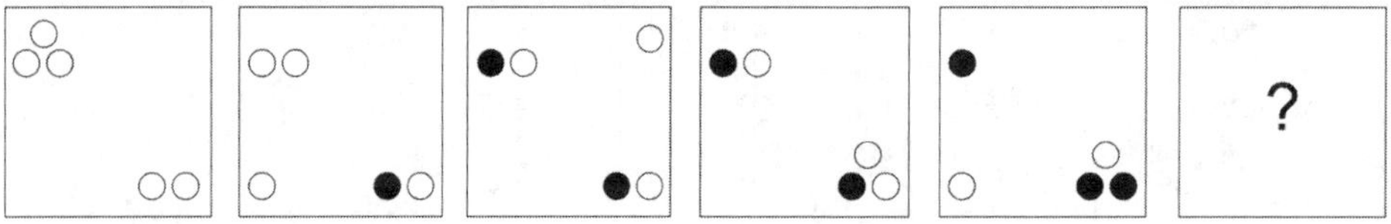

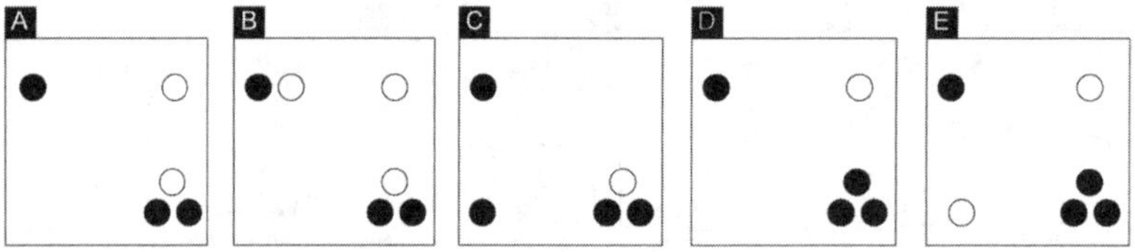

159 Which figure completes the series below?

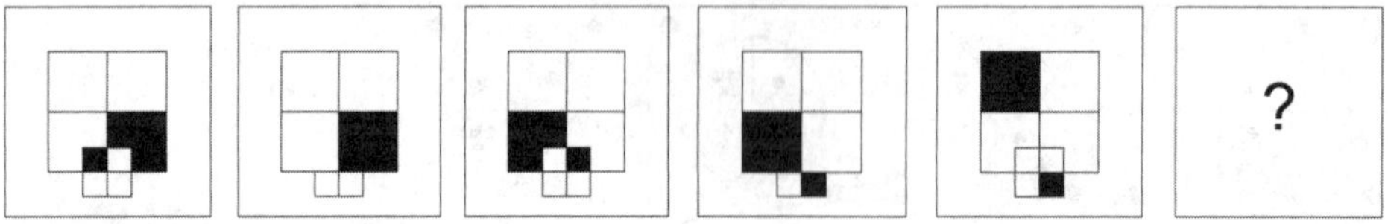

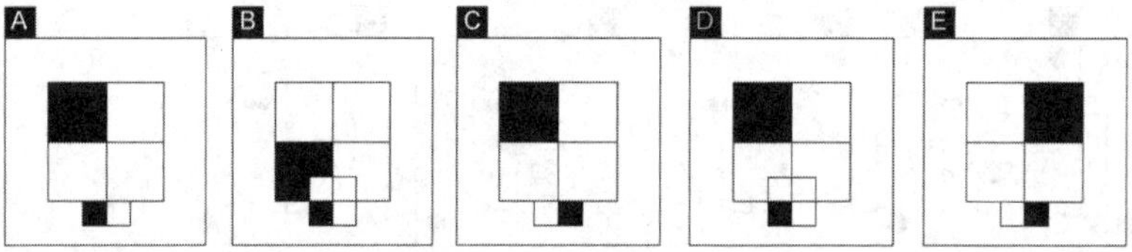

160 Which figure completes the series below?

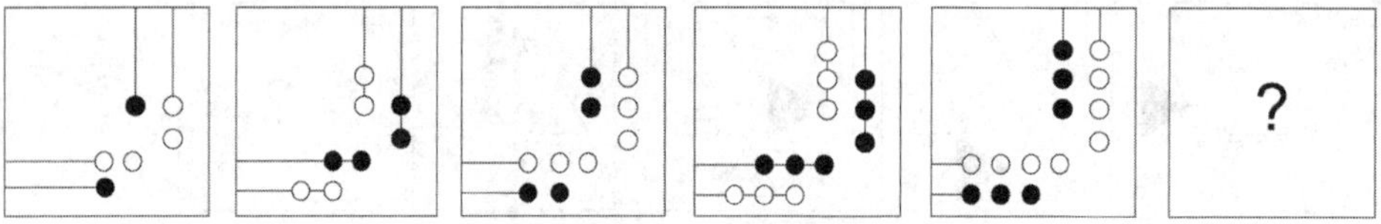

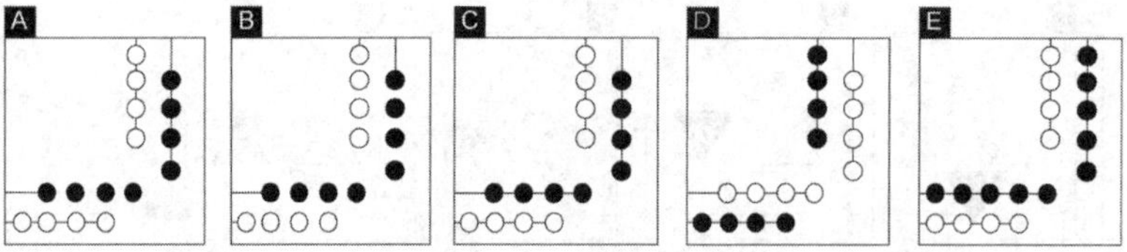

ANSWERS

1. E

Rule 1: The arrow rotates anti-clockwise 90° each time round the shape in the middle.

Rule 2: The shapes are shaded in the repeating pattern 2 black, then 2 white.

Rule 3: The shapes are in the repeating series triangle, circle, square.

2. C

Rule 1: The bent arrow rotates clockwise 90° each time round the centre.

Rule 2: The circles are shaded in the repeating pattern black, grey, white.

Rule 3: The circles move anti-clockwise around the centre, independently from the rotation of the bent arrow.

3. B

Rule 1: The triangle rotates 45° clockwise each time.

Rule 2: The fill of the square runs in the sequence black, striped, white (this leads to the square covering the triangle in the fourth of the series).

Rule 3: Which shape contains the other alternates (the square is big with triangle small, followed by triangle big with square small).

4. D

Rule 1: The arrow's position within the space moves around clockwise along the sides, progressing half the length of a side at a time (top right, middle right, bottom right, middle bottom etc.).

Rule 2: The arrow rotates anti-clockwise 90° each time.

Rule 3: The circle in the centre is shaded in the sequence black, grey, white.

5. D

Rule 1: The line connecting the arrow and the outside square rotates 45° clockwise each time.

Rule 2: The circle alternates between having a black and a grey centre.

Rule 3: The arrow points up if the circle is in the top half of the square and down if the circle is in the bottom half of the square.

6. A

Rule 1: The rhomboid moves left to right in equal steps, covering any shapes it passes over (two shapes when the rhomboid is fully visible, one shape when it is only half visible).

Rule 2: The small shapes rotate 45° each time (not visible for circle).

Rule 3: The small shapes alternate through the following shading sequence: white, striped, grey (they may have a fourth version as well but it never happens to be visible).

7. A

Rule 1: All the shapes rotate 45° each time even when not visible.

Rule 2: We move in the sequence star, smiley, triangle, arrow, ellipse one shape each time (only 3 are ever visible).

Rule 3: The slope alternates from white to black.

8. E

Rule 1: The waves move a half arc forward each time.

Rule 2: The shapes scroll horizontally two shapes at a time, through the sequence square, circle, triangle, pentagon, diamond.

Rule 3: The shapes are white in the repeating sequence second, third, first.

9. C

Rule 1: The shapes scroll one shape at a time through the sequence circle, triangle, rectangle, diamond (only 3 are ever visible).

Rule 2: The second visible shape is the largest, then the third, then the first, in a repeating pattern.

Rule 3: The shapes are white in the repeating sequence third, second, first.

10. D

Rule 1: The shapes alternate between being below or above the line.

Rule 2: The shapes are white in the repeating sequence second, third, first.

Rule 3: The shapes scroll one shape at a time through the sequence circle, triangle, square, rectangle, diamond (only 3 are ever visible).

11. D

Rule 1: The number of candles on the cake repeats through the sequence 2, 1, 3.

Rule 2: The number of circles is the number of candles plus 1.

Rule 3: The cake alternates between white and black.

12. B

Rule 1: The number circle changes size in the repeating sequence whole, three quarters, half, one quarter.

Rule 2: The shape at the top right alternates between a semi-circle and a heart.

Rule 3: The circle parts progress through the repeating shading sequence striped, grey, clear.

13. E

Rule 1: Starting with step one, every other step the number of shapes in the heart increases by one.

Rule 2: The heart is mirrored in the vertical plane after each step.

Rule 3: The number of pentagons changes in the repeating sequence 4, 1, 0.

14. D

Rule 1: The number of sides of the shape or shapes in the centre increases by two each time (6, 8, 10, 12, 14, etc.).

Rule 2: The clock hand rotates 90° each time in a clockwise direction.

Rule 3: As the clock hand reaches the black square at the top, the number of shapes in the middle increases by one.

15. C

Rule 1: The number of whiskers on each side of the animal's face goes through the sequence 2, 1, 0, 3.

Rule 2: The eyes alternate between slits and circles.

Rule 3: The nose changes shape in the sequence triangle, square, circle.

16. E

Rule 1: The circle rotates 45° each time.

Rule 2: A line is added to the circle each time in equal spacing on the right side and then the left.

Rule 3: The circle is half shaded in the sequence grey, clear, black.

17. A

Rule 1: The top left shape changes in the sequence circle, pentagon, star.

Rule 2: The top right shape alternates in the sequence between triangle and diamond.

Rule 3: The bottom left shape changes in the sequence 3 quarters shaded, 1 half shaded, 1 quarter shaded, all shaded.

18. C

Rule 1: Each shape appears once on its own, then once stacked on top of its double.

Rule 2: When the total number of sides on the central shapes is even, the top left arrow points down. When they are odd, it points up.

Rule 3: The bottom arrows alternate between pointing right and left.

19. C

Rule 1: The shapes on the star change in the sequence circle, square, pentagon.

Rule 2: The position of the shapes on the star moves two points anticlockwise each time.

Rule 3: The star smiles when the shape is on one of the top 3 points of the star.

20. B

Rule 1: The shape at the top left predicts the shape of the door of the house in the next figure.

Rule 2: The number of sides on the roof is the number of sides of the door plus one.

Rule 3: The doors are shaded in the sequence grey, clear, black.

21. E

Rule 1: The triangle rotates clockwise 45° each time.

Rule 2: If a heart is present, in the next figure the circles increase by one, otherwise they decrease by 2.

Rule 3: The shaded portion of the triangle shifts anti-clockwise each turn.

22. B

Rule 1. The shading of the grid piece changes in the repeating sequence grey, black, black.

Rule 2. The shapes in the upper parts of the figures are changing in the repeating sequence diamond, black circle and nothing.

Rule 3. The grid piece moves in a diamond pattern around the central rectangle.

23. E

Rule 1: The square, triangle and rectangle rotate 90° anti-clockwise and move along the following pattern around the corners. Rectangle: bottom left, bottom right, top right. Square/Triangle: top right, top left, bottom left, and then the cycle repeats.

Rule 2: If a star is present, the triangle is mirrored horizontally after the rotation from rule 1.

Rule 3: The number of smiley faces changes in the repeating pattern 3, 7, 1.

24. D

Rule 1: The ice cream colour changes in the repeating sequence black, light, stripy and grey.

Rule 2: The shapes at the bottom change in the sequence of sun, heart and moon.

Rule 3: A flake appears in the top of the ice cream in the sequence of no flake, no flake, flake, flake.

25. B

Rule 1: The top arrow rotates 120° anti clockwise each time (a third of a circle).

Rule 2: The bottom arrow alternates between rotating 90° and 180° clockwise each time.

Rule 3: If the arrows both point upwards, a moon is visible. If they both point downwards, a cloud is visible.

26. C

Rule 1: The hexagon jumps 2 spaces across the board each time, moving left to right, then down at the end of the row, before moving right to left until the end of the row. This is then repeated.

Rule 2: The board rotates 90° clockwise each turn.

Rule 3: If the hexagon would arrive on a star because of rule 1, it moves back 3 spaces, retracing where it came from.

27. E

Rule 1: The largest shape moves clockwise one each time.

Rule 2: If an extra shape appears near the middle, the shapes in the next turn change to be this shape, otherwise the shapes stay the same.

Rule 3: The largest shape alternates between rotating clockwise 45° and 90°, as seen via the shading.

28. B

Rule 1: The number of circles changes by the pattern: add two extra, take away one, add one.

Rule 2: If the number of circles is bigger than the number of triangles, crosses appear in the circles.

Rule 3: The number of triangles changes in the sequence 1, 4, 7.

29. A

Rule 1: The shapes (even when not visible) rotate 90° anti-clockwise each turn.

Rule 2: Presence of a double headed arrow in the centre means the shapes switch whether they are in the top half or bottom half within the same turn.

Rule 3: One shape vanishes each turn until there is just one shape. Then the other 2 reappear one by one (shapes continue to rotate while 'invisible'). The process then repeats.

30. D

Rule 1: A new random shape is added to the top of the cross each time.

Rule 2: The new shapes alternate between rotating clockwise around the cross and rotating anticlockwise.

Rule 3: The mouth on the face in the cross changes in the sequence straight, frowning, smiley.

31. B

Rule 1: If a star isn't present the circle and its internal shapes turn clockwise 45°, otherwise the shapes rotate anticlockwise 45°.

Rule 2: The number of triangles in the circle changes in the sequence 2, 4, 6.

Rule 3: The shapes inside the circle change in the repeating sequence clear, black, grey, stripy.

32. E

Rule 1: Balls shown at the top are added to balls at the bottom in the previous image in the repeating pattern 8, 4, 0.

Rule 2: After rule 1 is applied, balls at the bottom decrease by 3 each time.

Rule 3: If an explosion is present the balls are shaded grey.

33. A

Rule 1: The number of ears on the creature changes in the pattern 1, 4, 2.

Rule 2: Ears change shape in the pattern round, pointy, droopy, long.

Rule 3: If a nose is present, the ears go spotty.

34. D

Rule 1: The face rotates 45° clockwise each turn.

Rule 2: The eyes change shape in the pattern wide, point, slit.

Rule 3: If a smile appears, the glasses change to star shapes.

35. B

Rule 1: If the flower smiles, add a leaf.

Rule 2: The weather changes in the sequence sunny, cloudy, lightning, rain.

Rule 3: The angle of the leaves goes through the pattern down, middle, up.

36. C

Rule 1: The snake snakes down, adding a body section each time.

Rule 2: The shapes on the snake change in the repeating sequence diamond, oval, circle.

Rule 3: If the snake goes over (eats) a star, the shapes go grey.

37. D

Rule 1: The number of spots on the cat changes in the repeating sequence 1, 5, 2.

Rule 2: The number of sides of the cat's spots increases by one each time.

Rule 3: The cat's eyes look up, down, left, then right in sequence.

38. E

Rule 1: The elephant's trunk changes length from medium to long to medium to short in a repeating sequence.

Rule 2: The puddle in the dish grows by two squares each turn. See also Rule 3.

Rule 3: If the trunk reaches the puddle, it shrinks by 3 squares and the 3 squares appear in the elephant's stomach.

39. C

Rule 1: The 6-pointed star turns clockwise one point each turn.

Rule 2: The 4-pointed star turns anticlockwise one point each turn. The rope hangs off and moves with the 4-pointed star while holding onto the weight.

Rule 3: The weight changes colour in the pattern black, grey and clear.

40. D

Rule 1: The shapes scroll past one shape at a time through the sequence triangle, square, diamond.

Rule 2: The ball moves right to left covering one shape at a time until it reaches the far left and then reappears at the right.

Rule 3: The circle rotates 90° anticlockwise each time.

41. B

Rule 1: The arrow rotates 90 degrees in a clockwise direction in each turn.

Rule 2: If the arrow is at the top or left-hand side of the central shape, the central shape has an even number of sides. If the arrow is at the bottom or right-hand side of the central shape, the central shape has an odd number of sides.

Rule 3: If the arrow points to the bottom, the shape is unshaded.

42. E

Rule 1: The circle takes an increasing number of steps around the 'slots' of the central shape.

Rule 2: The circle is shaded if it's in one of the upper two 'slots'.

Rule 3: The arrow attached to the central shape points upwards if the circle is in one of the left-hand 'slots' – otherwise it points downwards.

43. A

Rule 1: The triangle and the square alternate between rotating 45 degrees in a clockwise direction and staying still: when the triangle rotates, the square stays still, and vice versa.

Rule 2: The shape which did not rotate from the previous turn is outside.

Rule 3: The triangle becomes shaded if it rotated compared to the previous turn.

44. C

Rule 1: The direction of the arrow shows in which direction the circle will move the following turn. If the circles reaches the edge of the image and is instructed by the arrow to move forward, it re-appears on the other side.

Rule 2: If the circle is shaded, the arrow itself will itself move in the direction in which it is pointing.

Rule 3: The arrow is shaded in every second turn.

45. E

Rule 1: The star rotates increasing multiples of 45 degrees in an anticlockwise direction.

Rule 2: The circle takes an increasing number of steps around the corners of the image in a clockwise direction.

Rule 3: The circle is shaded every time it's in one of the left corners.

46. A

Rule 1: The three shapes (triangle, circle and rhomboid) take one step to the right in each turn. When they reach the right edge of the image, they re-appear on the other side.

Rule 2: The shading starts at the rightmost shape and takes an increasing number of steps to the left in every turn.

Rule 3: The size of the leftmost shape is increased first. Then, the size increase moves an increasing number of steps to the right in every turn.

47. A

Rule 1: The four components (arrow, triangle, circle and empty space) move down the slope one step at a time.

Rule 2: The slope is shaded if all those three components that are actual, visible shapes, are visible.

Rule 3: The visible shapes become shaded the second time they appear.

48. D

Rule 1: The direction of the bottom curvy line changes from turn to turn, while the shapes underneath change randomly, without any specific pattern.

Rule 2: The only unshaded bottom shape is first the left one, then the right one and, finally, the middle one. This pattern then repeats throughout the series.

Rule 3: The top half copies the bottom half (the direction of the curvy line and the shading and arrangement of the shapes) from the previous turn.

49. C

Rule 1: The small square on the left-hand side alternates between being fully shaded, top-half shaded and unshaded.

Rule 2: The small square on the right-hand side alternates between being bottom-half shaded, unshaded and fully shaded.

Rule 3: The small squares are moving from the top to the bottom, reappearing at the top after reaching the bottom position.

50. A

Rule 1: The shapes have increasing numbers of sides from left to right when the black line is above them. They have decreasing numbers of sides from left to right when the black line is below them.

Rule 2: The shading takes an increasing number of steps to the right. When the shading reaches the rightmost shape, it reappears on the leftmost one, and so on.

Rule 3: The shape that was shaded in the previous turn is shown at the bottom of the image.

51. A

Rule 1: The circles at the bottom show how many candles will be on the cake in the following turn.

Rule 2: If a circle is shaded, the candle it represents will appear at the bottom of the cake.

Rule 3: The cake is shaded if it has an even number of candles on it (including candles at the bottom).

52. B

Rule 1: The location of the small heart determines the number of quadrants the circle at the centre will have. The top left corner means one quadrant and every other corner in a clockwise direction means an additional quadrant added.

Rule 2: The heart is shaded if it's in either of the left corners.

Rule 3: If the heart is unshaded, the quadrants it creates will be shaded and vice versa.

53. E

Rule 1: Unshaded circles outside the heart show how many circles will be inside the heart in the following turn.

Rule 2: If there are shaded circles outside the lower part of the heart, they will appear next to the unshaded circle(s) at the top in the following turn.

Rule 3: Circles inside the heart alternate between shaded and unshaded.

54. C

Rule 1: The clock hand's position shows whether the shape in the centre will have an odd or even number of sides – 12 and 6 o'clock = even number of sides, 3 and 9 o'clock = odd number of sides.

Rule 2: The shape of the previous turn is shown at the top in the current turn.

Rule 3: Shapes in the centre are shaded if they have more sides than the small shape at the top and vice versa.

55. D

Rule 1: If the cat has an even number of whiskers, its ears are farther away from each other – if it has an odd number of whiskers, the ears are closer to each other.

Rule 2: The cat's nose is shaded if it has more whiskers on the left side. It is unshaded in all other cases.

Rule 3: If the cat has more whiskers on the right side of its face, its nose turns into a triangle.

56. A

Rule 1: A new line is added to the circle in each turn, and the circle rotates in a way that the side which gets the line is always on top.

Rule 2: Every second line added gets a small circle on top of it.

Rule 3: The small circles turn shaded in their second turn of existence.

57. C

Rule 1: The shaded section of the square in the bottom left corner shows which corners of the figure have shapes in the same turn (the bottom left section of the square is always shaded as the square is always present).

Rule 2: Every shape in the corners starts as a triangle and they gain a side every consecutive turn they are present.

Rule 3: Shapes with an even number of sides are shaded.

58. E

Rule 1: The top left arrow shows which direction the shape will travel in the following turn.

Rule 2: If the top right arrow points upwards, the shape will gain a side, if it points downwards, the shape will lose a side.

Rule 3: If both arrows point in the same direction the shape is shaded in that turn.

59. B

Rule 1: Unshaded circles inside the star show how many steps (clockwise) along the points of the star the shape outside will take in the following turn.

Rule 2: Shaded circles inside the star mean an anti-clockwise movement.

Rule 3: Every time the shape crosses the top arm of the star, it gains a side.

60. D

Rule 1: The left 'window' of the house shows the shape of the 'door' in the following turn.

Rule 2: The right 'window' shows the shape of the left 'window' in the following turn.

Rule 3: 'Doors' with an even number of sides are shaded.

61. A

Rule 1: The number of circles by default shows how many 90 degree rotations the triangle will take in a clockwise direction in the following turn.

Rule 2: The number of hearts indicates how many steps the shading within the triangle will take in an anticlockwise direction in the following turn.

Rule 3: Shaded circles and hearts are 'disabled', that is, they do not exert any influence on the shape.

62. A

Rule 1: The number of sides the top left shape has indicates how many vertical steps the shaded section of the grid will take in the following turn. A shaded shape indicates moving upwards, an unshaded shape means moving downwards. When the shaded section reaches the edge of the grid, it re-appears on the other side.

Rule 2: The number of sides the top right shape has indicates how many horizontal steps the shaded section of the grid will take in the following turn. A shaded shape means moving left, an unshaded shape means moving right.

Rule 3: The shading alternates between black and grey.

63. E

Rule 1: The arrow in the top left corner shows whether a new line of smilies will be dropped on the current ones in the following turn (arrow pointing upwards) or an existing line will be removed (arrow pointing downwards) from the bottom. When new similies are added, they arrive in groups of 2-3-2-3.

Rule 2: Shaded arrows indicate that sad smilies will be dropped in the next figure.

Rule 3: Sad smilies will turn into happy smilies in the second turn of their existence.

64. C

Rule 1: The number of 'snowflakes' indicates how many balls of ice cream the cone will consist of in the following turn. Every time a snowflake appears in a figure, the cone will get an extra ball of ice cream in the following turn. Whenever a 'sun' is present, the cone will lose a random ball of ice cream in the following turn.

Rule 2: An unshaded ball of ice cream turns shaded in the second turn of its existence and then disappears in the third.

Rule 3: As long as there is a shaded ball of ice cream present, the cone becomes shaded as well.

65. B

Rule 1: The lower shape takes the posture (direction of arrow) of the upper one from the previous turn.

Rule 2: The upper circle is shaded for two turns, then the bottom one for one turn – this pattern then repeats.

Rule 3: Each time the arrow on the bottom circle is attached to the top half of the circle, a triangle appears in the image.

66. D

Rule 1: The star shows where in the grid the circle will appear next.

Rule 2: In every turn, the previous position of the circle is shaded.

Rule 3: The circle is shaded if it's next to the star.

67. A

Rule 1: The middle shape takes the form of the top right shape from the previous turn.

Rule 2: The bottom right shape shows what the middle shape will look like two turns from now.

Rule 3: The top and bottom shapes on the left do the same but with previous versions of the middle shape.

68. C

Rule 1: In each turn, both the top and the bottom row of circles start with 5 – 5 circles, but some of these circles are 'destroyed' by the shaded triangles pointing at them.

Rule 2: Circles will become shaded if they have unshaded triangles pointing at them.

Rule 3: Figures in the series alternate between having more circles than triangles and vice versa.

69. D

Rule 1: The shaded section of the circle in the top left corner shows where the shape in the middle was pointing in the previous turn. The shaded section of the circle in the middle shows where the shape is pointing in the current turn, while the shaded section of the last circle shows where the shape will be pointing in the following turn.

Rule 2: The shape in the middle is shaded for two turns then unshaded for a single turn. This pattern then repeats.

Rule 3: A second row of circles appears at the bottom, with the same rules applying to them.

70. E

Rule 1: The shape in the top arm of the cross will appear in the left arm in the following turn. This shape then will be "judged" by the smiley face. If the face is smiling, the shape will transfer to the right arm without change. If the face is frowning, the shape will transfer with one fewer side, while if the face is sad, the shape will transfer with two sides taken away.

Rule 2: Each time the face is smiling, a small dot will appear at bottom of the cross which then stays there for the rest of the series.

Rule 3: Each time the face is sad, a dot is removed.

71. E

Rule 1: The circle is divided into two halves with shapes in both. The total number of sides is always larger in the top half of the circle.

Rule 2: A shaded shape's sides are not counted towards the total number of sides.

Rule 3: In even-numbered turns (2,4, etc.), the total number of shapes (in both halves) is odd, while in odd turns, this number is even.

72. A

Rule 1: Vertical arrows within the circles indicate whether the given circle will appear/remain in the upper row or the bottom row in the following turn.

Rule 2: Circles with arrows pointing to the right will become shaded in the following turn.

Rule 3: Circles with arrows pointing to the left will be removed in the following turn.

73. E

Rule 1: The number of circles increases by two in each turn (eyes and eye segments are counted as circles).

Rule 2: In every even turn, a single circle becomes shaded.

Rule 3: The nose, starting as a triangle, gains an additional side in each odd turn.

74. D

Rule 1: The number of unshaded circles indicates how many times the smaller shape will rotate 45 degrees in a clockwise direction in the following turn, becoming the larger shape at the same time. In the next figure, the rule again applies to the smaller shape, the larger shape is always only the result of the rotation.

Rule 2: Shaded circles cause an anticlockwise 45 degree rotation similarly to the mechanism described in Rule 1.

Rule 3: The number of circles alternates between odd and even.

75. A

Rule 1: The number and location of the suns indicate how many leaves the flower will gain in the following turn. The side on which a given sun appears will determine the side on which the corresponding leaf will appear. The leaves are not cumulative, that is, leaves are removed before the new leaves are added in each turn.

Rule 2: Clouds have an effect opposite to that of suns. A sun and a cloud cancel each other out.

Rule 3: A lightning bolt will turn all the leaves black (if any) on the side on which it appears in the following turn.

76. C

Rule 1: The triangle takes an increasing number of steps down the shape. When it reaches the bottom of the shape, it re-appears at the top, continuing its movement.

Rule 2: The triangle gains a new side each time it lands on an odd section of the shape (counting from the top).

Rule 3: In each turn, the previous position of the triangle is shaded.

77. C

Rule 1: The shape within the structure gains an additional side for two turns then loses one in the third. This pattern then repeats.

Rule 2: The structure rotates 45 degrees in a clockwise direction after each turn where the shape within it was unshaded. If it was shaded, the structure rotates in an anticlockwise direction.

Rule 3: A circle appears under the structure each time the shape within has an odd number of sides.

78. A

Rule 1: In each turn, the shape above the bowl has as many sides as the number of unshaded squares in the bowl in the previous turn.

Rule 2: In each turn, the shape under the bowl has as many sides as the number of shaded squares in the bowl in the previous turn.

Rule 3: Shapes (with the exception of the squares in the bowl) change their shading from turn to turn.

79. B

Rule 1: The circle attached to the six-headed star takes an increasing number of steps around the points of the star in a clockwise direction, while the circle on the four-headed star does the same, but in an anticlockwise direction.

Rule 2: The circle on the six headed star is shaded if situated on any of the three upper arms of the star, while the circle on the other star is shaded when situated on the top or the bottom arm.

Rule 3: The triangle becomes shaded if one circle is shaded.

80. A

Rule 1: The shape shown at the base of the arrow will appear in the following turn in the position where the arrow is pointing.

Rule 2: Shapes turn shaded and rotated 45 degrees clockwise in the third turn of their existence.

Rule 3: Shapes disappear in the fourth turn of their existence.

81. E

Rule 1: A circle is surrounded by two other shapes, one of them shaded. The shaded shape will either gain a side in the following turn (when the straight line is above the shapes) or lose one (when the straight line is below the shapes).

Rule 2: If the circle is shaded, the shapes switch places in the following turn.

Rule 3: The shading goes left-right-left-right, etc.

82. C

Rule 1: Circles at the top and the bottom indicate how many 'chimneys' will be visible in the following turn. The shading of the circles changes from turn to turn.

Rule 2: Counting from the left, even numbered chimneys are shaded at the top, and odd numbered ones are shaded at the bottom.

Rule 3: If three or more chimneys are shaded, the rectangle becomes shaded as well.

83. A

Rule 1: The shape in the middle is the same as that shape from the corners from the previous turn which had the most sides (see also Rule 2).

Rule 2: Shaded shapes in the corners cannot become shapes in the middle.

Rule 3: The central shape becomes shaded every second time it appears.

84. B

Rule 1: The shape within the circle is first the shape that was to the left from the circle then to the right of the circle in the previous turn. This pattern then repeats.

Rule 2: Shapes on the left are shaded if they have on odd number of sides, while shapes on the right are shaded when they have an even number of sides.

Rule 3: The shape within the circle is shaded in every second turn.

85. A

Rule 1: An arrow pointing upwards shows that the shape will gain a side; if the arrow is pointing downwards, the shape will lose a side. An arrow pointing to the left signals that a new shape will appear, while an arrow pointing to the right shows that the shape will disappear. All transformations take place in the following turn.

Rule 2: Every second shape that appears is shaded.

Rule 3: No two arrows can point in the same direction in a given figure.

86. B

Rule 1: If a horizontal unshaded arrow points to a circle, it will be shaded in the following turn.

Rule 2: If an arrow is pointing downwards, both circles will be shaded in the given row in the following turn, while if it's pointing upwards, neither of them will be.

Rule 3: If an arrow is shaded, its effect is the opposite of the default effect described above. In the case of horizontal arrows, this means that the circle 'behind' the arrow will become shaded.

87. D

Rule 1: The top lane scrolls to the right, while the bottom one scrolls to the left. See also Rule 3.

Rule 2: Shapes change their shading if they disappear on one side and reappear on the other.

Rule 3: If a circle appears in the middle, the lanes switch scrolling direction from the next turn.

88. E

Rule 1: The top left pie chart rotates 45 degrees in a clockwise direction in each turn, while the bottom left is showing the position of the top one from the previous turn. The pie charts on the right do the same but the rotations happen in an anticlockwise direction.

Rule 2: Each time a pie chart points upwards, a circle appears which then stays there for the rest of the series.

Rule 3: The number of shaded circles equals the number of pie charts pointing downwards in the current turn.

89. A

Rule 1: The shading switches between being on the left arm – in the middle – on the right arm of the structure.

Rule 2: Each time the big central oval is shaded, the whole construction rotates 90 degrees in a clockwise direction.

Rule 3: In each turn, a small circle appears in the circle that was previously shaded.

90. C

Rule 1: The small shape in the top right corner starts as a triangle, then gains a single side for two turns, then loses one on the third. This pattern then repeats.

Rule 2: For as long as the top left shape is gaining sides, a new section is also added to the circle.

Rule 3: The circle is shaded during the turns in which the top left shape is gaining sides.

91. D

Rule 1: An increasing number of circles appear within hearts. Once a heart has three circles, a new one appears.

Rule 2: Every second added circle (circles are added as following: Left – Bottom – Right) in a given turn will be shaded.

Rule 3: A heart with more shaded than unshaded circles stand upside down.

92. A

Rule 1: An increasing number of circles are added to the bottom each turn. The circles next to the arrow show how many circles will be shaded the following turn.

Rule 2: If a circle next to the arrow is shaded, it does not have a 'shading effect' on the circles in the bottom.

Rule 3: If the total number of circles next to the arrow is even, a large triangle is added to the image.

93. C

Rule 1: The inner square is rotating 45 degrees in an anticlockwise direction while the outer one is doing the same in a clockwise direction.

Rule 2: In each turn, the number of circles increases by one.

Rule 3: In even turns, there is an even number of shaded circles, while in odd turns there is an odd number of shaded circles.

94. E

Rule 1: The snake grows by two segments in each turn and the total number of circles in it also grows by two in each turn. There will always be an odd number of total circles as the circle in the first segment is alone.

Rule 2: First, an odd number of circles are shaded, then an even number. This pattern then repeats.

Rule 3: The snake segments alternate between being shaded and unshaded.

95. B

Rule 1: The large central shape assumes the form of the shape in the left then top then right position from the previous turn.

Rule 2: The small shape that will become the large shape in the following turn is shaded.

Rule 3: The big shape is shaded every second time it appears as the same shape.

96. D

Rule 1: The arrows on the left mirror the previous turn's arrows on the right, while the arrows on the right rotate 45 degrees in a clockwise direction every turn.

Rule 2: Arrows pointing upwards or downwards are shaded.

Rule 3: A triangle appears if only one arrow is shaded.

97. A

Rule 1: Shaded shapes will rotate 45 degrees in an anticlockwise direction in the following turn, while unshaded shapes will rotate 45 degrees in a clockwise direction. There is no rule governing the shading of the shapes or which shape is removed.

Rule 2: First, two shapes are added, then one gets taken away. This pattern then repeats.

Rule 3: A star appears every time there is an even number of shapes in the image.

98. C

Rule 1: The structure rotates 90 degrees in a clockwise direction in each turn while circles fall on the spikes (as shown by the single circle atop the construction).

Rule 2: A given spike loses its circle when facing downwards.

Rule 3: Circles that fell off the spikes are collected at the bottom of the figure and will have the shading of the spike they fell off of.

99. E

Rule 1: The three shapes scroll vertically downwards one at a time.

Rule 2: Shapes switch their shading each time they reappear at the top.

Rule 3: The arrows show whether a shape will gain a side (pointing to the right), lose one (pointing to the left) or stay the same (no arrows) in the following turn. The number of arrows indicates how many sides the shape will gain.

100. B

Rule 1: Based on how many circles were shaded in a given turn, the central shape is rotating that many times 45 degrees in the following turn.

Rule 2: During even-numbered turns, there is an odd number of unshaded triangles within the shape, while during odd-numbered turns, there is an even number.

Rule 3: The total number of shaded and unshaded triangles within the shape changes in the sequence 2, 3, 4, 5, 4, 3, etc.

101. D

Rule 1: One clock hand and clock face alternate between black on white and white on black each time.

Rule 2: The hand of the alternating colour clock moves backwards by 2 hours (60°) each time.

Rule 3: When the hand is black and the clock face is white, the clock moves as far as possible within the figure in the direction indicated by the arrow on the hand. When the hand is white and the clock face is black, the clock moves as far as possible within the figure in the opposite direction to that indicated by the arrow on the hand. It always moves in a straight line in that direction from its current position.

Rule 4: The grey clock with the dashed outline mirrors the alternating colour clock face, with the mirroring alternating between mirroring in the vertical plane and mirroring in the horizontal plane. When overlap occurs, the grey clock is positioned behind the alternating colour clock.

102. A

Rule 1: The number of sides on the black shape increases by 1 every time.

Rule 2: The number of sides on the white shape decreases by 2 every other time, beginning with staying the same the first time.

Rule 3: The black shape moves in the following pattern within the figure, which is then repeated: top left corner, bottom right corner, bottom left corner.

Rule 4: The white shape moves in the following pattern within the figure, which is then repeated: bottom right corner, top left corner, bottom left corner, top right corner. When the white shape and the black shape occupy the same space, the white shape is visible in front of the black shape.

103. B

Rule 1: The overall number of squares increases by 2 each time.

Rule 2: The overall number of triangles increases by 3 then decreases by 1. This pattern is then repeated.

Rule 3: The number of black squares is 1 fewer than the overall number of triangles in the previous figure.

Rule 4: The number of white triangles in a figure is the same as the number of black squares in the same figure.

104. E

Rule 1: The white triangle is reflected in a manner which alternates between the vertical plane and the horizontal plane.

Rule 2: The number of black circles increases by 1 every time.

Rule 3: The black circles are positioned at the same side as the triangle, starting from the edge of the figure. When there is an even number of circles, they are split equally above and below the triangle. When there is an odd number of circles, the extra circle is positioned near the shortest edge of the triangle rather than near the sharpest point.

Rule 4: The arrow points to the edge that the next arrow will start from.

105. D

Rule 1: The black compass point moves round clockwise by 135° each time.

Rule 2: The grey point moves round anti-clockwise by 90° each time. When it occupies the same space as the black point, the grey point is completely obscured by the black one.

Rule 3: The grey pie chart slice in the bottom left reflects the angle in the previous figure, going clockwise, from the black compass point to the grey compass point. In the first figure shown, the pie chart slice reflects where the black and grey compass points would have been in the previous figure, based on Rules 1 and 2. Please note that as the black and grey compass points shared the same point on the compass in the third figure, there is an angle of 0° between them for that figure, so consequently the pie chart slice does not appear in the fourth figure in the sequence.

Rule 4: The shaded circle appears at the centre of the compass whenever the angle of the grey pie chart slice is greater than 180°.

106. C

Rule 1: The black star moves 1 space horizontally each time. When it hits the edge of the grid it goes back in the opposite direction, following the same rule.

Rule 2: The white star moves 2 spaces to the left every time. When it reaches the edge of the grid, it continues moving left by 2 spaces from the opposite edge of the grid.

Rule 3: The black circle moves 2 spaces horizontally and 1 space vertically each time. When it hits the edge of the grid it goes back in the opposite direction, still following this same rule.

Rule 4: A white triangle appears to the right of every row and underneath every column every time there are two symbols in that row or column.

107. E

Rule 1: There are always three arrow heads, one on a single-headed arrow and two on a double-headed arrow. Whilst the left-to-right position of the arrows is arbitrary, the head of the single-headed arrow alternates between pointing up and pointing down.

Rule 2: If an arrow points to a black circle, that circle is changed into a white circle until pointed at again.

Rule 3: If an arrow points to a white circle, that circle vanishes until the space is pointed at again.

Rule 4: If an arrow points to a space, a black circle appears until that location is pointed at again.

108. C

Rule 1: The solid black line rotates through 45° clockwise each time, joining either the opposite corners or the middle of the opposite edges of the figure.

Rule 2: The line comprising alternating long and short dashes rotates through 45° clockwise every other turn. Like the solid line, it joins either the opposite corners or the middle of the opposite edges of the figure. This line is not visible if it is in the same position as the solid line.

Rule 3: The dotted line of dashes of equal length rotates through 90° every time. It always joins the opposite corners of the figure. This line is not visible if it shares a position with either of the other lines.

Rule 4: When only two lines are visible in a figure, one or two additional circles are added in order to take the total number up to the first even number that is higher than the number of circles present in the last figure. When all three lines are visible, one or two additional circles are added in order to take the total number up to the first odd number that is higher than the total number of circles present in the last figure. The positioning of the circles is purely arbitrary.

109. C

Rule 1: The circles move left to right in the top panel.

Rule 2: The circles move top to bottom in the rest of the panels.

Rule 3: The circles move in the shaded vertical panels on odd turns and in the unshaded vertical panels on even ones.

110. B

Rule 1: The white triangle rotates through 90° anti-clockwise every time.

Rule 2: The black square always appears in the space that is just outside where the shortest edge of the white triangle was in the previous figure.

Rule 3: The grey circle always appears in the space to which the narrow point of the triangle was pointing two figures earlier. When the grey circle shares any space with the black square, the grey circle is positioned in front of the black square.

Rule 4: The black cross alternates between being absent and present.

111. D

Rule 1: The cloud colour alternates between black and white.

Rule 2: White clouds produce an odd number of raindrops, whilst black clouds produce an even number of raindrops.

Rule 3: The rain falls on a diagonal from left to right for two figures then on a diagonal from right to left for two figures. This sequence then repeats.

Rule 4: The shaded circle next to the raindrops is present whenever there are 6 or more raindrops.

112. B

Rule 1: The number of white circles is increased by 2 or 1 each time in an alternating sequence, starting with 2.

Rule 2: The number of black circles decreases by 1 less than the previous time every time, starting with 5, then 4, then 3, then 2, then 1.

Rule 3: The total number of sides on the three white shapes is equal to the combined number of white and black circles.

Rule 4: Reading from top to bottom, the three white shapes are always presented in order of their number of sides, with the lowest number at the top and the highest at the bottom. Shapes with an equal number of sides are presented consecutively in the downwards sequence rather than being positioned at the same height as each other.

113. A

Rule 1: The circle with a cross in it that is located in the top left corner rotates by 45° every time.

Rule 2: The circle with a cross in it that is located in the bottom left corner of the figure rotates by 45° every other time, starting with the first time.

Rule 3: The circle with a cross in it that is located in the bottom right corner of the figure rotates by 45° every other time, starting with the second time.

Rule 4: The black circle appears in the top right corner whenever all 3 circles with a cross are oriented the same way.

114. C

Rule 1: The black triangle moves one place at a time on a diagonal line down and to the right. When it reaches the bottom of the grid, it starts at the top of the next set of upward-pointing triangles to the right and follows the same type of diagonal movement as before.

Rule 2: The grey triangle pointing upwards moves by one place in a straight line from right to left. When it reaches the end of the grid, it starts again on the same line from the right hand side.

Rule 3: The grey triangle pointing downwards starts by moving by one place at a time in a diagonal up and to the left. When it reaches the top edge of the figure, it follows the path it would take if it was a snooker ball bouncing off the cushion of the table, and describes a diagonal down and to the left. Following the same logic, when it reaches the bottom of the figure it should next follow a diagonal that goes up and to the left.

Rule 4: The small white circle moves one triangle to the right every time, whether that triangle is pointing upwards or downwards. When it is positioned over a black or grey triangle, the circle remains visible over the top of it.

115. D

Rule 1: Although they start at different points in the sequence, the top two shapes change colour in the order black, grey, white. This sequence then repeats. The bottom shape remains black at all times.

Rule 2: The shape at the top left has one fewer side each time.

Rule 3: The shape at the top right loses one side then gains two sides. This pattern then repeats.

Rule 4: The shape at the bottom has the same number of sides as the difference between the number of sides of the other two shapes. The orientation of the shape does not matter.

116. E

Rule 1: The segmented circle alternates between being large and being small.

Rule 2: The segmented circle rotates by 120° anti-clockwise each time.

Rule 3: The segmented circle moves around the edge of the figure in an anti-clockwise direction, alternately taking up position at the corners and the mid-point of the edges. When the circle is large, it occupies the corners of the figure, when it is small it is half-way along the edge.

Rule 4: Whenever the shaded part of the segmented circle points down, a white star appears at the opposite edge or corner to the face.

117. B

Rule 1: The number of points on the star determines the number of shapes in the next figure, including the star itself. There is no fixed sequence regarding which star will be in the next figure.

Rule 2: If there are an odd number of shapes (including the star), the non-star shapes are triangles. If there is an even number of shapes, the non-star shapes are squares.

Rule 3: Half of the shapes are black and half are white. If there are an odd number of shapes, the "extra" shape is always white.

Rule 4: The star alternates between being white for two figures and black for two figures.

118. E

Rule 1: The arrow heads alternate between pointing left and right and pointing up and down. The position of the arrow heads is at the top right and bottom left for two figures, then at the top left and bottom right for two figures. After four figures, the sequence repeats.

Rule 2: The arrows on the left half of the figure have the effect of changing the fill of the shape they point to between a downward right diagonal stripe and a downward left diagonal stripe. The change itself takes place in the next figure in the sequence.

Rule 3: The arrows on the right half of the figure have the effect of changing the shape they point to. Triangles change into squares, squares change into hexagons and hexagons change into triangles. The change itself takes place in the next figure in the sequence.

Rule 4: The shapes on the right hand side of the figure all alternate between black and white each time.

119. E

Rule 1: The small and medium circles take an increasing number of steps around the large one.

Rule 2: The small circle takes a single anti-clockwise step around the medium circle in each turn.

Rule 3: The large circle changes shading each time the medium circle is in the 12 o'clock position.

Rule 4: The medium circle changes shading in every second turn.

Rule 5: The small circle changes shading in every turn.

120. C

Rule 1: The two triangles rotate by 45° anti-clockwise each time.

Rule 3: Looking at them from where their bases are joined (i.e. treating them like the left and right ears of a rabbit), the two triangles are both white, then white and black, then both black, then black and white. This sequence then repeats.

Rule 4: The black circle's position alternates between being at the corner of the figure that is closest to where the two triangles are pointing and being in the corner that is diagonally opposite to where the triangles are pointing.

121. C

Rule 1: The square alternates between jumping diagonally between opposite corners and taking two clockwise steps.

Rule 2: The circle and the square swap their shading in every other step.

Rule 3: The group of dots follows the square, indicating the square's position in the previous step.

122. D

Rule 1: The circles at the top left corner migrate from the left to the right corner one by one in every other step. The migration starts between the first and second steps.

Rule 2: The circles at the bottom right corner migrate from the right to the left corner one by one in every other step. The migration already started before the start of the series, and continues from between the second and third steps.

Rule 3: Circle clusters are shaded when there is an odd number of circles and unshaded when an even number.

Rule 4: The triangle alternates between pointing up and pointing down.

123. A

Rule 1: The shading within the triangle moves from top to bottom, alternating between the left and right side between steps. When the shading reaches the bottom level, it resets to the top level in the next step (as on the right-hand side between the first and second steps).

Rule 2: The two circles show where the shading will be the following turn.

Rule 3: The circles' shadings are the opposite of the triangle segment they are next to in a given turn.

124. E

Rule 1: The circle takes a clockwise step each turn.

Rule 2: The square the circle lands in will either move away from or towards the middle (based on its current position) the next turn.

Rule 3: The circle is unshaded when it is in squares that are in the middle.

125. A

Rule 1: The square with the connector lines to neighbouring squares moves from left to right in each step. When it reaches the right edge of the figure, it moves onto the next row down.

Rule 2: The squares which were connected to the moving square in the previous step become shaded in the next step.

Rule 3: The 9-square grid is framed in every other step.

126. E

Rule 1: The set of rectangles rotates 90 degrees clockwise in each step.

Rule 2: Every second time that either a single horizontal or vertical rectangle lies on top of the 2 lower layers of rectangles, it is shaded.

127. B

Rule 1: In each step, one or two shapes move either to the middle or to the edge. Movement starts with the two shapes on the left, and then proceeds in a clockwise direction in a 2-1-2-1 sequence (two shapes move, then one shape moves…).

Rule 2: One shape in each figure is connected with lines to the two shapes in the opposite half (top or bottom) of the figure. This connection travels clockwise from one shape to the next, starting from the shape in the top right corner.

Rule 3: Shapes that are not aligned horizontally with their pairs (i.e. if the two rectangles or circles are not in the same horizontal line) are shaded, otherwise they are not.

128. E

Rule 1: The shading of the larger circles takes a step clockwise each turn, moving from circle to circle to reach the next segment in the sequence.

Rule 2: The small circles within the circles take a clockwise step each turn.

Rule 3: The small circles are alternately either shaded or unshaded, based on whether the large circle they are in has the large shading or not.

129. B

Rule 1: Small circles move clockwise as a group (not one by one) in each step from one segment of the large shapes to another.

Rule 2: As the small circles move to and through the segments of the top right shape, they increase by 1 in each step.

Rule 3: As the small circles move to the bottom shape, their number resets to 1.

Rule 4: As the small circles move to and through the segments of the top left shape, they change their shading.

130. B

Rule 1: Circles hanging from the top move from top to bottom, stopping at the bottom for a step before starting to move upwards again.

Rule 2: The shading of the circles moves from left to right. Once it reaches the rightmost position, it reappears on the left side.

Rule 3: When a circle is shaded, it will move two positions (up or down) in the following step.

131. C

Rule 1: The setup of shapes alternates between 3 columns with 2 dividing lines and 2 columns with 3 dividing lines.

Rule 2: The shading of the columns moves one space from left to right from each 3-column shape to the next 3-column shape, and one space from left to right from each 2-column shape to the next 2-column shape.

Rule 3: The circles also move from left to right along the top and bottom points of the dividing lines. When they reach the rightmost point, they reset to the leftmost position.

132. E

Rule 1: The setup of shapes alternates between 3/4/3 and 4/3/4 rows of squares.

Rule 2: The shading in each row moves left to right but only when the given row is visible.

133. B

Rule 1: Going anticlockwise, a circle in each step has an increasing number of connections to subsequent circles in an anticlockwise direction. This resets to 1 connection after reaching 4.

Rule 2: The number of shaded circles increases by one and the shading moves in an anticlockwise direction in each step. When the number of shaded circles reaches 5, it resets to 1.

Rule 3: The connections alternate between reaching the middle or only the edge of the circles.

134. A

Rule 1: In each square, the number of circles increases by 1 in each step, resetting to 1 after it has reached a maximum of 4.

Rule 2: Starting from 2 in the first figure, the number of shaded circles increases by 1 in each step from left to right, resetting to 1 after reaching a maximum of 4.

Rule 3: The number of shaded circles in a given step dictates how many anticlockwise steps the shading of the rectangle will take between the current and next steps.

135. D

Rule 1: Each small circle can have the following states, in the following order: unshaded, shaded, shaded with an intersecting line. When a circle reaches the third state, it remains in that state until affected another rule.

Rule 2: The shading of the large half circles moves from top left to bottom left and top right to bottom right.

Rule 3: When a large half circle becomes shaded, the small circle in that sector resets to its starting (unshaded) state.

136. D

Rule 1: The shading of the squares moves from left to right and from top to bottom in both columns. When the shading reaches the bottom, it resets to the top left positon and continues from there.

Rule 2: Shaded squares move away from the column in the following step.

Rule 3: Squares that moved away from the column in a given step move back to their original position in the next step.

137. C

Rule 1: The shaded circle takes a diagonal step towards the bottom right, then a vertical step downwards, then a diagonal step towards the top right, then a vertical one upwards, and then this pattern repeats. Diagonal steps are indicated by diagonal lines pointing to where the circle was in the previous step. When the circle reaches the right edge of the figure, the left-right direction of movement switches to right-left (although this is not visible in the series).

Rule 2: The unshaded circle takes a diagonal step towards the top right, then a vertical step upwards, then a diagonal step towards the bottom right, then a vertical one downwards, and then this pattern repeats. Diagonal steps are indicated by diagonal lines pointing to where the circle was in the previous step. When the circle reaches the right edge of the figure, the left-right direction of movement switches to right-left (although this is not visible in the series).

138. C

Rule 1: In even-numbered steps (e.g. 2,4), a circle on the vertical arm changes position, going from left to right or right to left, alternating between the top and bottom circles. In odd-numbered steps (e.g. 3,5), a circle on the horizontal arm changes position, going from top to bottom or bottom to top, alternating between the left and right circles.

Rule 2: The circles are shaded when they are in opposite positions on the same 'arm', i.e. when one is on the right, the other on the left, or when one is pointing to the bottom and the other to the top. Another way to think about it is to say that the circles follow the shading pattern of none shaded, outer two shaded, all shaded, inner two shaded, and so on.

139. E

Rule 1: The square that is three-quarters shaded moves 1-2-1 positions clockwise between steps.

Rule 2: The square that is one-quarter shaded moves 2-1-2 positions clockwise between steps.

Rule 3: The shaded circle in the middle moves 1-2-1 positions anticlockwise between steps.

140. C

Rule 1: The lines originating from the top of the figure lengthen until they reach the bottom, and then start to shorten again. The number of steps a line takes is equal to the numbers of circles on it and the line only changes length in the step after a circle has landed on it.

Rule 2: The unshaded circle jumps one step from left to right while the shaded circle jumps two steps from left to right. When circles reach the right edge of the figure, they reappear on the left side and the movement continues.

141. D

Rule 1: The unshaded circle takes left-to-right and then diagonal steps across the left/right points of the right angles.

Rule 2: The shaded circle takes diagonal and then left-to-right steps across the top/bottom points of the right angles.

Rule 3: When an unshaded circle lands on a right angle, it is mirrored vertically in the next step.

Rule 4: When a shaded circle lands on a right angle, it is mirrored horizontally in the next step.

142. A

Rule 1: Circles (both shaded and unshaded) move from top to bottom, reappearing at the top after they have reached the bottom.

Rule 2: The squares switch shading in every step.

Rule 3: When a circle 'jumps' through a square, it assumes the shading of the square in the next step. If it already had the same shading as the square, nothing changes.

143. B

Rule 1: The shapes containing the circles flip vertically one by one, going from left to right.

Rule 2: Once a shape has flipped, the circles contained in it start 'falling' out of it and into the next shape, one by one, starting with the bottom one first.

Rule 3: Falling circles change shading.

144. E

Rule 1: The line with the circle on the outside is rotated 90 degrees anticlockwise and then mirrored horizontally, then the pattern repeats.

Rule 2: The rectangular shape is mirrored vertically between each step.

Rule 3: The shaded circles at the points of the rectangle move clockwise in a 1-2-1 steps pattern.

145. A

Rule 1: The entire shape rotates 90 degrees clockwise in each step.

Rule 2: The shading takes a clockwise step across the three sections.

Rule 3: The shaded and unshaded circles swap positons in each step.

146. D

Rule 1: The arrows move from left to right between steps. Once they reach the rightmost position, they reappear on the left-hand side.

Rule 2: The arrows follow a down-up-up-pointing pattern.

Rule 3: Each shading takes one step in each row, from left to centre to right. When they reach the end of the row they move to the left position of the next row (top or bottom).

147. C

Rule 1: The shaded square moves from left to right along the row of squares in a 2-1-2 steps pattern, switching between rows when it reaches the right edge of the figure.

Rule 2: The circle is shaded while in the top row, unshaded while in the bottom row.

Rule 3: The circle moves around the rows, by two steps at a time from left to right when its starting position is in the bottom row, and by one step at a time from right to left when its starting position is in the top row.

148. E

Rule 1: The shaded triangle within the small square moves two positions and then one position clockwise between steps.

Rule 2: The circle in the small square moves clockwise around the four triangles.

Rule 3: A circle appears in a segment of the large square in each step going clockwise.

Rule 4: If the shading and the small circle appear in the same segment in a given step, the circle added to the large square will be shaded.

149. C

Rule 1: In successive steps, the blank circles become minus (–) circles, the – circles become plus (+) circles and the + circles become blank.

Rule 2: When blank circles become – circles, they move to the middle; when – circles become + circles they move to the corners, and stay in the corners when reset to blank, moving to the middle again when they become – circles.

150. E

Rule 1: In each step, a new circle is added, alternating between the left and the right columns. When a new circle is added in one of the columns, it pushes all previously added circles on that side down one row.

Rule 2: Each circle starts on the outside and then takes one step towards the centre, and then the cycle repeats.

Rule 3: The shading of the rectangle moves from left to right and top to bottom in a 1-2-1 pattern. When it reaches the bottom right corner, it continues from the top.

Rule 4: Circles become shaded when they are co-located with the shaded rectangle.

151. D

Rule 1: The circle groups move according to the following pattern: (1) the circles at the top take a step from left to right; (2) the circle at the connecting vertical line drops to the bottom; (3) the circles at the bottom take a step from right to left; (4) the circle at the connecting vertical line ascends to the top. This cycle then repeats.

Rule 2: Circles that either dropped or ascended change their shading and stay that way.

Rule 3: The shading of the large circles changes (separately) in every other turn, i.e. the left circle changes shading in the second, fourth and sixth figure, while the right circle changes shading in the 3rd and 5th figures.

152. C

Rule 1: The two shaded circles move one position clockwise in each step.

Rule 2: The short double lines at right angles to the main connecting lines flip direction when there are two shaded circles at either end of the main line they connect to.

Rule 3: Shaded / unshaded, shaded / shaded, unshaded / unshaded circles are connected (with a line in bold), then it repeats. An additional connecting line appears in each figure, connecting the shaded to the unshaded circle first, then shaded to shaded, and finally unshaded to unshaded, and then the cycle repeats.

153. E

Rule 1: The shaded triangles in both the bottom and top rows alternatingly take a left to right step.

Rule 2: Those triangles in the top row that are pointed at by the shaded triangles in the bottom row rotate 90 degrees anticlockwise in the next step.

154. E

Rule 1: The arms on the top side of the horizontal line change orientation one by one from left to right, and then right to left.

Rule 2: The arms on the bottom side of the horizontal line change orientation one by one from right to left, and then left to right.

Rule 3: Arms that are mirrored horizontally have circles on their endpoints.

155. A

Rule 1: The inside shaded circle on the left travels from top to bottom. When it reaches the bottom, it resets to the top position.

Rule 2: The inside shaded circle on the right travels from bottom to top. When it reaches the top, it resets to the bottom position.

Rule 3: Outer circles next to shaded inner ones will become shaded themselves the following turn.

Rule 4: The direction of the arms changes whenever the two inside circles next to each other are both either shaded or unshaded.

156. B

Rule 1: The groups of circles within the sectors of the large circle move clockwise from sector to sector.

Rule 2: The two shaded circles in the corners of the figure alternate in taking single steps clockwise.

Rule 3: One circle from each inner circle group that falls in the same position as either of the shaded outer circles becomes shaded in the next step. If a circle from the group is already shaded, an additional one becomes shaded (if there are additional circles in the group).

157. D

Rule 1: Going clockwise, one triangle is rotated by 180 degrees in each step.

Rule 2: The shading travels along the triangles in a clockwise direction, starting from the top.

Rule 3: When the shading lands on a triangle, the triangle is rotated 90 degrees clockwise; then, in the subsequent step, it is rotated 90 degrees clockwise again.

158. A

Rule 1: A single circle from the top left moves to the bottom left, then top right, then bottom right. Then another circle start its journey along the same path.

Rule 2: When a circle lands in the bottom left corner, a circle in the bottom right corner becomes shaded for the rest of the series.

Rule 3: When a circle lands in the top right corner, a circle in the top left corner (if available) becomes shaded for the rest of the series.

159. A

Rule 1: The shaded quarters of both the large and small squares take alternating clockwise steps. This means that the shading in either square only moves every other step.

Rule 2: The small square alternates between being in front of or behind the large square.

160. C

Rule 1: All circles alternate between being shaded and unshaded. Those 'hanging' from the top have a left-right alternation while those connected to the side have a bottom-top alternation.

Rule 2: In each step, two circles are added to the figure. In even steps, they are added to the bottom group on the side and to the left group on the top; in odd steps, they are added to the top group on the side and the right group on the top.

Rule 3: The lines connecting the circles alternate between being visible and invisible.

11. Succeeding in Situational Judgement Tests

Although many AD competitions do not include situational judgement tests, they may be used, especially in the annual AD5 graduate competition, where they can be an important element in the scoring (see page 27). Note that situational judgement tests are taken in your language 2.

Situational judgement tests (or SJTs for short) present candidates with a series of hypothetical but realistic work-based scenarios in which they are required to make a decision. It is important to understand that even though called "tests", they are very different in nature from the verbal, numerical and abstract reasoning tests you will face during the selection process as they measure how you evaluate certain situations instead of testing your harder analytical skills and behaviours.

Situational judgement tests are employed because they can be used to consistently and fairly assess at an early stage behavioural attributes such as decision-making ability and interpersonal skills that are difficult to measure by other techniques.

SJTs are a fast-growing area in the selection and development field. The basic idea of presenting a relevant hypothetical situation has been in use in recruitment since the early 1900s, but SJTs in a format comparable to today's SJTs have been more prevalent since the 1940s, used in particular for predicting supervisory and managerial potential.

More recent research has found that SJTs are strong predictors of real-life job performance. This means that in the development or review of SJTs, those people doing well in the tests were also the people who performed well in role. Not only that, but SJTs seem to measure an additional aspect of performance that is not measured by other assessment tools such as ability tests or personality questionnaires. This suggests that the SJTs are tapping into a different skill, and one that is highly relevant to job performance.

In AD competitions the following competencies are measured by means of situational judgement tests:

- Analysis and Problem Solving
- Delivering Quality and Results
- Prioritising and Organising
- Resilience
- Working with Others

Theory behind Situational Judgement Tests

At the heart of social psychology is the idea that what makes us human is our ability to make sense of social situations. When we evaluate an important or new situation most of us try to understand the intentions of others in the situation, and possible causal explanations, to guide our response (e.g. "How would you react if you discovered that your colleague had leaked some confidential information to the press?").

Social psychology theory also holds that there is a similarity in how people evaluate situations, and that most people will have a shared expectation of what is an *appropriate* response. This theory forms the basis of why situational judgement tests can be used to provide an indicator of our likely behaviour in an EU job-context or elsewhere. By presenting the candidate with relevant hypothetical scenarios and a set of responses which have been previously scored for their level of effectiveness, it is possible to assess how appropriate the candidate's response selection is, and to use this information to predict their likely behavioural response if faced with similar situations in the role.

What They Measure

The name "situational judgement test" suggests that what is being measured is indeed "situational judgement", actually tapping into an aspect of "practical intelligence" or "general intelligence". It is likely that SJTs are indeed multi-dimensional; they measure a number of different constructs including social or behavioural judgement, practical or general intelligence and aspects of personality such as conscientiousness. In the EPSO assessment process the SJT has been specifically developed for the purpose of measuring the candidate's situational judgement in relation to selected EPSO competencies.

How They Are Developed

Robust situational judgement tests are developed in the same way as other psychometric tests. The particular job profiles EPSO is seeking to select for are analysed by experts to understand what type of workplace situations occur that are critical to achieving good performance outcomes. This was done by interviewing current EU officials, heads of unit, directors and subject matter experts to gain a number of perspectives on what is important and what would be effective behaviour.

At the same time, examples of how less effective behaviour could lead to less desirable outcomes are gathered. Once these situations are identified, they are written up as possible test scenarios: a paragraph or two that summarises the situation and a range of four or more response options (from *most effective* or *desirable* to *least effective* or *least desirable*). The scenario and response options are crafted so that there is no "obvious" answer and even the "undesirable" options sound plausible. This is of course necessary to avoid the risk that candidates would be able to identify the "desired" answer too easily.

Careful consideration is given to the design of the test introduction and instructions and the scenario wording, format and content. It is well known that in the case of public opinion surveys, how the question is formulated will significantly influence the answer. As this is certainly true for SJTs as well, even subtle details of presentation must be thought through carefully.

It is important that the SJT design fits within the organisational setting and the assessment process, and that it reflects realistic elements of the job role in question. However, EPSO has said that its situational judgement tests are designed so that they require no specialist knowledge to complete: they are purely behaviourally-based assessments.

How They Work

The theory of planned behaviour states that an individual's behaviour in the past is a good predictor of their likely behaviour in the future. As with a standard competency based interview, this is the basis on which a situational judgement test is used to predict a candidate's job performance or suitability for the given job profile.

For each given situational judgement test, a *scoring key* is developed so that the candidate's response can be compared against this key. Initially, this can be developed by making rational judgements as to which are the most and least preferred responses to each scenario, based on the job analysis data collected in the design process and from additional evaluations made by subject matter experts.

The SJT can then be *validated* by demonstrating a clear relationship between good performance in the test and real-life good performance in the role. In order to validate the test design, and to select which scenarios will be in the final test, groups of existing job holders such as – for example – Administrators in the European Commission or Assistants in the Committee of the Regions will be tested on the sample scenarios and their responses will be compared to their real-life competency-based job performance (as judged by their superior's appraisal ratings).

Those scenarios for which the high performers have consistently selected the most preferred response as their *own* most preferred response will be selected as good ones for the final test. If there are scenarios for which high performers consistently select different responses, these will be brought into question as to their appropriateness and dropped from the test. When used in the organisation's assessment process, the candidate's score in the SJT will be based on their performance across all scenarios within the test and a score will be given to each competency in question.

What They Look Like

When sitting the test, you will be presented with a number of workplace scenarios, or "situations", together with options for how you should respond to the problem in the situation. You will have to choose which of the options in your view represent the most and the least appropriate responses. The scenarios will not be specifically limited to tasks and roles in the EU institutions, but instead will relate to more generic workplace situations of the sort that can arise in many jobs, involving working with colleagues and within hierarchies.

Each of the situations measures one of the key competencies for the job (although you would not be informed which is being measured when answering each question) and also cross-checks the consistency of your answers. Consequently, each competency will need to be measured more than once in order to reliably estimate your ability and therefore more than one scenario will relate to each competency. The test will have been designed especially for EPSO by expert occupational psychologists and it typically might contain 20 questions with 2 points per question though this can vary.

You have been approached by your superior and asked to deliver a project within a very tight deadline. You are pleased that your head of unit has approached you to work on the project but are concerned about delivering it within the timeframe given. What do you do?

A. Review and reprioritise the projects you are currently involved in so you can start work on the new project straight away.

B. Schedule a meeting with your head of unit to discuss options for delivering the project, suggesting colleagues that you would like to involve to ensure the project is delivered within the timeframe given. (**Most Effective**)

C. Develop a plan outlining how you intend approaching the project and use this to emphasise to your head of unit your concern about the deadline and ask if it can be extended.

D. Delegate the task to another person, stressing to them the importance of meeting the deadline. Retain an overview so that you can track progress and keep the ultimate credit for the work. (**Least Effective**)

On the previous page is a sample SJT test scenario, designed to measure a generic "planning"-type competency (which is not itself a specific EPSO competency, but see the next chapter for a comprehensive sample test and explanations based on the EPSO competency framework). It also includes what can be judged to be the most and least effective courses of action (although this could vary according to exact competency definitions):

The Candidate Experience

SJTs contribute to the assessment by being a two-way process for EPSO and the candidate.

EPSO can evaluate the candidate's responses to the scenarios against the structured scoring key and evaluate the extent to which the candidate's behaviour is likely to fit in with the competencies and way of working at the EU institutions.

The candidate is also able to take a view of what it would be like to work with the EU by reflecting after the test on the types of scenarios and response options presented. These may provide a general insight into what situations or behaviours might be expected in the role. Reviewing this chapter and trying out some of the practice questions in the next chapter will prove beneficial for you: those candidates who are familiar with SJTs have been found to view the experience of completing SJTs as part of an assessment process more positively than those without that familiarity.

How to Prepare

It is a bit challenging to prepare in advance of taking an SJT: a response to a situation that may be appropriate in one role may be inappropriate in another (e.g. the way you would react to a critique from your supervisor is very different from your reaction to an issue raised by an EU citizen affected by a policy you are covering). Therefore, your answers should draw from your intuitive, *honest* responses about how you would address such situations.

However, doing some practice questions on the lines of those in the next chapter can help to alleviate stress and allow you to focus on the *content* of the questions once you start the real test, rather than spending time becoming familiar with the *format*. Also, ensure that you are familiar with the EPSO competencies, as each scenario will be based around one of these. By doing this, you will be more aware of what is likely to be looked for across all the questions. Once again, however, it should be reiterated that you must be honest in your responses and not spend time trying to second-guess what is being looked for.

If you wished to, you could look up some reference material on current best practice thinking on areas related to the competencies being assessed. Ideas for research topics on the competencies measured by EPSO through SJTs are as follows:

- **Analysis and Problem Solving** – *Identifies the critical facts in complex issues and develops creative and practical solutions.* Research areas such as troubleshooting techniques, how to approach dealing with large amounts of information, techniques to stimulate creative problem solving, how to gather appropriate information.
- **Delivering Quality and Results** – *Takes personal responsibility and initiative for delivering work to a high standard of quality within set procedures.* Research areas such as how to effectively balance quality and deadlines, how to judge when rules or procedures might be bent or broken.
- **Prioritising and Organising** – *Prioritises the most important tasks, works flexibly and organises own workload efficiently.* Research areas such as project management tools and techniques, how to prioritise effectively, how to distinguish the important from the urgent, how to respond to shifting deadlines and goalposts, when and how to delegate.

- **Resilience** – *Remains effective under a heavy workload, handles organisational frustrations positively and adapts to a changing work environment.* Research areas such as how to stay calm under pressure, how to keep an optimistic outlook, how to respond to criticism, how to balance work and home life, how to cope with ambiguity.
- **Working with Others** – *Works co-operatively with others in teams and across organisational boundaries and respects differences between people.* Research areas such as effective team working, working across organisational boundaries, how to support others.

However, it should be noted that this will be a lot of background work and it would be unrealistic to expect to become an expert in all of these areas prior to the test if you are not already. A better tactic might be to decide which one or two competency areas are your prime areas for development and focus upon these.

Tips for the Assessment itself

Several tips mentioned in the verbal reasoning chapter can be successfully applied for SJTs as well. Review and adapt those hints to match the specialties of SJTs.

- **Read Everything**: Read the scenario and each of the possible answers fully before responding. You may find that the answer that originally seemed to be the best does not turn out to be upon closer inspection. Remember that the options will be carefully worded and watch out for subtle differences in wording that could differentiate a truly exceptional response from an adequate one. If possible, try to judge which EPSO competency is being assessed so you have a good idea about what qualities they will be looking for you to emphasise.
- **Relative Answers**: Bear in mind that you are being asked to make *relative* judgements: you are not asked to say which courses of action are right or wrong. In other words, you may find that *all* of the possible responses are appropriate to some degree. In this case, just rank them in order of appropriateness to help you make the "most effective" and "least effective" decision.
- **Limited Context**: As with verbal reasoning exams, try not to bring in outside knowledge – base your responses solely on the information contained within the scenario itself. This is because your outside experience may colour your response in a way that means it is not relevant to the question being posed. To take a light-hearted example, you may know that in your team at work, they are all huge fans of pizza and therefore this would be a good way of motivating them. However, in the SJT test item, there may be no reference to this and the best way to motivate a team may well be to give a motivational talk. Therefore, your outside experience might negatively impact on your ability to perform well in the test.
- **Outcome Focus**: Take the time to consider what the possible *outcomes* would be, both positive and negative, of each of the courses of action you are considering. This will help you to narrow down the choices.
- **Communication is Key**: When a situation is described where you need to choose between handing responsibility for discussing an issue to your superior or discussing an issue with another party face-to-face, it is likely that the latter option will be preferred.
- **Internal Issues**: In a situation involving a conflict, try to look for options that favour keeping a certain issue in-house and involve only those affected by it; your loyalty to your unit or institution is highly valued.
- **Stay Positive**: When faced with a problem that may be resolved by making someone

take the blame, avoid the temptation and try to act as fair as possible even if that means a disadvantage for you in the short term.

Though the primary focus of situational judgement tests is not your factual knowledge of EU procedures or administrative practice, it is advisable to read through the Code of Good Administrative Behaviour of EU officials. This includes fundamental principles such as lawfulness, proportionality, non-discrimination, consistency, objectivity and others which can *indirectly* help in your judgement of the questions. Another valuable source is EPSO's very own statement of the values based on which it aims to conduct its mission : integrity, ambition, professionalism, quality service, diversity and respect. If you bear these in mind when making your "situational judgement", it will surely yield the best result.

In the following chapter, you can find a sample Situational Judgement Test with detailed explanations, based on EPSO's competency framework.

12. Situational Judgement Test

The following practice situational judgement test questions have been developed to test the types of behaviours assessed by EPSO with specific exercises (rather than only by observation of behaviour in other assessment exercises). By completing this test you will gain an insight into the question types you will face and subject matter areas that will be invaluable in your preparation for the real test.

Each of the "situations" below is designed to relate in particular to one of the following EPSO competencies, and the answers at the end of the chapter tell you which one it was:

- Analysis and Problem Solving
- Delivering Quality and Results
- Prioritising and Organising
- Resilience
- Working with Others

Please complete these questions in a quiet place with few distractions. You have a series of scenarios and then four possible ways to approach that scenario. It is your task to decide which of the answers you think would be most effective and which would be the least effective.

There is no time limit in this exercise (at the EPSO exam timings can vary but in the 2018 AD5 graduate competition candidates had 30 minutes for 24 questions). However you should try not to ponder too long on any one question: your first reaction to each of the possible approaches is usually the most honest one. Try to identify which competency you think is being assessed to help focus your response, but aim to give your honest response rather than attempting to "second guess" the examiners.

If you feel that you agree or disagree with ALL of the possible options, then please choose the ones that you think are the most and least effective from those presented in a RELATIVE sense.

Remember: For each of the following situations you should pick the MOST and the LEAST effective of the options listed.

The answers come after Situation 30.

Situation 1

You have spent a lot of time putting together a long and very detailed EU report. A more experienced colleague in your Unit offered to review it for you before submission. Although they were not directly involved in the project it covers, you accepted this offer. Their review has come back to you and is highly critical of the report content and its structure. You believe that the critique is unnecessarily negative, and that many of the criticisms are unjustified. How do you respond to this criticism?

A. Submit the report as it stands. You were the person initially given the task of producing the report and were personally involved in the project.

B. Ask your colleague to explain his criticisms so you can better understand which of them to address.

C. Make all of the changes recommended by your colleague, as his experience is likely to contribute to the validity of his criticisms.

D. Dispassionately analyse the criticisms to determine which of the recommendations are sensible and which should be ignored.

Situation 2

You have been assigned a fairly lengthy project which will require you to work closely with a teammate who you have previously found to be distant and stand-offish. You have also previously overheard him saying negative things about your abilities to another team member. You are concerned about having to now work closely with him. How do you proceed?

A. Try to approach working with the teammate with an open mind.

B. Discuss your concerns with your Superior prior to starting the project.

C. Ask the teammate to explain the negative comments you overheard.

D. Adopt a high degree of caution in your interactions with the teammate.

Situation 3

You are part of a project team that provides data to DIGIT, the Commission's IT Directorate-General, which they then utilize in implementing a complex computer generated report about performance against agreed monthly targets. They are dissatisfied with the format in which your team provides the data and provide details of the alternative format they would prefer instead. This format would require additional analysis from your team and would not be viable within the timescales your team has to turn the data around. How do you proceed?

A. Continue to use the existing format in order to ensure that timescales are appropriately managed.

B. Adopt the elements of the new format that you know can be easily changed and that would not impact on timescales.

C. Adopt the new format in its entirety whilst explaining that timescales for getting the data to them will need to be longer as a result.

D. Ask the IT Unit to explain which elements of their preferred format are of greatest value to them and adopt these if timescales are not dramatically impacted.

Situation 4

You are responsible for preparing key aspects of a presentation for a more senior colleague. These will be inserted into the overall presentation, some aspects of which are already written, some of which are being prepared by other members of your Unit. The senior colleague has provided everyone with a clear overview document and she has promised to inform the relevant individuals if aspects of their part of the presentation require any changes. How do you tackle this task?

A. Frequently telephone your colleagues who are also working on the presentation to understand how the presentation is coming together.

B. Work primarily from the overview document provided by the senior colleague and from any changes that come directly from her.

C. Request that colleagues inform everyone involved in preparing the presentation of any changes affecting their area using e-mail or similar.

D. Arrange regular meetings for everyone involved in preparing aspects of the presentation where changes can be discussed collectively.

Situation 5

You have been finding your work relatively unchallenging recently and asked your Superior for more opportunities to challenge yourself. In response to your request, he put you in charge of a project, the output of which has clear visible benefits to EU policy. However, the work is taking up more time than you initially anticipated and you are finding much of the work even more tedious and mundane than your regular responsibilities. How do you act?

A. Continue to deliver the work without commenting on the fact that you are finding it tedious as the policy benefits are clearly evident.

B. Continue to deliver the work as requested, whilst informing your Superior that it is not actually challenging you as much as you had hoped.

C. Point out to your Supervisor that the work is more time consuming than anticipated and request some assistance from another team member to share the time commitment.

D. Tell your Superior that you would like someone else to take on this work as you are finding it time consuming without being challenging.

Situation 6

There are unconfirmed rumours that the roles within your Directorate are being reviewed and people's responsibilities will be changed. Your Superior has confirmed that a major restructure will take place, and although the final details are not yet clear, from the information provided it seems that your role will be affected. As a result of this uncertainty, morale is low across the Directorate. How do you approach this situation?

A. Spend some time putting together an outline of your skills so you can align them with any new responsibilities that may come your way.

B. Put most of your energy into performing your existing role as effectively as possible, thus demonstrating how much you can achieve and await further clarity.

C. Offer to contribute to tasks that are similar to those that you believe are likely to be required after the restructure has taken place.

D. Request a meeting with your Superior to understand the nature of the restructure more fully and how it will affect you.

Situation 7

One of your colleagues has become very erratic in their time-keeping, which is very out of character. In addition he is apparently trying to avoid another member of your Unit with whom he previously appeared to have a close working relationship. This behaviour is impacting on the performance of the team and the team dynamic on a project that involves all three of you. How do you act in this situation?

A. Ask your colleague in private if there are any issues underlying his time-keeping and the deterioration in both performance and dynamic in the team.

B. Ask the team member that the colleague may have difficulties with if they know of any issues that might be affecting your colleague.

C. Raise your concerns about your colleague with your Superior as you feel they ought to know and may be able to advise on how to proceed.

D. Decide that the matter is none of your business and allow the two individuals concerned to deal with the issue themselves.

Situation 8

You are in a meeting, trying to get your point of view heard, when another person interrupts you saying that you are "talking nonsense" and then puts forward his views instead. The group all agree with the other person's idea even though you did not finish describing yours and you feel it still has merit. Moreover, the other person's plan has some obvious flaws. The group is about to move onto another topic of conversation; what are you most likely to do?

A. State that you, likewise, feel that the other person's idea is "nonsense" and that if he hadn't interrupted so rudely, he might have had a chance to hear your idea as well. Then proceed to give your views.

B. As the group is about to move on, don't hold up the meeting by disagreeing now, but send round an email that outlines your alternative idea afterwards, asking for feedback and whether you could call a subsequent meeting to discuss.

C. Let them proceed with the other person's idea, as it is the group consensus decision. However, do some preparation in advance to manage the fall-out when things go wrong.

D. Despite holding up the meeting, you state clearly and firmly that whilst you appreciate the other person's idea has merit, there are some drawbacks and you would like to suggest an alternative. Then proceed to give your views.

Situation 9

You have conducted analysis on some anonymous staff satisfaction surveys relating to your Unit's output, and are writing a report on the key findings. Whilst most of the data demonstrates clear trends, responses relating to the courtesy with which the end users were treated by your Unit vary wildly, and there are no discernible trends as to who provided the poor levels of courtesy or who was on the receiving end of it, and no consistent explanations as to why that may be the case. What do you do?

A. Write your report, highlighting in it the fact that there is no discernible trend around courtesy and that no obvious explanations are apparent.

B. Inform your Superior that this part of the analysis lacks discernible trends before you produce your report and ask their advice on how to proceed.

C. Send out a short, more targeted request to those who completed the surveys to ascertain the reasons for the lack of a clear trend in this area.

D. Highlight that there are no overall trends around courtesy in your report, but choose also to include those explanations that best support your understanding of why that may be the case.

Situation 10

You are working as part of a team to discuss how to resolve a problem that has occurred with a technical system. The conversation seems to be going nowhere, with lots of people suggesting their own solutions but no-one listening. About halfway through you notice that the technical expert who was responsible for the problem has been quiet for most of the meeting, only contributing the occasional fact when asked by others. You know he is shy as you have worked with him for a while, but you definitely feel he could be contributing more. What do you do?

A. Explain that you feel the meeting is not achieving its objectives and you are running out of time. Summarise what has been discussed and then say that you want to make sure that everyone's views are heard. Then ask for the technical expert's views directly in front of the rest of the group.

B. Make a note of the fact that the technical expert not only caused the problem, but was also unhelpful in resolving the issue. Feed this back to him and his superior following the meeting.

C. Ask him for his views immediately and assertively. The meeting is already halfway through and you do not wish to waste any more time on discussions that might be irrelevant.

D. Suggest that the group pause for a moment and refocus on the purpose of the meeting. Then ask if anyone would like to comment on what we have covered so far whilst looking at the technical expert in the hope that they will take the opportunity to speak.

Situation 11

You are new to the role and one of your team members comes to you for an urgent decision. Apparently, they are in a heated debate with someone from another team about the best way to implement a new piece of software. Your team member has presented you with a large amount of information that they say backs up their case and asks you to give them your support at a project meeting tomorrow. What do you do next?

A. Demonstrate your faith in your team member's judgement and promise to give your full support at the meeting.

B. Ask if the meeting can be postponed so that you have a chance to look through the information and analyse it in more detail before arriving at a decision about what to do.

C. Go and see the individual from the other team to get their side of the story before making up your mind about what to do.

D. Start from scratch in analysing the situation for yourself and see if you can suggest something that meets both party's needs.

Situation 12

You have just been given responsibility for overseeing a special project team that has been put together to work on a large piece of translation work over the next 6 months. You have worked with everyone before and you feel you know their strengths and weaknesses. They are all hard workers and you are confident they have the motivation to do an excellent job. However, you do know that the commissioning client is likely to change the specification of the project as time progresses, so you want to keep things flexible. How would you approach the management of the team?

A. Gather the team together at the start and reiterate the faith you have in their ability to deliver. Avoid patronising them by telling them exactly what is expected of them. Ask for regular updates from them and hold ad hoc meetings to check on progress.

B. Identify the key milestones, risks and contingencies facing the project in partnership with the team and pull together a formal project plan that you can all refer to as the project progresses.

C. Instruct the team to begin by working towards the first deadline target, without looking too far into the future so that you can respond flexibly to the client's changing requests.

D. Start with a broad plan, but then arrange one-to-one meetings with every team member on a daily basis in order to check on progress and assign new tasks and responsibilities as they arrive from the client.

Situation 13

You are responsible for compiling the results of an important opinion survey that is running behind schedule and you are due to present the findings in two days' time. The work required is fairly basic data entry with some simple calculations required to get average scores. You already have a full diary and are feeling exhausted, your superior is away on holiday and you have no additional budget to spend. How do you approach the situation?

A. Decide to request an extra temporary member of staff anyway and worry about the budget later: delivering the project on time is the most important issue.

B. Scale back the scope of the project and report on what you have been able to complete in the available time and then give a follow-up presentation at a later date that covers subsequent work.

C. Work additional hours yourself in order to get the data entered, even if you already have a very busy schedule.

D. See if some extra resource is available from another team to help with the data entry.

Situation 14

You have been asked to manage the transition from an old database system to a newer replacement, a task that will require many people's contributions and cooperation. The new system has improved search facilities but data input is more complicated and time-consuming. You have a target date several weeks down the line for when the entire task must be completed, but it is up to you to determine how best to meet this deadline. How do you approach the task?

A. Break the task down into a series of smaller processes, complete with individual deadlines and targets for each task.

B. Concentrate on engaging with those required to input data into the system as these are likely to be the people most resistant to the transition.

C. Heavily publicise the target date to ensure that everyone affected is aware of when it must all be completed.

D. Focus on examining in detail the elements of the task you expect to be most challenging.

Situation 15

You submitted a report making several efficiency recommendations to your Unit and you received a lot of praise for your work. However, you recently reread your report and noticed an error in your analysis of one key process, upon which one of your main recommendations was founded. As a result of this recommendation, which has already been adopted, savings in time and money have been great. Unfortunately a previous stage for checking data has now been omitted and there is an increased risk of errors continuing into later stages. Although this has not happened so far, if it did, bad policy decisions could be made or, if the mistake was spotted, delays could be severe, as much work would need to be redone using the correct data. As your recommendations resulted in a complex process overhaul rather than tackling processes in isolation, the stage cannot easily be reinserted in its previous form. How do you act?

A. Continue with the revised processes without saying anything as they are delivering savings in both time and money.

B. Alert everyone using the process to your oversight to ensure they are especially careful in inputting the data first time round.

C. Say nothing but explore ways to address the omission which, once identified, you can include in a second set of recommendations.

D. Point out your oversight and suggest reverting to the original processes until you can formulate a new set of recommendations.

Situation 16

It is your first week back at work after two weeks of annual leave. You come back to find that a large amount of work has been set for you by different people in your Unit. All of the work is to be completed by the end of the day and you feel overwhelmed. Each of the people who set you work has asked what time you will complete it by and insists that their work is of the utmost importance. Your Superior then reminds you of another important task you have with a non-negotiable deadline of tomorrow morning. What do you do?

A. Arrange to see your Superior, explain that you are feeling overwhelmed due to the unrealistic amount of work you have been set, and discuss together how to move forward.

B. Speak straight away to each person in your Unit who set you work; explain the situation and ask them whether the deadlines can be extended, apologising for the inconvenience.

C. Take 5 minutes to reflect on the situation and take hold of your emotions before persevering with the tasks as they were set. Ask for support from your colleagues if needed.

D. Tell each person that due to a lack of communication, you have an unrealistic workload. Explain that it is not just their work which is important and if they need the work completed by today, they need to see if someone else is available.

Situation 17

You have been tasked with creating a presentation based on a project which you and some colleagues from your Unit recently undertook. Your Superior will give the presentation to the Directorate tomorrow. You want to show your Superior that you are personally capable of producing the necessary content so that your efforts and skills will be recognised. Ultimately, the most important thing is that a high quality presentation is produced. How do you proceed?

A. Create the presentation yourself based upon what you learnt during the project. Run the final version by your colleagues for feedback before sending it to your Superior.

B. Ask the other people you worked with to send you any notes they made about the project when working on it, but decide on the content yourself.

C. Invest some time reflecting on the project and deciding what is the most relevant content. Create the presentation based upon your own experiences and expertise.

D. Call together the colleagues who worked on the project with you and discuss it in order to get their views on the most suitable content for the presentation.

Situation 18

Your Superior has compiled some data for you to analyse and then include in a report. After looking at the data, you start to think that something isn't right. You believe you may have identified an error in the dataset – however you are not certain at this stage. What approach do you adopt?

A. As you are not certain, and to avoid embarrassment, include the original data in the report and send it to your Superior to review.

B. Look at the dataset in more depth before raising the issue. Carry out the appropriate analysis to confirm or deny the suspected error.

C. In order to address the potential issue, notify your Superior of the possible error straight away and explore the dataset together.

D. Ask a colleague to look over the dataset and see if they identify an error. If an error is confirmed, raise the issue with your Superior.

Situation 19

It is a very busy period for your Unit, with everyone working to tight deadlines. You've been given three tasks by three different senior staff members, all of which are to be completed before tomorrow morning. You are finding it difficult to juggle all three tasks. What are you going to do?

A. Contact the people who set the tasks. Enquire about the urgency and importance of each task and ask whether the deadlines can be extended.

B. Complete the most important task to the very best of your abilities by the deadline. Move on to the other tasks later once you have the time.

C. Persevere with all three tasks and aim to get all of them to a fairly good standard by the deadline, despite the lack of time.

D. In order to complete all three tasks, work throughout the night until all of the tasks have been completed to a high standard.

Situation 20

You are about to embark on a new project. You have had a preliminary project briefing and are due to have one final meeting with your Superior before you start, just to confirm arrangements. The project is scheduled to start by the end of the week as the timeframe is quite tight. However, due to unforeseen circumstances, your Superior has been called away and will not be contactable until the middle of next week. How do you act?

A. So as not to begin the project before having had the final meeting with your Superior, postpone the start date until after your Superior returns.

B. Before you start the project, spend however long is needed consulting your colleagues in order to get ideas for how best to approach it.

C. Attempt the parts of the project where everything is confirmed and delay the rest of the project until your Superior is back.

D. Despite no final meeting, make a start on the project based on the information gathered from the initial briefing and your own ideas.

Situation 21

Your Superior asks you to finalise a report on a major new EU initiative because the person who started it has been called into an urgent meeting. When you finish the report, you send it to the Directorate as requested by your Superior. The Directorate complains that the data in the report is inaccurate and not what they originally produced. You are sure that the data is right as you did not change it. When your Superior learns of the Directorate's reaction he is very disappointed and asks you to explain what happened. How do you handle this situation?

A. Approach the person who started the report when you next see him. Ask him to explain his approach when compiling the report and use this to see if he made any errors.

B. Contact the Directorate yourself and apologise for what happened, assuring them that you will investigate to ensure this does not happen again.

C. Inform your Superior that you used the data you were given. Suggest that he asks the person who started the report if he made a mistake or altered the data.

D. Request a meeting with everyone involved in compiling the report and try to understand what happened. Take the necessary actions and apologise where necessary.

Situation 22

You are running a Unit project and hold weekly meetings for your Unit members. One of the members repeatedly arrives late to the meetings and then wastes time and makes disrespectful comments to you whilst you are asking for input from the group on your ideas. The person is appearing increasingly agitated as the weeks go by. How do you act in this situation?

A. In order to resolve the issue, contact the person's manager and ask them to speak to the individual: he may be more likely to listen to a more senior individual.

B. Send an email to the whole project team which stresses how important the meetings are and how everyone needs to arrive on time and be fully committed.

C. Meet with the individual on a 1:2:1 basis and ask him why he is often late. Ask him for feedback on how he thinks the meetings could be improved.

D. The next time the Unit member arrives late or is disruptive, stop the meeting and challenge the person there and then to try and prevent it happening again.

Situation 23

You recently started to think that your Unit would benefit from having someone who is tasked with generating new systems and ways of working, and improving existing ones. You believe that this would benefit everyone in the Unit and the majority of people appear in favour of your suggestion. However the senior Unit managers you approach say that adding the cost of an additional role is not currently feasible. What do you do?

A. Put together a site in the intranet where all Unit members can share new ways of working. This way, all members have easy access to them and can adopt them if useful.

B. Arrange to meet with the most senior person in your Unit and put together a proposal for your ideas which is tailored to her, in order to win her support.

C. Look at other ongoing projects within your Unit that could benefit from new ways of working. Use these examples to support your case and approach the senior managers again in a few months.

D. Due to the seniority and knowledge of the managers you approached, accept their decision for now. Share ideas informally with colleagues as they arise.

Situation 24

You are managing a group of colleagues on a key project. You are eager to prove to your Superior that you are capable of leading the group to success. One way you want to show your ability is to finish the project 3 days ahead of the deadline, which means there will be ample review time for your Superior. You are aware that some of the group members have other fairly demanding tasks to complete within this timeframe, but you believe your aim to be achievable. However, you then receive a request from your Superior for the project to be completed a whole 14 days prior to the deadline. How do you respond?

A. In order to show your Superior what you are capable of, agree to the new deadline and ask the group members to invest additional hours in the project if required in order to complete it on time.

B. Agree to the new timeframe and ask other colleagues from your department not already involved in the project if they have any spare time to assist with the workload.

C. Explain that due to your group members' other commitments, you don't think that the requested deadline is feasible; however, say that you aim to complete the project 3 days ahead of schedule.

D. Inform him you are unsure whether or not you could achieve the new deadline. Work on the project as planned and let him know nearer the deadline if you think it is realistic.

Situation 25

There is a set of internal procedures that you have abided by since working for the EU. When you first started, you were told that it was important that organisational rules and procedures were followed, and any instances where they were breached should be highlighted upwards. When speaking to a Senior Manager from another Unit, he asks you if you can find a way around one of the procedures in order to help him get a report completed before an important deadline. He presents a strong rationale for his argument. How do you proceed?

A. Help the Senior Manager as he put forward a good argument and this will strengthen your working relationship.

B. Inform your Superior of the situation and ask him to respond to the Senior Manager on your behalf.

C. Explain to the Senior Manager that you cannot help him and inform your Superior of the situation that has occurred.

D. Refuse to bypass the procedure and remind the Senior Manager of the importance of following organisational procedures.

Situation 26

You have been asked to take responsibility for writing a complex policy document within the next month. One of your colleagues has offered to support you as he has experience in the subject area. There is a very large amount of available information that you could use to write the document, including a series of documents of different styles such as spreadsheets, slides and reports. A lot of the information is unfamiliar to you and you are concerned about your experience in the overall topic you are looking at. How do you respond?

A. Figure out some of the key documents and focus on understanding them first, as these may give you a good understanding of the area overall.

B. Ask your colleague to put together a plan for how to tackle the information, to ensure your approach is based on his experience.

C. Create a detailed list of all the different documents that could possibly be used so that you have a clear reference for these.

D. Meet with your colleague to propose an approach to tackle the data, stating that he is welcome to contribute insight to your plan.

Situation 27

You have been working closely with a colleague on putting together a review of recent international legislation. There are only a couple of days before the review is due. You have just found out that your colleague is unwell and will not be in the office today. While the review is almost complete, you feel that your colleague could still add value to the process. What do you do?

A. Wait until your colleague returns tomorrow to finalise the review to make sure you don't make incorrect changes to the report.

B. Focus on finishing off the review yourself and try to send it to the relevant people today, a day before the expected deadline.

C. See whether anyone else can help you finalise the review and then run the work past your ill colleague tomorrow if they return.

D. Contact the relevant people in your Unit, explaining the situation and ask for an extension to make sure the review is finalised.

Situation 28

You are responsible for managing an important project which requires input from several of your colleagues. You are reaching an important point in the project's progress and, while it is mostly running well, a few of the team have not delivered everything you expected and needed from them by this stage. While you are still on schedule overall, this may well have a knock-on impact on the rest of the team's work and change their schedules. How do you deal with this?

A. Re-work your timeline for the project and then communicate new goals for the different team members.

B. Immediately look for additional resources to ensure that you can meet your timelines comfortably.

C. Meet with the team members who were not able to meet their targets and ask how you can support them.

D. Write to the whole project team, highlighting the incomplete work and how it will negatively impact the project.

Situation 29

At a weekly meeting you are making a presentation to a large number of members of your Unit, including several senior staff. You prepared well for the presentation, but halfway through you realise you are working from an incomplete version of the slides and you do not have the final few slides that show the conclusion. There are still some slides remaining in your slideshow that you know are not missing. You have about 15 minutes left to talk, and know that it will take about 5-10 minutes to find the updated version of the slides.

A. Apologise and state that you will need to complete the talk next week as you are missing important slides.

B. Apologise and ask a colleague to find the correct slides while you continue to talk on the available slides.

C. Continue the talk but focus mainly on the slides available, discussing the conclusion briefly where possible.

D. Call a break while you find the slides, locate them, then return and talk through what you can in the remaining time.

Situation 30

You are leading a small team putting together a significant risk assessment for a piece of proposed legislation. Two of your team members are constantly getting into disputes and this is distracting other members of the team. In your current meeting you are discussing who will do what work. The two team members quickly get into an argument regarding how you have allocated the work, with one agreeing with the way you have suggested and the other stating he disagrees. They are raising their voices and this is clearly upsetting the other members of the team. How do you deal with this?

A. Assertively tell the whole team that you are leading the project so they need to follow your instructions to ensure that it is a success.

B. Ask both team members to stop raising their voices as it is having a negative impact on the meeting rather than helping with the task.

C. Try to solicit the views of each team member independently and ensure they are presenting their ideas to you rather than arguing with each other.

D. Allow the debate to continue for the meanwhile, but make a note to talk to both team members after the meeting.

Answers with Explanations

Situation 1. EPSO competency: RESILIENCE

The most appropriate answer in this case is **Option D**. A dispassionate approach to criticism demonstrates great resilience, whilst the analysis will ensure that effort expended in amending the report is more likely to be in areas where amendments are genuinely needed.

Option A is probably the least desirable as it simply dismisses the criticisms out of hand, in spite of your colleague's experience, and also means that his review of your work has been a waste of his time.

Option C, in contrast, whilst demonstrating a desire to take criticism on board, assumes that overall experience is everything; your colleague may not have sufficient knowledge of your particular project to be able to advise on all aspects of content.

Option B is arguably the second best option, but requires your colleague to invest more of his time having already done you a favour.

Situation 2. EPSO competency: WORKING WITH OTHERS

The most appropriate answer in this case is **Option A**. An open minded approach is the best way to give the working relationship a decent chance, and for you also to ultimately disprove their negative opinions of you.

Option D, in contrast, risks damaging the relationship.

Option B has some merits, in that your Superior will be aware of the potential issues should anything go wrong; however your teammate has not said anything negative to you directly, so it is difficult to raise this issue.

The least desirable option, however, is probably **Option C**; it means your teammate knows you may have a problem with him, which risks damaging the relationship, and also involves admitting to listening in on other people's conversation.

Situation 3. EPSO competency: ANALYSIS AND PROBLEM SOLVING

The most appropriate answer in this case is **Option D**. This option balances meeting the needs of the end user of the data (i.e. DIGIT) whilst recognising that timescales cannot be greatly affected if the data is used to analyse performance against monthly targets.

Option B also demonstrates a pragmatic approach, but without knowledge of how the data is converted into the final report, it would be difficult for you to make a call as to which elements of the proposed format should be retained and which are less critical.

Option A demonstrates a desire to maintain the status quo and disregard the request.

However, **Option C** is probably the least desirable option; if the reports are produced monthly, a delay in their production will make it difficult for DIGIT to react swiftly enough to the messages they contain.

Situation 4. EPSO competency: PRIORITISING AND ORGANISING

The most appropriate answer in this case is **Option C**. This makes the most effective use of everyone's time whilst ensuring that everyone is kept informed via a clear written record.

Option B is the least desirable option, as it does not keep track of any changes to other people's parts of the presentation that may impact on your own.

Option A involves time-consuming chasing of information and multiple communications of the same information.

Option D includes the benefit that changes can be discussed in a single forum, but may prove a waste of time; it can always be added into the process if changes prove to be very frequent and complex, but as a starting point is less sensible than the e-mail approach of Option C.

Situation 5. EPSO competency: DELIVERING QUALITY AND RESULTS

The most appropriate answer in this case is **Option B**. Your Superior will be made aware that the work is not challenging you, whilst the work continues to be done.

Option A also ensures that the important work is completed, but your Superior may believe that it is challenging you if you do not speak up, and future tasks may be at a similar level.

Option C could be seen as a rather underhand attempt to share the dull duties and could also make you look less capable in the eyes of your Supervisor.

However **Option D** is probably the least desirable option, as it is an attempt to shirk any personal responsibility for delivering output that is important to EU policy.

Situation 6. EPSO competency: RESILIENCE

The most appropriate answer in this case is **Option B**. It demonstrates great resilience to continue to work effectively under difficult circumstances.

Option C is probably the least desirable as everyone will wish to demonstrate their skills on tasks that will be relevant, and not everyone can do them at once. Your Superior will have assigned tasks with people's skills in mind and chasing the ones that will exist after the restructure may not be in alignment with your Superior's wishes and without further information your guesses as to what will be required may be wrong.

Option A contains some good qualities (it is always useful to be aware of your skills and consider how they could be applied), but without further knowledge of what the new responsibilities will look like, this exercise could lack focus at this stage.

Option D is also a reasonable reaction, but your Superior will likely have shared as much as they can already, and will wish to inform others according to a timetable set by the organisation.

Situation 7. EPSO competency: WORKING WITH OTHERS

The most appropriate answer in this case is **Option A**. A private discussion with your colleague where you seek to better understand any potential underlying issues and give the opportunity to talk about them both demonstrates concern for their well-being and potentially enables the issues to be addressed.

Option B is probably the least desirable option; if there are issues between the two teammates, it is not advisable to talk to one about the other as this could appear to be taking sides with the one you have the discussion with rather than the one who is externally exhibiting behaviours that are out of character.

Option C does allow you to get advice about how to proceed, but it also involves you highlighting someone else's potential personal issue to your Superior without their knowledge that you are doing so.

Option D is not an accurate reading of the situation; your project is being affected, and this option does not address it in any way.

Situation 8. EPSO competency: RESILIENCE

The most appropriate answer in this case is **Option D**. It demonstrates great resilience to not only come back against a challenger that everyone else has agreed with, but also to do so in a calm and measured manner. It will be far more efficient to raise the point now, even if it means extending the meeting, as it ensures all subsequent discussions are relevant.

Option A is likely to simply cause antagonism by being equally rude in return. Although your views will be heard by the group, they will also note your emotional reaction and may hesitate about engaging with you or challenging you in the future. Additionally, the person you were originally in conflict with may then feel obliged to argue back just because of the approach you adopted, in order to maintain his pride.

Option B may be acceptable, depending upon the timescales available, but it would show greater resilience to address the issue there and then, face to face. It also runs the risk of the rest of the meeting being unproductive because it will be based on the premise that the alternative idea will be adopted.

However, **Option C** is probably the least desirable as because you failed to speak out, now an entire project's success is at risk: Option C almost feels like you are getting your own back on the other person through spite. It also shows a tendency to shy away from confrontation, which shows a lack of personal confidence.

Situation 9. EPSO competency: ANALYSIS AND PROBLEM SOLVING

The most appropriate answer in this case is **Option C**. A lack of clear explanation in this case warrants trying to better understand the underlying reasons, and this targeted approach is a reasonably optimal way of achieving that.

Option D is probably the least desirable option; it would be inappropriate to present only the information that supports one explanation rather than presenting a balanced picture.

Option A is at least more honest than Option D, but raises a question that goes unanswered.

Option B has the benefit of keeping your Superior informed, but as this task has clearly been assigned to you, there is no reason why you should need your Superior's views on how to proceed and it is up to you to find an appropriate solution.

Situation 10. EPSO competency: WORKING WITH OTHERS

The most appropriate answer in this case is **Option A**. By pausing the meeting and summarising, this gives the chance to ensure everyone has the same understanding so far and also allows a pause for the technical expert to speak. Choosing Option A not only demonstrates empathy on your part, it also shows a certain drive to help the team achieve its goals.

Option B shows no real attempt to aid the team-working process and is therefore the least desirable option. It also abdicates responsibility for resolving the issue there and then yourself which would have aided the team-working process.

Option C shows a certain lack of appreciation for the technical expert's current mindset: this action may embarrass him and/or lead to him being unable to contribute by feeling too exposed. Introducing a pause in proceedings and then asking the technical expert to contribute in a non-threatening way shows far greater emotional intelligence.

Option D is unlikely to be successful as it seems from the scenario information that the technical expert is so shy or embarrassed they may not pick up on your cue to speak. More direct action is needed to encourage their contribution.

Situation 11. EPSO competency: ANALYSIS AND PROBLEM SOLVING

The most appropriate answer in this case is **Option B**. It is likely to be unrealistic for you to make a sound judgement before you have reviewed the evidence and it sounds like there is not only complex data to analyse, but also some internal politics to consider before reaching a conclusion. There does not seem to be an urgent deadline for a decision, other than the scheduled meeting, and therefore a delay would probably be acceptable.

The least effective is **Option A**: this shows perhaps a tendency to shy away from detailed analysis and does not take into account the possible biases of your team members in presenting their views to you. Although it may demonstrate unwavering loyalty to your team, it may result in a less than optimum outcome – especially considering you are new to the role and you presumably know little about your team members' trustworthiness to date.

Option C would be a potentially good course of action at some point, as it will help not only give you a balanced view but also build bridges with the other team and help reduce conflict. However, to go and see them before having first reviewed your team member's documentation and doing some preparation may result in you not having all the facts to hand. Therefore it would be better to do Option B first.

Option D is a possibility if you had a lot of time, but it seems an uneconomical way of problem solving if a lot of the research has already been conducted. It would be better to capitalise on the existing information, even if it is biased, and then once you have reviewed all the evidence you can then decide if a full analysis from scratch is required or not.

Situation 12. EPSO competency: PRIORITISING AND ORGANISING

The most appropriate answer in this case is **Option B**. Despite the fact that project scope is likely to change, in order to stand the best chance of successful delivery, an initial project plan with milestones, risks and contingencies is required. By involving the project team, not only will you formulate a better plan but you will gain their buy-in to it and show how you value their expertise. You can always build contingencies into the plan from an early stage to try and pre-empt any difficulties.

Option A reflects too much of a relaxed approach and this lack of planning is likely to lead to difficulties later on due to a lack of clarity over deliverables. Whilst you may expect this to lead to your team feeling empowered, it is actually likely to make them feel a little directionless and therefore possibly demotivated and certainly less productive.

Option C reflects a very "short-termist" approach. It may mean that some time is saved in planning, but it would be more effective to consider all the steps required in the lead up to the ultimate objective rather than dealing with each in isolation. Without a view of the bigger picture, it is impossible to plan effectively for each stage in isolation. Option C is therefore probably the least effective course of action.

Option D reflects a micro-management approach that is likely to make the team members feel a lack of empowerment, as well as taking up a lot of your time. If you are meeting that regularly with your team and issuing frequent changes of direction or new tasks, this may cause frustration: better to meet less frequently and have time to consolidate all the feedback from the commissioning client into coherent, larger pieces of information that could be fed back to all – e.g. at a team meeting.

Situation 13. EPSO competency: DELIVERING QUALITY AND RESULTS

The most appropriate answer in this case is **Option D**. If extra resource is available from another team, this should help to ensure the deadline is met and with no additional cost implications. If the extra resource is not available, you are still free to pursue one of the other options, meaning that this gives you the most possible flexibility.

Despite demonstrating drive and determination, **Option C** runs the risks of errors being made due to fatigue. There is the additional risk that the other work you have on the go will also suffer as a result. Therefore, this answer falls down on the quality focus aspects.

Choosing **Option B** means that you fail to deliver the project objective. There is no indication that this course of action will be acceptable in the scenario and it is likely to be unsatisfactory to the stakeholders. Therefore it is probably the least appropriate answer.

Option A shows initiative, and should get the project delivered on time and with less chance of mistakes than working extra hours yourself (although a temp will still need to be fully briefed). However the extra budget goes beyond the remit of the project and this is therefore not an ideal solution as you will not have worked within the project objectives.

Situation 14. EPSO competency: PRIORITISING AND ORGANISING

The most appropriate answer in this case is **Option A**. This converts the single overall deadline into a practical project plan that everyone involved in the transition can make use of in order to ensure that targets are being met.

Option C is probably the least desirable option, as it focuses on just one key date that will initially seem relatively distant, so will not create any urgency. As a result, the project may drift from a lack of focus in the initial stages and the final deadline may either be missed or else the latter stages may involve working under pressure with a greater risk of mistakes being made as a result of that pressure.

Option B recognises where the resistance to the project may come from, which is always useful, but concentrating too much on this aspect may result in the bigger picture being ignored.

Option D is similarly useful in so far as understanding the most complex elements will be important, but as with Option B, too much focus here could result in ignoring the bigger picture, and indeed in ignoring other elements that may be challenging but which you have not identified as such.

Situation 15. EPSO competency: DELIVERING QUALITY AND RESULTS

The most appropriate answer in this case is **Option D**. The impact of errors creeping into later stages is potentially great, so temporarily reverting to the original processes is safer than continuing with the new ones.

Option A is the least desirable option, as it does not involve any attempt to address the oversight.

Option B at least ensures everyone is aware of the issue but still relies on the data being handled accurately in the first place without a later independent check, and would probably slow down the process anyway.

Option C relies on no errors being made until you find a solution, and once you have found the solution you will need to explain why you are proposing a second set of recommendations anyway, thus demonstrating your recklessness and the fact you were not open about the issue once you had identified it.

Situation 16. EPSO competency: RESILIENCE

The most appropriate answer in this case is **Option B**. Addressing the issue yourself without showing emotion shows an ability to remain calm under pressure and to persevere with a task.

Option D is probably the least desirable as it could be seen as being defensive and shifting the blame onto the people who set the work.

Option C, in contrast, demonstrates an ability to control one's emotions and know when to take some time out. However, persevering with the workload when it is unrealistic may lead to greater pressure in the long run.

Option A is also a plausible option as a solution is being sought, but it involves passing the problem on to someone else to help resolve your issues.

Situation 17. EPSO competency: WORKING WITH OTHERS

The most appropriate answer in this case is **Option D**. Including your colleagues in the decision making process and the creation of the presentation not only allows for a greater breadth of ideas to be generated and therefore a better outcome, but the collaboration could also help to strengthen relationships.

The least desirable option is probably **Option C**: it involves no collaboration with the relevant people, thereby losing the chance of getting help in making the presentation better.

Option A is a plausible answer as feedback is sought on the presentation before it is sent off; however, collaboration during the creation of the presentation could have benefited both the presentation and team relationships further.

Likewise, in **Option B**, the colleagues are consulted but there is no direct collaboration.

Situation 18. EPSO competency: ANALYSIS AND PROBLEM SOLVING

The most appropriate answer in this case is **Option B**. This shows an ability to challenge presented data, analysing it further rather than taking it at face value. Taking responsibility is also evident in investigating whether there is an error or not before consulting others.

Option A is probably the least desirable as the issue is not being addressed but simply being avoided: further analysis/investigation should be carried out.

Option C has its merits in raising the issue, but more analysis should ideally be carried out first in an attempt to see whether or not there is an error.

Option D shows an ability to consult others in order to get a second opinion, but the data still could have been looked at in more depth first.

Situation 19. EPSO competency: PRIORITISING AND ORGANISING

The most appropriate answer in this case is **Option A**. Finding out which task is the most important/urgent, and exploring whether there is a way to reduce the workload, will lead to prioritisation and allow a high standard to be maintained on all three tasks.

Option C is the least desirable option, as although all three tasks may get completed within the timeframe, they are likely to be rushed and not completed to the same standard as if more time had been spent on them.

Option B focuses on the right priority, but without a clear plan for the remaining tasks, this could result in disappointing the other stakeholders.

Option D includes the possibility that all tasks could be completed to a high standard before the deadline. However, working throughout the night may lead to a reduction in performance levels which could lower the standard of work. Time management and task prioritisation would be better options.

Situation 20. EPSO competency: DELIVERING QUALITY AND RESULTS

The most appropriate answer in this case is **Option D**. It shows an ability to act and start the project without receiving complete instructions, using the information already gathered and one's own initiative.

Option A is probably the least desirable option, as it shows a reluctance to take the initiative and start the project despite the tight deadline.

Option B has its merits as there is an element of proactivity shown by consulting others in order to start the project before your Superior returns. However, there is a danger of over-consulting and this delaying the start date.

Option C shows proactivity in starting the project; on the other hand, not progressing past the areas confirmed with your Superior is likely to impact on completion by the deadline and again misses an opportunity to take the initiative.

Situation 21. EPSO competency: RESILIENCE

The most appropriate answer in this case is **Option D**. It demonstrates an ability to assume a degree of responsibility in trying to find out what happened but without being defensive.

Option C is probably the least desirable as it demonstrates an element of defensiveness in reaction to the Superior's disappointment and request for an explanation. Potentially, blame is also passed onto the colleague.

Option B contains some good qualities as it shows the ability to apologise and investigate an issue regardless of fault; however there is less emphasis on taking action on the current report.

Option A is also a reasonable reaction as again some responsibility is taken. But the potential blame is simply passed on to the colleague, rather than a more objective, holistic approach being taken.

Situation 22. EPSO competency: WORKING WITH OTHERS

The most appropriate answer in this case is **Option C**. By trying to find out why they are behaving in that way you are more likely to be able to find a solution. Asking the member for their feedback shows an ability to listen to others and to involve them in reaching a resolution.

Option D is probably the least desirable option – confronting the member in front of the rest of the group is unlikely to resolve the issue. It is possible that the member has some personal issues outside work, or is faced with other pressures at work: therefore trying to address the issue in front of others could be quite insensitive.

Option A does at least ensure that someone speaks to the problematic member and that his behaviour is addressed. But by not speaking to the team member yourself, you are failing to take full responsibility for your group.

Option B may be a good way of avoiding conflict, but it is not getting to the root cause of the issue or allowing the member to explain his actions.

Situation 23. EPSO competency: ANALYSIS AND PROBLEM SOLVING

The most appropriate answer in this case is **Option A**. Coming up with a different way of enabling all members to benefit, despite the rejection of the initial idea, demonstrates an ability to produce creative ideas and effective solutions.

Option B is probably the least desirable: the senior managers have already said the idea would not be feasible on cost grounds, therefore a 1:2:1 meeting is likely to be a waste of time as the resources are simply not available at the moment.

Option C is more practical than option B and budgets may have changed in a few months; however this still does not address the issue in the short term.

Option D shows respect and understanding for the views expressed by the senior managers, but there is no structure to the proposed idea-sharing, and this may well make it less likely to succeed.

Situation 24. EPSO competency: PRIORITISING AND ORGANISING

The most appropriate answer in this case is **Option C**. Being realistic about what can be achieved and by when, allows both your Superior and your colleagues to know where they stand and what the outcome is likely to be.

Option A is probably the least appropriate, as the desire to impress overrides the ability to set a realistic timeframe. You know that the other people involved in the project have other demanding tasks; therefore it is unrealistic to suppose that the project could be completed so far ahead of the original deadline.

With **Option B**, although there is recognition that the suggested deadline is not realistic without additional support, it is risky to agree to the new timeframe without arranging extra support beforehand.

Option D does not commit to the deadline; on the other hand, it fails to confirm a deadline at all, therefore creating ambiguity for both the Superior and rest of the project team.

Situation 25. EPSO competency: DELIVERING QUALITY AND RESULTS

The most appropriate answer in this case is **Option C** as it shows adherence to set procedures and a willingness to escalate situations where there is an attempt to breach procedures.

Option A is the least desirable, as it is clearly involves breaking procedures put in place by the organisation.

Whilst **Option B** demonstrates an ability to raise the issue with your Superior, asking them to deal with the situation abdicates responsibility.

Option D correctly refuses to go against organisational rules; however the issue is not raised with anyone else to prevent this happening in future.

Situation 26. EPSO competency: ANALYSIS AND PROBLEM SOLVING

The most appropriate answer in this case is **Option D**. This shows that you are thinking about how to break down the data into something manageable, but also looks to run your idea past someone who may well have insight into how effective it will be.

Option A is an acceptable response. This does not draw on your colleague's existing expertise at all but is still likely to be a logical way to tackle large amounts of data.

Option C is also an acceptable response. This detailed list could serve as a useful resource; however, it's not clear how much information there is. If there is a manageable number of documents this may well be a good starting point, but if there are a lot and some are less relevant you risk wasting valuable time.

Option B is the least effective response. You are responsible for this project and there are several ways you can tackle the information yourself rather than passing the responsibility on to your colleague. You risk losing control of the project at an early stage by handing over such a major task to your colleague entirely.

Situation 27. EPSO competency: DELIVERING QUALITY AND RESULTS

The most appropriate answer in this case is **Option C**. This ensures that you hit your original deadline and get the input of others wherever possible – while also leaving your colleague with the opportunity to contribute final comments if they are back to work in time.

Option A is the least effective response. You do not know whether your colleague will return tomorrow and you risk falling behind in finishing off the report. You should be prepared to take responsibility for getting this finished in your colleague's absence.

Option B could be seen as an acceptable response as it means you are taking full responsibility for delivering the report. However, while it is admirable that you are striving to deliver ahead of schedule, it may still be worth seeing if your colleague returns tomorrow to add additional value and, if not, seeking input from elsewhere. That way, you may add something to the quality while still delivering on time.

Option D has the merit of being open and clear about the situation. It also gives the relevant people the opportunity to insist on getting the job finished faster, if that is their priority. However, it would be better if you took the initiative yourself for meeting the deadline.

Situation 28. EPSO competency: PRIORITISING AND ORGANISING

The most appropriate answer in this case is **Option A**. This shows that you can adjust plans as needed while still setting clear timelines. By communicating clear goals, you will let your colleagues know exactly what is needed of them. It will be important to think about how to communicate the importance of meeting the new deadlines to everyone involved so as to leave no doubt about the need to stick to the plan.

Option B could help in keeping the project on track. However, you are still on schedule overall, so while this step may help the group to successfully complete the project, it may not actually be necessary. Furthermore, adding extra resources may not be possible without affecting other work, may make the project not stretching enough to get the most out of the team, and does not tackle the fact that some members of the team are not currently pulling their weight – it may even encourage the idea that if the work doesn't get done, someone else will be brought in to do it.

Option C has the merit that you are trying to get the most out of the team and this approach could well help your underperforming colleagues improve if handled well. However, it is important that you ensure that they fully understand the importance of their input to the project as a whole.

Option D is the least effective response. Sharing this information may have a deleterious effect on the team's morale. It is possible that the underperforming team members may not know what you expected of them. This is especially true as you are still on target overall, so the team are likely to feel positive about their output overall and that things are on track. A better approach is to look forward and ensure it is clear what is needed for the rest of the project.

Situation 29. EPSO competency: RESILIENCE

The most appropriate answer in this case is **Option B**. While this involves admitting that a mistake was made with the slides, it should not undermine confidence in what you have to say. By talking off script (if you have to) while the slides are located, you can demonstrate your breadth of knowledge in the topic which could actually add credibility to your talk.

Option A is the least effective response. While it is a difficult situation to find yourself in, you should seek to resolve it now. You risk losing impact and interest if you resume in a week's time. You also risk wasting the time of those who are unable to attend the meeting both weeks.

Option C is a possible response and it may actually help the presentation appear to go the most smoothly to your audience. However, it has the downside that you risk losing impact by not addressing the conclusion in as much depth as you could. You are also potentially wasting important slides that you spent time developing and could illustrate your key conclusions well.

Option D is an appropriate response. This shows a determination to fix the issue despite the difficult situation. However, by breaking off your presentation you may damage the flow of the talk, and you may also need to rush your final slides to keep to time. Thus, it would be better to ask a colleague to locate the slides.

Situation 30. EPSO competency: WORKING WITH OTHERS

The most appropriate answer in this case is **Option C**. It shows an interest in their input while managing the situation actively and ensuring the team know that you are leading the project. By getting them to address you rather than argue with each other, you are aiming to keep a focus on the task itself rather than their individual dispute.

Option A is the least effective response. This authoritarian approach may prevent you from getting potentially valuable input from team members – including those who are not involved in the argument. And it does not deal properly with the core ongoing issue of the two disputing team members.

Option B is an appropriate response in the sense that it is likely to help with the immediate issue and highlight the damage that they are doing to the meeting. It does not, however, take account of the possibility that they might both have valid points to make that you can listen to and try to understand.

Option D has the benefit that it may allow you to tackle the issue with the sensitivity it deserves, rather than choosing an inappropriate response in the heat of the moment when tempers are high. However, it does not deal with the immediate situation, which may have a damaging impact on morale and could undermine your credibility in leading the team.